Managerial Economics

Ana and Strategy

3rd Edition

Evan J. Douglas

Bentley College

Prentice Hall, Englewood Cliffs, New Jersey 07632

10 9 8 7 6 5 4 3 2 1

ISBN 0-13-551060-0

Prentice-Hall International (UK) Limited, *London*
Prentice-Hall of Australia Pty. Limited, *Sydney*
Prentice-Hall Canada Inc., *Toronto*
Prentice-Hall Hispanoamericana, S.A., *Mexico*
Prentice-Hall of India Private Limited, *New Delhi*
Prentice-Hall of Japan, Inc., *Tokyo*
Prentice-Hall of Southeast Asia Pte. Ltd., *Singapore*
Editora Prentice-Hall do Brasil, Ltda., *Rio de Janeiro*
Prentice-Hall, Inc., *Englewood Cliffs, New Jersey*

PRENTICE-HALL INTERNATIONAL, INC.

© 1987, 1983, 1979 by Prentice-Hall, Inc.
A division of Simon & Schuster
Englewood Cliffs, New Jersey 07632

Printed in the Republic of Singapore

10 9 8 7 6 5 4 3 2

ISBN: 0-13-551060-0

Prentice-Hall International (UK) Limited, *London*
Prentice-Hall of Australia Pty. Limited, *Sydney*
Prentice-Hall Canada Inc., *Toronto*
Prentice-Hall Hispanoamericana, S.A., *Mexico*
Prentice-Hall of India Private Limited, *New Delhi*
Prentice-Hall of Japan, Inc., *Tokyo*
Prentice-Hall of Southeast Asia Pte. Ltd., *Singapore*
Editora Prentice-Hall do Brasil, Ltda., *Rio de Janeiro*
Prentice-Hall, Inc., *Englewood Cliffs, New Jersey*

Contents

PART 2   DEMAND THEORY, ANALYSIS, AND ESTIMATION

✕ **5   Estimation of the Demand Function 156**

PART 3   PRODUCTION AND COST ANALYSIS

6   Production Functions and Cost Curves   211

7 Cost Concepts for Decision Making 279

PART 5   TOPICS IN MANAGERIAL ECONOMICS

Preface

Managerial Economics is concerned with the application of economic principles and methodologies to the decision-making process of the business firm operating under conditions of risk and uncertainty. My approach to managerial economics can be summarized by the following four points. First, I believe that economic theory establishes important principles for business practice. I have tried to include the economics that is more readily applicable in business situations and to exclude or subordinate the economics that is less applicable.

Second, business practice must be recognized and incorporated into the discipline of managerial economics. For example, if firms choose to use markup pricing policies rather than take the marginalist approach, then the task of the managerial economist is to assist the decision maker in finding the optimal level of the markup, rather than to harangue for marginalism.

Third, as the subtitle of the book suggests, managerial economics should be concerned with the firm's competitive strategy, rather than simply costs and revenues. Thus this book is concerned with not only cost and price decisions, but also quality and advertising/promotional decisions, and it integrates all these in the chapter on product quality and competitive strategy.

Finally, the concepts and issues involved in managerial economics must be put into the context of real-world business decision problems in order to demonstrate methods of identifying problems and finding solutions. Thus each chapter incorporates business examples and is followed by provocative discussion questions and case-study problems.

A NOTE TO THE STUDENT

Welcome to managerial economics! You are about to embark on what I hope will be an interesting and rewarding learning experience. When you finish this book, and the course in which this book is used, you will have a much clearer view of the applicability and relevance of economics to decision making within the business firm. You will know a lot more economics and, just as importantly, will have developed your analytical skills to a higher level. You will also know more about how businesses operate and about the types of problems managers face. You will more readily identify the nature of a decision problem, and you will know where to start looking for the answers to that problem. You will be armed with analytical techniques and conceptual insights that will make you a better business decision maker.

Managerial economics is a serious course that will require a serious effort on your part if you want to achieve the benefits noted in the previous paragraph, not to mention a respectable grade in the course. You will have to read a lot of material, answer the end-of-chapter discussion questions, and work your way through the case-study problems assigned by your instructor. The rewards will be worth the effort. To assist you, I have written short answers to all the case-study problems; these appear in Appendix C at the back of the book. Unfortunately, space does not permit more detailed answers, but these brief answers will let you know if you are on the right track. Your instructor will have the more detailed answers in the *Instructor's Manual*.

There is a *Study Guide/Workbook* available through your bookstore that some of you might really appreciate. In the study guide each chapter is broken down into section summaries, followed by self-test questions and their answers. Case-study problems are then worked through in steps before you are asked to work one through by yourself and compare your answers with mine. Potential midterm and final exam questions are provided for you to practice on. Also, if you have access to a personal computer and the Lotus 1–2–3 software package, you may be interested in the *Computer Courseware Package and Manual* that contains a variety of "templates" that help with the calculations involved in many of the case-study problems. Ask your instructor about this learning aid (details are in the *Instructor's Manual*).

I wish you good luck, in this course and in your future career. If you have any comments on this book, or on any of the supplementary learning aids, please write and share them with me.

A NOTE TO THE INSTRUCTOR

As in the earlier editions, this book is designed for use in a one-semester or one-quarter course at the undergraduate or MBA level, in courses with names like "Managerial Economics," "Economics of the Firm," or "Microeconomics for Business." The third edition allows the instructor a wider range of options in adapting this book to suit his or her preferred curriculum. As described in more detail under "Changes in the Third Edition," the book now has one additional chapter and four more appendices. There is expanded coverage of topics previously included only briefly, and there is new material that will better serve the curricular preferences of some instructors. Some of the more complex intermediate microeconomic theory has been shifted into Appendices 3A, 6A, and 9A, where it can be bypassed without difficulty if doing so best suits a specific curriculum. New material has been added to the book and other material has been culled, in an effort to keep the book up-to-date with the evolving nature of the field.

The only prerequisite course assumed is a principles course in microeconomics, and even this is not necessary in M.B.A. programs where students are typically more mature and more highly motivated. Each concept is developed from the basics, presuming that students will need refreshing on their micro principles in any case. If intermediate microeconomics is a prerequisite in the curriculum, Chapters 3, 4, 6, and 9 can be covered more quickly or bypassed altogether, but note that Chapter 3 includes the "attribute" approach to consumer behavior, which students may not yet have encountered.

A basic statistics course as a prerequisite may make students more secure initially, but its absence does not seem to materially affect grades in this course, in my experience. The same applies to basic mathematics and algebra. All statistics and mathematics used in this book are explained in basic terms at the point of first usage, and a more detailed review of functions, graphs, algebra, and differential calculus is provided in Appendix A at the end of the book. Some instructors may wish to cover this material in class, and others will prefer to assign it as initial reading and preserve class time for more applied material.

OUTLINE OF THIS BOOK

Part 1 of the book contains two chapters that lay the groundwork for decision making under risk and uncertainty. Chapter 1 introduces the student to the field of managerial economics and the use of models and other analytical concepts in the decision-making process. Then, the concept of "value" is addressed, involving both present-value and expected-value analysis. The firm's objective is then related to its planning period and time horizon. Chapter 2 introduces the concept of "risk and uncertainty," measurement of risk, and the adjustment of decisions to reflect the decision maker's attitude toward risk.

Part 2 is concerned with consumer behavior and the demand side of the firm's business. Chapter 3 considers the utility-maximizing behavior of consumers in response to changes in prices, incomes, tastes and preferences, and perceptions of product quality. Attribute analysis is introduced at a basic level to allow the qualitative differences between products to be distinguished. Chapter 4 examines the determinants of market demand, the elasticities of demand with respect to price, income, other product prices, and so on. Chapter 5 is concerned with the estimation of the firm's demand and involves both marketing research and statistical (regression) techniques that are introduced and developed from basics.

Part 3 considers the production and cost side of the firm's business. Chapter 6 examines production and cost theory, linking them together for pedagogical effectiveness. Chapter 7 is concerned with cost concepts for decision making and considers accounting versus economic cost and profit concepts, stressing incremental or contribution analysis of decision problems. Chapter 8, which is concerned with cost estimation, uses the gradient method, regression analysis, and the engineering technique to ascertain both short- and long-run costs. The learning curve is also estimated here.

Part 4 looks at the firm's pricing decisions. Chapter 9 examines several relevant economic models of firm behavior, and Appendix 9A extends this to several more-complex models. Chapter 10 looks at pricing in practice and examines markup pricing for its optimality in view of the firm's objectives, as well as other empirical pricing practices. Chapter 11 considers the pricing of new products and serves to reinforce many of the concepts introduced in Chapters 9 and 10. Chapter 12 analyzes competitive bid markets, and it also draws together elements from throughout the course in a pricing context that is observed in the markets for a wide variety of products.

Part 5 considers three topics that many instructors will strive to include in their course, despite the limitation of class time. Chapter 13 concerns advertising and promotional decisions faced by the firm, including the joint determination of price and advertising expenditures. Chapter 14 examines the firm's choice of product quality, as well as price and advertising strategy, in the context of its chosen competitive strategy. Finally, Chapter 15 considers capital budgeting, building on the expected-present-value concept that was introduced in Chapter 1 and used throughout the book.

CHANGES IN THE THIRD EDITION

Chapter 14 is entirely new; it is concerned with the firm's quality decisions in the context of its chosen competitive strategy. Also incorporated is the issue of the cost of the information the consumer needs to evaluate product quality, an issue that has definite implications for the firm's quality decisions, as well as its pricing and advertising decisions, which are considered jointly. Many instructors will find that this is a good "capstone" chapter for their courses and that it will whet students' appetites for a course in competitive strategy or business policy.

Chapters 9, 10, and 11 have been totally reorganized. Chapter 9 and Appendix 9A now contain much of what was previously in Chapters 9 and 10. Many instructors will prefer to bypass the appendix to allow them time to cover material in later chapters, but those preferring more microeconomics will continue to cover all this material. New topics in Appendix 9A include transfer pricing and delivered prices (spatial competition). Chapter 10 now includes most of the former Chapter 11. The material on product line pricing has been expanded, and new topics include the impact of consumer search costs on pricing decisions, pricing product bundles, quantity discounts, and promotional pricing. Chapter 11 is now concerned with the pricing of new products, a topic of increasing applicability in this technological age.

Several other chapters also have new material incorporated. Chapter 1 considers daily interest discount factors, reflecting the availability of daily interest as the firm's opportunity cost of funds in many situations. The principal-agent problem and the issue of incentive contracts are considered briefly in the context of the potential divergence between the firm's (shareholders') objectives and those of management. Chapter 6 discusses the learning curve in the context of changing input productivity as cumulative output grows. Chapter 9 considers contestable markets in the context of barriers to entry. Chapter 12 now considers cost-plus-fee and incentive (risk-sharing) bids as well as the fixed-price bid or quote. Recent examples have been added in many places throughout the book.

There are six new appendices, as well as Appendix 7A, "Breakeven Analysis," which has been carried over. Appendix 3A applies indifference curve analysis to the separation of the income and substitution effects of a price change, a topic formerly in Chapter 3. Appendix 5A examines demand forecasting in much more detail and coverage than before, including regression models, moving averages, exponential smoothing, time-series decomposition, macroeconomic indicators, and intention surveys. Appendix 6A considers isoquant-isocost analysis of production problems, formerly in Chapter 6. Appendix 6B examines linear programming in some detail, in the context of a firm's product-mix decision. Appendix 9A examines several more-complex models of the firm's pricing decision. Appendix 10A is concerned with pricing practices that may be illegal under the Sherman and Robinson-Patman Acts.

In general, the chapters are shorter in this edition, because of editing and reorganization to improve the flow of the material, as well as the shifting of material to appendices. The book is longer because of the additional chapter and appendices and the addition of many new case-study problems at the end of the chapters and appendices. There are now more than 170 of these short case-study problems, and brief answers to all of them are found in the back of the book to assist students in their learning process. A *Study Guide/Workbook* and a *Computer Courseware Package and Manual* are offered for the first time publicly, although both have been student-tested for three years.

DISTINCTIVE FEATURES OF THIS TEXT

In my view this book has several distinctive features, as compared to other books available in this field, as follows:

1. Flexibility

Many of the chapters and all of the appendices can be included or excluded at the instructor's discretion. Whatever the prerequisites for your course, and whether your approach is predominantly quantitative, theoretical, or practical, there is likely to be a suitable combination of topics here, in short, self-contained chapters and appendices, that will facilitate coverage of the material you want to cover. (In the *Instructor's Manual* I suggest several sequences that might be chosen, based on input from a large number of instructors teaching this course.)

2. Currency

This text incorporates recent advances in economics that seem indispensible to the study of managerial economics. For example, Lancaster's attribute analysis is included for its profound implications for consumer behavior, pricing, the quality choice, advertising, and competitive strategy. The principal-agent problem, arising from the separation of ownership and control, is considered before assuming that managers will strive to maximize the firm's net worth. Learning by doing, and the impact of learning on costs, is incorporated into production and cost analysis. The notion of "contestable" markets and the impact of barriers to entry on pricing decisions are incorporated into the theory of markets. The consumer's cost of information, which influences the quality decision, the desirability of price competition, and the extent and type of advertising expenditures, is incorporated into these subjects in this book. The three generic strategies of competitive strategy analysis are considered in the context of the joint determination of the firm's quality, price, and advertising strategies.

3. Breadth and Depth of Coverage

In addition to the topics mentioned before, several other issues that are neglected or treated superficially in other books are covered in depth in this text. Pricing in practice is covered in more detail than in any competing book, and the discussion includes in-depth analysis of markup and other practical pricing strategies, new product pricing, and competitive bid pricing. The economics of advertising and promotion decisions are afforded a complete chapter. In Chapter 14, the firm's quality decision is considered in the context of the firm's competitive strategy. Yet this text also covers the bases, including all of the topics that are found in the core of typical managerial economics curricula. It economizes on space (and class time) by combining production and cost theory into one chapter, concentrating on business firms, and by treating some topics more concisely in chapters and appendices.

4. Capstone Chapters

Each of the last five chapters in the book can be regarded as a "capstone" chapter for the course. In Chapters 11, 12, 13, 14, and 15, material from earlier chapters is reiterated and consolidated in the context of another extension of managerial economics into new territory. At whatever point your course runs out of time, your students will have been able to revise and consolidate their understanding of earlier material and apply it in a new context, thus "rounding out" the course.

5. More and Better Case-Study Problems

Reviewers have said that one of the major strengths of this book is the case-study problems at the end of each chapter. Now there are more than ever; some are new, some are revised, and others are carried over because "if it ain't broke, don't fix it." These problems are "not simply plug and chug," as one reviewer said, but require analysis, judgment, and sensitivity analysis. They are designed to reinforce the material and apply it in business contexts.

6. Learning and Teaching Aids

Within the text, definitions and examples are highlighted to aid student comprehension. Short (essential) answers are provided in Appendix C for all the case-study problems to allow immediate feedback and reinforcement. A *Study Guide/Workbook* is available separately that will help the student who is having difficulty, as well as the one who wants to "ace" the course. A *Computer Courseware Package and Manual* that uses Lotus 1–2–3 is available to the instructor and to students and may be used in class or in the lab to set or to solve assigned problems. Details of the courseware package are found in the *Instructor's Manual,* which in turn has detailed answers to all discussion questions and case-study problems, as well as many other questions and several problems suitable for assignments and exams.

ACKNOWLEDGMENTS

I thank all the people once again who were mentioned, or should have been mentioned, in the two earlier editions of this book. In particular, I will mention my former teachers Cliff L. Lloyd, Peter E. Kennedy, and Brian L. Johns and my former colleagues Stephen P. Robbins, Gary W. Johns, and Kenneth D. Riener. Their input lives on, as does my gratitude.

Instrumental in the third edition were my colleagues at Bentley College, in particular, Andrew Stollar, Stephen Grubaugh, William Clarke, Stephen Silver, and Dale Kuntz. Sincere thanks also to Duncan Holthausen, Jr., and Steve Margolis (North Carolina State), John N. Stevens (Franklin College of Indiana), Masako Darrough (Columbia), George Garman (Loyola), Doug Wilson (University of Massachusetts, Boston), John E. Rowcroft (University of New Brunswick, Canada), Michael Pickford (Massey University, New Zealand), Harold Hotelling (Kentucky), Houston Stokes (Illinois–Chicago Circle), R. M. Addudell (Loyola), Marvin Frankel (Illinois–Urbana), Frank Hood (Mississippi College), Jung Lim (Wingate College), Scott Smith (Arizona State), Michael Brendler (Louisiana State), F. E. Weldon (William Carey College), John Marcis (Virginia Commonwealth), George Brower (Connecticut–Storrs), Paul Schoofs (Ripon College), and others whose contributions I will no doubt recall only after this goes to press.

My thanks also go to my graduate assistant Andrew Mara and work-study student Irene Canino, whose efforts helped materially in the revision of this manuscript. Many other students, too many to mention separately, have assisted with feedback on the earlier editions and on draft material. Secretarial support from Kathy Lynch and her band of work-study students has been excellent. The support of Bentley College, through my chairman Dale Kuntz and Deans John Burns and Jeremiah O'Connell, is also greatly appreciated. I thank you all.

At Prentice-Hall, my thanks go to my editor, Linda Frascino, and her assistant Zsuzsa Neff, who have been very helpful and cooperative. My production editor, Scott Huler, who was ultimately responsible for transforming the manuscript into this fine book as you see it, also receives my sincere thanks.

Finally, my family continues to sustain me. My mother and father have always been a great source of inspiration and encouragement. My wife and children, Shelley, Meghan, and Andrew, have my love and gratitude for their love and support, particularly over the past few months when this project took so much of their time.

Evan J. Douglas

Department of Economics
Bentley College
Waltham, Massachusetts

1 Introduction to Managerial Economics

1.1 INTRODUCTION

This chapter introduces the reader to the field of managerial economics and builds the foundation necessary for decision making under uncertainty. In the next section we examine the *definition and scope* of managerial economics in order to establish the nature and direction of the discipline you are about to study. This leads to a discussion of the use of *models* in managerial economics. We will see that models depicting the behavior of consumers and business firms can be of substantial assistance in decision analysis.

In the third section we consider the multiperiod nature of decision making. Decisions made now typically have cost and revenue implications not only for the present period but also for future periods. This necessitates the use of *present-value analysis*, also known as discounted cash flow analysis, to allow the proper weighting of future profits against present profits for effective decision making.

In the fourth section we introduce *expected-value analysis* to allow the proper evaluation of decision alternatives when the decision must be made under conditions of risk and uncertainty—the usual situation in the real world.

Which decision is optimal depends on the firm's *objective*. In the fifth section of this chapter we consider the appropriate objective function for the firm and the *decision criterion* indicated under each of four different scenarios. Finally, we provide a brief summary of the chapter.

1.2 DEFINITION AND SCOPE OF MANAGERIAL ECONOMICS

■ *Definition:* *Managerial economics* is concerned with the application of economic principles and methodologies to the decision-making process within the firm or organization. It seeks to establish rules and principles to facilitate the attainment of the desired economic goals of management. These economic goals relate to costs, revenues, and profits and are important within the business and the nonbusiness institution.

1

Profits are at the heart of the study of managerial economics. Profits are defined as the excess of revenues over costs. If this difference is negative, it is called a *loss*. For a nonprofit institution, an excess of revenues over costs is called a surplus, while a shortfall of revenues compared to costs is called a deficit. No economic organization, not even the United States government, can continue forever incurring losses or deficits. The objective of a business firm usually requires profit maximization over its time horizon, which may be short term or long term depending on the firm and its circumstances. Nonprofit institutions typically do not seek to make a surplus, but wish to spend their available funds to maximum effect. The decision problems facing business and nonbusiness institutions are therefore essentially similar, involving revenue enhancement (if possible) and cost control, with profit (or the avoidance of a deficit) seen as a measure of managerial effectiveness.

Some people think that profit is a dirty word, associating profit making with "profiteering." In the normal course of economic activity, seeking profit is a thoroughly honorable activity. Without the promise of profit, there would be no private business firms, and all business activity would have to be organized by the government. History has shown us that this approach is not a superior alternative. Competition for profits among private business firms leads to the ongoing availability of high-quality goods and services at reasonable prices, to increasing productivity, and to continuing economic growth and well-being for the nation's people. Profit should be seen as the reward for enterprise, the reward for risking capital, and the reward for superior insight and judgment concerning market conditions. Profiteering, or "gouging" the consumer when supply is limited, is typically not a good business strategy (whether or not it is immoral), because consumer ill will is likely to hurt the firm in the longer term.

The scope of managerial economics is quite wide and extends into what some might call accounting, marketing, and finance. There are economic issues of importance to managers in each of these areas, and each decision made will be a better decision if the economics of the problem is clearly understood. Decision making in the areas of revenue enhancement and cost control are the two major concerns of the managerial economist. Chapters 1 and 2 are concerned with effective decision-making methods. Revenue enhancement requires a clear understanding of consumer behavior and of the reactions of consumers to changes in prices, advertising and promotion, and product quality. Estimation and forecasting of demand are of critical importance for the practicing manager. Chapters 3, 4, and 5 are concerned with these issues. Effective cost control requires a clear understanding of cost behavior, the components of cost, the relevant costs for a particular decision, techniques to estimate costs, and cost forecasting. Chapters 6, 7, and 8 are concerned with these issues.

Pricing the firm's products for optimal revenue enhancement requires a sound knowledge of the theory of markets, pricing under uncertainty, pricing new products, and pricing in markets where price quotes or bids are submitted without knowledge of rivals' prices. Chapters 9, 10, 11, and 12 address these issues. Advertising and promotion decisions intended to enhance revenue are analyzed in Chapter 13. The quality of the firm's products and the competitive strategy of the firm (typically involving a distinct tradeoff between low-cost production and revenue enhancement) is the topic of Chapter 14. Decisions to increase or reduce plant capacity in order to control costs or enhance revenues are covered in Chapter 15.

Thus managerial economics covers a range of topics of critical interest to the practicing manager. Although it is mainly economics, the managerial economics course is to some extent an interdisciplinary and integrative course in the business school curriculum, since it draws upon elements of accounting, finance, marketing, statistics, and quantitative methods for many of its concepts and analytical tools. The economic principles and methodologies of managerial economics are derived largely from *microeconomics*, the branch of economics that is concerned with the behavior of individual consumers, producers, and suppliers of capital, raw materials, labor, and services. In this book it is assumed that, while you may have taken courses in microeconomics, statistics, accounting, and so on, you are probably pretty rusty on the specifics. Thus each concept is developed from basic principles, presenting little difficulty for those who have no prior experience in these areas and allowing a quick review for those who have.

A review of basic calculus and analytical geometry (graphs), with extension to various optimization techniques, is provided in Appendix A at the end of this book. Your instructor may wish to cover this material at this point, or you may simply be asked to refer to it as needed throughout the course in order to better understand the material being covered.

Certainty versus Uncertainty

In simple microeconomics, economists use models of consumer and firm behavior that assume full information, or *certainty*, about the shape and location of demand curves, cost curves, and so on. That is, they presume to know exactly how much will be demanded at each price, and exactly what the cost of production will be at that output level. In the real world, however, business firms typically operate under conditions of incomplete information, or *uncertainty*, and must estimate or forecast the quantity demanded at any price and the costs, based on the limited information they have at hand or can obtain by conducting information-search activity.

Managerial economics has evolved out of microeconomics to provide guidance for business decision making in an environment of uncertainty. In managerial economics we nevertheless examine several microeconomic models that assume full information, as a prelude to the incorporation of uncertainty into the decision problem. In many cases we can effectively estimate the demand and cost data necessary to apply the microeconomic model, but in other cases the information search cost is prohibitive and we must look for an alternate solution procedure.

Positive versus Normative Economics

In economics, the distinction is made between those areas that are "positive" and those areas that are "normative." Positive economics is descriptive: it describes how economic agents or economic systems *do operate* within the economy or society. Normative economics, on the other hand, is prescriptive: it prescribes how economic agents or systems *should operate* in order to attain desired objectives.

Managerial economics is primarily normative, since it seeks to establish rules and principles to be applied in decision making to attain the desired objectives. But managerial economists must always be mindful of the actual practices in the business or institutional environment. For example, if firms choose their price level by applying a markup to their direct costs rather than by equating marginal revenue and marginal costs as implied by microeconomic principles, managerial economics should be concerned with determining the *optimal level* of the markup rather than attempting to persuade decision makers to use the marginalist principles. The approach taken in this textbook is to integrate business practice with economic principles. Thus, business practices, even if divergent from the strictures of normative microeconomics, are discussed in terms of the microeconomic principles. By reference to the microeconomic principles, the business practice can be evaluated in terms of its efficiency in attaining the desired objectives.

The Use of Models in Managerial Economics

■ *Definition:*   A *model* is defined as a simplified representation of reality. Models abstract from reality by ignoring the finer details which are not essential to the purpose at hand. They therefore concentrate on the major features and interrelationships existing among those features without obscuring the picture with less important details.[1]

Symbolic models use words and other symbols to represent reality, and they include descriptive speech, diagrams, and mathematical expressions. Descriptive speech usually simplifies or abstracts from reality, such as in the statement "A horse is a four-legged animal with a long brushy tail." Such a statement is a symbolic model of the members of the equine family, giving the general idea of what a horse is without mentioning the complexities involved in the physical or psychological makeup of a horse or the differences between a Thoroughbred and a Percheron. Diagrams similarly represent a situation of reality by means of lines, shading, and other features, and they abstract from the finer details. Mathematical models are usually further removed from reality and are used because reality is very difficult to depict visually or verbally or because it involves interrelationships that are extremely complex.

In this book we shall use mostly verbal and diagrammatic models to explain concepts and to analyze decision problems, although some mathematical models will be used, mainly in footnotes where these are appropriate. Diagrams (and mathematical expressions) are a very *efficient* means of representing reality; they are quicker to make and comprehend (once you understand them), and there is less ambiguity in

---

[1]This discussion relies on the excellent discussion in I. M. Grossack and D. D. Martin, *Managerial Economics* (Boston: Little, Brown & Company, 1973), pp. 5-10.

such models, as compared to descriptive speech. A diagram (or mathematical expression) states precisely and concisely the relationships assumed to exist among facts, observations, or variables. If these assumed relationships are inaccurate, the inaccuracies will be exposed by later testing the model against reality; and our model may be modified to reflect the feedback received from this testing.

The Purposes of Models.   There are three main purposes of models. First, models are used for *pedagogical* purposes: They are a useful device for teaching individuals about the operation of a complex system, since they allow the complexity of reality to be abstracted to a framework of manageable proportions. By excluding from consideration the minor details that do not affect the basic features or relationships that are at issue, the model allows us to deal with the central issues of the problem without the added complexity of relatively minor influences.

Second, models are used for *explanatory* purposes. They allow us to relate observation of objects and subsequent events in a logical fashion. The assumed link between the objects and the events may be tested for its authenticity by reference to real-world situations. If an observation that contradicts the link is made, then this link is refuted, while the link is supported (although not proved) by the repeated observation of supporting evidence. Models may aid the researcher in discovering relationships that exist between and among variables. If a high correlation is found to exist between two variables, the researcher may then attempt to discover the reasons for this relationship, construct a model incorporating the assumed relationship, and test for this relationship with future observations.

Third, models are used for *predictive* purposes. The predictive value of a model is usually based upon the ability of that model to explain the past behavior of a system, and it uses this past relationship to predict the future behavior. Suppose we have found that two events are causally related, such as low winter temperatures and high consumption of heating oil; we may predict increased consumption of heating oil the next time we observe temperatures falling. The model should specify the extent to which heating oil consumption is related to the temperature so that we may predict with some degree of accuracy the consumption of heating oil during a particular cold spell. This model will remain a good predictor as long as the relationships it represents stay constant. For example, if many households were to change to electric heating, the model would no longer represent reality as well as it did, and its predictions would be less accurate than before. A new or revised model would then be called for.

Friedman has argued that it is not necessary that the assumptions underlying a predictive model be valid and testable.[2] For example, a spurious model of the behavior of a sunflower, which twists around to follow the sun each day, is that the sunflower swivels at the base in response to a heat sensor located in the petals. This model,

---

[2]Milton Friedman, "The Methodology of Positive Economics," in his *Essays in Positive Economics* (Chicago: The University of Chicago Press, 1953). See also Lawrence A. Boland, "A Critique of Friedman's Critics," *Journal of Economic Literature*, 17 (June 1979), pp. 503-22.

although simplistic, would nevertheless allow us to use the direction which the sunflower is facing to predict the location of the sun on a partly cloudy day.

For predictive purposes such a model could be quite useful, although for pedagogical and explanatory purposes such a model has no virtue. Even for predictive purposes, however, we may be somewhat cautious and skeptical about the model's ability to predict accurately on its *next* test. If the relationship postulated is obviously false and the real determinants are unknown, the latter could change and our prediction would turn out to be wrong. For example, the installation of a bright light nearby might cause the sunflower to look at the light all day and to wrongly predict the location of the sun. Thus we need to be more cautious in using such a model to predict, since it may fail as a predictor at any time if the underlying (true) relationship changes without our knowledge or observation.

How Do We Evaluate Models?   It should be clear from the preceding discussion that a model must be evaluated with an eye to its purpose. If a model is intended for pedagogic purposes, then it must be evaluated on this basis. For example, simple models of oligopoly (an oligopoly is a small group of competing firms) do not perfectly explain the actual behavior of real firms in the real world, yet they do introduce students to the problems of mutual interdependence in business situations. Criticisms of such models as being too simplistic or unrealistic are thus unwarranted to the extent that such models best introduce these concepts to the student.

Models designed for explanatory purposes must be evaluated on the basis of how well they explain reality. If an observation is generated that is at variance with the model, then that model is refuted as an explanatory device. If there are two or more separate models that purport to explain a sequence of events, the best model is the one that most accurately depicts the important variables and relationships between and among these variables.

Models designed for predictive purposes must be judged by the accuracy of their predictions in subsequent tests. A predictive model is superior to an alternate predictive model if its predictions are more accurate more of the time. As the situation being depicted changes or evolves, we would expect existing models to become less accurate, since they must be modified to represent the evolving or changed situation.

In all cases when evaluating models, it is important to keep in mind that the model is a simplified representation of reality and is thus intended to represent the general features of reality rather than the specific features of a particular instance in reality. The model is an abstraction that loses some of the finer points and details; consequently, the predictive or explanatory power of a model will generally not be exact for any particular instance, because variables and relationships have been excluded from the model for the sake of simplicity or expedience. For example, a model may predict that firms will increase the size of their inventories of raw materials when the price of those raw-material components is seasonally reduced. If such a model abstracts from the cash-flow situation of the firm, it may imperfectly predict the behavior of certain firms that are facing a liquidity problem at that particular time.

In the following chapters you will notice the considerable use of graphical models to explain and analyze economic phenomena. Understanding graphs requires a basic knowledge of analytical geometry and calculus, and specifically, an understanding of such concepts as slopes, intercepts, linear functions, curvilinear functions, convexity, concavity, maximums, and minimums, among others. If your analytical geometry and basic calculus is rusty, I'd suggest you take half an hour to read about functions, graphs, and derivatives in Appendix A. Doing so may save many hours later, since graphs are an efficient tool for both understanding and expressing managerial economics. Someone once said "a picture is worth a thousand words." A graph is worth at least as much.

Jargon: The Use of Verbal Models for Efficient Communication.   The study of managerial economics involves a lot of specialized words, or *jargon*. Since the start of this book, you have been bombarded with "new" words, in the sense that these words convey a special meaning or connotation. Even words like *costs*, *revenues*, *profits*, *labor*, *capital*, and *risk* have special, more precise, meanings in the jargon of economics. Each of these jargon words and many others are formally defined at appropriate points in this book. We use a lot of jargon in managerial economics (as do all other disciplines of inquiry) to facilitate our discussion of complex phenomena.

Jargon words are really only verbal models of things or phenomena. They allow us to communicate with each other more efficiently, since they offer a concise and precise means of conveying the information we wish to convey. For example, "utility" is substantially quicker to say than is "the psychic satisfaction which a consumer expects to derive from the consumption of a product or service." And since jargon words are definitional terms, there should be no ambiguity about the precise meaning of these words. Thus communication between economists, between managers, or between you and me through the medium of these printed pages is facilitated and greatly enhanced by the use of jargon.

1.3 PRESENT-VALUE ANALYSIS AND THE FIRM'S TIME HORIZON

Many decisions involve a flow of revenues extending beyond the present period. In choosing between or among various alternatives, it is important to distinguish between revenues that are received immediately and those that are received at some later date. A dollar received today is worth more than a dollar received next year, which in turn is worth more than a dollar received the following year. The reason for this is that a dollar held today may be deposited in a bank or other interest-earning security, and at the end of one year it will be worth the original dollar plus the interest earned on that dollar. Hence, if the interest rate is, say, 10 percent, a dollar today will be worth $1.10 one year from today. Looking at this from the reverse aspect, a dollar earned one year from today is worth less than a dollar that is held today. Thus the future earnings must be discounted by the interest rate they could have earned had they been held today.

In this section we introduce and examine the concept of the present value of cash flows that occur beyond the present period. Both revenues to be received and costs to be incurred in the future must be reduced to present-value terms for proper evaluation of decision alternatives. Net present value is found by subtracting the present value of costs from the present value of revenues and can be expressed alternatively as the present value of profits. The major convention used for discounting future cash flows to their present value is to treat all flows as if they arrive, or are incurred, at the end of year one, year two, and so on. We look also at other cash flow patterns, such as the receipt of funds as an annuity, or on a daily, weekly, or monthly basis.

Present Value and Future Value

■ *Definition:*   The *future value* in one year of $1.00 presently held is equal to $1.00 plus the annual rate of interest times $1.00. That is,

$$FV = PV(1 + r)$$

where FV denotes future value, PV denotes present value, and r is the rate of interest available.

Example: If the interest rate is 10 percent, $r = 0.1$, the future value of a principal sum of $1.00 is

$$FV = \$1(1 + 0.1)$$
$$= \$1.10$$

Now suppose we could leave this money in the bank for a second year, also at 10 percent interest. The future value would be

$$FV = \$1.10(1 + 0.1)$$
$$= \$1.21$$

If a third year were possible, we would find

$$FV = \$1.21(1 + 0.1)$$
$$= \$1.331$$

and so on for future years. Note that the principal sum each year was simply multiplied by $(1 + r)$. In effect, the dollar was multiplied by $(1 + r)$ initially, then the resulting product was multiplied by $(1 + r)$, and then the product of that was multiplied by $(1 + r)$ again.

That is, for the three-year deposit

$$FV = PV(1 + r)(1 + r)(1 + r)$$

which simplifies to

$$FV = PV(1 + r)^3$$

Generalizing for any number of periods into the future, we have

$$FV = PV(1 + r)^n \qquad (1\text{-}1)$$

where *n* represents the number of years into the future that the principal sum plus interest will be returned.

Example: Suppose we lend $2,500 for a period of five years at 8.5 percent interest. What is the future value of the presently held $2,500?

$$
\begin{aligned}
FV &= \$2,500\,(1 + 0.085)^5 \\
&= 2,500\,(1.085)^5 \\
&= 2,500\,(1.50366) \\
&= \$3,759.15
\end{aligned}
$$

Thus $2,500 saved at 8.5 percent for five years will return the saver $3,759.15 at the end of the five-year period.

Note: The above process is known as *compounding* the principal sum plus annual interest over the period of the loan. It tells us that $2,500 held today is worth $3,759.15 in five years if we can obtain 8.5 percent interest compounded annually. The *compound factor* which we used to multiply the $2,500 to obtain $3,759.15 was 1.50366. This compound factor effectively says that $1.00 today is worth $1.50366 in five years if the interest rate is 8.5 percent.

Now let's do it in the reverse direction. The *present* value of a *future* value can be found by manipulating equation (1-1). Dividing both sides by $(1 + r)^n$ we find

$$PV = \frac{FV}{(1 + r)^n} \qquad (1\text{-}2)$$

Example: Although we already know the answer, let's find the present value of $3,759.15 available in five years during which the available interest rate is 8.5 percent.

$$
\begin{aligned}
PV &= \frac{\$3,759.15}{(1 + 0.085)^5} \\
&= \frac{3,759.15}{1.50366} \\
&= \$2,500.00
\end{aligned}
$$

What we have just done is to *discount* \$3,759.15 (future value) back to present-value terms and demonstrate that the discounting process is simply the inverse of the compounding process. Whereas future value equals present value multiplied by the compound factor, present value equals future value divided by the compound factor. Alternatively, let us call the reciprocal of the compound factor the *discount factor* and say equivalently that present value is equal to future value multiplied by the discount factor. The reciprocal of 1.50366 is 0.66504, which is the discount factor when the interest rate is 8.5 percent. (Note that \$3,759.15 multiplied by 0.66504 equals \$2,500.00.)

■ *Definition:*   The *present value* of a sum of money to be received or disbursed in the future is the value of that future sum when discounted at the appropriate discount rate. Alternatively, it is the sum which would grow to that future sum when compounded at the appropriate interest rate.

The decision maker must choose the rate of discount quite carefully, since use of the "wrong" discount factor could cause a poor decision to be made in cases where the time profiles of future profit streams associated with alternative decisions differ markedly. The appropriate discount rate is the "opportunity" discount rate.

The Opportunity Discount Rate

■ *Definition:*   The *opportunity discount rate* is the rate of interest or return the decision maker could earn in his or her best alternative use of the funds at the same level of risk. Note that we require that the alternative use of the funds must involve the same level of risk or uncertainty, since many other alternative uses of the funds will be more or less risky or uncertain and are thus not strictly comparable with the present proposal.

Example: Suppose that a firm intends to invest \$10,000 in an expansion of its facilities but might otherwise invest the funds in a bond issue, which is considered to have similar risk and which would pay 12 percent interest compounded annually. The opportunity discount rate to be used when evaluating the future returns from the project under consideration is, therefore, 12 percent.

How do we ascertain whether the alternative investment or savings opportunities have similar risk? This issue is discussed in detail in Chapter 2. It is enough to say here that the risk in any decision lies in the dispersion of possible outcomes. Finding the equal-risk, best-alternative use of the funds, therefore, involves finding the alternative savings and investment opportunities which have the same or very similar dispersions of possible outcomes, and noting the highest rate of interest or rate of return on investment available within this subset. If the project or decision is risk free, the appropriate comparison would be treasury bills or guaranteed bank deposits, which are also risk free. More likely, the project or decision does involve risk, and we must look around for other investment opportunities that involve similar risk and note the highest rate available among these investments in the same risk class. That rate is the opportunity discount rate to be used when discounting future cash flows associated with the decision under consideration.

It is important to see that the higher is the opportunity rate of interest (or opportunity discount rate), and the longer the time period, the lower is the discount factor. In Table 1–1 we show the discount factors associated with several different opportunity interest rates and several different periods of time. Each discount factor is calculated using the expression $1/(1 + r)^n$, and you can calculate the discount factor appropriate to any other opportunity interest rate and time period using the same expression. Note that the discount factor is inversely related both to the length of the time period and the opportunity interest rate. Discount factors effectively tell you the value of $1.00 at the end of a given period for any opportunity interest rate. Thus, at 10 percent opportunity interest rate, $1.00 is worth $0.9091 if received after one year; $0.6209 if received after five years; and $0.0923 if received after twenty-five years. Similarly, with a 20 percent opportunity interest rate, $1.00 is worth only $0.4019 if received after five years; $0.0649 after fifteen years; and only a fraction over one cent if received after twenty-five years!

Example: Which would you prefer, $5,000 now, $20,000 in ten years, or $100,000 in 25 years? If the opportunity discount rate is 10 percent, the present values of these alternatives are $5,000, $7,710, and $9,230, respectively. Thus, you would prefer to take $100,000 in 25 years over the other opportunities. But note that if the opportunity discount rate is 15 percent, the present values become $5,000, $4,944, and $3,040, respectively. In the latter case it is preferable to take the $5,000 now. This example demonstrates the powerful effect that higher opportunity discount rates have upon future cash flows, and it shows that the selection of the appropriate discount rate is critical for the effective evaluation of decision alternatives.

TABLE 1–1.   Discount Factors for Several Different Opportunity Interest Rates and Time Periods

Time Period (years hence)	OPPORTUNITY INTEREST RATE (%)			
	5	10	15	20
0	1.0000	1.0000	1.0000	1.0000
1	0.9524	0.9091	0.8696	0.8333
2	0.9070	0.8264	0.7561	0.6944
3	0.8638	0.7513	0.6575	0.5787
4	0.8227	0.6830	0.5718	0.4823
5	0.7835	0.6209	0.4972	0.4019
10	0.6139	0.3855	0.2472	0.1615
15	0.4810	0.2394	0.1229	0.0649
20	0.3769	0.1486	0.0611	0.0261
25	0.2953	0.0923	0.0304	0.0105

Table 1-1 is excerpted from Table B-1 in Appendix B of this book. The table in the appendix shows the discount factors for all opportunity interest rates from 1 percent to 28 percent over periods from one year to 25 years. This table is provided for your convenience, although with the aid of a calculator you can find the discount factor for any opportunity interest rate over any period of time using the formula supplied by equation (1-2). For discount rates involving fractions, such as 16.5 percent, you will have to use your calculator, although an approximation can be obtained by a simple interpolation between the discount factors given in the appendix.[3]

Net-Present-Value Analysis

When a decision involves both revenues and costs in future periods, we net the costs of each year against the revenues of each year to find the present value of the net revenues, or net costs. Since profits are the excess of revenues over costs, and losses are the excess of costs over revenues, this procedure amounts to finding the present value of the profits (or losses) associated with the decision in future years.

Using symbols, we can write

$$NPV = C_o - \sum_{i=1}^{n} \frac{FV_i}{(1 + r)^i}$$

where *NPV* is the net present value, C_o is the initial (present period) cost of the project or decision, and the FV_i are the future net revenues (profits) to be received in each of the *n* years over which cash flows are expected. The Σ (sigma) connotes the sum of the discounted future values from $i = 1$ (the first year) to $i = n$ (the last year).

Example: Suppose we are considering the installation of equipment to manufacture a gift item, and we anticipate the cost and revenue streams shown in Table 1-2. The cost stream includes the initial capital cost and the annual operating costs of the equipment and associated labor and material costs. The revenue stream shows the revenue expected from sales of the product and includes the salvage value of the equipment in the last year, when we assume the market will become saturated and production will cease. Since there is some uncertainty about the future revenue and cost streams, we must identify the opportunity discount rate. Suppose we investigate and conclude that it is 18 percent. We can then calculate the present value of the profits from the project as shown in Table 1-2 using the discount factors from Table B-1 in Appendix B.

Note that this example includes year zero, or the present period, in the calculations, since the capital expenditure on the equipment ($744,850) must be made in the

---

[3]Interpolation is the imputing of values between two points in a data set. We stress that this interpolation is approximate because it is a linear approximation of a curvilinear relationship. Considerations of accuracy aside, for more complex interpolations (such as for 16.335 percent), you would most likely use a calculator and would find it more simple to compute the exact discount factor using equation (1-2).

TABLE 1-2. Net Present Value of a Proposed Decision

Year	Revenue Stream ($000)	Cost Stream ($000)	Profit (Loss) Stream ($000)	Discount Factor (@ 18%)	Present Value ($000)
0	–	744.85	(744.85)	1.0000	−744.85
1	400.00	224.62	175.38	0.8475	148.63
2	1,085.00	648.22	436.78	0.7182	313.70
3	872.50	456.98	415.52	0.6086	252.89
4	220.00	131.43	88.57	0.5158	45.68
5	380.00	58.35	321.65	0.4371	140.59
				Net Present Value	156.64

present period. Thus, the appropriate discount factor is one, since this sum is *already* in present-value terms. For each year in which there are both revenues and costs, the net revenues (profits) are discounted by the appropriate discount factor to find the present value of each year's profits from the proposed decision. Adding up the present values of each year's profits or losses results in a net present value of the decision of $156,640. If this is the best alternative open to the firm, we would certainly advise them to go ahead with it, since it represents $156,640 more than the firm could earn if it invested the funds elsewhere at the opportunity interest rate.[4]

Annuities. A simplification can be applied if the stream of cash flows is regular and uniform for a number of periods. Such a uniform cash flow over several consecutive time periods is known as an annuity. You are probably aware of the concept of annuities. Retirement savings can be used to purchase an annuity which pays the owner a given sum of money every year or every month for a prescribed number of years. Any regular and uniform stream of payments can be treated like an annuity. For example, a firm expecting to earn $50,000 each year for five years as the result of a particular decision, is, in effect, expecting an annuity.

---

[4]If the NPV of a project is positive, it implies that the project yields a higher *internal rate of return* (IRR) than the opportunity rate at which its profit stream was discounted. The IRR is the discount rate that would reduce the net present value of the project to zero. Alternatively, it is the discount rate that would reduce the future stream of profits to equality (in present-value terms) with the initial cost of the project. That is,

$$C_o - \sum_{i=1}^{n} \frac{FV_i}{(1 + k)^i} = 0$$

where k is the internal rate of return. Most calculators with preprogrammed financial functions can quickly calculate the IRR, as well as the NPV, after the data have been entered. A method for calculating IRR is shown in Chapter 15. The IRR of the above project is 26.89 percent. A firm will wish to compare the IRR of potential projects with its cost of capital (the interest rate at which it borrows funds). Note, however, that if the NPV is positive, the IRR will exceed the opportunity discount rate, which in turn will be equal to or higher than the firm's cost of capital.

It can be shown that the present value of an annuity can be calculated as the amount to be received in each period times the sum of the discount factors for each period. That is,

$$PV = \frac{FV_1}{(1 + r)^1} + \frac{FV_2}{(1 + r)^2} + \frac{FV_3}{(1 + r)^3} + \cdots + \frac{FV_n}{(1 + r)^n} = \sum_{i=1}^{n} \frac{FV_i}{(1 + r)^i}$$

$$= FV \sum_{i=1}^{n} \frac{1}{(1 + r)^i}$$

since all the *FV*s have the same value.

Example: A firm expects to receive $50,000 at the end of each year for five years as a result of a decision it is about to implement. What is the present value of this annuity if the firm's opportunity discount rate is 16 percent? In Table 1-3 we find the present value of the revenue stream of $50,000 each year for five years, given 16 percent discount factors. The sum of the present values of the annual payments is $163,720. Now, notice that the sum of the discount factors is 3.2744 and that this figure multiplied by $50,000 equals $163,720. The sum of the discount factors is known as the *present-value factor* for an annuity over that period of time.

Table B-2 in Appendix B shows the present-value factors for annuities up to periods of 25 years and for opportunity interest rates of 1 percent through 28 percent. It is certainly much quicker to find the present value of an annuity in a single calculation rather than to find the present value of each annual cash flow and then add these to find the present value of the revenue stream. Referring to Table B-2, we find the present-value factors for a 16 percent discount rate over five years to be 3.2743. (This is the more accurate figure, since the sum of the discount factors used above includes a discrepancy caused by rounding off at the fourth decimal place.) Thus, the present value of the annuity is 3.2743 times the periodic payment of $50,000, or $163,715.

Discounting Using Daily Interest Rates. Most of the cash flows paid and received by firms do not occur in lump sums at the end of the year, but instead occur at more frequent intervals. Cash receipts from customers may be received daily, wages may be

TABLE 1-3. Present Value of an Annuity

Year	Revenue Stream $	Discount Factor (@ 16%)	Present Value $
1	50,000	0.8621	43,105
2	50,000	0.7432	37,160
3	50,000	0.6407	32,035
4	50,000	0.5523	27,615
5	50,000	0.4761	23,805
	Totals	3.2744	$163,720

paid weekly, and management salary, payments to suppliers, and other expenses usually occur monthly. It makes a significant difference to the present value if the payments and receipts are received and disbursed frequently during the year, rather than being delayed until year end. Money received during the year can be put in the bank and will earn interest between now and the end of the year. Daily-interest savings and checking accounts are now common, and our analysis should reflect the greater present value of a sum if it is received during the year as a stream of payments rather than being received at the end of the year as a lump sum. The end-of-year convention is a simplification that is often quite appropriate. In many cases, the cash flows do occur annually in lump sums. For example, the firm's cash flow may be highly seasonal (such as around Christmas), and the end-of-year assumption is a tolerable approximation. In other cases, however, the cash flows of a decision are expected to occur more or less evenly throughout the year, and it is more appropriate to use discount factors based on daily interest rates.

The present-value formula is easily modified to reflect higher frequencies of receipt or disbursement of funds. Let m be the number of times that the payment period fits into the year, that is $m = 365/d$ where d is the number of days in the payment period. For example, $m = 365$ for daily cash flows, $m = 52$ for weekly cash flows, $m = 12$ for monthly cash flows, and $m = 4$ for quarterly cash flows. The modified present-value formula would then read

$$PV = \frac{FV/m}{(1 + r/m)^{1m}} + \frac{FV/m}{(1 + r/m)^{2m}} + \frac{FV/m}{(1 + r/m)^{3m}} + \cdots + \frac{FV/m}{(1 + r/m)^{nm}}$$

$$= \sum_{i=1}^{n} \frac{FV/m}{(1 + r/m)^{im}}$$

where FV again represents the future sum received during the year but is received in a series of payments, each equal to FV/m. In effect, the firm receives an annuity of $1/m$ of the FV value every d days during the year. For the daily interest case, and assuming $FV = \$1$, that dollar is presumed to arrive in 365 equal instalments, each equal to $1/365$ of one dollar. Note that the above expression for PV is also the formula for the daily interest rate discount factor when $FV = \$1$.

Discount factors based on daily interest rates are provided in Table B-3 in Appendix B. We can see the impact of using daily interest discount factors if we redo the NPV calculations of the cashflows shown in Table 1-2, now assuming that the cash flows occur on a more or less daily basis throughout each year.[5] The results are shown in Table 1-4.

---

[5]Strictly speaking, the salvage value of the equipment should have been separated from the sales revenues of year five, since the revenue from salvage is doubtless received in lump sum at the end of year five. It should, therefore, be discounted using the end-of-year discount factors, while the sales revenue received during year five is more appropriately discounted using the continuous-cash-flow convention. Our purpose here was simply to demonstrate that the difference in the cash-flow conventions can make a substantial difference in the present-value calculation.

TABLE 1-4. **Net Present Value of Proposed Decision Using Daily Discount Factors**

Year	Profit Stream ($000)	Discount Factor (@ 18%)	Present Value ($000)
0	-744.85	1.0000	-744.850
1	175.38	0.9150	160.473
2	436.78	0.7643	333.831
3	415.52	0.6384	265.268
4	88.57	0.5333	47.234
5	321.65	0.4454	143.263
		Net Present Value	205.219

Note that each discount factor is slightly higher than the year-end discount factor for the same year and opportunity rate, and it reflects the greater value of a dollar received as a stream of payments during the year rather than as a simple payment at the end of the year. Consequently, the NPV is higher (by $48,579) when we account for the daily cash flow pattern rather than assuming year-end payments and receipts. This could be a critical consideration in deciding between two decision alternatives. If they both have the same annual cash flows, but one series of cash flows occurs at the end of each year, while the other series occurs more or less evenly throughout each year, then the latter will be the preferred option. NPV analysis should use the discount factors that are appropriate for the cash flow pattern expected. End-of-year discount factors will be appropriate for some decision alternatives, whereas daily discount factors will be more appropriate for others.

The Firm's Planning Period and Time Horizon

■ *Definition:* The firm's *planning period* is the period of time over which the firm takes into account the cost and revenue implications of its decisions. The firm's *time horizon* is the point in the future at which the firm no longer considers the cost and revenue implications of its decisions. The time horizon is, therefore, the end of the firm's planning period.

Example: Suppose a firm is considering investing in a new building and calculates the present value of the initial cost and future maintenance costs for the next fifteen years and sets against these costs the present value of the revenues it expects to receive from the building over the same fifteen-year period. This firm's planning period is, thus, fifteen years, since it has taken into account the cost and revenue implications of its decision to buy the new building only up to the fifteenth year into the future. The sixteenth and subsequent years' costs and revenues are ignored. The firm, in effect, considers them to occur so far into the future that they are insignificant to the decision.

A firm's time horizon, and, thus, the length of its plan: vary among firms for various reasons. Firms involved in intense day-to-day survival are less likely to worry about the longer-ter. implications of their decisions. Immediate or short-term costs and i. given full weight in their decision making, to the complete exclusion of the . profit implications of their actions. Conversely, a firm that is well establish. secure in its market, without the constant pressure of day-to-day price competit. can afford the luxury of taking into consideration the future profit implications of its current decisions.

Another reason for differing planning periods among firms is the motivation of the manager. A manager who expects to retire in six months, or who is actively seeking a promotion within the year, may be expected to prefer actions which have greater short-term profit implications over those that promise greater longer-term profits. Conversely, managers who wish to make a career out of their position, or who prefer longer-term stability of employment and salary income, may be expected to take the longer view, preferring to take actions which promise greater profits over an extended planning period.

Finally, the firm's planning period may be inversely related to the general level of interest rates, because the present value of future profits declines as the opportunity discount rate increases. This presumes that the decision maker decides to suspend the search for information (concerning future costs and revenues associated with a particular decision) when the present value of $1.00 earned at the time horizon falls below a predetermined level.

Example: A firm that places its time horizon at fifteen years when the opportunity discount rate is 10 percent may shorten its planning period to ten years when the opportunity discount rate is 15 percent, since the present value of $1.00 falls below $0.25 at the time horizon in each case. (You may confirm this in Table 1–1.)

The reason a firm may adopt a cutoff rule like this is related to the cost of obtaining information, or *search costs*, which we examine in Chapter 2. It will suffice to say here that if the firm expects to pay $0.25 now to find out that it will earn $1.00 in ten years, it is profit maximizing to suspend search activity at that point if the present value of the $1.00 is less than $0.25.

The firm's time horizon will occur either within the present period or in some future period. If it occurs in the present period, we can treat all cash flows at face value, since they will already be in present-value terms. If the firm's time horizon lies beyond the present period, we must discount future cash flows back to present-value terms in order to compare them properly with present-period costs and revenues.

How long is the present period? Strictly it should be very short indeed, and should end before the value of a dollar to be received in the present period depreciates at all. Note that $1,000 to be received next week is worth fractionally less than $1,000 to be received today, because a lesser sum could grow to $1,000 (in a daily-interest savings account) by next week. Realistically, however, there is a cost involved in converting every cash flow into its present-value equivalent, and it is not worth doing for most cash flows that will arrive or will be disbursed in the near future. For our purposes it is probably sufficient to treat cash flows that occur within the coming year in nominal terms, ignoring the fact that doing so will slightly overstate their present value. But when the dollar amounts are very large and the interest rates are relatively high, we should certainly discount the nominal values to present values for cash flows occurring within the present year.[6]

1.4 EXPECTED-VALUE ANALYSIS OF UNCERTAIN OUTCOMES

In this section we consider risk and uncertainty, and we describe the method for evaluating decision alternatives when the decision maker faces risk and uncertainty. We first clarify what is meant by risk and uncertainty, and note that the phrase implies a probability distribution of outcomes related to each decision alternative. Expected-present-value (EPV) analysis is then introduced to summarize each probability distribution of outcomes into a single number such that the decision alternatives may be compared and an optimal decision may be selected.

Certainty, Risk, and Uncertainty

The state of information under which a decision is made has important implications for the predictability of the outcome of that decision. If there is *full* information, the outcome of a decision will be foreseen clearly and unambiguously. In this situation (of certainty) the firm can accurately predict the outcome of each of its decisions. When there is less than full information, however, the decision maker may foresee several potential outcomes to a decision and, therefore, will be unable to predict consistently which outcome will actually occur. In this case we say that the individual or firm is operating under conditions of risk and uncertainty.

■ *Definition:* Certainty exists if the outcome of a decision is known in advance without a shadow of a doubt. Under conditions of certainty, a decision leads to a single possible outcome, which is perfectly foreseen. *Risk and uncertainty* are involved when a decision leads to one of several possible outcomes but the exact outcome is not known in

---

[6]To discount a cash flow to be received within the current year, use the same formula

$$PV = \frac{FV}{(1 + r)^n}$$

where n is the number of years as before, except that it can take fractional values. For example, a lump-sum payment due in six months would have $n = 0.5$, and a lump-sum payment due in two and a half years would have $n = 2.5$.

advance. Instead, there will be a probability distribution of possible outcomes, which the decision maker must identify.[7]

The Probability Distributions of Possible Outcomes

Risk is involved when one flips a coin, throws dice, or plays a hand of poker. The probability of flipping a coin and having it land "heads" is $1/2$, since there are only two possible outcomes (ruling out the coin landing on its edge), and each is equally likely to occur, given an unbiased coin. Similarly, when one throws two dice, the probability that they will turn up "snake eyes," or any other pair of numbers, is $1/6 \times 1/6 = 1/36$. The probability of drawing a "royal flush" in poker, or any other combination of cards, can likewise be calculated.

In each of the illustrations above the probability of each outcome is known *a priori*. That is, on the basis of known mathematical and physical principles, we can deduce—prior to the act—the proportion of the total number of outcomes that should be attained by each particular outcome. We can confirm this calculation by undertaking a number of trials. Although "heads" might appear three or even four times out of the first four tosses of a coin, given a sufficiently large number of trials, the proportions will converge upon $1/2$ for each of the two possible outcomes.

A second class of risk situations is that in which probabilities are assigned *a posteriori*, or on the basis of past experience under similar circumstances. The business of insurance is based upon this type of risk situation. The possible outcomes are known: for example, a particular vehicle will or will not be involved in an accident. Insurance companies keep extensive data on previous policies and claims and other pertinent data; from these they compile actuarial tables, which show the relative incidence of the various outcomes in past situations or trials. On the presumption that a particular driver and vehicle are similar in all important respects to those of the data base, the companies are able to form an expectation (or assign a probability) of the chances of that particular driver having an accident in that vehicle.

In perhaps the great majority of decison-making problems, the precise nature of the potential outcomes cannot be foreseen clearly in advance. Instead the decision maker must estimate a range of potential outcomes. Similarly, there is typically no data bank of past decisions that are sufficiently similar to the one at hand to allow the assignment of probabilities based on past observations. In these situations, the decision maker must assign the probabilities subjectively, based on experience, intuition and judgment.

---

[7]Many economists, following Frank Knight, *Risk, Uncertainty and Profit* (Boston: Houghton Mifflin, 1921), distinguish between risk and uncertainty. Under risk, the probabilities of each outcome can be assigned on an objective basis, based on either *a priori* or *a posteriori* data. Under uncertainty, no such data are available, and the probabilities must be assigned on a subjective basis. In this book we shall use the terms risk and uncertainty interchangeably.

The Expected Value of a Decision

Under conditions of risk and uncertainty the decision maker looks at each of the potential solutions to a problem and, for each of these possible decisions, foresees a probability distribution of outcomes. That is, several different levels of profit (or loss) are perceived as possible, and each of these is assigned a probability of occurring. How does the decision maker summarize all this data so that they can be compared with other potential solutions to the same problem?

■ *Definition:* The *expected value* of an outcome is the value of that outcome multiplied by the probability of that outcome occurring. Since several outcomes are possible under risk and uncertainty, the expected value of a decision is the sum of the expected values of all the possible outcomes that may follow the decision.[8] The expected value of a decision thus allows the probability distribution of possible outcomes to be characterized by a single number, which can then be compared with the expected values of other potential solutions to the problem.

Example: In Table 1-5 we show a hypothetical probability distribution of profit levels that are expected to be possible outcomes of a decision to invest in a particular investment project. The first column shows the possible profit levels, ranging from a loss of $50,000 to a profit of $250,000. The second column shows the probability of each profit (or loss) level, as assigned by the decision maker. Thus there is considered

TABLE 1-5. The Expected Value of a Decision

Possible Profit Levels ($)	Probability of Each Occurring (P)	Expected Value of Each Profit Level ($)
−50,000	0.05	−2,500
0	0.10	0
50,000	0.15	7,500
100,000	0.20	20,000
150,000	0.25	37,500
200,000	0.15	30,000
250,000	0.10	25,000
Totals	1.00	117,500

[8]Formally, we define the expected value of a decision as

$$EV = \sum_{i=1}^{n} R_i P_i$$

where Σ connotes "the sum of"; R_i is the return of the ith outcome; $i = 1, 2, 3, \ldots, n$ identifies each separate possible outcome; n is the total number of possible outcomes; and P_i the probability of the ith outcome occurring.

to be a 5 percent chance of losing $50,000, a 10 percent chance of only breaking even, a 15 percent chance of making $50,000 in profits, and so on. Note that the probabilities must total 1.00, since all possible outcomes are included and these outcomes are mutually exclusive.

The third column in the table is the product of columns one and two. The expected value of each possible outcome is equal to the possible profit (or loss) associated with each outcome, multiplied by the probability of that outcome's occurring. The sum of the expected values of all the possible outcomes is $117,500. This is the expected value of the decision to invest in this particular investment opportunity. Note that the *actual* outcome will not be known until after the investment is made and all returns are in. The expected value is an *a priori* measure of the decision that allows the probability distribution of outcomes to be summarized as a single number. This expected value is actually a weighted average of the possible profit levels, with each possible outcome weighted by the probability that it will occur.[9]

Thus, if a firm is faced with a decision problem, the decision maker(s) should investigate all potential solutions to that problem and evaluate the probability distribution of each potential solution in terms of its expected value. The firm should choose that alternative which promises the highest expected value, subject to adjustment for risk, which we examine in Chapter 2.

1.5 THE OBJECTIVES OF THE FIRM

Any decision problem should be approached with the firm's objectives clearly in mind, so that the actual decision taken will best serve the firm's objectives. What are the objectives of the business firm? Is it profit maximization, or would the firm sacrifice some current profitability for an enlarged market share? Does the firm wish to maximize its rate of growth, or is management content to attain profit, market share, and growth targets, while maximizing their own benefits and the quality of their lives?

At this point we shall confine ourselves to the assumption, which is well supported in the literature and the related disciplines of finance and accounting, that the decision maker's objective is to maximize the net worth of the firm over its time horizon, subject to considerations of risk and uncertainty. The other objectives mentioned above will be incorporated into the analysis and reconciled with this objective in later chapters.[10]

---

[9]The actual outcome might be, for example, $67,964.45, a value that does not appear as a possible outcome in the table. The potential outcomes each represent a range of outcomes, and this (actual) outcome falls within one of those ranges. In this case the potential outcome of $50,000 represents the range from $25,000 to $75,000, in which the actual outcome fell. The probability distribution is continuous in reality, but we have "summarized" it using, in this case, seven points along the continuum.

[10]We shall see in Chapter 9 that sales, or market share maximization, growth maximization, managerial utility maximization, and even "satisficing," can be regarded as real-world approximations for the maximization of the expected present value of profits.

■ *Definition:* *Net worth*, also known as *owner's equity*, is measured as the excess of the firm's assets (cash, securities, land, buildings, plant and equipment, and so on) over its liabilities (amounts owed to creditors, short-term and long-term loans, and so on). There are three groups of items on the firm's balance sheet, namely, assets, liabilities, and owner's equity. Assets are equal to the sum of the other two. Thus, maximization of the net worth of the firm requires maximizing the difference between assets and liabilities, or, what amounts to the same thing, maximizing the owner's equity.

The preceding simple statement of the firm's objective function implies slightly different decision criteria for each of the different scenarios in which a firm may find itself. In the foregoing we have established two separate dichotomies, one referring to the time horizon (the present period versus future periods) and the second referring to the state of information (certainty versus uncertainty). There are four combinations of these circumstances, and we now proceed to specify the decision criterion which will allow the maximization of net worth under each scenario.

The Present Period with Certainty

The most simple scenario is that in which the firm's time horizon falls inside the present period and the firm enjoys full information, or certainty, about the outcome of all decisions. Thus there is no need for either present-value analysis or expected-value analysis. Rather, the firm may maximize its net worth by the pursuit of short-run profit maximization. Profits are calculated as the excess of total revenues over total costs. Total revenues add to asset accounts, such as cash and debtors, while total costs represent outflows of funds for materials, labor, and other services, and, if these costs remain unpaid, there will be an increase in the liabilities accounts for various creditors. When profits are made, assets increase more than liabilities, to the extent of the profits made. Owner's equity, or net worth, therefore, rises by the same amount. Maximization of profits thus ensures the maximization of the firm's net worth.

Rule: For the firm operating in an environment of *certainty* and with its time horizon falling within the *present period*, short-run profit maximization is the appropriate decision criterion to maximize the firm's net worth.

Future Periods with Certainty

If the firm has full information concerning revenues and costs but its time horizon falls in a future period, the firm must use present-value analysis in order to evaluate its decision alternatives properly. A decision that causes immediate profits and no future profits can be compared with another decision promising a stream of future profits only if both are expressed in present-value terms. The firm wishing to maximize its net worth in present-value terms, or its *net present worth*, should always choose the decision alternative that promises the greater net present value of profits.

Rule: For the firm operating in an environment of *certainty*, and with its time horizon falling in a *future period*, maximization of the present value of (present and future) profits is the appropriate decision criterion to maximize the firm's net (present) worth.

The Present Period with Uncertainty

Uncertainty means that decisions have more than one possible outcome that is foreseen, and that decisions must be made on the basis of the prior probability distribution of outcomes. Expected-value analysis is, therefore, required to summarize the probability distributions of the various decision alternatives and to allow the selection of that decision which will maximize the expected value of the firm's profits. If the firm always chooses the alternative that offers the greatest expected value of profits, it will sometimes receive less than the expected value and sometimes more, but after many decisions the firm will find its actual total profits to be greater than they would have been by following any other strategy. If the probability distributions are accurately estimated, the law of averages will ensure that after many decisions the probability distributions will be validated by the actual outcomes.

Rule: For the firm operating in an environment of *uncertainty*, and with its time horizon falling within the *present period*, maximization of the expected value of (short-run) profits is the appropriate decision criterion to maximize the firm's net (expected) worth.

Future Periods with Uncertainty

In the final scenario, the firm's time horizon falls in a future period, and the firm does not have full information about its potential costs and revenues. This is the predominant situation in the real world. Most firms consider the future cost and revenue implications of their decisions, and they face risk and uncertainty as to the possible outcomes of their decisions. Thus these firms should use both present-value analysis and expected-value analysis. First, all future cash flows must be discounted back to present-value terms, using the appropriate opportunity discount factor and the appropriate cash-flow convention. Then, the present value of each of the possible outcomes is weighted by the probability of its occurring, and the sum of these is the expected present value (EPV) of the decision. The decision maker then selects the decision alternative that promises the highest EPV of profits. (In Chapter 2 we shall proceed through several examples of EPV analysis with the aid of "decision trees.")

Rule: For the firm operating in an environment of *uncertainty* and with its time horizon falling in a *future period*, maximization of the expected present value of profits is the appropriate decision criterion to maximize the firm's net (expected present) worth.

uction

Thus we have seen that the decision criterion for pursuit of the maximization of firm's net worth is modified as the firm's time horizon moves from the present *iod* to a future period and as the state of information changes from certainty to uncertainty. These criteria are summarized in Table 1-6.

The Principal-Agent Problem

We have stated that the objective of the firm is to maximize its net worth in expected-present-value terms. By "the firm" we really mean the owners or shareholders of the firm, whose interests presumably lie in the maximization of their personal net worth. However, the owners of the firm are typically not the decision makers. The shareholders are most often excluded from the day-to-day process of making decisions, having delegated the authority to trained managers whose job is to make these decisions. As absentee owners, shareholders are unable to observe perfectly whether or not the managers' decisions are always consistent with the shareholders' objectives. Consequently, managers may pursue their own personal objectives, to some degree, rather than assiduously seek the maximization of net worth. Only in the case of owner-managed firms can we expect the objectives of the owners and the managers to coincide perfectly.

This difficulty has been called the principal-agent problem.[11] The manager is an agent of the shareholders (the principals), making decisions on their behalf. Although the principals may monitor the agents' actions, monitoring involves information-search costs, and it will not be taken to the ultimate degree, with the result that there remains an asymmetry of information—the actions of the agent are not perfectly ob-

TABLE 1-6. The Decision Criteria for Maximization of the Firm's Net Worth under Four Scenarios

The State of Information	THE FIRM'S TIME HORIZON FALLS WITHIN THE	
	Present Period	Future Period
Certainty	Maximize short-run profits	Maximize present value of profits
Uncertainty	Maximize expected value of profits	Maximize expected present value of profits

[11]See A. A. Alchian and H. Demsetz, "Production, Information Costs, and Economic Organization," *American Economic Review*, 57 (December 1972), pp. 777-95; M. C. Jensen and W. H. Meckling, "Theory of the Firm: Managerial Behavior, Agency Costs, and Ownership Structure," *Journal of Financial Economics*, 3 (October 1976). pp. 305-60; E. F. Fama, "Agency Problems and the Theory of the Firm," *Journal of Political Economy*, 88 (April 1980), pp. 272-84; and G. M. MacDonald, "New Directions in the Theory of Agency," *Canadian Journal of Economics*, 17 (August 1984), pp. 415-40.

served by the principal. Thus managers may make decisions that do not best serve the firm's (owners') objectives.

The manager may not select the decision alternative that maximizes EPV if another alternative better serves the manager's own objectives. These may include rapid promotion (served by highly visible decisions that make the decision maker look good), personal enrichment (served by allocating contracts to higher-cost suppliers who give kickbacks, or by channeling business to family members), aesthetics (served by choosing an alternative that has pleasant, rather than profit-maximizing, consequences), or avoidance of stress and competitive conflict both within the firm and in the firm's product markets (served by avoiding decision alternatives that may generate conflict or threaten job security).

A means of helping to ensure that the manager's efforts will serve the firm's objectives is to offer the manager an "incentive contract" that relates the manager's total compensation package to the profit performance of the firm.[12] Thus the manager would be offered a bonus equal to some share of the firm's profits. To encourage decisions that best serve the expected present value of net worth, the current year's bonus is often related to profits over the past several years. Such incentive contracts do not guarantee the manager's unflagging pursuit of shareholder objectives, however, because the problem of asymmetric information remains. Managers may continue to exert less than maximum effort (known as "shirking") and take nonmonetary benefits (known as "perks," or more correctly, perquisites), with the result that net worth is not maximized, and the shareholders may not be aware of these problems.

In this book we shall continue to speak of the firm's objectives, but it must be kept in mind that managers' objectives may be at variance with those of the firm and that decisions may be made that do not maximize the firm's net worth, to the extent that shareholders remain unaware of the divergence or are unable to discipline management effectively (through the board of directors).

1.6 SUMMARY

In this chapter we have introduced the subject of managerial economics and proceeded to build a framework for business decision making. Managerial economics was defined as the application of economic principles and methodologies to the decision-making process within the firm or organization. It is a normative discipline, seeking to provide rules that allow the firm to best pursue its objective function. The use of models in managerial economics was examined, and we noted that the purpose of models may be either pedagogical, explanatory, or predictive. In this course we will

---

[12]See S. A. Ross, "The Economic Theory of Agency: The Principal's Problem," *American Economic Review*, 58 (May 1973), pp. 134–39; M. Harris and A. Raviv, "Some Results on Incentive Contracts with Applications to Education and Employment, Health Insurance, and Law Enforcement," *American Economic Review*, 68 (March 1978), pp. 20–30; and S. Shavell, "Risk Sharing and Incentives in the Principal and Agent Relationship," *Bell Journal of Economics*, 10 (Spring 1979), pp. 55–73.

use symbolic models, including verbal, graphic, and some simple mathematical expressions.

Present-value analysis and expected-value analysis were introduced and examined in detail. The former involves the discounting of future cash flows so that they may be properly compared with present cash flows for decision-making purposes. The appropriate rate of discount is the opportunity interest rate, defined as the best rate of return available elsewhere at similar risk.

Expected-value analysis allows the summary of a probability distribution of outcomes in a single number, which may then be compared with the expected values of other decision alternatives. The expected value of a decision is the weighted mean of the possible outcomes, where the weight for each outcome is the prior probability of its occurring. Expected present-value analysis requires discounting the expected value of future profits back to present-value terms before aggregation to find the expected present value of each decision alternative.

If the firm's planning period is sufficiently short that its time horizon falls within the present period, the firm should maximize its profits within the present period (if it has full information) or maximize the expected value of its profits (if it operates under uncertainty). If the firm's planning period is longer, so that its time horizon falls in a future period, the firm should maximize the present value of its profit stream (under certainty) or the expected present value of its profit stream (under uncertainty).

DISCUSSION QUESTIONS

1-1. Distinguish between certainty, and risk and uncertainty.

1-2. Under what circumstances is it appropriate that a model be based on assumptions that are extremely simplistic? Could it, nevertheless, be a good model? Could a model be based on false assumptions and yet serve a purpose? Discuss.

1-3. What advantages are there in the graphical or algebraic representation of a model, as compared with a verbal representation of the same phenomena?

1-4. What is the firm's time horizon? What kinds of considerations determine the firm's time horizon?

1-5. What determines the opportunity discount rate to be used when evaluating the present value of a multiperiod profit stream?

1-6. Which discounting formula should be used to most accurately calculate the present value of a stream of revenues received each week throughout the year? If, instead, you used daily discount factors, would this cause an overestimate or an underestimate of the true present value? Would the difference be important?

1-7. What is a decision problem? Is it necessarily a situation in which there is a crisis or in which remedial action is necessary? What has the firm's objective function to do with the existence (or nonexistence) of a decision problem?

1-8. Explain the notion of uncertainty in terms of the probability distribution of outcomes associated with each decision alternative.

1-9. Summarize the modifications necessary to the firm's objective function as the firm's time horizon shifts from the present to a future period and as we relax the assumption of full information.

1-10. Briefly outline the "principal-agent" problem and what it might mean for the achievement of the firm's objectives.

PROBLEMS AND SHORT CASES[13]

1-1. A large internationally recognized manufacturer of soft drink products has announced it will establish a foundation to provide scholarships to business students at your university. The company acknowledges a slight cash-flow problem at the present moment and gives your university's president two choices: Either take a once-and-for-all grant of $10 million immediately or take $2.5 million immediately, $4 million more next year, and $5 million more in two years. Of course the president is euphoric and announces to the faculty that he intends to accept what he calls the "$11.5 million alternative." As an interested party, you are concerned that a complete analysis has not been made.

   (a) Assuming that the opportunity discount rate is 14 percent, what is the present value of the second alternative?

   (b) Explain to the president, in a memo of 200 words or less, what this revised estimate means and which alternative should be accepted.

   (c) Would your decision change if the opportunity interest rate were 12 percent, or 16 percent, instead of the assumed 14 percent? Explain.

1-2. The Words-Are-Cheap Publishing Company is considering extending a contract offer to an author who has written a book entitled *How to Deal with High Interest Rates in the Mid-1980s.* This project would involve reviewing, editing, artwork, and composition costs of $80,000, payable in full at the end of year one, before a single book has been printed. The publisher expects to sell 20,000 copies in year two, 17,500 in year three, 12,500 in year four, and 2,500 in year five. It plans to sell the rights to another publisher at the end of year five for $10,000. Its production, distribution, and royalty costs will be constant at $1.50 per copy, and it will receive $3.50 per copy for every copy sold.

   The finance vice-president advises that the funds involved could alternatively be invested in a corporate bond issue, considered no more or less risky than this book project, at an interest rate of 18 percent, the best rate available.

   (a) Calculate the net present value of the book project, assuming that all cash flows are received or disbursed at the end of the year in which they occur.

   (b) Advise the publisher whether or not to extend the contract offer to the author.

1-3. Your firm has called for bids for the fabrication and installation of a pollution-control system tailored specifically to meet the legal requirements applicable to your manufacturing process. The lowest bid is for $370,000, with delivery and installation in thirty-two months. Your firm plans to sign a contract with the supplier on the above terms, including a clause stating that the contract price of $370,000 is absolutely fixed (regardless of any cost overruns or production difficulties the supplier may encounter) and will be paid in full in thirty-two months' time, following the installation of the system. Between now and then your firm plans to invest its funds in the best available guaranteed, interest-bearing securities, which pay interest of 12 percent per annum.

   (a) What is the present value of the cost of the pollution-control system to your firm?

   (b) Why is 12 percent the appropriate discount rate?

1-4. Doreen Delights has invented a device that allows drinking drivers to self-test for excessive alcohol in their system. Rather than get into that business itself, the firm plans to license this device to the highest bidder. Company A has bid $40,000, payable $10,000 immediately, $15,000 after one year, $10,000 after two years, and $5,000 after three years. Company B has bid $42,500, payable $5,000 immediately, $10,000 after one year, $12,500 after two years, and $15,000 after three years.

---

[13]Short answers to all problems are provided in Appendix C at the back of this book.

The management of Doreen Delights considers that their opportunity discount rate is 9 percent. You are concerned that this is a little low, in view of recent upward movements in interest rates and foreseeable trends, and you feel that 11 percent is the appropriate discount rate.

(a) Calculate the present value of each proposal, using management's opportunity discount rate of 9 percent.

(b) Would the decision be different if the 11 percent discount rate was applied?

(c) Explain to management which option you feel should be chosen and the impact of the time profile of the cash flows on the relative present values.

1-5. The owner of a restaurant approaches you and offers you the following deal: You would manage his restaurant for two years while he goes back to his country to do his compulsory military service. He shows you all his records and you see that the restaurant has sales revenue of $100,000 spread more or less evenly over each year and operating costs of $80,000 similarly spread over each year. You expect the revenue and cost situations to remain stable for each of the next two years. The restaurant owner wants to sell you this opportunity on the following basis: You pay $30,000 initially to the owner but keep all the profits you make over the two years. You know that you could, alternatively, invest your $30,000 in corporate bonds for a 20 percent rate of return, and you consider that alternative no more or less risky than the restaurant venture.

(a) What is the present value of the opportunity to invest in the restaurant venture?

(b) Which alternative should you choose, presuming these are the best opportunities available? Are there any other issues involved?

1-6. You are reading the "Businesses for Sale" advertisements and notice a corner-store business offered for sale. Its assets comprise inventory of $50,000, equipment and plant of $80,000, and land and buildings of $120,000 (all assets are current market value). There are no debtors or creditors. The store's profit stream is $30,000 per year, received more or less evenly throughout the year. Your time horizon is five years; your opportunity discount rate is 16 percent per annum; and you will re-sell the assets after five years for the same *real* value (you expect inflation to average 8 percent over the five years).

(a) What is the net present cost of the assets of the business?

(b) What is the present value of the profit stream over the five years?

(c) What is the net present value of the decision to buy the corner store?

(d) What is the maximum you would offer for the business? If the present owner were asking $400,000, how would you explain your lower offer?

1-7. The Swiss Crest Embroidery Company is considering the installation of a computerized loom, which would be substantially more efficient than their existing equipment. They have two options. Machine A costs $100,000 initially; would earn net profits of $60,000, $80,000, $40,000, and $20,000 on a more or less continuous basis throughout years one to four, respectively; and would have salvage (resale) value of $20,000 at the end of the fourth year. Machine B costs $120,000, but payment for this machine can be deferred for twelve months. Machine B promises to earn net profits of $70,000, $60,000, $50,000, and $30,000 throughout the first, second, third, and fourth years, respectively, and it would have resale value of $30,000 at the end of the fourth year.

The firm is considering alternate areas for expansion, and the best of these other opportunities, which has the same degree of risk as the computerized loom project, promises to return 16 percent on the funds that might otherwise be invested.

(a) Evaluate the two machines in terms of the net present value of their cash-flow streams.

(b) Advise the management about which machine they should select.

1-8. Your firm is considering diversification into a new product line. After extensive investigation the two most promising possibilities have been isolated. Product A is a line of personalized stationery, and Product B is a line of paper party decorations. Annual production and marketing costs for A will be $90,000 and those for B will be $115,000; in both cases these costs are incurred on a weekly basis throughout the year. Annual sales for A will be $100,000, received on a daily basis, and those for B will be $125,000 and will be seasonally biased, being heavily concentrated in December of each year.

For each product, the market research team has predicted a five-year stream of costs and revenues, constant at the above levels. Rather than embark on this diversification, the firm's next best alternative, at equal risk, is to invest the funds in an expansion of the market share for its existing products, which is expected to yield an 18 percent return on investment.

(a) What are the present values of the decision alternatives A and B over the five-year planning period?

(b) Which alternative should the firm choose?

(c) How would you rank the alternatives open to the firm? Explain.

1-9. The Oxford Equipment Company has decided that it will "computerize" its inventory, billing, payroll, and so on. It has two choices. First, it could buy a computer, several terminals, and a variety of software packages and have several of its employees trained to use the hardware and the software, and so do it all "in house." The cost per annum of this alternative is uncertain, since the firm has not yet had experience with computers, and none of its executives know much about either the hardware available or the software packages. The estimated probability distribution of costs for the coming year is as follows:

Possible Cost Level ($)	Probability
20,000	0.15
30,000	0.20
40,000	0.30
50,000	0.25
60,000	0.10

Alternatively, it could contract with a specialist company that would keep contemporaneous records of inventory, handle the billing and payroll, and so on, at a fixed fee of $42,000 per annum. This fee would be payable at the end of the year, whereas the in-house alternative would involve cash outflows on a more or less daily basis throughout the year. Rather than invest the money in either alternative, Oxford could leave the money in bonds, where it is currently earning 15 percent interest per annum.

(a) Calculate the expected value of the in-house alternative.

(b) Calculate the expected present value of the in-house alternative.

(c) Calculate the expected present value of the outside contract alternative.

(d) Advise the management of Oxford Equipment which alternative you think they should select, making explicit any reservations that underlie your recommendation.

1-10. The manager of the Fearless Ambition Racing Team is faced with the following decision problem: There is one race left in the series, and his driver could win the championship with a win or a second placing in the final race. He is concerned that the engine of the race car may be a little "tired" and is considering either a complete rebuilding of the engine or the purchase of a new engine. There is uncertainty involved in both alternatives. In a complete rebuilding of the engine the cost will vary, depending upon the mechanical components that must be replaced after inspection shows them to be worn beyond acceptable tolerances. Similarly, a new engine will be partially dismantled, examined, and subject to mechanical work and replacement of parts that are unlikely to withstand the rigors imposed by race conditions. Either option (to rebuild or to buy new) will result in an engine of the same power and durability. Based on past experience, the following probability distribution of costs associated with each option has been established:

REBUILD		BUY NEW	
Cost ($)	Probability	Cost ($)	Probability
25,000	0.05	35,000	0.05
30,000	0.15	36,000	0.10
35,000	0.40	37,000	0.30
40,000	0.25	38,000	0.35
45,000	0.10	39,000	0.15
50,000	0.05	40,000	0.05

If the team manager decides to rebuild the existing engine, the parts and labor expenses will be incurred more or less evenly throughout the next year, because he will be able to keep suppliers waiting for their money for various lengths of time, up to a maximum of twelve months. If he purchases the new engine, the supplier will give the team a special deal in lieu of direct sponsorship: payment for the engine itself ($35,000) can be deferred twelve months. The other expenses can be spread out over twelve months, as in the rebuild option. The opportunity interest rate is 14 percent per annum.

(a) What is the expected value of the costs for each option?

(b) What is the expected present value of the costs for each option?

(c) Which option should be selected? Explain.

SUGGESTED REFERENCES AND FURTHER READING

Baumol, W. J. "What Can Economic Theory Contribute to Managerial Economics?" *American Economic Review*, 51 (May 1961), pp. 142–46. Reprinted in T. J. Coyne, *Readings in Managerial Economics* (3rd ed.), chap. 1. Plano, Tex.: Business Publications, 1981.

Clayton, G. E., and C. B. Spivey. *The Time Value of Money*. Philadelphia: W. B. Saunders Company, 1978.

Fama, E. F. "Agency Problems and the Theory of the Firm," *Journal of Political Economy*, 88 (April 1980), pp. 272–84.

Gordon, G., and I. Pressman. *Quantitative Decision Making for Business*, chaps. 1, 2. Englewood Cliffs, N.J.: Prentice-Hall, Inc., 1978.

Grossack, I. M., and D. D. Martin. *Managerial Economics*, chap. 1. Boston: Little, Brown & Company, 1973.

Huber, G. P. *Managerial Decision Making*, chaps. 1, 2, 3. Glenview, Ill.: Scott, Foresman & Company, 1980.

Jensen, M. C., and W. H. Meckling. "Theory of the Firm: Managerial Behavior, Agency Costs, and Ownership Structure," *Journal of Financial Economics*, 3 (October 1976), pp. 305–360.

Khoury, S. J., and T. D. Parsons. *Mathematical Methods in Finance and Economics*, chap. 2. New York: Elsevier North-Holland, Inc., 1981.

MacDonald, G. M. "New Directions in the Theory of Agency," *Canadian Journal of Economics*, 17 (August 1984), pp. 415–40.

Papps, I., and W. Henderson. *Models and Economic Theory.* Philadelphia: W. B. Saunders Company, 1977.

Radford, K. J. *Modern Managerial Decision Making*, chaps. 1, 4. Reston, Va.: Reston Publishing Company, Inc., 1981.

Simon, H. A. "Theories of Decision Making in Economics and Behavior Science," *American Economic Review*, 49 (June 1959), pp. 253-80. Reprinted in T. J. Coyne, *Readings in Managerial Economics* (3rd ed.), chap. 2. Plano, Tex.: Business Publications, 1981.

Williamson, O. E. "The Modern Corporation: Origins, Evolution, Attributes," *Journal of Economic Literature*, 19 (December 1981), pp. 1537-68.

2 Decision Making under Risk and Uncertainty

2.1 INTRODUCTION

In Chapter 1 we considered present-value analysis, which should be employed when decisions have cost and revenue implications for future periods, and expected-value analysis, which should be used when decisions must be made under conditions of risk and uncertainty. In this chapter we use PV and EV analysis together, known as expected-present-value (EPV) analysis, for cases where the firm has both future cash flows to consider and an uncertain environment. In the next section we introduce "decision trees" to facilitate multiperiod EPV analysis. These allow the cost and revenue consequences of each decision alternative to be arrayed so that all consequences are accounted for and the EPV of the decision can be properly calculated.

The degree of risk involved in each decision alternative, and its measurement, is considered in the third section, where we incorporate risk analysis into the decision-making process. The degree of risk is measured by the standard deviation of the probability distribution of possible outcomes. Most business decision makers are risk *averse,* meaning that they do not like bearing risk for its own sake. They will, however, bear risk if adequately compensated for doing so. Thus we see a tradeoff between risk and return—more risk will be borne only if it promises more return. This tradeoff has implications for the decision criteria introduced in Chapter 1; risk averters will wish to consider the risk involved in each alternative in conjunction with that alternative's EPV of profits.

In the fourth section we introduce several decision criteria that allow for the incorporation of risk into the decision process. These criteria include a modification to the EPV criterion; the coefficient of variation criterion; the certainty equivalent criterion; and the maximin criterion. We also consider some noneconomic factors which may enter the decision-making process.

Section 2.5 considers information-search costs and the value of information. The problem of incomplete information can be at least partly rectified by information-search activity, such as market research, cost analysis, and consultant's reports. Information-search costs should only be incurred if the decision maker has the prior expectation that the value of the information acquired will exceed the search costs. In many cases the information would cost more than it is worth, and the firm should proceed without seeking further information.

Finally, we look at the evaluation of the decision actually made by the decision maker. What is a good decision? Is a decision necessarily a bad decision if it results in a bad outcome? We shall see that decisions should be evaluated on the basis of whether sufficient search activity was undertaken, whether the information was fully and properly utilized, and whether the appropriate decision criterion was applied. The sensitivity of the final decision to the validity of the assumptions on which it is based is also discussed in this context.

2.2 DECISION TREES AND EXPECTED-PRESENT-VALUE ANALYSIS

Expected-present-value (EPV) analysis is multiperiod analysis because there will be cost and revenue implications of the decision in both the present period and at least one future period. Things can get complicated when there is also a probability distribution of outcomes in each period; possible outcomes in the second and subsequent periods will have *joint* probabilities of occurring. Decision trees greatly facilitate EPV analysis because they spread out the consequences of the decision, like the branches of a tree, so that we can see clearly all the consequences of the decision and easily calculate the joint probabilities and the EPV of the decision.

Decision Trees and Joint Probabilities

Imagine a tree with a trunk that forks into two or more branches, and these in turn each fork into two or more smaller branches. A decision tree has the decision problem at its base, and the first fork represents the decision alternatives, that is, potential solutions to the decision problem. The decision maker must choose one branch or another. In each period following the decision there may be several different "states of nature" that will influence the profits earned under each decision alternative in each period. These "states of nature" are alternative possible scenarios, determined by factors outside the firm's control, and one of them will be experienced by the firm in each subsequent year. The outcomes under each of the scenarios in each subsequent year are shown as higher branches on the tree. The final outcomes are shown as the uppermost branches on the tree, also known as the terminal branches. In Table 2–1 we show the decision tree of a manager who wants to install a metal stamping machine and must decide between a large machine and a small machine.[1]

---

[1]The number of terminal branches (possible final outcomes) is equal to the number of states of nature to the power of the number of years considered. Thus there are nine terminal outcomes for a decision problem involving three states of nature and a two-year horizon. The decision trees in this text are constrained to three states of nature in each of two years, to simplify calculations, although any number could be specified to fit a particular application. Three states of nature is typically sufficient, however, since under conditions of uncertainty the firm will have enough difficulty specifying a "high," "medium," and "low" profit estimate. For practical applications, the medium estimate would be the firm's best guess, or most likely outcome. The low and high estimates would be a pessimistic view and an optimistic view, respectively.

TABLE 2-1. The Decision Tree for the Metal Stamping Machine Decision

Machine Size	YEAR 1 Demand	Profits ($)	YEAR 2 Demand	Profits ($)
Large	Heavy	10,000	Heavy	12,500
			Medium	5,000
			Light	1,000
	Medium	4,000	Heavy	12,500
			Medium	5,000
			Light	1,000
	Light	−1,000	Heavy	12,500
			Medium	5,000
			Light	1,000
Small	Heavy	7,000	Heavy	8,000
			Medium	6,000
			Light	2,000
	Medium	5,000	Heavy	8,000
			Medium	6,000
			Light	2,000
	Light	1,000	Heavy	8,000
			Medium	6,000
			Light	2,000

The branches of the decision tree show the outcomes that are expected in the first and second years after the decision is made. Three demand situations are thought possible; these are characterized as "heavy," "medium," and "light" demand. The profits associated with each demand situation, in nominal dollars, are shown in the table. With the large machine the expected outcomes for year one are profits of either $10,000 or $4,000, or a loss of $1,000. In the second year demand may change as compared with the first year. For example, the demand may be light the first year, yet be heavy, medium, or light in the second year. In this case we say that the second year's outcomes are *independent* of the first year's outcomes.[2] Profits under each of the possible demand situations in the second year, for each decision alternative, are shown in the table. The level of profits that is expected to occur in each of the possible outcome situations apparently reflects the different cost situations of the large and small machines and the different prices that may be obtained under differing demand conditions. For the purposes of this simple example we shall assume that the product has a market life of only two years; that the large machine costs $2,000 initially, as compared

---

[2]In many cases, the probability distribution of profits in the second year will depend on the outcome in the first year. For example, if demand is heavy in the first year, the probability distribution of profits in the second year may be different from what it would be if demand was either medium or light in the first year. In these cases, we say that the probability distribution in the second year is *conditional* on the earlier outcome. Decision trees are even more useful for these more complex decision problems.

with an initial cost of $1,700 for the small machine; that neither machine has any scrap value after two years; and that depreciation expense is not tax deductible.[3]

To decide which machine the firm should install, we must evaluate the EPV of the profits promised by each alternative. First, we need to assign probabilities to the possible situations of heavy, medium, and light demand in each of the two years, and then we must choose the appropriate discount rate. Let us suppose that the results of market research into the demand for this particular product indicate that in the first year there is a 20 percent chance that demand will be heavy, a 30 percent chance that it will be medium, and a 50 percent chance that it will be light. The same research, however, indicates that in the second year there is a 40 percent chance that demand will be heavy, a 40 percent chance that it will be medium, and a 20 percent chance that it will be only light. Concerning the discount rate, we shall suppose that the firm could have earned 10 percent per annum by investing the necessary financial outlay in other assets of comparable risk. Therefore, we shall use a 10 percent opportunity discount rate (ODR) in evaluating the future profits from the enterprise. For the purposes of the discounted cash-flow analysis let us suppose that the first year's profits are received in lump sum at the end of year one and that the second year's profits are received at the end of year two.

The calculation of the expected present value from each of the two machines is shown in Tables 2-2 and 2-3. In each table, column 1 indicates the size and initial cost of the alternatives. Column 2 details the demand possibilities and the probabilities that these demand situations will occur, and column 3 shows the profits expected under each of the demand and plant combinations. Column 4 shows the present value of these profit levels, given a discount rate of 10 percent, which implies a discount factor of 0.909. The demand situations in year two and the profits derived from them are listed in columns 5 and 6. Column 7 shows the present value of the profits in column 6 using a discount factor of 0.826, since this is the present value of $1.00 received two years hence, given the 10 percent ODR. Column 8 shows the aggregate present value of the profits of years one and two, minus the initial cost of the machine (which is already in present-value terms). Column 9 shows the probability that each of these total present values will be achieved. Note that these probabilities are *joint* probabilities, since being at each particular branch of the tree depends upon the preceding year's activity. The appropriate probability, then, is the product of the probability that demand will be heavy in the first year and, for example, also heavy in the second year. Thus the joint probability of the uppermost branch is 0.08, which is the product of 0.2 times 0.4. In column 10 the expected present value of the alternatives is calculated by summing the weighted present values. It can be seen that the large machine has an expected present value of $6,401.50, as compared with the small machine's $6,346.60. The EPV criterion would therefore suggest the installation of the large machine.

---

[3]The significance of these simplifying assumptions, if not known to you now, will become clear in Chapter 15 where the issue of capital budgeting is treated in more detail.

TABLE 2-2. Calculation of Expected Present Value for the Large Machine

Machine (cost) [1]	YEAR 1			YEAR 2			CALCULATION OF EPV		
	Demand (prob.) [2]	Profits [3]	PV (DF = 0.909) [4]	Demand (prob.) [5]	Profits [6]	PV (DF = 0.826) [7]	Total PV [8]	Joint Prob. [9]	Weighted PV [10]
Large ($2,000)	Heavy (P = 0.2)	$10,000	$9,090	Heavy (P = 0.4)	$12,500	$10,325	$17,415	0.08	$1,393.20
				Medium (P = 0.4)	5,000	4,130	11,220	0.08	897.60
				Light (P = 0.2)	1,000	826	7,916	0.04	316.64
	Medium (P = 0.3)	4,000	3,636	Heavy (P = 0.4)	12,500	10,325	11,961	0.12	1,435.32
				Medium (P = 0.4)	5,000	4,130	5,766	0.12	691.92
				Light (P = 0.2)	1,000	826	2,462	0.06	147.72
	Light (P = 0.5)	-1,000	-909	Heavy (P = 0.4)	12,500	10,325	7,416	0.20	1,483.20
				Medium (P = 0.4)	5,000	4,130	1,221	0.20	244.20
				Light (P = 0.2)	1,000	826	-2,083	0.10	-208.30
							Expected present value		$6,401.50

TABLE 2-3. Calculation of Expected Present Value for the Small Machine

Machine (cost) [1]	YEAR 1			YEAR 2			CALCULATION OF EPV		
	Demand (prob.) [2]	Profits [3]	PV (DF = 0.909) [4]	Demand (prob.) [5]	Profits [6]	PV (DF = 0.826) [7]	Total PV [8]	Joint Prob. [9]	Weighted PV [10]
	Heavy (P = 0.2)	$7,000	$6,363	Heavy (P = 0.4)	$8,000	$6,608	$11,271	0.08	$ 901.68
				Medium (P = 0.4)	6,000	4,956	9,619	0.08	769.52
				Light (P = 0.2)	2,000	1,652	6,315	0.04	252.60
Small ($1,700)	Medium (P = 0.3)	5,000	4,545	Heavy (P = 0.4)	8,000	6,608	9,453	0.12	1,134.36
				Medium (P = 0.4)	6,000	4,956	7,801	0.12	936.12
				Light (P = 0.2)	2,000	1,652	4,497	0.06	269.82
	Light (P = 0.5)	1,000	909	Heavy (P = 0.4)	8,000	6,608	5,817	0.20	1,163.40
				Medium (P = 0.4)	6,000	4,956	4,165	0.20	833.00
				Light (P = 0.2)	2,000	1,652	861	0.10	86.10
							Expected present value		$6,346.60

2.3   RISK ANALYSIS OF DECISION ALTERNATIVES

We now consider the *degree* of risk and uncertainty and the appropriate measure of risk which allows us to quantify and compare the risk of competing decision alternatives.

The Degree of Risk and Uncertainty

■ *Definition:*   The *degree of risk* associated with a particular decision is defined as the dispersion of the prior probability distribution of possible outcomes around the expected value of those outcomes. By dispersion of outcomes we mean the spread or range of outcomes within which the actual outcome may fall after the decision is made. Before the decision is made, some decision alternatives will exhibit greater dispersion of possible outcomes than will other decision alternatives, and we say that these have a greater degree of risk involved, or that they are more risky.

Look back at Tables 2-2 and 2-3 and note the dispersion of outcomes that is possible under each decision alternative. Note that the possible outcomes are shown in column 8 in each table. These are the potential profit (or loss) levels after two years. The dispersion of possible outcomes is substantially greater for the large machine, which has outcomes ranging from $17,415 profit to a loss of $2,083, as compared to the small machine's range of profits from $11,271 to $861. If the decision maker is risk averse, it is not clear that the larger machine should be the one selected. We shall see in the next main section how the risk-averse firm might make its decision between these two decision alternatives.

The range of outcomes is a rather crude measure of the dispersion of a probability distribution, primarily because it ignores the relative probabilities. The extreme points on the probability distribution may be only remotely possible—for example, have probabilities of only 0.0001—yet the range will stay the same. A superior measure of dispersion around the expected value is the standard deviation of the probability distribution.

The Standard Deviation of a Probability Distribution

■ *Definition:*   The *standard deviation* of a probability distribution shows the weighted average absolute deviation of all possible outcomes from the expected value of that probability distribution. The deviation of each possible outcome from the expected value is weighted by the probability of each outcome occurring to find the weighted-average deviation. We seek the absolute deviations—that is, without regard to whether they are positive deviations (above the expected value) or negative deviations (below the expected value)—because we do not want the negative deviations to offset the positive deviations. We get rid of the minus signs on the negative deviations by first squaring the deviations and later taking the square root of the sum of weighted deviations. Symbolically,

$$\sigma = \sqrt{\sum_{i=1}^{n} (X_i - \text{EPV})^2 P_i}$$

where σ (lowercase sigma) is the conventional symbol used to denote standard deviation; Σ (uppercase sigma) connotes the sum of the series of squared and weighted deviations from $i = 1, 2, 3, \ldots, n$; X_i represents the ith possible outcome; P_i the probability of that outcome; and EPV is the expected value of the probability distribution.

Example: Let us calculate the standard deviation for each of the probability distributions in the large-machine/small-machine decision problem introduced earlier. We show the full calculations in Table 2–4. Column 1 lists the possible outcomes for each decision alternative (repeated from column 8 in Tables 2–2 and 2–3), and column 2 shows the EPV that was calculated for each decision alternative. Column 3 shows the deviation of each possible outcome from the EPV, and column 4 shows the squares of these deviations. Column 5 repeats the joint probabilities of each outcome occurring (from column 9 in Tables 2–2 and 2–3), and column 6 shows the deviations weighted by the joint probabilities.

The next step, as evident in the equation, is to find the sum of these weighted squared deviations, known as the *variance* of the probability distribution. The final step is to calculate the square root of the variance to find the standard deviation of the probability distribution.

The standard deviation for the large machine decision alternative is $5,395.70, and it is $2,903.60 for the small machine. Thus the degree of risk associated with the large machine is substantially greater.

Risk Aversion, Risk Preference, and Risk Neutrality

■ *Definition:* *Risk aversion* is defined as the feeling of disutility caused by uncertainty. That is, the dispersion of possible outcomes of an act causes the risk averter to experience psychic dissatisfaction, or disutility. In general, we expect business decision makers to be risk averse; that is, they do not like risk *per se* and are only prepared to undertake risky situations if adequately compensated for bearing the risk involved. Risk averters regard risk as a "bad"—an item which gives them disutility—as compared with a "good"—one which gives them utility. Risk averters accept risk only if they at the same time expect to gain sufficient utility from the return (or profits) associated with the proposed investment project. The greater the risk perceived, the greater the return the investor requires to offset that risk. Conversely, risk averters are willing to accept lower expected returns if these are associated with lower degrees of risk. This risk-return tradeoff is the characteristic of a risk averter: he or she is prepared to take risks, but only if there is sufficient compensation expected.

We can depict a risk averter's preference structure between risk and return in terms of indifference-curve analysis, which we shall examine in detail in the following

TABLE 2-4.   Calculation of the Standard Deviation for the Large and Small Machine Decision

Large Machine

X_i ($000)	EPV ($000)	$X_i - $ EPV ($000)	$(X_i - $ EPV$)^2$ ($000)	P_i	$(X_i - $ EPV$)^2 P_i$ ($000)
17.415	6.4015	11.0135	121.297	0.08	9.7038
11.220	6.4015	4.8185	23.218	0.08	1.8574
7.916	6.4015	1.5145	2.294	0.04	0.0917
11.961	6.4015	5.5595	30.908	0.12	3.7090
5.766	6.4015	−0.6355	0.404	0.12	0.0485
2.462	6.4015	−3.9395	15.520	0.06	0.9312
7.416	6.4015	1.0145	1.029	0.20	0.2058
1.221	6.4015	−5.1805	26.838	0.20	5.3675
−2.083	6.4015	−8.4845	71.987	0.10	7.1987
				1.00	

Variance = 29.1136

Standard Deviation = $\sqrt{\text{Variance}}$ = 5.3957 or $5,395.70

Small Machine

X_i ($000)	EPV ($000)	$X_i - $ EPV ($000)	$(X_i - $ EPV$)^2$ ($000)	P_i	$(X_i - $ EPV$)^2 P_i$ ($000)
11.271	6.3466	4.9244	24.250	0.08	1.9400
9.619	6.3466	3.2724	10.709	0.08	0.8567
6.315	6.3466	−0.0316	0.001	0.04	0.0000
9.453	6.3466	3.1064	9.650	0.12	1.1580
7.801	6.3466	1.4544	2.115	0.12	0.2538
4.497	6.3466	−1.8496	3.421	0.06	0.2053
5.817	6.3466	−0.5296	0.281	0.20	0.0561
4.165	6.3466	−2.1816	4.759	0.20	0.9519
0.861	6.3466	−5.4856	30.092	0.10	3.0092
				1.00	

Variance = 8.4310

Standard Deviation = $\sqrt{\text{Variance}}$ = 2.9036 or $2,903.60

chapter. It will suffice to say here that indifference curves are lines joining combinations of variables that give the consumer, or decision maker in this case, the same amount of utility. Thus the decision maker will be indifferent as to which combination is chosen. We shall show in Chapter 3 that higher indifference curves are preferred to lower indifference curves, that indifference curves do not meet or intersect, and that they are convex to the origin. Indifference curves showing combinations of goods from which the consumer derives utility will be negatively sloping throughout, since more of one good must be combined with less of the other good in order for the consumer to remain indifferent between the combinations. But, since a risk averter gains utility from returns (or profits) and disutility from risk, the indifference curves are not like the negatively sloped ones of consumer-behavior analysis. Rather, they are *positively* sloping to reflect the fact that risk is a "bad" and that it generates disutility rather than utility.

In Figure 2-1 we show risk—measured by the standard deviation of possible profit levels—on the horizontal axis, and we show returns—measured by the expected present value of the possible profit levels—on the vertical axis. Three arbitrarily chosen indifference curves are shown as I_1, I_2, and I_3. The direction of preference, shown by the arrow, is upward and to the left—that is, I_1 is preferred to I_2, and I_2 is preferred to I_3. Notice that the indifference curves are convex from below, just as in the regular case, reflecting diminishing marginal utility of expected profits and increasing marginal disutility of risk.

Example: Suppose the decision maker is considering four different solutions to a particular decision problem, which we shall identify as decision alternatives A, B, C, and D. Point *A* in Figure 2-1 represents decision A, which has expected present value E_2 and standard deviation σ_2. The decision maker is indifferent between this project and the status quo (with the funds invested in the best alternative investment), which is represented by the origin. You can see that the decision maker requires E_2 dollars of expected return to compensate for bearing σ_2 dollars of standard deviation, or risk. Note that decision A is preferred to decision B, which has the same expected value but higher risk, σ_3. It follows that the status quo (and the best alternative investment) is also preferred to decision B, since decision A and the status quo are on the same indifference curve. Decision C is preferred to both A and B, since it has the same expected value but lower risk, σ_1. Finally, decision D is regarded as equally desirable to decision B, but it is inferior to both A and C, as well as to the status quo. Decision D has the same risk as A but lower expected profits, and it has both more risk and less re-

FIGURE 2-1.   Indifference Curves for a Risk Averter in Risk-Return Space

turn than decision C. In this case the decision maker's only desirable alternative is decision C.

Note: The slopes of the indifference curves between risk and return indicate the individual's degree of risk aversion. The slope of an indifference curve represents the individual's *marginal rate of substitution* (MRS) between the two variables under consideration. In this case, the decision maker's MRS is the amount of expected return he or she requires before accepting an extra unit of risk. You can see that the individual's MRS between risk and return is positive and increases as the level of risk and return increase, because the slope of each indifference curve becomes progressively steeper as the decision maker "moves along" the curve. Accordingly, a decision maker who is already bearing high levels of risk will require an even greater increment of expected profits before agreeing to accept any more risk. This relationship reflects the assumptions of diminishing marginal utility of wealth and increasing marginal disutility of risk, which underlie the analysis and appear reasonable for most decision makers.

Differing Degrees of Risk Aversion.   Different people have different degrees of risk aversion. Graphically these differences are reflected in steeper or flatter indifference curves in risk-return space. In Figure 2-2, we show a person with a relatively high degree of risk aversion contrasted with a person whose preferences indicate a relatively low degree of risk aversion. Points A and D are the same on both graphs. Project D is inferior to project A, since for the same expected return, E_0, it has the larger risk, σ_1. In both cases the person would accept the risk level σ_1 only if this is accompanied by an expected profit larger than that of project A. How much additional expected profit would it take to make each person indifferent between project A and a project containing σ_1 units of risk? The more risk-averse person in the left-hand graph requires an

FIGURE 2-2.   Different Degrees of Risk Aversion

additional *DB* dollars in order to remain at the same level of utility and thus has a relatively high MRS of return for risk, measured by the ratio *BD/AD*. The less risk-averse person on the right-hand side requires only the considerably smaller amount of extra expected profit, *DC* dollars, for the extra risk, $\sigma_1 - \sigma_0$, and thus exhibits a relatively low MRS of return for risk measured by the ratio *CD/AD*.

Risk Preference and Risk Neutrality.   Risk preference and risk neutrality are not common among business decision makers. Consumers, on the other hand, may show risk preference or neutrality in such situations as gambling, sporting, and recreational activities. Risk preference means that risk is viewed as a utility-producing good, and so the individual's indifference curves are negatively sloping as in the left-hand graph of Figure 2-3. Such an individual is prepared to give up expected profits for a larger amount of risk. For example, a gambler might prefer a game in which the odds are poorer and the expected value of gains is lower, over a safer bet on another game in which the expected value is somewhat higher.

Risk neutrality means that the individual is completely indifferent to risk, receiving neither utility nor disutility from risk regardless of the amount of risk involved. Such an individual's indifference curves would be horizontal, as in the right-hand graph of Figure 2-3. The arrow shows the direction of preference—more expected profit is preferred to less, regardless of the risk. Consider an athlete who desperately wants to win the final event of the season. Some athletes will do whatever is necessary to help their teams score or to prevent the opposition from scoring. Thus hockey players block shots on goal with their faces and bodies, football players make plays that could easily result in broken bones, and racing drivers attempt that final pass on the last turn before the checkered flag.

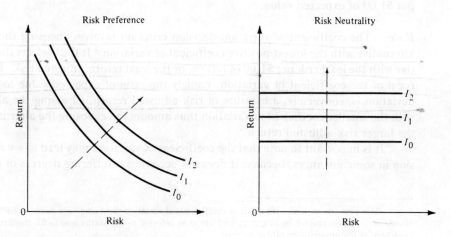

FIGURE 2-3.   Risk Preference and Risk Neutrality

2.4 ADJUSTMENT FOR RISK IN DECISION MAKING

In this section we examine several methods by which the risk-averse decision maker can compare decision alternatives on a *risk-adjusted* basis and select the alternative that best serves the firm's objective function, subject to the decision maker's degree of risk aversion. The first two methods, the coefficient-of-variation criterion and the expected-value criterion using different discount rates, are relatively crude measures conceptually, but at least they can be calculated and compared with little difficulty, thus saving search costs. The third method, the certainty-equivalent criterion, is conceptually elegant, but its application presents certain problems. The fourth method, the maximin criterion, is appropriate in only a limited range of situations.

The Coefficient-of-Variation Criterion

- *Definition:* The *coefficient of variation* is defined here as the ratio of the standard deviation to the expected present value. The coefficient of variation for a probability distribution thus indicates the amount of standard deviation, or risk, per dollar of expected present value, or return.

  Example: In the large-machine/small-machine example discussed earlier we calculated both the EPV and the standard deviation for each decision alternative. For the large machine the standard deviation was $5,395.70 and the expected value was $6,401.50. The ratio of these figures, or the coefficient of variation, is 0.8429. For the small machine the standard deviation was $2,903.60 and the expected value was $6,346.60. The coefficient of variation for the small machine is, thus, only 0.4575. In effect, these figures say that the large plant promises a little over $0.84 average dispersion from the expected value, per $1.00 of expected value. The small machine, on the other hand, offers a little less than $0.46 average dispersion from the expected value, per $1.00 of expected value.

  Rule: The coefficient-of-variation decision criterion involves choosing the decision alternative with the lowest positive coefficient of variation.[4] It thus selects the alternative with the least risk per $1.00 of return, or the least return-adjusted risk. The reciprocal of the coefficient of variation, namely the ratio of expected value to standard deviation is, conversely, a measure of risk-adjusted return. Choosing the alternative with the smaller coefficient of variation thus amounts to choosing the alternative with the larger risk-adjusted return.

      It is important to note that the coefficient of variation may lead to a wrong decision in some instances, because it does not account for differing degrees of risk aver-

---

[4]Decision alternatives with negative coefficients of variation must also have negative EPVs, since the standard deviation cannot be negative, and are thus inferior to the status quo (with the funds invested elsewhere at the opportunity rate of return).

sion. We shall return to this issue after discussing the certainty-equivalent criterion, later in this section.

The Expected-Value Criterion Using Different Discount Rates

An alternative method of adjusting the expected-value criterion for risk is to use higher discount rates for the more risky decision alternatives. Recall that the opportunity discount rate (ODR) is the best rate of interest that could be earned elsewhere at the same degree of risk. Thus, if one decision alternative has a dispersion of outcomes (and resulting standard deviation value) similar to a corporate bond issue yielding 10 percent and another decision alternative has a dispersion of outcomes similar to a 12 percent corporate bond issue, the appropriate ODRs are 10 percent and 12 percent, respectively.

Example: Looking back at the large-machine/small-machine decision, we note that the dispersions (and the standard deviations) of the two alternatives are significantly different. Suppose 10 percent is the correct ODR for the small machine, but that the risk of the large machine's expected outcomes is similar to that of a 12 percent bond issue. In Table 2–5 we show the calculation of the EPV of the large-machine decision using the 12 percent discount factors shown. As you can see, discounting the expected cash flows by the higher rate reduces the EPV to $6,150.67. This is now somewhat less than the small machine's $6,346.60. Thus the expected-value criterion using different ODRs now favors the decision to purchase the small machine, just as the coefficient-of-variation criterion did.

Rule: The expected-value decision criterion, adjusted for differing risks of decision alternatives, involves selecting the alternative with the greatest expected value (or EPV), after each alternative has been discounted using the opportunity discount rate that is specifically appropriate for that particular decision alternative.

Note: You may be wondering why we didn't discount the large-machine/small-machine alternatives at different discount rates in the first instance. Essentially, there are two different ways to adjust the EPV criterion for risk. One is to discount both (or all) decision alternatives at the same discount rate and then use the coefficient of variation as the risk-adjusted EPV criterion. The second method is to foresee the different degrees of risk involved in the different decision alternatives and to discount each alternative at its appropriate ODR. One method or the other may be used but not a combination of the two. For example, if you discount two alternatives at different ODRs and then calculate the coefficient of variation, you will have doubly adjusted for risk and may choose the wrong alternative.

These two methods are basically similar and would normally rank decision alternatives in the same order. But which one is superior? In terms of data required to use

TABLE 2-5. Expected Present Value of the Large-Machine Decision Using 12 Percent ODR

Initial Cost ($) [1]	YEAR 1			YEAR 2			CALCULATION OF EPV		
	Demand (prob.) [2]	Profits ($) [3]	PV (DF = 0.8929) [4]	Demand (prob.) [5]	Profits ($) [6]	PV (DF = 0.7972) [7]	Total PV ($) [8]	Joint prob. [9]	Weighted PV [10]
−2,000	Heavy (P = 0.2)	10,000	8,929	Heavy (P = 0.4)	12,500	9,965	16,894	0.08	1,351.52
				Medium (P = 0.4)	5,000	3,986	10,915	0.08	873.20
				Light (P = 0.2)	1,000	797	7,726	0.04	309.05
	Medium (P = 0.3)	4,000	3,572	Heavy (P = 0.4)	12,500	9,965	11,537	0.12	1,384.39
				Medium (P = 0.4)	5,000	3,986	5,558	0.12	666.91
				Light (P = 0.2)	1,000	797	2,369	0.06	142.13
	Light (P = 0.5)	−1,000	−893	Heavy (P = 0.4)	12,500	9,965	7,072	0.20	1,414.42
				Medium (P = 0.4)	5,000	3,986	1,093	0.20	218.62
				Light (P = 0.2)	1,000	797	−2,096	0.10	−209.57
							Expected Present Value		$6,150.67

the criterion, the coefficient-of-variation criterion can be used with much lower search costs, as compared to the proper implementation of the "different ODR" criterion. The latter requires that a study be made of the dispersion of possible outcomes of a broad range of alternative investments, so that the correct ODR may be ascertained for each decision alternative. The coefficient-of-variation criterion is usually implemented using the firm's *cost of capital* as the discount rate. Since the firm knows its cost of capital (the rate of interest which the firm pays to borrow funds), the firm does not need an extensive search procedure each time it makes a decision.[5]

The Certainty-Equivalent Criterion

■ *Definition:* The *certainty equivalent* of a decision alternative with more than one possible outcome is the sum of money, available with certainty, that would cause the decision maker to be indifferent between that decision alternative and accepting the certain sum of money.

Example: Suppose that I offer to give you either $0.50 or "toss you" for double or nothing. If you accept the $0.50, that means you prefer the certain sum ($0.50) to the gamble which has two possible outcomes ($1.00 or nothing). To find your point of indifference I would now offer you the choice of $0.30 with certainty or the toss for $1.00 or nothing. Suppose you now prefer to take the gamble. Somewhere between $0.30 and $0.50 is your certainty equivalent of the gamble. Suppose that after several more offers I find that you are indifferent between accepting $0.42 with certainty and taking the gamble. Thus, your certainty equivalent (CE) for that gamble is $0.42. In effect, the CE is the sum of money that will *almost* bribe you to give up the gamble.

The notion of an individual's certainty equivalent involves the concept of utility and indifference, and it incorporates the decision maker's degree of risk aversion (or risk preference). The more risk-averse decision maker would exhibit a lower CE than a less risk-averse (or a risk-preferring) decision maker for the same gamble. Moreover, it can incorporate other considerations as well. If the gamble is to be repeated many times, we would expect the CE to be equal to the expected value (in this case $0.50). If the gamble is to be taken just once or a few times, we expect a risk averter's CE to be less than the EV. In effect, the risk averter is trading off expected return for removal of the risk. Conversely, a risk preferrer's CE is expected to exceed the EV, since this

---

[5]See Eugene F. Brigham, *Financial Management Theory and Practice*, 2nd ed. (Hinsdale, Ill.: The Dryden Press, 1979), pp. 555–93.

Note that the firm's cost of capital (CC) may or may not be equal to the firm's opportunity discount rate. The rate at which the firm borrows reflects the lender's view of the risk of the firm, rather than the firm's view of the risk of the decision alternative. If the current decision involves a higher degree of risk than the degree of risk already borne by the firm, the CC will understate the ODR. Conversely, if the current decision involves a lesser degree of risk than the degree of risk already borne by the firm, the CC will overstate the ODR. When the current decision involves the same degree of risk, and the firm and its lenders view the situation identically, the CC is an accurate measure of the ODR.

person gets utility from risk and will require more than the gamble's EV to be bribed into giving it up. Finally, suppose a person is desperate for a given sum of money. For example, a student needs $0.75 to wire home and ask for more money: That individual's CE is likely to be $0.75. Any lesser sum doesn't solve the problem, and the student will be prepared to gamble for the best payoff unless assured of the $0.75 with certainty. This person, whatever his or her usual attitude toward risk, would be acting like a risk preferrer in this instance.

Expressed in terms of indifference-curve analysis, the certainty equivalent of a decision alternative can be shown as the point on the vertical axis joined by an indifference curve to the point representing the decision alternative under consideration.

Example: In Figure 2-4 we show the two decision alternatives introduced as the large-machine/small-machine decision problem earlier. Note that we have shown the small machine as the preferred alternative, since it lies on the higher indifference curve. The point CE_S on the expected-value axis is the certainty equivalent of the combination of expected value and risk represented by point S. It is the certainty equivalent because *risk,* on the horizontal axis, has been reduced to zero and, thus, the decision maker is indifferent between $$CE_S$ with certainty and $6,346.60 with risk (standard deviation of $2,903.60). Similarly, the certainty equivalent of the large machine, point L, is $$CE_L$.

Rule: The certainty-equivalent criterion involves selecting the decision alternative which has the highest certainty equivalent. Note that since indifference curves neither meet nor intersect and since higher curves are preferred to lower curves, the certainty-

FIGURE 2-4.   Certainty Equivalents of the Large-Machine/Small-Machine Decision

equivalent criterion is entirely consistent with the utility theory of rational consumer (or decision-making) behavior.

Unfortunately, we are now in a position to see that the earlier methods of adjusting for risk, namely, the coefficient-of-variation and the EPV criterion using different discount rates, are not entirely consistent with utility theory and may sometimes indicate the choice of a decision alternative that would not be optimal in terms of the decision maker's utility. Consider Figure 2–5 in which the points S and L for the small and large machine alternatives are shown on rays emanating from the origin. The slopes of these rays reflect the ratio of expected value to standard deviation, or what we have earlier called risk-adjusted return. The slope of each ray is equal to the reciprocal of the coefficient of variation. Thus, as we saw earlier, the small machine, point S, is preferred to the large machine, point L, on the basis of both the coefficient-of-variation and the certainty-equivalent criteria.

But consider points M and P which have the same value for their coefficient of variation as point S, yet are ranked differently in terms of their certainty equivalents: M is preferred to S, which in turn is preferred to P. The coefficient-of-variation criterion is unable to distinguish between M, S, and P and ranks them as equals. In effect, it says that the ray from the origin $0PSM$ is an indifference curve, with all points on it giving equal utility (or certainty equivalent) to the decision maker. Similarly, it effectively says that the ray $0TRL$ is a *lower* indifference curve, with all points on that ray regarded as equal, but inferior to any point on the higher ray $0PSM$. The curvilinear indifference curves shown in Figure 2–5 indicate that this is untrue for the case presented: L is preferred to R, which in turn is preferred to T, and, moreover, L is pre-

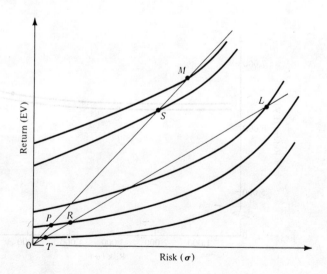

FIGURE 2-5. **Conflict between the Coefficient-of-Variation Criterion and the Certainty-Equivalent Criterion**

ferred to *P*, and *R* is equivalent to *P*, despite *P*'s lower coefficient of variation (or higher risk-adjusted return).

Thus, although the coefficient-of-variation criterion correctly ranked points *S* and *L*, it incorrectly ranked most of the other points shown! In fact, the coefficient-of-variation criterion may incorrectly rank *S* and *L* for a particular decision maker. In Figure 2-6 we show a decision maker who is only slightly risk averse (with very low marginal rate of substitution of expected return for risk) who *prefers* point *L* over point *S*. Point *L* lies on a higher indifference curve for this individual and, accordingly, has a higher certainty equivalent. Note that the expected-value criterion with different discount rates also incorrectly ranked the small versus large machine alternatives for this particular decision maker and would similarly make mistakes between other pairs of decision alternatives.

Why does this problem arise? Essentially, the coefficient-of-variation criterion and the EV criterion using different ODRs assume a linear and constant tradeoff between risk and return. In fact, most risk averters exhibit a nonlinear risk-return tradeoff. In economic terms we explain this as diminishing marginal utility of wealth and increasing marginal disutility of risk. The more wealth (expected return) one is offered, the less utility one receives from the marginal dollar, and the more risk one is offered, the greater the disutility one receives from the marginal unit of risk.

Should we throw away the coefficient-of-variation and the EV criterion using different ODRs and simply use the certainty equivalent? Without doubt the certainty equivalent gives the better answers for maximizing the decision maker's utility function. This might be quite different from maximizing the firm's objective function, however. For the firm with a single owner-manager, maximizing net worth and maxi-

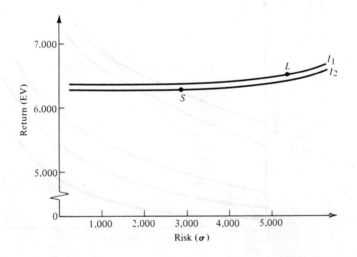

FIGURE 2-6.   Coefficient-of-Variation Criterion Refuted for a Slightly Risk-Averse Decision Maker

mizing the decision maker's utility may well amount to the same thing, but for a widely held firm with a variety of decision makers within the management team, it is not at all clear that maximizing managerial utility will lead to the maximization of net worth. One could argue that the firm *does* have a constant tradeoff between risk and return. More importantly, perhaps, the coefficient-of-variation criterion, and the EV using different ODRs to a lesser extent, can be calculated and subjected to scrutiny, whereas certainty equivalents and utility are more cerebral and intuitive notions that are more difficult to defend quantitatively.

Rule: The solution to this apparent impasse is to use all three methods with caution and with reservations. For example, one would say that the small machine appears to be preferable on a risk-adjusted basis, unless the firm is only very slightly risk averse, to the extent that the firm would be willing to accept an additional $2,492.10 standard deviation (that is $5,395.70 − $2,903.60) for an additional $54.90 expected return (that is, $6,401.50 − $6,346.60). The caveat attached to this recommendation can be settled by management consensus (or by the boss's opinion). If the consensus is that the extra risk should be undertaken for the extra expected return, the simple risk-adjustment criterion is overturned. Alternatively, if the consensus (or the owner's opinion) is not to accept the extra risk for the extra return, the simple risk-adjustment criterion is supported.

Note: In many cases there will be no doubt which decision alternatives dominate others for the risk-averse decision maker or firm. Consider Figure 2-7 in which we show one of several possible outcomes, labeled point A. Relative to point A, we show quadrants I, II, III, and IV. Any point in quadrant IV is unambiguously superior to point A (for a risk averter) since it has either more return for the same or less risk, or less risk for the same return. Similarly, any point in quadrant II is unambiguously

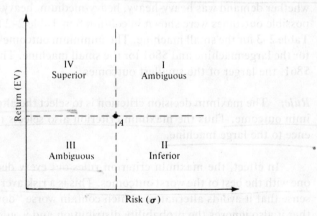

FIGURE 2-7. Superior and Inferior Quadrants with Respect to a Particular Decision Alternative (Point A)

inferior to point A, having either less return for the same or more risk, or more risk for the same return. Quadrants I and III, relative to point A, on the other hand, do represent potential areas of conflict between the coefficient-of-variation and the EV criteria using different ODRs, on the one hand, and the certainty-equivalent criterion on the other. Points in quadrant I have both more risk and more return, and in quadrant III there is both less risk and less return. When decision alternatives fall in quadrants I and III with respect to each other, one must use the "caution and reservation" rule suggested above.

The Certainty-Equivalent Factor. To find the certainty equivalent of an uncertain venture without involving indifference curves, decide what *fraction* of the EPV would make you indifferent between (a) the EPV of the uncertain venture and (b) that fraction of the EPV if it were available with certainty. One way to do this is to decide "how many cents in the dollar" you would consider to be equivalent if these were available with certainty. This fraction, say 0.75, is known as the certainty-equivalent factor (CEF). Multiplying the CEF by the EPV will give you the CE of the gamble. Riskier ventures will have smaller CEFs, but the CE is the product of the CEF and the EPV, such that the CE may be greater or smaller for the more risky venture. The decision rule remains the same: choose the alternative with the greatest (positive valued) certainty equivalent.

The Maximin Decision Criterion

- *Definition:* The *maximin* is the term given to the largest (the maximum) of the smallest outcomes (the minimums) associated with each decision alternative.

Example: Using the large-machine/small-machine decision outlined earlier, there are nine possible outcomes after two years for each alternative, depending upon whether demand was heavy-heavy, heavy-medium, heavy-light, and so forth. The nine possible outcomes were shown in column 8 in Table 2-2 for the large machine and in Table 2-3 for the small machine. The minimum outcomes are expected to be $-\$2,083$ for the large machine and $\$861$ for the small machine. The maximin outcome is, thus, $\$861$, the larger of the smallest outcomes.

Rule: The maximin decision criterion is to select the alternative containing the maximin outcome. Thus the maximin criterion also selects the small machine in preference to the large machine.

In effect, the maximin criterion rules out every decision alternative except the one with the best of the worst outcomes. This is a risk averter's decision criterion in the sense that it avoids alternatives which contain worse "downside" outcomes. But note that it also ignores the probability distribution and would have chosen the small machine even if its worst outcome probability was high and the large plant's worst outcome probability was very low. Note also that the maximin criterion ignores all other outcomes. The large machine shows several relatively high outcomes, yet these don't enter into consideration at all.

When is the maximin criterion appropriate? For repeated decisions it is clearly too pessimistic, always expecting the worst to happen, when, in fact, the law of averages should cause the EPV to be attained (on average) over many trials. For a one-shot deal, however, where the firm simply cannot afford to suffer the worst outcomes associated with some of the decision alternatives, the maximin criterion may be appropriate.

Example: In the large-machine/small-machine decision, suppose that any loss over $1,000 would cause the firm to go bankrupt and be liquidated by its creditors. The decision maker might then be unwilling to take the risk of the $2,083 loss associated with the large machine and choose the small machine to avoid to possibility of a loss exceeding $1,000.

Similarly, a decision maker looking for a promotion in the near future may reason that a loss resulting from one of his or her decisions will most likely prevent that promotion, and may decide to apply the maximin criterion. Thus, in particular situations, usually involving relatively short time horizons in which the law of averages cannot be relied on and in which the firm or the decision maker cannot afford the outcomes associated with some of the decision alternatives, the maximin criterion may be appropriate.

Which Criterion Should Be Applied?

The choice among the various decision criteria available depends upon three major factors. First, one must consider the *frequency* with which one is confronted by the particular decision. Second, one must consider the *magnitude* of the gamble. Third, the decision maker's *attitude toward risk* and uncertainty is important. To illustrate each of these factors we shall consider another example, that of insurance.

Example: Suppose a firm has two major insurance contracts: one for collision damage to its fleet of automobiles and the other for fire damage to its plant and buildings. The firm is considering whether it should renew these contracts or carry the risk itself. The risk is known to the firm from insurance company data. The odds are 5 in 100 that each of the company's vehicles will be damaged to a mean value of $5,000. Hence, the expected value of the damage is $250 per vehicle. The insurance company, however, charges a premium of $275 per vehicle, since it wishes to contribute to its overhead expenses and profits. The odds are 1 in 1,000 that the company's plant will burn down. The value of the plant is $10 million, and thus the expected value of the possible loss is $10,000. The insurance company's premium for this policy is $11,000. Will the firm carry its own insurance? Let us consider the three factors mentioned previously.

First, regarding the frequency with which the company takes the particular gamble, we must remember that risk involves the law of averages. If one runs the risk a large number of times, one might reasonably expect to win and lose in the same proportions as the general population. On the other hand, if one runs the risk only once, then one might be fortunate enough to avoid the unhappy event of an accident or a fire; but, on the other hand, one might suffer all the bad luck all at once. In the case of the firm deciding to carry its own insurance, the automobiles represent a high frequency of taking the gamble. The company has, say, 100 vehicles, and this is a sufficiently large number that it might expect the probability of any one being damaged to be similar to the population of vehicles at large. On the other hand, the firm has only one plant and the frequency of this gamble is only once. It does not have 100 plants; it does not take this gamble at a large number of locations; and, therefore, it should not expect the average vulnerability to fire damage.

Concerning the second factor, the magnitude of the gamble, the important point to consider here is whether or not the decision maker can afford the worst possible outcomes. That is, can it afford the loss it would sustain if things turned out very badly? In the case of our company considering its insurance, it is possible that it could withstand the (unlikely) loss of all its vehicles for a total loss of $500,000. On the other hand, the loss of the plant and buildings to the tune of $10 million would probably represent a significant setback to that company. Thus the second factor would militate in favor of the company renewing its insurance policy for fire damage to the plant and buildings, but not for the automobile fleet.

The third factor, the decision maker's attitude toward risk and uncertainty, involves the individual's degree of risk preference or aversion. The crucial factor is the willingness of the decision maker to accept risk *and its consequences*. Thus, even though the first two factors above indicate that the firm should perhaps bear the risk on its motor vehicles, the attitude of the decision maker might be such that the policy will be renewed. Alternatively, even though the first two factors above indicate that the firm should probably renew its insurance for fire damage for that plant, a risk-preferring decision maker might decide to cancel that policy.

Tables 2-6 and 2-7 show the payoffs, expected values, standard deviations, and coefficients of variation for each of the two problems confronting the firm. From these data we can choose the appropriate decision using each of several criteria discussed above. Using the expected-value criterion, the decision maker would insure neither the fleet of automobiles nor the plant and buildings. Under the maximin and coeffi-

TABLE 2-6.   Auto Fleet Insurance Problem

	INSURE			NOT INSURE		
	Cost	Prob.	EV	Cost	Prob.	EV
Accidents	$-27,500	0.05	$- 1,375	$-500,000	0.05	$-25,000
No accidents	-27,500	0.95	-26,125	0	0.95	0
Expected value			$-27,500			$-25,000
Standard deviation			0			119,895.75
Coefficient of variation			0			4.80

TABLE 2-7. Plant and Buildings Insurance Problem

	INSURE			NOT INSURE		
	Cost	Prob.	EV	Cost	Prob.	EV
Fire	$-11,000	0.001	$- 11	$-10,000,000	0.001	$-10,000
No fire	-11,000	0.999	-10,989	0	0.999	0
Expected value			$-11,000			$-10,000
Standard deviation			0			316,701.75
Coefficient of variation			0			31.67

cient-of-variation criteria, the decision maker would insure both the fleet and the plant buildings. Under the certainty-equivalent criterion, we are unable to say, since this criterion depends upon the decision maker's individual attitude toward bearing risk and uncertainty. On the basis of the three factors considered above, however, we may hazard a guess that under this criterion a risk-averse decision maker would choose to renew the insurance policy on the plant and buildings, and possibly to allow the collision policy on its fleet of cars to lapse. This information is summarized in Table 2-8.

Nonmonetary Factors in Decision Making. The objectives of the firm's owners and managers may include particular nonmonetary goals, such as concern for the protection of the natural environment, and philanthropic considerations relating to the impact of layoffs of workers during periods of low demand. Similarly, managers may prefer decision alternatives that allow the avoidance of highly competitive markets and high-stress management situations. Concern for these nonmonetary issues may induce the managers to forgo the decision alternative that would best serve the purely monetary objectives of the firm and, perhaps also, its managers.[6]

TABLE 2-8. Comparing Decision Criteria

Criterion	Auto Fleet	Plant and Buildings
Expected value	Not insure	Not insure
Maximin	Insure	Insure
Coefficient of variation	Insure	Insure
Certainty equivalent	(Not insure?)	(Insure?)

---

[6]See A. R. Cohen, H. Gadon, and G. Miaoulis, "Decision Making in Firms: The Impact of Non-Economic Factors," *Journal of Economic Issues,* 10, No. 2 (June 1976), pp. 242–58.

2.5   SEARCH COSTS AND THE VALUE OF INFORMATION

Search Costs

In an environment of uncertainty the firm lacks full information about the actual outcomes of its decision. If it chooses, it may engage in search activity to improve its information. Information can be improved by various means, starting with simple surveys of potential customers and progressing all the way to complex computer modeling and simulation. Advice and information can be purchased from consultants, or the firm can engage its own personnel in search procedures. The information which decision makers often need will not simply be the raw data but will usually require adjustment in some way, such as finding the expected values and present values of the raw data. In addition, raw data will often need to be seasonally adjusted or deflated by a price index, in order to be in the form most useful to the decision maker. Naturally, this search process costs money, and the costs of obtaining information are usually inversely related to the speed with which the information must be generated.

■ *Definition:*   *Search costs* are defined as the costs of obtaining information in the form needed by the decision maker and within the time constraints required by the decision maker.

The Value of Information

■ *Definition:*   The *value of information* is the difference between what you can earn with the information already held and what you could earn if you were to know with certainty the outcome prior to making the decision. In cases where the search costs are expected to be greater than the value of the information, the decision maker should proceed on the basis of the information already held and should not undertake the cost of obtaining any extra information, since its cost outweighs the benefits derived.

Example: Recall once more the decision problem of the firm considering the installation of either the large metal-stamping machine or the small machine. Now, suppose that a market research firm offers to undertake some intensive studies in order to tell the firm what the state of demand will be over the two-year period, before the firm has to make its decision. The market research firm advises that its fee will be $1,000, including all expenses. Should the firm incur these search cost or not?

If the firm did know in advance the exact state of demand over the next two years (for example, that it would be medium in year one and heavy in year two), it would simply choose the alternative that offers the greatest net present value under those circumstances. Similarly, for any other state of demand—if known in advance—it becomes a simple decision that can be made under conditions of certainty, since a single outcome follows each decision.

In Table 2–9 we repeat the outcomes for each decision alternative under each of

TABLE 2-9. Expected Value of Choosing the Best Alternative Given Full Prior Information

| State of Demand [1] | PRESENT VALUE OF PROFITS IF | | Choice with Certainty (machine) [4] | Present Value of Profits ($) [5] | Joint Probability [6] | Weighted PV ($) [7] |
	Large Machine ($) [2]	Small Machine ($) [3]				
Heavy-heavy	17,415	11,271	Large	17,415	0.08	1,393.20
Heavy-medium	11,220	9,619	Large	11,220	0.08	897.60
Heavy-light	7,916	6,315	Large	7,916	0.04	316.64
Medium-heavy	11,961	9,453	Large	11,961	0.12	1,435.32
Medium-medium	5,766	7,801	Small	7,801	0.12	936.12
Medium-light	2,462	4,497	Small	4,497	0.06	269.82
Light-heavy	7,416	5,817	Large	7,416	0.20	1,483.20
Light-medium	1,221	4,165	Small	4,165	0.20	833.00
Light-light	−2,083	861	Small	861	0.10	86.10
				Expected Present Value		$7,651.00

the nine jointly possible states of demand. Given the prior information concerning the actual state of demand, the firm would select the machine with the highest PV of profits under that state of demand. The machine that should be chosen under each possible state of demand is indicated in column 4 of Table 2-9, with the resultant profits in column 5.

What is the probability that the market researchers will advise the firm that the actual state of demand will be heavy-heavy, for example? Prior to receiving the additional information the firm still has only its joint probability distribution shown in column 6. The firm's decision maker would weight each of the payoffs in column 5 by its prior probability of occurring and add these weighted payoffs to find the expected present value of the decision under conditions of certainty. As we can see, this sum is $7,651.00.

Note: The expected value of information is the difference between this sum, $7,651.00, and the expected value of the best alternative with the information already held. The large machine had the higher EPV of profits, namely $6,401.50, and the difference is, therefore, $7,651.00 — $6,401.50 = $1,249.50. Thus the expected value of information is $1,249.50, and the cost of that information is $1,000. The firm should hire the market researchers, since it expects to be $249.50 ahead by doing so.[7]

---

[7]We are assuming that the researchers' findings will be borne out by the firm's experience. Typically, the firm would require a substantial margin for error in case the "full information" turns out to be wrong.

2.6 EVALUATION OF THE DECISION MADE

How do we evaluate decisions? What is a good decision? Is a decision a bad one if the actual outcome is bad? For example, if the firm chooses the large machine and the actual outcome is −$2,083 (the worst possible outcome foreseen), should the decision maker be castigated for the quality of his or her decision? The answer is "not necessarily." The quality of the decision depends on three main issues.

Three Basic Considerations

First, was the information search undertaken to the point where it would not be marginally profitable to continue the search procedure? Second, was the information obtained used in the appropriate form—for example, expected-present-value terms? Third, was the appropriate decision criterion used? If the answer is yes to all three questions, it *was* a good decision regardless of the actual outcome.

Note: The quality of decisions must be judged a *priori*, before the actual outcomes. Decision making under risk and uncertainty necessarily involves unsatisfactory outcomes from time to time. You win some and you lose some, but consistent application of the appropriate decision criterion, using as much good information as it seemed profitable to purchase, should ensure maximization of the firm's net worth, subject to risk considerations, over a series of decisions made. A bad decision will be made if the decision maker doesn't seek information when its cost is expected to be less than its value, if the decision maker ignores or discards information, or if an inappropriate decision criterion is used to make the decision. If such a decision turns out to be very profitable, the decision maker was just lucky and should not expect this luck to hold forever.

The Timing of the Decision

Since information tends to grow with the passage of time, decisions should not be made irrevocably before they *must* be made. A commitment made too early cannot (easily) be altered if new information comes along a little later. For example, if bids are solicited for a contract and the deadline for the submission of bids is at noon on the last day of the month, the firm should work through all the analysis and make a tentative decision (on the price of its bid), but it should delay submitting the bid until just before the deadline in case new information, such as a substantial increase in a major cost item or the bankruptcy of a major competitor, should come to light and cause the firm to want to change its commitment.

Rule: Whether or not there is a specific deadline, the timing rule is to defer the decision until the expected value of deferring the decision further is equal to the expected profits forgone by not making the decision. This deferral is not the same as procrastination, but rather, it means that the decision maker should consider and attempt to quantify the advantages of waiting and actually make the decision when it is apparent that more would be lost than gained by further waiting.

What if important additional information does arrive after the decision is made? Such things happen all the time. At that point a new decision problem occurs: Should the decision maker stick with the decision just made or make another decision. This new decision should be evaluated on the basis of the EPVs of each alternative, their relative risks, and so on. Even if the new decision is to change the earlier decision, this change does not make the earlier decision a bad one. If it was made on the basis of all information available at the time (after search had been carried to the optimal point), by the application of the appropriate decision criterion, and at a time when it appeared optimal to actually make the decision, then it was a good decision.

Sensitivity Analysis

Finally, the decision maker should consider the *sensitivity* of the decision to the assumptions on which it is based. All decisions are based on some assumptions—for example, that the data are accurate, that probability distributions will be validated by future events, that the discount rate used is appropriate, that fixed cost categories do not, in fact, vary with output levels, and so on.

■ **Definition:**   *Sensitivity analysis* is defined as the examination of a decision to find the degree of inaccuracy in the underlying assumptions that can be tolerated without causing the decision to be inappropriate.

Sensitivity analysis involves a systematic examination of the decision alternative selected, to see if that alternative would still be chosen under somewhat different assumptions concerning the cost and demand conditions and the opportunity discount rate. If these assumptions can be varied over a relatively wide range and the selected decision still remains optimal, we can be confident that it is not very sensitive to the underlying assumptions. If, on the other hand, a slightly different set of assumptions causes another decision alternative to be the chosen one, then the choice under the initial assumptions is very sensitive to those assumptions.

To conduct sensitivity analysis one proceeds systematically to vary one assumption at a time and notes whether any changed assumption causes a change in the recommendation. You might start with the discount rate, and recalculate the EPV assuming a discount rate that is, say, two points higher, and a third time assuming a discount rate that is two points lower, to see if the optimal decision would change if interest rates were to rise or fall in the near future.[8] Interest rates are potentially quite volatile and have been known to move dramatically in relatively short periods. The

---

[8]I can see you wincing at the thought of having to repeat all those calculations several more times! With the increasing availability of personal computers and spreadsheet software like Lotus 1-2-3, such recalculations are a simple matter. The *Computer Courseware Package and Manual* that is ancillary to this textbook contains a variety of templates, including an EPV decision tree template that allows you to enter

wise decision maker will be aware that significantly higher or lower interest rates either would or would not change the decision selected. If the decision is sensitive to the opportunity interest rate assumed, the decision maker should consider undertaking information-search activity to be assured which is the most likely interest rate scenario over the duration of the project.

Similarly, you should be assured that your decision is not sensitive to the accuracy of the estimate made of the initial costs. Since the initial costs are typically in present-value terms already, it is a simple matter to see how much of a cost overrun could be tolerated by looking at the EPV. If a small percentage variation in the initial costs would wipe out the EPV, then the decision is sensitive to the assumption that initial costs are estimated accurately. Again, more information should be sought on the cost situation if the decision is sensitive to that assumption.

Finally, your estimates of the probability distributions relating to the demand situations in the future periods are assumed to be accurate. In case they are not, you could look at a more pessimistic set of demand probabilities, as well as a more optimistic one. Here, you could either revise the profit figures downward (and later upward) using the same probabilities, or alternatively, shift the weighting toward the lower outcomes (and later toward the high outcomes) to reflect a more pessimistic (and later, more optimistic) demand scenario. If, under either the pessimistic or optimistic scenario, the chosen decision becomes suboptimal, information should be sought to assure the decision maker of the most likely demand situations.

2.7 SUMMARY

In this chapter we have continued our examination of the basic foundations of economic decision making. The expected-present-value analysis of Chapter 1 was extended to incorporate risk analysis. Most business decision makers appear to be risk averse; that is, they derive disutility from risk and uncertainty. The degree of risk can be measured by the standard deviation of the probability distribution of outcomes, and the degree of risk aversion can be measured by the rate at which the decision maker is willing to trade off expected value (or profits) for reduced risk. For complex decision alternatives with probability distributions of outcomes in each year there will be a joint probability distribution of outcomes at the end of the planning period. Such

---

the cost, demand, probability, and discount rate data and then instantly calculates the EPV and the coefficient of variation and selects the minimum and maximum possible outcomes. Sensitivity analysis is greatly facilitated by this template, since you simply enter the new data and the new solution values are displayed instantly. To use the courseware you need an IBM (or compatible) or Hewlett-Packard personal computer with at least 256K bytes of RAM, and a copy of the Lotus 1-2-3 software package. The *Courseware Manual* is included in the back of both the *Study Guide/Workbook* and the *Instructor's Manual*. Ask your instructor how to get a copy of the disk containing the Lotus templates that will help you with the great majority of the problems at the ends of the chapters (details are in the *Instructor's Manual*). The *Study Guide/Workbook*, which you may order through your bookstore, has full details on solving the problems, as well as chapter summaries, self-tests, and answers to all the discussion questions at the ends of the chapters.

decision problems are best handled by the use of decision trees, which array the possible outcomes and joint probabilities in a manner that facilitates the understanding and the solution of the problem.

Four more decision criteria were introduced, each incorporating some method of adjustment for risk. The coefficient-of-variation criterion effectively makes the decision on the basis of the least risk per dollar of expected value. The expected-value criterion can be adjusted for risk by the use of differing discount rates for alternatives with differing degrees of risk. The certainty-equivalent criterion is more comprehensive than the other two and adjusts for risk by choosing the decision alternative with the combination of risk and return that gives the decision maker the highest level of utility. Finally, the maximin-decision criterion adjusts for risk in a crude way by avoiding the decision alternatives that have inferior "downside" outcomes. The appropriate criterion for any particular decision depends on the firm's and the decision maker's objectives, the frequency and magnitude of the decision, and the firm's and the decision maker's attitudes toward risk.

Decisions should be evaluated on an *ex ante* basis, rather than on an *ex post* basis. Good decisions are those that are (1) based on properly adjusted EPV information; (2) obtained from a search procedure taken to the point where the value of additional information falls to equal the costs of obtaining that information; (3) found by applying the appropriate decision criterion; (4) made at the optimal point of time; and (5) suitably qualified by a statement of the sensitivity of the decision to the assumptions on which it is based.

DISCUSSION QUESTIONS

2-1. Define risk and uncertainty. How do we measure risk and uncertainty? Can you think of any other, more appropriate, measure of risk and uncertainty?

2-2. Define risk aversion. Does a risk averter refuse to take risks? Will a risk averter ever select the more risky alternative? Explain.

2-3. Explain why a risk preferrer might prefer a high-risk, low-stakes gamble to a low-risk, high-stakes gamble. Are you a risk averter, a risk preferrer, or are you risk indifferent? How do you know?

2-4. Demonstrate that the investor's *degree* of risk aversion (or preference) is an important element in determining his or her choice among investment alternatives.

2-5. Go through the thought process of determining your own certainty equivalent for a fifty-cent lottery ticket that is one of 100,000 sold for a $10,000 prize.

(a) What is the expected value of the ticket?

(b) Would you buy such a ticket? Why?

(c) How much more or less expensive would the ticket need to be to *just* induce you to buy it?

(d) Is that price your certainty equivalent for the gamble? Explain.

2-6. The product manager of a large company has had a series of disastrous new-product offerings. He fears that another failure will cost him his job. He is currently trying to make up his mind between two rather different new products for his next new-product launching. Product A has the greater expected value and has both a smaller minimum outcome and a larger maximum outcome as compared with Product B. Which product do you think the product manager will choose, and why?

2-7. In some cases the coefficient-of-variation criterion ranks decision alternatives in a different order, as compared to their ranking by the certainty-equivalent criterion. Explain.

2-8. Explain how the value of additional information is calculated.

2-9. Discuss the factors you would consider when evaluating a decision made by somebody else. Is it possible that you might conclude that it was a "good" decision even if the actual outcome was a disaster? Explain.

2-10. What is sensitivity analysis? How would you incorporate this into your recommendation to management concerning the choice between several decision alternatives?

PROBLEMS AND SHORT CASES

2-1. Sounds True, Inc., a small company producing stereo amplifiers, has found that its leading model has suffered substantial market-share losses because of the competition from other producers' newer models. The company is considering two alternatives for the coming year: either to give the existing product a minor facelift or to introduce a totally new model. The success or failure of these strategies will depend ultimately upon the state of the economy, as is evident from the payoff matrix:

State of the Economy	DECISION ALTERNATIVES	
	Minor Facelift	New Model
Downturn	10	−20
Constant	30	20
Upturn	80	150

The payoffs shown represent thousands of dollars net profit. The company considers that the probabilities of a downturn, a constant economy, and of an upturn, are 30 percent, 50 percent, and 20 percent, respectively.

(a) Calculate the expected value, standard deviation, and coefficient of variation for each decision alternative.

(b) Apply the expected-value, coefficient-of-variation, and the maximin decision criteria to find which alternative is indicated under each criterion.

(c) Which alternative will have the greater certainty equivalent? Explain.

2-2. To help pay your way through college you plan to operate either a hot-dog stand or an ice-cream stand at every home game of your local baseball team. The actual outcomes associated with each decision alternative depend to a large degree on the weather, since hot dogs will be in greater demand on cloudy and rainy days, whereas ice cream will be in greater demand on sunny days. The following payoff matrix shows the expected value of profits for each baseball game and for each decision alternative, under the three different states of nature considered possible. Your research at the local meteorological office indicates that over the past ten baseball seasons it was raining for 15 percent of the home games, cloudy for 55 percent of the games,

State of Nature	DECISION ALTERNATIVES	
	Hot Dogs	Ice Cream
Rain	$300	$ 75
Cloud	250	150
Sun	100	400

and sunny for 30 percent of the games. You must decide which product to choose for the entire season, either hot dogs or ice cream.

(a) Calculate the expected value and coefficient of variation of each decision alternative. Which alternative would you choose? Explain, including a statement about your certainty equivalent for each of the two alternatives.

(b) Suppose that you could purchase, for $50 per game, the right to choose between hot dogs and ice cream on the day of each game, so that you could always have the appropriate product for the state of nature encountered each time. (Someone else would take the other product on each occasion.) (1) What is the value of the information to be gained (about the weather) by delaying your decision until the day of the game? (2) Assuming you must, before the season starts, decide among option A (to sell hot dogs), or option B (to sell ice cream), or option C (to buy the right to sell either hot dogs or ice cream, depending on the weather for each game), which option would you choose? Explain.

2-3. Safeguard Stores is a relatively small chain operation in the retail supermarket industry. The area manager for Montreal, Nick Wolkowski, is considering opening a new store in a rapidly expanding suburb. Two sizes of store have been suggested: the regular size of 27,000 square feet and the superstore size of 40,000 square feet. The initial costs, expected-demand situation, profits, and probabilities are as follows:

Store Size	Initial Cost	Demand Situation	YEAR 1		YEAR 2	
			Profits	Prob.	Profits	Prob.
	$ 000		$ 000		$ 000	
Regular	850	Low	300	0.2	500	0.2
		Medium	500	0.5	800	0.4
		High	800	0.3	1,000	0.4
Super	1,000	Low	300	0.6	600	0.4
		Medium	600	0.3	900	0.3
		High	1,000	0.1	1,200	0.3

Mr. Wolkowski is considering only a two-year horizon, since he hopes to be regional manager by then. He feels that the appropriate discount rate is 10 percent. (Treat the profits as though they are received in lump sum at the end of year one and year two. The costs are incurred immediately.)

(a) Which store size promises the larger expected net present value?

(b) What do you think Mr. Wolkowski's decision will be, and why?

2-4. The Express Delivery Company operates a courier and parcel delivery service between the major cities in southern California. Management is considering whether to lease or buy an additional truck it needs in order to extend its services. Careful analysis of costs and the potential demand situation has led to the following estimates of net cash flows (NCF) for each of the first two years:

Lease Option:

YEAR 1		YEAR 2	
NCF	Probability	NCF	Probability
−5,000	0.25	5,000	0.30
5,000	0.40	10,000	0.50
15,000	0.35	15,000	0.20

Buy Option:

YEAR 1		YEAR 2	
NCF	Probability	NCF	Probability
−10,000	0.20	10,000	0.30
0	0.50	15,000	0.50
10,000	0.30	20,000	0.20

The management considers that a two-year time horizon is appropriate, since it would replace this truck with a new one in two years whether it was leased or purchased. If purchased, the truck will have a salvage value of $5,000 at the end of the second year, and this value is included in the above NCF figures. The lease agreement is for two years with no possibility of cancellation once signed. Management could alternatively invest the funds involved in corporate bonds, considered to be of similar risk to the strategy of expanding its services, and these bonds would yield 15 percent of current prices. Assume that all cash flows are spent or received at the end of each year in a single lump sum and ignore any tax considerations.

(a) Using decision-tree analysis, find the expected net present value of each alternative.

(b) Calculate a measure of risk for each alternative.

(c) Apply several decision criteria and make your recommendation to management.

(d) State any qualifications and reservations you would wish to add to your recommendation.

2-5. The Keene Construction and Real Estate Development Company buys tracts of land, builds residential home units on the land, and sells them to home buyers. Keene is currently considering the development of Loon Swamp Estates, which is a tract of land it has owned and used as a dump for landfill for several years.

   The potential development of Loon Swamp Estates has been narrowed to two alternatives. Project A is to build single-family houses, and project B is to build condominiums. In each case there would be immediate outlays to establish the streets, drainage, electrical and sewerage systems, and other amenities. For project A these initial costs will be $1 million, while for project B these costs will be $1.5 million because of the additional costs of a swimming pool, tennis courts, security services, and other features of the condominium project.

   For either project there would be costs incurred throughout the following two years as the home units are constructed. Building would start at the main entrance and proceed in stages toward the back of development. As units (either houses or condominiums) are completed, they will be sold at current market value. Keene faces uncertainty on the revenue side since market value might be high or low depending on various factors. This uncertainty is reflected in the following probability distributions of net cash flow (not including the initial costs) for each project:

PROJECT A NET CASH FLOWS				PROJECT B NET CASH FLOWS			
Year 1 (million dollars)	Prob.	Year 2 (million dollars)	Prob.	Year 1 (million dollars)	Prob.	Year 2 (million dollars)	Prob.
−1.5	0.30	2.0	0.20	−1.5	0.35	2	0.20
0.25	0.50	2.5	0.50	0.5	0.40	3	0.50
1.5	0.20	3.0	0.30	2.5	0.25	4	0.30

Rather than invest in either of these projects at all, Keene could alternatively invest in bonds being issued by another real estate developer in a nearby city, which promise 14 percent interest on funds invested.

(a) Using decision-tree analysis, calculate the expected net present value and standard deviation of each project.

(b) Conduct sensitivity analysis with respect to your input data.

(c) Apply several decision criteria to this problem, and make your recommendation to Keene management.

(d) State explicitly any qualifications and assumptions which underlie your recommendation.

2-6. Your firm is considering the introduction of a new product, and you are required to set the price. You are considering three price strategies: high ($6), medium ($4), and low ($2.50). Your market research team has indicated that the probability distribution of sales at these prices is as follows:

	HIGH PRICE		MEDIUM PRICE		LOW PRICE	
	Sales	Prob.	Sales	Prob.	Sales	Prob.
First year	3,500	0.1	5,000	0.2	10,000	0.4
	2,500	0.3	4,000	0.5	7,500	0.3
	1,500	0.6	3,000	0.3	5,000	0.3
Second year	5,000	0.2	8,000	0.3	12,000	0.3
	4,000	0.3	6,500	0.4	9,000	0.5
	3,000	0.5	5,000	0.3	7,500	0.2

The initial investment will be $22,000, and per-unit variable costs will be constant at $1 regardless of volume. You are advised by the finance department that the $22,000 could otherwise be invested (at comparable risk) in a forthcoming bond issue at 12.5 percent per annum.

(a) Using decision-tree analysis, find which pricing strategy promises the greatest net present value over the two-year period.

(b) Should the investment funds be used to buy the bonds instead? Why?

(c) Rank the strategies in order of their risk. Explain the basis for your ranking.

(d) Rank the strategies in order of their risk-adjusted expected value.

(e) Is the coefficient-of-variation criterion contradicted by the certainty-equivalent criterion in this case? Explain.

2-7. Noble Neckties is considering investing in another machine to produce neckties. It is considering the joint decision of the price and quality of the single type of necktie it will market. Three possibilities are considered feasible: (A) lower-quality materials and workmanship, resulting in a per-unit direct cost of $5 and priced at $8 per unit; (B) better-quality materials and workmanship, with direct cost of $6 per unit and priced at $11; and (C) top-quality materials and workmanship, with direct cost of $7 per unit and priced at $14. The firm has a planning horizon of two years, after which time the machine will be worthless. The machines will cost $10,000, $15,000, and $25,000, respectively. (Treat all cash flows as arriving at the end of the year.) The firm considers its opportunity discount rate to be 10 percent.

To help in the decision, the firm employed the Astigmatic Research Company to generate estimates of probable sales for each of the above-mentioned price/quality modes. A.R.C. has produced the following carefully estimated projections of sales volumes for the next two years:

	SALES VOLUME	PROBABILITIES	
	Each Year	Year 1	Year 2
Necktie A	2,000	0.10	0.50
	6,000	0.60	0.30
	10,000	0.30	0.20
Necktie B	2,000	0.40	0.30
	6,000	0.40	0.50
	10,000	0.20	0.20
Necktie C	2,000	0.50	0.40
	6,000	0.30	0.50
	10,000	0.20	0.10

(a) Apply the expected-value, maximin, and coefficient-of-variation criteria to these alternatives to find which alternative is indicated under each criterion.

(b) Which price/quality mode should the firm choose, in your judgment?

2-8.   The Walwyn Widgets Company operates a thriving mail-order business and has achieved considerable success using television advertisements to promote new products, novelty items, record and tape collections of music, and so forth. The Director of New-Product Development, Charles van Winkle, has presented to the Executive Committee three new product suggestions, one of which will be the next product produced and sold. Because of limited availability of television time, sales personnel, and production facilities, only one of these projects can be implemented now. The other two will be set aside and will compete with any new possibilities that arise in the future.

Product A is an electronic message board that is preprogrammed to roll a series of messages across the screen, including "Have a Nice Day!" and "God Loves You." This product is expected to encounter very stiff competition after two years. The initial setup cost of Product A is $40,000. Product B is a collection of country music on a videotape album, initially costing $250,000, because of the permissions that must be purchased. Market research indicates that the market for this product will be saturated after two years. Product C, initially costing $30,000 is an antitheft alarm system for automobiles which is also expected to have only a two-year life because of rapid technological advances. Mr. van Winkle has obtained estimates of profits and probability distributions associated with each product, as shown on page 67.

Assume that these profits are received at the end of the year and that Walwyn Widgets could otherwise invest the funds at 14 percent in a mutual fund, judged by Mr. van Winkle to be roughly equal in risk to the three proposals presented.

(a) Using decision-tree analysis, find the expected net present value of each proposal and calculate a measure of risk for each proposal.

Product	YEAR 1		YEAR 2	
	Profits	Probability	Profits	Probability
A	$ 30,000	0.60	$ 30,000	0.65
	80,000	0.30	60,000	0.25
	100,000	0.10	80,000	0.10
B	100,000	0.30	50,000	0.35
	300,000	0.50	100,000	0.40
	500,000	0.20	150,000	0.25
C	−25,000	0.20	15,000	0.30
	50,000	0.40	50,000	0.40
	100,000	0.40	75,000	0.30

(b) Apply several decision criteria to the choice problem and advise Mr. van Winkle which product he should choose.

(c) State any qualifications and reservations you would wish to add to your decision.

2-9. The Venture Startup Company (VESCO) solicits capital from investors and uses this capital to start new business ventures. It pays 14 percent on the capital it borrows, and invests in new ventures that promise to make a return on investment higher than that. At the present time VESCO has $700,000 to invest and is considering two alternative ventures. Alternative A is a Christmas-tree farm, already operating, and alternative B is a new fast-food restaurant chain, specializing in South American food. For each venture, VESCO has considered three demand scenarios for each of the first two years. VESCO typically sells its ventures after two years, presuming either a successful startup or rejuvenation of an existing business.

The initial cost of the Christmas tree farm is $550,000, and profits in the first year are expected to be either $600,000, $400,000, or $200,000, with probabilities 0.25, 0.6, and 0.15, respectively. The profit in the second year will depend on what happened in the first year: it will be the same as the first year, with probability 0.4; 50 percent greater, with probability 0.4; or 50 percent less, with probability 0.2. This business is highly seasonal, of course, with the great bulk of the profits being generated at the end of each year. Assume that it is now January, and you would pay for the farm immediately.

The initial cost of the fast-food chain is $700,000, also payable immediately. First-year profits are expected to be $600,000, $500,000, or $400,000, with probabilities 0.3, 0.4, and 0.3, respectively. In the second year profits may be the same as they turn out to be in the first year, with probability 0.5, or $100,000 higher or lower, with probabilities 0.3 and 0.2, respectively. These profits flow in throughout each year in a more or less continuous stream.

(a) Calculate the EPV of each alternative.

(b) Using several decision criteria, advise VESCO as to which alternative they should choose.

(c) Qualify your recommendation with sensitivity analysis with regard to the discount rate used, VESCO's attitude toward risk, and the estimated demand scenarios.

(d) What other assumptions and qualifications underlie your recommendation?

2-10. Houston Homewares has suffered a declining market share over the past year, and management has considered various means of reversing the trend. Extensive analysis has narrowed the options to two.

Plan A is to conduct a point-of-purchase promotion campaign involving the manufacture of special samples and the disbursement of these in shopping centers and on city streets. This plan would take a year to set up and would cost $100,000 during the first year. Implementation of this plan is expected to increase the firm's existing profits in the second year by $40,000, $60,000, or $80,000 (with probabilities of 0.2, 0.5, and 0.3, respectively), depending upon whether the promotion is fairly, moderately, or highly successful, respectively. If fairly successful in year two, year-three profits will be increased by either $50,000, $100,000, or $150,000, with probabilities of 0.4, 0.3, and 0.3. If moderately successful in year two, year-three profits will be increased by either $80,000, $120,000, or $160,000 with probabilities of 0.3, 0.4, and 0.3. If highly successful in year two, year-three profits will be increased by either $100,000, $150,000, or $200,000, with probabilities of 0.2, 0.5, and 0.3. All cash flows under plan A will occur more or less continuously throughout each year.

Plan B is to contract out to an advertising agency that would prepare a series of campaigns for use predominately in the print media. This would cost $150,000 in the first year, and increased profits of $50,000, $100,000, or $150,000 are expected in the second year, with probabilities of 0.1, 0.5, and 0.4, depending upon whether the campaign is fairly successful, moderately successful, or highly successful. If year two is fairly successful, increased profits in year three will be $50,000, $100,000, or $150,000, with probabilities of 0.2, 0.4, and 0.4. If year two is moderately successful, year three's increased profits will be $100,000, $150,000, or $200,000, with probabilities of 0.2, 0.5, and 0.3. If year two is highly successful, profits in year three will be increased by $150,000, $200,000, or $250,000, with probabilities of 0.1, 0.5, and 0.4. Because of the financial arrangements associated with plan B, all cash flows will occur at the end of each year. The firm's opportunity discount rate for both projects is 18 percent.

(a) Construct the decision tree for each decision alternative and calculate the expected present value of profits for each plan.

(b) Calculate the standard deviation of the outcome for each plan.

(c) Apply the expected-value, maximin, and coefficient-of-variation criteria to find the plan favored by each criterion.

(d) Discuss the application of the certainty-equivalent criterion to this problem, on the presumption that management is risk averse.

SUGGESTED REFERENCES AND FURTHER READING

Arrow, K. J. "Risk Perception in Psychology and Economics," *Economic Inquiry,* 20 (January 1982), pp. 1–19.

Baumol, W. J. *Economic Theory and Operations Analysis* (4th ed.), chaps. 18, 19, 25. Englewood Cliffs, N.J.: Prentice-Hall, Inc., 1977.

Brigham, E. F. *Financial Management Theory and Practice* (2nd ed.), chaps. 5, 12, 15. Hinsdale, Ill.: The Dryden Press, 1979.

Dean, G., and A. Halter. *Decisions Under Uncertainty.* Cincinnati, Ohio: South-Western Publishing, 1971.

Friedman, D. "Why There Are No Risk Preferers," *Journal of Political Economy,* 89 (June 1981), p. 600.

Friedman, M., and L. J. Savage. "The Utility Analysis of Choices Involving Risk," *Journal of Political Economy,* 56 (August 1948), pp. 279–304.

Gordon, G., and I. Pressman. *Quantitative Decision Making for Business,* chaps. 3, 4, 5. Englewood Cliffs, N.J.: Prentice-Hall, Inc., 1978.

Hirshleifer, J. "Investment Decisions Under Uncertainty: Choice-Theoretic Approaches," *Quarterly Journal of Economics,* 79 (November 1965), pp. 509–36.

Horowitz, I. *Decision Making and the Theory of the Firm.* New York: Holt, Rinehart & Winston, 1970.

Huber, G. P. *Managerial Decision Making.* Glenview, Ill.: Scott, Foresman & Company, 1980.

Loomes, G., and R. Sugden. "Regret Theory: An Alternate Theory of Rational Choice under Uncertainty," *Economic Journal,* 92 (December 1982), pp. 805–24.

Miller, E. "Decision-Making under Uncertainty for Capital Budgeting and Hiring," *Managerial and Decision Economics,* 6 (March 1985), pp. 11–18.

Radford, K. J. *Modern Managerial Decision Making.* Reston, Va.: Reston Publishing Company, Inc., 1981.

Raiffa, H. *Decision Analysis: Introductory Lectures on Choices under Uncertainty.* Reading, Mass.: Addison-Wesley Publishing Co., Inc., 1970.

3 Utility Analysis of Consumer Behavior

3.1 INTRODUCTION

In the first two chapters we established the basis for decision making under conditions of risk and uncertainty. In those chapters we spoke generally of costs, revenues, and profits, and we utilized those concepts to find the decision alternative which best served the firm's objectives. Now, we go back to basics to examine the principles underlying consumer demand and, hence, the firm's revenues. Our objective is to examine the behavior of consumers to determine their most likely response to changes in variables that the firm can control, such as prices, product design, and promotional expenditures, as well as to examine the probable response of consumers to changes in variables that the firm cannot control, such as consumer incomes and the prices (and other competitive strategies) of other sellers. With a strong understanding of the principles underlying consumer behavior, we are then in a better position to explain and predict the impact on the firm's revenues of changes in the factors that operate to determine the level of those revenues.[1]

The next section of this chapter examines the traditional approach to economic consumer behavior, that is, indifference-curve analysis of consumer choice between and among products. The third section examines an alternative and relatively new approach to consumer behavior: the *attribute* approach to consumer choice. Whereas the traditional approach assumes that consumers derive utility from the consumption of products, the attribute approach assumes that consumers derive utility not from the products *per se* but from the attributes (or characteristics) embodied in or attached to the products. Using the example of an automobile, the traditional view is that the consumer derives utility from the automobile itself, while the attribute approach is

---

[1]This chapter may be bypassed without serious loss of continuity if, for example, the instructor deems it necessary to do so because of limited course length or appropriate because the students already have a strong background in the underlying principles of demand theory. Chapter 4 looks at *aggregate* consumer demand and is written so that it can stand alone without the necessity of understanding all the underlying principles of *individual* consumer demand.

that utility is obtained from the benefits derived from the automobile, such as transportation, comfort, prestige, power, economy, and other features perceived and appreciated by the consumer.

The attribute approach has important implications for managerial economics, especially in the pricing and product quality areas. Since attributes have utility value to consumers, prices of products should be chosen with regard to the presence, absence, or degree of desirable attributes associated with the product. Similarly, products should be developed to include the attributes that are considered desirable by potential buyers. The attribute approach to consumer behavior provides the bridge that links the economic analysis of consumer behavior with the pricing practices and the product development strategies of business firms, as we shall see in Chapters 10, 11, and 14.

3.2 INDIFFERENCE-CURVE ANALYSIS OF CONSUMER BEHAVIOR

The indifference-curve model of consumer behavior is not an *explanatory* model of consumer behavior. The reasons people buy what they do and react to changes in economic variables the way they do are buried deep in their psyches, and we leave it to psychologists to investigate the actual thought processes that culminate in the decision to purchase any particular product. Instead, the indifference-curve model is a *predictive* model of consumer behavior; although consumers do not think in terms of their indifference curves, they act as if they do. In fact, the predictions of the indifference-curve model are usually remarkably accurate, and consequently this model is of great assistance to the managerial economist.

Economists postulate that consumers derive *utility*, or psychic satisfaction, from the consumption of goods and services. Different products give different amounts of utility, and for a given product the consumer is assumed to receive diminishing utility from consecutive units consumed during a given period. Suppose a consumer buys an ice cream and enjoys it immensely. We might speculate that the consumer received, say, 10 units of utility. A second ice cream then consumed would also be enjoyed, but probably not as much as the first one. We might speculate that the consumer received 6 units of utility from the second ice cream. A third ice cream might give only 2 units of utility, since the consumer would by now be quite full, and the taste is no longer as pleasing as it first was. The consumer's *total utility* would be 18 units of utility from the three ice creams. The change in total utility for each additional ice cream is known as the *marginal utility* of those ice creams.

■ **Definitions:** *Utility* is the psychic satisfaction, or feeling of well-being, that a consumer derives from the consumption of goods and services. *Total utility* is the sum of all utility received from all goods and services consumed. The *marginal utility* of a good is equal to the change in total utility as the consumption of that good is changed by one unit. We assume *diminishing marginal utility*—that is, declining values for marginal utility as the rate of consumption increases during any given consumption period—for all goods and services.[2]

We postulate that consumers are basically hedonists and wish to maximize their utility. Thus they choose products for consumption on the basis of the utility they expect to receive from each product. But since most goods and services cost money and since the income, or wealth, of most consumers is limited, consumers must allocate their available funds among the goods and services, taking account of the differing prices and differing utility expected from different products so that their utility is maximized, given the income constraint. A consumer who is pursuing the maximization of utility is said to be acting "rationally."

Preference and Indifference

Since consumers are assumed to be seeking utility maximization, they will *prefer* combinations of goods and services that give them higher levels of total utility over combinations that give them lower levels of total utility. They will be *indifferent* among combinations that give exactly the same level of total utility. In order to depict the indifference-curve model using two-dimensional graphs we restrict the analysis to combinations of only two goods. This simplification does not limit our conclusions, however: you may rest assured that this model can be extended to any number of goods, using mathematical techniques, and the major conclusions stay the same. Thus we assume that the consumer may consume any combination of two particular goods. Some of these combinations will be preferable to others, and some combinations will give the same level of total utility, leaving the consumer indifferent among those combinations. Now imagine these combinations on a graph, with quantities of one product measured along the horizontal axis and quantities of the other product measured on the vertical axis.

■ *Definition:*   An *indifference curve* is defined as a locus of points in a graph representing combinations of two products (or any two variables, such as risk and return) that give the same total utility to a particular person.

---

[2]Products for which it is said one must "acquire a taste," such as caviar, frogs' legs, and truffles, are often suggested as contradictions to the principle of diminishing marginal utility, since, as you eat more and more caviar, for example, you may enjoy it more and more. But the principle of diminishing marginal utility is only contradicted if, at any one meal, you enjoy subsequent spoonfuls of caviar more than you enjoyed preceding spoonfuls. Trying caviar again a week later and enjoying it more this time is not the same as having a second serving on the first occasion. The principle of diminishing marginal utility refers to the decline of marginal utility during a particular period of time when more than one unit of the product is consumed. Thus we expect marginal utility to decline as the consumer increases the *rate* of consumption during a given time period. Even if you like caviar more the second time you try it (for example, a week later), your MU is expected to decrease as you increase your rate of consumption.

Example: Let us consider a particular consumer's demand for two particular products. Suppose a college student buys hamburgers and milkshakes for lunch and we wish to know what weekly combination of hamburgers and milkshakes would maximize her utility from those two products. Figure 3–1 shows hamburgers on the vertical axis, measured in physical units, and milkshakes on the horizontal axis, also measured in physical units. The lines I_1 and I_2 are two of the student's indifference curves. The combinations of hamburgers and milkshakes represented by indifference curve I_1, such as five burgers/one shake and three burgers/two shakes, gives her the *same* level of expected utility. Combinations that lie to the right and above indifference curve I_1 promise a *higher* level of utility, and combinations that lie to the left and below that curve promise a *lower level* of utility.

For each point in the product space represented by Figure 3–1 there will be a series of other points among which the student is indifferent. Consider point C on indifference curve I_2, which represents two burgers/four shakes. Starting from this point, we could find the other points on indifference curve I_2 by a process of questioning the student about her preference or indifference between other combinations of burgers and shakes.

Suppose we ask the student which would she prefer: two burgers and four shakes (point C) or three burgers and three shakes? If she prefers the latter combination, it is

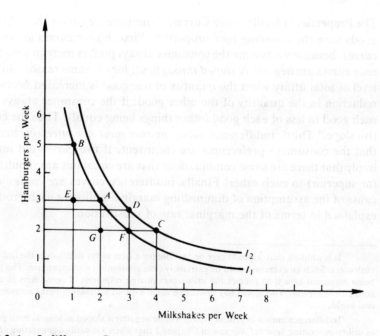

FIGURE 3–1. Indifference Curves between Products

evident that the extra burger in the latter combination more than compensates her in terms of utility for the shake that was taken away. If we then offer this consumer the choice of the initial combination C, or of two and one-half burgers and three shakes, and she expresses preference for the initial combination, we know that the extra half burger does not compensate her for the loss of the one shake. Continuing this process, we would find a new combination of burgers and shakes for which the consumer is indifferent when faced with a choice of this combination or with the combination represented by point C. Suppose this occurs at point D, which is two and three-quarters burgers and three shakes. When confronted with this choice, the student says that she has no preference between the two combinations, that either one is as good as the other. Hence points D and C are on the same indifference curve. By the same process we could generate a multitude of combinations that this consumer feels are identical (in terms of utility derived) to points D and C and which, therefore, also lie on indifference curve I_2.

Since we could start this process from any combination of hamburgers and milkshakes, it follows that there is an indifference curve passing through every point in the figure. We have shown simply two of the infinite number of indifference curves that represent this particular consumer's taste and preference pattern between the two products. To the right of those curves shown there will be curves that depict progressively higher levels of utility; and to the left and below indifference curve I_1 there will be curves that depict progressively lower levels of utility.[3]

The Properties of Indifference Curves.   Indifference curves showing combinations of goods have the following four properties. First, *higher curves are preferred to lower curves*, because we assume the consumer always prefers more to less. Second, indifference curves are *negatively sloped throughout*, for the same reason. To stay at the same level of total utility when the quantity of one good is increased necessarily requires a reduction in the quantity of the other good, if the consumer always prefers more of each good to less of each good (other things being equal). Thus the curve has a negative slope.[4] Third, indifference curves *neither meet nor intersect*, because we assume that the consumer's preferences are consistent. If two curves did intersect, it would imply that there are some combinations that are equal but are simultaneously inferior (or superior) to each other! Finally, indifference curves are *convex from below*, because of the assumption of diminishing marginal utility for each product. This is best explained in terms of the marginal rate of substitution.

---

[3]It is unlikely that it would ever be feasible for a firm to try to discover the indifference curves of its customers. Such an exercise would be extremely time consuming and expensive. The purpose of the model being employed here is to predict the utility-maximizing responses of consumers to changes in their economic environment. The model has predictive value without necessarily being economically feasible in the real world.

[4]Indifference curves in product space will be negatively sloped as long as both products are regarded as utility-generating "goods." We saw in Chapter 2 that when a disutility-generating "bad," such as risk, is placed on one axis, the indifference curves will be positively sloping. Note that the other three properties hold true for the risk-return indifference curve discussed in Chapter 2.

■ *Definition:*   The *marginal rate of substitution* (MRS) is defined as the amount of one product that the consumer will be willing to give up for an additional unit of another product, in order to remain at the same level of utility. The proviso that the consumer remains at the same level of utility makes it clear that the MRS refers to a movement along a particular indifference curve. By convention we define the MRS between two products for a movement *down* a particular indifference curve. Thus the MRS is the ratio of the amount given up of the product on the vertical axis, to the one-unit increment of the product on the horizontal axis.

The MRS is thus equal to the *slope* of an indifference curve at any point on that curve, since it is defined in terms of the vertical rise (or fall) over the horizontal run. Symbolically, and in terms of our example,

$$\text{MRS} = \frac{\Delta H}{\Delta M}$$

(3-1)

where ΔH is the decrement to hamburger consumption necessary to maintain utility at the same level given the one-unit increase in milkshake consumption, ΔM. (The Greek letter Δ, uppercase delta, is the conventional symbol for denoting a change in a variable.)

Since convexity of an indifference curve means that the slope will decrease progressively as we move from left to right along the indifference curve, it also means that the MRS will diminish progressively as we move down each indifference curve. In terms of Figure 3-1 the MRS between points B and A on indifference curve I_1 is the ratio $BE/EA = 2$. The MRS for the next (third) milkshake per week is equal to the ratio $AG/GF = 1$. Observing Figure 3-1 you can see that the MRS for the fourth milkshake is approximately 0.5 and that the MRS continues to diminish as the consumer exchanges more hamburgers for milkshakes along indifference curve I_1.

Note: The MRS declines because it is equal to the ratio of the marginal utility of the product on the horizontal axis divided by the marginal utility of the product on the vertical axis. That is,

$$\text{MRS} = \frac{MU_m}{MU_h}$$

(3-2)

To appreciate this, note that the movement from point B to point A along indifference curve I_1 in Figure 3-1 left the consumer at the same level of utility after substituting one milkshake for two hamburgers. The marginal utility attached to the milkshake received must have been equal to the marginal utility given up by sacrificing *two* hamburgers. Thus the ratio of the marginal utility of milkshakes to the marginal utility of hamburgers is equal to two. Similarly, from point A to point F, total utility stays constant as the consumer gives up one more hamburger for one more milkshake. Thus the marginal utilities attached to the two products must be equal, and their ratio is equal to one. Since the MRS is equal to the ratio of the MU of the product being acquired to the MU of the product given up, and since we have assumed diminishing marginal utility for all products, it is clear that MRS must diminish, since MRS is the ratio of a numerator that is falling and a denominator that is rising, as we move down along any given indifference curve. Thus the assumption of diminishing marginal utilities causes indifference curves to be convex to the origin.[5]

The Consumer's Budget Constraint

Since the consumer prefers higher indifference curves to lower indifference curves, it is evident that to maximize utility the consumer would proceed to the highest indifference curve possible. The limits of possibility are defined by the consumer's ability to afford the combinations desired. Were it not for a constraint upon income, wealth, and other financial resources, the consumer might proceed upward and to the right to a state of infinite euphoria! The budget constraint, however, keeps our consumer's feet on the ground, since certain combinations of the two products are simply not affordable.

■ *Definition:*   The *budget constraint* is defined as the total income or wealth the consumer is able to spend on goods and services per period. In the simple two-commodity situation we can write the budget constraint as

$$B = P_h \cdot H + P_m \cdot M \tag{3-3}$$

where B is the total dollar budget available to the consumer; P_h and P_m are the prices per physical unit of hamburgers and milkshakes; and H and M are the number of physical units of hamburgers and milkshakes purchased by the consumer.[6]

In this equation three symbols (B, P_h, and P_m) represent parameters that will be known to the consumer, namely, the budget available, the price of hamburgers, and the price of milkshakes. The remaining symbols (H and M) are variables that will take on the values necessary to maximize the consumer's utility. Equation (3-3) is actually a linear equation in those two variables. This will be more obvious if we rearrange terms

---

[5]In the case of indifference curves in risk-return space the marginal utility of return (a "good") is assumed to diminish, while the marginal *disutility* of risk (a "bad") is assumed to *increase* as the risk averter accepts more and more units of risk. The slope of an indifference curve in risk-return space is MD-risk/MU-return = MRS. As the risk averter accepts more risk in conjunction with more expected return, MD-risk rises and MU-return falls. Thus the MRS ratio rises and the indifference curve becomes progressively more steep as we move along it to the right. Consequently, the indifference curve is convex from below, as in the regular case of negatively sloped indifference curves between combinations of goods.

[6]The model does not preclude savings; the consumer is free to "spend" money on savings if this contributes to utility maximization. Savings are like any other product in the sense that the consumer expects to derive utility by allocating part of available income to that end.

and express the equation in terms of one of the variables. Subtracting B and $P_h \cdot H$ from both sides, and dividing both sides by $-P_h$ gives us

$$H = \frac{B}{P_h} - \frac{P_m}{P_h} \cdot M \tag{3-4}$$

In this form H is a linear function of the variable M and three parameters, where B/P_h is the intercept term, and the coefficient to M (namely, $-P_m/P_h$) is the slope term.

Example: Suppose the parameters take the values B = \$5.00, P_h = \$1.00, and P_m = \$0.50. To solve for the intercept we set M = zero and find B/P_h = 5. Thus, if the consumer spends her entire budget on hamburgers, she will be able to purchase 5 units weekly. Alternatively, if she spends her total available income on milkshakes, she can purchase 10 units weekly. In Figure 3-2 we show equation (3-4) plotted in product space. Note that it intercepts the vertical axis at 5 units and the horizontal axis at 10 units. Starting from the vertical intercept, if milkshake consumption is increased from zero to 1, we note from equation (3-4) that the value of H is drawn down in the ratio $-P_m/P_h$. This ratio of prices is of course the slope of the line and is constant throughout the length of the line, since prices are constant.

All combinations of hamburgers and milkshakes that occur on that line cost exactly \$5, as may be verified from Figure 3-2. All combinations that lie above and to

FIGURE 3-2. The Budget Constraint between Products

the right of the income constraint line are unattainable combinations, since they cost more than $5, and all combinations lying below the line cost less than $5.

Utility Maximization

Let us now superimpose the indifference curves of Figure 3-1 upon the budget constraint line of Figure 3-2. This combined graph is shown in Figure 3-3. Suppose the consumer is at point E, spending all her available income on three hamburgers and four milkshakes and enjoying a utility level denoted by indifference curve I_2. It can be seen that point F is superior to point E and, moreover, that it allows the consumer to attain the highest possible indifference curve. Any higher indifference curve would not touch any of the attainable combinations and therefore is not affordable. The combination of hamburgers and milkshakes that appears to maximize our consumer's utility is thus approximately two and one-third hamburgers and five and one-third milkshakes.[7] By a quick calculation we can confirm that this combination does not break the consumer's income constraint. The two and one-third hamburgers will cost approximately $2.33, and the five and one-third milkshakes will cost approximately $2.67, making a total expenditure of $5.00.

FIGURE 3-3. Maximization of Utility from Products

---

[7]These fractional units should not bother us, since we can eliminate them by extending the time period. For example, every three weeks the consumer should purchase seven hamburgers and sixteen milkshakes.

Rule: Utility maximization therefore requires that the consumer choose the combination on the budget constraint line where this line is tangent to an indifference curve. Tangency between the budget line and an indifference curve requires that their slopes be equal. Recalling that the slope of an indifference curve is the marginal rate of substitution and that the slope of the budget line is the price ratio, we can express the condition for utility maximization as

$$\text{MRS} = \frac{P_m}{P_h} \qquad (3\text{-}5)$$

given that all available income is spent. We have previously seen that

$$\text{MRS} = \frac{MU_m}{MU_h} \qquad (3\text{-}2)$$

Therefore, we may alternatively express the maximizing condition as

$$\frac{MU_m}{MU_h} = \frac{P_m}{P_h} \qquad (3\text{-}6)$$

Rearranging terms, we have

$$\frac{MU_m}{P_m} = \frac{MU_h}{P_h} \qquad (3\text{-}7)$$

Thus the condition for maximizing utility is to spend the available income such that the ratio of marginal utility to price is the same for all products purchased. In the hamburger/milkshake example it is clear that the consumer must expect to derive twice as much utility from the marginal hamburger, as compared with the marginal milkshake, since its price is twice as great.[8]

The preceding analysis is concerned with the consumer's utility maximization given a set of available products, their prices, and the consumer's income. We turn now to an analysis of the consumer's utility-maximizing *response* to *changes* in the price of a product.

---

[8]Generalizing to n products, the condition for utility maximization is

$$\frac{MU_1}{P_1} = \frac{MU_2}{P_2} = \frac{MU_3}{P_3} = \ldots = \frac{MU_n}{P_n}$$

given the equality of

$$B = \sum_{i=1}^{n} P_i Q_i$$

where the subscripts $i = 1, 2, 3, \ldots, n$ represent the identity of the n products available.

The Price Effect and the Law of Demand

■ *Definition:* The *price effect* is defined as the change in the quantity demanded of a particular product that is due to a change in the price of that product, *ceteris paribus*.[9] Let us investigate the reaction of a particular consumer to changes in the price level of a particular product.

Example: In the upper part of Figure 3-4 we show the indifference curves of an individual consumer between self-service and full-service gasoline.[10] Suppose the initial prices of self-service gas (SSG) and full-service gas (FSG) and the consumer's income level are such that the appropriate budget line is N_1M_1. Thus the consumer maximizes utility at point A, at which he purchases X_3 units of FSG and the indicated amount of SSG.

Let us now suppose that the price of FSG is reduced. This price change causes the budget line to swing around to that shown as N_1M_2 since its vertical intercept is unchanged while the slope coefficient falls. The consumer responds by moving to point B with a higher level of utility. Notice that after the price reduction for FSG, the consumer's consumption of this product was raised from X_3 to X_4. Let us now suppose that the price of FSG is *raised* such that the appropriate budget line is N_1M_3. The consumer will now maximize utility by attaining the point C, where consumption of FSG has fallen to X_2 units. If the price of this product were raised still further, such that the appropriate budget line was N_1M_4, the consumer would select point D on that budget line and would maximize utility by consuming X_1 units of FSG and the indicated amount of SSG.

If we join the points A, B, C, and D, we obtain what is known as the *price consumption curve* (PCC), which is the locus of the points of tangency between the appropriate budget constraint line and the highest attainable indifference curve at various price levels of the product on the horizontal axis. It shows how the consumption of one product (and implicitly of the other as well) changes as the price of that product varies. It is apparent that the relationship between the price of a product and the quantity demanded of that product is an inverse one.

■ *Definition:* The *law of demand* states that as the price is raised the consumer demands progressively less of the product and, conversely, as the price is reduced the

[9]If you have forgotten, *ceteris paribus* means "all other things remaining the same," which means in this case that the consumer's monetary income and the price of all other available products must remain the same. The price effect requires a constant *monetary* income, while the substitution effect, explained on page 82, requires a constant *real* income.

[10]We can legitimately regard these as separate products since they are composed of different attributes. Full-service gas comes complete with smiling attendant eager to check your oil, fan belt, filters, radiator water and hoses, and tire pressures and to wash your windows, headlights, and taillights. (This is clearly a *textbook* example.) Self-service gas comes without the above but with a significant saving per tankful and no anxiety about lost filler caps. Many consumers will demand both types of gas since they desire the attributes of each at different times.

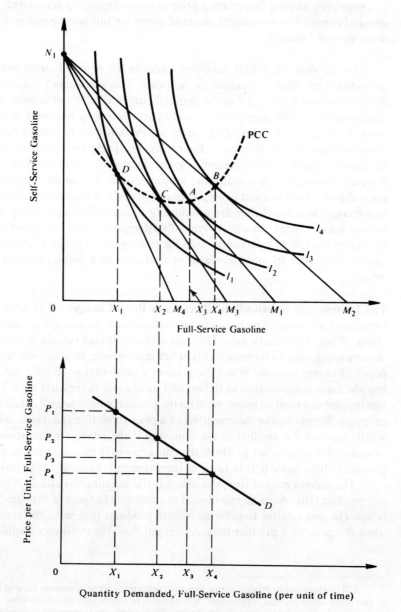

FIGURE 3-4. The Price Consumption Curve and the Demand Curve

consumer demands progressively more of the product. It is an empirical law, meaning that it is commonly observed in practice. The law of demand is expressed graphically as a negatively sloping line relating price to units of quantity demanded; this line is the *demand curve*. The consumer's demand curve for full-serve gasoline is shown in the lower part of Figure 3-4.

Notice that the actual data that underlie the demand curve depend upon the individual's reaction to changes in the price. This consumer's demand curve is not likely to be exactly the same as the demand curves of other consumers, who have their own taste and preference patterns and hence their own reactions to changes in the price of the product. These differences in reaction may be traced back to different marginal rates of substitution in their taste and preference patterns, as reflected in indifference curves having greater or lesser degrees of curvature. The above analysis, however, serves to demonstrate that although other consumers may not react to the *same degree* as our present example, they will react in the *same direction* in response to a change in price if they are attempting to maximize their utility from a limited income source. Since consumers typically attempt to get the most out of their money, we expect the law of demand to hold for consumers in general, although some consumers may react to price increases or decreases to a greater or lesser degree than others.[11]

The Income and Substitution Effects of a Price Change.   The price effect can be thought of as comprising two separate effects—an income effect and a substitution effect. When a product's price falls and all other things remain unchanged, the consumer experiences an increase in his or her real income. Real income is the purchasing power of money income. When the price of a particular good falls, the consumer can buy the same combination as before and have some money left over. This additional real income can then be spent, both on the product whose price has fallen and on other products. Normally, the income effect of a price reduction causes the consumer to buy a little more of the product in question, but if the product in question is an inferior substitute for some other product, the consumer may reduce purchases of the inferior product (whose price fell) in favor of increased purchases of the superior substitute.

The second part of the price effect is the substitution effect. When the price of any product falls, consumers will tend to substitute in favor of that product because it is now cheaper relative to other substitute products that serve the same need. Thus, when the price of a product falls, *ceteris paribus*, the consumer would normally buy

---

[11]It is important to remember that demand curves presuppose a constant value of the monetary unit as part of the *ceteris paribus* requirement. When there is inflation, such that the value of the dollar declines as time passes, one should correct for the change—for example, by dividing the nominal prices by an index of the price level, such as the Consumer Price Index, before using observations of price and quantity demanded that are collected in different time periods. Such time-series data are always suspect in economics, since a variety of other things are likely to have changed during the period of the data collection, and these changes must be controlled for. We consider this problem further in Chapter 5.

more of that product, first, because his or her real income has increased, and second, because he or she substitutes toward that product and away from other substitutes that are now relatively more expensive. A detailed treatment of the income and substitution effects of a price change, using indifference-curve analysis, is presented in the appendix to this chapter.

The Impact of Changes in Consumer Income

When the consumer's money income, also known as nominal income, rises and all other things remain the same, there is necessarily a rise in the consumer's real income to the same extent. The preceding discussion concerning the income effect thus applies. Normally, increases in money income, *ceteris paribus*, will lead to increased demand for the products available to the consumer. We show a situation in Figure 3–5 where the consumer's income has increased and the consumer subsequently purchases more of both products available. Note that at the initial prices and income level, and given the consumer's taste and preference pattern (indicated by the indifference curves), the consumer maximizes utility at point A. An increase in money income causes the budget constraint line to shift outward, parallel to its earlier position, since the intercept term increases while the slope term remains constant. In this case the quantity demanded of both products increases as a result of the increase in the consumer's income. Since income and quantity demanded moved in the same direction, we say that the income effect was positive for both goods. We call such products "superior" or "normal" goods.

FIGURE 3–5. Income Consumption Curve for Normal Goods

For some products the income effect is negative, meaning that if income increases, the quantity demanded of those products actually declines. As mentioned above, this may happen to a product that is an inferior substitute for some superior product. As people become richer, they tend to switch away from the "inferior" good to a superior substitute. Conversely, as incomes fall, in a recession for example, people tend to switch back to the inferior substitutes as they find themselves unable to afford the superior substitutes.

In Figure 3-6 we show the income effect for an inferior good. The product on the horizontal axis, travel by train, is assumed to be an inferior good for this particular consumer. Travel by air is assumed to be the superior substitute. Note that when the consumer's income increases and the budget line moves outward, the quantity demanded of travel by train actually decreases while travel by air increases. This consumer, now able to afford more air travel, substitutes away from the inferior good and in favor of the superior good. Looking at this from the opposite perspective, if the consumer's income were to fall from the higher level to the lower level, the consumer would reduce consumption of the superior good and increase consumption of the inferior good.

For any particular product at any particular point of time, it is apparent that some consumers may regard that product as a superior good while others may regard it as an inferior good. This difference in attitude toward a particular product stems from either a difference in income levels or a different pattern of tastes and preferences. Just as the price effect varies between and among consumers, the income effect should also be expected to vary between and among consumers, being high and positive for some, perhaps, while being low, or even negative, for others.

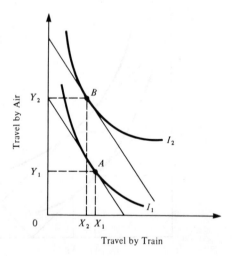

FIGURE 3-6.   Income Consumption Curve Where X Is an Inferior Good

Changes in Consumer Tastes and Preferences

In the preceding analysis consumer tastes and preferences were a̲~
constant while changes took place in price and income levels. We must recu̲~
ever, that consumer tastes and preferences may change from time to time, eı̲~
line with the latest fashions or trends, or as the result of the advertising and promotion
expenditures of business firms. However induced, changes in consumer tastes and
preferences have an impact on the quantity demanded of particular products.

Example: Suppose the sellers of product X institute an advertising campaign to promote the demand for their product. In the absence of simultaneous new campaigns
from the sellers of other products, we would expect this campaign to influence at least
some buyers in the direction of product X. Referring to Figure 3-7, suppose the initial
situation is represented by the tangency at point A on the dotted indifference curve I_1.
An advertising campaign that causes product X to be regarded more favorably than
previously would cause that particular level of utility represented by indifference curve
I_1 to be attained by the consumption of fewer units of product X, since X is now regarded more highly. Suppose that, whereas consumers previously required X_1 units of
product X to attain the utility level depicted by indifference curve I_1, it now takes only
X_1' units of product X to attain the *same level* of utility, in conjunction with Y_1 units of
product Y. In effect, then, indifference curve I_1 has swung downward and to the left,

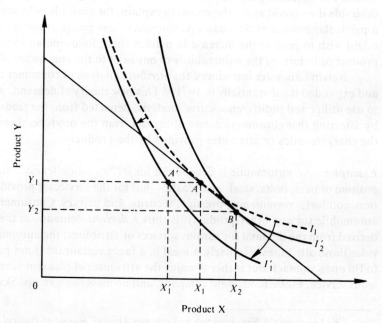

FIGURE 3-7.   **A Change in Tastes and Preferences in Favor of Product X**

since the same level of utility can be obtained with lesser combinations of X and Y due to the new appreciation the consumer has for product X. Under the new taste and preference conditions, indifference curve I_1 is irrelevant, since it refers to a previous pattern of tastes and preferences.

Thus the consumer *could* derive the same level of utility by shifting back from point A to point A'. Instead the consumer will wish to reallocate his or her budget such that utility is maximized under the new circumstances. Indifference curve I_2' is the highest attainable indifference curve given the budget constraint, and hence the consumer reallocates his or her income between products X and Y such that he or she is located at point B. Notice that the change of tastes and preferences in favor of product X has led to an increase in the consumption of product X, from X_1 to X_2, and to a reduction in the consumption of product Y from Y_1 to Y_2. In this simple two-commodity model the gain of product X necessarily came at the expense of product Y, whereas in a multicommodity system the shift of tastes and preferences in favor of product X would be at the expense of some, but not necessarily all, of the other products.

3.3 THE ATTRIBUTE APPROACH TO CONSUMER CHOICE

The traditional model of consumer choice among products suffers from several shortcomings that have prevented its widespread use as an explanatory, or predictive, model. For practical purposes, such as the marketing of a firm's products, it would be desirable if we could apply the model to explain, for example, why some consumers in a particular market prefer brand A, whereas others prefer brand B. Alternatively, we might wish to predict the increase in market share following an improvement of our product or to foresee the vulnerability of our sales to the emergence of a new product.

Kelvin Lancaster introduced the *attribute analysis* of consumer behavior in 1966 and expanded it substantially in 1971.[12] This new theory of demand, while continuing to use utility and indifference-curve analysis, departed from the traditional approach by asserting that consumers derive utility not from the products themselves but from the characteristics or attributes provided by the products.

Example: An automobile is desired not for its "automobileness"—its physical composition of nuts, bolts, steel, and plastic—but for the services it provides—transportation, comfort, convenience, prestige, security, and privacy. Consumer demand for an automobile (or any other product) is thus a *derived* demand, in the sense that it is derived from the demand for various services or attributes; the automobile simply provides those attributes. Similarly, a meal in a fancy restaurant is not purchased simply to fill one's stomach but rather to enjoy the attributes of pleasant surroundings, courteous service, exotic food, good company, and no mess to clean up. Skydiving is under-

---

[12]K. Lancaster, "A New Approach to Consumer Theory," *Journal of Political Economy*, 74 (April 1966), pp. 132-57; and *Consumer Demand: A New Approach* (New York: Columbia University Press, 1971).

taken not by those wishing to fall out of an airplane but by those in search of danger, exhilaration, solitude, exclusiveness, an outlet for their courage, or a conversation opener.

If it is the attributes that are desired, rather than the products in which they are found, it is instructive to examine the consumer's demand for the attributes *directly*, rather than *indirectly* as in the products approach. This is especially useful when a particular attribute—excitement, for example—is available in a wide variety of products, such as automobiles, skydiving, and roller coasters. In such a case the consumer derives an "excitement quota" from some but not necessarily from all of the available sources of supply. The attribute approach allows us to explain this behavior. Unlike the product approach, which takes the consumer's preferences between and among products as an imponderable fact, the attribute approach looks behind these preferences to explain them in terms of the attributes of those products. The attribute approach greatly facilitates the explanation of consumer choice within groups of substitutes and readily allows us to incorporate new products into the analysis.

Depicting Products in Attribute Space

The consumer derives utility from the consumption of attributes but must buy products in order to obtain the desired attributes. The products are simply the means by which the attributes are supplied to the consumption process. Each product will supply one or more attributes in a particular ratio.

Example: To demonstrate how a consumer might choose among products in order to maximize utility derived from the attributes, consider the case of Mr. Magnus Corpus, who dines out frequently and has a choice of six nearby restaurants. Mr. Corpus chooses among six products (the meal and its associated attributes at each of six restaurants), so that his utility is maximized. In order to treat the problem graphically, let us suppose that he seeks only two attributes: exotic atmosphere and haute cuisine. The six restaurants provide these attributes in differing proportions and at different prices. Let us suppose that after visiting all six restaurants Mr. Corpus rates each one on a scale of 100 for both exotic atmosphere and haute cuisine, as shown in Table 3-1.

TABLE 3-1. Attributes and Prices of Meals at Six Restaurants

Restaurant	Price of Meal ($)	ATTRIBUTE RATING		Ratio of Atmosphere to Cuisine	Meals per $100
		Atmosphere	Cuisine		
A	22.22	89	22	4.05	4.50
B	25.00	94	50	1.88	4.00
C	27.30	76	86	0.88	3.66
D	26.47	57	90	0.63	3.78
E	18.95	18	72	0.25	5.28
F	19.74	10	77	0.13	5.07

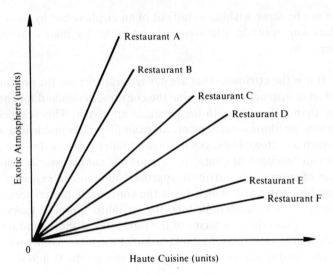

FIGURE 3-8. **Depicting Products in the Attribute Approach**

In Figure 3-8 the six products are depicted in attribute space as rays from the origin. The slope of each ray is determined by the ratio of exotic atmosphere to haute cuisine, as listed in Table 3-1. If Mr. Corpus has a meal at restaurant *A*, he "travels out" along the steepest ray, absorbing the two attributes in the ratio of 4.05 : 1—that is, 4.05 units of exotic atmosphere to each unit of haute cuisine. The other restaurants (products) are indicated by the lower rays. These offer atmosphere and cuisine at a lower ratio. Notice that a product for which one of the attributes was completely absent, such as home cooking, would be represented by one of the axes. (*You* decide which axis!)

The Budget Constraint and the Efficiency Frontier

How far along each ray would the gourmet go? That is, how much of Product A, or any other product, is it possible to purchase? The answer of course is up to the limit of his budget constraint. Suppose Mr. Corpus examines his finances and decides to allocate $100 monthly to eating in one or more of the six restaurants. The prices at the restaurants for a given meal are not identical, as shown in Table 3-1. If Mr. Corpus spends his entire $100 in restaurant A, he could have 4.5 meals at the price of $22.22 per meal (including taxes and tip) before exhausting his budget. Now 4.5 meals at restaurant A produce $4.5 \times 89 = 400.5$ units of the attribute exotic atmosphere and $4.5 \times 22 = 99$ units of the attribute haute cuisine. This point in attribute space is marked as point *A* in Figure 3-9. It shows the maximum intake of the two attributes that can be obtained by consuming product A, given the budget constraint of $100. Repeating this procedure for each of the other five restaurants, we find the limiting

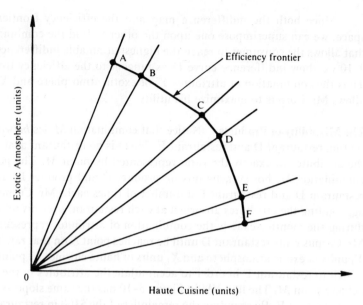

FIGURE 3-9. The Efficiency Frontier in the Attribute Approach

points B, C, D, E, and F on each product ray, which represent the entire budget (hypo-thetically) spent at each of the restaurants. Joining the points $ABCDEF$ we have what is known as the efficiency frontier in attribute space.

- **Definition:** The *efficiency frontier* is the outer boundary of the attainable combina-tions of the two attributes, given the budget constraint. We shall presently see that any point on the frontier is attainable by consuming combinations of the two adjacent products; it is called *efficient* because a rational consumer will prefer a combination of attributes on the frontier rather than any combination inside the frontier.

Maximizing Utility from Attributes

Just as consumers were able to express preference or indifference between combina-tions of products, they will be able to express preference or indifference between com-binations of attributes. At any given combination of exotic atmosphere and haute cui-sine, our gourmet will be able to express a marginal rate of substitution between the two attributes: an extra unit of haute cuisine will be worth giving up some amount of exotic atmosphere in this consumer's mind. Thus Mr. Corpus will have an indifference map in attribute space expressing his tastes and preferences between the two attrib-utes at all levels of those attributes. As before, higher curves are preferred to lower curves, the curves have negative slopes throughout, they neither meet nor intersect, and they are convex to the origin.

Since both the indifference map and the efficiency frontier are in attribute space, we can superimpose one upon the other to find the combination of attributes that allows the consumer to reach the highest attainable indifference curve. In Figure 3-10 we show indifference curve I^* as tangent to the efficiency frontier at point M. Thus the combination of attributes Y_2 of exotic atmosphere and X_2 of haute cuisine allows Mr. Corpus to maximize his utility.

The Mixability of Products.   Notice that combination M lies *between* the rays representing restaurant D and restaurant E. There is no restaurant available that provides the attributes in exactly the ratio represented by point M. The gourmet can attain combination M, however, by mixing product D and product E. That is, by visiting restaurant D and restaurant E a number of times each, Mr. Corpus can absorb—by aggregating the attributes absorbed at each restaurant over his total number of visits during the month—exactly the combination of attributes represented by point M. If Mr. Corpus visits restaurant D until he reaches point N on that ray, he will accumulate Y_1 units of exotic atmosphere and X_1 units of haute cuisine. At point N he should then switch to restaurant E in order to accumulate the attributes in the ratio necessary to achieve point M. The line NM in Figure 3-10 has the same slope as the ray representing restaurant E. By spending the remainder of the $100 in restaurant E, the gourmet derives an extra $Y_2 - Y_1$ units of exotic atmosphere and $X_2 - X_1$ units of haute cuisine, bringing his total to Y_2 units of the former and X_2 units of the latter, thereby maximizing his utility.

Alternatively, the gourmet could attain point M by visiting restaurant E until he had in effect reached point P on the ray representing restaurant E, and he could then switch to restaurant D to accumulate the remaining units of the two attributes in the ratio necessary to reach point M. The two paths to maximum utility are thus $0NM$ or $0PM$ in Figure 3-10. Since $0NMP$ is a parallelogram, however, the path $0PM$ is equivalent to $0NM$, because $0N = PM$ and $0P = NM$. Mr. Corpus may visit either restaurant first or in whatever sequence suits his whims, as long as the attributes accumulate to the combination M without exceeding the $100 budget constraint.[13]

Note: You may think it strange that the consumer patronizes only two of the six restaurants. This result is a function of our two-attribute model. The more attributes the consumer desires, the more products one would expect to be necessary to supply the optimum combination of those attributes. In the two-attribute case, the optimum combination of attributes could have been supplied by just one of the available products if the highest attainable indifference curve had touched one of the corners of the

[13]The consumer could arrive at point M by combining nonadjacent products, for example, D and F. This is inefficient, however, since it would cost more than $100. One hundred dollars spent on some combination of D and F brings the consumer to a point on a straight line joining points D and F, since it is a linear combination of those points. The straight line joining D and F must necessarily lie below the section of the frontier DEF, and therefore does not include point M. To reach point M by combining nonadjacent products, therefore, costs more than $100. See Lancaster, "A New Approach to Consumer Theory."

Haute Cuisine (units)

FIGURE 3-10. Maximization of Utility from Attributes

efficiency frontier. (In Figure 3-10 these corners are the points A, B, C, D, E, and F.) Where the highest attainable indifference curve is tangent to a flat section of the efficiency frontier, a combination of two goods is necessary, as in the above case. If, for example, the consumer desires n attributes, as many as n products (restaurants) might be required to provide the optimal combination of attributes.[14]

Indivisibility of Products.   Where products cost a large amount of money in relation to the consumer's income or are otherwise available only in discrete units, the consumer may have to settle for a suboptimal combination of attributes. With a very large and indivisible purchase, such as an automobile, the consumer must choose one product or another and is therefore constrained to one of the corners on the efficiency frontier. Consider Figure 3-11, in which we show three automobiles in economy-comfort attribute space. Brand A automobile offers a relatively high ratio of economy to comfort, followed by brands B and C. If these products were mixable, the efficiency frontier would be the kinked line ABC, and the consumer would maximize utility by mixing brands A and B at point W to attain indifference curve I^*.

---

[14]The assumption that products are mixable has drawn criticism from Reuven Hendler, "Lancaster's New Approach to Consumer Demand and Its Limitations," *American Economic Review*, 65 (March 1975), pp. 194-199. It is clear that in some cases a consumer is not indifferent to combinations of goods that give identical combinations of attributes at the same price. Among other examples Hendler cites two medium-sweet apples versus one extremely sweet apple and one completely unsweet apple. Both combinations offer the same sweetness but the consumer is not likely to be indifferent to them.

FIGURE 3–11. Indivisibility of Products Necessitating a Suboptimal Combination of Attributes

However, if the consumer cannot mix brands A and B (by renting both cars or by agreeing with another person to buy the other car and then share), the consumer must be content to attain either point A, point B, or point C. Of these options, point A allows the attainment of the highest indifference curve, shown as I_0. The indivisibility of the products thus prevents the consumer from reaching indifference curve I^*, and the consumer must be satisfied with the suboptimal point A on indifference curve I_0. Given the constraint imposed by the indivisibility of the product, the consumer chooses the best available option.

Thus the efficiency frontier will be a series of facets joining the affordable-limit points on each product ray, given the mixability and divisibility of products. Note that the location of the frontier depends on three things, namely, the prices of the products, the consumer's income, and the consumer's perception of the attribute content of each product. To appreciate this fact more fully, we shall examine the impact of changes in these parameters of the model. As might be expected, a change in any one of these things causes a shift of the efficiency frontier.

Changes in Price and the Law of Demand

The affordable-limit point on each ray is given by the ratio of income to the product's price multiplied by the attribute content of each unit of the product. Given constant consumer perceptions and income, a change in the product's price will therefore shift the affordable-limit point, and, consequently, the efficiency frontier. If the product's price were reduced, the frontier would shift outward along the product ray, and, conversely, the frontier would shift inward along the product ray if the price were increased.

Example: Consider an audiophile who has a tape deck and frequently purchases new tapes. She desires two major attributes in these tapes, namely, "clarity of sound reproduction" and "reliability of tape operation." There are five brands available, and we show the efficiency frontier and two of the audiophile's indifference curves in Figure 3–12.

Initially, the prices of the five brands are such that the efficiency frontier is *ABCDE*, and the consumer is able to maximize utility at point *C*, where indifference curve I_1 just touches the frontier. Now suppose that the price of brand B is reduced, such that the efficiency frontier moves out along the brand-B ray to point *B'* and is now represented by *AB'CDE*. The audiophile can now attain a higher indifference curve (I_2) by switching to brand B tapes. Product B offers the attributes in a different ratio to the previously preferred product C, but the consumer exhibits a marginal rate of substitution between the attributes and is willing to trade off some "reliability" for more "clarity" at the lower price in order to increase her total utility derived.

In Figure 3–13 we show a different case in which a different consumer is initially mixing two products in order to obtain the desired combination of attributes. Our second consumer has a different taste and preference pattern between the two attributes, as compared with the consumer depicted in Figure 3–12. The second audiophile's indifference map is such that his highest-attainable indifference curve, given the initial efficiency frontier *ABCDE*, is tangent to the frontier at point *N*. This consumer

FIGURE 3-12. The Price Effect Shown by the Attribute Approach: Audiophile 1

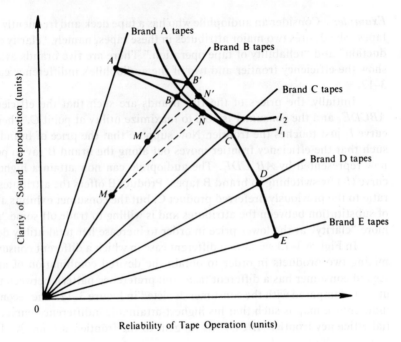

FIGURE 3-13.   The Price Effect Shown by the Attribute Approach: Audiophile 2

prefers to purchase both brand B and brand C tapes, presumably using the brand B tapes for applications where "clarity" is relatively more important. Let us suppose his path to the frontier is $0MN$.

Again we reduce the price of brand B tapes, and the new efficiency frontier becomes $AB'CDE$. Our second audiophile is able to increase utility by moving to point N' on indifference curve I_2. He still purchases both brand B and brand C tapes, but he now will purchase more brand B tapes and fewer brand C tapes. Whereas his previous path to the frontier was $0MN$, it is now $0M'N'$. The segment $0M'$ exceeds $0M$, indicating the consumer's greater absorption of the attributes from product B and hence greater purchases of product B. The segment $M'N'$ is shorter than MN, indicating the consumer's reduced purchases of product C. Thus the law of demand is demonstrated by the behavior of both audiophiles: each one responded to the reduced price of brand B tapes by buying more of that brand and less of a substitute brand.

Pricing a Product out of the Market.   Given a consumer's perception of the attributes embodied in a particular product, there is a maximum price that the consumer will pay for that product even if it exactly mirrors his taste and preference pattern. In Figure 3-14 we show a simple case where three products offer the two desired attributes X and Y. The initial price situation generates the efficiency frontier ABC, and the consumer maximizes utility on indifference curve I_2 by purchasing only product B.

Suppose the price of product B is now increased such that the efficiency frontier becomes $AB'C$. The consumer is now unable to reach indifference curve I_2 and must be content with the lower curve I_1 at point B', still purchasing only product B but necessarily purchasing fewer units of product B because of its higher price and the consumer's unchanged budget.

If the price of product B is raised still further, such that the consumer's entire budget spent on product B would purchase only the combination of attributes shown by point B'' for example, this consumer will no longer buy any units of product B. The efficiency frontier remains at $AB'C$, and product B has fallen inside the frontier. Purchase of product B would now be an inefficient use of the consumer's budget, since the other products provide the desired attributes more inexpensively. The consumer is still able to attain point B' on the efficiency frontier and on indifference curve I_1, but will now travel via the path $0MB'$ or $0NB'$ rather than along the ray representing product B. That is, the consumer will now prefer to combine products A and C in order to maximize utility from a given budget rather than purchase any of product B. Thus product B has been priced out of reach for this consumer, even though it provides the attributes in exactly the preferred ratio. (I feel the same way about Ferraris.)

Thus we see that the price effect, or the law of demand, still applies to products even though they are purchased as a means of acquiring desired attributes. As price falls, consumers already purchasing the product in question will purchase more units, and other consumers will begin to buy their first units of that product. Alternatively, as

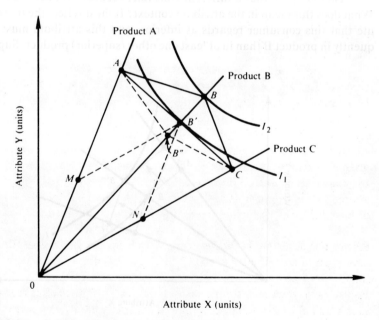

FIGURE 3-14. Pricing a Product out of the Market

price is increased, consumers will buy fewer units or will drop out of the market for that product completely. Substitute products will tend to sell more units when the price of a product on an adjacent ray increases and will tend to sell fewer units when the price of that product is reduced.

Changes in Income for Superior and Inferior Goods

Given the consumer's perception of attribute content in each product and the prices of the products, an increase in the consumer's income or budget constraint will shift the efficiency frontier outward; a reduction in income will shift the frontier inward. The new frontier shifts in a parallel fashion, since the affordable combinations of attributes change in the same proportion for each product.

We have noted earlier that the income effect may be either positive (for superior or normal goods) or negative (for inferior goods). That is, the change in quantity demanded of a product may be in the same direction as the change in income, indicating a superior good, or in the opposite direction, indicating an inferior good. In Figure 3-15 we show an increase in the consumer's income, *ceteris paribus*, that leads to an increase in the quantity demanded of product B. The initial frontier is ABC, the highest attainable indifference curve is I_0, and the consumer purchases only product B. Then an increase in the consumer's income shifts the frontier out to $A'B'C'$, allowing the attainment of indifference curve I_1. The consumer's utility-maximizing response to the increase in income is to purchase a larger quantity of product B.

Now suppose that a different consumer regards product B as an inferior good. What does this mean in the attribute context? It must reflect the presence of an attribute that this consumer regards as inferior, and this attribute must occur more frequently in product B than in at least one other (superior) product. Suppose that attrib-

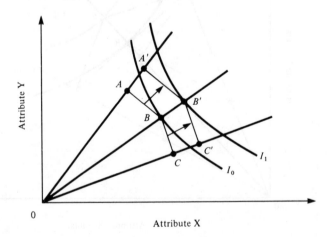

FIGURE 3-15. The Income Effect Where Product B Is a Normal Good

ute X is "sweetness," attribute Y is "nutrition," and the products shown in Figure 3-16 are candy bars A, B, and C. As before, the increase in income shifts the frontier out from ABC to $A'B'C'$. In this case, however, the consumer switches from product B at the lower income to product A at the higher income. This consumer is apparently nearing his or her saturation point for sweetness and maximizes utility by reducing sweetness intake slightly in favor of a substantial increase in nutrition. Since candy bar A has a higher ratio of nutrition to sweetness, it is regarded as a superior product, and candy bars B and C are viewed as inferior products, when rising income brings the consumer nearer to his or her saturation level for sweetness.

Approaching the saturation point for an attribute is just another way of saying that the consumer's marginal utility is very close to zero for that attribute. Thus the income effect for a product may be positive or negative, depending on the consumer's relative marginal utilities derived from the attributes contained in the product. As the marginal utility of an attribute approaches zero—while the marginal utility of other attributes remains relatively high—that attribute becomes inferior, and products containing a relatively high ratio of that attribute become inferior as a consequence.[15]

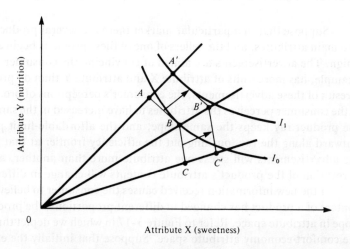

FIGURE 3-16. The Income Effect Where Product B Is an Inferior Good

---

[15]Note that the indifference curves are drawn to indicate this consumer's decreasing fondness for attribute X relative to attribute Y, as he or she is able to afford more of both. The higher indifference curve is markedly flatter than the lower curve as we move out along any ray from the origin. This change in shape indicates that the consumer's marginal rate of substitution of attribute Y for attribute X is falling as the quantity of both is increased, in turn because of the more rapidly falling values of the marginal utility of attribute X relative to attribute Y.

Changes in Consumer Perceptions

The attribute content of a product depends critically upon the consumer's perception of those attributes. In the production process a product may be endowed with great strength and durability, but if a consumer thinks it looks "flimsy," then this strength and durability are not perceived. Advertising and promotional activity by sellers of particular products, as well as information from other sources (word of mouth or published reports by consumer testing agencies), may change the consumer's perception of the quantity of particular attributes embodied in each unit of a particular product. We now examine the impact that such changes might have on the demand for the product.

Note: The first thing we must do is make the distinction between changes in perceptions and changes in tastes. A consumer's perceptions relate to the amount of each attribute perceived to exist in each unit of the product. A consumer's tastes refer to the amount of utility expected from each unit of the product. Attribute analysis allows us to separate these quite neatly: a change in perceptions shifts one or more of the product rays and may shift the efficiency frontier, whereas a change in tastes shifts the indifference curves (through changes in marginal utilities that are involved in the marginal rate of substitution and hence the slope of indifference curves).

Suppose that in a particular market there are several products characterized by two main attributes, and the sellers of one of these products begin a promotional campaign. The advertisements are aimed at convincing the consumer that product B, for example, has more units of attribute X and attribute Y than do products A and C. As a result of these advertisements, the consumer's perceptions of product B may change. If the consumer perceives the attributes to have increased in the same proportion, then the product ray keeps the same slope, and the affordable-limit point simply moves outward along the ray, pushing out the efficiency frontier at that point. More likely, the advertisements will stress one attribute more than another, and the consumer's perception of the product's attribute contents will change in different proportions.

If the new information received causes the consumer to believe that the attribute content of a product has changed in different proportions, the product ray changes its slope in attribute space. Refer to Figure 3–17 in which we depict three economy cars in the comfort-economy attribute space. Suppose that initially the efficiency frontier is *ABC* and the consumer chooses product C, attaining indifference curve I_0. Now suppose that Volkswagen begins to advertise their diesel-engine Rabbit using the theme that economy means more than just fuel economy. Operating economy includes the savings on electrical parts and tune-ups one expects with a diesel engine. Diesel engines have no carburetor, no spark plugs, no points, no condenser, no distributor (and no power, too!). The absence of these parts saves money since they do not have to be recalibrated and replaced.

Let us assume the consumer is convinced by this reasoning and now perceives the Rabbit to contain the same amount of comfort as before, but more economy. In terms

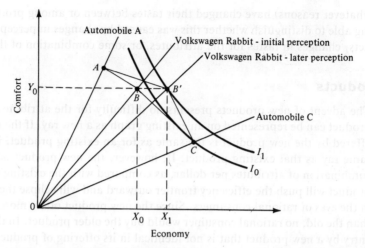

FIGURE 3-17. Changed Consumer Perception of a Product: The Volkswagen Rabbit Diesel Example

of Figure 3-17 the consumer perceives an extra $X_1 - X_0$ units of economy in the Rabbit. This causes the Rabbit's product ray to shift from $0B$ to $0B'$, and the efficiency frontier to move from ABC to $AB'C$. In the case depicted the consumer can now attain a higher indifference curve by switching to the Rabbit from product C. Thus a changed perception of the attribute content of one or more products may change the shape or location of the efficiency frontier, without affecting the consumer's indifference curves.[16]

It is possible that consumers' tastes for attributes could change at the same time or in response to different stimuli. Suppose a consumer suddenly becomes more aware of the energy shortage and wants to be more socially responsible by using less fuel. This desire is reflected by a steepening of the consumer's indifference curves in comfort-economy space. The consumer's MRS between comfort and economy would increase as a result of this change in taste for the attributes. A change in the indifference map is likely to cause a new point of tangency, of course, and the consumer may rearrange his or her purchases as a result.

Note: It is important to see that this change in tastes is independent of any change in perceptions of the attribute content of the products. The attribute approach allows us to make this distinction, whereas the product approach simply says consumers (for

---

[16]If a product is an inefficient supplier of the desired attributes, changed perceptions of this product do not change the efficiency frontier, unless these changes are sufficient to cause the product to be viewed as an efficient supplier of the attributes. Conversely, of course, new information or experience with a product may cause a consumer to view a product as inefficient for the first time. A distasteful or boring advertising campaign could change a consumer's perceptions of attribute content downward.

ver reasons) have changed their tastes between or among products, without be-
ble to distinguish whether this was caused by changes in perceptions of the prod-
, changes in tastes for the attributes, or some combination of the two.

New Products

The advent of new products presents no difficulty for the attribute approach; a new
product can be represented on an existing graph as a new ray. If the ratio of attributes
offered by the new product is the same as for an existing product, it will occupy the
same ray as that existing product. If, however, the new product offers more of this
combination of attributes per dollar, as compared with the existing product, the new
product will push the efficiency frontier outward and will eclipse the existing product
in the eyes of rational consumers. Since the new product offers more utility per dollar
than the old, no rational consumer would buy the older product. In the case of market
entry by a new product that is not identical in its offering of product attributes when
compared with existing products, there will be a new ray in the figure. If the highest
affordable point on that ray occurs outside the existing frontier, the new product will
serve to push the frontier outward at a point where it was previously flat. In both these

FIGURE 3-18. Addition of a New Product to an Existing Group of Products

cases, where the new product extends the frontier, some consumers will change their consumption in favor of the new product, since the new frontier will now poke through their previously attained indifference curves and allow them to reach a higher curve.

Example: In Figure 3-18 we show an initial situation of only three products—A, B, and C. The initial efficiency frontier perceived by the consumer is thus *ABC*, and he or she attains indifference curve I_1 by purchasing product B. We now suppose a new product is launched that competes with products A, B, and C in the sense that it also offers attributes X and Y. The new product offers these attributes in a different ratio, however, between those of products B and C. The new product is priced so that the efficiency frontier is extended to *ABNC*. The consumer is now able to reach indifference curve I_2 by switching to the new product. Notice that the new product steals sales from both B and C, but does not affect A unless there are more than two attributes desired by consumers. In the real world, of course, consumers do demand more than two attributes simultaneously, and we should expect the advent of a new product (or new model of an existing product) to affect the sales of a range of other products.

Market Segments

- ***Definition:***   *Market segments* are groups of consumers who have similar taste and preference patterns and who therefore tend to buy similar products. Groups of consumers with similar marginal rates of substitution, at a particular combination of attributes, will tend to find their highest-attainable indifference curve tangent to the efficiency frontier at similar points. Consumers with relatively *low* MRS between the attributes will tend to buy products with relatively *high* attribute ratio rays, and vice versa.

Example: In the case of the audio tapes discussed earlier, we may characterize the "music clarity" segment as consisting of those who will have low marginal rates of substitution (relatively flat indifference curves) between clarity and reliability and who therefore tend to purchase brands A and B. On the other hand, consumers with relatively high marginal rates of substitution (relatively steep indifference curves) will tend to buy brands D and E and may be characterized as the "reliability" segment. Similarly, consumers with a low MRS between exotic atmosphere and haute cuisine tend to eat at restaurants A, B, and C and might be characterized as the "exotic" segment of the market, whereas the patrons of restaurants D, E, and F might be called the "gourmet" segment.

Knowledge of the tastes of consumers for the various attributes allows firms to design their products to incorporate the attributes in the ratios desired by a particular group of consumers. This group of consumers becomes the firm's *target market*. Similarly, consumers in a particular market segment seek out firms that supply products providing the attributes in the desired ratios.

Problems of Identifying and Measuring Attributes

Some attributes are readily identifiable and measurable, such as the "power" and "economy" associated with an automobile. Objective measurement of "power" might proceed on the basis of engine horsepower, horsepower divided by vehicle weight, or some similar measure. Economy likewise can be measured by a standard unit of measure, such as miles per gallon or liters per hundred kilometers. Problems arise, however, with attributes that are measurable only subjectively, such as "modern styling," "prestige," "status," "comfort," and "security." The consumer will typically have an intuitive evaluation of these attributes and will be able to make what appears to that consumer as an optimal decision in the light of the information held.

The identification and measurability problems arise when we attempt to explain or predict consumer behavior in real-world situations. As you will appreciate, the implications of attribute analysis for the pricing, promotion, product, and distribution strategies of the business firm are profound. If the firm is able to identify *which* attributes consumers base their choices upon and on *what basis* they evaluate the attributes, it is in a better position to increase sales and profits by adjusting one or more of its marketing strategies.[17] We return to this issue in the contexts of pricing policy in Chapter 10 and product design in Chapter 14.

3.4 SUMMARY

In this chapter we have demonstrated how the rational consumer is expected to adjust to changes in economic variables. The price effect gives rise to the individual's demand curve for individual products. In general, these demand curves show an inverse relationship between the price of the product and the quantity demanded by a particular consumer. This price effect can be divided into two component parts: the income effect and the substitution effect. The income effect may be either positive or negative, depending upon the taste and preference pattern of the consumer in question and the level of income of each consumer. The substitution effect is always negative; that is, the relationship between price and quantity demanded, with real income constant, is an inverse one. The net effect of a price change, given *ceteris paribus*, is that quantity demanded will increase when price is reduced and decrease when price is raised. This relationship is known as the law of demand. We caution that in the real world the law of demand may sometimes be obscured by the effects of inflation or by the simultaneous movement of another variable that influences demand.

Changes in the consumer's income will change the quantity demanded at a given price level. The quantity demanded of superior (or normal) goods will move in the

---

[17]In marketing research the technique of *conjoint analysis* is being used to establish consumers' perceptions and tradeoffs between attributes embodied in competing products. See, for example, Paul E. Green and V. Srinivasan, "Conjoint Analysis in Consumer Research: Issues and Outlook," *The Journal of Consumer Research*, 5 (September 1978), pp. 103-23. Also Albert Madansky, "On Conjoint Analysis and Quantal Choice Models," *Journal of Business*, 53 (July 1980), pp. S37-S44.

same direction as income, whereas the quantity demanded of inferior goods will move in the opposite direction to income. Similarly, changes in the consumer's taste and preference pattern will cause changes in the quantity demanded of goods, given the prevailing price and income levels. If tastes change in favor of a product, for example, its quantity demanded will increase at the expense of substitute products.

The attribute approach to consumer behavior gives several valuable insights into consumer choice which are not so readily apparent using the product approach. The attribute approach allows the entire range of substitutes available to the consumer to be depicted on the same graph. It is thus able to explain quite clearly why a consumer buys one brand of a product in preference to the other brands available: the preferred brand offers the consumer the greatest amount of the preferred attribute mix per dollar. Moreover, the analysis easily explains why a consumer will purchase combinations of substitute products: doing so allows the consumer to obtain the desired attribute ratio even when there is no product that offers the attributes in this ratio. New products are easily handled by the attribute approach, since they are simply added to the existing analysis. The implications for marketing policy are more obvious under the attributes approach: the price level determines the degree to which the product extends the efficiency frontier, and the firm's promotion, product, and distribution policies determine the combination of attributes and hence the product's placement on the frontier.

Studying individual consumer behavior is important, for it explains why consumer responses to changes in economic variables are basically predictable, in *direction* if not always in *magnitude*. When price changes are regarded in the real, or purchasing power, sense and when the impact of other variables can be accounted for, we must expect a negative price effect to prevail. The ramifications of this expectation for revenues, profits, and general business decision making are explored in subsequent chapters.

DISCUSSION QUESTIONS

3-1. Explain the diminishing marginal rate of substitution between two products in terms of the marginal utilities of those products.

3-2. Explain how the MRS, at a particular combination of the two products, would differ between two consumers—one who "likes" hamburgers and "loves" milkshakes and another who "loves" hamburgers and merely "likes" milkshakes.

3-3. Demonstrate that an increase in a consumer's income could lead to either an increase or a decrease in the consumption of a particular product, using first the product approach and then the attribute approach.

3-4. Show how a change in the consumer's tastes and preference pattern will cause a change in the quantity demanded of any two products, using first the product approach and then the attribute approach.

3-5. In the self-service versus full-service gasoline example used in the text, how would the indifference map of a person who is knowledgeable about preventive maintenance, economy-minded, and not lazy, compare with that of another person who is the opposite in these respects?

3-6. How would the indifference map between X and Y look different for a consumer who regards X as a normal good (or attribute) as compared with another who regards X as an inferior product (or attribute)?

3-7. What attributes do you think are being sought by a consumer who chooses to fly somewhere for a holiday as compared with another consumer who would drive the same distance for the same holiday?

3-8. Why would a consumer not be acting "rationally" in purchasing a product that fell short of the efficiency frontier in attribute space?

3-9. Distinguish between a change in consumer perceptions and a change in consumer tastes.

3-10. How would new-product policy benefit from an analysis of the attributes demanded by consumers in the overall market for several substitute products?

PROBLEMS AND SHORT CASES

3-1. Show graphically the effect of a price *increase* on the quantity demanded of a product by a particular consumer. Verbally explain the income and substitution effects of this price change.

3-2. Explain why the *ceteris paribus* assumption is so important in the economic analysis of consumer behavior? Then, using graphs, show the effects of the following series of events: a price reduction for product X, followed by an increase in the consumer's income, followed by a change in the consumer's tastes away from product X.

3-3. Company A sells product X, which has several close substitutes. At its present price, however, it is not making a sufficient contribution to the firm's profitability. A price rise is contemplated. The marketing manager is adamant that an advertising campaign must be undertaken before the price is raised. The finance department says that this expenditure is unnecessary. Explain the marketing manager's reasoning in terms of the attribute approach to consumer behavior.

3-4. Imagine two consumers—Mr. A, who simply appreciates classical music, and Ms. B, who is wildly enthusiastic about it. Suppose that in a simple two-product situation both buy classical music records in conjunction with some other product Y.

  (a) Using the indifference maps you think are appropriate for each consumer, derive each of their demand curves from their price consumption curves. (Assume that they have the same income and face the same prices.)

  (b) Aggregate their individual demands to find their total demand for the records at each price.

3-5. In the automobile market, various segments of the market are catered to by the manufacturers. Show graphically why three different consumers might choose three different automobiles in the simple case where they desire only two attributes, "power" and "economy." Verbally explain the *n*-attribute case, where *n* is a large number.

3-6. In a western region two brands of beer are sold which between them share almost all the market. Through careful research it has been found that their main differences are perceived to be in the attributes "lightness" and "thirst-quenching." Brand A is perceived to contain 10 "units" of thirst-quench and 5 "units" of lightness and costs $0.80 per bottle. Brand B is perceived to contain 5 "units" of thirst-quench and 10 "units" of lightness and costs $0.67 per bottle.

  Research has also indicated that a significant share of the market would become available if a third beer were introduced, as long as its price was not too high. The Norbert Brewing Company has a new "premium" beer that incorporates 10 "units" of each attribute in each bottle.

  For a consumer who has $10 monthly to spend on beer and who perceives the attributes in the ratios implied above,

(a) what is the maximum price that may be charged for Norbert's beer such that $10 will buy a combination of the attributes that lies on the efficiency frontier? (An approximate answer derived from your graph will suffice.)

(b) Supposing that Norbert prices the new beer at $0.72 per bottle, will the above consumer necessarily switch to Norbert's beer or stay with one or the other of the initial brands? Why?

3-7. The MacFarlane Chocolate Company has a product called Snackers in the health-food segment of the candy bar market. Each Snackers bar contains 150 grams of protein and 150 calories. The two rival products are Healthnut bars, containing 200 grams of protein and only 100 calories, and Hi-energy bars, containing 50 grams of protein and 200 calories. Each of these bars weighs 4 ounces. Snackers bars sell for $1.75, compared to $2 for Healthnut bars and $1.50 for Hi-energy bars.

Recently the cost of peanuts and chocolate has been increasing while the cost of sugar has been falling substantially. As a consequence, MacFarlane's management is considering changing the composition of Snackers to include less protein and more calories. In effect they are considering repositioning their product in the market. The proposal being considered is to make Snackers contain only 100 grams of protein but raise the caloric content to 200. The price would stay the same, but promotional efforts would stress the extra energy packed into the Snackers bar. Market research indicates that the typical customer spends $10 weekly on these so-called health-food bars.

With the current Snackers bar, MacFarlane has about 30 percent of the market. Healthnut has 25 percent, and Hi-energy has the remaining 45 percent. The protagonists of the new bar argue that the new Snackers bar will steal sales from Hi-energy bars. The antagonists argue that it will lose more sales to the Healthnut bar than it will gain from the Hi-energy bar.

(a) Using attribute analysis, show how the Snackers bar would be repositioned in nutrient-calorie space, and how this would change the efficiency frontier for the typical consumer.

(b) Given the current market-share information, advise management whether or not to reposition the Snackers bar. Do you have any other suggestions?

(c) State all assumptions and reservations underlying your conclusion.

3-8. One of the domestic auto manufacturers (which we shall call company D) is considering some strategic changes to its "luxury-subcompact" model. Its research indicates that consumers consider two main attributes when purchasing a subcompact car, namely, fuel economy and comfort. It recognizes that in the design of a subcompact car there is a tradeoff between fuel economy and comfort, since features that increase fuel economy (such as smaller size, better aerodynamics, and lighter weight) have the opposite impact on comfort. Similarly, features that improve comfort, like a longer wheelbase, more soundproofing, and larger seats, come at the expense of reduced fuel economy.

Fuel economy is measured by the EPA's fuel economy rating (average for city and highway driving), and comfort is measured by an index that industry insiders have developed to incorporate interior dimensions, the weight of sound-deadening materials, and so on. Based on these two scales, the current competitors in the luxury subcompact segment of the market are rated as follows:

Competitor A: fuel economy, 55; comfort 40.
Competitor B: fuel economy, 45; comfort 90.
Competitor C: fuel economy, 30; comfort 120.

Company D's luxury subcompact is rated at 40 miles per gallon and has a comfort index of 100. Each of these cars is priced within a few dollars of $10,000 in basic trim (as rated here). The current market shares of the firms in this segment are as follows: A has 40 percent, B has 25 percent, C has 15 percent, and D has 20 percent.

Two competitive strategies are being considered for the next model year. Plan A is to keep fuel economy the same through improvements in engine efficiency while increasing the comfort index to 110 by additional sound deadening. Plan B is to lighten the car dramatically and incorporate an electronic fuel management system, such that the car will be rated at 50 miles per gallon with a comfort index of 80. In either case the price would be left at its current level, because of consumers' high degree of price sensitivity in this market.

(a) Show graphically how plan A and plan B differ from the status quo.

(b) Speculate, on the basis of the market-share data given, which would be the better strategy, assuming that the new model would cost the same as the current model once it got into production, that the initial costs of the two plans would be roughly the same, and that these costs would equal the usual costs of the annual model change.

(c) State all assumptions and reservations that underlie your analysis.

3-9. Richard Poirier has recently graduated from college, and upon receipt of his first paycheck he began planning to buy a sports car. He is considering four major attributes: prestige, performance, reliability, and resistance to rust. The value he attaches to these attributes varies depending upon whether he will drive the car all year round or in the summer only. The latter decision depends upon whether he is to be transferred 1,500 miles north by his employer. If he moves north he will use the car in the summer only.

If he is to drive the car only in the summer, Richard considers performance to be twice as important as reliability, prestige to be three times as important as reliability, and rust resistance to be only half as important as reliability. For year-round driving, he considers rust resistance to be three times as important as reliability, performance half as important as reliability, and prestige twice as important as reliability.

Richard has found three sports cars for sale; each one is secondhand and costs $5,000. All are in good condition, and he decides to buy one of the three. After considering the problem and talking with some experts, he has rated each car on a scale of 10 for each of the four attributes, as follows:

	Car A	Car B	Car C
Prestige	8	9	6
Performance	8	8	9
Reliability	7	6	9
Rust resistance	8	7	6

(a) Please advise Richard about which sports car he should buy to maximize his expected utility if he is in fact transferred 1,500 miles north.

(b) Which car should he buy if he is sure that he will not be transferred?

(c) Which car should he buy if the probability of his being transferred north can be reliably estimated at 0.7? (Explain your reasoning in each case.)

3-10. The demand for telephone installation peaks around the first day of each month, since many subscribers request service on that day because they are moving to a new house or apartment. The Tanguay Telephone Company (T.T.C.) is examining a means to reduce this monthly demand peak, which accounts for 40 percent of all installations. The problem has been aggravated in recent years by the increasing hourly cost of labor, the reluctance of unionized employees to work overtime, the increased "no access" problems caused by the greater number of working households, and the decline of profitable auxiliary sales to the subscriber (colored telephones, extension phones, etc.) due to access being given by a third party (landlord, neighbor, etc.).

T.T.C. is considering opening several "Phoneshops" in its area, so that customers may obtain their telephones and install them in their own homes. The company would prewire all homes in its territory, installing one or two phone jacks in each room; the installation by the customer would simply involve plugging in the sets where desired. The company would continue to offer home installation for those unable or unwilling to visit the Phoneshops. Two types of Phoneshop are being considered: more conveniently located stores which would offer a moderate saving as compared with the traditional home installation and less conveniently located stores which would offer a more substantial saving due to the lower overhead costs in the less convenient locations.

A market survey has found that telephone subscribers want two major attributes in their purchase of a new installation—"convenience" and "economy." A "typical" customer has been found who rates the three options on a scale of 100 for "convenience" as follows: Home Installation 100; More Convenient Store 75; and Less Convenient Store 25. The "economy" of the second and third options will be measured by the savings from the $20 it will continue to cost to have home installation. Thus "economy" will be determined by prices that T.T.C. decides to charge for the latter two options.

(a) Supposing initially that T.T.C. prices the More Convenient (MC) Phoneshop service at $16 and the Less Convenient (LC) Phoneshop service at $12, show the consumer's options in attribute space, with "convenience" on the vertical axis and "dollars saved" on the horizontal axis. (Since the consumer wants *one* unit only of *one* of the three services, these options will be represented by points in attribute space, not rays.)

(b) For a consumer who has an MRS = 10 at the point represented by the MC Phoneshop (i.e., who is prepared to give up 10 units of convenience for $1 saved), which of the three options should be selected?

(c) For a person who has an MRS = 15 at the point represented by the MC Phoneshop, which of the three options should be selected?

SUGGESTED REFERENCES AND FURTHER READING

Auld, Douglas. "Imperfect Knowledge and the New Theory of Demand," *Journal of Political Economy*, 80 (November, December 1972), pp. 1287–94.

Baumol, W. J. *Economic Theory and Operations Analysis* (4th ed.), chap. 9. Englewood Cliffs, N.J.: Prentice-Hall, Inc., 1977.

Cornell, B. "Relative vs. Absolute Price Changes: An Empirical Study," *Economic Inquiry*, 19 (July 1981), pp. 506–14.

Green, P. E., and V. Srinivasan. "Conjoint Analysis in Consumer Research: Issues and Outlook," *The Journal of Consumer Research*, 5 (September 1978), pp. 103–23.

Hendler, R. "Lancaster's New Approach to Consumer Demand and Its Limitations," *American Economic Review*, 65 (March 1975), pp. 194–99.

Hirshleifer, J. *Price Theory and Applications* (2nd ed.), chaps. 3 and 4. Englewood Cliffs, N.J.: Prentice-Hall, Inc., 1980.

Hyman, David N. *Modern Microeconomics: Analysis and Applications*, esp. chaps. 3 and 4. St. Louis: Times Mirror/Mosby College Publishing, 1986.

Lancaster, K. "A New Approach to Consumer Theory," *Journal of Political Economy*, 84 (April 1966), pp. 132–57.

————. *Consumer Demand: A New Approach.* New York: Columbia University Press, 1971.

Leibenstein, H. "Bandwagon, Snob and Veblen Effects in the Theory of Consumer Demand," *Quarterly Journal of Economics*, May 1950, pp. 183–207.

Mansfield, E. *Microeconomics: Theory/Applications*, esp. chaps. 3 and 4. New York: W. W. Norton & Company, 1985.

Ratchford, Brian T. "The New Economic Theory of Consumer Behavior: An Interpretive Essay," *Journal of Consumer Research*, 2 (September 1975), pp. 65–75.

————. "Operationalizing Economic Models of Demand for Product Characteristics," *Journal of Consumer Research*, 6 (June 1979), pp. 76–84.

Rosen, Sherwin. "Hedonic Prices and Implicit Markets: Product Differentiation in Pure Competition," *Journal of Political Economy*, 82 (January, February 1974), pp. 34–45.

Roth, Timothy P. "On the Predictive Power of the New Approach to Consumer Theory," *Atlantic Economic Journal*, 7 (July 1979), pp. 16–25.

Schoemaker, P. J. H. "The Expected Utility Model: Its Variants, Purposes, Evidence and Limitations," *Journal of Economic Literature*, 20 (June 1982), pp. 529–63.

Appendix 3A: Indifference-Curve Analysis of the Income and Substitution Effects of a Price Change

In the chapter we noted that the price effect has two components, namely, the income effect and the substitution effect of the price change. The income effect is the change in the quantity demanded that is due to the change in the consumer's real income, which in turn is due to the change in the price level. We expect the income effect to be positive for superior (or normal) goods and negative for inferior goods. That is, income and quantity demanded will move in the same direction for superior goods, and they will move in opposite directions for inferior goods. The substitution effect is the change in the quantity demanded that is due solely to the change in relative prices of goods, given a constant real income. We expect the substitution effect to always be negative; that is, the quantity demanded of a particular product will always move in the direction opposite to the price change.

Note: It is important to make the distinction between a consumer's monetary, or *nominal*, income and his *real* income. Nominal income is the amount of money the consumer has to spend. Given a set of product prices, the consumer can buy certain amounts of various products. Suppose the price of one product is now reduced. The consumer is thus able to buy the same combination of goods and services as before but now spends a *smaller* amount of nominal income. The consumer thus has some money left over to purchase more of the commodity whose price has decreased or any other product. This increase in purchasing power, which follows the reduction of any product price, represents an increase in the consumer's *real* income. Real income, or the purchasing power of nominal income, may be expressed as the ratio of nominal income to a price index that represents the prices of all commodities. Hence, if the price index is reduced because of the lowering of any particular price, the consumer's real income is increased. Conversely, if the price of any product is raised, the consumer's real income is reduced.

Since the substitution effect requires constant real income, we need to adjust the consumer's nominal income to compensate for the change in real income that follows a price change. In Figure 3A-1 we illustrate the isolation of the substitution effect. Suppose that the consumer's initial point of equilibrium is point *A* on the indifference curve I_1 and budget line *MN*. At this point the consumer chooses to purchase X_1 units of product X. Suppose now that the price of X is reduced, such that the income constraint line swings around to the new line *MN '*, allowing the consumer to attain point *B* on indifference curve I_2. The consumer now chooses to purchase X_2 units of product X, and the total effect of the price change is to increase his consumption of product X by the distance $X_2 - X_1$. It can be seen that this total effect of the price change is what we have called the price effect, since a line joining points *A* and *B* would be part of the consumer's price consumption curve. We are now aware, however, that some part of this price effect is caused by an increase in the consumer's real income, which we have called the income effect. Thus the price effect is comprised of the income effect and the substitution effect.

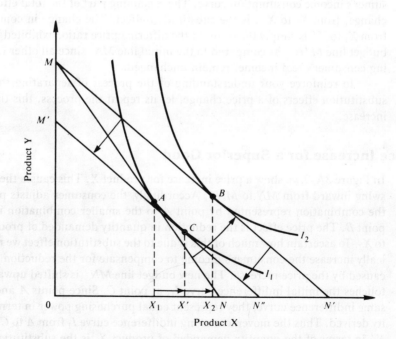

FIGURE 3A-1.   Income and Substitution Effects of a Price Reduction for a Superior Good

How to Separate the Income and the Substitution Effects

If we can account for and eliminate the income effect, we will be able to identify the remainder of the price effect as the substitution effect. We can account for the income effect by adjusting the consumer's monetary income until it allows the same level of real income as it did before the price change. To eliminate the increase in the real income, we must reduce the consumer to his previous level of real income. A method of comparing levels of real income is to compare the utility that may be derived from particular levels of nominal income. Hence, if we were to reduce this consumer to the initial level of utility by a reduction in his nominal income, we would, in effect, have reduced the consumer to the initial level of real income. Thus we wish to move the consumer from the level of utility at point B in Figure 3A–1 down to a level of utility which is equivalent to point A and therefore lies on the indifference curve I_1.

By hypothetically reducing the consumer's nominal income, we begin to move the MN' budget constraint line downward and to the left, such that it remains parallel to MN'. When this hypothetical budget line is tangent to indifference curve I_1, the consumer's level of utility is reduced to a level of real income equivalent to that previously derived from point A. This occurs with budget line $M'N''$ at the tangency point C. At the hypothetical point C the consumer would choose to purchase X' units of product X. The movement from point C to point B, or from X' units to X_2 units, is the income effect, since a line joining points C and B would, in fact, be part of this consumer's income consumption curve. The remaining part of the total effect of the price change, from X_1 to X', is the substitution effect. The change in consumption of X from X_1 to X' is simply the result of the differing price ratio, exhibited by the slope of budget line $M'N''$ as compared to the initial line MN, since all other factors, including consumer's real income, remain unchanged.

To reinforce your understanding of the process of separating the income and substitution effects of a price change, let us repeat the process, this time for a price increase.

A Price Increase for a Superior Good

In Figure 3A–2 we show a price increase for product X. This causes the budget line to swing inward from MN to MN'. Accordingly, the consumer adjusts purchases from the combination represented by point A to the smaller combination represented by point B. The price effect is the reduction in quantity demanded of product X from X_1 to X_2. To ascertain how much of this is due to the substitution effect we must hypothetically increase the consumer's income to compensate for the reduction in real income caused by the price increase. The new budget line MN' is shifted upward until it just touches the initial indifference curve I_1, at point C. Since points A and C are on the same indifference curve, they represent equal purchasing power in terms of total utility derived. Thus the movement along indifference curve I_1 from A to C, or from X_1 to X' in terms of the quantity demanded of product X, is the substitution effect, since real income is held constant and the only difference is the price ratio. The remaining

FIGURE 3A-2. **Income and Substitution Effects of a Price Increase for a Superior Good**

part of the price effect, from C to B, or from X' to X_2 in terms of the quantity demanded of product X, is the income effect of the price change. Note that the income effect and the substitution effect both work in the same direction to reduce consumption of X when its price increases, and in Figure 3A-1 both worked to increase consumption of X when its price fell.

Inferior Goods

In Figure 3A-3 we show the income and substitution effects of a price change for an inferior good.[1] Again the initial point is a tangency between budget line MN and indifference curve I_1 at point A. The price of product X is reduced such that the budget line swings around to MN', allowing the consumer a new higher level of utility at point B on indifference curve I_2. The total effect of the price change, or the price effect, is the movement from A to B, which in terms of product X is a change in consumption from X_1 to X_2. To isolate the income effect we hypothetically reduce the consumer's income until a budget line with the same slope (that is, with the same price ratio) as budget

---

[1]The indifference-curve map must reflect the inferiority of product $\overset{\shortmid}{X}$ in order for our graphs to "work out" correctly. When product X is regarded as inferior, the indifference curves will not be parallel but will be closer together at the top end than they are at the bottom end, as shown in Figure 3A-3. While indifference curves are everywhere dense (meaning that one passes through every point on the graph), they are also infinitely narrow, so that the multitude of indifference curves that exist between the lower parts of curves I_1 and I_2 have no problem squeezing through the more narrow space at the top end of those curves.

FIGURE 3A-3.   Income and Substitution Effects of a Price Reduction for an Inferior Good

line MN' is just tangent to the original indifference curve. This occurs at point C. The income effect is thus the movement from C to B, or in terms of product X from X' to X_2.

In this case the income effect is negative, since the increase in real income caused by the price reduction was accompanied by a decrease in the quantity demanded of product X. A line drawn between the points C and B, which is part of the consumer's income consumption curve, would have a negative slope, confirming that product X is regarded by this consumer as an inferior good. The substitution effect is once again the movement along the initial indifference curve from point A to point C. The substitution effect of a price reduction for product X is thus an increase in the quantity demanded of product X from level X_1 to X'. This is partly offset by a negative income effect from X' to X_2, such that the total effect (or the price effect) is from X_1 to X_2.

Note: Notice that in both the normal goods case and the inferior goods case the substitution effect was negative. Given the general validity of the assumptions that underlie the construction of a consumer's indifference curve, the substitution effect is *always* negative; that is, for price reductions corrected for the income effect the consumer will always purchase more of the product, while for price increases corrected for the income effect the consumer will always purchase less of the product. The income effect, however, may be either positive or negative, and, if negative, it offsets part of the substitution effect.

Giffen Goods. It is theoretically possible that a large negative income effect could more than offset the substitution effect, in which case a price reduction would be followed by a decline in the quantity demanded, or a price increase would be followed by an increase in the quantity demanded. A product that behaved in this way would exhibit a positive price effect and would therefore run counter to the empirical law of demand. Such a product is known as a *Giffen good.*[2] A modern-day example of a Giffen good is difficult to find, keeping in mind that we require *ceteris paribus* to hold when the price of the product in question is changed. A situation that may seem to indicate a Giffen good is one in which a product sells for a while at one price and later sells more units at a higher price. If and only if *ceteris paribus* prevailed over the entire period of the observations would the product be a Giffen good. More likely, however, one or more of the underlying factors has changed during the period (such as consumer tastes, incomes, and the prices and availability of other products). If so, the two observations are not on the same demand curve but are on separate demand curves, because of a shift of the demand curve caused in turn by a change in an underlying determinant.

Example: Suppose a merchant offers hand towels for sale at $0.59 each and demand for these towels is somewhat less than enthusiastic. If the merchant now raises the price to $0.99 and customers eagerly purchase the towels, does this mean that those hand towels are a Giffen good? The answer is probably no. Consumers tend to make price-quality associations when they are unable to judge quality on any other basis. At the lower price the hand towels were perceived as "low-quality" hand towels, whereas at the higher price they were perceived as "better-quality" hand towels. The consumers' taste and preference patterns between low-quality and high-quality hand towels are probably the same as they were when they first confronted by the hand towels. The error in calling hand towels a Giffen good rests upon failing to distinguish that consumers regard the higher-priced hand towels as a different product from the lower-priced hand towels. Our analysis of the income and substitution effects of a price change for a particular good depends upon successive units of that product being identical with the preceding and following units.

In the above example the two observations are most likely part of two separate negatively sloping demand curves, rather than of a single positively sloping demand curve. "Shifts" versus "movements along" demand curves are discussed in detail in

---

[2]The existence of such perverse price effects was noted in the case of potatoes during the Irish famine of 1846 to 1849. Although the price of potatoes had increased as a result of a blight affecting the crops and reducing supplies, many families were consuming more potatoes than they were at earlier prices. The Irish peasant was typically so poor that potatoes formed the major part of the family diet, supplemented by meat and other foodstuffs. When the price of potatoes was increased, the demand for potatoes actually increased, since the money left over for meat and other foodstuffs (after buying the same quantity of potatoes) was insufficient to buy enough of these less-bulky items to satisfy the family appetite. Thus demand for the more-filling potato was increased despite its higher price. See G. J. Stigler, "Notes on the History of the Giffen Paradox," *Journal of Political Economy*, 55 (April 1947), pp. 152–56.

Chapter 4, and the "identification problem," which causes confusion between shifts and movements along demand curves in practice, is discussed in Chapter 5.

Summary

The price effect is composed of an income effect and a substitution effect. The income effect is the change in quantity demanded because of the change in real income which accompanies a price change, given *ceteris paribus*. The substitution effect is the change in quantity demanded because of a change in the relative prices of two products, given *ceteris paribus*. To isolate the income effect we move the new budget line into tangency with the initial indifference curve to return the consumer to the initial level of real income. The change in quantity demanded that this would cause is the income effect, and the remainder of the price effect is the substitution effect.

DISCUSSION QUESTIONS

3A-1. What is the income effect of a price change? Does the change in the price of one product have income effects on other products as well?

3A-2. What is the substitution effect of a price change? How is its definition different from the definition of the price effect?

3A-3. Why is the same level of total utility (at points *A* and *C*, for example) taken as a proxy for the same level of real income?

3A-4. Why is the (hypothetical) compensating change in income always shown as a parallel shift of the budget line?

3A-5. What do we mean when we say that the substitution effect is always negative, regardless of whether the price increases or decreases?

PROBLEMS AND SHORT CASES

3A-1. The Consumer Price Index is derived by comparing the cost of a given combination of the many products that are usually included in the household's budget. For example, if the price of any one of those goods decreases and other things remain unchanged, the CPI decreases. Explain how the income and substitution effects would work in a multiproduct case like this, with reference to a change in the CPI.

3A-2. Using graphs, show the separation of the income and substitution effects of a price *increase* for an *inferior* good, and explain why the consumer reacts in the way shown.

3A-3. See if you can devise a set of indifference curves that show product X to be a Giffen good. Using these curves, show the separation of the income and substitution effects of a price reduction for that Giffen good. (Hint: Giffen goods are extremely inferior goods, and the indifference curves must reflect this fact.)

SUGGESTED REFERENCES AND FURTHER READING

Hirshleifer, Jack. *Price Theory and Applications*, 2nd ed., esp. chaps. 3 and 6. Englewood Cliffs, N.J.; Prentice-Hall, Inc., 1980.

Hyman, David N. *Modern Microeconomics: Analysis and Applications*, esp. chaps. 3 and 4. St. Louis: Times Mirror/Mosby College Publishing, 1986.

Mansfield, E. *Microeconomics: Theory/Applications*, esp. chaps. 3 and 4. New York: W. W. Norton & Company, 1985.

Stigler, George J. "Notes on the History of the Giffen Paradox," *Journal of Political Economy*, 55 (April 1947), pp. 152–56.

4 Market Demand Analysis for Decision Making

4.1 INTRODUCTION

In Chapter 3 we examined the behavior of individual consumers who make utility-maximizing decisions to purchase goods and services.[1] They make these decisions on the basis of their own incomes and preferences and on the basis of the price and availability of various products. When discussing individual consumer behavior, we do not expect the actions and reactions of any individual consumer to change the environment for subsequent behavior by that consumer. Consumers in aggregate, on the other hand, can and do influence the prices and availability of goods and services. Their collective actions constitute the demand side of the product markets, and as such they are responsible, in conjunction with the supply side of each market, for the determination of the price and output levels in each of the product markets.

The total demand in any particular product market, or market demand, as it is commonly called, is an important force in the economic system because it enters the product markets supported by the income that consumers expect to spend in order to maximize their utility. These consumer expenditures become sales revenue from the firm's point of view. In this chapter we consider the major factors likely to influence the total demand and sales revenue for a product as well as the probable direction of the influence in each case. We then examine the interrelationships among the important revenue concepts, namely total revenue, marginal revenue, and average revenue (or price per unit). A means of measuring and summarizing the direction and magnitude of the influence that each variable has on the total demand for a particular product is provided by the concept of elasticity of demand, and we consider several different elasticity measures and their application to decision-making problems.

---

[1] Chapter 3 is not a prerequisite to this chapter, although it does allow a more thorough understanding of individual consumer behavior. In Chapter 4 the consumers' reactions to change in their economic environment are restated briefly, and this will allow a sufficient understanding of market demand analysis.

4.2 THE DEMAND FUNCTION AND THE DEMAND CURVE

Note: Let us immediately make the following distinction. The demand *function* refers to the relationship that exists between the quantity demanded of a particular product and *all factors* that influence that demand. The demand *curve* refers to the relationship that exists between the quantity demanded of a particular product and the *price* of that product, with all other influencing factors held constant. The demand curve is thus a subset of the demand function in the case where *ceteris paribus* applies to all of the independent variables except price.

The Independent Variables in the Demand Function

The demand function is a specification of the relationship existing between the quantity demanded of product X and the variables influencing the demand for that product. The quantity demanded of X, or Q_x, is known as the dependent variable in the demand function, since its value depends on the values of the influencing variables, which are known as the independent variables. What are the independent variables that influence Q_x? Let us discuss them one by one.

Price. We have seen in the preceding chapter that quantity demanded varies inversely with the price of the product, given *ceteris paribus*. For increases in the price of X we expect the quantity demanded to fall, and for decreases in the price of X we expect the quantity demanded to rise.

Prices of Related Products. The price of *substitute* products enters the demand function for product X because of the willingness of consumers to purchase products that are substitutes for product X, given changes in the relative prices of this group of products. If the price of one of the substitute products increases, we expect the demand for product X to increase, since individual consumers tend to switch from the substitute products to product X. We expect the converse for reductions in the prices of substitute products.

Complementary goods, on the other hand, are products that are typically consumed in conjunction with product X. For example, coffee and cream, gasoline and tires, and beer and peanuts are pairs of complementary goods for many people. If the prices of complementary goods rise, we expect the quantity demanded of product X to decrease, since the consumption of product X and its complementary products is now more expensive. Conversely, if the prices of complements decrease, the quantity demanded of X should increase, since the "package price" for X and its complements is now reduced.

Advertising and Promotional Efforts. Advertising and other promotional efforts by the sellers of product X can be expected to influence the quantity demanded of that product, since these efforts are designed to influence the taste and preference patterns of consumers. Advertising related to product X is expected to be followed by an increase in the quantity demanded of product X. On the other hand, advertising of substitute products is expected to have a negative influence on the quantity demanded of X, since it should be expected to induce consumers to switch their consumption from product X toward one of the substitute products. Conversely, advertising of a complementary good is expected to have a positive influence on the quantity demanded of product X, since consumers tend to buy product X and that complementary good in some proportionate way.

Product Quality and Design.   Consumers typically appreciate quality and good design and are expected to purchase more of a product when they perceive it to be of higher quality or of a more functional or fashionable design, given similar prices. Conversely, if the quality is judged inferior to other products or represents a reduction in quality, as compared to the firm's earlier production, consumers are expected to reduce their aggregate demand for the product. Quality can be designed into the firm's product itself, or it can be attached as a peripheral attribute like courteous service, a comprehensive guarantee, or a convenient and well-trained service network. In addition, consumer perceptions of quality and design may be influenced by the firm's advertising and promotional efforts.

Distribution Outlets and Place of Sale.   Total demand for the firm's product is directly influenced by the number of sales or distribution outlets and by the location of these outlets. Having a larger number of outlets allows the firm to reach consumers who may not otherwise be exposed to the product, to make it more convenient for consumers to purchase the product, and to offer ancillary services (such as technical advice, repairs, and warranty service) which help to augment total sales. Of course, the location of sales outlets is an important consideration. A retail store in a busy shopping center may have triple the sales volume of a similar store on a low-traffic side street. Thus firms choose the locations of their wholesale and retail outlets with an eye to the potential sales volume (and hence sales revenue) that is expected to result from each location.[2]

Consumer Incomes.   The relationship between consumer income and quantity demanded of product X can be expected to be either positive or negative, depending on the product in question and the level of consumer income. We saw in Chapter 3 that for some consumers at some income levels a particular commodity could have a negative income effect, whereas for other consumers at other income levels the income effect might be positive. We are interested here in the *aggregate* income effect. Thus,

---

[2]Distribution strategy is covered in detail in marketing courses. See Philip Kotler, *Principles of Marketing* (Englewood Cliffs, N.J.: Prentice-Hall, Inc., 1980), chapters 14 and 15. Marketers speak of the four P's—price, promotion, product design, and place of sale—as the firm's controllable variables among those that influence consumer demand. Other influencing variables, such as actions by competitors, consumer incomes, and population are uncontrollable, and others, such as tastes and preferences and expectations, may be regarded as partially controllable by the firm through its product design and promotional strategies.

if to most purchasers the product is an inferior good, its demand will decrease when income levels rise or increase when income levels fall. On the other hand, if it is a normal or superior product for most purchasers, quantity demanded and income levels move in the same direction.

Consumer Tastes and Preferences.   The tastes and preferences of consumers may be expected to be in a continual state of flux, with some people shifting their purchases toward a particular product and others shifting away. In explaining aggregate demand we are interested in the net effect of changing tastes and in the general trend of tastes and preferences toward or away from the product in question. An index of consumer preferences for a particular product may be constructed and periodically updated by surveys of consumer attitudes toward that product. If random samples of consumers indicate that the product is, for example, becoming more widely appreciated, or that the strength of consumers' desire for the product is increasing, this shift would be captured by an increase in the value of the index.

Consumer Expectations.   Consumer expectations about the future price, availability, and substitutability of product X influence their present demand for product X. For example, if you expect gasoline to be significantly more expensive or less readily available in the near future, you may be motivated to increase your current demand for gasoline, by keeping your tank full most of the time or even by filling extra containers with gasoline. Similarly, if you expect a new model of product X to be released in the near future and if you expect this new model to be a significant improvement, you may reduce your purchases of X now and wait for the new model. Thus consumer expectations have a positive impact on current demand for product X if the expectations are pessimistic with respect to future prices, availability, or quality of product X. Conversely, consumer expectations have a negative impact on current demand if the expectations are optimistic.

Other Factors.   Every demand function will have its own particular set of determinants, reflecting the reasons people purchase the product. For example, the demand for umbrellas in a particular market depends on the amount of rainfall in that area. The demand for many other products, including clothing, sporting equipment, and types of transportation demanded, is also dependent on the weather. Government policy affects the demand for many products. The government may be pursuing an industrial strategy that encourages production of the firm's products, such as high-technology goods, for example. Tariff protection for the firm's product may be increased or reduced as part of government policy, or the government may act to reduce the external value of the dollar, with subsequent impacts on the firm's demand. Reduced or increased surveillance of the firm's pricing and advertising policies by the Federal Trade Commission may impact upon the effectiveness of the firm's policies. Finally, we should note that the demand for most products is positively related to the number of people in the market, or the size of the population. Still other factors may be significant determinants of the demand for particular products.

The determinants of demand are summarized in Table 4-1. Note that we can categorize them into four main groups. The firm's "strategic" variables are those it can adjust to influence demand directly. We also call these the "controllable" variables. The remaining three groups of determinants are not controllable by the firm, although the firm may be able to influence some of them, including consumer tastes and preferences, the actions of competitors (including the producers of complementary products), and government policy.

The *specific* form of the demand function for a particular product is an empirical question. That is, collection and analysis of data may reveal Q_x to be a linear function of its determinants or, alternatively, a multiplicative function of several independent variables. The linear form of the demand function is exemplified by the following:

$$Q_x = \alpha + \beta_1 P_x + \beta_2 P_y + \beta_3 A_x + \beta_4 A_y$$
$$+ \beta_5 Y_c + \beta_6 T_c + \beta_7 E_c + \beta_8 N \tag{4-1}$$

TABLE 4-1.   The Determinants of Demand for a Product

where

Q_x is quantity demanded of product X, per period.
P_x is price of product X
A_x is advertising/promotion for product X
D_x is design/style/quality of product X
O_x is outlets for distribution of product X
I_c is incomes of consumers/customers/clientele
T_c is tastes and preference patterns of consumers
E_c is expectations of consumers re future prices, etc.
P_y is prices of related goods (substitutes, complements)
A_y is advertising/promotion for related goods
D_y is design/style/quality of related goods
O_y is outlets for distribution of related goods
G is government policy, industrial strategy
N is number of people in the economy
W is weather conditions

where α (the Greek letter alpha) is that part of quantity demanded determined exogenously or by other variables not explicitly mentioned in the demand function, and β_1, $\beta_2, \ldots, \beta_8$ (β is the Greek letter beta) are the coefficients of the demand function indicating the marginal impact of each independent variable upon the quantity demanded.

Alternatively, two or more variables may be found to have a multiplicative impact on Q_x, as follows:

$$Q_x = \alpha P_x^{\beta_1} N^{\beta_2} O_x^{\beta_3} \qquad (4\text{-}2)$$

In this case, quantity demanded for product X is the product of the variables for the price of X, total market population, and number of outlets for product X.

The coefficients in the demand function (namely α, β_1, β_2, β_3, and so on) may be estimated using regression analysis and other techniques, as we shall see in Chapter 5. Equations (4–1) and (4–2) are, in effect, symbolic models of the demand function for product X. Each one is an explanatory model used to explain the demand for X in terms of the levels of each of the independent variables. Such models explain changes in the value of Q_x as the result of a change in one or more of the independent variables. A model of the demand function can also be used for predictive purposes, given estimates of all the β coefficients and the residual term α.

Example: Suppose the demand function for product X has been estimated using regression analysis to be as follows:

$$Q_x = 5{,}030 - 3{,}806.2P_x + 1{,}458.5P_y + 256.6A_x - 32.3A_y + 0.18Y_c \qquad (4\text{-}3)$$

where the symbols for the independent variables are the same as introduced previously, and the coefficients are replaced by their numerical equivalents. Note that the positive or negative sign preceding each independent variable indicates the direction of the influence that variable has on Q_x. Given this specification of the demand function, we can predict the sales level for product X, given the values of the independent variables. Suppose $P_x = \$8$; $P_y = \$6$; $A_x = \$168$ (in thousands); $A_y = \$182$ (in thousands); and $Y_c = \$12{,}875$. Substituting for these variables in Equation (4–3), we find

$$Q_x = 5{,}030 - 30{,}449.6 + 8{,}751.0 + 43{,}108.8 - 5{,}878.6 + 2{,}317.5$$
$$= 22{,}879.1$$

Thus we predict that at the current values of the independent variables, quantity demanded of product X should be 22,879.1 units, given *ceteris paribus*.

The Demand Curve Derived from the Demand Function

The demand curve is a special subcase of the demand function in which *ceteris paribus* applies to all independent variables except the price of the product in question. Since none of the other independent variables or the residual term α vary when *ceteris paribus* is in force, we can compress them all into a single term A and express the demand function as follows:

$$Q_x = A + \beta_1 P_x \quad (4\text{-}4)$$

where the parameter A includes the influence of all the other independent variables and the residual term α on Q_x, and is, therefore, equal to $\alpha + \beta_2 P_y + \beta_3 A_x + \dots$ and so forth, from equation (4-1).

Note: The demand curve expresses the relationship between Q_x and P_x with all other things remaining the same, and equation (4-4) is, therefore, an expression of the demand curve. But economists, following the convention set by Alfred Marshall, the great classical economist, traditionally place the independent variable (price) on the vertical axis for their graphical analysis.[3] Given this convention, it is important for efficient communication that we also observe this practice, keeping in mind that Q_x is the dependent variable and P_x is the independent variable. Economists typically state the demand curve in this form:

$$P_x = a + bQ_x \quad (4\text{-}5)$$

Equation (4-5) is easily obtained from equation (4-4) by a couple of manipulations and substitutions. Working on equation (4-4), subtract A from both sides and divide both sides by β_1 to find

$$P_x = -\frac{A}{\beta_1} + \frac{1}{\beta_1}Q_x \quad (4\text{-}6)$$

Letting $a = -A/\beta_1$ and $b = 1/\beta_1$, we have $P_x = a + bQ_x$. Note that the numerical value of β_1 is expected to have a negative sign because of the law of demand. Thus the parameter a will be a positive number, and b will be a negative number.

Example: From the numerical example introduced earlier, we can find:

$$Q_x = 53{,}328.7 - 3{,}806.2P_x \quad (4\text{-}7)$$

The number 53,328.7 is the sum of the α term (5,030) and the influence of all other independent variables except P_x. It is usually more convenient when dealing with large numbers to express them in larger units, such as thousands or millions, in order to simplify calculations. Expressing Q_x in thousands of units, we have:

$$Q_x = 53.3287 - 3.8062P_x \quad (4\text{-}8)$$

---

[3]See Alfred N. Page, "Marshall's Graphs and Walras' Equations: A Textbook Anomaly," *Economic Inquiry,* 18 (January 1980), pp. 138-43.

To invert this expression to the form $P_x = a + bQ_x$ we add $3.8062P_x$ to both sides, subtract Q_x from both sides, and divide both sides by 3.8062, as follows:

$$3.8062P_x = 53.3287 - Q_x$$

$$P_x = \frac{53.3287}{3.8062} - \frac{1}{3.8062}Q_x$$

$$P_x = 14.011 - 0.26273Q_x \qquad (4\text{-}9)$$

Thus we have derived an expression for the demand curve from the estimate of the demand function. Note that we have price expressed as a linear function of quantity demanded, *ceteris paribus*, where a is the intercept term on the vertical (price) axis and b is the slope term. In Figure 4-1 we show the market demand curve for product X. Note that the curve intercepts the price axis at the value a, and slopes downward at the rate b, or $1/\beta_1$. The intercept on the horizontal axis is, of course, the value A, since this is the value of Q_x when P_x is zero.[4] Note that when $P_x = \$8$, $Q_x = 22,879.1$, as calculated earlier. That price-quantity combination is shown as point M on the demand curve in Figure 4-1.

FIGURE 4-1.   The Market Demand Curve for Product X

---

[4]We should be cautious about extending the analysis to extreme values of P_x and Q_x. It is sufficient to say that the intercept terms a (on the vertical axis) and A (on the horizontal axis) simply *locate* the demand curve at its appropriate height. We expect the demand curve to depict the relationship between P_x and Q_x adequately only within the relevant range of observations, which is in the vicinity of the current price and demand levels. For the same reason it is a sufficient approximation to show the demand curve as linear through the relevant range, although for extreme values of P_x and Q_x the demand curve is likely to become curvilinear.

Movements Along versus Shifts of the Demand Curve

A *movement along* the demand curve will occur when there is a change in price (and consequently quantity demanded) while all other determinants of demand remain constant. In Figure 4-1 we show a price change from $8 per unit to $5 per unit, which causes quantity demanded to increase from 22,879.1 units to 34,297 units. (This value of quantity demanded was calculated by substituting the value 5 for P_x in equation 4-8 or 4-9.) In effect, there has been a movement along the demand curve from point M to point N as a result of the price change, given *ceteris paribus*.

A *shift* of the demand curve will occur when *ceteris paribus* does not apply, and thus the value of the intercept term changes. In Figure 4-2 we show shifts of the demand curve which are the result of changes in one or more of the other factors while price is held constant. Suppose that the initial demand curve is that shown as D, such that at price P_1, quantity demanded is Q_1. If, for example, consumer incomes increased (or there was an increase in some other variable that has a positive coefficient in equation (4-3) or a decrease in a variable that has a negative coefficient), the demand curve would *shift* to the right, as shown by the movement to demand curve D'. For the same price level P_1 the quantity demanded is now Q'; the additional quantity demanded is caused by a change in one or more of the other variables. On the other hand, had there been a reduction in consumer incomes (or a shift in consumer tastes away from product X or any of a number of other changes in the determining factors), the demand curve would shift to the left, to a position such as that shown by demand curve D''.

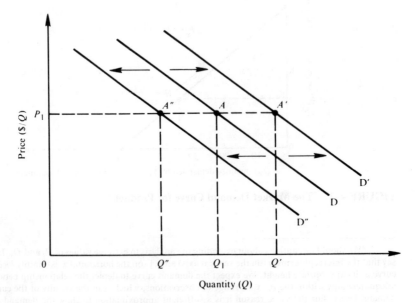

FIGURE 4-2.   Shifts of the Demand Curve for Product X

Note: Thus changes in price will, *ceteris paribus*, lead to a *movement* along an existing demand curve, whereas changes in any of the other variables will cause a *shift* of the demand curve. Given the new set of the other variables, there will be a new demand curve that is appropriate, and the initial demand curve will now be inappropriate. Given this new set of the other variables, we may now speak of movements along the new demand curve in response to changes in the price level, *ceteris paribus*. When analyzing the effect on quantity demanded of a change in the price level, it is therefore extremely important to ascertain whether or not any of the other factors have changed before concluding that there has been a movement along the demand curve.

Example: To illustrate the combined impact of movements along demand curves and shifts of demand curves, consider the substantial price increase of coffee during 1977, caused by the price increase of imported coffee beans by exporting countries (who had earlier seen the oil-producing countries do the same thing). The left-hand part of Figure 4–3 shows the price and quantity demanded of coffee in supermarkets before and after the increase in coffee bean prices (P_1, Q_1 and P_2, Q_2, respectively). A superficial analysis of this situation might lead to the conclusion that the supply curve for coffee had shifted from S_1 to S_2, causing a movement along the market demand curve from point A to point B. This interpretation would indicate that consumers' demand for coffee was not very sensitive to price increases and may lead to consideration of further price increases.

Closer analysis reveals that the substantial change in the price level was the result of both a movement along *and* a shift of the demand curve. The right-hand part of the figure shows the supply curve having shifted from S_1 to S_2 as a result of the increase in coffee bean prices. This change alone would cause supply and demand to be equal at price P', considerably below the actual price that eventuated (P_2). The actual price was higher because there had been a *shift* of the demand curve as well: fearing that coffee might not be available in the near future, many consumers bought

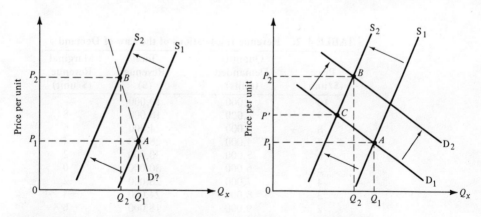

FIGURE 4–3.   Shifts Distinguished from Movements along Demand Curves

more than they normally would in order to build personal stockpiles. This reaction manifested itself as a shift of the demand curve from D_1 to D_2, resulting from a change in consumers' expectations concerning future prices and availability of the product. Thus the price change was the result of two separate influences: from P_1 to P' as the result of a movement along the initial demand curve and from P' to P_2 as a result of the shift of the demand curve from D_1 to D_2.

This example points out the danger of assuming that the change in quantity demanded is entirely due to the variable the manager has adjusted (in the case of a controllable determinant of demand) or has seen move (in the case of an uncontrollable determinant of demand). A naive view of what happened in the coffee market (the interpretation in the left-hand side of Figure 4–3) would lead the manager to conclude that the demand for coffee is really quite unresponsive to changes in price—the quantity demanded seemed to fall only slightly after the price rose substantially. This manager might be inclined to raise the price further, expecting quantity demanded to fall only slightly. A more informed view, recognizing that *ceteris* was not *paribus*, would lead to the conclusion that quantity demanded would fall very substantially for such a price increase, if other things did remain the same. If nothing happens to shift the demand curve, the further price increase would amount to a movement along the new demand curve D_2, and this would come as a great surprise to the naive manager who mistakenly believes the demand curve to be much steeper than it is.

Relationships among Price, Total Revenue, and Marginal Revenue

Why are we interested in the variation between price and quantity of a particular commodity? Our concern is to see what happens to total sales revenue when prices and quantities are varied. Whatever the decision maker's objective function, total revenue is likely to play a major role in the optimization of that objective function. In Table 4–2

TABLE 4–2.   Revenue Implications of the Law of Demand

Price ($/unit)	Quantity Demanded (units)	Total Revenue ($)	Marginal Revenue ($/unit)
10	1,000	10,000	—
9	2,000	18,000	8
8	3,000	24,000	6
7	4,000	28,000	4
6	5,000	30,000	2
5	6,000	30,000	0
4	7,000	28,000	−2
3	8,000	24,000	−4
2	9,000	18,000	−6
1	10,000	10,000	−8

we demonstrate the variation of total revenue for the demand curve specified by $P_x = 11 - 0.001\ Q_x$.

Example: Suppose this formula represents the demand curve for a carton of twelve cans of dog food at a discount supermarket during a particular month. For this simple demand curve the intercept on the price axis is thus $11, and the slope is -0.001. Thus, for every price reduction of $1.00, quantity demanded will increase by 1,000 cartons. Substituting different values of price into this equation, we are able to determine the quantity that will be demanded at all prices, as shown in the second column of Table 4–2. Total revenue at each price is derived by multiplying the price by the quantity demanded at that price, to find the total revenue associated with each price (or quantity) level. It can be seen that total revenue increases progressively as price is lowered from $10 to $6, that the price reduction to $5 leaves the total revenue unchanged, and that further price reductions cause total revenue to decline.

Note that high prices are not necessarily the best prices. By progressively lowering the price, we were able to increase total revenue up to a point. Similarly, neither is a very low price necessarily a good strategy; although it does expand the quantity demanded, it causes a smaller total revenue, as compared with that which may be earned at a higher price level. In Table 4–2 the fourth column shows the marginal revenue associated with each price level.

■ *Definition:* *Marginal revenue* is defined as the change in total revenue that results from a one-unit increase in quantity demand. Since quantity demanded increases by blocks of 1,000 units in Table 4–2, marginal revenue is calculated here as the row-to-row difference in the total revenue column divided by the change in quantity demanded. It can be seen that marginal revenue falls progressively to zero and becomes negative as price is reduced.

In Figure 4–4 we plot the values for the demand curve (given by the price/quantity combinations) and the total revenue and marginal revenue curves to illustrate the relationships that exist between and among these curves. These relationships hold for any demand curve that is negatively sloped. Total revenue increases at first as prices are lowered, reaches its maximum, and thereafter declines as prices are reduced further. Marginal revenue will always be less than price at each output level; will fall to zero at the point where total revenue reaches its maximum; and will take negative values if price is reduced any further, since this causes an absolute reduction in total revenue.[5]

---

[5]The price reductions shown in Table 4–2 were made by discrete $1.00 units, and hence the changes in quantity-demanded observations were in blocks of 1,000 units. Marginal revenue calculated from these data is strictly the *average* change in total revenue per one-unit change in quantity demanded for each of the 1,000-unit blocks. If we had shown smaller price reductions, we would have found that the price generating the highest revenue would be $5.50. At this price level, 5,500 units would be demanded and total revenue would be $30,250. Strictly, then, marginal revenue is zero at these price and quantity levels, as shown in Figure 4–4, rather than the more crude approximations shown in Table 4–2.

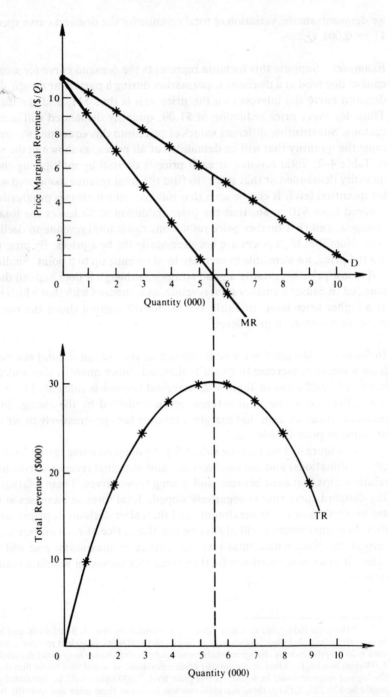

FIGURE 4-4. Relationships between Demand, Marginal Revenue, and Total Revenue

Price and Marginal Revenue.   The relationship between the demand curve and the marginal revenue curve bears further observation. Since both may be derived from the total revenue curve, it is clear that there must be a relationship between them. To find this relationship we begin by expressing the total revenue as the product of price and quantity:

$$TR_x = P_x \cdot Q_x \qquad (4\text{-}10)$$

Equation (4–5) gave us the following expression for P_x:

$$P_x = a + bQ_x \qquad (4\text{-}5)$$

Substituting for P_x in equation (4–10), we obtain

$$TR_x = aQ_x + bQ_x^2 \qquad (4\text{-}11)$$

Since *marginal revenue* is defined as the change in total revenue for a one-unit change in quantity demanded, it can be expressed as the first derivative of equation (4–11) with respect to Q_x. Thus,[6]

$$MR_x = a + 2bQ_x \qquad (4\text{-}12)$$

Now compare the expression for the demand curve, equation (4–5), with the expression for the marginal revenue curve, equation (4–12). The intercept term of each is a, indicating that both curves must emanate from the same point on the vertical axis of the graph, and the slope term in the marginal revenue expression is exactly twice the slope term in the price or demand curve expression.

Note: Thus the marginal revenue curve does have a fixed relationship with the demand curve from which it is derived. It begins at the same point on the price axis, and its slope is twice that of the demand curve.[7]

---

[6] The derivative of Equation (4–11) with respect to Q_x was obtained using the *power rule*. If this is unfamiliar to you it is explained in Appendix A.

[7] In the above, we have confined our discussion to *linear* demand curves. A linear specification of the demand curve is typically a sufficient approximation over the relevant range of prices and outputs. It is nevertheless also true that the marginal revenue curve for a *curvilinear* demand curve will have the same intercept and twice the slope of the demand curve at any given output level. That is, a tangent to the (curvilinear) marginal revenue curve will have twice the slope of a tangent to the curvilinear demand curve at any given output level. This assumes that the demand curve is *convex* to the origin, which is in keeping with the economic theory of consumer behavior. Horizontal demand curves, such as in pure competition, are coextensive with the marginal revenue curve and thus have the same intercept and the same slope. But since the slope of a horizontal line is zero and since twice zero is still zero, the general rule (that MR has the same intercept and twice the slope of the demand curve) is not violated.

Example: From the estimated demand function provided earlier, we had derived the following expression for the demand curve:

$$P_x = 14.011 - 0.26273 Q_x \qquad (4\text{-}9)$$

The marginal revenue curve associated with this demand curve will have the same intercept term on the price axis and twice the slope and can, therefore, be expressed as

$$MR_x = 14.011 - 0.52546 Q_x$$

The above relationships between price, quantity demanded, total revenue, and marginal revenue can be summarized in a single number known as the "price elasticity" of demand. The concept of elasticity is used widely in economics and expresses the responsiveness of one variable to a change in another variable. Stated a little more rigorously, an *elasticity* is the percentage change in the dependent variable occasioned by a 1 percent change in an independent variable. It thus shows the proportionate response of one variable to a change in one of the variables that influence that variable. In the following sections the dependent variable is the quantity demanded, and the independent variables are a selection of the independent variables shown in Table 4-1.

4.3   PRICE ELASTICITY OF DEMAND

■ *Definition:*   *Price elasticity of demand* is defined as the percentage change in quantity demanded divided by the percentage change in price which caused the change in quantity demanded. That is,

$$\epsilon = \frac{\% \text{ change in } Q_x}{\% \text{ change in } P_x} \qquad (4\text{-}13)$$

where ϵ (the Greek letter epsilon) is the conventional symbol for price elasticity of demand. Expanding equation (4-13) we have

$$\epsilon = \frac{\dfrac{\Delta Q_x}{Q_x} \cdot \dfrac{100}{1}}{\dfrac{\Delta P_x}{P_x} \cdot \dfrac{100}{1}} \qquad (4\text{-}14)$$

where Δ (the Greek letter delta) connotes a change. Rearranging terms and cancelling the 100/1 terms, we have

$$\epsilon = \frac{\Delta Q_x}{Q_x} \cdot \frac{P_x}{\Delta P_x}$$

or

$$\epsilon = \frac{\Delta Q_x}{\Delta P_x} \cdot \frac{P_x}{Q_x} \qquad\qquad (4\text{-}15)$$

Note that $\Delta Q_x/\Delta P_x$ is equal to the reciprocal of b, the slope term in the demand curve. Hence price elasticity is equal to the reciprocal of the slope multiplied by the ratio of price to quantity demanded, P_x/Q_x. On a linear demand curve the slope term is constant, and therefore the term $\Delta Q_x/\Delta P_x$ is constant in equation (4-15). Note, however, that the P_x/Q_x term in the elasticity expression is not constant, but varies throughout the length of the demand curve. At points high on the demand curve, the ratio of P_x to Q_x is relatively large, whereas for points low on the demand curve, the ratio of P_x to Q_x is relatively low. In fact this ratio approaches infinity as we move toward the intercept on the price axis. It approaches zero as we move toward the intercept on the quantity axis. Since elasticity is the product of a constant and a number that varies from infinity to zero, it is apparent that the value for price elasticity must vary from infinity to zero as we move from the price intercept down a linear demand curve to the quantity intercept.

Note: Strictly, the value of price elasticity varies from *minus* infinity to approach zero from the *negative* side, because $\Delta Q_x/\Delta P_x$ has a negative sign. Either ΔQ_x or ΔP_x is negative, depending on whether we move up or down the demand curve. By convention, however, we speak of price elasticity in *absolute* terms, saying for example that $\epsilon = -5$ is greater than $\epsilon = -3$.

Now, since elasticity varies from minus infinity to zero as we move down the demand curve, it must at some point be equal to -1. Let us assert and then prove that $\epsilon = -1$ at the midpoint of the demand curve. Take a specific demand curve, such as $P_x = 5 - 0.625Q_x$. You can visualize this demand curve as having a vertical intercept of \$5, since $P_x = 5$ when $Q_x = 0$, and a horizontal intercept of 8 units, since $Q_x = 8$ when $P_x = 0$. The slope of the demand curve is $\Delta P_x/\Delta Q_x = -0.625$, which is of course, equal to $-5/8$, the negative ratio of the vertical intercept value over the horizontal intercept value. The reciprocal of the slope, $\Delta Q_x/\Delta P_x$, which enters the elasticity calculation, is therefore $-8/5$, or -1.6. This demand curve is shown in Figure 4-5.

For the value of price elasticity to be equal to -1, and given $\Delta Q_x/\Delta P_x = -8/5$, and other half of the elasticity formula—the price-quantity ratio—must equal $5/8$. The *only* pair of price-quantity observations on the demand curve $P_x = 5 - 0.625Q_x$ having the ratio $5/8$ is $P_x = 2.50$ and $Q_x = 4$. Thus elasticity is equal to -1 at price \$2.50 and quantity demanded of 4 units. Now notice that these are the midpoint values between the origin and the intercept on each axis. It follows (by proof for congruent triangles) that the coordinates $P_x = 2.50$ and $Q_x = 4$ are the midpoint of the demand curve.[8]

Note: Thus elasticity ranges from 1 to infinity above the midpoint and from 1 to zero below the midpoint. By convention, we say demand is *elastic* when ϵ is greater than 1 and it is *inelastic* when ϵ is less than 1 (in absolute terms). At the midpoint there is *unitary* elasticity. The knowledge that the midpoint divides the demand curve into these two ranges of elasticity is quite useful, since we can, by inspection of any point on a demand curve, immediately conclude whether its elasticity exceeds, is equal to, or is less than 1. Let us demonstrate the significance of elasticity being greater than, equal to, or less than 1.

Price Elasticity, Marginal Revenue, and Total Revenue

We now examine the relationship that exists between price elasticity and marginal revenue. Since the marginal revenue curve begins at the same intercept on the price axis as the demand curve but has twice the slope of the demand curve, it must intersect the quantity axis in half the horizontal distance from the origin to the point where the demand curve intersects the quantity axis. Thus, in terms of Figure 4-5 the marginal

FIGURE 4-5. Price Elasticity Equals 1 at the Midpoint of the Demand Curve

---

[8]Prove that $AB = BC$. Proof: $AD = BE$
$$DB = EC$$
Angle ADB = Angle BEC
$\therefore$ Congruent triangles
$\therefore AB = BC$

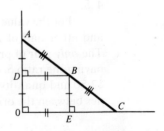

TABLE 4-3. Relationship between Price Elasticity and Total Revenue

Elasticity Value	Price Increases	Price Decreases
$\infty > \lvert\epsilon\rvert > 1$	TR falls	TR rises
$\infty > \lvert\epsilon\rvert = 1$	TR constant	TR constant
$0 < \lvert\epsilon\rvert < 1$	TR rises	TR falls

revenue curve must pass through the point where $Q_x = 4$. It is therefore apparent that the marginal revenue is negative when elasticity is less than unity.

Let us now look at the relationship between price elasticity of demand and *total* revenue. Referring back to Figure 4-4, recall that when marginal revenue is positive (that is, when elasticity exceeds unity), total revenue increases for successive increases in quantity, and when marginal revenue is negative (that is, when elasticity is less than unity), total revenue decreases for successive increases in quantities. In Table 4-3 we summarize what happens to total revenue when price is either increased or decreased and when elasticity is greater than 1, equal to 1, and less than 1.

The relationship between price changes and price elasticity and the change in total revenue should be intuitively obvious when one recalls our initial definition of price elasticity. We defined it as the percentage change in quantity demanded divided by the percentage change in the price. Elasticity exceeds unity when the percentage change in quantity exceeds the percentage change in price. Hence it should be obvious that if, for example, a price is raised by 10 percent and the quantity demanded falls by 15 percent, that total revenue must fall, since the reduction in quantity demanded is proportionately greater than the increase in the price level. The extra revenue per unit from the quantity actually sold is outweighed by the loss of the revenue from the units that were previously being sold but that are not now being sold.

Point versus Arc Elasticity

We distinguish between *point* elasticity of demand and *arc* elasticity of demand on the basis of the size of the change in price and quantity represented by Δ in the preceding elaboration of the elasticity concept. We use point elasticity when the changes in price and quantity are infinitesimally small, since such a small price change represents a virtual point on the demand curve. For more substantial price changes we speak of arc elasticity, since we are considering a discrete movement along, or an arc of, the demand curve.

For point price elasticity, the formula is modified to read

$$\epsilon = \frac{dQ_x}{dP_x} \cdot \frac{P_x}{Q_x} \qquad (4\text{-}16)$$

where the letter d is substituted for Δ to reflect the infinitesimally small change in the variables P_x and Q_x.

Point price elasticity is the appropriate concept for finding the elasticity value at a particular price level if the demand curve is *known*. That is, if you know the slope of the demand curve, you simply weight the reciprocal of that slope by the price-quantity ratio to find the elasticity.

Example: In the example introduced earlier we found that when $P_x = \$8.00$, $Q_x = 22,879.1$. What is the price elasticity of demand at this price-quantity combination on the demand curve? Using the formula for point price elasticity, Equation (4–16), we insert the known values for P_x and Q_x and recall that dQ_x/dP_x is the reciprocal of b, the slope of the demand curve. From equation (4–9) we know $b = -0.26273$. Thus,

$$\epsilon = \frac{1}{-0.26273} \cdot \frac{8}{22,879.1}$$

$$= -1.33$$

Alternatively, we could have multiplied the dQ_x/dP_x term, which was given in the initial estimate of the demand function as $-3,806.2$, by the price-quantity ratio to arrive at the same value for point price elasticity. Thus demand is "elastic" at the price of $8.00—total revenue would increase if price were reduced or would decrease if price were raised.

In the real world, however, a firm may not know how its demand curve slopes through its present price-quantity coordinate. To find out, they must change the price and see what happens to the quantity demanded. But infinitesimally small price changes are not likely to attract the attention of consumers in the marketplace: *discrete* price changes, or significant and noticeable movements of the price level, are necessary to overcome consumer thresholds of price awareness. Thus we are unable, in many real-market situations, to generate the data required to calculate point price elasticity. In order to use the data we can generate, we must modify the formula to reflect the fact that $\Delta Q_x/\Delta P_x$ is relatively large, as compared with the infinitesimally small dQ_x/dP_x used in the point elasticity formula.

■ *Definition:*   *Arc price elasticity,* therefore, is defined as the relative responsiveness of quantity demanded to a *discrete* change in price, whereas point price elasticity is defined as the relative responsiveness of quantity demanded to an *infinitesimal* change in price.

Example: Let us illustrate the arc price elasticity of demand with reference to the following example. Suppose a small store has been selling hanging flowerpots over the last few months at a price of $8 per unit and sales appear to be stabilized at about 32 units per week. The store now reduces the price of those flowerpots to $7 per unit and after a couple of weeks finds that sales have stabilized at a new level of 44 units per week. If all other factors entering the demand function have remained constant, we expect that the two price-quantity combinations above are points on the demand curve for those flowerpots. The small store is, therefore, able to estimate the $\Delta Q_x / \Delta P_x$ term required for its elasticity calculation as follows:

$$\frac{\Delta Q_x}{\Delta P_x} = \frac{Q_1 - Q_2}{P_1 - P_2} \tag{4-17}$$

where the subscripts refer to the sequence of the observations. Substituting for the two price and quantity observations, we have

$$\frac{\Delta Q_x}{\Delta P_x} = \frac{32 - 44}{8 - 7}$$

$$= \frac{-12}{1}$$

$$= -12$$

Given this estimate of the $\Delta Q_x / \Delta P_x$ value, we can conclude that point price elasticity at the price of \$8.00 is

$$\epsilon = \frac{-12}{1} \cdot \frac{8}{32} = -3.00$$

and that point price elasticity at price \$7.00 is

$$\epsilon = \frac{-12}{1} \cdot \frac{7}{44} = -1.9091$$

As we should expect, the point price elasticity is lower for the lower price, because it represents a point further down the demand curve.

Thus point elasticity has provided us with *two* figures for the responsiveness of quantity demanded to changes in the price level. Arc elasticity, on the other hand, provides a *summary measure* of price elasticity over the range of prices between \$7.00 and \$8.00 per unit. For the arc elasticity calculation, we weight the $\Delta Q_x / \Delta P_x$ term by the *average* price and *average* quantity demanded.[9] That is,

$$\epsilon_{\text{arc}} = \frac{\Delta Q_x}{\Delta P_x} \cdot \frac{\dfrac{P_1 + P_2}{2}}{\dfrac{Q_1 + Q_2}{2}}$$

---

[9]We choose the average price and quantities as the weights to calculate arc elasticity because these represent the midpoint of the arc. The midpoint values of price and quantity minimize the variance from all other price and quantity points on the arc, as compared to any other point on the arc. Other formulas have been suggested for arc elasticity, such as using the new price and the old quantity or the old price and the new quantity. These formulations are inferior, since they base the elasticity calculation on a combination of P and Q which does not lie on the demand curve.

Substituting for ΔQ_x and ΔP_x and allowing the 2's to cancel out, we have

$$\epsilon_{arc} = \frac{Q_1 - Q_2}{P_1 - P_2} \cdot \frac{P_1 + P_2}{Q_1 + Q_2} \qquad (4\text{-}18)$$

Inserting the values for P_1, P_2, Q_1, and Q_2 into equation (4-18), we find

$$\epsilon_{arc} = \frac{32 - 44}{8 - 7} \cdot \frac{8 + 7}{32 + 44}$$

$$= \frac{-12}{1} \cdot \frac{15}{76}$$

$$= -2.368$$

It can be seen that the value of the arc price elasticity of demand lies between the two values of the point elasticities calculated above. We should expect this, of course, since the arc elasticity is actually the point elasticity at the midpoint of the arc. It is, however, a better *summary measure* of the elasticity over the arc than are the point elasticity values at either extreme on that arc. The arc elasticity value becomes progressively less accurate as we move toward the end of the arc, but the degree of inaccuracy is much less than the value given by the point elasticity at the *other* end of the arc.

Implications for Optimal Prices

Having obtained an estimate of the slope of its demand curve, what can the flowerpot seller do with this information? The seller can derive an expression for its demand curve and check to see if the present price level is optimal, given its objectives. Let us assume that the firm wishes to maximize profits and knows that its marginal costs are constant at $5.00 per unit regardless of output levels. Is the price of $7.00 profit maximizing? That is, is marginal cost equal to marginal revenue at that price level? To find out we must derive an expression for the demand curve and then for the marginal revenue curve.

We know from equation (4-5) that the firm's demand curve is of the form $P_x = a + bQ_x$, and that P_x is currently $7.00, Q_x is forty-four units, and $b = \Delta P_x/\Delta Q_x = 1/-12 = -0.08333$. Substituting these into equation (4-5), we have

$$7 = a - 0.08333(44)$$

Solving for a, we find $a = 10.6667$, and the expression for the firm's demand curve is therefore

$$P_x = 10.6667 - 0.08333Q_x$$

The marginal revenue expression (with the same intercept and twice the slope) is therefore

$$MR = 10.6667 - 0.16667Q_x$$

Setting MR = MC = $5.00 and solving for Q_x, we have:

$$5 = 10.6667 - 0.16667Q_x$$
$$Q_x = 34$$

This is the profit-maximizing output level where MC = MR. To find the profit-maximizing price, we substitute for $Q_x = 34$ in the demand curve expression:

$$P_x = 10.6667 - 0.08333(34)$$
$$= 10.6667 - 2.8333$$
$$= 7.8333$$

Thus the profit-maximizing price is $7.83 rather than the current price of $7.00 per unit.

Suppose instead that the firm wishes to maximize total revenue from the sale of the flowerpots. What price level would serve this objective? To maximize total revenue we know that marginal revenue must fall to zero. (See Figure 4-4.) Setting the expression for MR (obtained above) equal to zero and solving for Q_x, we find

$$0 = 10.6667 - 0.16667Q_x$$
$$\text{Therefore } Q_x = \frac{10.6667}{0.16667}$$
$$= 64.00$$

Substituting for $Q_x = 64$ in the demand curve expression, we find:

$$P_x = 10.6667 - 0.08333(64)$$
$$= 10.6667 - 5.3333$$
$$= 5.333$$

Thus the total revenue-maximizing price is $5.33, at which 64 units of the flowerpot are expected to be sold. We can verify this by observing that this price-quantity combination represents the midpoint of the demand curve. The price, $5.33, is halfway to the intercept on the price axis, and the quantity, 64 units, is halfway to the intercept on the horizontal axis ($Q_x = 128.00$ when $P_x = 0$).

A Priori Guestimation of Price Elasticity

The theory of consumer behavior points to the following two major factors as determinants of the value of price elasticity:

1. The substitutability of the product.
2. The relative expense of the product.

We saw in the preceding chapter that the substitution effect of a price change is always negative; that is, a price change in one direction will lead to a quantity-demanded response in the opposite direction. This substitution effect is the result of consumers' seeking alternative means of satisfying a particular desire by switching to an available substitute product. Thus the greater the number of substitute products and the more closely substitutable those products are, the more we would expect consumers to switch away from a particular product when its price rose or toward that product when its price fell. Thus the more substitutes and the more closely these substitutes resemble the product in question, the greater we expect the price elasticity of demand for that product to be.[10]

Note: We should distinguish between substitutability of products from within the same group of products and substitutability from other groups of products. For example, coffee is a group of products in the larger family of beverages; but within the product group of coffee there are many different brands and types. If we are concerned with the price elasticity of a particular brand of coffee, such as Maxwell House, and the prices of all other coffees and other beverages remain unchanged, we should expect the price elasticity for Maxwell House coffee to be relatively high. On the other hand, if all coffee prices were likely to rise in unison (owing to an increase in the price of the imported coffee beans, for example), there would be little or no substitutability between or among coffee brands, but there may be substitutability away from coffee as a class toward other groups of beverages. Therefore, in the case where all close substitutes are expected to follow a similar price strategy, we expect the price elasticity to be somewhat lower, since the substitutability will be toward only the more distant substitutes.

The relative expense of the product as a determinant of price elasticity is related to the income effect of a price change. You will recall from the preceding chapter that for any product, when price is increased for example, the consumer suffers a loss in real income. The consumer is thus able to buy less of all products, including the prod-

[10]A feature of products that is related to this substitutability is their versatility, or the number of uses to which they may be put. A product is more versatile if it can serve two or more purposes rather than only one purpose. A *more versatile* product is likely to be *less substitutable*, since it may require two or more other products to serve the purposes of the more versatile product. Hence, the more versatile the product is, the less sensitive to price changes its demand is likely to be, and vice versa.

uct for which the price has risen. The larger the fraction of the consumer's budget that the price of this product represents, the larger the influence on the consumer's real income level that we would expect from a given percentage change in price in that product. A 10 percent change in the price of an automobile, for example, would cause the consumer's real income to be changed considerably, whereas a 10 percent change in the price of bread would have a minimal impact.

In view of the factors influencing elasticity, would you expect the price elasticity of demand for kitchen salt to be high or low? With regard to substitutability it would seem that salt has few close substitutes for its kitchen uses. The relative expense, or proportion of the consumer's income spent on that commodity, is always very low. Thus both the substitutability and the relative expense factors militate in favor of salt having a relatively low price elasticity of demand. On the other hand, consider the demand for a particular automobile, such as a Chevrolet Cavalier. There are numerous substitute automobiles, many of them quite close substitutes while others are more distant substitutes. The proportion of the consumer's income that is involved in the purchase of an automobile is typically high. Hence, both determinants militate in favor of the price elasticity for a particular automobile being quite high. If the price of all automobiles rises simultaneously, such as at the start of a new model year, the elasticity of demand faced by the Chevrolet Cavalier will be somewhat lower, since the substitutability toward other products is limited to the more distant substitutes such as mass transit, bicycles, and walking.

In some cases the substitutability of a product will indicate high price elasticity, while the relative expense will indicate low price elasticity, or vice versa. Guestimation of the value of price elasticity must then proceed on the basis of judgment about which factor will be stronger if a decision must be taken immediately. If the decision can be delayed, research into the nature of the demand function and its elasticities should be undertaken. This, however, is the subject matter of the following chapter. We now turn to some other important elasticity measures.

4.4   INCOME ELASTICITY OF DEMAND

■ *Definition:* The *income elasticity* of demand may be defined as the percentage change in quantity demanded divided by the percentage change in consumer income, *ceteris paribus*. That is,

$$\Theta = \frac{\%\Delta Q_x}{\%\Delta B} \qquad (4\text{-}19)$$

where Θ (the Greek letter theta) is the conventional symbol for income elasticity and B is the consumer's budget, or income constraint. Expressing this in terms of proportionate changes, we have

$$\theta = \frac{\dfrac{\Delta Q_x}{Q_x}}{\dfrac{\Delta B}{B}} = \frac{\Delta Q_x}{\Delta B} \cdot \frac{B}{Q_x} \qquad (4\text{-}20)$$

Notice that the size of $\Delta Q_x/\Delta B$ is undefined as yet. If we know the relationship between income and quantity demanded of X, we could find point income elasticity as follows:

$$\theta = \frac{dQ_x}{dB} \cdot \frac{B}{Q_x} \qquad (4\text{-}21)$$

If, on the other hand, we need to observe a significant income change to ascertain the effect on Q_x, we would find the arc income elasticity as follows:

$$\theta = \frac{Q_1 - Q_2}{B_1 - B_2} \cdot \frac{B_1 + B_2}{Q_1 + Q_2} \qquad (4\text{-}22)$$

where the subscripts reflect the sequence of the observations of the two quantity and income levels.

Example: Recall the numerical example introduced early in the chapter. The demand function had been estimated as

$$Q_x = 5{,}030 - 3{,}806.2P_x + 1{,}458.5P_y + 256.6A_x - 32.3A_y + 0.18Y_c \qquad (4\text{-}3)$$

where the variable Y_c represents the average disposable income of consumers or some other measure of spending power, such as gross national product (GNP) per capita.

From the demand function we can calculate the *point* income elasticity of demand, given our knowledge of the current value of Y_c, which we said was \$12,875, and the current value of Q_x, which we calculated to be 22,879.1.

$$\theta = \frac{dQ_x}{dY_c} \cdot \frac{Y_c}{Q_x}$$

$$= 0.18 \cdot \frac{12{,}875}{22{,}879.1}$$

$$= 0.101$$

Note that the coefficient to the income term in the demand function represents the dQ_x/dY_c term we need to calculate the income elasticity. (Strictly, the coefficient to Y_c is the *partial* derivative, $\partial Q_x/\partial Y_c$, but this is equivalent for our purposes.)

As an example of *arc* elasticity, suppose that in a different situation per capita disposable income is \$15,650 and that the quantity demanded of stereo amplifiers is 36,000 per month. Now, suppose that (real) per capita disposable income rises to \$17,215, because of cuts in personal income taxes. As a result (with *ceteris paribus*), we observe an increase in the quantity demanded of stereo amplifiers to 40,320 units per month.

Using Equation (4-22) for the arc income elasticity calculation, we find:

$$\theta = \frac{36,000 - 40,320}{15,650 - 17,215} \cdot \frac{15,650 + 17,215}{36,000 + 40,320}$$

$$= \frac{-4,320}{-1,565} \cdot \frac{32,865}{76,320}$$

$$= 1.189$$

Now, what do these numbers mean? Calculating the income elasticity of demand allows us to classify products as either luxuries, necessities, or inferior goods, and gives insights into the shift of the demand curve that will follow changes in consumer incomes.

Luxuries, Necessities, and Inferior Goods

■ *Definition:* Luxuries are defined as products for which the proportionate change in quantity demanded is greater than the proportionate change in consumer income levels; income elasticity is, therefore, positive and greater than unity. The arc elasticity calculation in the preceding section indicates, therefore, that stereo-amplifiers are luxury goods, since $\theta = 1.189$. Other examples of luxury goods are items such as fur coats, travel by air, and the use of hotel accommodations. Note that *luxury good* is now a definitional term, a piece of our jargon. In common usage you might refer to something as a "luxury," but here the connotation is that it is a product whose quantity demanded responds more than proportionately to changes in consumer incomes.

Graphically, the impact of a change in consumer incomes is reflected by a *shift* of the demand curve for product X. Recall that the quantity demanded of product X that is caused by the income variable becomes part of the intercept term of the demand curve. If consumer incomes change, the intercept term of the demand curve changes, and we must have a shift of the demand curve. In Figure 4–6 we show that the demand curve for the luxury good has shifted from D to D' as a result of an assumed increase in consumer incomes.

■ *Definition:* Necessities are defined as products which have an income elasticity of demand which is positive but less than 1. The first example calculated above is, therefore, classified as a necessity good, since its income elasticity is 0.101. This means that the quantity demanded increases as income increases but that the change in Q_x is less than proportionate to the change in income. In this example, if income changed by 10

FIGURE 4-6.   A Shift of the Demand Curve for a Luxury Good, Given an Increase in Income

percent, we would expect Q_x to change by only 1.01 percent. Examples of necessities are some foodstuffs and items of apparel.

Graphically, the impact of an increase in income on the demand for a necessity good, given *ceteris paribus,* can be shown as a shift outward of the demand curve. The extent of the outward shift will be less than for a luxury good, of course, since the demand for necessities is less responsive to changes in income than it is for luxury goods. Note that both luxuries and necessities exhibit a positive income effect, and they are what we have called superior (or normal) goods. In fact, we have now divided superior goods into two subclasses, depending upon whether the demand for these items responds more or less than proportionally to changes in income.

■ *Definition: Inferior goods* are products which exhibit a negative income effect and, consequently, an income elasticity which is negative. These products experience a decline in quantity demanded as real income levels rise. Conversely, if real income levels decline, the quantity demanded of an inferior good will increase. Examples of inferior goods may be items such as potatoes, baked beans, ground beef, bologna, low-quality clothing, and travel by train. As incomes rise, people tend to switch away from these items to more desirable substitutes. As incomes fall, people (reluctantly) switch back to these cheaper alternatives and away from the more desirable but typically more expensive substitutes.

Note: The shift of the demand curve for an inferior good will be in the opposite direction to the change in incomes. In Figure 4-7 we show the demand curve shifting back to the left, following an increase in consumer incomes. Consumers now buy *less* of this product than they did before, as a result of the increase in their incomes. The extent of the shift depends, of course, on the value of income elasticity—small negative values mean small shifts to the left while relatively large negative income elasticities mean

**FIGURE 4-7.   A Shift of the Demand Curve for an Inferior Good, Given an
Increase in Income**

relatively large shifts to the left, in both cases in response to an increase in real incomes.

Table 4-4 summarizes the relationships that are indicated by a calculated income elasticity that is greater than 1, between zero and 1, and less than zero.

Business Implications of Income Elasticity

The implications of income elasticity of demand to the business decision maker are considerable. If the income elasticity for your product exceeds unity, the demand for your product will grow more rapidly than does total consumer income or it will fall more rapidly than does total consumer income when income levels are generally falling. Hence, while income elasticity greater than 1 in a growing economy indicates a "growth industry" it also indicates a greater susceptibility to fluctuations in the level of aggregate economic activity. On the other hand, if the income elasticity of demand for your product is positive but less than 1, the demand for your product will grow more slowly than the gross national product or consumer income, but it will be relatively "recession proof" in the sense that the demand will not react in the volatile fashion of luxury goods. Third, if your product is regarded by the market as a whole as

TABLE 4-4.   Income Elasticity and Luxuries, Necessities, and Inferior Goods

Income Elasticity	Product Class	Increased Income	Decreased Income
$\infty > \theta > 1$	Luxuries	Q_x increases by greater percentage	Q_x decreases by greater percentage
$1 > \theta > 0$	Necessities	Q_x increases by lesser percentage	Q_x decreases by lesser percentage
$0 > \theta > -\infty$	Inferior goods	Q_x decreases	Q_x increases

an inferior good, you must expect the quantity demanded of your product to decline as the gross national product rises, yet increase during economic downturns. Good corporate and product planning would therefore indicate the desirability of having all three types of products in your product mix.

4.5   CROSS ELASTICITIES AND OTHER ELASTICITIES

We now consider the responsiveness of quantity demanded of product X to changes in the prices of related products. *Related* products are either substitutes or complements, and cross elasticity of demand provides a measure of the *degree* of substitutability, or complementarity, between product X and some other product.[11]

■ *Definition:*   *Cross elasticity of demand* is defined as the percentage, or proportionate, change in quantity demanded of product X, divided by the percentage, or proportionate, change in the price of some product Y. That is,

$$\eta = \frac{\% \Delta Q_x}{\% \Delta P_y} \qquad (4\text{-}23)$$

where η (the Greek letter eta) is the conventional symbol for cross elasticity. Following our earlier analysis, we can restate this as a *point* cross elasticity measure, as follows:

$$\eta = \frac{dQ_x}{dP_y} \cdot \frac{P_y}{Q_x} \qquad (4\text{-}24)$$

In practice it may be necessary to have a significant change in P_y before an impact is noticed on Q_x. In this case, we would use the *arc* cross elasticity formula, as follows:

$$\eta = \frac{Q_1 - Q_2}{P_1 - P_2} \cdot \frac{P_1 + P_2}{Q_1 + Q_2} \qquad (4\text{-}25)$$

Note that the Q symbols refer to Q_x, the P symbols refer to P_y, and the subscripts reflect the sequence of the data collection.

Example: From the earlier example of the estimated demand function for product X (equation 4-3) we can calculate the point cross elasticity of demand between products

---

[11]Cross elasticity is the abbreviated name for cross-price elasticity, since we are concerned with the impact of a change in P_y on Q_x. Given that product Y is a substitute, we should also expect a cross-*advertising* elasticity, for example, indicating the impact of a change in Y's advertising efforts on Q_x. By convention, cross elasticity means cross-price elasticity, unless specifically noted otherwise.

X and Y, because the term dQ_x/dP_y has already been estimated. It is, of course, the coefficient to the term P_y in the demand function for Q_x and was seen to be 1,458.5. Using Equation (4–24) and substituting for variables P_y and Q_x, we have

$$\eta = 1{,}458.5 \cdot \frac{6}{22{,}879.1}$$
$$= 0.382$$

What does this number tell us? It says that for a 1 percent change in the price of product Y the quantity demanded of product X will change by 0.382 percent. Note that the changes will be in the same direction since the sign of the cross elasticity is positive. The positive sign indicates that there is a movement of consumers from product Y, as its price rises, across to product X, given *ceteris paribus*, and that, hence, products X and Y must be substitutes for each other.

Substitutes

- **Definition:** *Substitutes* are defined as products among which the cross elasticity of demand is positive. Suppose that the price of a product Y is reduced from $10 to $9, and that this reduction induces a change in the quantity demanded of a product X from 100 units to 85 units, as shown in Figure 4–8. Since these are discrete price changes, the arc cross elasticity formula is appropriate. Inserting these values into Equation (4–25), we see that the cross elasticity between product X and product Y is

$$\eta = \frac{100 - 85}{10 - 9} \cdot \frac{10 + 9}{100 + 85}$$
$$= \frac{15}{1} \cdot \frac{19}{185}$$
$$= 1.54$$

In terms of Figure 4–8 it is clear that products X and Y must be substitutes for each other, since when the price of product Y was reduced the quantity demanded of product X was reduced from 100 units back to 85 units. Given that *ceteris paribus* prevails, the gain of quantity demanded for product Y must have been at the expense of the demand for product X. Recall that the price of product Y enters the demand function for product X as a shift parameter; a reduction in the price of product Y would cause the demand curve for product X to shift to the left, such that at price P_x the quantity demanded for product X would be somewhat less. Examples of a pair of substitute products include the product groups of tea and coffee or pairs of products within either of these groups, such as Maxwell House coffee and Yuban coffee.

FIGURE 4-8.   Cross Elasticity between Substitute Products

Complements

- *Definition:* *Complements* are defined as products among which the cross elasticity of demand is negative. Suppose that a 10 percent price reduction for product Y leads to a 20 percent increase in demand for product X. For example P_y is reduced from $1.00 to $0.90 and Q_x increases from 100 units to 120 units. The value of cross elasticity is

$$\eta = \frac{100 - 120}{1.0 - 0.9} \cdot \frac{1.0 + 0.9}{100 + 120}$$

$$= \frac{-20}{0.1} \cdot \frac{1.9}{220}$$

$$= -1.73$$

Such a situation is illustrated in Figure 4-9. In this case the price reduction in product Y, while accompanied by an increase in the demand for product Y, was also accompanied by an increase in the demand for product X. Given *ceteris paribus*, it is clear that the increase in consumption of product Y called forth an increase in the consumption of product X, notwithstanding that the price of product X did not change. Hence, products X and Y are complementary goods in that they are apparently used jointly in consumption and in some predetermined ratio. Notice that in this case the cross elasticity of demand between product X and product Y must have a negative sign. Examples of products with negative cross elasticity are coffee and cream, beer and pretzels, and gasoline and tires.

Of course, a change in price of product Y may have zero or minimal impact upon the demand for product X. In this case we conclude that products X and Y are unre-

FIGURE 4-9.   Cross Elasticity between Complementary Products

lated in consumption. That is, products X and Y are neither substitutes nor complements. Table 4–5 summarizes the relationships existing between the cross elasticity of demand and the relationship that apparently exists between the two products under examination.

At what level do we define cross elasticity as indicating that we have a pair of "strong" substitutes as compared with "weak" substitutes? Alternatively, how large and negative must the cross-elasticity value be before we decide that the products are "strong" complements rather than simply "weak" complements? In fact, the answer is quite arbitrary. A cross elasticity value of 2 will mean that a competitor's price adjustment will have a significant impact upon your quantity demanded, but whether we would call this a strong or a weak relationship is essentially a matter of taste. Certainly if another product shared a cross elasticity of 5 with your product, for example, we would be able to say that the latter product is a *stronger* substitute for your product than is the former product.

Advertising and Cross-Advertising Elasticities

We know from the demand function that the quantity demanded of product X will be responsive to both the advertising in support of product X and the advertising in support of related products. The advertising elasticity of demand for product X measures

TABLE 4-5.   Substitutes, Complements, and Cross Elasticity of Demand

Cross Elasticity	Relationship	Increase in P_y	Decrease in P_y
$\infty > \eta > 0$	Substitutes	Q_x rises	Q_x falls
$\eta \simeq 0$	Unrelated	Q_x unchanged	Q_x unchanged
$0 > \eta > -\infty$	Complements	Q_x falls	Q_x rises

the responsiveness of the change in quantity demanded to a change in advertising budget expended for product X. We expect a positive relationship between advertising and quantity demanded, but we also expect that the responsiveness of sales to advertising will decline as advertising expenditure continues to increase. There will be a lower limit on the value of the advertising elasticity if advertising expenditure is not to be carried beyond an optimal level. We defer this issue until Chapter 13 where we will see that the critical value of advertising expenditure (and hence advertising elasticity) depends upon the profit contribution expected from each additional unit sold as a result of the advertising.

Cross-advertising elasticity measures the responsiveness of quantity demanded (sales) of product X to a change in the advertising efforts directed at another product, Y. We expect cross-advertising elasticity to be negative between substitute products and positive between complementary products. For example, increased advertising efforts for a particular movie would be expected to reduce the quantity demanded (sales) of admission tickets to other movies and attractions but to increase the sales of the refreshment kiosk in the lobby of that particular movie theater. In effect, the increased advertising would have shifted the demand curves to the left for all substitute attractions and would have shifted the demand curve to the right for the refreshment kiosk.

It is clear that we might calculate the elasticity of demand with respect to any of the independent variables in the demand function. Using the general concept of elasticities, we can construct the appropriate formula and measure any elasticity that may be useful for decision-making purposes.

The Value of Elasticities

Many would argue that the various elasticities of demand simply summarize information that is already known to the decision maker and that if one has the information necessary to calculate the elasticities of demand, the elasticity value is redundant. (In the case of price elasticity for example, if one knows the two price and quantity coordinates, one can quite simply calculate the change in total revenue that results when moving from one coordinate to the other.) So the question arises, Why calculate elasticities?

Note: Essentially the value of elasticities is twofold. First, they are useful as a summary measure which indicates at a glance the direction of change in total revenue given a price change and shows whether products are substitutes, complements, luxuries, necessities, or inferior. The magnitude, and in some cases the sign, of the various elasticity measures says in the briefest way possible what there is to know about the relationship between the two variables. Second, by categorizing this relationship in terms of a single number, we are able to reduce a variety of relationships between products to a common denominator, such that we may rank the values of elasticity for comparison purposes. Hence, if product X is related to a number of other products, we might rank those other products in order of their cross elasticity with product X. Those with the highest value of cross elasticity would be the strongest substitutes, and those with the largest negative values would be the strongest complements.

Moreover, we shall see in Chapter 10 that the calculation of price elasticity facilitates selection of the optimal markup to be applied to costs in order to determine the profit-maximizing prices of various products. In fact, the value of price elasticity provides the link between the pricing theory of economics and the pricing practice of the marketplace!

4.6 SUMMARY

In this chapter we examined the *demand function*, which expresses the dependence of the quantity demanded (or sales) of a particular product upon a variety of independent variables. We examined the impact we would expect changes in these variables to have upon the quantity demanded of a particular product. The *demand curve* was defined as part of the demand function when price is the only variable independent factor. That is to say, when all other factors remain constant and price changes *along* a particular demand curve. If any other factor does not remain constant we must expect a *shift* of the demand curve, which will cause a differing quantity to be demanded at the prevailing price level.

The relationship between price, quantity demanded, total revenue, and marginal revenue was examined, and it was determined that for any negatively sloping demand curve, total revenue would initially increase as a price is reduced but would later decline. Consequently, marginal revenue would initially be positive and later negative.

Several measures of the elasticity of quantity demanded were discussed. Price elasticity of demand is particularly useful for indicating the direction of change in total revenue when there is a particular directional change in price. Moreover, when a firm has several products, the relative price elasticities of these products will indicate which of these products can best sustain a price increase versus those for which a price increase would be a poor strategy. Income elasticity of demand is important for growth and stability considerations in the firm, since the demand for luxury products will tend to be relatively responsive to changes both up and down in the aggregate level of activity. Similarly, we argued that necessity goods are relatively recession proof and that inferior goods are expected to exhibit countercyclical demand patterns.

Cross elasticities of demand allow the summary and classification of the relationships existing between a particular product and all other products. The decision maker should be interested in knowing which of the other products on the market represent the most serious competition for his or her product. Similarly, negative values of cross elasticity indicate product complementarity and the relative strength of this complementarity.

The concepts and principles outlined in this chapter will be called upon in subsequent chapters. Pricing the firm's product requires a strong knowledge of the demand conditions existing in a particular market, and an understanding of the responsiveness of demand to the various factors that influence that demand is therefore of considerable importance.

DISCUSSION QUESTIONS

4-1. Which factors do you think should be held constant in a discussion about the demand curve for season tickets to the home games of a National Football League team?

4-2. What is the relationship between the coefficient of price in the demand function and the slope term in the demand curve? Explain.

4-3. Set up a matrix with $|\epsilon| > 1$, $|\epsilon| = 1$, $|\epsilon| < 1$ down the left-hand side and "TR increases" and "TR decreases" along the top. Fill in the six parts of the matrix to indicate whether the coordinates imply an increase or a decrease in the price level.

4-4. Summarize the methodological error and the resultant overestimate or underestimate that is involved when the point elasticity formula is used to calculate elasticity from observations of discrete price and quantity changes.

4-5. Explain how you could calculate the price elasticity at any particular price if you know the parameter values in the mathematical expression for a particular demand curve.

4-6. Classify the probable price elasticity value of the following products as either "relatively high" or "relatively low":

(a) soft drinks

(b) Coca-Cola

(c) Diet Pepsi

(d) compact automobiles

(e) Levi jeans

(Support each classification with your reasoning.)

4-7. Explain how you would derive the demand curve for a particular product X, given the information that $P_x = \$4.50$; $Q_x = 25$; and price elasticity of demand is -1.5.

4-8. Explain why you would expect the demand for luxury goods such as fur coats and jewelry to be more volatile in periods of fluctuating incomes as compared with items such as groceries and meat.

4-9. How would you explain a situation in which two products have both a positive cross-price elasticity of demand and a positive cross-advertising elasticity of demand?

4-10. Define the "rainfall elasticity" of demand for umbrellas, using your knowledge of the elasticity concept. What possible usefulness could such an elasticity have?

PROBLEMS AND SHORT CASES

4-1. The Silverstein Coffee Company faces the following demand schedule in the relevant price range for one of its products.

Price (lb)	Quantity Demanded (lbs/wk)
$5.00	970
4.95	1,000
4.90	1,026
4.85	1,049
4.80	1,071
4.75	1,085
4.70	1,095
4.65	1,105
4.60	1,114
4.55	1,122

(a) Plot the associated demand curve, marginal revenue curve, and total revenue curve on a graph.

(b) Calculate the price elasticity for each price change.

(c) Over what range is demand (1) elastic, (2) inelastic, (3) unitary elastic?

4-2. Billabong Boomerangs, Inc., and Swahili Spears are direct competitors in the fast-growing segment of the hunters' equipment market. Because of recent intense competition, both companies have redeveloped their main product, requiring the users' skills to be less developed than before and thus avoiding extensive field trips by company representatives for on-the-job training. This also reduced the need for costly instruction manuals. Stephen Pesner, president of Billabong Boomerangs, has decided to hire a local market research company to assist his company in planning its strategy. After extensive research using modern methods of data collection and statistical analysis, the researchers came up with Billabong's demand function:

$$Q_B = -1,700P_B + 750Y_H + 350A_B - 250A_S + 1,585P_S + 1.05H + 7.25W$$

where Q_B is the quantity demanded of boomerangs; P_B is the price of boomerangs; Y_H is the average income of hunters (in thousands); A_B is the advertising budget for Billabong Boomerangs (in thousands); A_S is the advertising budget for Swahili Spears (in thousands); P_S is the price of spears; H is the total number of hunters (in millions); and W is the estimated population of wildlife (in hundreds). The current values of the independent variables are $P_B = 29.95$; $Y_H = 12.5$; $A_B = 680$; $A_S = 525$; $P_S = 32.25$; $H = 24.68$; and $W = 8.75$.

(a) What is the current level of demand for Billabong boomerangs?

(b) Calculate the values of price elasticity, cross-price elasticity, and advertising elasticity.

(c) Is the price of boomerangs too high or too low in view of Mr. Pesner's desire to maximize profits? Explain.

4-3. The demand function for Fritz Reinhart premium beer has been estimated as

$$Q_x = 2,486.5 - 1,931.6P_x + 283.9P_y + 168.2A_x - 18.8A_y$$

where Q_x is the demand for the Reinhart beer (in cases); P_x is the price of the Reinhart beer (in dollars); P_y is the price of the main rival beer (in dollars); A_x is the advertising expenditure for Reinhart ($000); and A_y is the expenditure for the rival beer ($000). The current values of the independent variables are $P_x = 4.50$; $P_y = 4.39$; $A_x = 168$; and $A_y = 182$.

(a) Calculate the price elasticity of demand for Reinhart beer.

(b) Calculate the advertising elasticity of demand for Reinhart beer.

(c) If the marginal cost of producing Reinhart beer is constant at \$2.00 per case, should the firm change its price in order to maximize profits? Explain.

(d) Suppose instead that the Reinhart company wishes to maximize sales revenue from this beer. What price should it set?

4-4. The demand function for Crispie Chips has been estimated to be as follows:

$$Q_x = -27.6887 + 0.2315A_x + 44.1177P_s - 37.73585P_x$$

where Q_x represents thousands of packets of chips; A_x is thousands of advertising dollars; P_s is the average price of substitute-brand chips; and P_x is the price of Crispie Chips (all prices in dollars per packet). The current values of the independent variables are $A_x = 216.0$; $P_s = 0.85$; and $P_x = 0.79$.

(a) What is the price elasticity of demand at the current price level? Explain what this value implies.

(b) Derive an expression for the demand curve from the estimated demand function.

(c) Supposing that marginal costs are constant at \$0.19 per unit, what is the profit-maximizing price for Crispie Chips?

(d) What is the sales-revenue maximizing price for Crispie Chips?

(e) Explain in detail the assumptions and qualifications which underlie your price and output predictions.

4-5. The Belcher Brewing Company has undertaken market research for the purpose of ascertaining the responsiveness of consumers to changes in the price level for their premium beer. Analysis of the results has led to the following estimate of the demand relation:

$$Q = 15.9996 - 1.47297P$$

where Q represents thousands of cases of one dozen bottles, and P represents the price per case in dollars. Belcher's present price is \$5.95 per case at the retail level, and the marginal cost of production is \$3.00 per case regardless of volume (within the foreseeable range of possible volumes).

(a) What is the price elasticity of demand at the current price level? Comment on this figure.

(b) Express the demand relation in terms of a conventional demand curve.

(c) Is the current price profit maximizing? If not, what is the profit-maximizing price?

(d) What is the total revenue maximizing price?

(e) State explicitly all assumptions and qualifications which underlie your answers.

4-6. The Gutowski Grocery Company markets a brand of a particular food item for which there are a number of reasonably similar substitutes. The company has been subject to a series of cost increases recently but feels that the present level of costs is expected to continue in the near future. These recent cost increases have caused the monthly profit to fall below the target of \$15,000, and the management feels that this target could be attained if the price were reduced to \$3.99 per unit, presuming that rivals are unlikely to retaliate. Average variable costs are constant up to the maximum output level of 120,000 units. The following data refer to this month's operations:

Variable costs per unit	\$2.74
Fixed costs per unit	1.57
Price per unit	4.45
Total profit for month	\$11,431.28

(a) What is the price elasticity of demand for the product in the vicinity of the present and contemplated price levels?

(b) Find the profit-maximizing price and the maximum profit level. (Show all calculations and defend your methodology.)

(c) What qualifications and assumptions underlie your analysis?

4-7. The Thompson Textile Company has asked you for advice about the optimality of its pricing policy with respect to one of its products, product X. The following data are supplied:

Sales (units)	282,500
Price per unit	$2.00
Marginal cost per unit is constant at	$1.00
Price elasticity of demand	−3.25

(a) Is the present price level optimal if the firm wishes to maximize profits? If not, can you say what price it should charge?

(b) What is the sales revenue maximizing price for product X?

(c) Explain to the management of Thompson Textile Company the assumptions underlying your analysis and the sensitivity of your price recommendations to these assumptions.

4-8. The Bustraen Company is one of five firms that manufacture washing machines. The five firms are all about the same size, have approximately equal market shares, and produce very similar products. Bustraen sells approximately 200,000 washing machines per annum. The company has engaged a market research consultant to provide estimates of the price elasticity and cross elasticity of demand for its product. These estimates have just been received and are as follows: price elasticity of demand for Bustraen's washing machine, −1.85; cross elasticity of demand for Bustraen's washing machine, 0.45, vis-à-vis any one of the other firm's machines; and price elasticity of demand for all washing machines (if all prices changed together), −0.55.

(a) Explain what Bustraen should expect to happen to its sales if it were to raise prices by 10 percent and no other firm changed its price.

(b) Explain what Bustraen should expect to happen to its sales if one of its rivals were to raise its price by 10 percent, with *ceteris paribus*.

(c) Explain what would happen if Bustraen raised its price 10 percent and all other firms did the same.

(d) What assumptions and qualifications underlie your analysis?

4-9. Paul McLaughlin recently purchased the MFF Company, a large company that specializes in the manufacture of minifreezers. Mr. McLaughlin has a reputation for revitalizing companies and reselling them, and he has purchased this company with the intention of holding onto it for a period of two years, after which he would sell the entire operation. The management of the MFF Company gave Mr. McLaughlin the following demand function for their product, which they said was based on a number of years of experience:

$$Q = 3000 - 800P + 0.05A + 2Y$$

where Q represents the quantity demanded each quarter; P is the price; A represents advertising expenditures (dollars per quarter); and Y is personal disposable income per capita (dollars per annum).

As Mr. McLaughlin's special consultant, you are faced with the following problems:

(a) Mr. McLaughlin wishes to maximize sales revenue. He informs you that he is allocating $23.5 million each quarter for advertising expenditures and that the estimated personal disposable income per capita is $11,000. In order that he might maximize his sales revenue, what price should be charged for his product, and how many minifreezers can he expect to sell at this price level? Illustrate this both mathematically and graphically.

(b) Alternatively, let us assume that Mr. McLaughlin had originally priced his product at $450 and had set his sales goal at 2 million minifreezers for the four quarters of the first year. Price ($450) and personal disposable income ($11,000) have remained constant throughout the first three quarters and are not expected to change during the fourth quarter. His advertising expenditures were as follows:

First quarter	$18,000,000
Second quarter	$15,000,000
Third quarter	$23,000,000

Given these figures, what should his advertising expenditures be for the fourth quarter so that he will be able to reach his goal of 2 million products sold?

4-10. The Alpha Beta Company produces and sells toaster ovens. Mr. Learmonth has just been appointed marketing vice-president and is determined to be the first VP to guide the company past the million-dollar sales mark. To do so, ABC must average $84,000 per month for the last nine months of the year.

Mr. Learmonth has been given a free hand to run the marketing side of ABC, subject to the following constraints:

1. Perceived social responsibilities dictate that ABC, as the town's largest employer, produce a minimum of 5,800 units per month to avoid layoffs. With overtime the plant can turn out a maximum of 8,100 units per month.

2. Budgetary considerations have limited increases in advertising to 15 percent above current monthly levels ($5,000). ABC has already contracted for a minimum of $5,000 per month with local media.

Mr. Learmonth's first move as VP was to have the Con-Sulting Company, a local marketing research firm, do some analytical work, and this company has developed the following normative model based on statistics supplied by Mr. Learmonth:

$$Q = 3000 + 0.3A + 0.4Y - 300P$$

where Q represents the number of ovens demanded; A represents the monthly advertising expenditure; Y represents the per capita income; and P represents the selling price of the ovens. Current selling price is $14, and current values of A and Y are $5,000 and $14,000, respectively. You have been given the assignment of recommending a strategy for the remainder of the year.

(a) What price level do you recommend?

(b) What do you recommend with regard to advertising?

(c) Calculate the income elasticity. What does this indicate about the nature of the product?

(Make any assumptions required for the solution of the problem, indicating why they were made. Show all calculations.)

SUGGESTED REFERENCES AND FURTHER READING

Ferguson, C. E., and S. C. Maurice. *Economic Analysis: Theory and Application* (3rd ed.), chap. 2. Homewood, Ill.: Richard D. Irwin, Inc., 1978.

Hirshleifer, J. *Price Theory and Applications* (2nd ed.), chap. 5. Englewood Cliffs, N.J.: Prentice-Hall, Inc. 1976.

Johnson, A. C., Jr., and P. Helmburger. "Price Elasticity of Demand as an Element of Market Structure," *American Economic Review.* December 1967, pp. 1218-21.

Leftwich, R. H. *The Price System and Resource Allocation* (7th ed.), chaps. 3, 5. Hinsdale, Ill.: The Dryden Press, 1979.

Mansfield, E. *Microeconomics* (5th ed.), chap. 5. New York: W. W. Norton & Co., Inc., 1985.

Martin, R. L. "Price Elasticity and a Shifting Demand Curve," *Economic Inquiry*, 17 (January 1979), pp. 153-54.

Miller, R. L. *Intermediate Microeconomics*, chap. 5. New York: McGraw-Hill Book Company, 1978.

Nicholson, W. *Intermediate Microeconomics and Its Application* (2nd ed.), chaps. 4, 5. Hinsdale, Ill.: The Dryden Press, 1979.

Simon, H. "Dynamics of Price Elasticity and Brand Life Cycles: An Empirical Study," *Journal of Marketing Research,* 16 (November 1979), pp. 439-52.

Thompson, A. A., Jr. *Economics of the Firm* (3rd ed.), chap. 5. Englewood Cliffs, N.J.: Prentice-Hall, Inc., 1981.

Wan, F. C. "Elasticities and Effects of Price Change on Revenue," *Atlantic Economic Journal.* 11 (September 1983), p. 115.

5 Estimation of the Demand Function

5.1 INTRODUCTION

This chapter examines the methods by which we may obtain the demand data for real-world decision problems. In preceding chapters we presumed to *know* the impact on the quantity demanded of changes in the price level, in consumers' incomes, in prices of related products, and so forth. It is obvious, however, that this information may not be readily available. Given the prior expectation that the value of the information will exceed the search costs of obtaining that information, the decision maker must generate the data using a variety of techniques from market research and statistical analysis.

Note: We distinguish between demand estimation and demand forecasting on the basis of the period for which demand data are sought. *Demand estimation* will be taken to mean the process of finding *current* values for the coefficients in the demand function for a particular product. *Demand forecasting* will be taken to mean the process of finding values for demand in *future* time periods. Current values are necessary to evaluate the optimality of current pricing and promotional policies and in order to make day-to-day decisions in these strategy areas. Future values are necessary for planning production, inventories, new-product development, investment, and other situations where the decision to be made has impacts over a prolonged period of time. This chapter is confined to the issue of demand estimation. Demand forecasting is treated in the appendix to the chapter. Although we shall treat estimation and forecasting separately, demand estimation often forms the basis for demand forecasting. We shall examine the major methods of both estimation and forecasting and indicate the major problems and pitfalls one may expect to encounter.

In Chapter 4 we considered the demand function in the form where demand (or sales) is expressed as a function of the variables price, advertising, consumer incomes, consumer tastes and preferences, and whatever other variables are thought to be important in determining the demand for a particular product.

$$Q = \alpha + \beta_1 P + \beta_2 A + \beta_3 Y + \beta_4 T + \ldots + \beta_n N \qquad (5-1)$$

The β coefficients represent the amount by which sales will be increased (or decreased) following a one-unit change in the value of each of the variables. The present level of each of the variables is known or can be found with some investigation. It is the coefficients of these variables that are the mystery and that are important to us for decision making. That is, we wish to know what will happen to the sales level if we change a particular independent variable by a certain amount, holding all other variables constant. Stated alternatively, we wish to know whether or not a change in the value of any of these variables from their present levels would have a beneficial impact on the firm's profits, or net worth.

Of course, not all of these independent variables are controllable, in the sense that we have the ability to adjust their level. The *controllable* variables are price, promotional efforts, product design, and the place of sale, which may be known to you as the "four P's" of marketing. The *uncontrollable* variables in the demand function are those that change independently of the firm's efforts, and they include such variables as consumer incomes, taste and preference patterns, the actions of competitors, population, weather, and political, sporting, and social events or happenings. However, even if the firm is unable to influence these variables, knowledge of the probable value of the coefficients is useful, since it reduces the uncertainty of the impact of changes in those variables. Given an expectation of the effect of increased consumer incomes, for example, the firm is able to plan more effectively its production, inventories, and new-product development, in view of expected changes in the affluence of consumers.

Direct versus Indirect Methods of Demand Estimation

Methods of estimating the values of these beta coefficients may be classified as either direct or indirect. *Direct* methods are those that directly involve the consumer, and they include interviews and surveys, simulated market situations, and controlled market experiments. Thus consumers are either asked what their reactions would be to a particular change in a determining variable, or they are observed when actually reacting to a particular change. *Indirect* demand estimation proceeds on the basis of data that have been collected and attempts to find statistical associations between the dependent and the independent variables. The techniques of simple correlation and multiple-regression analysis are employed to find these relationships. Direct methods of demand estimation are covered in detail in marketing research courses, while indirect methods are examined in quantitative methods courses. In this chapter we confine ourselves to the application of these methods to the problem of estimating the parameters of the demand function, and we refer the reader to the sources cited at the end of the chapter for more detailed treatments and other applications.

5.2 INTERVIEWS, SURVEYS, AND EXPERIMENTS

Interviews and Surveys

Problems :-

The most direct method of demand estimation is simply to ask buyers or potential buyers how much more or how much less they would purchase of a particular product if its price (or advertising, or one of the other independent variables) were varied by a certain amount. "Focus groups" may be assembled for discussions, or questionnaires may be administered to a sample of buyers. Although seemingly simple, this approach is fraught with difficulties. The first problem is that the individuals interviewed or surveyed must represent the market as a whole so that the results will not be biased. Thus a sufficiently large sample, generated by random procedures, must be interviewed in order to form a reasonable estimate of the market's reaction to a proposed change.

A second problem is interviewer bias, defined as the distortion of the interviewee's response caused by the presence of the interviewer. Where the true answer would make the respondent feel a little stupid, imply gluttony or drug dependence, expose the person as a tax cheat, or involve any other potential embarrassment, the respondent may give an incorrect answer to avoid the embarrassing moment. Interviewer bias will occur in personal interviews, telephone interviews, and even mailed-in questionnaires (because someone reads them). Telephone and mailed questionnaires avoid eye contact and lessen the potential embarrassment to a large extent, but at the same time the repondents may be less well chosen and their responses less well considered, as compared to personal interviews. Anonymous written or telephone responses may be more accurate in terms of interviewer bias, but less accurate in terms of deep thought given to the responses.

Third, there is the gap between intentions and action. The consumer may have truly intended to buy the product at the time of interview, but by the time the marketing strategy is implemented something may have intervened to change the consumer's mind. Other things may not stay equal long enough for the action to have the anticipated result. Finally, the responses may be unreliable if any question is confusing or misinterpreted or if it involves things beyond the realm of the respondent's imagination. New products, for example, when described briefly for the first time, cannot easily be pictured as part of the consumer's lifestyle. Early estimates of personal computer sales underestimated the dramatic growth of business demand for them in the early 1980s. Later predictions were wildly optimistic about the continuing penetration of the business and household markets, as evidenced by the excess inventories held by the major manufacturers by the mid-1980s (despite falling prices).

A great deal of research has gone into the problems of questionnaire formulation in order to derive reliable results from interviews, surveys, and focus groups. Rather than asking questions directly, researchers may derive the answers to a specific question from the respondent's answer to a number of other questions. Reliability of responses to specific questions may be checked by asking the same questions in a different form at a later point during the interview or on the questionnaire.[1] The form of the question can influence the nature of the results: open-ended questions allow the consumer to express in his or her own words what the response may be, while structured questions, such as multiple-choice questions where the respondent must use one of four or five specific responses, suggest an answer to the consumer and may bias the results toward something the researcher expected to find. The choice of words is an important consideration, since nuances may be involved and some words have different meanings to different people. The questions must be sequenced in a way that creates and holds the subject's interest, provokes accurate responses, and does not create an emotional reaction that may influence subsequent answers or cause the respondent to refuse to continue.[2]

In summary, considerable care and thought must be included in the construction of the questionnaire, and reasoned analysis must be involved in interpreting the results of the survey. Let us consider the results of a particular market survey.

Example: The Sylvain Leather Products Company intends to introduce a new wallet and wishes to estimate the demand curve for the new wallet. Members of the market research department have conducted a questionnaire survey of one thousand people interviewed while shopping for goods of a similar nature. The interviewees were each asked to choose one of six responses as to whether they would actually purchase the new wallet at each of five price levels. The responses were (a) definitely no; (b) not likely; (c) perhaps, maybe; (d) quite likely; (e) very likely; and (f) definitely yes. The number of people responding in each category at each price level is shown in Table 5-1. The analysts have determined that the probabilities of actually buying the product for each of the six responses are 0.0 for response (a); 0.2 for response (b); 0.4 for response (c); 0.6 for response (d); 0.8 for response (e); and 1.0 for response (f).

TABLE 5-1.   Sylvain Leather Products Company: Summary of Questionnaire Responses

Price ($)	NUMBER OF PEOPLE RESPONDING AS						Expected Quantity
	(a)	(b)	(c)	(d)	(e)	(f)	
9	500	300	125	50	25	0	160
8	300	225	175	150	100	50	335
7	100	150	250	250	150	100	500
6	50	100	100	300	250	200	640
5	0	25	50	225	300	400	800

---

[1]See, for example, P. E. Green and D. S. Tull, *Research for Marketing Decisions,* 3rd ed. (Englewood Cliffs, N.J.: Prentice-Hall, Inc., 1975), esp. chaps. 4 and 5; and D. J. Luck, H. G. Wales, and D. A. Taylor, *Marketing Research,* 4th ed. (Englewood Cliffs, N.J.: Prentice-Hall, Inc., 1974), esp. chaps. 9 and 10.

[2]See P. Kotler, *Marketing Management,* 3rd ed. (Englewood Cliffs, N.J.: Prentice-Hall, Inc., 1976), pp. 430-31.

From these data, we can find the expected value of quantity demanded at each price level. At a price of $9, for example, the expected value of quantity demanded is the sum of the expected value of sales to each group of respondents. That is,

$$E(Q) = 500\,(0.0) + 300\,(0.2) + 125\,(0.4) + 50\,(0.6)$$
$$+ 25\,(0.8) + 0\,(1.0) = 160 \text{ units}$$

Proceeding similarly, we can calculate the expected quantity demanded at prices of $8, $7, $6, and $5, as shown in Table 5–1. Plotting these price-quantity coordinates on a graph, as in Figure 5–1, we see that they trace out a demand curve which intercepts the price axis at approximately $10.00, and which has a slope of approximately −5/800, or −0.00625. This quick estimate of the slope is obtained by noting that as price falls from $10 to $5 (rise = −5), quantity demanded increases from zero to 800 units (run = 800). This relation indicates that for quantity demanded to increase by 100 units, price must be reduced by 62.5 cents.

Thus the estimate of the demand curve is $P_x = 10.00 - 0.00625 Q_x$; and from this the firm can easily find $\text{MR}_x = 10.00 - 0.0125 Q_x$, since the marginal revenue curve has the same intercept and twice the slope as the demand curve.

Note: This estimate of the demand curve and the marginal revenue curve depends upon the sample of shoppers being a *random* sample that is representative of people who are in the market for leather wallets. It also presumes that the responses were free from interviewer bias and that their intentions would actually culminate in purchases to the extent indicated by the probabilities. We also require *ceteris paribus* with regard to consumer incomes, tastes, perceptions, prices of rival products, and so forth. In particular, if any of these factors change between the time when the data were col-

FIGURE 5–1.   Sylvain Leather Products Estimated Demand and Marginal Revenue Curves

lected and analyzed and the time when the wallet is actually offered for sale, we should expect the above specification of the demand curve to be inaccurate because of a *shift* in the actual demand curve.

Simulated Market Situations

Another means of finding out what consumers would do in response to changes in price or promotion efforts is to construct an artificial market situation and observe the behavior of selected participants. These so-called consumer clinics often involve giving the participants a certain sum of money and asking them to spend this money in an artificial store environment. Different groups of participants may be faced with different price structures among competing products and differing promotional displays. If the participants are carefully selected to be representative of the market for these products, we may—after observing their reactions to price changes of different magnitudes and to variations in promotional efforts—conclude that the entire market would respond in the same way.

Results of such simulated-market test situations must be viewed carefully, however. Participants may spend someone else's money differently from the way they would spend their own money, a phenomenon amply demonstrated by business executives' use of expense accounts. Alternatively, participants may feel that they are expected to choose a particular product when its price is reduced in order to demonstrate that they are thrifty and responsible shoppers. Consumer clinics are likely to be an expensive method of obtaining data, however, since there is a considerable setup cost, participants must be provided with the products they select, and the process is relatively time consuming. Given these factors, it is likely that the samples involved will be quite small, and hence the results may not be representative of the entire market's reaction to the pricing and promotional changes. Nevertheless, such experiments may provide useful insight into the price awareness and consciousness of buyers and into their general reaction to changes in specific promotional variables.

Example: The Brazilian Gold Coffee Company wished to ascertain the responsiveness of consumers to changes in the price of its coffee. Six groups of one hundred shoppers each were organized for a simulated market experiment. The membership of the groups was chosen such that the socioeconomic characteristics of the groups were roughly equal and similar to the market in total. Within one afternoon each group was allowed thirty minutes to shop in a simulated supermarket. Each participant was given $30 in "play money" to purchase any items on display in the simulated supermarket. Brazilian Gold coffee was displayed prominently alongside the best-selling brand of coffee. For each of the six groups, Brazilian Gold was priced at different levels while the prices of all other products were held constant. The price levels and the resultant quantities demanded are shown in Table 5-2.

In Figure 5-2 we plot the price-quantity coordinates for Brazilian Gold coffee and sketch in the demand curve which seems to be indicated by these data points. Note that we have not simply joined the observations with a jagged line but have, instead,

TABLE 5-2.   Simulated Market Experiment for Brazilian Gold Coffee

Group	Price ($ per lb)	Quantity Demanded (lbs)
1	3.39	112
2	3.29	123
3	3.49	94
4	3.19	154
5	3.69	37
6	3.59	71

superimposed a "line of best fit." In the next section we shall see how to calculate the exact line of best fit using regression analysis. In the present example, we have simply "eye-balled" the line of best fit across the data points. That is, we have sketched in the demand curve that seems visually appropriate to the points shown. We show it as a straight line for simplicity and because the data do not clearly indicate a nonlinear relationship between price and quantity demanded. The intercept of the line of best fit occurs at approximately $3.88 on the price axis, and the slope of the line is approximately 0.0045, which can be calculated by taking a particular vertical change (e.g., $3.88 to $3.38, or $0.50) and dividing this by the horizontal change indicated by the line of best fit (in this case, from zero to about 110 units). Thus, $0.50/110 = 0.0045$.

✳ Thus the simulated market experiment has generated data that allow the demand curve for Brazilian Gold coffee to be estimated as $P = 3.88 - 0.0045Q$, *ceteris paribus*. The firm can then determine the expression for its marginal revenue curve or calculate the price elasticity of demand at any price level. Note that for the price-elasticity calculation one would use the reciprocal of the slope term, namely $1/-0.0045$, or -222.22, as the term dQ_x/dP_x and read the coordinates P_x and Q_x

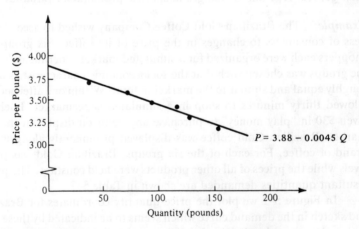

FIGURE 5-2.   Estimated Demand Curve for Brazilian Gold Coffee

from the line of best fit. For example, the price elasticity at price $3.59 would be calculated as

$$\epsilon = -222.22 \cdot \frac{3.59}{65}$$

$$= -12.27$$

Note that we have used the *estimated* quantity demanded (at a price of $3.59) of 65 units, read from the demand curve (line of best fit) rather than from the *observed* quantity (in the experiment) of 71 units. We do this because we recognize that all the observations probably contain random errors and we expect (from consumer behavior theory) that the demand curve will be a smooth line between price-quantity combinations. The next time we set price at $3.59 the random disturbances may cause demand to be, for example, only 58 units. Our *best estimate* of demand at price $3.59 is given by the line of best fit, and therefore our best estimate of price elasticity at that price should be based on the estimated demand curve rather than on the actual data observed.[3]

Direct Market Experiments

Direct market experiments involve real people in real market situations spending their own money on the goods and services they want. The firm will select one or more cities, regional markets, or states and conduct an experiment in these "test markets" that is designed to gauge consumer acceptance of the product and to identify the impact of a change in one or more of the controllable variables on the quantity demanded. In a regional market, for example, the firm might reduce the price of its product by 10 percent and compare the reaction of sales in that market over a particular period with previous sales in that market or with current sales in a similar but separate regional market. Alternatively, the firm may increase its advertising in a specific area or introduce a promotional gimmick or campaign in a particular market to judge the impact of that change before committing itself to the greater expense and risk of instituting this change on a nationwide basis.

Example: Many firms in the United States launch new products and conduct experimental promotional campaigns in regional test markets. San Diego, California, was used by the Miller Brewing Company as a test market for its new "Special Reserve"

---

[3]Note that if we had only two pairs of price-quantity observations, such as those for the prices $3.69 and $3.59, we would calculate *arc* elasticity of demand and we would have to use the observed price-quantity points in that calculation. Given more observations, however, we are able to see that the slope of the line joining the two coordinates above is not our best estimate of the slope of the demand curve. Given more than two data points, we are able to estimate the line of best fit (demand curve) and use the information provided by this curve (rather than the raw data containing probably random disturbances) for our elasticity calculations.

beer during 1981, prior to the nationwide availability of that beer. Similarly, light (low calorie) wines were test marketed first in the San Diego area by Taylor California Cellars to evaluate market acceptance of the product and to judge consumer reaction to the price level and promotional campaign. San Diego is used as a test market because it is demographically representative of southern California. Similarly, Denver, Baltimore, Phoenix, and Providence were chosen as test markets by Miller for the new beer since they are representative of other areas of the United States in terms of demographics, income levels, lifestyles, and so forth.[4] Similarly, in the last quarter of 1985, Time, Inc., tested the market acceptability and price of a new weekly photo-news magazine called *Picture Week* in thirteen cities stretching from Portland, Oregon, to Portland, Maine. The new magazine was heavily promoted in those cities, and was priced at 95 cents in nine of those cities and 79 cents in the remaining four cities.[5]

"Direct marketing," probably better known by the obsolete term "mail-order marketing," is a channel of communication between buyers and sellers that is ideally suited to market experiments. The consumer responds to an advertisement placed by the seller in any of several media, including newspapers, magazines, radio, television, and direct mailings to consumers. The mail and telephone orders that follow a firm's advertisement or direct mailing represent cash up front and are much more reliable indicators of market demand than are simple statements of consumer intentions. By placing different advertisements and price offers in different regions or by making different offers to different samples within the same region (using direct mailings to randomly selected samples of the target market), the impact of different prices and promotional strategies on the entire target market can be reliably estimated. As a bonus, the feedback is usually fairly quick—responses to television advertisements requiring mail or telephone orders are concentrated within the next few days following the advertisement, while magazine advertisements and direct mailings generate the great majority of the total responses within six or eight weeks. Note, however, that direct marketing represents a different channel between the producer and the consumer and may appeal to a different type of consumer, with the result that the findings from experiments using direct marketing may not be generally applicable to other marketing channels, such as retailing through suburban and city stores.[6]

Note: With any change in price or other marketing strategy there is likely to be an initial or "impact" effect followed by a gradual settling of the market into the new longer-term relationship between price (or other controllable variable) and the sales level. Consumers will eagerly try a new product or respond to a price reduction or a

---

[4]Lanie Jones, "San Diego's Role as Test Market Toasted as Cap Comes off New Beer," *Los Angeles Times,* August 17, 1981, pt. 2, pp. 1, 10; also Dan Berger, "Miller Introduces New Beer Here," *San Diego Union,* August 13, 1981.

[5]"Time Inc. Is Testing a Photo Magazine in 13 U.S. Markets," *Wall Street Journal,* September 23, 1985.

[6]See Bob Stone, *Successful Direct Marketing Methods,* 2nd ed. (Chicago: Crain Books, 1979).

promotional campaign, but having tried the product, many will go back to the rival product they were previously purchasing. Consumers may respond to a price reduction by purchasing several cartons of the product to build up their personal inventory of the product in the belief that the lower price is only temporary. The initial surge in consumer demand for a new product or for an established product at a lower price (or following a promotional campaign) may substantially overstate the sales gain the firm can expect in several weeks or months after consumers have finished making their adjustments in response to the change in prices, product availability, promotion, or in some other variable.

In order to observe more than the impact effects of a change, market experiments must be conducted over a reasonably prolonged period of time. During this period, however, one or more of the uncontrollable variables are likely to have changed, and thus the observed change in sales over the period will not be due simply to the change in the controllable variable. To separate the effects of changes in other variables the firm should also observe a "control market," which should be chosen to exhibit a similar socioeconomic and cultural profile and be subject to the same climatic, political, and other uncontrollable events as is the "test market." The change in sales in the control market over the period of the experiment will be solely the result of the uncontrollable factors. Assuming that the same change would have occurred in the test market, this magnitude is deducted from (if positive) or added to (if negative) the change in sales in the test market to find the change in sales caused by the manipulation of the controllable variable(s).

If an uncontrollable variable changes in the test market but remains constant or changes to a different degree in the control market, the results of the market experiment will be less reliable. Even when the control market is nearby, the climatic influence may vary, local politics may intervene, or some other event may cause an impact on the sales level. Competitors may react to the change in the test market by lowering prices or increasing promotional efforts, for example, while maintaining the status quo in the undisturbed control market. Under such circumstances the market experiment could prove to be worthless.

Thus direct market experiments must be implemented with caution; some luck must be forthcoming so that uncontrollable variables do not distort the results, which must be interpreted with care. If the pitfalls are largely anticipated and subsequently avoided, such experiments may provide information whose value (in terms of the present value of the additional future sales revenue) far exceeds its cost. We now turn to a means of estimating the demand coefficients from secondary data, in contrast to the previous reliance on primary data.

5.3 REGRESSION ANALYSIS OF CONSUMER DEMAND

■ *Definition:* *Regression analysis* is a statistical technique used to discover the apparent dependence of one variable upon one or more other variables. It is thus applicable to the problem of determining the coefficients of the demand function, since these express the influence of the determining variables upon the demand for a product. For regression analysis we require a number of sets of observations, each consisting of the value of the dependent variable Y plus the corresponding values of the independent X variables. Regression analysis allows conclusions to be drawn from the pattern that emerges in the relationships between these pairs or sets of observations, and it can be applied to either time-series or cross-section data.

Time-Series versus Cross-Section Analysis

- *Definition:*   *Time-series analysis* uses observations that have been recorded *over time in a particular situation.* For example, monthly price and sales levels of a product in a particular firm may have been collected for the past six or twelve months. A problem with time-series analysis is that some of the uncontrollable factors that influence sales tend to change over time, and hence some of the differences in the sales observations will be the result of these influences rather than the result of any changes in the price level. If the changes in the uncontrollable variables are observable and measurable, we may include these variables as explanatory variables in the regression analysis. Actions of competitors and changing consumer income levels, for example, should be quantified (either directly or by use of a suitable proxy variable) and incorporated into the analysis.

    Changing taste and preference patterns, on the other hand, are difficult to observe and measure, but they are likely to change over time. Using time as an explanatory variable in the regression analysis will pick up the influence of tastes and any other factors (not otherwise included in the analysis) that tend to change over the period.

- *Definition:*   *Cross-section analysis* uses observations from different firms in the same business environment at the *same point or period of time.* Hence cross-section analysis largely eliminates the problem of uncontrollable variables that change over time, but it introduces other factors that may differ between and among firms at a particular point of time. If factors such as the effectiveness of sales personnel, cash-flow position, level of promotional activity, and objectives of management differ among firms, they should be expected to have differing impacts on the sales level. Again, if these factors can be quantified and data obtained, they may be entered into the regression analysis to determine their impact upon the dependent variables.

Linearity of the Regression Equation

Having hypothesized that Y is a function of X or of several X variables and having collected data on the variables, we must then specify the form of the dependence of Y upon the X variables. Regression analysis requires that the dependence be expressed in the linear form   *Beyond scope Non-linear*

$$Y = \alpha + \beta_1 X_1 + \beta_2 X_2 + \ldots + \beta_n X_n + e \tag{5-2}$$

where the e term is added to represent the error or residual value that will arise as the difference between the *actual* value of each Y that has been observed in association with each set of X values, and the *estimated* value of each Y that the regression equation would predict for the X values given. For individual observations we should expect either a positive or a negative residual term, because of random variations in the value of Y.[7]

Nonlinear relationships between the Y and X values, such as quadratic, cubic, exponential, hyperbolic, and power functions, may be used if these best fit the data, since these forms may be converted to linear form by mathematical transformation. The most commonly used nonlinear form is the power function, such as

$$Y = \alpha X_1^{\beta_1} X_2^{\beta_2} \tag{5-3}$$

where the independent variables, X_1 and X_2 in this case, have a multiplicative (rather than additive) influence on the dependent variable Y. This curvilinear relationship can be expressed as a rectilinear relationship by logarithmic transformation. Taking logarithms of the values for Y, X_1, and X_2, we can express equation (5-3) as

$$\log Y = \log \alpha + \beta_1 \log X_1 + \beta_2 \log X_2 \tag{5-4}$$

In this form, the equation is linear, and the coefficients β_1 and β_2 can be found directly using regression analysis. The coefficient α in equation (5-3) can be found by reversing the transformation (that is, taking the antilog) of the $\log \alpha$ value provided by the regression analysis. We shall work through an example of this procedure in Chapter 8, in the context of cost forecasting.

Alternatively, you may feel that the appropriate functional form between the dependent variable and the independent variables is quadratic, like the form for the total revenue curve. A quadratic function can be expressed linearly as follows:

$$Y = \alpha + \beta_1 X_1 + \beta_2 X_1^2 \tag{5-5}$$

Note that the last variable in this expression is the same independent variable (X_1) squared. Similarly, if the appropriate functional form is thought to be cubic, as in the case of the production function or total cost function to be discussed in Chapter 6, we can postulate the relationship to be

$$Y = \alpha + \beta_1 X_1 + \beta_2 X_1^2 + \beta_3 X_1^3 \tag{5-6}$$

and use regression analysis to determine the values of the α, β_1, β_2, and β_3 parameters.

---

[7]For the accurate calculation of the coefficients in the regression equation, we require that the residuals occur randomly, be normally distributed, have constant variance, and have an expected value of zero. When the pattern of residuals does not conform to these restrictions, several problems arise, as we shall see later in this section.

Estimating the Regression Parameters

The "method of least squares" is used to find the α and β parameters such that the regression equation best represents or summarizes the apparent relationship between the X_i values and the dependent variable Y. To illustrate this method, we shall proceed using a simple example of only one independent variable. (This is usually referred to as "simple regression" analysis, or "correlation" analysis rather than "multiple regression" analysis, which is used when we have two or more independent variables.)

Example: Suppose that we have collected ten pairs of observations on the variables Y and X—that is, the Y value and its associated X value on each of ten different occasions in a single situation (time-series data) or from ten different situations during the same period of time (cross-section data). These data points are shown as the asterisks in Figure 5-3. Observing these data points, we hypothesize a relationship of the form $Y = \alpha + \beta X$ and use regression analysis to estimate the α and β parameters, which allow the line $Y = \alpha + \beta X$ to *best fit* (or represent most accurately) the apparent relationship between the variables Y and X.

The method of least squares, often called ordinary least squares (OLS), is a mathematical process which chooses the intercept and slope of the line of best fit such that the sum of the squares of the deviations (or errors) is minimized. These deviations are shown in Figure 5-3 as the vertical distance between the line of best fit and the actual value of Y observed for a particular value of X. For example, given X_1 in Figure 5-3, the estimated value of Y is $\hat{Y}_1$ (known as Y_1 *hat*, where the *hat* [circumflex] over the Y_1 indicates the estimated, or expected, value of Y_1, given X_1). The vertical difference between the observed Y_1 and the estimated $\hat{Y}_1$ is known as the deviation, residual, or error term, and was connoted as e in equation (5-2).

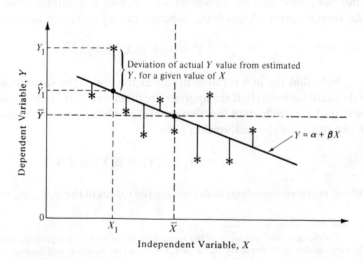

FIGURE 5-3. The Line of Best Fit

Thus the regression equation specifies the line of best fit. It is selected by a mathematical procedure that positions the line such that the sum of the squared errors is minimized. We square the errors to avoid the positive deviations (points above the line of best fit) canceling out against negative deviations (points below the line of best fit), and to weight more heavily the larger deviations.[8] Note that the line of best fit passes through the point representing the mean values ($\bar{Y}$ and $\bar{X}$) of the variables. The regression equation "explains" part of the variation of each Y observation from the $\bar{Y}$ value, in terms of the difference between the associated X observation and the $\bar{X}$ value. In Figure 5–3, when $X = X_1$, the regression equation predicts $\hat{Y}_1$, explaining the variation from Y (that is, $\bar{Y} - \hat{Y}_1$), in terms of the variation in X (that is, $\bar{X} - X_1$). The "unexplained" residual, or error term, is the difference between the actual observation of Y and the predicted value of Y (that is, $Y_1 - \hat{Y}_1$).

Since computer programs (and preprogrammed or programmable hand calculators) for obtaining correlation and regression equations are becoming readily available and since the theory underlying regression analysis is typically covered in other courses, we shall not go too deeply into the theory or calculation of regression equations. It is instructive, however, to work through a simple two-variable case to demonstrate some of the issues and problems involved. Without proof, we state the following expressions for α and β:[9]

$$\alpha = \bar{Y} - \beta\bar{X} \tag{5-7}$$

and

$$\beta = \frac{n\Sigma XY - \Sigma X\Sigma Y}{n\Sigma X^2 - (\Sigma X)^2} \tag{5-8}$$

where $\bar{Y}$ is the arithmetic mean of the Y values; $\bar{X}$ is the arithmetic mean of the X values; Σ (sigma) connotes the sum of the term indicated (for example, ΣXY is the sum of the products of X and Y for all pairs of X and Y observations); and n is the number of observations or data points.

Given a set of X and Y observations, we can use these equations to solve for the line of best fit for the relationship that appears to exist between those two variables. Let us introduce a hypothetical example.

Example: Suppose a chain of department stores sells its own brand of frozen broccoli in each of its six stores. The chain is interested in knowing the price elasticity of

[8]See Richard I. Levin, *Statistics for Management*, 2nd ed., (Englewood Cliffs, N.J.: Prentice-Hall, Inc. 1981), pp. 463–65.

[9]See J. Johnston, *Econometric Methods* (New York: McGraw-Hill Book Company, 1963), pp. 9–19. Note that your calculator, if it has a regression-equation program, may be programmed for a simplified formula, and you may, as a consequence, arrive at a slightly different answer. The degree of inaccuracy is usually very small, however.

demand for this product. Its six stores are in similar middle-income suburban neighborhoods, and all are currently selling the item at $0.79 per package. Monthly sales at the six stores average 4,625 units per store, with no store's sales being more than 150 units away from this level. Suppose the management decides to conduct an experiment: it will set the prices at different levels in each of the six stores to observe the reactions of sales to the different price levels. As a control it will maintain the price at $0.79 in the first store. The prices set for the other stores and the sales levels (in thousands) at each of the six stores over the one-month period of the experiment are shown in Table 5-3.

The table includes the calculations necessary for the solution of the α and β parameters. Using equation (5-8), we have

$$\beta = \frac{6(19.506) - 4.96(26.1)}{6(4.5094) - (4.96)^2}$$

$$= \frac{-12.42}{2.4548}$$

$$= -5.0595$$

and from equation (5-7), we have

$$\alpha = \bar{Y} - \beta\bar{X}$$

$$= 4.35 - (-5.059)(0.8267)$$

$$= 8.5327$$

TABLE 5-3.   Price/Sales Observations for Broccoli at Six Stores and the Calculations for Least-Square Analysis

Store No.	Price X ($)	Sales Y (000)	XY	X^2	Y^2
1	0.79	4.650	3.6735	0.6241	21.6225
2	0.99	3.020	2.9898	0.9801	9.1204
3	1.25	2.150	2.6875	1.5625	4.6225
4	0.89	4.400	3.9160	0.7921	19.3600
5	0.59	6.380	3.7642	0.3481	40.7044
6	0.45	5.500	2.4750	0.2025	30.2500
	4.96	26.100	19.5060	4.5094	125.6798
	(ΣX)	(ΣY)	(ΣXY)	(ΣX^2)	(ΣY^2)

$$\bar{Y} = \frac{\Sigma Y}{n} = \frac{26.1}{6} = 4.35$$

$$\bar{X} = \frac{\Sigma X}{n} = \frac{4.96}{6} = 0.8267$$

Thus, $Y = 8.5327 - 5.0595X$ is the "line of best fit" to the data, when sales (Y) are measured in thousands of units. As shown in Figure 5-4, the intercept of this line is thus 8,532.7 units on the Y axis, and the slope is $-5,059.5$ units of sales per dollar increase in price (which is to say, 50.595 units for each cent the price is increased). The intercept value should not be interpreted as the sales level that would be expected at the price of zero, since the range of price observations is from \$0.45 to \$1.25, and the values of α and β are estimated only for that range. Outside this range a different relationship may hold between X and Y. The intercept parameter serves only to locate the line of best fit such that it passes through the observations at the appropriate height. To interpret the intercept as the sales value when price is zero would be an example of the dangerous practice of extrapolation.

Note: The regression equation calculated above shows the dependence of quantity demanded on the price per unit. We can easily convert this into the form $P = \alpha + bQ$ traditionally used to represent the demand curve. Substituting for Q and P in the regression equation, we have

$$Q = 8.5327 - 5.0595P \tag{5-9}$$

Subtracting Q from both sides, adding $5.0595P$ to both sides, and dividing both sides by 5.0595, we have:

$$5.0595P = 8.5327 - Q$$
$$P = 1.6865 - 0.19765Q \tag{5-10}$$

FIGURE 5-4.   **Graphical Plot of Price/Sales Observations**

The marginal revenue curve is obtained from this estimate of the demand curve, based on our knowledge that it has the same vertical intercept and twice the slope. Thus,

$$MR = 1.6865 - 0.3953Q \qquad (5\text{-}11)$$

Price elasticity of demand at any price level may be estimated using $dQ/dP = -5.0595$ from the regression equation (5-9) and the estimated quantity demanded at that price level. For example, given $P = 0.85$, we find $\hat{Q}$ by substituting for P in equation (5-9) as follows:

$$\hat{Q} = 8.5327 - 5.0595\,(0.85)$$
$$= 4.2321$$

Inserting these values into the point price elasticity expression, we find

$$\epsilon = \frac{dQ}{dP} \cdot \frac{P}{Q}$$
$$= -5.0595 \cdot \frac{0.85}{4.2321}$$
$$= 1.0162$$

The price elasticity of demand at the price level of $0.85 is, therefore, fractionally above unity, indicating that total revenue would be virtually constant for either (very small) price increases or price reductions from the price of $0.85.

The Coefficient of Determination

■ *Definition:* The *coefficient of determination*, conventionally expressed as R^2, is a number indicating the proportion of the variation in the dependent variable which is explained by the variation in the independent variable(s).

In effect, the R^2 value tells us *how well* the regression equation fits the data. An R^2 value of 0.98, for example, indicates that changes in the value(s) of the independent variable(s) account for 98 percent of the changes in the dependent variable. An R^2 value of 1.0 would indicate that *all* the variation in Y is explained by the variation in the X variable(s), and consequently, all data points would actually lie on the line of best fit. Conversely, an R^2 value of, for example, 0.32, would indicate a broadly scattered set of data points with relatively large deviations from the line of best fit and a relatively weak relationship between the dependent and independent variables.

The coefficient of determination can be calculated using the following formula:[10]

$$R^2 = \left(\frac{n\Sigma XY - \Sigma X \Sigma Y}{\sqrt{[n\Sigma X^2 - (\Sigma X)^2][n\Sigma Y^2 - (\Sigma Y)^2]}} \right)^2 \qquad (5\text{-}12)$$

Example: Inserting the values as calculated in Table 5-1, we have

$$R^2 = \left(\frac{6(19.506) - 4.96(26.1)}{\sqrt{[6(4.5094) - (4.96)^2][6(125.6798) - (26.1)^2]}} \right)^2$$

$$= \left(\frac{-12.42}{\sqrt{178.8783}} \right)^2$$

$$= \left(\frac{-12.42}{13.3745} \right)^2$$

$$= (-0.9286)^2$$

$$= 0.8624$$

Thus we are able to say that slightly more than 86 percent of the variation in the sales observations was due to the influence of the differences in the price levels. The remaining unexplained variance is due to some other influence on sales. This remaining variability could be due to differences in promotional activity, consumer incomes, consumer tastes, or other factors that may differ between and among the six stores.

---

[10]See Johnston, *Econometric Methods,* pp. 30–32. This formula facilitates hand calculation of the coefficient of determination, but it does little to explain why this statistic indicates the proportion of variation in Y explained by X. Note that the OLS method minimizes the sum of the squared residuals, or the total variation of the Y observations from the mean value of Y, namely $\Sigma(Y_i - \bar{Y})^2$, where Y_i represents the ith observation of the variable Y (where $i = 1,2,3, \ldots ,n$). In turn,

$$\Sigma(Y_i - \bar{Y})^2 = \Sigma(\hat{Y}_i - \bar{Y})^2 + \Sigma(Y_i - \hat{Y}_i)^2$$

That is, the total variation is equal to the variation in Y (the difference from the mean) that is explained by the regression equation, plus the residual variation (the difference of the actual observation from the value predicted by the regression equation). Now, dividing through by the total variation, we have

$$\frac{\Sigma(Y_i - \bar{Y})^2}{\Sigma(Y_i - \bar{Y})^2} = \frac{\Sigma(\hat{Y}_i - \bar{Y})^2}{\Sigma(Y_i - \bar{Y})^2} + \frac{\Sigma(Y_i - \hat{Y}_i)^2}{\Sigma(Y_i - \bar{Y})^2}$$

The coefficient of determination is the term following the equal sign, since it is the ratio of the variation explained to the total variation. Since the term on the left is equal to 1,

$$R^2 = 1 - \frac{\Sigma(Y_i - \hat{Y}_i)^2}{\Sigma(Y_i - \bar{Y})^2}$$

Thus R^2 is equal to 1 minus the proportion of the total variation not explained by the regression equation. When $\Sigma(Y_i - \hat{Y}_i)^2$ is zero (meaning all observations lie on the line of best fit), R^2 is equal to 1, signifying a perfect fit of the line to the data. When $\Sigma(Y_i - \hat{Y}_i)^2$ is relatively large, R^2 is relatively small, signifying a poor fit to the data and showing that X is a relatively unimportant determinant of Y.

The Standard Error of Estimate

Most computer regression programs include as standard output several other statistics that allow the decision maker to evaluate the confidence that may be placed in certain predictions. The first of these is the standard error of estimate.

■ *Definition:* The *standard error of estimate* is a measure of the dispersion of the data points from the line of best fit. Given the standard error of estimate (S_e), we can calculate the confidence interval (around the estimated value for the dependent variable) for different levels of confidence. The *confidence interval* is the range of values within which we expect the actual observation to fall a given percentage of the time. For example, we can be confident at the 95 percent level that the actual value of Y for a given X will fall within a certain range of outcomes above and below the estimated value (that is, $\hat{Y}_i$) if we know that 95 percent of the time it *should* fall within this interval.

Assuming that the error terms (deviations or residuals) are normally distributed about the line of best fit, we can use the properties of a normal distribution to say that there is a 68 percent probability that actual observations of the dependent variable will lie within the range given by the estimated value plus or minus one standard error of the estimate. Furthermore, there is a 95 percent probability that the future observations will lie within plus or minus *two* standard errors of its predicted value and a 99 percent probability that the observed value will lie within plus or minus *three* standard errors of the estimated value.

By adding and subtracting the standard error to and from the estimated value of $\hat{Y}_i$ for each value of X_i, we establish a band within which we can expect the value of Y to fall for a particular value of X. A broader band is established when we add or subtract two standard errors of the estimate, and as noted previously the probability is raised to 95 percent that the actual observation will lie within this band. The latter band is perhaps the most widely used in decision making, and it establishes what are known as the upper and lower 95 percent confidence limits. That is, we can be 95 percent confident that the actual observation will lie in the band and that the best and worst outcomes associated with the particular value of the independent variable will be no further than the limits of the band.

We can calculate the standard error of estimate using the following expression:[11]

---

[11]See Levin, *Statistics for Management*, pp. 471-77. Again this formula facilitates computation. Equivalently,

$$S_e = \sqrt{\frac{\Sigma(Y_i - \hat{Y}_i)^2}{n - k}}$$

where k is the number of parameters estimated (the intercept and the slope). In this form you can see that the standard error of estimate is effectively the average absolute value of the deviations (corrected for de-

$$S_e = \sqrt{\frac{\Sigma Y^2 - \alpha \Sigma Y - \beta \Sigma XY}{n - 2}}$$

(5-13)

Example: For the broccoli example introduced earlier we can insert the values that were calculated in Table 5-3 and the α and β values subsequently derived to find the standard error of estimate associated with the line of best fit:

$$S_e = \sqrt{\frac{125.6798 - (8.5327)(26.1) - (-5.0595)(19.506)}{6 - 2}}$$

$$= \sqrt{\frac{1.66694}{4}}$$

$$= \sqrt{0.41673}$$

$$= 0.64555$$

Thus the standard error of estimate is 0.64555, or 645.55 units, since the sales data were in thousands. To find the 95 percent confidence interval, we would simply add twice this figure to $\hat{Y}$ to find the upper confidence limit and subtract twice this figure to find the lower confidence limit. Selecting a price near $\bar{X}$, such as $0.85, we estimate sales to be

$$\hat{Y} = 8.5327 - 5.0595 \,(0.85)$$
$$= 8.5327 - 4.3006$$
$$= 4.2321$$

Thus, when the price is $0.85, our best estimate of sales is 4,232.1 units. However, we don't really expect the actual sales to fall at exactly that number because the

---

grees of freedom). Again, when $\Sigma(Y_i - \hat{Y}_i)^2$ is zero, then $S_e = 0$, signifying a perfect fit to the data. When S_e is relatively large, it signifies a poor fit to the data. Note that the value of S_e calculated using equation (5-13) is only accurate at the mean values of X and Y and that it understates the confidence intervals by progressively more as we move away from $\bar{X}$ and $\bar{Y}$. The *exact* value of the standard error for each value of X_i can be calculated using

$$S_p = \sqrt{S_e^2 \left(1 + \frac{1}{n} + \frac{(\bar{X} - X_i)^2}{\Sigma X^2 - n\bar{X}^2}\right)}$$

From this expression, you can see that S_p diverges from S_e as n becomes smaller and X_i is more distant from $\bar{X}$. Thus the confidence intervals given by the rule of thumb (for example, plus or minus $2S_e$ around $\hat{Y}$ indicates the 95 percent confidence interval) are accurate at $\bar{X}$ and for reasonably large values of n, but *understate* the confidence intervals for X_i more distant from $\bar{X}$ and when n is relatively small. For greater accuracy when using small samples, the S_e should be multiplied by the appropriate t-statistic (rather than simply 2) to find the 95 percent confidence interval. See Levin, pp. 476-77.

estimate is derived from data that exhibited deviations from the line of best fit. The standard error of estimate uses the observed deviations to establish confidence intervals on the presumption that later observations will similarly contain random disturbances and tend to scatter around the line of best fit. The upper bound of the 95 percent confidence interval is equal to

$$\hat{Y} + 2S_e = 4.2321 + 2\,(0.64555)$$
$$= 5.5233$$

and the lower bound of the 95 percent confidence interval is equal to

$$\hat{Y} - 2S_e = 4.2321 - 2\,(0.64555)$$
$$= 2.9409$$

Thus we can be confident at the 95 percent level that when price is set at $0.85, sales will fall within the range 2,940.9 units to 5,523.3 units. Clearly, we would prefer to discover a smaller standard error of estimate, since the confidence interval would then be smaller, and we could be more confident of experiencing an actual outcome close to the expected outcome $\hat{Y}$.

The Predictive Power of the Regression Equation.   If the confidence interval is relatively narrow, because of a relatively small value of the standard error of estimate, we say that the regression equation has greater predictive power than it would if the value of S_e were relatively large and the confidence interval relatively broad. How do we judge whether the S_e value is relatively large or small? Relative to what? A convenient rule of thumb is to relate it to the mean value of the Y observations. If the ratio of $S_e/\bar{Y}$ is less than 0.05, then the average absolute deviation from the predicted value of Y should be less than 5 percent of the predicted value of Y. Note that the S_e value increases as the predicted value $\hat{Y}$ diverges from the mean value $\bar{Y}$ (see footnote 11), so that this rule of thumb becomes progressively less accurate as the value of $\hat{Y}$ diverges from $\bar{Y}$. If the ratio of $S_e/\bar{Y}$ is less than 0.05, then we have a reasonably accurate predictive equation with relatively tight confidence limits (or a relatively narrow confidence interval) at the desired level of confidence. Note that if we want to be even more secure in our predictions, we could set the $S_e/\bar{Y}$ "test" at 0.02, for example, and only use predictive equations that have an $S_e/\bar{Y}$ ratio less than 0.02.

For the broccoli case we note that $S_e/\bar{Y} = 0.64555/4.35 = 0.148$, or that the standard error of estimate is nearly 15 percent of the "typical" value of sales. This result, in conjunction with the relatively broad confidence interval calculated, indicates that the predictive accuracy of our regression equation will not be especially good.[12]

The Standard Error of the Coefficient

- *Definition:* The *standard error of the coefficient* is a measure of the accuracy of the calculated value of $\hat{\beta}$, the coefficient estimating the marginal relationship between the variables Y and X. The standard error of the coefficient S_β, if relatively small, allows us to express confidence that the calculated value of $\hat{\beta}$ is very close to the "true" value of β. The true value of β could be verified if we had the entire population of observations linking the variables Y and X, rather than just a sample. In short, S_β is the standard deviation of the sampling distribution of $\hat{\beta}$.

  Assuming that the deviations are normally distributed, we can use the features of a normal distribution to say that there is a 68 percent probability that the true coefficient will lie in the interval of the estimated coefficient plus or minus one standard error of the coefficient; a 95 percent probability that the true coefficient will lie in the interval given by the estimated coefficient plus or minus two standard errors of the coefficient; and a 99 percent probability that the actual relationship will be within plus or minus three standard errors of the coefficient of the estimated marginal relationship. Clearly, the smaller the standard error of the coefficient, the greater the confidence we can have in the regression coefficients generated by the data as reliable indicators of the true marginal relationships between the X_i values and the Y value.

  The standard error of the coefficient can be calculated using the formula[13]

$$S_\beta = \frac{S_e}{\sqrt{\Sigma X^2 - n\bar{X}^2}} \tag{5-14}$$

Example: For the broccoli example, the estimated coefficient $\hat{\beta}$ was -5.0595. What are the 95 percent confidence limits associated with this estimate? Inserting the data calculated earlier into equation (5-14), we find

---

[12]Other, very similar, measures of predictive power, are the mean absolute deviation (MAD) and the mean square error (MSE). MAD $= \Sigma |Y_i - \hat{Y}_i|/n$ and MSE $= \Sigma (Y_i - \hat{Y}_i)^2/n$. Note that the MAD is a simple average absolute measure of the deviations without correction for degrees of freedom, but the MSE squares the deviations to give greater weight to the larger deviations. The square root of the MSE, known as the root mean square of errors (RMS), is then very similar to the standard error of estimate formula shown in footnote 11, except that the RMS is not corrected for degrees of freedom. Thus, for relatively small sample sizes, the MAD and the RMS would both underestimate the standard error of estimate.

[13]See Levin, *Statistics for Management*, pp. 491-93.

$$S_\beta = \frac{0.6456}{\sqrt{4.5094 - 6(0.8267)^2}}$$

$$= \frac{0.6456}{0.4088}$$

$$= 1.5792$$

Thus the 95 percent confidence limits for the estimated coefficient are $-5.0595 + 2(1.5792)$ and $-5.0595 - 2(1.5792)$, or -1.9009 and -8.2181.

A simple rule of thumb to test for confidence in the regression coefficient is to take twice the value of the standard error of the coefficient and compare it with the estimated regression coefficient. If the regression coefficient exceeds twice its standard error, we can be 95 percent confident that the estimated coefficient is significantly different from zero and that there is a statistically significant relationship between the variables. In the present example, $\beta = -5.0595$ and is substantially more than twice the size of S_β, so we *can* be confident at the 95 percent level that the price level is a statistically significant determinant of the quantity demanded of the broccoli.[14]

The foregoing discussion in the context of simple regression, or correlation, analysis applies *mutatis mutandis* to multivariate regression analysis. The formulas for calculating the regression parameters for multivariable situations are given below.[15] The calculations become increasingly more complex and time consuming as the number of variables is increased and are thus a problem ideally suited to computer solution. The wide availability of computer programs for regression analysis means that essentially we need to know only how to enter the data and to interpret the results rather than to know the mechanistic processes of obtaining the results.

---

[14]Alternatively, if the regression program generates t-statistics for each independent variable, we would require that the t-value exceed 2, since the t-statistic is calculated as the correlation (or regression) coefficient divided by its standard error adjusted for the degrees of freedom. See Levin, *Statistics for Management*, pp. 491–93.

[15]For the multivariate regression equation $Y = \alpha + \beta_1 X_1 + \beta_2 X_2$, we can find α, β_1, and β_2 by simultaneous solution of the equations:

$$Y = n\alpha + \beta_1 \Sigma X_1 + \beta_2 \Sigma X_2 \tag{1}$$

$$\Sigma X_1 Y = \alpha \Sigma X_1 + \beta_1 \Sigma X_1^2 + \beta_2 \Sigma X_1 X_2 \tag{2}$$

$$\Sigma X_2 Y = \alpha \Sigma X_2 + \beta_1 \Sigma X_1 X_2 + \beta_2 \Sigma X_2^2 \tag{3}$$

See Levin, *Statistics for Management*, pp. 511–16. For more than two independent variables the equations are commensurately more complex. Using computer programs, such as the STATPAK Multiple Regression Program, complex regression equations can be solved much more quickly and accurately. The *Computer Courseware Package and Manual* that is ancillary to this text includes a multiple-regression program, named MULTREG, available on disk for IBM and compatible personal computers. Your instructor can get a copy of the disk from Prentice-Hall, Inc., and you may copy it. Details of the Courseware package are included in both the *Study Guide/Workbook* and the *Instructor's Manual*.

Problems in Regression Analysis: Six Major Pitfalls

There are six major problem areas likely to be encountered in regression analysis. If one or more of these problems do arise, the mechanistic regression analysis will still provide parameter estimates and statistics, but these results may well be spurious and therefore give misleading explanations and poor predictions. (Computers act in good faith, presuming that researchers know what they are doing.) We shall address the major problems in turn.

Specification Errors.   The first place to create unreliability in the results is in the specification of the relationship that is hypothesized to exist between the dependent variable and the independent variable(s). Two main types of problems occur under this heading: first there is the use of the wrong functional form of the relationship, and second there is the omission of important independent variables. We noted previously that the regression equation must be calculated in linear form, but that this could be achieved for nonlinear relationships by logarithmic transformation of the function to linear form. The first specification error is to specify the relationship as linear when in fact it is nonlinear of some form, or vice versa. How do we know which functional form is the "true" relationship? We find which functional form "best fits" the data by comparing the coefficient of determination (R^2) for various functional forms. By running the data in both the linear form (equation (5-2)) and, for example, the power form (equation (5-3)), the R^2 statistics can be compared to determine which functional form best explains the variance in the dependent variable. For bivariate correlation analysis, of course, a simple plot of the Y values against the X values should allow a visual assurance that the relationship is either linear or nonlinear.

The second specification error involves the omission of an important explanatory variable. This leads to probable unreliability in the regression coefficients and the likely violation of the restrictions that we place upon the error terms. Essentially, since one or more of the explanatory variables are not included in the regression equation, the influence of these variables is attributed to the variables that *are* included, or it shows up as an unexplained residual.

Example: To illustrate this problem, recall the broccoli example discussed earlier. Suppose we now learn that *ceteris paribus* did not hold for the period of the experiment: the promotional activity of the six stores differed during the period because of differences in the availability of advertising space in the suburban weekly newspapers and differences in the circulation of these newspapers. Multiplying pages of advertising by circulation in each area, we obtain a proxy measure of advertising exposure for each store as shown in Table 5-4 with the original price and sales data.

We now hypothesize that $Y = \alpha + \beta_1 X_1 + \beta_2 X_2$, and we use a computer to estimate the α and β parameters. The regression equation that "best fits" the data in Table 5-4 is

$$Y = 5.71802 - 5.80262X_1 + 0.000153X_2$$

TABLE 5-4. **Price, Sales, and Advertising Exposure for Six Stores during the Experiment**

Store No.	Sales Y (000)	Price X_1 ($)	Advertising X_2 (proxy units)
1	4.650	0.79	23,000
2	3.020	0.99	18,500
3	2.150	1.25	24,600
4	4.400	0.89	26,200
5	6.380	0.59	25,100
6	5.500	0.45	16,800

and we are provided with the following statistics:

Standard error of estimate: 0.23838
Standard error of the X_1 coefficient: 0.39975
Standard error of the X_2 coefficient: 0.00298
Coefficient of determination (R^2): 0.986

Note that the relative magnitudes of these standard errors indicate that the independent variables are reliable for predictive purposes, according to the rules of thumb mentioned earlier. The coefficient of determination indicates that the two variables, price and advertising exposure, jointly explain 98.6 percent of the variance of Y. Note also that the coefficient to X_1 has changed by the addition of the second explanatory variable, and that the R^2 value has increased, when compared with our earlier bivariate correlation analysis. Thus the omission of a significant determining factor in the earlier analysis led to a misleading coefficient for the price variable and to a subsequently misleading estimate of the price elasticity of demand.

Measurement Errors. The next pitfall to be avoided is the improper measurement of the variables. In the broccoli problem, for example, does the proxy measure of advertising exposure *accurately* depict the determining variable we wish to measure? To the extent that some suburban weeklies may have a superior advertising format or to the extent that the newspaper tends to lie neglected on the porches (or under the Porsches!) of some suburbs, the simple measure of advertising exposure may not accurately depict the influence of advertising efforts on sales.

The price variable is notorious for its problems of measurement. The most readily available measure of price is usually the "list price" or "manufacturer's suggested price," but in many instances this may not accurately depict the actual price paid. Whenever bargaining, discounts, or trade-ins are involved, the actual money changing hands may be somewhat less than the list price. For all variables, if the data used do not accurately measure the level of the variables, the programmer's adage "garbage in, garbage out" is likely to be appropriate.

Simultaneous Equation Relationships. Regression analysis proceeds on the assumption that a single equation explains the entire relationship. One problem with demand estimation arises because the price level is the result of the solution of the simultaneous equations for both demand and supply.

Example: Suppose we have three price/quantity observations that have been collected over a period of time and are as shown in Figure 5-5. They seem to indicate a negative relationship between price and quantity and hence may be thought to trace out the demand curve shown in part (a) and be the result of a shifting supply curve that has moved to the right over time, causing progressively lower intersection points on the demand curve. Alternatively, the three observations may be a result of the scenario depicted in part (b) of the figure. The first price/quantity observation may be the result of the intersection of supply and demand curve S_1 and D_1, while the subsequent price/quantity observations are the result of shifting demand and supply curves as indicated. Regression analysis, however, would conclude that part (a) is the appropriate interpretation of the data, which, if erroneous, would give a misleading view of the slope and placement of the demand function.

The problem arises because there are insufficient data in the regression analysis to identify the shifts of the demand curves, and hence this is often called the *identification problem*. This problem arises particularly with time-series data in demand estimation, since we cannot expect the demand function to remain stable for any extended period of time, because of changing influences such as consumer incomes and prefer-

FIGURE 5-5. The Identification Problem

ence patterns. In this case the problem may be avoided by inclusion of the determining variables which cause the demand curve to shift.

Multicollinearity.   The problem of multicollinearity arises when the independent variables are not independent (of each other) at all. If two or more of the explanatory variables vary together because of their dependence on each other or on another variable, the $\hat{\beta}$ coefficient assigned to each of the variables by the regression solution may have no relationship to the "true" marginal influence of these variables upon the dependent variable. The regression analysis is unable to detect the true relationships and will assign an arbitrary value to the coefficients. Besides reducing the explanatory and predictive power of the regression equation, the presence of multicollinearity is likely to cause the standard error of the coefficient (or t-test) to be an unreliable indicator of the statistical significance of the coefficients.

The presence of multicollinearity may be uncovered by checking the correlation coefficients between pairs of independent variables. Most computer regression programs will generate a correlation matrix. If any two independent variables are found to be highly correlated with each other, one of the two should be excluded from the regression equation, and a new, more reliable estimate of the intercept and slope parameters may then be obtained.[16]

Note: Multicollinearity can be tolerated in the regression equation if the purpose of that equation is simply *predictive*. Recall that we have acknowledged three purposes of models: namely, pedagogical, explanatory, and predictive. The demand function estimated by regression analysis is in effect an explanatory and predictive model—explaining and predicting the value of Q_x in terms of the independent variables. As an explanatory model, it is important that there be no multicollinearity in the data, since we ascribe importance and significance to the individual coefficients in the regression equation. For example, the β coefficient to price is used to calculate price elasticity and to find the slope of the demand curve. Consequently, it is important that this β coefficient be an accurate estimate of the marginal relationship between Q_x and P_x and that it not be distorted by the presence of multicollinearity. However, when the estimate of the demand function is used to *predict* Q_x in a subsequent period, given the values of all the independent variables, we look at the impact of the independent variables as a *group* rather than individually. Thus it does not matter if individual coefficients are inaccurate because of multicollinearity, since it is the total effect on Q_x which interests us. Recall from Chapter 1 that predictive models do not have to be realistic or based on accurate assumptions—the test of a predictive model is how well it predicts. Thus, if the presence of multicollinearity increases the R^2 and makes the regression equation a better predictor, it can be tolerated as long as the equation is used only for predictive purposes, with the independent variables viewed as a group rather than individually.

---

[16]See Levin, *Statistics for Management.* pp. 201–6; or see A. S. Goldberger, *Topics in Regression Analysis* (London: Macmillan, Inc., 1968), pp. 79–83.

Heteroscedasticity.   The regression analysis presumes homoscedasticity of the error terms; that is, it assumes that the residuals or deviations from the line of best fit occur randomly with respect to the magnitude of the independent variables. When the error terms do not occur randomly but exhibit a systematic relationship with the magnitude of one or more of the independent variables, we have the condition of heteroscedasticity. The presence of heteroscedasticity is likely to cause the standard error of the coefficient to give misleading indications and cause the coefficient of determination to overstate the explanatory power of the regression equation.

A simple means to discover the presence of heteroscedasticity is to plot the values of the residuals against the values of the independent variable(s). Many regression programs will produce these graphs for visual inspection: any systematic relationship that appears will indicate the presence of heteroscedasticity. For example, the residuals associated with each of the X observations may become progressively larger (or smaller) as the value of X is larger. This problem may be removed by respecifying the independent variables, by changing the functional form of the relationship, by a transformation of the data, or by using a weighted least-squares regression technique.[17]

Autocorrelation.   Autocorrelation is another problem that arises when the error terms do not conform to the restrictions required for regression analysis. Autocorrelation (also known as serial correlation) can only occur in time-series data and is indicated by a sequential pattern in the error terms. That is, if the size of the error term becomes progressively larger or smaller, or exhibits a cyclical or any other pattern, as the X observations are arrayed in chronological order, this pattern indicates that some other variable is changing systematically and influencing the dependent variable. Autocorrelation may be removed by adding to the regression equation the variable thought to explain the systematic pattern. For example, if the residuals appear to follow a cyclical pattern over time, "dummy" variables might be required to account for seasonal variation. If the cycles are longer, and appear to be related to the state of the economy, a variable to reflect national income, such as GNP, might be added in an attempt to eliminate the autocorrelation. A continuing upward or downward trend in the residuals could be eliminated by adding time as an explanatory variable.

Most regression programs will produce either a sequence plot of the residuals or the Durbin-Watson statistic, which is calculated to indicate the presence or absence of autocorrelation. A Durbin-Watson statistic around the value of 2 indicates the absence of autocorrelation, while values significantly greater or less than 2 indicate that the residuals do not occur randomly and, therefore, that the results are likely to be unreliable.[18]

In summary, regression analysis is an extremely useful tool for estimating the coefficients of the demand function. But precautions must be taken with the use of

---

[17]This takes us into the big league. These rectifications are discussed in advanced statistics texts, such as in N. R. Draper and H. Smith, *Applied Regression Analysis* (New York: John Wiley & Sons, Inc., 1966), pp. 77-81.

[18]See Johnston, *Econometric Methods*, chap. 7.

this tool. Most regression programs will produce the various statistics mentioned above and will plot the residuals such that the experienced researcher can readily discover the presence of one or more of the major problems that may occur. Clearly, the greatest care must be taken in the initial steps of specifying the assumed relationship and collecting the data. Once the regression analysis has been conducted, the researcher must carefully interpret the results before concluding that these results are a sufficient basis for decision-making purposes.

5.4 SUMMARY

Demand estimation is concerned with finding the values of the parameters in the demand function that are currently appropriate. This information is important for current decision making and in evaluating whether decisions are optimal in terms of the current demand situation.

Buyers' reactions to changes in the independent variables in the demand function may be gauged by interviews and surveys, simulated market situations, or direct market experiments. Care must be taken to ensure the selection of a random sample that properly reflects the target market, and the size of each sample should be large enough to allow confidence in the findings. Questionnaire design is critical to the accuracy of the predictions from interviews and surveys. Consumer intentions do not always accurately translate into actions at a later point. Interviewer bias and lack of consumer interest or information may also distort the estimates derived.

Simulated market situations and direct market experiments allow the observation of the consumer during the consumption-decision process, and conclusions may be drawn from the actual behavior of consumers. Care must be taken to isolate impact effects from longer-term effects and to ascertain whether the behavior of people in consumer clinics accurately reflects their usual behavior patterns. Direct marketing techniques provide an ideal opportunity to test the impact of different levels of price or other strategic variables, and regional test markets have proved useful for ascertaining the impact of different strategies at the retail level.

Regression analysis of data collected allows the calculation of the coefficients in the demand function, as well as the calculation of several statistics which indicate the confidence that can be attached to the estimates derived. Regression analysis is a powerful tool, when used correctly, for estimating the parameters of the demand function, on the basis of the statistical association that appears between and among variables in either time-series or cross-section data observations. The pitfalls that may invalidate this technique were outlined in some detail so that the researcher can better set up the problem for analysis and better interpret the results of that analysis.

DISCUSSION QUESTIONS

5-1. Why is it useful to the decision maker to have an estimate of the impact (on the quantity demanded) of variables that are not controllable by the decision maker?

5-2. List the problem areas that one must be cautious about when using interviews and surveys to derive estimates of the market demand function for a particular product.

5-3. List ten questions you would ask a sample of people in order to estimate their demand function for a specific brand of toothpaste.

5-4. Suppose you were to interview a large number of people, asking each person whether he or she would buy a particular product at a series of prices starting from a relatively low price and then raising the price until each person would *not* buy the product. How would you translate this information into an estimated demand curve?

5-5. Design a simulated market situation intended to ascertain customers' responses to changes in prices, packaging, and point-of-purchase promotion for a particular product.

5-6. What factors must be monitored while conducting a direct market experiment in order to allow confidence that the results obtained give reliable information about the demand function?

5-7. Suppose you had data on the annual quantity demanded of newsprint and the price per ton of newsprint over the past twenty years and that you had found the regression equation relating quantity demanded to price. Why would this be an unreliable estimate of the demand curve?

5-8. Explain the importance of the assumptions concerning the residuals, or error terms, to the accuracy of the estimate of the demand function derived using regression analysis.

5-9. Explain how you would satisfy yourself that your analysis did not contain any specification errors.

5-10. Summarize the issues you would need to check before concluding that the results of a regression analysis were a reliable basis for estimating the demand function.

PROBLEMS AND SHORT CASES

5-1. Jose Hermanos Liquors has conducted a simulated market experiment aimed at finding the price that would maximize total revenue from the sale of one item in its product line, namely Hermanos Gold Tequila. Six samples of 100 persons each were assembled at intervals one hour apart and allowed to select bottles of liquor up to a total value of $50 from a simulated liquor store display. The Hermanos tequila was displayed prominently between two major brands of tequila and its price was different for each sample of shoppers. All other prices and promotional variables remained the same over the six tests.

After the six groups of shoppers had finished the experiment, the following results were tabulated:

Group	Price $	Quantity Demanded
1	9.55	17
2	7.85	24
3	8.25	21
4	10.75	10
5	6.45	32
6	6.95	28

(a) Sketch the line of best fit representing the demand curve for Hermanos Tequila for market size of 100 consumers. Estimate the intercept and slope terms of this demand curve.

(b) Generalize this demand curve to the total market in the region, estimated to be 1 million people. What changes does this process cause in your demand curve expression?

(c) What price promises to maximize total revenue for Hermanos Tequila?

(d) What is the value of the price elasticity of demand at that price? Explain what this value indicates.

5-2. The Direct Deal Marketing Company operates a mail and telephone order business, selling products directly to consumers who order DDMC's products after seeing advertisements in magazines or after receiving informational materials and samples through the mail. At the present time, DDMC is considering a mailing to 500,000 subscribers of *Road and Track* magazine, offering custom-fitted sheepskin seat covers to fit most automobiles sold in North America. Before incurring the major expense associated with this large mailing, however, DDMC has conducted a market experiment in order to ascertain consumer responsiveness to price. It has rented four separate lists of names of *Road and Track* subscribers, each list randomly generated by computer from the total subscription list and each containing 2,500 names and addresses. In its mailing to these four subsamples all other promotional and information material was the same, but each sample was offered a different price. After two months DDMC has received orders from each of the subsamples, as shown below, and considers that all orders are in after waiting this long:

Subsample	Price	Pairs Ordered
A	$179.95	51
B	$199.95	38
C	$219.95	26
D	$239.95	14

(a) Estimate the intercept and slope term for DDMC's demand curve for the seat covers, given that the proposed mailing will reach 500,000 subscribers.

(b) What is the price elasticity of demand at each of the four price levels indicated?

(c) Suppose that the marginal cost to fulfill each order is $150 per pair, including postage and handling costs. What price should DDMC establish for the proposed mailing in order to maximize its profits from this particular product?

(d) State all assumptions which underlie your analysis and predictions.

5-3. The Karich Electronics Corporation manufactures stereo equipment and has recently developed a distinctly new-looking stereo receiver. As a result of surveying several thousand people about their perceived quality and expected price level, the marketing department of Karich has estimated the probabilities of sales at several levels for each of five price levels (see table).

Karich Electronics Corporation

Price ($)	Sales (units)	Probability of Sales
	7,500	0.20
	6,000	0.25
100	4,500	0.40
	3,000	0.10
	1,500	0.05
	6,000	0.10
	5,000	0.20
125	4,000	0.45
	2,500	0.20
	1,000	0.05

Price ($)	Sales (units)	Probability of Sales
	4,500	0.10
	4,000	0.20
150	3,000	0.40
	2,000	0.20
	750	0.10
	3,500	0.05
	3,000	0.10
175	2,500	0.50
	1,000	0.20
	500	0.15
	3,000	0.05
	2,500	0.15
200	1,500	0.30
	1,000	0.25
	500	0.25

(a) Calculate the expected value of quantity demanded at each price level.

(b) Use these expected values to estimate the demand curve for the new product.

(c) If the marginal cost of the stereo receivers is $112.50 per unit, regardless of volume, what price would you recommend?

(d) What qualifications would you add to your recommendation?

5-4. Wido Heck, manager of the Red Baron Flying School, is wondering how many instructional hours will be demanded during the coming season. He needs to have an estimate of demand in order to hire instructors. He has just completed a survey by questionnaire among the students and has summarized the results, as shown in the table. He feels that any influx of new students will do no more than balance the attrition of existing students and that their demands for flying time will be similar to those of the students they replace.

Demand for Flying Instruction

Price per Flying Hour ($)	Hours per Day Demanded
10	64
15	53
17	43
20	37
27	29
30	23

(a) Plot prices against quantity demanded and establish an estimate of the demand curve by a freehand smoothing line.

(b) Using regression analysis, calculate and state the demand curve equation and calculate the coefficient of determination.

(c) Using the regression equation calculated above, estimate the flying hours per day demanded at a price of $23/hr. Comment on the probable degree of accuracy of this estimate.

(d) If Mr. Heck is now charging $25/hr. and his marginal cost is constant at $10/hr., should he raise or lower his price? At what price is his profit maximized?

5-5. The Lifestyle Leisure Company produces and sells hot tubs for the southern California market. It has recently been varying the price of its best-selling unit and observing the quantity sold at each price level. Based on these data the following regression equation has been calculated:

$$Q_x = 38,658.235 - 8.667P_x$$

where Q_x is quantity sold and P_x is price per unit. The regression analysis also produced the following statistics: coefficient of determination, 0.723; standard error of estimate, 3,251.625; and standard error of the coefficient, 5.213.

Lifestyle Leisure's marginal cost of producing these hot tubs is constant at $1,500 per unit for all foreseeable output levels.

(a) What is the profit-maximizing price for the hot tubs?

(b) What is the sales-revenue-maximizing price?

(c) Calculate the price elasticity of demand at the profit-maximization price and comment on the value obtained.

(d) At the profit-maximizing price, what is the 95 percent confidence interval for sales?

(e) What other qualifications and assumptions underlie your prediction?

5-6. Ambivalent Autronics has commissioned a study to quantify the determinants of the demand for its cruise-control device. This device is installed in an automobile to allow the vehicle to maintain a constant cruising speed, with subsequent fuel economy advantages.

Based on the data available to it from sources, the Demand Data Research Company has calculated the following regression equation:

$$Q_x = 125,062.85 - 1,862.52P_x + 1,226.94P_s + 524.18A_x + 28,672.74Y + 0.035S$$

where Q_x is quantity demanded of the cruise-control unit per month; P_x is the price per unit set by Ambivalent Autronics (in dollars); P_s is the average price (in dollars) of the three other cruise control units that are considered the closest substitutes for AA's unit; A_x is AA's advertising budget per month (in thousands of dollars); Y is the level of per capita disposable income per month (in thousands of dollars); and S is the level of sales of new automobiles per month. The regression analysis also provided the following statistics:

Coefficient of determination (R^2):	0.8675
Standard error of estimate:	6,432.75
Standard errors of the coefficients:	for P_x, 725.6; for P_s, 482.8; for A_x, 106.2; for Y, 188.1; for S, 0.015.

AA's cost of production of the cruise-control units has stabilized, and it can produce for all foreseeable demand situations at a constant marginal cost of $132.50 per unit. The current values of the independent variables are $P_x = 189.95$; $P_s = 195.00$; $A_x = 12.65$; $Y = 1.53$; and $S = 895.645$.

(a) Calculate the price elasticity, the cross elasticity, and the income elasticity of demand for the product and comment on the values obtained.

(b) Derive expressions for the firm's demand and marginal revenue curves for the product.

(c) Calculate the profit-maximizing price for the cruise-control unit.

(d) At that price, in what range of figures do you expect quantity demanded to fall at the 95 percent confidence level?

(e) What other qualifications underlie your analysis?

5-7. The demand function for product X has been established, using regression analysis, as follows:

$$Q_x = -5,154.605 - 35.83P_x + 82.97P_y + 78.67P_z - 64.03P_w$$

where P_x, P_y, P_z and P_w are the prices of products each identified by the subscript. The current price levels are as follows: $P_x = \$188.50$; $P_y = \$103.75$; $P_z = \$119.25$, and $P_w = \$32.50$.

The regression program also generated the following statistics: $R^2 = 0.92$; $S_e = 80.01$; Standard errors of the coefficients: for P_x, 8.62; for P_y, 33.91; for P_z, 60.82; and for P_w, 35.82.

(a) What price would maximize sales revenue from the sale of product X?

(b) Suppose the marginal cost of producing X is constant at $100 per unit. What price would maximize profits from the sale of product X?

(c) Suppose the price of product Y is raised to $114.95. Does this increase have any impact on the profit-maximizing price for X? Explain.

(d) What qualifications and/or assumptions underlie your analysis?

5-8. The Jumping Jack Flash Company has developed a new lightweight camera with an automatically triggered flash which (naturally) pops up and flashes just as you press the shutter-release button. This product was introduced last year and a follow-up survey has just been completed, giving rise to the following regression equation:

$$Q_x = -190.1366 - 1.0475P_x + 3.9824A_x + 3.6145Y + 1.8794P_s$$
$$(32.11) \qquad (0.18) \qquad (1.25) \qquad (1.92) \qquad (0.63)$$

where Q_x is the quantity demanded in thousands; P_x is the price per unit in dollars; A_x is the advertising budget per month in thousands; Y is per capita disposable income in thousands; and P_s is the price per unit (average) of competing cameras. The figures in parentheses represent the standard errors of the coefficients. The coefficient of determination was 0.922, and the standard error of estimate was 0.3871.

Jumping Jack's cost of production for these cameras has stabilized at $25 per unit and the current price is $48.88. The current values of the other variables are $A_x = 36$, $Y = 15.865$, and $P_s = 46.86$.

(a) Calculate the price elasticity, the income elasticity, and the cross elasticity of demand for JJF's camera, and comment on the values obtained.

(b) Derive expressions for the firm's demand and marginal revenue curves.

(c) Suppose JJF wishes to maximize total revenue—what price should be set for these cameras? At that price, what is the expected sales volume?

(d) What qualifications and assumptions underlie your analysis?

5-9. The demand function for compact Hertz rental cars at Boston's Logan Airport has been estimated, using regression analysis, to be

$$Q_x = 26.0071 + 2.4490P_{cc} + 1.8233P_{sc} - 3.6075P_x$$
$$(8.624) \qquad (0.816) \qquad (0.631) \qquad (1.508)$$

where Q_x represents the number of compact cars rented per day by Hertz; P_{cc} is the average rental price of competitor's compacts; P_{sc} is the rental price of Hertz's subcompacts; P_x is the rental price of Hertz's compacts; and the figures in parentheses are the standard errors of the coefficients. The regression analysis also provided the coefficient of determination, which is 0.8325, and the standard error of estimate, which is 2.5613. The current values of the independent variables are $P_{cc} = 24.50$; $P_{sc} = 21.95$; and $P_x = 24.95$.

(a) What are the cross elasticities of demand between Hertz's compact cars and the other cars, and what do these figures indicate?

(b) Derive an expression for the demand curve for Hertz's compact cars.

(c) What is the sales-revenue-maximizing price (daily rate) for the Hertz compact car?

(d) At that price, what range of sales volumes can be expected at the 95 percent confidence limits?

(e) Outline all the assumptions and qualifications which underlie your sales predictions.

5-10. The demand function for Blitz brand economy beer at a major suburban supermarket has been estimated, using regression analysis, to be

$$Q_x = -109.093 - 2.8985 P_x + 10.044 P_y + 5.126 P_z + 41.665 A_x - 25.631 A_y + 0.0581 M$$
$$\quad\quad (8.62)\quad\quad (0.86)\quad\quad\quad (1.03)\quad\quad (1.58)\quad\quad\quad (15.33)\quad\quad (10.88)\quad\quad (0.12)$$

where Q_x represents the number of cases of Blitz sold per week; P_x is the price per case of Blitz economy beer; P_y is the price per case of Sudds economy beer; P_z is the price per case of the store's generic (no brand) beer; A_x is the advertising expenditure per week (in thousands of dollars) for those weeks when Blitz beer was featured as a special; A_y is the advertising expenditure per week (in thousands of dollars) for those weeks when Sudds beer was featured as a special; and M is the mean weekly take-home income per household for the store's customers (in dollars). The figures in parentheses are the standard errors of the coefficients. The coefficient of determination is 0.85, and the standard error of estimate is 0.75. The data were collected weekly over a six-month period within the store. Mean income of customers was estimated by the average response to the income question on the questionnaire required from those wishing to enter the store's weekly lottery. (The winner is given a refund for the money spent in the store in the preceding week.) The store prepares a weekly advertising supplement to accompany the Sunday newspaper and always features either Blitz or Sudds beer. The generic beer is never advertised.

The current values of the independent variables are $P_x = 7.99$; $P_y = 8.49$; $P_z = 6.49$; $A_x = 1.25$; $A_y = 1.5$; and $M = 350.96$.

(a) Calculate the elasticities of demand for Blitz beer, with respect to the its own price, the prices of the other beers, and consumers' incomes. What do these figures indicate?

(b) Derive an expression for the demand curve for Blitz beer, and express this in the conventional way.

(c) What is the sales-revenue-maximizing price for Blitz beer?

(d) Supposing the store's marginal cost is $2 per case, what is the profit-maximizing price for Blitz beer?

(e) At that price, what range of sales volumes can be expected at the 95 percent confidence limits?

(f) Outline all the assumptions and qualifications which underlie your sales predictions.

SUGGESTED REFERENCES AND FURTHER READING

Baumol, W. J. *Economic Theory and Operations Analysis* (4th ed.), chap. 10. Englewood Cliffs, N.J.: Prentice-Hall, Inc., 1977.

Bennett, S., and J. B. Wilkinson. "Price-Quantity Relationships and Price Elasticity under In-Store Experimentation," *Journal of Business Research*, 2 (January 1974), pp. 27–38.

Draper, N. R., and H. Smith. *Applied Regression Analysis*. New York: John Wiley & Sons, Inc., 1966.

Goldberger, A. S. *Topics in Regression Analysis*. London: Macmillan, Inc., 1968.

Green, P. E., and D. S. Tull. *Research for Marketing Decisions* (3rd ed.), esp. chaps. 3–5. Englewood Cliffs, N.J.: Prentice-Hall, Inc., 1975.

Johnston, J. *Econometric Methods*, chaps. 1, 2, 4, 7, and 8. New York: McGraw-Hill Book Company, 1963.

Kotler, P. *Marketing Management* (3rd ed.), chap. 19. Englewood Cliffs, N.J.: Prentice-Hall, Inc., 1976.

Levin, R. L. *Statistics for Management* (2nd ed.), chaps. 11 and 12. Englewood Cliffs, N.J.: Prentice-Hall, Inc., 1981.

Luck, D. J., H. G. Wales, and D. A. Taylor. *Marketing Research* (4th ed.), esp. chaps. 9, 10, 12, and 14. Englewood Cliffs, N.J.: Prentice-Hall, Inc., 1974.

Pessemier, E. A. "An Experimental Method for Estimating Demand," *Journal of Business*, 33 (October 1960), pp. 373–83.

Stone, B. *Successful Direct Marketing Methods* (2nd ed.), esp. chap. 15. Chicago: Crain Books, 1979.

Appendix 5A: Demand Forecasting

Forecasting the future level of demand is an issue of concern not only to business firms but also to governments, banks, and other institutions. Consequently, there is a considerable amount of forecasting activity at the aggregate, sectoral, and industry levels. Decision makers in firms and institutions have access to the results of much of this forecasting activity and should utilize this material in forming their own forecasts. If the demand for their particular products is closely correlated with GNP or some other measure of aggregate activity, the published forecasts, such as those in the *Business Conditions Digest* issued by the U.S. Department of Commerce, will serve as an inexpensive source of data on future demand levels. On the other hand, the firm's demand may move against the general trend, or it may exhibit lags or leads, and the decision maker must construct a forecast to suit the specific circumstances of the individual firm.

A full discussion of the methods and techniques of demand forecasting constitutes a course in itself and would take us far beyond the space constraints of this appendix. We shall therefore confine ourselves to a brief discussion of the major methods of demand forecasting and refer the reader who requires more detail to the suggested readings listed at the end of this appendix.

We start by extending regression analysis to forecast future values of quantity demanded, given estimates of future values of the determinants of the firm's demand. This is a *causal* forecasting model, since we attempt to model the causes (determinants) of future demand based on our prior observations and explanatory models of demand. Next, we consider time-series analysis and the decomposition of a time series into its trend, seasonal, cyclical, and random components. Future values can then be predicted by projection of the trend and adjustment for the expected seasonal and cyclical effects. Exponential smoothing is considered as a technique to improve predictions of future demand. Finally, we examine several methods of predicting the state of the economy, and, from this prediction (and prior knowledge of a relatively stable relationship between the firm's demand and some aggregate variable), we derive a forecast for the firm's demand.

Regression Analysis as a Forecasting Tool

Regression analysis was utilized in Chapter 5 both as an explanatory model of the determinants of demand and as a predictive model of the quantity demanded, given estimates of the coefficients and known values of the variables that determine quantity demanded. Estimation of the firm's demand function in the present period allowed the regression equation to be used as a predictive model to predict the impact of changes in the firm's price (or any other determining variable) on the quantity demanded of the firm's product. The predictive power of the regression equation is easily applied to future periods as well. If we can generate predicted values for the determining variables in a future period and can be confident that the coefficients estimated in the present period remain reliable in the future period, we can derive a forecast of demand in the future period.

The future-period values of the determining variables may be estimated by a variety of means, each involving information-search activity. The most simple procedure would be to project any trend displayed by each variable into the future period and insert the projected value of each variable in the regression equation. A simple trend projection for each variable may be established by regressing the variable against time and using the line of best fit to provide an estimate of the variable's value in the future period. The regression equation for the variable as a function of time should be checked for its predictive power (the R^2, standard errors, and $S_e/\bar{Y}$ ratio) before using the projected value in the regression equation to forecast demand.

A second method is to establish a probability distribution for the uncertain future value of each variable and insert the expected value of each variable in the regression equation. For such variables as competitor's prices and advertising budgets, which might have been constant throughout the period of the time-series data, the decision maker might estimate the probability distribution relating to possible levels of that variable in the next period. For example, you might estimate that the firm's main competitor may raise its price by 10 percent with probability 0.40, may maintain its price at the same level with probability 0.50, or may reduce its price by 5 percent with probability 0.10; you would then use the expected value of the competitor's future price in the regression equation representing the demand function.

Third, one might use published sources to establish a consensus forecast—that is, one might average the values forecast by several well-known forecasting firms or individuals—for those variables that are widely discussed and predicted, such as the consumer price index (CPI), interest rate, gross national product (GNP), imports and exports, and industrial production. If these variables are significant determinants of your firm's demand, you might use the consensus, or average, prediction of the various "experts" who routinely follow and forecast these variables. Alternatively, their forecasts of these variables may assist in determining your estimate of the variables in your demand function. The forecast value of CPI may be the most likely indicator of movements in competitor's prices in the next period, or forecast values for GNP may be the best information you have about the likely movement in consumer incomes.

Finally, for other variables that are specific to your demand function, marketing research and professional forecasting firms employ high-powered people and techniques to generate their forecasts of these variables, and it may well be cost-effective to utilize their services rather than attempt to duplicate their efforts.

In addition to an explanatory model of the demand function for current-period decision-making purposes, the firm may be able to develop a separate predictive model that has greater predictive power when used to forecast future values of quantity demanded. For predictive purposes only, a regression model may safely fall into some of the pitfalls of regression analysis. Collinear variables, spurious and illogical dependences, and autocorrelation may be permitted to exist if the regression equation is to be used only to forecast future quantity demanded. Essentially, any variable (with any lag applied) may be included in the regression equation as long as it increases the value of the R^2 and consequently reduces the standard error of estimate. This is not to say that the firm's forecasting model should be totally unrealistic; such a situation would carry with it the danger that if the true causes of quantity demanded are not incorporated to a large extent, their values might change and cause the forecast to be substantially wide of the mark.

The multiproduct firm may be more interested in its total sales revenue in a future period, rather than the quantity demanded (and hence sales) of a particular product or product line. A regression model can be constructed to predict the firm's total sales in a future period, using independent variables suggested by consumer behavior theory. For example, the next period's sales should be expected to depend on the next period's general price level and consumer incomes. The CPI is a measure of general prices that is applicable here, and GNP is a broad measure of total consumer incomes. (A better measure is disposable income [DI], which is aggregate personal income after taxes, estimates of which are also readily available.) If the firm's products are often bought on credit, then the cost of borrowing money, or the interest rate

r, is a likely determinant of future sales. Estimates of future interest rates are published regularly in the financial pages. Thus an explanatory (or causal) model to forecast the firm's total sales revenue (TR), might be

$$TR = \alpha + \beta_1 CPI + \beta_2 DI + \beta_3 r \qquad (5A\text{-}1)$$

The constant term α and the β coefficients may be estimated using past data. For example, using data collected for each year since 1975, actual sales revenues would be regressed on the independent variables to establish a regression equation that best fits the data. The R^2 and standard errors also generated will indicate the predictive power of the model. If this is not high enough, then other probable determinants of sales should be entered into the regression equation until an acceptable predictive equation is obtained. Then, using current estimates of the next period's CPI, DI, and r, a predicted value of the next period's total sales may be calculated from the regression equation.

Time-Series Forecasting Models

Time-series forecasting models generate a forecast of future values based entirely on past values of the variable to be predicted. They therefore exclude any changes in the current period or those expected in the next period which the manager may be aware of, since these changes will not yet be reflected in the past data. In this sense, these models are "naive." In terms of complexity they run all the way from simple projections through moving averages, exponential smoothing, and time-series decomposition.

Simple Projections.   The simple trend projection method takes the present period's value of the time-series variable and multiplies it by the trend that has become evident in the past to obtain a forecast of the next period's quantity demanded, or sales, level. That is,

$$\hat{Y}_{t+1} = (1 + b)Y_t \qquad (5A\text{-}2)$$

where the subscripts indicate the period (t is the present period, $t + 1$ is the next period, $t - 1$ would be the preceding period, and so on). The coefficient b is the slope term derived from the regression of past Y values against time. Of course it is unlikely that the value of Y_{t+1} will fall exactly on the trend line, since a multitude of influences may operate to cause the observed value to fall above or below the trend line. Cyclical, seasonal, and random variations about the trend will be discussed below. For longer-term projections, simple extrapolation of trend may be useful, but it is unlikely to be very reliable for short- to medium-term forecasts. For *very* short term forecasts, such as for next month's sales, it may be relatively useful, since the cyclical and seasonal factors may not be expected to change much in the very short term.

✴ **Moving Averages.**   If the time series is subject to unexpected fluctuations, a moving average may generate an acceptable prediction of future period values of the variable. Supposing that sales have fluctuated over the past six periods as shown in Table 5A-1. Taking a four-period moving average of sales in column 4 (equal to the value in column 3 divided by 4) we see that the moving average rises and then falls. We take the moving average for periods t to $t - 3$ (namely, \$7,068,000) as our forecast of sales in period $t + 1$, the next period. Adding this figure into the four-period total (and dropping the $t - 3$ sales figure), we find a new four-period total and a new moving average of \$7,070,000, which becomes our forecast of sales in period $t + 2$. The use of a forecast value of a variable to generate the forecast of the following value of that variable is called "recursive" forecasting.

If a trend exists within the data, the moving average would tend to move up or down over time. Note, however, that the moving-average method weights equally each of the past periods that are included in the moving average. Thus the moving average would systematically underestimate the future values if there is an upward trend, or overstate future values if the trend is downward. A *weighted* moving average, weighting the more recent periods more heavily, would show the trend effect and more accurately predict future values of the variable. One could experiment with the weights assigned to the past periods until one found the combination that minimizes the sum of the squared deviations of the forecast values from the actual values in past periods, and then use these weights to forecast the value of the variable in future periods. However, one would probably be better off using an exponential smoothing model, as we shall see below.

Exponential Smoothing Models.   These models attach exponentially declining weights to the past observations, starting with the largest weight being assigned to the most recent period. A major advantage of these models over weighted-moving-average models is that exponential smoothing models adjust each prior forecast to reflect its

TABLE 5A-1.   Forecasting Using Moving Averages

Period [1]	Sales ($000) [2]	Four-Period Total ($000) [3]	Four-Period Moving Average ($000) [4]
$t - 6$	7,000		
$t - 5$	7,200		
$t - 4$	6,820		
$t - 3$	7,060	28,080	7,020
$t - 2$	7,120	28,200	7,050
$t - 1$	6,872	27,872	6,968
t	7,220	28,272	7,068 (forecast for $t + 1$)
$t + 1$	7,068*	28,280	7,070 (forecast for $t + 2$)
$t + 2$	7,070*		

*Forecast values based on four-period moving average.

forecast error. Thus these models adjust more quickly to changing conditions than do moving-average models. The forecast value of $\hat{Y}_{t+1}$ can be written as

$$\hat{Y}_{t+1} = \hat{Y}_t + a(Y_t - \hat{Y}_t) \qquad (5A-3)$$

This equation says that the forecast for period $t + 1$ is equal to the forecast for period t plus a times the difference between the actual Y_t and the previously forecast $\hat{Y}_t$. Thus the new forecast is adjusted by some proportion a of the error involved in the prior forecast. If a is chosen to be close to 1, a relatively large weight is placed on the most recent observation. Conversely, if a is close to 0, more weight is placed on the previous forecast than on the previous outcome, reflecting the belief that the most recent outcome probably contains a significant random fluctuation. This is seen more easily if we rewrite the above equation as follows:

$$\hat{Y}_{t+1} = aY_t + (1 - a)\hat{Y}_t \qquad (5A-4)$$

Thus the forecast value of $\hat{Y}_{t+1}$ is the sum of the actual outcome in period t (that is, Y_t) weighted by a and the forecast value of $\hat{Y}_t$ (made in period $t - 1$) weighted by the complement of a. The value of a is chosen, after experimentation with past data, to minimize the sum of the squared deviations of the predicted Y values from the actual values. Note that the estimate of $\hat{Y}_t$ must have been

$$\hat{Y}_t = aY_{t-1} + (1 - a)\hat{Y}_{t-1} \qquad (5A-5)$$

and the estimate of $\hat{Y}_{t-1}$ in turn must have been

$$\hat{Y}_{t-1} = aY_{t-2} + (1 - a)\hat{Y}_{t-2} \qquad (5A-6)$$

Thus the forecast value of $\hat{Y}_{t+1}$ can be rewritten, after substituting for $\hat{Y}_t$, $\hat{Y}_{t-1}$, and $\hat{Y}_{t-2}$, as

$$\hat{Y}_{t+1} = aY_t + (1 - a)Y_{t-1} + a(1 - a)^2 Y_{t-2} + a(1 - a)^3 Y_{t-3} + \ldots$$
$$(5A-7)$$

Thus $\hat{Y}_{t+1}$ is a weighted average of the prior levels of Y, where the weights decline exponentially as the prior period goes further back into the past. Since the previous values of Y are all involved in the Y_{t+1} forecast, we may simply use equation (5A-3) or, equivalently, (5A-4) to calculate the new forecast for $\hat{Y}_{t+1}$. A major practical advantage of the exponential smoothing model is that one does not need to keep, or retrieve, data going back a large number of years. One simply modifies last year's forecast by a proportion of its error.

If we were going to start using an exponential smoothing model, we would need to collect the actual Y value data for several years back in order to generate the optimal value for the weight a. Alternatively, we might simply begin with any forecast of

$\hat{Y}_t$, start with $a = 0.5$, and refine the model over the next several periods. Note that the weights decline exponentially, which means quite rapidly. If $a = 0.5$, for example, the weights in equation (5A–7), shown as a, $a(1 - a)$, $a(1 - a)^2$, and so on, are 0.5, 0.25, 0.125, 0.0625, 0.03125, 0.015625, and so on. Placing a greater weight on the most recent outcome means that the influence of past outcomes diminishes even faster.

There are many more complex time-series forecasting models, such as double exponential (and several other) smoothing models, and the Box-Jenkins model, but we have probably gone far enough for our purposes here. Hopefully your appetite is whetted for a course in business and economic forecasting, which would complement this course very nicely. If you cannot wait for that, I refer you to a good forecasting text.[1]

Time-Series Decomposition. A time series may be decomposed into four potential elements, namely, the trend, cyclical, seasonal, and irregular components of the series. The trend is the general rate of increase or decrease of the variable's value as time passes, and it is captured by the line of best fit to the observations when plotted chronologically. The cyclical component is the oscillation around the trend that results from alternating expansions and recessions in general business activity. Seasonal variation in the data, represented by a cycle within each year, is caused by the influence of weather and by events that take place on an annual basis, such as pre-Christmas sales and Thanksgiving weekend. The irregular component is the residual, which is not explained by the other three components. We expect the irregular component to be positive or negative and to depend on random events. Since these components interact with each other to determine the value of the time-series variable, we can specify the model in multiplicative form as follows:

$$Y_t = T_t \cdot C_t \cdot S_t \cdot I_t \qquad (5A–8)$$

where Y_t is the value of the time-series variable in time period t (such as quantity demanded in the fourth quarter of 1986). Essentially, the future value of $\hat{Y}_{t+1}$ is equal to the projected trend value T (calculated using the line of best fit), multiplied by three index numbers representing the cyclical, seasonal, and random variation expected. The cyclical index will be greater than 1 if the variable is above the trend line, less than 1 if below the trend. The seasonal index will be greater than 1 if the current observation is above the quarterly (or monthly) average, and less than 1 if below the quarterly (or monthly) average. The irregular component will have an expected index value of 1 if indeed the residual component is due to random events.

To isolate the components we would first deseasonalize the data. Deseasonalizing requires calculation of a moving average, over four quarters if the observations are quarterly, or over twelve months if the observations are monthly, for example. The

[1]See, for example, Dale G. Bails and Larry C. Peppers, *Business Fluctuations: Forecasting Techniques and Applications* (Englewood Cliffs, N.J.: Prentice-Hall, Inc., 1982).

ratio of the actual observation in a particular period to the moving average centered[2] on that period is the seasonal index number S for that period. Dividing each Y observation ($Y = T \times C \times S \times I$) by the seasonal index number leaves us with the deseasonalized data ($Y/S = T \times C \times I$). The next step is to calculate the trend line of the deseasonalized data by regressing $T \times C \times I$ against the period number in which each data point was observed (1 for the first quarter, 2 for the second quarter, and so on). From the resulting regression equation a series of predicted $T \times C \times I$ values will be generated. The ratio of the observed $T \times C \times I$ value to the predicted value, for each observation, is the cyclical index number C. Dividing each observed $T \times C \times I$ value by its cyclical index number we have $T \times I$, or the trend component multiplied by the irregular index number. Since we are unable to predict the irregular component's direction or magnitude, we expect $I = 1$, and hence we are left with the trend component that is subject to unexpected variations caused by random events. This method of decomposing a time series is shown in more detail in elementary statistics and business forecasting textbooks.[3]

Suppose we have the following regression equation for the firm's (deseasonalized) quantity demanded:

$$Q_t = 12,586.83 + 452.39t$$

---

[2]To *center* a moving average on a period means to locate it opposite the middle period of those periods included in the moving average. For example, a three-period moving average would be centered on the second period and include the previous period and the next period. To center an even-numbered moving average requires an extra step, namely, to average the moving averages. For example, to center a four-period moving average we proceed as follows:

Period	Observation	Four-Period Total	Four-Period Moving Average	Centered Moving Average
1	100			
2	105			
		423	105.75	
3	110			106.25
		427	106.75	
4	108			106.375
		424	106.00	
5	104			
6	102			

Note that the moving average centered on period 3 (106.25) is the average of the first two values in the preceding column, and that the moving average centered on period 4 (106.375) is the average of the last two values in the preceding column. Note also that calculation of a four-period centered moving average involves the "loss" of two periods at each end of the time series.

[3]See Robert R. Johnson and Bernard R. Siskin, *Elementary Statistics for Business,* 2nd ed. (Boston: Duxbury Press, 1985), chap. 18. See also Bails and Peppers, *Business Fluctuations,* esp. chap. 4.

where t is the number of the periods over which the observations were collected. Suppose further that this equation was estimated over twenty periods and we wish to forecast $\hat{Q}_{21}$, the value in the twenty-first period, which is, say, the first quarter of the sixth year. Inserting 21 for t in the equation, we find $\hat{Q}_{21} = 22,087.02$, which is the trend value (subject to irregular variation) expected for quantity demanded in the future period. In other words, this is the $T \times I$ value of Q.

Now suppose that the cyclical index C has been rising over the past several quarters and a reasonable projection of it for the future period is the value 1.035, indicating that demand will be 3.5 percent above trend because of the expansion of the economy during this period. Multiplying the $T \times I$ value of Q by the cyclical index number we find the $T \times C \times I$ value of $\hat{Q}_{21} = 22,860.07$. Finally, assume that the seasonal index number S for the first quarter is given as 0.925 (that is, quantity demanded is typically only 92.5 percent of the four-quarter moving average during the first quarter of the year). Multiplying the $T \times C \times I$ value of Q by $S = 0.925$ we have $\hat{Q}_{21} = 21,145.56$. Thus the firm's forecast quantity demanded ($T \times C \times S \times I$) for the future period is 21,145.56 units. The standard error of estimate associated with the regression equation would be used to establish the confidence interval (caused by the irregular component) in which the actual observation is expected to fall with a particular level of confidence.

Macroeconomic Forecasting

We turn now to the forecasting of macroeconomic aggregates, such as gross national product (GNP) and other measures of national income, the "general" price level, and the level of interest rates. Our interest in these variables is a derived interest: they may provide information that allows the firm to make better forecasts of the demand for its products. National income, or more appropriately, disposable income (national income less net taxes) measures aggregate consumer income, and it may be the best indicator of changes in the income of the firm's clientele.

Indices of the price level, such as the consumer price index (CPI) and the wholesale price index (or producer price index), indicate the general trend of prices of products purchased by consumer and producers, respectively. These price indices, along with the measure of disposable income, may prove useful to the firm considering whether or not to raise its own prices.

Forecasts of "the" interest rate, actually a structure of interest rates based on the treasury bill rate (with more risky securities and longer term loans typically carrying higher risk premiums), may be important determinants of sales for firms in "interest-rate-sensitive" markets. Demand for much of construction, housing, automobiles, and other consumer durables, including furniture and appliances, depends on the prevailing and forecast borrowing rate, since much of this demand is supported by credit.

Readers of the *Wall Street Journal, Business Week, Fortune*, and other business periodicals will already be familiar with the ongoing discussion of the trends in the above macroeconomic variables. For the forecaster, and for managers in general, I believe these periodicals should be mandatory reading. They report on virtually everything of interest to the business decision maker, including the presentation of periodic forecasts of disposable income, prices, and interest rates.

The following discussion is confined to two related issues. First we shall examine the "intention surveys" conducted monthly, quarterly, or semiannually by a variety of government and private sources. Second we examine the use of "barometric indicator forecasting" to track and forecast the general level of economic activity.

Intention Surveys.   Two main intention surveys are conducted periodically: the survey of consumer intentions and the survey of investor intentions.[4] Both are used to judge the level of confidence the consumer or investor feels concerning the desirability of spending for consumption or investment in the future. If consumers are hesitant about continuing their purchases of consumer durables or semidurables in the near or not-too-distant future because of pessimistic expectations about the state of the economy (and indirectly the likelihood of their incomes remaining at high levels), we might forecast an attenuation of the demand for these products in future periods. For many purchases, especially nondurables such as food, the consumer's purchases may be expected to continue at a relatively constant level almost regardless of the level of aggregate economic activity. For durables and semidurables, however, the consumer may postpone such purchases if the immediate outlook is less promising. If consumer expectations take a general turn toward the pessimistic, we would expect demand for such products to fall in the ensuing period.

Investors' intentions are important not only as an indicator of the future level of aggregate economic activity but also for the implications these intentions have for the demand for a variety of products, such as construction materials, office supplies, and plant and equipment. Decision makers interested in the demand for these products must therefore remain aware of such intentions for the implications that these will have on the demand for their own products.

Investors' intentions are similarly highly dependent upon their expectations about the future levels of aggregate activity. Investors will feel more confident about investing if they expect aggregate activity to remain high or to increase from its present level, since this expectation has implications for the degree of idle capacity in future periods. If the investors' expectations are relatively pessimistic, we might expect investment projects to be postponed or canceled, with subsequent impacts upon the level of aggregate economic activity. The ironic feature about both consumers' and investors' expectations is that these expectations tend to become self-fulfilling prophecies.

---

[4]Consumer intentions to purchase homes, automobiles, and a variety of consumer durable goods are surveyed by the Census Bureau, and also by the Survey Research Center at the University of Michigan. Investor's intentions are surveyed quarterly in the *Survey of Current Business* by the U.S. Department of Commerce, as well as by the Securities and Exchange Commission and the National Industrial Conference Board. Purchasing plans of business executives are surveyed monthly by the National Association of Purchasing Agents. Business periodicals report on these surveys on an ongoing basis.

To counter this phenomenon, governments, banks, and business leaders often express great confidence in the future levels of aggregate economic activity at times when all other indications imply the opposite.

The problems with intention surveys as a forecasting device are similar to those that occur when surveys are used to estimate present levels of the demand parameters, except that some of these problems are increased by our asking the consumers or investors to predict their actions far into the future instead of our simply observing their current actions. A continuing survey of intentions does serve, however, as an ongoing "finger on the pulse" of the people who make the demand decisions. Any change in the expectation of these decision makers, and by association a change in expected future demand levels, should become immediately apparent. Thus decision makers have an advance warning of likely changes and can plan their production, inventories, and other matters more effectively.

Barometric Indicators: Leading Indicators and Diffusion Indices.   *A barometer* is a device that predicts changes in one variable (weather) by measuring the change in another variable (air pressure). Since falling air pressure foretells the arrival of relatively inclement weather and rising air pressure indicates that the weather will begin to improve, the barometer is able to predict tomorrow's weather on the basis of today's air pressure. Barometric indicators in forecasting are named for the same ability: Movements in the barometric indicator typically lead movements in the variable that we wish to predict. Thus by observing the level of the barometric time series and its changes we are able to predict changes in the variable of interest, based on the previous association between these two time series.

Leading Series Indicators.   The first type of barometric indicator consists of a single leading series. In this case the firm will attempt to find a particular time series that tends to consistently lead the performance of the demand for its products.[5] By "lead the performance" we mean that the barometric indicator will experience turning points (the changes in direction from growth to contraction or from contraction to growth) in advance of the turning points of demand for a firm's products. In addition, a pattern may emerge between the rate of growth or decline of the barometric series and the rate of change of the demand. Examination of time-series data for various industries and sectors should unearth a time series that tends to act as a leading indicator for the sales of a company's products. We may find, for example, that the shipments of coal and the production of steel vary as indicated in Table 5A-2.

In Table 5A-2 it can be seen that reductions in steel production (the negative percentage changes) tend to precede the reductions in coal shipments by two quarters, just as the increases in steel production tend to precede the increases in coal shipments by two quarters. We can rationalize this as the time period it takes for the steel pro-

---

[5]For an extensive listing of leading, lagging, and coincident indicators, see the *Business Conditions Digest,* a monthly publication of the U.S. Department of Commerce.

TABLE 5A-2. Steel Production as a Leading Indicator for Cost Shipments (hypothetical)

Year	Quarter	Steel Production—% Changes (qtr. to qtr.)	Coal Shipments—% Changes (qtr. to qtr.)
1984	1	2.5	1.6
	2	3.1	3.2
	3	1.8	2.4
	4	−0.2	1.8
1985	1	−1.4	1.2
	2	−1.8	−0.4
	3	0.6	−3.8
	4	2.4	−4.1
1986	1	3.0	1.6
	2	−1.2	3.2
	3	−2.1	3.6
	4	0.8	−2.5

ducers to become aware of the reduction in demand for their product and to organize a reduction in their orders for coal. Producers of coal thus have a six-month warning for turning points in the demand for their product, which should aid their production and inventory planning considerably. In this case, then, steel production acts as a barometric indicator of changes in the level of demand for coal.

Single-series leading indicators are unlikely to *consistently* lead the series they are intended to, and moreover they are unlikely to lead by a consistent *lead period.* A multitude of other factors influence the demand for steel in the above example or the barometric indicator in the general case. It is difficult in practice to find a leading indicator that leads even 90 percent of the time, since random factors intervene to cause the barometric indicator to sometimes indicate continued growth when in fact the dependent time series is already falling, or vice versa.

Composite Leading Indices. To avoid the problem of the unreliability of a single indicator, composite barometric indices have been established. Several leading indicators are aggregated to form an index, with the result that the random movements in any one series tend to be offset by opposite movements in one or more of the other series. The result is that the composite index provides a more reliable indication of actual turning points in the series we are attempting to predict. Table 5A-3 shows the major leading, coincident, and lagging indicators, as identified by the National Bureau of Economic Research and by other sources. The value of the latter two categories for forecasting is their ability to indicate when the peak or trough has in fact passed. Since the coincident indicators are expected to turn at about the same time as GNP or aggregate economic activity and since lagging indicators are expected to turn after the GNP has turned, we may be confident when we observe these series turning that GNP has in fact turned as indicated by the leading indicators, without having to wait for actual measurement of GNP to confirm that there has been a turning point.

TABLE 5A–3.   Selected Leading, Coincident, and Lagging Indicators

Leading Indicators

1. Average workweek, production workers, manufacturing
2. Nonagricultural placements
3. Index of net business formation
4. New orders, durable goods industries
5. Contracts and orders, plant and equipment
6. New-building permits, private-housing units
7. Change in book value, manufacturing and trade inventories
8. Industrial materials prices
9. Stock prices, 500 common stocks
10. Corporate profits after taxes
11. Ratio, price to unit labor cost, manufacturing
12. Change in consumer debt

Roughly Coincident Indicators

1. Employees in nonagricultural establishments
2. Unemployment rate, total (inverted)
3. GNP in constant dollars, expenditure estimate
4. Industrial production
5. Personal income
6. Manufacturing and trade sales
7. Sales of retail stores

Lagging Indicators

1. Unemployment rate (unemployment > 15 weeks, inverted)
2. Business expenditure, new plant and equipment
3. Book value, manufacturing and trade inventories
4. Labor cost per unit of output, manufacturing
5. Commercial and industrial loans outstanding
6. Bank rates on short-term business loans

From Table 2 in J. Shiskin and L. H. Lempert, "Indicator Forecasting," in W. F. Butler, R. A. Kavesh, and R. B. Platt, *Methods and Techniques of Business Forecasting* (Englewood Cliffs, N. J.: Prentice-Hall, Inc., 1974), pp. 48–49.

The Diffusion Index.   A third category of barometric indicators involves the diffusion index, which shows the proportion of the total number of series in a chosen collection that are rising at any point of time. For prediction of GNP, for example, when the diffusion index exceeds 50 percent we expect that GNP will be rising, and when it is less than 50 percent we expect that GNP will be falling. We can construct a diffusion index to predict the sales of any product by using past data to choose the series to be included in the index so that it will best predict turning points of the sales for that product. In Figure 5A–1 we show the relationship between the diffusion index and the variable that we are hoping to predict by the use of the diffusion index. In the ideal situation where the series in the diffusion index are weighted by the exactly appropriate amounts, as the diffusion index rises to 50 percent and above the variable to be predicted reaches its lower turning point and continues to rise. When the diffusion index reaches a maximum the variable to be predicted should exhibit an inflection point, and as the diffusion index drops below 50 percent the variable to be predicted will attain a maximum and thereafter fall. There are likely to be random shocks to the diffusion index such that it will not appear smooth, as in Figure 5A–1. To better judge the direction of change of the diffusion index we may need to use a moving average of the past few weeks or months.

The major limitation of barometric indicators generally is that they predict turning points only and not the magnitudes of the change, so that we must use some other method to find the likely magnitude of the change in the variable to be predicted. Thus barometric indicators, like surveys, are more suited to short-run forecasting, since they require little lead time and indicate turning points rather than the general longer-term direction of sales. Projection techniques, on the other hand, require substantial preparation time in some cases, and in all cases they generate the general trend of the data and may incorrectly predict the immediate direction and magnitude of the change in the variable.

Summary

Demand forecasting is concerned with the future values of the parameters and independent variables of the demand function, and it is clearly vital for decision problems where expected sales in future periods must be forecast.

Regression analysis is an important forecasting tool. A regression equation may be a causal (or explanatory) model of the relationship between the demand for a prod-

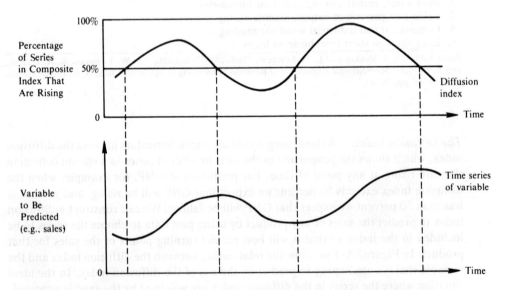

FIGURE 5A–1.   Relationship between a Diffusion Index and a Time Series

uct and its major determinants. Alternatively, the regression equation may be simply a predictive model that best explains the variation in the firm's demand or sales, without necessarily being completely logical and without necessarily avoiding all the pitfalls that may apply to explanatory regression models.

Time-series forecasting models naively project future values of the time-series data based solely on the past values of the data. Moving average forecasts allow the average of the most recent observations to be used as the forecast value of the next period. Weighted moving averages must be used if a trend is apparent in the data, to weight the most recent observations more heavily. Exponential smoothing models weight the more recent observations more heavily and also adjust the forecast for errors in previous forecasts. The time-series decomposition technique decomposes the time series into its trend, cyclical, seasonal, and irregular components. The projected trend value is then adjusted up or down by the use of cyclical and seasonal indices (calculated on the basis of past observations), to arrive at the forecast value for the next period.

Forecasts of macroeconomic variables and surveys of consumer and producer intentions are also useful in helping the firm forecast its future demand situation. The technique of barometric indicator forecasting was examined in some detail. Such forecasts and survey results are published periodically and should be incorporated into, or at least checked for consistency with, the firm's own forecast of its future demand.

DISCUSSION QUESTIONS

5A-1. Distinguish between causal forecasting models and time series forecasting models. How can a complex model be naive?

5A-2. When is a moving average forecast likely to be better than the simple projection of the current period value plus a trend factor?

5A-3. What are the advantages of exponential smoothing models over weighted average forecasting models?

5A-4. Explain how the forecaster would arrive at the weight to be used in an exponential smoothing model.

5A-5. Explain how a time series may be decomposed into its four components and how a forecast value for the next period may be arrived at.

5A-6. What are leading indicators? Name several, and speculate as to why they are leading indicators.

5A-7. Why is the use of a composite leading index usually preferable to a single leading index? What is the advantage of a diffusion index?

5A-8. Outline how you might generate a demand forecast for a particular product group, such as for automobiles.

PROBLEMS AND SHORT CASES

5A-1. The Leiberman Plastics Company wishes to predict sales for its plastic pails for the 1987 year. It has recorded data for its past ten years' demand and has obtained data on the number of households within its market area. This information is listed in the accompanying table.

Leiberman Plastics Company

Year	Sales of Pails (units)	Number of Households (000)
1977	7,000	350
1978	6,750	462
1979	7,150	548
1980	8,300	610
1981	8,000	694
1982	9,200	830
1983	9,050	985
1984	10,100	1,080
1985	10,300	1,210
1986	10,600	1,330

(a) Plot the annual sales data against the number of households in the market area and draw in the "line of best fit" that seems to be visually appropriate.

(b) Measuring the intercept and slope of the above line of best fit, state the approximate functional relationship between the two variables.

(c) Suppose the number of households is projected as increasing by 165,000 in 1987. Use the above functional relationship to forecast the demand for plastic pails during 1987.

(d) Comment upon the probable accuracy of your forecast.

5A-2. The Johnston Raymond Corporation has established a "composite index of demand" which has been relatively accurate in predicting the annual quantity demanded of its cement products. A number of variables are included in the index, such as GNP in current dollars, the index of industrial production, personal disposable income, manufacturing and trade sales, and industrial materials prices. Also included is the average price of JRC's cement products and the prices of substitute products. By trial and error, JRC has adjusted the weights to each of these variables such that composite index has performed very well in predicting sales in the recent past. Historical data for the past twelve years are shown in the following table:

Johnston Raymond Corporation: Historical Data

Year	Sales (units) (Y)	Demand Index (X)
1975	1,950	500
1976	2,570	658
1977	3,140	801
1978	3,280	843
1979	3,360	853
1980	3,570	917
1981	3,750	953
1982	3,980	995
1983	5,800	1,485
1984	6,170	1,567
1985	6,650	1,729
1986	7,130	1,854

(a) Calculate the regression equation showing the relationship between the quantity demanded and the value of the composite index.

(b) How reliable is the composite index as an explanatory variable?

(c) Form a projection of the value of the composite index over the next five years.

(d) Use this projection in the regression equation to forecast the quantity demanded in each of the next five years.

5A-3. A large cosmetics company markets its products directly to customers in eighteen separate campaigns annually. Sales brochures are prepared and printed for each campaign and are sold to the sales representatives, who are paid by commission only. In order to allow time for printing and distribution and to give the sales representatives sufficient time to utilize the brochures while making their normal rounds to clientele, it is necessary to forecast sales of the brochures three campaigns in advance. The quantity of brochures sold to representatives in a particular territory for each campaign during 1984, 1985, and the first six campaigns of 1986 are shown in the accompanying table, along with the scheduled print runs for campaigns 7, 8, and 9.

Actual Brochure Sales

Campaign	1984 (000)	1985 (000)	1986 (000)
1	1,013	865	997
2	923	811	965
3	779	712	877
4	897	712	877
5	819	774	965
6	874	831	1,051
7	879	845	1,091*
8	885	878	1,122*
9	906	840	1,100*
10	869	824	
11	844	800	
12	823	803	
13	834	786	
14	789	847	
15	833	878	
16	986	1,011	
17	1,027	1,090	
18	1,024	1,141	

*Scheduled production based on sales forecasts.

(a) Have you any comments on the levels of the printing runs for the seventh, eighth, and ninth campaigns?

(b) Forecast the sales of brochures for the tenth, eleventh, and twelfth, campaigns of 1986, using trend projection.

5A-4. Halley Appliances has determined that quarterly sales of their household appliances depend on changes in consumers' incomes, the general price level, and the rate of interest. (Halley always sets its prices roughly equal to its major competitors, so these prices do not show up as significant determinants of quantity demanded.) Halley has generated the following regression equation:

$$S = 34,586.29 + 108.97INC - 28.73CPI - 15.43INT$$
$$(681.22) \quad (23.86) \quad (9.71) \quad (11.84)$$

where S is sales revenue per quarter, INC is the number of percentage points by which aggregate disposable income has changed in the prior quarter, CPI is the (percentage points) change in the consumer price index in the prior quarter, and INT is the (percentage points) change in the three-month treasury bill rate in the prior quarter. The coefficient of determination is 0.858, and the standard error of estimate is 1,238.77. The standard errors of the coefficients are shown in parentheses underneath the coefficients in the equation.

The estimates of this quarter's INC, CPI, and INT have just come in, and are 1.85, 0.65, and 1.25, respectively.

(a) Using this equation, forecast sales for the next period.

(b) What is the 95 percent confidence interval for that forecast?

(c) What comments do you have on the predictive power of this regression equation?

(d) What suggestions do you have that might improve the predictive power of the regression forecasting technique used by Halley?

5A-5. The demand for stereo and video equipment repair depends on breakdowns occurring, and thus the demand for Ace Electronic Service (AES) varies unexpectedly from month to month. This variability creates extra costs for AES's owner, since his two repair technicians always seem to be either too busy or not busy enough. Each technician can handle about 1.5 jobs per seven-hour working day (there are, on average, 20 working days per month). With an extra three hours of overtime per day, which costs AES $10 per hour instead of the regular $7, each technician can do two complete jobs per day. Over the past year, AES has employed two technicians on a full-time basis and has used overtime when necessary. The owner of AES would like you to set up a forecast of the number of repair jobs that they might expect in November, based on the past twelve months' data supplied:

Period	Service Calls	Revenue Generated*
November	42	$2,060
December	80	3,840
January	58	3,016
February	24	1,392
March	66	2,904
April	44	2,376
May	72	4,032
June	64	3,200
July	38	2,390
August	53	2,862
September	76	3,572
October	28	1,624

*Revenue generated is net of the actual cost of parts installed, which are charged to the customer at actual cost plus a markup which varies depending on the type of part. This revenue thus contributes toward labor and overhead costs. Overheads, comprising only rent, utilities, and depreciation, average $500 per month.

(a) Construct a three-period moving average of the number of repairs, and use the last one to forecast the number of repairs in November. Comment on this forecast.

(b) Based on the past year's demand, should AES employ any more, or any fewer, full-time repair technicians? Explain and defend your answer.

(c) The productivity of the technicians could be improved if they did not have to continually answer the phone and receive customers. They say they could do three jobs each, in the normal seven-hour workday, if a receptionist were employed. Overtime productivity would also be doubled. A receptionist would raise overhead by $750 per month. Should AES hire one?

(d) Alternatively, new diagnostic equipment would cost $4,000 but would raise the technicians' productivity to 2.5 jobs per day each, or 3.25 including overtime. This equipment will last at least a year. Should AES buy it? (Assume that monthly demand will fluctuate around the average of the past twelve months.)

(e) Finally, consider as an alternative a proposed incentive scheme that would pay each technician $10 for each job completed in addition to wages. This is expected to have the same impact on productivity as the new diagnostic equipment. Should AES implement this plan instead?

5A-6. Hubert Hockey Equipment faces cyclical, seasonal, and irregular variations in the trend for its hockey sticks. It has generated the following regression equation of past quantity demanded (deseasonalized) against time:

$$Q = 12,564.89 + 128.47t$$

where t is the month of the observation. The coefficient of determination for this equation is 0.933, and the standard error of estimate is 886.94. HHE has 72 months of data collected and wishes to forecast next month's ($t = 73$) quantity demanded. The cyclical index for next month, calculated on the basis of published forecasts of disposable income, is 0.956. The seasonal index, on the other hand is 1.122, since this one of the main months of the hockey season.

(a) Derive a forecast of the quantity of hockey sticks likely to be demanded next month, based on this information.

(b) Using the standard error, establish the 95 percent confidence interval around the *trend* value for quantity demanded next period.

(c) Suppose that 90 percent of the standard error is due to cyclical variation and the remainder to random deviations. Now establish a confidence interval around your *forecast* value of Q.

(d) What assumptions and qualifications underlie your forecast?

5A-7. The Four Squares Company has used exponential smoothing as a forecasting technique for several years and has established the optimal "weight" to be 0.85. The company's forecast value for sales last quarter was $1.265 million, and actual sales were $1.385 million.

(a) Derive a forecast of the current quarter's sales using their exponential smoothing model.

(b) Does the size of the optimal weight tell you anything about the pattern of their sales? Can you deduce why they would get better forecasts by using a relatively heavy weight like this, rather than weighting the most recent observation less heavily?

(c) For what type of data pattern would a time-series decomposition model give better forecasts than an exponential smoothing model?

(d) What kind of data pattern would cause a simple moving-average model to give better forecasts than an exponential smoothing model?

SUGGESTED REFERENCES AND FURTHER READING

Bails, D. G., and L. C. Peppers. *Business Fluctuations: Forecasting Techniques and Applications.* Englewood Cliffs, N.J.: Prentice-Hall, Inc., 1982.

Butler, W. F., R. A. Kavesh, and R. B. Platt. *Methods and Techniques of Business Forecasting,* esp. pts. 1, 2, and 4. Englewood Cliffs, N.J.: Prentice-Hall, Inc., 1974.

Chisholm, R. K., and G. R. Whitaker, Jr. *Forecasting Methods.* Homewood, Ill.: Richard D. Irwin, Inc., 1971.

Granger, C. W. J. *Forecasting in Business and Economics.* New York: Academic Press, 1980.

Hanke, J. E., and A. G. Reitsch. *Business Forecasting.* Boston: Allyn and Bacon, 1981.

Johnson, R. R., and B. R. Siskin. *Elementary Statistics for Business,* 2nd ed. Boston: Duxbury Press, 1985.

Nelson, C. R. *Applied Time Series Analysis for Managerial Forecasting.* Oakland, Calif.: Holden-Day, 1973.

U.S. Department of Commerce. *Survey of Current Business and Business Conditions Digest.* Springfield, Va.: National Technical Information Service, current issue.

6 Production Functions and Cost Curves

6.1 INTRODUCTION

■ *Definition:* *Production* can be defined as the transformation of resources into products, or the process whereby inputs are turned into outputs. In this chapter we introduce several new terms and concepts in order to better understand the relationships involved in the production process. We are concerned with the economic efficiency of production—that is, we wish to minimize the cost of producing any particular output level during a given period of time.

The efficiency of the production process depends upon the proportions in which the various inputs are employed, the absolute level of each input, and the productivity of each input at each input level and ratio. Since inputs are generally not free but have a cost attached, the degree of efficiency in production translates into a level of costs per unit of output. Production and costs are thus intimately related. In this chapter the theory of production and costs is presented in a way that both underscores this interrelationship and demonstrates the impact of changing efficiency in production upon the shape and placement of the cost curves. We examine the theory of production and costs in order to lay a sufficient conceptual foundation for the discussion of practical cost concepts and techniques of cost estimation in the two subsequent chapters.[1]

Capital and Labor: The Short-Run versus Long-Run Distinction

■ *Definition:* In production and cost theory the distinction is made between the *short run*, in which the quantities of some inputs are variable while others are in fixed supply, and the *long run*, in which all factors may be varied. Consequently, it is useful to

---

[1]In this chapter we confine our attention to a production process that has a single output. This allows us to demonstrate all the concepts in a relatively simple manner. The technique of linear-programming analysis deals with the problem of choosing the optimal product mix in the multiple-output situation. In Appendix 6B following this chapter we consider linear programming analysis in the context of the optimal input combination (allowing cost minimization) for a particular level of output.

classify the inputs on the basis of whether or not they are variable in the short run. Since labor has traditionally been variable and capital is typically fixed in the short run, these headings are commonly used to denote, respectively, *all* variable and *all* fixed resources.[2] When using the terms *labor* and *capital* in this sense we should think of one unit of labor as including, say, one hour of a worker's time plus a "package" of all the necessary raw materials, fuel, and other variable inputs, and we should think of capital as including all the plant, equipment, land, buildings, managers' salaries, and other expenses that do not vary with the level of output.

Note: It is important to understand that "the long run" does not refer to a long period of time. It is a peculiarity of the economists' jargon that the term has no direct connection with time at all, and that the firm is likely to be in a long-run situation for relatively short periods of time. When intending to change its scale of production, the firm must continue to operate in a short-run situation until its most-fixed factor becomes variable. At this point of time the firm is in a long-run situation, since it can vary the input levels of all factors. As soon as the firm is committed to new levels of plant, buildings, and other fixed facilities, it is back in a short-run situation, since the input of these factors cannot be varied from their chosen level. Notice that the short run could be a few days for some very simple types of firms (such as a street vendor selling flowers from a wheelbarrow) or as much as five years for large manufacturing concerns (such as steel mills or automobile producers). Thus the phrase "in the long run" should be taken to mean "when factors that are currently in fixed supply can be increased or decreased." Since the long run may be either a short or a long time coming, we will use the alternate phrase "the long term" to refer to an extended period of time and reserve "the long run" for its specific connotation in the jargon of economics.

Our simple pedagogical model abstracts from some of the complexities of the real world. In most real production processes there is a *gestation period*, or a time lag, between the conception of the idea to change plant size and the birth of the new plant. This time lag means that the firm must make its long-run decision (choice between available plant sizes) during a short-run period and continue in that short-run situation until the new plant is fabricated and installed, at which time it shifts into the new short-run situation. Also, firms with multiple outputs tend to be continually changing plant size for one or another of their multiple production processes.

Example: Consider the production process for the assembly of an automobile. Which inputs are fixed and which are variable? Remember that the criterion is whether or not the inputs vary in order to cause changes in the output level. Certainly the land and building are fixed inputs and are not varied from day to day in order to

---

[2]Note that with labor unions, labor input is more or less fixed in many production processes. In cases where reductions in the labor supply may be made only through attrition, labor tends to be varied by using overtime work for existing employees rather than hiring and firing extra workers as volume fluctuates. Whenever labor is hired by contract over a period of time, this labor must be classified as a fixed expense in the sense that it is independent of output levels for the duration of the contract.

cause changes in the output level. So too are the assembly lines, the computerized plant and equipment, and the various tools and machines used to assemble the cars. What about the assembly workers themselves? To the extent that management can increase or decrease the input of labor as production needs dictate, assembly labor is a variable input. But if these workers are strongly unionized and threaten to strike if some are laid off, management cannot reduce their input at short notice, and labor, in this case, is fixed, at least in the downward direction. Increases in labor input can usually be effected by paying overtime rates to workers who continue into the next shift or by hiring new workers on a strictly temporary basis. Other inputs, such as component parts, fuel, and power, are certainly fully variable inputs to the production process.

6.2 PRODUCTION IN THE SHORT RUN

The Production Function

- *Definition:* The *production function* is a technical specification of the relationship that exists between the inputs and the outputs in the production process. In general form it says simply that output is dependent upon the inputs in an unspecified way. That is, quantity produced is a function of the inputs of capital and labor, as follows:

$$Q = f(K, L) \qquad (6-1)$$

where Q is the quantity of output; f represents the functional relationship existing between the inputs and the output; and K and L are the conventional symbols representing the input levels of capital and labor, respectively.

In specific form the functional relationship is stated explicitly, and the functional form of the equation is the one that best expresses the actual relationship between the inputs and the output. Output may be expressed, for example, as a linear additive function of the inputs or alternatively as a multiplicative power function of the inputs. The exact mathematical specification of the production function depends upon the productivity of the input factors at various levels of all inputs.

The State of Technology. The productivity of the factors of production depends on the state of technology. Labor can be more productive if it works with modern mechanical and computer-assisted equipment. Similarly, the plant or equipment can be more productive if it is being operated by highly skilled and well-trained workers. Thus the *state of technology* refers to the inherent ability of factors of production to produce output, given the simultaneous efforts of all other inputs to the production process. For example, three units of labor and two units of capital may combine to produce fourteen units of output. If technology improves, that is, if either or both labor and capital become more productive, the same combination of labor and capital may then be able to produce, say, eighteen units of output. Thus the state of technology is incorporated into the specification of the production function and is reflected by the precise mathematical form taken by any particular production function.[3]

Given the specific form of the production function, we can insert values for labor and capital and find for every combination of labor and capital the output that would result. A tabular array of the output levels associated with various input levels of all factors for the hypothetical case of automobile assembly by a small company that produces sports cars is shown in Table 6-1. The numbers in the body of the table show how many vehicles can be assembled by each combination of capital and labor. For example, when capital is set equal to 2 units (2,000 machine hours) and 5 units of labor (500 labor hours) are added to this capital, the number of assembled vehicles produced will be 23.

Note that there is another combination of capital and labor that will also produce 23 assembled vehicles, namely, $K = 4$ and $L = 2$. This combination is clearly a more capital-intensive production process, apparently involving more automated techniques, such as robot welders and other mechanical and computer-assisted processes, and fewer units of labor per unit of output. This example demonstrates the *substitutability* of capital and labor in the production process. The same output level can usually be attained by several different combinations of capital and labor. This substitutability is also evident for the production of 8 assembled vehicles: these may be produced either by setting $K = 3$ with $L = 1$ or by setting $K = 2$ with $L = 2$. In fact there are other combinations of capital and labor that will also produce 8 vehicles. Note that $K = 1$ with a labor input somewhere between 3 and 4 (say, $L = 3.4$) could also produce 8 vehicles. So too could $L = 3$ with capital input somewhere between 1 and 2 units (say, $K = 1.15$). The same could be found for any other output level.

TABLE 6-1.   Motor Vehicle Assembly Production Function

		LABOR UNITS (hundreds of person-hours) (L)							
		1	2	3	4	5	6	7	8
Capital	1	1	3	7	10	12	13	13½	13
Units	2	3	8	14	19	23	26	28	29
(machine-	3	8	18	29	41	52	62	71	79
hours, 000)	4	11	23	36	50	65	78	90	101
(K)	5	12	26	42	60	80	98	112	124

---

[3]A linear production function can be expressed as $Q = \alpha + \beta_1 K + \beta_2 L$, where the α and β parameters are estimated from observed input and output data using regression analysis. A power function such as $Q = AK^{\alpha}L^{\beta}$ enables us to compute the multiplicative effect of capital and labor, if it exists. Regression analysis using logarithmic transformation of the observed data can be used to estimate the parameters A, α, and β. This power function is often referred to as the Cobb-Douglas production function, named after the writers who developed this concept. See C. W. Cobb and P. H. Douglas, "A Theory of Production," *American Economic Review*, 16 (1928), pp. 139–65. Also Paul H. Douglas, "Are There Laws of Production?" *American Economic Review*, 38 (March 1948), pp. 1–41.

Thus there are typically a variety of input combinations, ranging from the relatively labor intensive to the highly capital intensive, which can be utilized to produce any given output level. In Appendix 6A, following this chapter, we introduce isoquant-isocost analysis to demonstrate that the input combination chosen by the firm depends upon the relative cost of the capital and labor inputs. Suffice it to say here that when the cost of labor is cheaper, relative to the cost of capital, firms will choose more labor-intensive production methods. Conversely, when the cost of labor is high relative to the cost of capital, firms will choose more capital-intensive production methods.

Note: Table 6-1 depicts both the short run and the long run. In the short run the level of capital input would be fixed at a particular level, and output is constrained to that shown in the *row* opposite that level of capital. In the long run, that is, when all input quantities are variable, any point in the table may be achieved. Thus if only 3,000 machine-hours were available, output levels would vary as shown along the third row of Table 6-1 as we added or subtracted labor. Given the opportunity to change its plant size, the firm could move to any other row of the table to which it would be constrained for the duration of the following short-run period.

The Law of Diminishing Returns

■ *Definition:* The *law of diminishing returns* states that as additional units of the variable factor are added to the fixed factors in the short run, after some point the increment to total product will decline progressively.

The law of diminishing returns is concerned with the relative productivity of the marginal units of the variable factors as we progressively add units of the variable factors to the fixed inputs. Prior to the point where diminishing returns set in, there may be *increasing* returns to the variable factors followed by *constant* returns to the variable factors. The law of diminishing returns can be stated more broadly as the "law of variable proportions," which states that as more and more of the variable factors are added to a given quantity of the fixed factors, the increment to output attributable to each of the additional units of the variable factor will increase at first, will later decrease, and will eventually become negative.

Notice that this phenomenon relates to the short run, since fixed inputs are involved, and can be witnessed in any row of Table 6-1, where the differences between the adjacent numbers increase at first and later decrease as more labor is added to a particular level of capital. In Table 6-2 we show the increments to output as we move along the third row of the production function exhibited in Table 6-1. Notice that increasing returns prevail up to and including the fourth unit of labor when applied to three units of capital, after which point diminishing returns to the variable factor prevail.

**TABLE 6-2.   The Law of Variable Proportions Exhibited
by the Marginal Product of the Variable Factors**

Units of the Variable Factor (L)	Units of Output (for $K = 3$) (Total Product)	Increment to Output over Preceding Row (Marginal Product)	Returns to the Variable Factor (for $K = 3$)
0	0	—	—
1	8	8	Increasing
2	18	10	Increasing
3	29	11	Increasing
4	41	12	Increasing
5	52	11	Diminishing
6	62	10	Diminishing
7	71	9	Diminishing
8	79	8	Diminishing

Total Product and Marginal Product Curves

The total output from a production process is also known as the *total product* of the inputs to that production process. Thus the second column in Table 6-2 shows the total product for several levels of labor input (given capital input fixed at 3 units). In Figure 6-1 we plot the total product data on the vertical axis against the number of units of labor input on the horizontal axis. Note that for higher input levels (beyond that shown in Table 6-2) total product reaches a maximum and actually falls as still more labor input is added to the fixed capital inputs. This indicates that the ratio of variable to fixed inputs is "too high," causing congestion of the workplace which results in total output falling despite the additional units of the variable inputs.

Note that the law of variable proportions is evident from the shape of the TP curve shown in Figure 6-1. It is convex from below at first, showing output increasing at an increasing rate as labor units are added. After the point of inflection the curve is concave from below, reflecting diminishing returns to the variable factor. Note that we are talking about the rate of change of total product as the variable factor input is changed. This change in total product, as the result of a one-unit change in the variable input, or the rate of change of total production in relation to that of labor, is defined as the "marginal product of labor." In Figure 6-1 we show the total product curve along with the marginal product curve which can be derived from the total product curve.

■ *Definition: Marginal product* is defined as the rate of change of total product as labor is increased, and it is equal in mathematical terms to the first derivative of the total product function with respect to labor. This is the same as saying that marginal product is given by the *slope* of the total product curve at every level of labor input. Note that at the point of inflection, where the total product curve changes from being concave upward to concave downward, the total product curve is at its steepest, and

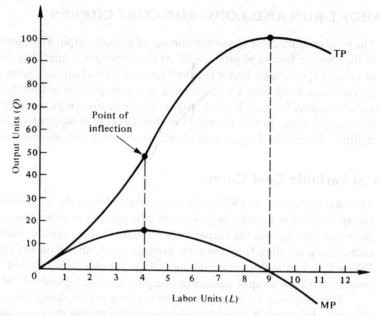

FIGURE 6-1.   The Total Product and Marginal Product Curves

marginal product attains its maximum value. Similarly, at the input level where total product reaches its maximum and later falls, marginal product falls to zero and becomes negative. The law of variable proportions can thus be expressed in terms of the behavior of the marginal product of the variable factor: there are increasing returns to the marginal unit of the variable factor while marginal product is rising, and there are decreasing returns thereafter as the marginal product falls.

   The law of variable proportions is an "empirical" law, which is to say it has frequently been observed in actual production situations. This empirical law is not a judicial law, however, and hence there is no compulsion for every production function to exhibit the pattern described above. The range of increasing returns to the variable factors may be quite brief or indeed absent in many production processes. The point of inflection may be extended to exhibit a prolonged range of constant returns to the variable factor. Decreasing returns to the variable factor are a necessary feature of all short-run production situations, however. Sooner or later, as units of the variable factor are added to the fixed supply of capital resources, the marginal product of the variable factor must begin to decrease, because of simple overcrowding if for no other reason. Hence, this law is more commonly referred to as the law of diminishing returns. But note that the law of diminishing returns refers only to the section of the total product curve that is concave from below, after the point of inflection, or to the negatively sloped portion of the marginal product curve.

6.3   SHORT-RUN AND LONG-RUN COST CURVES

The total product curve shows the number of units of output associated with each level of the variable factors of production. At the same time it implicitly shows the number of units of the variable factor required for each level of output. Since each unit of the variable factor will have a cost attached, it is a simple step to find the total cost of the variable inputs for each level of output, otherwise known as the *total variable cost* of each output level. To find the total variable cost of each output level, we would simply multiply the required input level of the variable factor by its cost per unit.

The Total Variable Cost Curve

The total variable cost (TVC) curve can be derived from the TP curve simply by multiplying the level of variable inputs by the cost per unit of those inputs and by plotting these cost data against the output level. Suppose that the variable factor units cost $10 each. Using the data from the total product curve, shown on the right-hand side of Figure 6-2, and multiplying each unit of the variable factor by $10, we can plot the cost of the variable input against the output, in the left-hand side of Figure 6-2.

For simplicity we have chosen the scale on the left-hand side of the horizontal axis to be ten times that on the right-hand side, so that the curve which reflects the total cost of the variable factors for all levels of output is a mirror image of the total product curve. Note that three units of the variable factors, or $30 spent on the variable factors (which amounts to the same thing), will produce Q_1 units of output. Similarly, five units, or $50 spent on the variable factors, will produce Q_2 units of output. Thus the shape of the total variable cost curve derives directly from the form of the

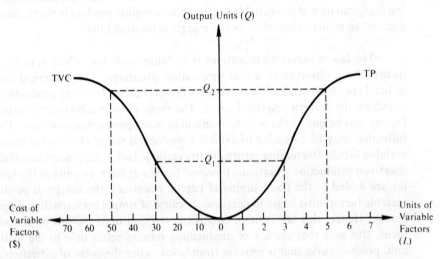

FIGURE 6-2.   Relationship between the Total Product and Total Variable Cost Curves

production function and the number of units of capital employed, since these factors underlie the shape of the total product curve.

Average Variable and Marginal Costs

■ *Definition:* *Average variable cost* is equal to TVC divided by output Q at every level of Q. That is,

$$\text{AVC} = \frac{\text{TVC}}{Q}$$

(6-2)

In Figure 6-3 we show the TVC curve tipped on its side—rotated 90° to the right— with the associated average variable and marginal cost curves. The AVC for each output level is equal to the ratio of the *vertical distance* from the quantity axis to the TVC curve to the *horizontal distance* from the cost axis to the TVC curve. In terms of the graph, this amounts to the vertical rise over the horizontal run, or to the slope of a ray from the origin that joins the point on the TVC curve. Average variable cost at point A on the TVC curve is equal to the ratio AR/OR, or the value of the slope of the line $0A$, and is shown as point A' on the AVC vertically below.

It can be verified that the slopes of lines between the origin and points on the curve become progressively flatter as we begin to move up the TVC curve away from the origin. Thus the AVC, which is equal to the value of these slopes, must fall over this range. A point is reached, however, where the ray from the origin can become no flatter and still touch the TVC curve. Point C, where the ray is just tangent to the TVC curve in Figure 6-3, signifies the lowest value for AVC. Since the rays become steeper for points on the TVC to the right of the tangency point, AVC must rise after this output level, as shown in the figure.

■ *Definition:* *Marginal cost* is the change in total costs caused by a one-unit change in output:

$$\text{MC} = \frac{\Delta TC}{\Delta Q}$$

(6-3)

where $\Delta Q = 1$. Since output changes cause only variable costs to change, we can equivalently define marginal costs as the change in total variable costs for a one-unit change in output. Hence,

$$\text{MC} = \frac{\Delta TVC}{\Delta Q}$$

(6-4)

where $\Delta Q = 1$. In this form you see that marginal cost is defined as the vertical rise over the horizontal run represented by a movement along the TVC curve that results

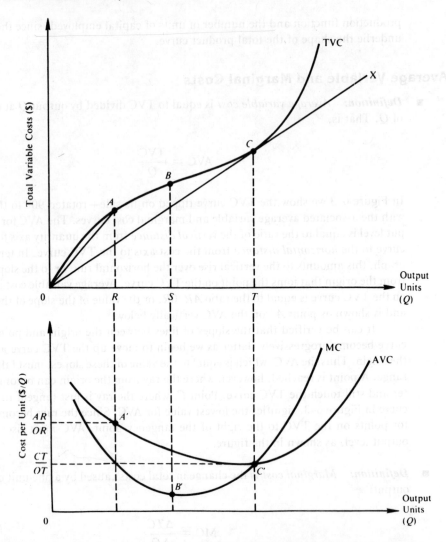

FIGURE 6-3.   Derivation of Average Variable and Marginal Cost Curves from Total Variable Cost Curve

from a one-unit change in output. MC is thus equal to the slope of the TVC curve at each output level.

If we were to put tangents against the TVC curve at every output level, we would see that the slopes of these tangents would fall at first, up to the point of inflection on the TVC curve, and would then rise. In Figure 6-3 the point of inflection occurs at point *B*, where the TVC curve changes from convexity from above to concavity from above. The slope of the TVC becomes progressively flatter until point *B*, and it becomes progressively steeper after point *B* as output is increased. This indicates that the marginal cost curve is U-shaped, falling to a minimum at the output level where the TVC exhibits its inflection point and rising thereafter.

Note: It is important to note that when the marginal cost curve lies below the average variable cost curve, the latter is falling. In effect, the lower marginal cost is pulling down the average. Conversely, when the MC curve lies above the AVC curve, the latter must be rising, being pulled up by the marginal costs. It follows that when the MC crosses the AVC, the AVC must be at its minimum value. This can be verified in Figure 6-3 at point *C* on the TVC curve. Marginal costs and average variable costs must be equal, since both are given by the slope of the tangent to the TVC curve at that point.

Marginal costs are the value counterpart of the marginal product of the variable factors. When marginal productivity of labor is falling, marginal cost of output is rising, and *vice versa*. If the efficiency of the marginal units of the variable factor is constant, output can be produced at a constant level of marginal cost.

These relationships can be confirmed by another look at Figure 6-2. Notice that when the TP curve is concave from above, exhibiting increasing marginal productivity of the variable factor(s), the TVC curve is indicating decreasing marginal costs per unit of output. Alternatively, when diminishing returns set in for the variable factor(s) after the inflection point, the TVC curve begins to increase at an increasing rate, and marginal costs are increasing over this range.

Short-Run Average Costs

■ *Definition:* *Short-run average costs* (SAC) are defined as total costs (TC) per unit of output.

$$SAC = \frac{TC}{Q}$$

$$(6-5)$$

Total costs are the sum of TVC and total fixed costs (TFC). To complete the short-run cost picture, therefore, we need to add the costs of the fixed factors. TFC is a horizontal line when plotted against output, as shown in Figure 6-4, since these costs are constant whatever the level of output. To find the total of fixed and variable costs, we add vertically the TFC and TVC curves on the graph. This procedure, in effect, causes the TVC curve to be moved upward a constant distance equal to the total fixed costs. Thus the total cost (TC) curve and the TVC curve have the same shape, as is evident in Figure 6-4. As noted previously, the marginal cost curve can thus be derived from the TC curve instead of the TVC curve.

Average total costs, or short-run average costs (SAC), may be derived from the TC curve by the same technique as was used to derive the AVC curve. The slope of a ray from the origin to a point on the TC curve gives the value of SAC for each output level. Thus at point *B* in the upper part of Figure 6-4, SAC is equal to the ratio *BF/0F*,

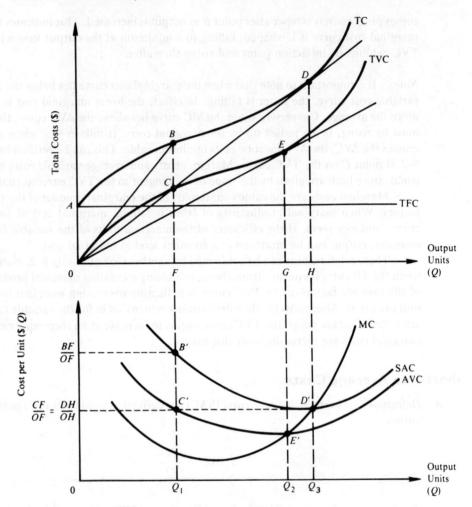

FIGURE 6-4.   Derivation of Short-Run Average Cost Curve

or the slope of the line $0B$. At the same output level, $AVC = CF/0F$, or the slope of the line $0C$. In the lower part of the figure these values are shown as points B' and C', respectively. Given the shape of the TC curve, SAC must fall at first, reach a minimum, and then rise. Note that at the minimum point, found where the ray from the origin is just tangent to the TC curve, the slope of the ray is equal to that of the TC curve, and hence SAC and MC are equal at that output level.[4]

---

[4]An alternative method of deriving the SAC curve is to find the average *fixed* cost (AFC) curve and add that to the AVC curve. The AFC curve must slope downward to the right as output is increased. Since TFC is constant, AFC will decline progressively as output increases, since the fixed costs are spread over progressively more units of output. Note that the SAC curve and the AVC curve converge on each other as output increases, as they differ by a decreasing margin—namely, the declining value of AFC.

Different Production Functions Cause Different Cost Curves

The total product curve is not necessarily a cubic function of the inputs of the variable factors, as indicated by the S-shaped curves in Figures 6-1 and 6-2. The shape of the TP curve is an empirical question—for some plants it may be cubic, for others quadratic or a power function, and it may even be sufficiently approximated by a linear function (over the relevant range) in other plants. Estimation procedures (to be considered in Chapter 8) will ascertain the shape of the TP curve in any particular production process. The cubic function we have been using is the most general case, since it allows for the entire range of returns to the variable factors: it shows increasing returns at first, then constant returns momentarily at the point of inflection, and finally diminishing returns after the point of inflection.

In some production processes we may expect diminishing returns to set in immediately—that is, for marginal product to decline from the outset. This may be true of very small plants which allow the variable inputs to be most efficient at low output levels. In Figure 6-5 we demonstrate that diminishing returns from the outset imply a quadratic TP curve (or other curve which increases at a decreasing rate, such as a power function). The TVC will take its shape from the TP curve and the resulting AVC and MC curves must be upward sloping throughout. Note that the SAC curve falls at

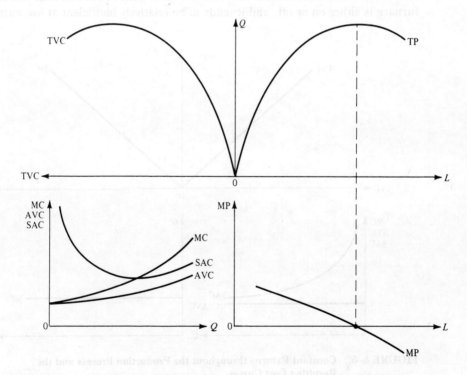

FIGURE 6-5. Diminishing Returns throughout the Production Process and the Resulting Cost Curves

first because of the influence of falling average fixed costs, but rises later as the rising AVC outweighs the falling average fixed costs.

Finally, there are cases in which it can be argued that constant returns to the variable factors prevail throughout, or at least over an extended range of output levels. This may occur in a production process in which the variable inputs interact primarily with each other and there is minimal impact with the fixed inputs. For example, the marginal product of the variable inputs in a basket-weaving production process may be constant over a wide range of outputs, since the variable inputs (labor and the straw) interact with each other virtually independently of the fixed factors (which pro-vide shelter, marketing support, and so on). In Figure 6-6 we show a linear TP and MP curve and the resulting linear TVC curve. The cost-per-unit curves which are asso-ciated with the linear TVC curve are shown in the lower left-hand part of Figure 6-6. Note that MC is constant from the outset and is, therefore, coextensive with the AVC curve. And note further that SAC falls to converge on AVC because of the influence of the falling average fixed costs.

Linear TVC Curves Resulting from Plant Divisibility

In many production processes the plant, or fixed factors, are indivisible in the sense that the firm must utilize all of the fixed factors or none at all. In a steel mill the blast furnace is either on or off, and it tends to be relatively inefficient at low output vol-

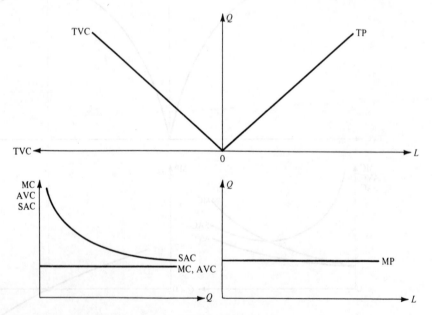

FIGURE 6-6.   Constant Returns throughout the Production Process and the Resulting Cost Curves

umes. Similarly, the assembly line in an automobile plant is either moving or not moving. The TVC curve associated with such plants might reasonably be expected to be a cubic function of the variable inputs, reflecting falling marginal costs at first and rising marginal costs later.

In other production processes, however, the plant, or some parts of it at least, are divisible in the sense that the variable inputs are not obliged to work with the entire plant but may instead work with a more efficient subset of the plant. In these cases the firm may be able to avoid situations in which "too few" units of the variable factors are working with "too much" capital and may instead be able to maintain the capital-labor ratio at the most efficient level over a considerable range of output levels.

Example: Consider the situation of a firm that manufactures stuffed satin toys. Its variable inputs are labor (cutting-machine and sewing-machine operators), satin material, filler, cotton thread, and electrical energy to power the machines. Its fixed inputs, or plant, include four cutting machines, eight sewing machines, the building, fixtures, all related overhead costs, and the inputs of the managers, administrators, secretaries, clerks, and so on. Some part of the plant is divisible—namely, the cutting and sewing machines. At low levels of output, that is, low levels of the variable inputs, it is clear that some cutting and sewing machines would not be used at all. As demand for the product grows, the firm would hire more labor, order more materials, and expand output by starting up its idle machines.

In terms of Figure 6-7, suppose that L_1, L_2, L_3, and L_4 represent the first four "units" of the variable factors. For example, L_1 might represent 1 cutting-machine operator, 2 sewing-machine operators, 30 yards of satin cloth, 50 pounds of filler, 100 yards of cotton thread, and the electrical energy to run one cutting machine and two sewing machines. These variable inputs, if applied to all four cutting machines and eight sewing machines, might produce only Q' units of output on the curvilinear total product curve shown as TP. Doubling the inputs of the variable factors to L_2 would

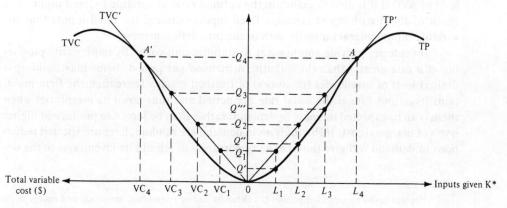

FIGURE 6-7. Linear TP and TVC Curves Due to Divisibility of Plant

increase output to Q''; tripling inputs to L_3 would produce Q'''; and quadrupling inputs to L_4 is the level of variable inputs that maximizes the average product of the variable inputs (Q_4/L_4). The average product of the variable inputs is given by the slope of the ray from the origin to a point on the total product curve and is maximized at the point where this ray is tangent to the curvilinear TP curve. From the total variable cost (TVC) curve on the left-hand side of the figure, we see that average variable cost (AVC) is also minimized at the output level Q_4 and the underlying input level L_4.

Note that at input level L_4 there are four cutting-machine operators operating four cutting machines and eight sewing-machine operators operating eight sewing machines. (The most efficient ratio of operators to machines is assumed to be one to one for both the cutting and the sewing machines.)

Now, suppose output had to be reduced because of a drop in demand. The firm would reduce its variable inputs back to L_3 units, but instead of asking the remaining workers to operate *all* the machines, it would close down one cutting machine and two sewing machines, maintaining the most efficient ratio of operators to machines. Thus output would fall only to Q_3 rather than to Q'''. Thus AVC stays at the minimum level. Similarly, if variable inputs were reduced to L_2 units, the firm could maintain AVC at its minimum level by shutting down another cutting machine and two more sewing machines.

Thus, if the firm can divide its fixed factors into units which may or may not be operated depending on the demand for its product, it may be able to maintain the most efficient ratio of its variable factors to those divisible fixed factors, such that it regards the straight lines TP' and TVC' as its total product and total variable cost curves, respectively. In this case the firm's marginal and average variable costs will not be U-shaped but will be linear, for output levels up to Q_4,[5] as shown in Figure 6–6.

Other Ways to Stabilize Costs per Unit. Stable marginal and average variable costs are highly desirable, since they facilitate the firm's pricing decisions and its profit planning. We have just seen that the firm may keep AVC equal to MC at the minimum level of AVC if it is able to maintain the optimal ratio of variable to fixed inputs as a result of the divisibility of strategic fixed inputs (namely, the fixed inputs that the variable inputs interact directly with in the production process).

Inventories provide another way to stabilize unit costs. By temporarily producing at a rate greater than the quantity demanded per period, firms may build up a desired level of inventories (or stocks) of finished goods. Thereafter, the firm maintains its output rate at the usual rate per period and runs down its inventories when there is an unexpected increase in demand, rather than be forced to produce at higher levels of marginal cost. If fluctuations in demand are random, later unexpected reductions in demand will give the firm an opportunity to rebuild its inventories to the de-

---

[5]Output could be increased beyond Q_4, either by adding more labor, materials, and energy to the existing plant (in which case, AVC would rise) or by also adding more cutting and sewing machines, in which case AFC (and SAC) would shift upward. The latter option implies a long-run plant size adjustment.

sired levels. Thus, when demand is uncertain, a firm may choose to produce the expected value of quantity demanded in each period, adding to inventories when demand falls short of expectations and selling from inventories when demand exceeds expectations. Its desired inventories should be such that the marginal cost of holding an item in inventory does not exceed the additional production cost avoided by not producing the item on demand.[6]

Another way to avoid rates of output that involve higher marginal and average variable costs is to have the firm "contract out" for additional production rather than produce this output itself. If producing the output would cause the firm's MC values to rise steeply, the firm may be able to purchase the items at lower cost from another firm that has excess capacity and can produce the same product at a similar quality level. Initial setup costs may be involved, if the subcontractor has to imprint the firm's logo or follow the firm's special design, for example. But if the sum of these costs, plus the subcontractor's price per unit times the number of units, is less than the additional cost to the firm of producing those units itself, the firm should contract out rather than produce the additional units. We consider this "make or buy" decision in more detail in Chapter 7.

Finally, unit costs can be kept constant by maintaining output rates and putting customers on a "backlist," or "waiting line," when demand exceeds the firm's capacity to supply. That is, customers are asked to wait for delivery until the firm can catch up with orders during periods when demand is abnormally or unexpectedly high. This approach may only be feasible if the firm's products are unique or customized, or if the delay causes the customer no problems, or if all rival suppliers are similarly operating with a backlist or waiting line. It may pay the firm to offer a discount for delayed delivery rather than incur the additional cost of producing the item on demand. This discount would encourage advance orders, which would help the firm in its production planning. If customers will wait for varying lengths of time, "queuing theory" may be utilized to calculate the optimal length of the queue, or waiting line. Queuing theory balances the sales lost because some customers will not wait at all (or not any longer than a certain time) against the cost of additional facilities that would allow the queue to be shortened.[7]

The Short-Run Supply Decision

In the short run the firm must incur its fixed costs, since it cannot, by definition, change the input of these factors of production. The firm's variable costs, on the other hand, are *discretionary*, in the sense that the firm may decide whether or not to incur

---

[6]Inventory control theory is beyond the scope of this text. Suffice it to say that it is only worth holding an item in inventory if the cost of holding that item does not exceed the difference between the marginal cost of producing an item at the time it is demanded and the marginal cost of producing it in advance.

[7]Queuing theory is also beyond the scope of this text and may be encountered in production management or optimal control theory texts.

these costs, since the input of variable factors can be varied all the way back to zero. What induces a firm to incur costs? We argued briefly in Chapter 1 that the firm is profit-oriented and incurs costs when it expects to more than cover those costs with revenues. Thus a firm will set up a plant and incur fixed and variable costs to produce a particular product because it expects to more than cover these fixed and variable costs with revenues and thereby make a profit.

Once committed to its present size of plant, however, the firm is obliged to incur the fixed costs of that plant in the short run. Variable costs, on the other hand, will be incurred only if the firm expects revenues to exceed these variable costs. Suppose price exceeds average variable cost but is less than the average total cost, meaning that the firm makes a loss. If the firm ceases production, it incurs no variable costs, earns no revenues, and therefore makes a loss equal to its fixed costs, which must be paid whether or not the firm produces anything. If the firm continues production when P is greater than AVC but is less than SAC, there is, for each unit sold, some excess of revenue over variable costs that contributes toward the fixed costs. Therefore, the firm reduces its losses by producing the product when $\text{SAC} > P > \text{AVC}$, rather than by ceasing production.

Rule: Thus the firm decides to incur variable costs and hence supply the product to the market, whenever price exceeds the firm's average variable cost level. If price also exceeds the SAC level, the firm makes a profit. If price falls below SAC, the firm suffers a loss, but it can minimize its loss by staying in production as long as $P > \text{AVC}$. If price slips below AVC, the firm minimizes losses by ceasing production and waiting until either the price rises above AVC again or until it can liquidate its fixed factors and terminate the associated fixed costs. The latter option implies a long-run situation, of course.

In most business situations the rule governing the decision "to supply or not to supply" is more clearly stated in terms of total revenues and total variable costs, rather than in terms of (per unit) $P > \text{AVC}$. That is, if $\text{TR} > \text{TVC}$, the firm should supply its product(s), whereas if $\text{TR} < \text{TVC}$, it should not incur the variable costs and, consequently, not supply the product(s). This rule is equivalent to the $P > \text{AVC}$ rule, since totals divided by quantity demanded equal the per-unit values. But in the real world, quantity demanded tends to vary day by day and month by month because of seasonal factors, chance circumstances, weather conditions, and competing attractions. In effect, the demand curve shifts back and forth in response to these shift factors. Most firms cannot change their prices daily to reflect the differing states of demand that eventuate. Rather, they set prices on the basis of some notion of the average, or normal, demand situation and hold these prices steady as sales fluctuate daily, monthly, or seasonally around this conceptually normal volume. Hence price is constant while AVC varies substantially from day to day depending on the volume produced. In such a situation the firm may find it easier to decide whether or not to supply its product in the short run on the basis of whether or not it expects TR to exceed TVC.

The four SAC curves represent the available plant sizes, with the subscripts indicating the maximum number of seats in each plant size. Note that each SAC becomes vertical at the point where it reaches its maximum output (passenger) level. The LAC curve is the envelope curve of these four SAC curves; it contains kinks at points A, B, and C, where it becomes less costly (per passenger) to choose the next largest plant size.

Note that if there were an aircraft available that seated 5 passengers (including the pilot), the SAC curve of that plant size would have nestled between SAC_4 and SAC_6, and it would have caused the kink in the LAC curve at point A to disappear. Similarly, if planes were also available with 7 and 9 seats, the other kinks might be removed or at least replaced by smaller kinks. With plant size continuously variable, the LAC curve would be a smooth line. In the real world, however, the LAC curve is most likely to exhibit kinks because plant size is not continuously variable.

Choice of Plant Size in the Long Run. In the short run the firm is confined to the plant size it is currently operating, but in the long run it will be able to either enlarge or reduce its plant to the size that best serves its objectives. Thus, if a firm finds itself with a plant that is either too large or too small in relation to its current quantity demanded, it may undertake the steps necessary to reduce or increase plant size. If it wants to reduce plant size, it has to find buyers for plant and buildings, wait until employment and other contracts expire, and so on. If the firm wishes to increase its plant size, it may need to order the fabrication and construction of new plant and buildings, search for new managers, hire and train more workers, and so on. All these things are possible; they simply take time to accomplish.

Given the freedom to choose any size of plant in the long run, which one should the firm choose? It should choose the plant size that minimizes the average cost of producing the firm's desired output level. Refer back to Figure 6-8 and suppose that the firm wishes to produce output level Q_1 (because Q_1 is the net-worth-maximizing output level, for example). Three different plant sizes that can produce output level Q_1 are shown in Figure 6-8, but the plant size chosen will be the one that produces this output level at the lowest average cost. Note that the plant size chosen will be the one with its SAC curve just tangent to the LAC curve at the desired output level. For "kinky" LAC curves, as shown in Figure 6-9, the plant size chosen will be the one with its SAC curve coextensive with the LAC at the desired output level. For example, when quantity demanded is expected to be 8 passengers (including the pilot), the optimal plant size is the 10-seat aircraft.

In many cases the costs are known, but demand is uncertain. How then does the firm select its plant size? We can apply expected value analysis to find the plant size that minimizes the *expected value* of average costs. Since the uncertain demand may be represented by a probability distribution of potential demand outcomes, we can transfer those probabilities to the output levels necessary to satisfy each of those demand levels, and note that each output level has a known average cost level in any particular plant. This process is demonstrated in Table 6-3. The probability distribu-

TABLE 6-3. The Expected Value of Average Costs: Choice of Plant Size When Costs Are Known but Demand Is Uncertain

QUANTITY DEMANDED		PLANT A		PLANT B	
Potential Outcome [1]	Prob- ability [2]	Average Cost [3]	Expected Value [4] = [2] × [3]	Average Cost [5]	Expected Value [6] = [2] × [5]
500	0.05	3.00	0.15	5.00	0.25
1,000	0.15	2.50	0.375	3.00	0.45
1,500	0.25	2.00	0.50	1.75	0.4375
2,000	0.35	2.75	0.9625	1.50	0.525
2,500	0.15	3.50	0.525	2.00	0.30
3,000	0.05	4.50	0.225	3.00	0.15
		Expected Values	2.7375		2.1125

tion of quantity demanded is shown in the first two columns. The average cost at each of those output levels in a particular plant (plant A) is shown in column 3, and the expected value of average cost in that plant is calculated in column 4, where each value is the product of the value in column 3 multiplied by the probability of its occurring, from column 2. The expected value of average cost in an alternate plant (plant B) is calculated in columns 5 and 6.

Note that plant A has lower average costs for smaller output levels but higher average costs for the larger output levels. Further inspection shows that where the weights (demand probabilities) are highest, plant B has the lower average costs. Thus we see that the weighted average costs, or the expected values of average costs, are lower (at $2.1125 per unit) in plant B. Assuming that these are the best two plant sizes available, the firm should install plant B based on this expected demand situation.[8]

Note: A totally erroneous procedure would be first to calculate the expected value of quantity demanded (in this case 1,775 units) and then to base one's decision on the average cost level at that expected value of output in each plant. A quick interpolation between the average cost figures at 1,500 and 2,000 units in Table 6-3 will confirm that this procedure would give an underestimate of average costs in both cases, since larger and smaller outputs tend to have higher costs per unit.

---

[8]Although the initial costs of plant B are probably higher than plant A, this difference is already incorporated into the analysis, since we are dealing with average costs. The fixed costs per unit include depreciation, which is an expense charged against revenues in each period to reflect the cost of the plant and equipment during the period. Also included would be any additional costs resulting from the larger size of plant B, such as additional salaries and maintenance expenses. Thus total cost per period is expected to be lower in plant B at the expected quantity demanded. In the following chapter we shall express some misgivings about the way that depreciation is typically calculated, since it involves an allocation of the nominal cost over a number of periods and may not accurately reflect the "economic" cost of the plant. Furthermore, the depreciation expense is deducted in nominal, rather than present-value, terms.

The firm's choice of its plant size to minimize the average cost (or expected value of the average cost) of production typically leads the firm to build a plant with production capacity greater than the level (or expected value) of quantity demanded. This *excess capacity* is evident in both the examples referred to previously (in Figures 6–8 and 6–9). In both cases the plant selected has the capacity to produce at a rate substantially higher than the (expected value of) quantity demanded. How do we measure excess capacity? In an absolute sense, the firm can continue to increase output until the SAC curve becomes vertical, but by the time that happens the marginal cost will be approaching infinity. Thus the *absolute capacity* is not a very useful reference point from which to measure excess capacity.

■ *Definition:*   The *full capacity* of a plant is usually referred to as the output level at which MC begins to rise above SAC. Although additional output could be produced by adding more units of the variable factors, MC would typically rise very steeply. Firms usually avoid such "overfull capacity" production wherever possible, preferring instead to produce at slightly less than full capacity so that they have in reserve some excess capacity that can be utilized if the firm's demand increases. When the market is growing, excess capacity buys the firm some time, allowing it to serve an expanding market without unit costs rising prohibitively (or at all) while it is in the process of building a larger plant. Excess capacity also allows a firm to produce at a rate higher than its current demand rate, to rebuild depleted inventories, to recover from a labor strike or mechanical breakdown, or to take advantage of a competitor's problem. Thus we measure excess capacity as the difference between the firm's current output level and the output level at which MC rises above SAC, and we recognize that after excess capacity is all used up the firm still has some overfull capacity it may wish to utilize, if it is profitable to do so.

The Long-Run Marginal Cost Curve

■ *Definition:*   The *long-run marginal cost* (LMC) curve shows the marginal cost of producing each additional unit of output when the firm is free to vary the inputs of all factors of production. As you should by now expect, the LMC lies below the LAC when the latter is falling, and it lies above the LAC when the latter is rising. In fact, LAC falls precisely because the LMC lies below it, pulling down the average cost. Similarly, LAC rises precisely because the marginal units cost more than the average to produce.

In Figure 6–10 we show the LMC associated with a particular LAC curve and three short-run cost situations. Notice that at output level Q_1, the short-run average cost is equal to the long-run average cost at point A. It follows that short-run marginal cost must equal LMC at this output level, since the two averages have converged upon each other precisely because the two marginals were converging on the same value (at point B). Similarly, at output level Q_2 we have $SAC_2 = LAC = LMC = MC_2$. We know that the LMC must pass through the minimum point of the LAC curve and that the short-run MC must pass through the minimum SAC point. Since SAC = LAC at

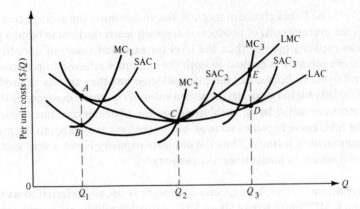

FIGURE 6-10. Long-Run Marginal Costs and Their Relationship to Other Cost Curves

the minimum points of both, we have the above four-way equality. Finally, at output level Q_3, average short-run and long-run costs are equal at point D, because marginal short-run and long-run costs are equal at point E.

Returns to Plant Size and Firm Size

■ *Definition:*   *Economies of plant size*, or increasing returns to plant size, are evident when the LAC curve slopes downward to the right, indicating that successively larger plant sizes have corresponding SAC curves lying lower and to the right. These economies arise because of such factors as an output level that is large enough to allow the firm to utilize more efficient capital-intensive methods—for instance, computer-controlled assembly lines—and that allows personnel to specialize in the areas of their greatest expertise. After some point, increasing inefficiencies in other areas, caused, perhaps, by the increasing bureaucracy of larger establishments, offset these cost advantages. The firm experiences *diseconomies of plant size* when successively larger plant sizes exhibit SAC curves that lie progressively higher and to the right.[9]

Note: The LAC curve is *not* the locus of the minimum points of each SAC curve. Since each SAC curve is tangent to the LAC curve, the minimum points would fall on

---

[9]One can make the distinction between economies of *scale* and economies of *plant size*. Economies of scale are found when *all* factors are increased in the same proportion. This involves a constant capital-labor ratio. Firms are unlikely to want to expand all inputs in the same proportion (as they increase their output under long-run conditions), because a different capital-labor ratio is likely to be cost minimizing because of differing marginal productivities of the inputs at different input levels. If the production function is *homogeneous*, the same ratio of inputs is optimal at all output levels. In this case there are both economies of scale and economies of plant size if proportional increases in all inputs lead to greater proportional increases in output, or there are both diseconomies of scale and diseconomies of plant size if output increases by proportionally less. See P. H. Douglas, "Are There Laws of Production?" *American Economic Review*, 38 (March 1948), pp. 1–41.

it only if the LAC curve were horizontal./If economies and diseconomies of plant size exist, the LAC curve will at first be negatively sloping and then positively sloping./ Thus tangencies with SAC curves must occur at first on negatively sloping parts of SAC curves and then on positively sloping parts. It follows that SAC curves are tangent to the left of their minimum points when there are economies of plant size and tangent to the right of their minimum points when there are diseconomies of plant size. Only for the SAC curve that is tangent to the minimum point of the LAC curve, often called *the optimum size of plant*, will the minimum point of an SAC curve be a point on the LAC curve. This is evident in Figure 6–10.

Economies of Firm Size and Multiplant Operation. Certain other economies arise as a result of the absolute size of the firm. For example, larger firms are usually able to obtain discounts for bulk purchases of raw materials, which gives them a cost advantage over smaller firms. These cost advantages are often referred to as *pecuniary economies* of plant or firm size; they are clearly different from the economies of plant size that are dependent upon increasing efficiency in production. Many large firms derive further pecuniary economies as the result of operating more than one plant. These cost savings are likely to result from spreading certain underutilized fixed costs, such as managerial talent, computer rental, and advertising expenditures, over more than one plant. The average cost curve for the first plant is, therefore, expected to sink downward to some degree as a result of opening a second and subsequent plants, since some part of the fixed costs previously charged to a single plant are now charged to one of the newer plants. This situation is illustrated in Figure 6–11.

FIGURE 6–11. Pecuniary Economies Causing Cost Curves to Sink Downward

Example: McDonald's fast-food restaurant chain is a good example. In a couple of decades this chain has burgeoned from a single fast-food restaurant to a worldwide network of almost identical restaurants. Whether in North America, Europe, Asia, or Australia one can walk right up to that familiar counter and place an order for a Big Mac, large order of french fries, an apple turnover, and a milkshake. Most of the phenomenal growth of McDonald's can be attributed to franchising, whereby local entrepreneurs supply a substantial capital investment in return for part ownership in a new outlet and several container loads of furniture, signboards, equipment, and fixtures that characterize a McDonald's restaurant. This familiar environment attracts customers who have tried McDonald's elsewhere and who know they can expect the same menu, the same quality, and the same prices. (This lack of uncertainty about prices and quality is very comforting to the wary consumer, who may have suffered disappointments and surprises at other fast-food restaurants.) In addition, McDonald's attracts new customers and reinforces preference patterns of regular customers by substantial expenditures on advertising and on other promotional efforts.

On the cost side there seems to be little indication that McDonald's benefits from economies of plant size, since all their restaurants seem to fall within a relatively small size range, although this is largely determined by the size of local markets for each outlet. On the other hand, there is little doubt that McDonald's benefits from economies of multiplant operation. Each additional plant (new outlet) probably allows McDonald's to reduce the per unit cost of its foodstuffs, since these are prepared in central locations and shipped to each franchised outlet. Advertising and promotion costs per outlet are reduced as the number of outlets sharing these costs is increased. Also the cost of replacing chairs, tables, and wall decorations is expected to decrease as the market (number of outlets) for these products increases. Thus we expect the cost curves of any particular McDonald's outlet to drift downward (in constant-value dollars, or *real* terms) over time as more and more outlets are opened.

The Learning Curve

It has been observed in particular production processes that the average costs per unit tend to decline over time as the factors of production learn the production process and become more efficient. K. J. Arrow called this relationship "learning by doing," and empirical studies have shown that costs per unit in many manufacturing processes do exhibit a downward trend (in real terms) over time.[10]

■ *Definition:*   The *learning curve*, also known as the experience curve, is a curve relating the cost per unit of output to the *cumulative* volume of output since that production process first started. Empirical studies indicate that unit costs tend to decline by a relatively stable percentage each time the cumulative output is doubled.[11]

---

[10]K. J. Arrow, "The Economic Implications of Learning by Doing," *Review of Economic Studies*, 29, No. 3 (1962). See also J. R. McGuigan and R. C. Moyer, *Managerial Economics*, 2nd ed. (St. Paul, Minn.: West Publishing Co., 1979), pp. 273-77; and "Selling Business a Theory of Economics," *Business Week*, September 8, 1973, pp. 86-88.

[11]See *Perspectives on Experience* (Boston: Boston Consulting Group, 1970).

Example: Suppose that after setting up the assembly process for a new calculator, Texas Instruments found that assembly time per unit had fallen to 100 minutes for each unit by the time 1,000 units had been assembled. Based on its previous experience that costs decline to 80 percent of their previous level each time output doubles, the company might predict that the 2,000th calculator would require 80 minutes assembly time; the 4,000th would require 64 minutes; the 8,000th 51.2 minutes; and so on. Given constant wages in real terms, the average cost per unit would be expected to decline along the learning curve depicted in Figure 6-12.

Note: The learning curve plots unit costs against *cumulative* output. Cumulative output grows over time and so the learning curve indicates that unit costs will decline over time as cumulative volume grows. The impact of this on the firm's SAC curves, which indicate costs per unit for different *rates* of output *per period* of time, will be to cause the SAC curve to sink downward as cumulative volume grows (and time passes). In Figure 6-13 we show the firm's SAC curves sinking downward as cumulative volume (indicated by the subscript to SAC) increases.

In terms of production and cost theory, the learning curve (and its manifestation as a sinking of the short-run cost curves over time) can be explained as a continuing improvement in the productivity of the variable inputs, given constant input prices. From one month to the next, the marginal product curve for the variable inputs shifts up, causing the marginal cost curve to shift down, bringing with it the AVC and SAC curves. Note that the learning effect is greatest when a production process first starts, and it diminishes as time passes. Mature production process will find very little learning effect, and subsequently the downward drift of the short-run cost curves from one month to the next will be negligible. Conversely, for new production processes (such as for the production of a new product, or a new way to produce an existing product), we

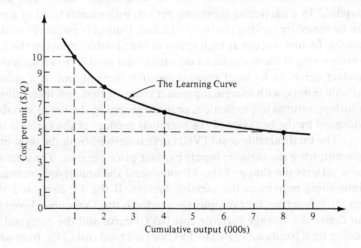

FIGURE 6-12. The Learning Curve: Declining Average Costs as a Function of Cumulative Output

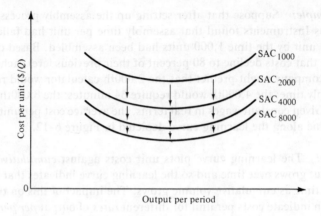

FIGURE 6–13.   Impact of the Learning Curve on the Firm's SAC Curve

should expect the learning effect to cause a significant downward movement in the short-run cost curves from one month to the next, until cumulative production grows to the level where the learning curve becomes relatively flat.

6.4 SUMMARY

The production process involves the interaction of inputs, or factors of production, to produce output. The inputs are categorized as either fixed or variable, depending upon whether or not their input can be varied in the short run. By convention, and for graphical simplicity, we call all the variable inputs "labor" and all the fixed inputs "capital." In a particular short-run period, with capital fixed at a given level, output can be varied by varying the input of labor. Output is positively related to input of the variable factors, except at high ratios of the variable inputs to the fixed inputs, when overcrowding of the workplace may cause total product to actually decrease. The total product curve, in its most general form, reflects output as a cubic function of the variable inputs, with marginal product rising at first and then falling. The law of diminishing returns in production, or more generally, the law of variable proportions, is evidenced by the behavior of the marginal product of the variable inputs.

The total variable cost (TVC) curve is derived from the total product (TP) curve by multiplying the variable inputs by their price per unit. Thus the shape of the TVC curve reflects the shape of the TP curve and the underlying increasing, constant, or diminishing returns to the variable factors. If the TP curve is a straight line, or a quadratic function, for example, then so too is the TVC curve. From the TVC curve we can derive the average variable cost (AVC) curve and the marginal cost (MC) curve. Adding total fixed cost (TFC) to TVC we find total cost (TC), from which we derive the short-run average cost (SAC). If production is a cubic function of the variable inputs, the SAC, AVC, and MC curves will be U-shaped, and the MC curve will pass through the minimum point on both the SAC and the AVC curves.

The AVC and MC curves may be horizontal if there are constant returns to the variable inputs or if the fixed inputs are divisible such that the ratio of variable to fixed inputs can be held at the optimal ratio (where AVC is minimized). Other ways to avoid fluctuations in the value of AVC and MC include keeping the output rate constant and using inventories to accommodate fluctuations in demand, contracting out for production, and having customers wait when demand is unexpectedly or abnormally high.

The long-run average cost (LAC) curve is the envelope curve of all the short-run AC curves. Larger plant sizes are reflected by SAC curves lying further to the right. The LAC curve is the locus of minimum average cost of production when the firm is free to choose any size of plant. If plant size is continually adjustable, the LAC curve will be a smooth line, and the long-run marginal cost (LMC) curve will lie below LAC when it slopes downward to the right (economies of plant size) and lie above it when LAC slopes upward to the right (diseconomies of plant size). If there are several discretely different plant sizes, the LAC curve will comprise elongated sections (rather than simply points) from each of the underlying SAC curves, and it will exhibit kinks where costs would be reduced by changing to a new plant size.

The firm's choice of plant size depends on its desired level of output. If demand is predictable with certainty, the plant size chosen is the one that allows the production of the quantity demanded at minimum average cost. If demand is uncertain, the plant size chosen is the one that minimizes the expected value of average cost, given the probability distribution formed by the meshing of the demand probabilities and the known cost values at each output level. Choosing plant size on this basis typically means that the firm builds in some excess capacity, which benefits the firm in case of market growth or successful competitive strategies that lead to sales gains at the expense of rivals.

The short-run cost curves of a particular plant, and thus the long-run cost curve as well, will shift downward if the firm benefits from reduced input prices, if it can spread some of its fixed costs over more than one plant through multiplant operation, or if the productivity of its inputs improves because of the learning effect.

DISCUSSION QUESTIONS

6-1. Explain how a tabular representation of a production function represents both the long-run and the short-run situations at the same time.

6-2. Suppose your production process has three inputs—machinery, highly skilled labor, and raw materials. If you wanted a new (larger or smaller) machine, it would take six months to be fabricated, delivered, and installed. Your present workers are all under contract for another eight months. New workers would take three months to acquire, because of the lengthy process of advertising, interviewing, and so forth. Raw-material supplies must be ordered four weeks in advance. How long is your short run? When can you make your long-run decision to expand or contract your plant size?

6-3. How does the law of variable proportions differ from the law of diminishing returns?

6-4. Why is the point of inflection on the total product curve the point where diminishing returns begin?

6-5. Explain why the shape of the short-run average variable cost curve depends on the specific form of the production function.

6-6. Discuss three ways that the firm may stabilize its costs per unit in the short run, rather than be forced to produce at varying levels of marginal cost.

6-7. Why would it be erroneous, when demand is uncertain, to choose plant size on the basis of the average cost level at the expected value of demand? What is the correct approach?

6-8. Distinguish between full capacity, absolute full capacity, overfull capacity, and excess capacity.

6-9. Explain the construction of the long-run average cost curve and its relationship with the long-run marginal cost curve and the various short-run average cost curves.

6-10. Distinguish between economies of scale, economies of plant size, and economies of firm size. Under what conditions would a firm's expansion be an example of all three phenomena at once?

PROBLEMS AND SHORT CASES

6-1. Donald K. Brown and Company operates a pearl-diving operation in the North Pacific Ocean. Mr. Brown owns a large trawler with all the required equipment. He hires local divers from the nearby islands and pays each of them on the basis of the weight of oysters recovered. He sells the pearls and the oyster meat separately. Over the past month he has been out pearling eight times in the same general area, taking all the divers who showed up for each trip. The particulars are as follows:

Trip Number	Divers Employed	Oysters Recovered (kg)
1	6	38
2	17	76
3	9	56
4	5	32
5	12	74
6	3	15
7	14	80
8	15	78

(a) Over what ranges do there appear to be increasing, constant, and diminishing returns to the variable factor?

(b) What number of divers appears to be the most efficient in terms of output per diver?

(c) What number of divers appears to be most efficient in terms of the utilization of the trawler and other equipment?

6-2. Taras Panache is the owner-manager of Panache Shirts Enterprises, which manufactures shirts by using rented space and equipment in a large warehouse. Because of the technical aspects of shirt production and the available equipment, separate production centers are used, each consisting of one cutting machine, two sewing machines, and three operators. Six months ago Mr. Panache had only one such production center, but recently he doubled, then tripled, and finally quadrupled the number of production centers by renting more space and equipment and by hiring more operators. Throughout the expansion Mr. Panache has personally supervised all the operators and has handled all other aspects of the business. He kept a record of the average daily output from the entire plant for each of the four situations, as follows:

> One production center: 20.6 shirts/day
> Two production centers: 42.4 shirts/day
> Three production centers: 60.8 shirts/day
> Four production centers: 76.3 shirts/day

Each production center costs $3,000 per month in fixed and variable costs. Mr. Panache pays himself $3,000 per month, and the remaining fixed costs are $1,000 per month. Assume there are 20 working days in a month.

(a) Can the expansion of Panache Shirts be regarded as a case of an increase in the *scale* of operations or simply an increase in the *size* of operations? Why?

(b) Are there economies and/or diseconomies of scale/size evident? Explain.

(c) Indulge in some speculation about the probable cause of the economies and diseconomies, if any.

6-3. The Superhealth Exercise Company has estimated its short-run production function to be as follows:

$$Q = 42L + 0.6L^2 - 0.08L^3$$

where Q represents output per hour and L represents units of the variable inputs, which cost $200 per unit. The firm's fixed inputs cost $100 per hour.

(a) Derive the firm's total product and marginal product schedules for $L = 1$ through $L = 10$.

(b) Transform the TP schedule into a total variable cost (TVC) schedule and calculate the average variable cost (AVC) and average cost (SAC) values.

(c) Plot the SAC and AVC curves and sketch in your estimate of the marginal cost (MC) curve.

(d) At what point do diminishing returns set in? Explain.

6-4. Silver Star Corporation has estimated its production function as follows:

$$Q = 38.6K + 3.2K^2 - 1.8K^3 + 16.3L + 2.8L^2 - 0.85L^3$$

where K represents units of the capital input (in $1,000 units) and L represents units of the labor input (in hundreds of labor hours).

(a) Construct the total product and marginal product curves for the case of $K = 5$.

(b) At what level of labor input do diminishing returns become evident?

(c) If labor were available at no cost (students wishing to gain work experience and willing to work without wages), what input level would you choose? Why?

6-5. Gewurz Fabricators Limited manufactures and assembles small aluminum buildings suitable for garden toolsheds, garages, and children's playhouses. Stephen Gewurz, the owner, is considering opening a new plant to diversify into the production of luxury dog kennels for the expanding large dogs' market. He has carefully considered the labor and capital requirements and the substitutability between these inputs at various output levels and has summarized the production function as follows:

Gewurz Fabricator—Production Function
(output in units per year)

		LABOR INPUTS (person-years)							
		1	2	3	4	5	6	7	8
Capital Inputs	1	30	52	80	110	130	145	155	162
(machine-years)	2	50	80	120	164	200	220	235	248
	3	80	124	175	226	260	274	282	287
	4	100	160	218	272	302	320	335	345

(a) Supposing that the cost of each unit of capital is $20,000 and the cost of each unit of labor is $10,000, derive the SAC curve for each of the four plant sizes indicated.

(b) What conclusions can you draw about the returns to increasing plant size in this example?

(c) Which of the four plants should be selected if demand is expected to be (1) 125 units? (2) 250 units? (3) somewhere within the range of 200–300 units? (Explain and defend your decision fully.)

6-6. The newly formed Beaudry Automobile Corporation plans to produce an expensive sports car and has asked your consulting firm for advice on the size of plant to construct. Because of the union contract and technical features of automobile production, labor must be paid $12,000 per person per annum, and each incremental change in plant size involves $900,000 in annual expenses for depreciation, interest, and other fixed costs. The maximum the firm will have available for expenditure on capital and labor is $9 million per annum. BAC has supplied the following details of its production function, meticulously derived by its chief engineer. (The data in the body of the table represent automobiles produced, in units.) Labor can be varied virtually continuously; the table shows units of 50 persons for convenience. All other variable expenses are constant at $2,500 per vehicle produced.

Capital (units of $900,000)	LABOR (units of 50 persons)					
	1	2	3	4	5	6
3	40	90	140	170	180	185
4	60	120	180	220	230	236
5	100	170	230	250	260	268
6	170	200	240	270	280	289

BAC's market research indicates that the new vehicle should be sold at around $50,000 per unit and that the expected demand situation is as follows:

Units Demanded (annually)	Probability
100	0.20
150	0.50
200	0.20
250	0.10

(a) Plot the SAC curves suggested by the production function and input cost figures.

(b) Comment upon the economies and diseconomies of plant size (if any) which are evident in your graph.

(c) Which plant do you suggest that BAC build, and why?

6-7. The Peachy Cosmetics Company has established the following relationship between the variable inputs and the output level for its production of its face cream products. Each unit of the variable product includes one person working 40 hours weekly, the necessary utilities, and a variety of ingredients in the required proportions, including the small glass jars and cardboard boxes in which the cream is packed. These variable inputs cost $600 per unit. Overhead (fixed) costs are $60,000 per week.

Variable Input (units)	Output (units)
100	6,500
200	14,300
300	20,200
400	24,400
500	27,800
600	30,000

(a) Use these data to derive the firm's AVC and SAC schedules for the output levels shown.

(b) Graph the AVC and SAC curves and sketch in your best estimate of the marginal cost curve.

(c) At what output level do you think diminishing returns first start? Explain with reference to the graph and reconcile this result with the input-output data.

(d) What is the full capacity output level? What is average cost at that level? Under what conditions would Peachy produce in the overfull capacity area of its cost curves?

6-8. Suppose that one of the very expensive ingredients in Peachy Cream (see problem 6-7) was suddenly found in abundance, and the cost of the variable units fell to $500 each.

(a) What is the impact of this discovery on the firm's AVC, SAC, and MC curves?

(b) Does it change the point where diminishing returns set in?

Now suppose that after the reduction in the price of that ingredient, worker productivity increases as a result of improvements in morale, such that output goes up by 10 percent at each input level.

(c) What is the impact of this improvement on the firm's AVC, SAC, and MC curves?

(d) What is the impact of both changes on the firm's full capacity output level?

6-9. Paxtronix Corporation is considering the installation of plant and equipment to manufacture a nonlethal stun gun for use by law enforcement agencies only. It has a choice of three plant sizes, A, B, and C. The average cost schedules for these plants are shown on page 244. Also shown is the estimated probability distribution of demand for each of the first two years.

(a) Plot the average cost curves for plants A, B, and C on the same graph.

(b) Calculate the expected value of average cost for each plant, given the probability distribution of demand.

(c) Which plant size should Paxtronix choose? Support your answer with sensitivity analysis.

(d) Given the plant size you have recommended, how much excess capacity will Paxtronix have?

Output Level (thousands)	Demand Probability	AVERAGE COST LEVEL ($)		
		Plant A	Plant B	Plant C
1	0.10	110	140	180
2	0.20	90	100	110
3	0.35	80	70	80
4	0.20	80	60	50
5	0.10	90	70	40
6	0.05	110	90	50

6-10. Magnocrunch Computer Company is currently producing at full capacity. This firm is fortunate to have fully divisible fixed inputs, such that its average variable cost is constant out to the full capacity level. Demand for the new Magnum computer is increasing, and the firm faces a backlog of orders. It cannot build inventories and fears that it will lose 20 percent of the buyers on the backlist if it cannot deliver within another month. The firm is considering two alternative plans. Plan A is to increase the rate of production to an overfull capacity situation, which would raise marginal cost from the present level of $1,500 by $300 for every 100 units beyond the current output rate of 500 computers per month. Alternatively, plan B is to contract out for the manufacture of various components, and then have these assembled into the finished unit by another firm. The firm estimates that these units will end up costing $2,200 per unit, regardless of volume. The present price of the computer is $2,995, and the firm's fixed costs per month are $250,000 per month. The firm's fixed costs are not expected to change, regardless of which plan is selected.

(a) Calculate the cost of solving the firm's immediate problem, under each of the plans taken separately.

(b) What strategy would you suggest to help Magnocrunch eliminate its backlist and begin to build up inventories?

(c) What assumptions and qualifications underlie your recommendation?

SUGGESTED REFERENCES AND FURTHER READING

Baumol, W. J. *Economic Theory and Operations Analysis* (4th ed.), chap. 11. Englewood Cliffs, N.J.: Prentice-Hall, Inc., 1977.

Chamberlin, E. H. "Proportionality, Divisibility and Economies of Scale," *Quarterly Journal of Economics*, 1948, pp. 229-57.

Cole, C. L. *Microeconomics: A Contemporary Approach*, chaps. 6 and 7. New York: Harcourt Brace Jovanovich, Inc., 1973.

Douglas, P. H. "Are There Laws of Production?" *American Economic Review*, March 1948, pp. 1-41.

Gold, B. "Changing Perspectives on Size, Scale, and Returns: An Interpretive Survey," *Journal of Economic Literature*, 19 (March 1981), pp. 5-33.

Hyman, David N. *Modern Microeconomics: Analysis and Applications*, esp. chaps. 6 and 7. St. Louis: Times Mirror/Mosby College Publishing, 1986.

Leftwich, R. H. *The Price System and Resource Allocation* (7th ed.), chaps. 8 and 9. Hinsdale, Ill.: The Dryden Press, 1979.

Mansfield, E. *Microeconomics: Theory/Applications*, esp. chaps. 6 and 7. New York: W. W. Norton & Company, 1985.

Appendix 6A: Isoquant-Isocost Analysis of Production and Costs

Introduction

In Chapter 3 we discussed indifference-curve analysis of the consumer's consumption problem, which is to choose the optimal values of the variables (goods and services) to enter the consumption process such that utility is maximized for a given budget constraint. The producer's production problem is analogous. That is, the producer must choose the optimal values of the variables (inputs) to enter the production process such that output is maximized for a given budget constraint. Alternatively, the producer may seek to minimize the cost of producing a given output level. Isoquant curves are the analogue to indifference curves, and isocost lines are the analogue to the consumer's budget constraint line.

Isoquant-Isocost Analysis

- **Definition:** An *isoquant* is a line joining combinations of inputs which generate the same level of output. The word *isoquant* comes from the Greek word *iso* meaning equal and the Latin word *quantus* meaning quantity. As with indifference curves, there will be a family of isoquant curves, with higher curves preferred to lower curves. Similarly, the curves do not cross, and they are convex to the origin. Unlike indifference curves, however, isoquant curves are not negatively sloped throughout their length. Isoquants may bend back, as shown in Figure 6A-1, at both relatively high and relatively low ratios of capital to labor. The reason for this difference is that in consumer theory we assumed that marginal utility would never be negative, whereas in producer theory we make no such restrictive assumption concerning marginal products.

We saw in Chapter 6 that the marginal product of the variable inputs will take on negative values when its input is "too large" relative to the fixed inputs. Conversely, the marginal product of the fixed inputs (in the long-run context) may become negative if the ratio of capital to labor becomes "too high." Just as the slope of an indifference curve is equal to the negative of the ratio of the marginal utilities, the slope of an isoquant is equal to the negative of the ratio of the marginal products. Specifically, with capital on the vertical axis, the slope of an isoquant is equal to the negative of the

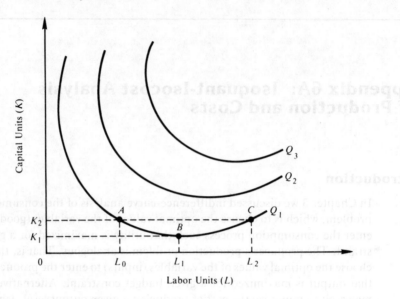

FIGURE 6A-1.   Isoquant Curves

marginal product of labor over the marginal product of capital.[1] When the marginal product of labor goes negative, at low capital-labor ratios, the slope term must be positive. Hence the isoquant bends upward at the right-hand end. Conversely, where the marginal product of capital goes negative, at relatively high capital-labor ratios, the slope of the isoquant must again take a positive value, and thus the curve bends back at the left-hand, or uppermost, end, as well. In between, where both marginal products are positive, the slope must be negative.

Technical and Economic Efficiency

A combination of capital and labor is *technically efficient* if none of either factor can be subtracted without reducing the output level, given *ceteris paribus*. All combinations on negatively sloped sections of the isoquant curves are technically efficient, since if one factor input is reduced while the other factor input is held constant, output will decline and the new input combination will lie on a lower isoquant curve. On the

---

[1]The slope of the isoquant curve can be represented by $\Delta K/\Delta L$, the vertical change over the horizontal change. Note that a negative ΔK, with L held constant, causes a reduction in output, ΔQ (a move to a lower isoquant curve). This $\Delta Q = \Delta K \times MP_K$, or the number of units of capital multiplied by the marginal product of those units. Now, to get back on the same isoquant curve, we need a positive ΔL, with K held constant, that causes the same absolute magnitude ΔQ (but in the other direction). This $\Delta Q = \Delta L \times MP_L$. Since the first ΔQ equals the negative of the second ΔQ, we know $\Delta K \times MP_K = -\Delta L \times MP_L$. From this relation we get $\Delta K/\Delta L = -MP_L/MP_K$. Thus the slope of an isoquant is equal to the ratio $-MP_L/MP_K$.

other hand, all combinations on positively sloped sections of isoquant curves are *technically inefficient*, since some of both factors may be subtracted without output being reduced. In terms of Figure 6A–1, output level Q_1 can be produced by different combinations of capital and labor at points A, B, and C. Combination C is technically inefficient, however, since the same output level could be produced at combination A by subtracting $L_2 - L_0$ units of labor or at combination B by subtracting both $L_2 - L_1$ units of labor and $K_2 - K_1$ units of capital. By the same process of reasoning, *all* points on positively sloped sections of the isoquants are technically inefficient combinations of the inputs.

The slope of an isoquant at any point can also be expressed as the ratio of the amount of capital that can be subtracted from the production process to the amount of labor that is added to the production process, such that output level remains constant. For a one-unit increment in the labor input, this ratio is known as the *marginal rate of technical substitution* of capital for labor.

■ *Definition:* The marginal rate of technical substitution (MRTS), is the rate at which labor can be substituted for capital in the production process, *such that output remains unchanged.* Note that it is equal to the amount of capital that can be subtracted from the production process for a one-unit increase in labor added to the production process. Thus,

$$\text{MRTS} = \frac{\Delta K}{\Delta L} \qquad (6A\text{–}1)$$

where ΔK is the decrement to capital that will just allow output to remain unchanged given a one-unit increment ΔL to the labor input. Thus the marginal rate of technical substitution reflects the slope of an isoquant curve, and the MRTS will be negative for all technically efficient combinations of the factors and positive for all technically inefficient combinations. Since the slope is also equal to the negative ratio of the marginal products, we can also say that $\text{MRTS} = -MP_L/MP_K$.

The combinations of capital and labor on the negatively sloped sections of the isoquants represent the range of possibilities open to the rational firm. The actual combination of capital and labor chosen to produce each output level (in the long-run situation where the firm is free to vary all inputs) will depend on the relative prices of the inputs. Only one of the technically efficient ways of producing each output level will be *economically* efficient; that is, only one will allow the lowest cost of producing that output level. To show this we need to introduce isocost lines which show combinations of capital and labor that cost the same amount.

■ *Definition:* An *isocost* line is a locus of combinations of inputs that require the same total expenditure.

Let us express the firm's expenditure on inputs as

$$E = K \cdot P_K + L \cdot P_L \qquad (6A\text{--}2)$$

where E is the total dollar expenditure; P_K and P_L are the unit prices of capital and labor, respectively; and K and L are the number of physical units of capital and labor that are to be employed in the production process. This can be rearranged to appear as

$$K = \frac{E}{P_K} - \frac{P_L}{P_K} \cdot L \qquad (6A\text{--}3)$$

in which form it is perhaps more recognizable as a linear equation explaining K in terms of L and three known values (E, P_L, and P_K). It can therefore be plotted in the same space as the isoquant curves. The intercept of the isocost line on the capital axis occurs when $L = 0$, and this intercept value of K is simply the total expenditure divided by the price of the capital units, resulting in a particular physical quantity of capital units. As we purchase units of labor, it is evident that our purchase of capital units, for the same expenditure (isocost) level, is drawn down in the ratio of the price of labor to the price of capital.

For each output level there will be a minimum-cost combination of the factors necessary to produce that output level. In Figure 6A-2 we show three isoquant curves representing 20, 40, and 60 units of output. The cost of producing 20 units is mini-

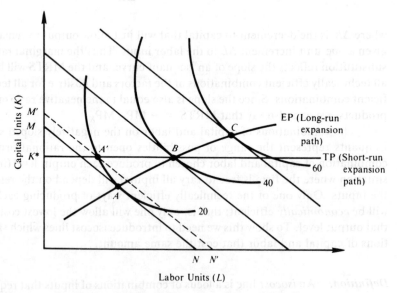

FIGURE 6A-2. Isoquant-Isocost Analysis Showing Short-Run and Long-Run Expansion Paths

mized at point A, since any other capital/labor combination producing 20 units, such as at A', will lie to the right of the isocost line MN and would thus require a larger total expenditure to purchase. Recall that the intercept on the capital axis is equal to E/P_K, where P_K is presumed to remain unchanged. Hence, larger total expenditures are represented by higher intercept points and higher isocost lines. Similarly, the output level of 40 units is produced at the least cost by the input combination represented by point B, and 60 units are produced at the least cost by the input combination at point C.

Rule: Output is maximized for a given input expenditure level where the isocost line representing that expenditure level is just tangent to the highest attainable isoquant curve. Equivalently, input cost is minimized for a given output level, where the isoquant curve representing that output level is just tangent to the lowest attainable isocost line. Note that at the point of tangency between the isoquant and the isocost curves the slopes of these curves are the same. The slope of the isoquant curve is the MRTS, and the slope of the isocost curve is equal to the negative of the input price ratio, $-P_L/P_K$. Thus MRTS $= -P_L/P_K$ at the point of tangency. Since MRTS $= -MP_L/MP_K$, we also have $-MP_L/MP_K = -P_L/P_K$. Rearranging terms we have $MP_L/P_L = MP_K/P_K$ as an alternative statement of the output-maximizing, or cost-minimizing, rule. Thus the firm should utilize all inputs such that the ratios of the marginal products to prices of all inputs are equal. This rule generalizes to the n input case, where n is any number of different inputs. That is, $MP_1/P_1 = MP_2/P_2 = \ldots = MP_n/P_n$.

The Expansion Path: Long Run and Short Run

■ *Definition:* A locus of the tangency points between various isoquants and various isocosts is called the *expansion path*, since it shows the least-cost combinations of labor and capital a firm would choose as it expanded its output level, if it were free to vary both labor and capital and if it were given constant factor prices and a constant state of technology. This expansion path is shown as the line EP in Figure 6A–2. Note that this must be the *long-run* expansion path, since all factors must be variable to allow the adjustment in both capital and labor involved in the movement along the line EP.

Suppose the firm wishes to produce 40 units of output and thus selects the combination of factors represented by point B on the long-run expansion path. The firm's capital input will now be fixed at K^* units, and the firm is in a short-run situation. If the firm wishes to vary its output level in the short run, it must simply add or subtract labor to or from the fixed capital input K^*. The *short-run expansion path* is therefore a horizontal line at the capital input level K^*, and we have shown it as the line TP in Figure 6A–2. This short-run expansion path is in fact the total product curve, viewed from a different perspective.

Notice that for every output level except the one where TP crosses EP, it costs more to produce the output in the short run than it does in the long run. Any isocost line that *intersects* an isoquant curve on the TP line must lie farther to the right when compared with the isocost line that is *tangent* to each isoquant curve. This statement is demonstrated in Figure 6A–2 for the output level of 20 units. In the long-run situation the optimal input combination is at point A, and the lowest attainable isocost line is shown as MN. In the short-run situation with capital input of K^*, 20 units must be produced by the input combination represented by point A', since the firm is constrained to the "short-run expansion path," TP. The minimum cost of producing 20 units with combination A', is shown by the isocost line $M'N'$, which lies to the right of the line MN. The short-run situation costs more than the long-run situation for all except one output level, because the firm is unable in the short run to change the input of capital and is thus forced to have an inappropriate factor combination for all except one output level. In the case shown, only at the output of 40 units does the level of capital (K^*) allow the tangency situation of economic efficiency to be attained.[2]

Factor Substitution Resulting from Changed Factor Prices

Economic efficiency depends upon the relative factor prices. If the price of one factor changes, with *ceteris paribus*, the profit-maximizing firm will attempt to substitute away from the factor that has become relatively more expensive and in favor of the factor that has become relatively less expensive. Suppose the initial situation in Figure 6A–3 is at point A. Output level Q_1 is being produced economically efficiently by the factor combination K_1 units of capital and L_1 units of labor, and factor prices are such that the lowest attainable isocost line is MN.

Suppose now that labor prices rise, for example, because of a new agreement with a labor union or because of legislation requiring the firm's contribution to an employee health scheme or to similar benefits. Imagine that the increase in the cost of labor is such that the isocost line swings down from MN to MN'. If the firm wishes to maintain its output level at Q_1, in order to hold its market share, for example, it will need to spend more money on the inputs in order to produce Q_1.

In the short run, the firm is constrained to the plant size indicated by K_1 and must produce Q_1 units of output at point A. This constraint necessitates the total expenditure indicated by the isocost line $M''N'''$. Given a long-run situation, the firm can adjust both capital and labor inputs and will increase its plant size to K_2 units of capital and reduce labor input to L_2 units in order to produce Q_1 units of output with economic efficiency at point B, given the new factor-price ratio. Thus the firm substi-

[2]We saw in Chapter 6 that each short-run average cost (SAC) curve is tangent to the long-run average cost (LAC) curve at a single point when plant size is continuously variable. Note that the long-run expansion path (EP) contains all the data necessary to derive the LAC curve, namely, the minimum total cost required to produce each output level, given the variability of both capital and labor. Similarly, the minimum total cost of producing each output level under short-run conditions can be derived from the values of the isoquants and isocosts crossing the short-run expansion path (TP). Thus the firm's SAC and LAC curve would be tangent at 40 units of output, and the SAC would lie above the LAC for all other output levels. Similarly, the TP curve for any other level of capital input would cross the EP line at a particular output level, and this would be the output level at which that plant's SAC curve was just tangent to the LAC curve.

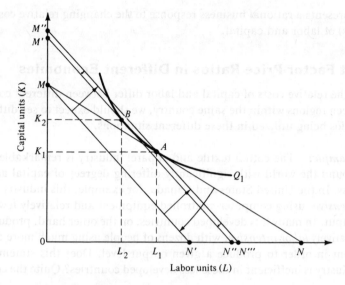

**FIGURE 6A–3. Factor Substitution Resulting from
Changed Relative Factor Prices**

tutes away from labor and in favor of capital when the price of labor increases relative to that of capital, given time to adjust the input of all factors. History has given us the opportunity to observe this phenomenon, of course: as the price of labor has increased relative to that of capital, we have observed that production processes have become relatively more capital-intensive with the introduction of labor-saving equipment such as mobile assembly lines by Henry Ford and the more recent use of computerized production technology.

Example: In the early 1980s there were thousands of robots working in American industry. These computer-controlled machines, which in some cases have visual and tactile skills, have replaced human labor for two main reasons. First, they are cheaper. General Motors reports that where robots are used in automobile assembly, they cost only about $6 an hour, compared with the average $20 an hour paid to assembly labor. Second, robots are more productive than the humans they replace. Hour after hour they methodically and precisely repeat their tasks, never stopping for coffee breaks, chats, washroom visits, and the like. Similarly, absenteeism and sick leave are human foibles. Should the robots break down, they are quickly repaired, since they can indicate which part needs replacing. General Electric (GE) found that robots were 10 percent to 35 percent more productive than humans in coating dish racks with polyvinyl. Although their initial cost averages $50,000 each, GE found that their first robot paid for itself in ten months as a result of its greater productivity. Estimates are that there will be 120,000 robots at work by 1990, replacing as many as 1 million workers. This represents a rational business response to the changing relative costs (and productivities) of labor and capital.[3]

Different Factor Price Ratios in Different Economies

If the relative costs of capital and labor differ between different countries or even between regions within the same country, we should expect to see differing capital-labor ratios being utilized in these different situations.

Example: The cotton textile and apparel industry is remarkable in that it is found around the world with significantly differing degrees of capital and labor intensiveness. In the United States and Canada, for example, this industry is relatively *capital intensive*, using computer-controlled equipment and relatively few people per unit of output. In many less developed countries, on the other hand, production processes are relatively *labor intensive*, with dozens of people using much more rudimentary equipment in order to produce a given output level. Does this statement mean that the industry is inefficient in these less developed countries? Quite the contrary, as we shall see.

In terms of isoquant-isocost analysis, firms in both situations are trying to attain tangency between their isocost line and the appropriate isoquant line. Suppose a firm in each group wishes to produce a particular output level, shown as Q^* in Figure 6A-4. In the less developed economy, labor is relatively cheap, whereas capital is relatively expensive, giving rise to an isocost line like M_2N_2. The economically efficient input combination for the firm in this situation is thus K_2, L_2, where the isocost curve is tangent to the isoquant at point *B*. In the more highly developed country, labor is relatively expensive, and capital is relatively cheap, giving rise to an isocost line like M_1N_1, which is tangent to the isoquant line at point *A*, indicating that K_1 and L_1 constitute the economically efficient input combination for the firm in the more developed economy.

Thus both situations are probably both technically and economically efficient given the factor productivities and factor prices facing the firm in each situation. The crunch comes for Americans when their economically efficient input combination for any given output level costs *more* than the economically efficient input combination in less developed economies. Hence the U.S. textile industry finds itself subject to the competition of imported textiles that are sold at a lower price in its market.

A similar example is found in the automobile industry. In the early 1980s, automobile assembly workers in Japan were paid only about $12 per hour in wages and benefits, compared with $20 per hour in the United States.[4] The cost of capital in these

---

[3]See Joann S. Lublin, "Steel-Collar Jobs: As Robot Age Arrives, Labor Seeks Protection Against Loss of Work," *Wall Street Journal*, October 26, 1981, pp. 1, 17.

[4]See Robert L. Simison, "Ford Asks for 50% Pay-Benefit Cut in Bid to Align Labor Costs with Japanese," *Wall Street Journal*, October 22, 1981.

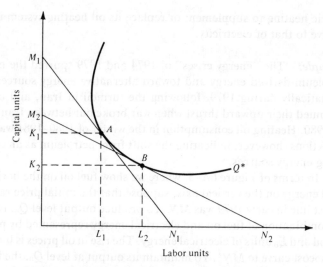

FIGURE 6A-4. **Different Economically Efficient Combinations in Different Economic Situations**

countries (and for large automobile companies) is more nearly equal, however, given the greater international mobility of capital and the international capital markets. Thus we should expect the Japanese automobile industry to be somewhat more labor-intensive than the U.S. automobile industry. Given their labor cost and other cost advantages, said to amount to $1,500 per car, the Japanese are able to compete very effectively in the American market and have enjoyed significant growth in their market share in recent years.

Isoquant-Isocost Analysis of Short-Run Production Problems

Isoquant-isocost analysis can be used to solve short-run production problems as well. Variable inputs are often substitutable for each other, and the firm faces a short-run decision concerning the combination of variable factors (in conjunction with fixed factors) which would minimize cost for a particular output level. A firm may have the choice of hiring either "generalist" labor (who can accomplish a sequence of tasks) or, alternatively, hiring "specialist" labor who can each do only one of the required tasks. Thus these two different types of labor are substitutable in the short run, presuming each can be hired or fired at management's discretion.

Similarly, labor may be substitutable for raw materials in some production processes. For example, three workers and ten yards of cloth may combine (along with the fixed factors) to produce five shirts per hour. Alternatively, five workers and eight yards of cloth may combine to produce five shirts per hour. The extra labor allows more careful cutting of the cloth so that there is less waste of the material. A further example is the substitutability among different sources of energy. A firm can install electric heating to supplement or replace its oil heating system if the cost of oil rises relative to that of electricity.

Example: The "energy crises" of 1974 and 1979 spurred the movement away from petroleum-derived energy and toward alternative energy sources. Oil prices shot up dramatically during 1979, following the turmoil in Iran, and after a short decline, continued their upward thrust when war broke out between Iran and Iraq in September 1980. Heating oil consumption in the winter of 1980–1981 was substantially below projections, however, indicating the shift from petroleum as an energy source to competing energy sources.[5]

In terms of Figure 6A–5, where we show fuel oil on the horizontal axis and electrical energy on the vertical axis, suppose that the initial price ratio was such that the isocost line in early 1979 was *MN*. To produce output level Q_0, the firm would choose the combination of fuel oil and electrical energy represented by point *A*, or F_0 units of fuel oil and E_0 units of electrical energy. The rise in oil prices is indicated by the shift of the isocost curve to *MN'*. To maintain its output at level Q_0, the firm (and households which had the ability to do so) would prefer to substitute away from fuel oil and toward electric energy to point *B* on isoquant Q_0. Thus, after the adjustment process, the firm would purchase E_1 units of electrical energy and F_1 units of fuel oil. In fact, we ob-

FIGURE 6A–5.   Response of Cost-Minimizing Firm to a Change in Fuel Oil Costs

[5]See Mary Greenebaum, "The Sudden Popularity of Heating Oil Contracts," *Fortune*, February 23, 1981, pp. 127, 130.

served a shift away from petroleum-derived energy and toward a variety of other energy sources, including solar and nuclear energy.

Summary

In this appendix we have used isoquant-isocost analysis to examine the firm's production problem. The firm should always operate on the negatively sloped section of an isoquant, to avoid technical inefficiency, which means the waste of inputs. While there are many technically efficient input combinations for every level of output, only one input combination will be economically efficient, given the cost of capital and labor.

The firm's choice of plant size in the long-run context is indicated by the tangency of the isoquant for the desired output level and the lowest attainable isocost line. The level of capital input indicated is the optimal plant size for that output level. Short-run fluctuations in the quantity demanded will cause the firm to move along a horizontal line which is effectively the total product (TP) curve. Except for the output level where the TP curve crosses the expansion path (EP), a given output level will cost more in the short run than in the long run, because the firm is unable to adjust its fixed inputs to the optimal level in the short run.

Isoquant-isocost analysis can also be used for short-run production problems—namely, the optimal combination of variable inputs when these are substitutable in production. Given the underlying fixed factors, a given output level will be attainable from a variety of combinations of the variable inputs, and the firm should choose the least-cost combination by reference to a tangency between the isoquant and isocost curves.

DISCUSSION QUESTIONS

6A-1. Distinguish between technical and economic efficiency in the production process.

6A-2. The smooth curve of an isoquant curve implies the ability to substitute small amounts of capital for small amounts of labor. Given that a person is not physically divisible, how can the firm use a fraction of a person's time? Similarly, how can it increase capital by very small increments?

6A-3. Why do isoquant curves bend back at relatively high and relatively low capital-labor ratios?

6A-4. What is the rule for the optimal input combination? State this rule verbally, and then symbolically. Generalize it to the *n* input case.

6A-5. Why would you expect the production of any particular product to be typically more capital intensive in more highly developed countries, as compared to less developed countries?

PROBLEMS AND SHORT CASES

6A-1. The Himam Foods Corporation is a relatively small firm producing grocery items. Recently its research department developed a new salad dressing. Production of this new dressing would involve the use of the firm's mixing machine, which combines, shakes, rotates, and warms the ingredients to a specified temperature before pouring the mixture into bottles which are then capped and labeled. Some of the above procedures can be done manually, however, and Himam wants to choose the optimal proportions of machine time and labor time. The production function has been estimated as shown below:

Himam Foods—Production Function
(output in thousands of units)

		LABOR-HOURS PER YEAR (000)					
		1	2	3	4	5	6
Machine Hours	1	25	80	110	120	125	115
per Year (000)	2	70	102	120	135	145	150
	3	86	117	140	160	175	182
	4	96	125	150	170	185	195
	5	95	130	155	175	192	205
	6	90	127	158	178	196	210

Machine-hours cost $25 per hour, and labor costs are $10 per hour. (Raw material costs are constant per bottle and are covered by a separate budget.) Because of the current difficult financial situation, Himam can allocate a budget of only $80,000 for the machine and labor costs of producing the new dressing.

(a) Plot these output levels in input space on a graph and sketch in several isoquant curves that are suggested by the data.

(b) Estimate from your graph the maximum output level which Himam can produce within its budget constraint and the factor combination that is required to achieve this level.

(c) Demonstrate what would happen if the cost of labor hours were to increase to $15 per hour. Estimate the new optimal factor combination and output level.

6A-2. The long-run production function for the Burnstein Apparel Company is represented by the following input-output table. Capital units cost $100,000 each, and labor units cost $50,000 each. The firm has an annual budget of $0.5 million.

Capital	LABOR UNITS					
Units	1	2	3	4	5	6
1	20	40	70	90	100	108
2	30	50	100	130	140	147
3	40	90	140	170	180	185
4	60	120	180	220	230	236
5	100	170	230	250	260	268
6	170	200	240	270	280	289

(a) Plot these output levels in input space, and sketch in the isoquant curves representing 50, 100, 150, 200, and 250 units of output.

(b) Superimpose the isocost line, and estimate the maximum output level that Burnstein can expect to achieve, given its budget constraint.

(c) Assuming capital is divisible, how much do you recommend that they spend on fixed factors of production annually?

(d) Given that they implement your recommended plant size, what change do you expect in their total variable costs if they expand output in that plant by 25 percent to meet an increase in their quantity demanded?

6A–3. The Vermont Maple Syrup Company has estimated the relationship between its inputs of fixed and variable inputs and the resultant output level, over the range shown in the following table. The units of fixed inputs cost $50,000 each, and the units of the variable inputs cost $10,000 each. The company believes it can sell 150 units of the product next year. (Each unit is 1,000 pints of grade A maple syrup.)

Fixed Inputs	VARIABLE INPUTS						
	1	2	3	4	5	6	7
1	30	52	80	110	130	145	155
2	50	80	120	164	200	220	235
3	80	124	175	226	260	274	286
4	100	160	218	272	302	320	335

(a) Plot these outputs in input space and sketch in your best estimate of the isoquants representing 50, 100, 150, and 200 units of output.

(b) Draw in the isocost line that represents the minimum cost level for the production of 150 units of output.

(c) What is your best estimate of the minimum total cost of producing 150,000 pints of maple syrup, based on this data?

(d) What will happen to total costs if the cost of the variable inputs goes up by 10 percent and the firm still wishes to produce 150,000 pints of syrup?

SUGGESTED REFERENCES AND FURTHER READING

Hyman, David N. *Modern Microeconomics: Analysis and Applications*, esp. chap. 6. St. Louis: Times Mirror/Mosby College Publishing, 1986.

Leftwich, R. H. *The Price System and Resource Allocation*, 7th ed., esp. chap. 8. Hinsdale, Ill.: The Dryden Press, 1979.

Mansfield, E. *Microeconomics: Theory/Applications*, 5th ed., esp. chap. 6. New York: W. W. Norton & Company, 1985.

Appendix 6B: Linear Programming Analysis

Linear programming is a solution technique that is applicable to a variety of problems encountered by the managerial economist. In this appendix we shall focus on the use of linear programming to solve a production problem, namely, the product mix problem. A multiproduct firm must allocate its labor, raw materials, and other variable inputs among the different products that it produces such that the firm's total profits are maximized. The problem is to find the optimal mix of products to be produced subject to the constraints imposed by the firm's fixed factors of production.

The Linearity Assumptions

To apply linear programming to a particular problem, both the decision maker's objective function and the constraints that confine the decision must be linear (or sufficiently approximated by linearity) over the range of outputs to which the decision applies. Supposing that the firm's objective function is the maximization of profits, this implies that the profit per unit of output must be constant in order for profit to be a linear function of output. This in turn requires that both price and average variable costs be constant over the range of outputs affected by the decision.

Under what circumstances would prices be constant over a range of output levels? This situation applies in markets in which the individual firm supplies such a small proportion of total industry output that it may presume that its output decision will not influence the market price. Clearly, as we consider progressively larger firms this assumption becomes more tenuous unless the range of outputs being considered is correspondingly reduced. Thus a relatively large firm may consider that for small variations in its output level it will not cause a change in the price level.

Constant average variable costs imply constant returns to the variable inputs. The statistical studies referred to in Chapter 8 indicate that constant AVC may be observed within many firms over limited ranges of output.

The second linearity requirement is that each of the possible outputs use each of the constraints as a linear function of the output of each product. If, for example, the first unit of product X uses twenty minutes of machine time,[1] so must all subsequent units of product X. Thus the efficiency of the fixed resources is constant and does not depend on the output level of each particular product to be produced. In any particular machine or plant facility, therefore, there will be a constant tradeoff between product X and product Y, or more generally between any two products that may be produced by that machine.

In the following sections the emphasis will be upon understanding the technique of linear programming so that it can be correctly applied to decision problems. Simple linear-programming problems may be solved either graphically or algebraically, but more complex problems demand the assistance of computer programs designed to search for the optimal solution.

---

[1]This should be interpreted as the first unit in the "relevant range" of outputs, rather than the very first unit produced. All we require is that, over the range of output levels likely to contain the optimal output level, the relationship between input usage and output rate is constant.

Graphical Solution of a Linear-Programming Problem

Suppose a small firm is in the business of making chromed shelf display units for city stores and boutiques. It has the necessary plant and equipment plus a small work force whose members regard their labor input as being fixed at certain weekly maximum levels. The firm has tapped a market for two particular shelf units and has found that demand exceeds its capacity to produce either product. It could specialize in either product X or product Y or produce some combination of the two products.

Suppose that product X involves a more complex design and has a constant per unit cost of $300 and that any feasible output of the firm can be sold at the current market price of $600 per unit. Product Y is a more simple design, has constant variable per unit costs of $200, and can be sold within the range of feasible outputs at a market price of $400. Thus product X contributes $300 per unit toward fixed costs and profits, whereas product Y contributes only $200 per unit. (We call the excess of price over AVC the per-unit "contribution" of the product in question. Similarly, the excess of TR over TVC is the total contribution of the product in question.)

The firm has three processes which have limited capacity to produce both product X and product Y. The first process consists of cutting the material to the appropriate size and configuration on the firm's power hacksaw. The power hacksaw is available for only thirty-two hours weekly, since the operator of this machine is available for this period only. The second process consists of welding the materials to construct the shelf units, and the availability of the welding equipment and its operator is limited to thirty hours per week. The third process involves immersing the units in the chrome bath, and this facility and its operator are available for forty hours a week only.

Representation of the Constraints. Product X requires eight hours per unit in the first process, six hours per unit in the welding process, and five hours per unit in the chrome bath. Product Y requires four hours of the hacksaw time per unit, five hours of the welding time, and eight hours of the chrome bath time per unit. It can be seen that while product Y contributes less per unit, its demands on two of the processes are less than the demands of product X. Alternatively, product X demands more time per unit for two of the three processes yet has a significantly higher contribution than does product Y. Thus it is not obvious that the firm should specialize in either product X or product Y, and in fact we shall see that a combination of the two products will allow a maximum contribution to overheads and profits. The linear-programming problem is to find the output mix that will achieve the maximum contribution to overheads and profits, given the constraints imposed upon the production of these two products.

Let us state the linear-programming problem in symbolic form. Supposing the firm wishes to maximize the total contribution of its operations, it thus wishes to maximize an objective function of the form:

$$\pi = AX + BY \tag{6B-1}$$

where π represents the total contribution to overheads and profits, X and Y are the number of units of each product to be produced, and the coefficients A and B represent the per-unit contribution expected from each of the two products. Using the price per unit and average variable cost data outlined above, we can deduce that the contribution per unit of product X is \$300, and for product Y it is \$200. Thus we can express the objective function as

$$\pi = 300X + 200Y \tag{6B-2}$$

The constraints upon the maximization of contribution can be expressed as follows:

$$Process~1:~8X + 4Y \le 32 \tag{6B-3}$$

$$Process~2:~6X + 5Y \le 30 \tag{6B-4}$$

$$Process~3:~5X + 8Y \le 40 \tag{6B-5}$$

Equation (6B-3) says in effect that the sum of the time utilized by the production of both product X and product Y must not exceed the time available in the first process. Since each unit of product X demands eight hours of the power hacksaw's time and each unit of product Y demands four hours, the number of units of products X and Y produced constrained to that which can be produced within thirty-two hours' utilization of the power hacksaw and its operator. Similarly for the welding process, where each unit of product X requires six hours and each unit of product Y requires five hours, the sum must not exceed thirty hours in total. Finally, for the chrome bath process, each unit of product X requires five hours and each unit of product Y requires eight hours, and the total utilization of this process must be less than or equal to forty hours weekly.

Since linear programming is a mathematical procedure, it is likely to assign both positive and negative values to the variables X and Y unless we instruct it otherwise. Since negative values of output for product X and product Y make economic nonsense, we must add the condition that

$$X \ge 0,~Y \ge 0$$

These are known as the nonnegativity requirements of linear-programming analysis.

The problem to be solved is thus to maximize profit contribution as shown by equation (6B-2) subject to the constraints indicated by equations (6B-3) through (6B-5) and the nonnegativity requirements on the variables X and Y. Thus we wish to choose values of X and Y such that none of the constraints are broken and π is maximized. We can solve this problem graphically by expressing the constraints and the objective function on a specific graph and finding the output level for which profits are maximized. To find the feasible combinations of X and Y, that is, those that it is possible to produce without violating one or more of the constraints, we must delineate between those combinations that are possible on each process and those that are impossible to produce given the total time available in each process. Beginning with the first process, it is clear that the limits of possible combinations will be achieved where all of the available thirty-two hours weekly are used in the production of X and Y. Thus we can remove the inequality from equation (6B-3) and state that

$$8X + 4Y = 32$$

or in terms of Y:

$$4Y = 32 - 8X$$
$$Y = 8 - 2X \qquad \text{(6B-6)}$$

We now have an expression that shows Y as a linear function of X. In a graph with product Y on the vertical axis and product X on the horizontal axis, the first term is the intercept on the Y axis, and the coefficient to the X term represents the slope of the line relating products Y and X. In Figure 6B-1 we show the first constraint graphed against products Y and X. Those combinations of Y and X that lie outside the line are clearly unobtainable, since they would demand more than thirty-two hours of the time available in process 1.

To find the feasible output combinations under the other two processes we proceed similarly. Thus for the second constraint:

$$6X + 5Y = 30$$
$$5Y = 30 - 6X$$
$$Y = 6 - 1.2X \qquad \text{(6B-7)}$$

and for the third process:

$$5X + 8Y = 40$$
$$8Y = 40 - 5X$$
$$Y = 5 - 0.625X \qquad \text{(6B-8)}$$

As shown in Figure 6B-1, the second constraint has an intercept value of 6 and a slope of -1.2, and the third constraint has an intercept value of 5 and a slope of -0.625.

The irregular area encompassing all combinations of X and Y that lie below all the constraint lines is known as the *feasible region* of the production problem and is shown as the shaded area $0ABCD$ in Figure 6B-1. The feasible region has several linear facets at its outer boundary, each corresponding to a particular constraint that is binding on the feasible combinations of X and Y.

Isoprofit Lines.   To find which of the feasible combinations allows the highest profit contribution we introduce the concept of isoprofit lines, which are analogous to the

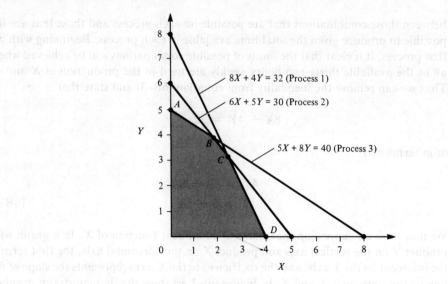

8X + 4Y = 32 (Process 1)

6X + 5Y = 30 (Process 2)

5X + 8Y = 40 (Process 3)

FIGURE 6B-1.   Feasible Region of Production Problem

isocost lines discussed in Appendix 6A. An isoprofit line is a locus of the combinations of products X and Y that allow the same total profit to be derived. Expressing the profit function, equation 6B-2, in terms of product Y, we have

$$Y = \frac{\pi}{200} - \frac{300}{200}X$$

or

$$Y = \frac{\pi}{200} - 1.5X \qquad (6B\text{-}9)$$

Thus we have represented the isoprofit function in terms of Y and X. On any given isoprofit line the value of π will be known, and hence we may find the combinations of X and Y that preserve the equality shown in equation 6B-9. Suppose we wish to find the combinations of X and Y that allow a profit level of \$1,000. Substituting in equation 6B-9, we have

$$Y = \frac{1,000}{200} - 1.5X$$

$$Y = 5 - 1.5X \qquad (6B\text{-}10)$$

Hence equation (6B–10) represents the equation for the isoprofit line along which profits are $1,000. We note that the intercept of this line on the Y axis must be at five units, and the slope of this line is -1.5 as the production of X is increased in one-unit increments. This isoprofit line is shown in Figure 6B–2 along with two other arbitrarily chosen profit levels. Notice that higher levels of profits are represented by higher isoprofit lines and that all isoprofit lines are parallel, since the slope of the isoprofit function is unchanged by variations in the value of π.

By superimposing the relevant isoprofit map upon the relevant feasible region, we are able to ascertain which of the combinations of X and Y allows the attainment of the highest possible isoprofit line. In Figure 6B–3 we reproduce the feasible region of the production problem from Figure 6B–1 and show that the highest isoprofit line that can be obtained is the line representing $1,350, which just touches point C on the feasible region. Any other point on the feasible region must lie on a lower isoprofit line, and any higher isoprofit lines will not touch the feasible region. Thus the optimal combination of Y and X is three units of Y and two and one-half units of X per week. (The fractional value of X does not worry us: every two weeks five complete units of Product X will be produced.)

Note that the solution occurs at one of the corners of the feasible region. Since the isoprofit lines are linear, and the constraints are linear, this must always be the case. In the event that the isoprofit line has the same slope as one of the constraint lines, the highest attainable isoprofit line would coincide with the facet of the feasible region that represents that particular constraint. In Figure 6B–4 we show such a situation. In this case the highest attainable isoprofit line coincides with the section CD of

FIGURE 6B–2.   Isoprofit Map for Production Problem

Hence equation 16B-10) represents the equation for the isoprofit line along which profits are $1,350. We note that the intercept of this line on the Y axis must be at five units, and the slope of this line is -1.63 as the production of X is increased by one unit, Y must . . . This isoprofit line is shown in Figure 6B-2 along with two other arbitrarily chosen profit levels. Notice that higher levels of profits are represented by higher isoprofit lines and that all isoprofit lines are parallel, since the slope of the isoprofit function is unchanged by variations in the value of π.

By superimposing the relevant isoprofit map upon the relevant feasible region we are able to ascertain which of the combinations of X and Y allows the attainment of the highest possible isoprofit line. In Figure 6B-3 we reproduce the feasible region of the production problem from Figure 6B-1 and show that the highest isoprofit line that can be obtained is the line represented by $1,350$, which just touches point C on the feasible region. Any other point on the feasible region A must lie on a lower isoprofit line, and any higher isoprofit lines will not touch the feasible region. Thus the optimal combination is 2 units of Y per week and one and one-half units of X per week. (The fractional value of X does not worry us, for over two weeks five complete units of product X will be produced.)

Note that the solution occurs at one of the corners of the feasible region. Since the isoprofit lines are linear, and the constraints are linear, this will often be the case. In the event that the isoprofit line has the same slope as one of the constraint lines, the feasible isoprofit line would coincide with the facet of the feasible region that represents that part of the boundary. In Figure 6B-4 we show such a situation. In this case the highest attainable isoprofit line coincides with the facet CD of

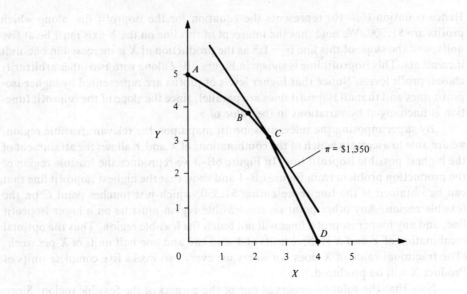

FIGURE 6B-3.   Solution to Production Problem

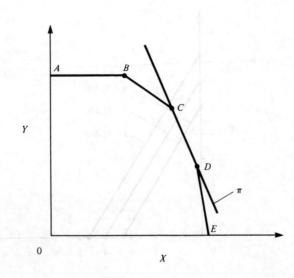

FIGURE 6B-4.   Isoprofit Line Coinciding with a Facet of the Feasible Region

the feasible region. Note that any output combination of X and Y along the facet CD allows the same level of profits to be attained. Thus the earlier statement that the solution will always occur at a corner of the feasible region is vindicated, since the corners represented by the points C and D represent equivalent levels of profit contribution when compared with any point on the facet of the feasible region, and thus either one will be an optimal solution.

A second interesting point depicted in Figure 6B-4 is the horizontal facet of the feasible region, labeled AB. This indicates a constraint that operates only on the production of product Y. It is thus a process that is not needed for the output of product X, and which when utilized fully by product Y allows $0A$ units of Y to be produced. Similarly, a process that is utilized only by product X would give rise to a vertical section on the feasible region (if it is a binding constraint).

Confirming the Solution Algebraically. The preceding discussion indicates that the slope of the constraint equations, in comparison with the slope of the isoprofit line, can be used to find the solution values for X and Y. Referring back to Figure 6B-3, notice that the slope of the isoprofit curve is greater than the slope of the third constraint (shown by the section AB of the feasible region) and is greater than the slope of the second constraint (shown by the segment BC), but it is less than the slope of the first constraint (shown by the segment CD). Thus we might have simply compared the slopes of the profit function with the slopes of the constraint lines to find, in comparison with the profit function, the next-steepest constraint line and the next-flattest constraint line. The intersection of these two constraint lines will thus define the point at which profit contribution is maximized, unless one of these constraints lies outside the feasible region. The comparison of the slopes of the objective function and the constraint functions that bound the feasible region thus acts as a check upon our graphical procedures.

Since the solution line lies at the intersection of the first and second constraint lines, we are able to confirm the graphical results by simultaneous solution of those two equations for the values of X and Y, as follows:

$$8X + 4Y = 32 \tag{6B-11}$$

$$6X + 5Y = 30 \tag{6B-12}$$

We proceed to eliminate Y by multiplying equation (6B-11) by 5 and equation (6B-12) by 4:

$$40X + 20Y = 160 \tag{6B-13}$$

$$24X + 20Y = 120 \tag{6B-14}$$

and subtracting equation (6B–14) from equation (6B–13), we have

$$16X = 40$$

or

$$X = 2.5$$

Substituting for X in equation (6B–11) to find Y:

$$8(2.5) + 4Y = 32$$
$$4Y = 12$$
$$Y = 3$$

To find the profit level, we substitute for X and Y in the isoprofit function, equation (6B–2):

$$\pi = 300(2.5) + 200(3)$$
$$= 750 + 600$$
$$= 1,350$$

It is clear that process 1 and process 2 are fully utilized by the production of the three units of Y and the two and a half units of X per week. Process 3, however, is not fully utilized, since this output combination requires less than forty hours of the third process. To confirm this, let us substitute the optimal values for X and Y into the constraint inequality given by equation (6B–5).

$$5X + 8Y \leq 40$$
$$5(2.5) + 8(3) \leq 40$$
$$12.5 + 24 \leq 40$$
$$36.5 \leq 40$$

Thus there are 3.5 units (hours) of the third process remaining unutilized at the optimal output combinations.

Algebraic Solution of the Linear-Programming Problem

Given the knowledge that the solution to linear-programming programs will occur at one of the corners, we could solve for the values of X and Y at each of the corners, substitute these values into the objective function, and choose that pair of values that generates the greatest value in the objective function. To solve the problem algebraically, however, all constraints must be expressed as equations rather than inequalities.

To cause all constraints to be expressed as equalities, we insert what are known as "slack variables" in each of the constraint expressions. The slack variables take up the slack if the constraint is not binding and are thus valued at the amount of idle capacity remaining in a particular process. Obviously, if a constraint is binding, the value of the slack variable is zero.

Algebraic solution of the linear-programming problem offers two main advantages over the graphical solution. First, it allows us to handle problems in which there are three or more variables; and second, the values of the slack variables provide information that is extremely useful for decision-making purposes. To demonstrate the algebraic solution of a linear-programming problem, suppose that the small firm making the shelf display units discovers that a market exists for a third product, product Z, which is essentially a smaller version of product X. Suppose that its price is expected to remain constant at $250 per unit and that its costs will be $150 per unit, such that the contribution will be $100 per unit. It will require two hours of hacksaw time, four hours of welding time, and three hours of the chrome bath time to produce each unit of product Z. Modifying the earlier objective function and constraints by the addition of the information relevant to product Z, and inserting slack variables, we may state the linear-programming problem algebraically as follows:

Maximize

$$\pi = 300X + 200Y + 100Z \qquad (6\text{B}-15)$$

subject to

$$8X + 4Y + 2Z + S_1 = 32 \qquad (6\text{B}-16)$$

$$6X + 5Y + 4Z + S_2 = 30 \qquad (6\text{B}-17)$$

$$5X + 8Y + 3Z + S_3 = 40 \qquad (6\text{B}-18)$$

with the nonnegativity requirements

$$X \geq 0,\ Y \geq 0,\ Z \geq 0,\ S_1 \geq 0,\ S_2 \geq 0,\ S_3 \geq 0$$

We wish to find the values of X, Y, and Z at each of the corners or peaks of a three-dimensional feasible region. The constraint equations (6B–16) to (6B–18) provide a system of three equations in six unknowns, and the system is therefore underdetermined. We know, however, that at each of the corners or peaks of the feasible region the values of some of the variables will be zero. In the three-dimensional case, three variables will be zero at each corner.[2]

----

[2]Imagine a three-dimensional surface, like a peaked roof. Where three planes intersect, as at the end of the roof, there will be a point. In a three-variable linear-programming problem this point corresponds to the intersection of three constraint planes. If the isoprofit surface sits on this point, then three of the processes will be fully utilized.

To identify each corner, we take the six variables (three output variables and three slack variables) and consider every combination in which three of these variables are zero and the other three have positive values. We then evaluate the profit function at each of these combinations. In Table 6B-1 we show the value of each of the variables at each corner of the feasible region. At corner 0, the origin, output of the three products is zero, and the slack variables must take the maximum values. At corner A, the values of X and Z are zero and the third constraint is binding, such that the slack variable S_3 is also zero. At this corner the value of Y is 5, and we find the values of S_1 and S_2 by substitution of $Y = 5$ in equations (6B-16) and (6B-17). Since X and Z are zero in each of these expressions, and Y is known, it is a simple matter to find $S_1 = 12$, and $S_2 = 5$. At corner B, $Z = 0$, $S_2 = 0$, and $S_3 = 0$. This procedure collapses equations (6B-17) and (6B-18) into the following system of two equations in two unknowns:

$$6X + 5Y = 30 \tag{6B-19}$$

$$5X + 8Y = 40 \tag{6B-20}$$

By simultaneous solution of equations (6B-19) and (6B-20) we find $X = 1.74$ and $Y = 3.91$. Substituting these values into equation (6B-16), we find the missing value of slack variable S_1, which is 0.44. Substituting the calculated values for X and Y into the objective function (6B-15), we find the total profit contribution at this corner to be $1,304. The values of the variables and the objective function at the other corners are calculated in similar fashion. The values of the objective function at the corners of the feasible region are calculated by substitution of the values of X, Y, and Z in the objective function equation (6B-15) and are shown in the next to the last column of Table 6B-1. It can be seen that contribution is maximized at corner C, as it was in the earlier two-dimensional case. Thus, the addition of product Z does not change the optimality of the earlier solution, since the contribution of product Z relative to its use of the

TABLE 6B-1.   Algebraic Solution of a Linear-Programming Problem

Corner name	VALUE OF VARIABLES						VALUE OF OBJECTIVE FUNCTION	
	X	Y	Z	S_1	S_2	S_3	Initial	Later
0	0	0	0	32	30	40	$ 0	0
A	0	5	0	12	5	0	1,000	500
B	1.74	3.91	0	0.44	0	0	1,304	870
C	2.5	3	0	0	0	3.5	1,350*	988
D	4	0	0	0	6	20	1,200	1,100
E	3.4	0	2.4	0	0	15.8	1,260	1,115*
F	0	4.12	2.35	10.8	0	0	1,059	588
G	0	0	7.5	17.0	0	17.5	750	563

*Maximum.

constrained processes is lower than for the original two products. Thus the firm would maximize total product contribution by producing 2.5 units of X, 3.0 units of Y, and ignoring the market opportunity for product Z.

Response to a Change in the Parameters of the Problem.   The above optimal combination of the three products depends upon their relative contributions to overheads and profits and their relative use of the three production processes. If either of these factors changed or if we were able to relax one of the constraints, we should expect a new combination of the three products to be optimal. To illustrate, let us suppose that market conditions change and the relative contributions of the three products change. Suppose a new firm begins making these units in direct competition with product Y, but causes the prices of products X and Z to be reduced also, such that the new objective function becomes

$$\pi = 275X + 100Y + 75Z \tag{6B-21}$$

Note that there has been no change in the availability of any of the production processes or in the usage rates of these processes by any of the products. Thus the corner solutions found earlier are still applicable. Inserting these values for the variables into the new objective function, we find the value of the objective function at each corner as shown in the last column in Table 6B-1. Note that profit contribution is now greatest at corner E rather than at corner C: under the new market conditions it is now more profitable to drop product Y and increase the production of both products X and Z. This result comes about because the isoprofit plane has shifted because of the change in the relative contributions of the three products, and the highest attainable isoprofit plane now touches the feasible region at the corner E, whereas previously the highest attainable isoprofit plane rested on point C.

If the capacity of a particular process could be increased, that is, if the constraint could be relaxed, would we expect a change in the optimal combination of outputs and the total profit contribution? The answer to this question is yes to both issues if the constraint is binding, but it is no if slack exists in the particular constraint. In order for additional availability of a constraint process to cause the solution to change, availability of additional capacity must cause the frontier of the feasible region to move outward and poke through the previously highest attainable isoprofit line or surface, such that a new higher isoprofit line or surface can be attained. This statement is demonstrated in the two-variable case in Figure 6B-5. Here the constraint represented by the facet BC has been relaxed by a certain amount to cause the feasible region to expand to the area bounded by $0AB'C'D'$. Whereas the previously highest attainable isoprofit curve was that shown by π, tangent at point C, the new feasible region allows the higher isoprofit line π' to be attained at point C'.

Shadow Prices of the Constraints.   The *shadow price* of a constraint is defined as the increment to the value of the objective function that results from that constraint being

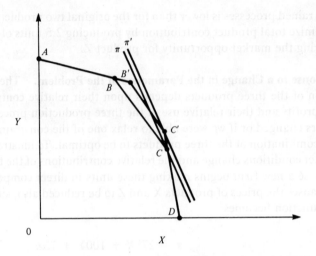

FIGURE 6B–5.   Relaxation of a Constraint and Its Impact on Profit Contribution

relaxed by one unit. From the preceding discussion it is clear that only those constraints that are binding will have positive shadow prices, since those constraints with slack remaining will add nothing to profit contribution if increased further.

Graphically we could find the shadow price of each constraint by expanding the frontier for each constraint, finding the new highest attainable isoprofit line, and calculating the value of this level of profit from the intercept value of this isoprofit line. Algebraically, the procedure is similar. We would expand one constraint by one unit—for example, $8X + 4Y + 2Z + S_1 = 33$—and solve for the optimal combinations of X, Y, and Z in conjunction with the other two constraint equations in their original form. We would then substitute the solution values for X, Y, and Z in the objective function to find the new profit-contribution level. A simple subtraction of the earlier maximum profit contribution from the new maximum profit contribution would generate the shadow price of the constraint that was augmented.

An alternative algebraic method of obtaining the shadow prices is to solve the "dual" of the linear-programming problem.

The Dual Problem

In the preceding discussion we have worked with what is by convention called the "primal" problem. A primal problem may be to maximize some variable subject to various constraints, as in the above example, or it may be to minimize a variable subject to several constraints in a different problem. Every primal linear-programming problem has a dual problem associated with it. For every maximization problem there is an associated (dual) minimization problem, and for every minimization problem there is an associated (dual) maximization problem. This relationship derives from the mathematical nature of the linear-programming technique. Although it may not be intuitively obvious, for every problem in which a particular variable is to be maximized (or minimized) subject to certain constraints, there is another variable that, if minimized (or maximized) subject to another set of constraints, will derive the same values for the crucial variables. In the case discussed above, we maximized profit contribution subject to the limited availability of three production processes, by choosing the optimal output mix of products X, Y, and Z. The dual to this problem is to minimize the value of these three production processes subject to the constraints that the value of the production processes used in the production of each unit of output do not exceed the contribution generated by each unit of each output. When this minimization problem is solved, the output mix of products X, Y, and Z will be the same as it would have been in the primal maximization problem. The virtue of solving the dual problem is that the solution imputes a value to the marginal units of each of the constraints, which of course are the shadow prices we seek.

Let us now return to the simple two-variable problem discussed previously, which was to maximize

$$\pi = 300X + 200Y$$

subject to

$$8X + 4Y + S_1 = 32$$
$$6X + 5Y + S_2 = 30$$
$$5X + 8Y + S_3 = 40$$

with the nonnegativity requirements that X, Y, S_1, S_2, and S_3 are all ≥ 0.

To establish the dual problem, we must define a number of new variables as follows:

$V =$ the total value of the three production processes,
$W_1 =$ the shadow price of the first process,
$W_2 =$ the shadow price of the second process,
$W_3 =$ the shadow price of the third process,
$R_1 =$ slack variable in the constraint that the value of the resources used in production of a unit of X should not exceed the contribution from a unit of X, and
$R_2 =$ the slack variable in the constraint pertaining to product Y.

We can now state the dual problem:

Minimize

$$V = 32W_1 + 30W_2 + 40W_3 \qquad (6B\text{-}22)$$

subject to

$$8W_1 + 6W_2 + 5W_3 + R_1 = 300 \qquad (6B\text{-}23)$$

$$4W_1 + 5W_2 + 8W_3 + R_2 = 200 \qquad (6B\text{-}24)$$

with the nonnegativity requirements that W_1, W_2, W_3, R_1, and R_2 are all ≥ 0.

Solving the Dual Problem. The objective function of the dual problem is thus to minimize the total value of the firm's fixed resources, measured in terms of the shadow prices of each resource times the availability of that resource in units. The constraints are that the total cost of the firm's resources involved in the production of each product should be less than or equal to the contribution from each of the products. We insert the slack variables to allow the constraints to be represented as equalities.

Equations (6B-23) and (6B-24) are a system of two equations in five unknowns, and this system is thus underdetermined. However, our knowledge of the nature of the solution to the linear-programming problem allows us to predict that at each corner of the feasible region three of the variables will take zero values, and hence we may iteratively assign zero values to combinations of three variables and find the combination that provides the minimum value of the objective function. We could array the values of the variables and the objective function in a table, as we did for the primal problem in Table 6B-1, where each line would represent the values of the variables and the objective function at one of the corners. That corner that meets all the nonnegativity requirements and shows the minimum value for V will represent the optimal solution. At that corner the values of the variables W_1, W_2, and W_3 will represent the shadow price of each of the constraints.

Rather than follow the above procedure, however, we shall use the knowledge gained from the solution of the primal problem to assign zero values to three of the variables in the system of equations (6B-23) and (6B-24) such that we may solve for the values of the shadow prices at the optimal solution. We know that in the primal problem the first and second constraints were binding. Thus W_1 and W_2 in the dual problem will have positive values, while W_3, R_1, and R_2 must take zero values. Eliminating the latter three variables from equations (6B-23) and (6B-24), we have

$$8W_1 + 6W_2 = 300 \qquad (6B\text{-}25)$$

$$4W_1 + 5W_2 = 200 \qquad (6B\text{-}26)$$

which is a system of two equations in two unknowns and can thus be solved by simultaneous solution. Multiplying equation (6B-26) by 2, we have

$$8W_1 + 10W_2 = 400 \qquad (6B\text{-}27)$$

Subtracting equation (6B-25) from (6B-27) to eliminate W_1, we have

$$4W_2 = 100$$

or

$$W_2 = 25$$

Substituting into equation (6B-25) to find W_1:

$$8W_1 + 6(25) = 300$$
$$8W_1 = 150$$
$$W_1 = 18.75$$

Thus the shadow prices of the two constraints that are binding are \$25 for the hacksaw process, and \$18.75 for the welding process. That is to say, an extra hour of utilization of either process would add those amounts to the total contribution to overheads and profits. If an additional hour of the hacksaw operator's time plus associated expenses could be employed for less than \$25, the decision maker should do so. Similarly, if an additional hour of the welding equipment's utilization could be employed for less than \$18.75, the decision maker would be advised to do so, since there would result a net increase in the contribution to overheads and profits.

An alternate method that finds both the optimal values of the variables and the shadow prices of the constraints is the simplex method.[3] Essentially, the simplex method uses the knowledge that the solution must occur at a corner of the feasible region, and that at each corner the number of nonzero variables is exactly equal to the number of constraints in the problem, to search for the solution. The simplex method starts at the origin of the feasible region and proceeds to compare the profitability of that corner point with an adjacent corner point. If the adjacent corner yields a greater profit, the next corner point is evaluated and compared. When the adjacent corner yields a lower profit, the procedure ceases, and the previous highest profit point is taken to be the optimal solution.

We shall not go into any detail concerning the simplex method, since it is a tedious method prone to error when calculated by hand. Computer programs are now readily available that use the simplex method to compute the optimal values of the variables and the shadow prices of the constraints quickly and accurately. It is impor-

---

[3]The simplex method is attributed to the mathematician George M. Dantzig. See Dantzig, *A Procedure for Maximizing a Linear Function Subject to Linear Inequalities* (Washington, D.C.: Headquarters U.S. Air Force, Comptroller, 1948). Although the word *simplex* might imply simplicity, a simplex is the *n*-dimensional analogue of a triangle. The simplex technique is named for its procedure of systematically evaluating the objective function at the simplexes of the feasible region.

tant for the decision maker to understand the underlying principles of linear programming, and then use the most cost-effective means of utilizing the linear programming technique.

Other Applications of Linear Programming

In this chapter we have confined our attention to the solution of a product-mix problem. Linear-programming analysis is applicable to a wide variety of decision problems that arise in the business firm or institutional environment. Linear programming is commonly used to solve transportation problems in which the shortest route must be found between a number of delivery points, subject to the constraints imposed by the highway or railroad system.[4] The classic diet problem involves minimizing the cost of supplying patients in a hospital with the minimum required amounts of certain vitamins and other nutrients which are contained in differing quantities in various foodstuffs, which in turn cost differing amounts.[5] This problem is analogous to a firm wishing to minimize the cost of meeting all specifications on a particular project when there is more than one way to meet each specification. In marketing, linear programming may be used to find the minimum costs of obtaining a certain level of advertising exposure given the different costs and availabilities of the various media. These examples serve to indicate the range of applications of linear-programming analysis. As long as the objective function and the constraints can be expressed linearly in terms of the variables, linear programming will serve as a valid solution procedure.

Summary

In this appendix we have outlined the application of linear programming to the product-mix problem. Linear programming allows the optimal combinations to be found, given the presence of certain absolute constraints. Simple two-variable cases can be solved graphically by graphing the constraints in the two-variable space and finding the corner solution that supports the highest attainable isoprofit line. At this corner solution two of the constraints will be equalities and thus can be solved for the values of the two variables at the optimal combination point, and the optimal level of profits will be found by substituting the solution values of the variables in the objective function equation.

More complex cases can be solved algebraically on the basis of the knowledge that the nature of the solution is such that the number of nonzero variables will equal the number of constraints at the solution point. Thus, if we have n constraints and m variables, we could set $m - n$ variables equal to zero and solve for the remaining n

---

[4]See, for example, W. J. Fabrycky and G. J. Thuesen, *Economic Decision Analysis* (Englewood Cliffs, N.J.: Prentice-Hall, 1974), pp. 324–32.

[5]See R. Dorfman, P. A. Samuelson, and R. M. Solow, *Linear Programming and Economic Analysis* (New York: McGraw-Hill, 1958), chap. 2.

variables in the n equations provided by the constraints. We would do this for all combinations of the variables. For each of the $m - n$ zero-valued variables and n positively valued variables that would result, we would evaluate the objective function and choose as a solution the combination that gave the optimal value to the objective function. The solution of the dual problem may be easier than solving the primal problem, but in any case it provides values for the shadow prices of each constraint, which provide valuable information for the decision maker.

The mechanistic nature of the linear-programming solution lends itself to computer programming, such that this technique is able to handle extremely complex decision problems. It has wide applicability in business situations, but the decision maker must be assured that the problem to be solved can be fairly represented by linear constraints and a linear objective function.

DISCUSSION QUESTIONS

6B-1. Outline the features necessary to make a problem suitable for solution by linear-programming analysis.

6B-2. When would a constraint line be horizontal or vertical in the graphical approach to linear programming analysis?

6B-3. Why is linear programming a technique suitable for short-run production problems rather than for long-run production problems?

6B-4. If a firm produces two products, both of which make exactly the same demands on resources and contribute the same to profits, how is the optimal product mix determined?

6B-5. What is the logic behind changing the inequality to an equality in order to depict each constraint graphically?

6B-6. For algebraic solution of the linear-programming problem, we insert slack variables in order to express the constraints as equalities. Why?

6B-7. Outline the process involved in the algebraic solution of the linear-programming problem. Why are we able to confine our attention to the corner solutions?

6B-8. What happens to the shape of the feasible region if a production process suddenly becomes more efficient in terms of the output of one product?

6B-9. What should the decision maker do after having ascertained the shadow prices of each constraint?

6B-10. Outline the relationship between the primal problem and its dual problem in linear-programming analysis.

PROBLEMS AND SHORT CASES

6B-1. Frank's Fish Packing Company produces two items, fish cakes (for human consumption) and fish meal (for animal consumption). The light-meat parts of the fish are separated from the rest of the fish for the fish cakes, and the rest of the fish is used for the fish meal. The ratio of fish cakes output to fish meal output can vary as more or less of the lighter meat is separated from the rest of the fish. As the fresh fish comes into the plant it goes through four processes: separating, shredding, packing, and canning. Each of these processes has a maximum input available because of the labor available with the required training for each process, and these workers' prior agreements with management as to the length of their workweek. The total time available in each process, and the time required in each process per 1,000 pounds of output for each of the products, is as follows:

Process	Total Time Available (hours weekly)	HOURS REQUIRED (PER 1,000 LB) Fish Cakes	Fish Meal
Separating	205	22.78	13.67
Shredding	106	10.60	8.83
Packing	188	14.46	17.09
Canning	65	5.00	5.00

Frank's sells the fish cakes for $0.80 per pound and the fish meal for $0.70 per pound. All costs, including the fresh fish, are joint costs, and hence these revenue figures can be treated as the per-unit contribution to joint (overhead) costs and profits.

Solve this product-mix problem using graphical analysis. Confirm your answers algebraically.

(a) What is the contribution-maximizing product mix?

(b) What is the maximum contribution attainable?

(c) Which processes are at full capacity?

6B-2. The Munchies Cake Company wishes to minimize the materials cost for its "Jumbo" fruit-and-nut cakes. The company has found that market acceptance of these cakes is maximized when they contain at least 250 grams of currants, 375 grams of sultanas, 150 grams of citrus peel, and 225 grams of nuts, and it consequently wishes to maintain at least these levels of these components in each cake. Neither of the two commercially available fruit and nut mixes comes in exactly these proportions, however, and Munchies combines these two mixes to achieve a mix that meets the above constraints on the minimum weight of each component. Brand A fruit-and-nut mix costs $2.15 per kilogram, and brand B fruit-and-nut mix costs $2.35 per kilogram. Each kilogram of these two mixes contains the following percentage breakdown of the four components:

	Currants	Sultanas	Peel	Nuts
Brand A	30%	40%	10%	20%
Brand B	15%	35%	25%	25%

(a) Using graphical analysis, find the combination of brand A and brand B fruit-and-nut mix that minimizes cost subject to the minimum weights being achieved for each of the four components. Confirm your answers algebraically.

(b) What is the minimum fruit-and-nut mix cost per Jumbo cake?

(c) Which constraints are binding? What would you suggest Munchies do? Why?

6B-3. The Grimes Gravel Company produces three mixtures of sand, pebbles, and rocks for eventual sale in 20-kg bags to the home handyperson for use in cement work. The sandy mixture is composed of 10 kg sand, 7 kg pebbles, and 3 kg rocks. The pebbly mixture is composed of 6 kg sand, 10 kg pebbles, and 4 kg rocks. The rocky mixture is composed of 2 kg sand, 8 kg pebbles, and 10 kg rocks. The market prices prevailing are $2.75 for the sandy mixture, $2.50 for the pebbly mixture, and $2.25 for the rocky mixture. Grimes Gravel feels that the market prices will hold regardless of the volume of each product it supplies.

Grimes Gravel wishes to maximize sales revenue from its present plant and equipment. The constraints on output are the limited size of the storage bins for the sand, pebbles, and rocks. These bins hold 2,000, 3,000, and 2,000 kilograms, respectively, and replenishment of supplies can only be made once weekly.

(a) Use the algebraic approach to find the optimal output of each of the three products.

(b) What is the maximum weekly revenue that Grimes Gravel can obtain?

(c) Which constraints are binding?

6B-4. Corpulent Foods, Inc., wishes to minimize the ingredient cost of its Krunchy-Karamel chocolate bar. This chocolate bar has become its major seller over the past year, but increasing costs have reduced the contribution margin below acceptable levels. The Krunchy-Karamel bar is now comprised of 45 percent chocolate, 35 percent caramel, and 20 percent nuts. It weighs 100 grams, and Corpulent Foods wholesales the bar at 10 cents apiece (in bulk) and expects to continue paying $1.25 per kilogram for chocolate, $0.85 per kilogram for caramel, and $0.50 per kilogram for nuts.

Corpulent Foods' marketing research department has been conducting tests with experimental compositions of the Krunchy-Karamel bar. Using bars with various combinations of chocolate, caramel, and nuts, it has ascertained that as long as the bars contain at least 30 grams of chocolate, 15 grams of caramel, and 10 grams of nuts, and score at least 150 on the "crunch" index and 300 on the "flavor" index, all consumers who initially preferred the (regular) Krunchy-Karamel bar over the rival bars will still prefer the (modified) Krunchy-Karamel bar. The score on the crunch and flavor indices reflects the average subjective evaluation given by the consumer-participants to each experimental bar, on a scale of zero to 500. Regressing these average crunch and flavor scores against the contents of the various experimental bars, it was found that chocolate gives 2 units of crunch and 3.3 units of flavor per gram, caramel gives 1 unit of crunch and 5 units of flavor per gram, and nuts give 7 units of crunch and 2 units of flavor per gram.

(a) Formalize the above problem by expressing its objective function and six constraints algebraically.

(b) Solve for that minimum cost combination of ingredients that satisfies all constraints by systematically assigning zero values to some variables and evaluating the objective function at each of the feasible corner solutions.

(c) Should Corpulent Foods change the present composition of its Krunchy-Karamel bar? Why?

6B-5. The P.M.D. Light Company produces and sells three standing lamps. The contribution to overhead and profit for these lamps is constant at the following levels regardless of output level: model A, $8.75; model B, $13.25, and model C, $16.80. All three models go through the basic assembly process, then models A and B go through the fabric installation process while model C goes through the antique-bronzing process. The requirements of each model in each process and the weekly availability of these processes are as follows:

Process	Hours Available	HOURS REQUIRED PER UNIT		
		A	B	C
Assembly	800	0.2	0.3	0.35
Fabric	480	0.1	0.12	—
Bronzing	160	—	—	0.8

278   *Production and Cost Analysis*

Using the simplex method, solve for the contribution-maximizing output mix, the maximum contribution available, and the shadow prices of the constraints.

(a) Should P.M.D. Light continue to produce all three models? Why?

(b) Suppose overtime labor was available in each process at a cost of $12 per hour compared with the regular $8 per hour. Would you advise P.M.D. Light to employ this overtime labor? Explain.

SUGGESTED REFERENCES AND FURTHER READING

Baumol, W. J. *Economic Theory and Operations Analysis* (4th ed.), chaps. 5 and 6. Englewood Cliffs, N.J.: Prentice-Hall, Inc., 1977.

Brigham, E. F., and J. L. Pappas. *Managerial Economics* (2nd ed.), chap. 7. Hinsdale, Ill.: The Dryden Press, 1976.

Charnes, A., and W. W. Cooper. *Management Models and Industrial Applications of Linear Programming*, vols. 1 and 2. New York: John Wiley & Sons, 1961.

Dano, S. *Linear Programming in Industry: Theory and Applications.* Vienna, Austria: Springer-Verlag, 1960.

Dantzig, G. M. *Linear Programming and Extensions*, esp. chaps. 1–5. Princeton, N.J.: Princeton University Press, 1963.

Dorfman, R. "Mathematical, or Linear, Programming: A Nonmathematical Exposition," *American Economic Review*, 63 (December 1953), pp. 797–825.

Dorfman, R., P. A. Samuelson, and R. M. Solow. *Linear Programming and Economic Analysis*, chaps. 1–7. New York: McGraw-Hill Book Company, 1958.

Fabrycky, W. J., and G. J. Thuesen. *Economic Decision Analysis*, chap. 15. Englewood Cliffs, N.J.: Prentice-Hall, Inc., 1974.

Heineke, J. M. *Microeconomics for Business Decisions: Theory and Applications*, chaps. 4 and 5. Englewood Cliffs, N.J.: Prentice-Hall, Inc., 1976.

Naylor, T. H., and J. M. Vernon. *Microeconomics and Decision Models of the Firm*, chaps. 6–8. New York: Harcourt, Brace & World, 1969.

7

Cost Concepts for Decision Making

7.1 INTRODUCTION

In this chapter we introduce cost concepts that are used in day-to-day decision making by the business executive. In some cases these are crude when compared with the theoretical nicety of the concepts discussed in the preceding chapter. Real-world business situations, however, seldom provide the data necessary for direct application of the theoretical concepts. Nevertheless, an understanding of the theoretical concepts is important to ensure the proper application of the concepts that will be discussed in this chapter. Decision makers sometimes apply convenient rules of thumb to problems that confront them without first examining the applicability of those rules to the particular problem at hand. The danger of incorrectly applying these shortcuts is perhaps nowhere greater than in the area of costs, since poor decisions here operate directly to erode profitability.

In this chapter we shall first examine the differences between economic and accounting concepts of costs and profits. We shall see that some accounting costs, such as the depreciation of an asset purchased in an earlier period or the cost of an item taken from inventory purchased at an earlier, lower price, must be evaluated in terms of the current or future cost for economic decision-making purposes. This subject leads to a discussion of the relevant costs for decision making—some costs are relevant and others are irrelevant to the decision problem at hand. The relevant costs are all "incremental" costs. The three main types of incremental costs are introduced and discussed. "Contribution analysis" is based on the incremental costs of a decision, and the last section before the summary uses contribution analysis in the context of several types of decision problems. The appendix to this chapter considers "breakeven analysis," with an examination of its applications and its limitations in the decision-making process.

7.2 ECONOMIC VERSUS ACCOUNTING CONCEPTS OF COSTS AND PROFITS

The data for decision making with respect to costs typically come not from economists but from accountants. In most cases these data are adequate and appropriate, but in some cases, since they were derived for different purposes, they are less suitable for direct insertion into economic decision-making procedures. We shall examine several different economic and accounting cost concepts and the relationships between them.

Direct and Indirect Costs

In the business firm some costs are incurred that can be directly attributed to the production of a particular unit of a given product. The use of raw materials, labor inputs, and machine time involved in the production of each unit can usually be determined. On the other hand, the cost of fuel for heating, electricity, office and administrative expenses, depreciation of plant and buildings, and other items cannot easily and accurately be separated and attributed to individual units of production (except on an arbitrary basis). Accountants speak of the *direct*, or *prime*, costs per unit when referring to the separable costs of the first category and of *indirect*, or *overhead*, costs when referring to the joint costs of the second category.[1]

Direct and indirect costs are not likely to coincide exactly with the economist's variable cost and fixed cost categories. The criterion used by the economist to divide cost into either fixed or variable is whether or not the cost varies with the level of output, but the criterion used by the accountant is whether or not the cost is separable with respect to the production of individual output units. To bring the accounting costs into line with the economic concepts we must find that part of the indirect or overhead costs that varies with the output level. Accounting statements often divide overhead expense into "variable overhead" and "fixed overhead" categories, in which case we would add the variable overhead expense per unit to the direct cost per unit to find what economists call *average variable cost*.

Example: Suppose that a company reports that during the past month it manufactured 1,480 units of output, and the accountant provides you with figures for the total expenditures on direct labor, direct materials, variable overhead, and fixed overhead, as shown in the left-hand side of Table 7-1. The sum of the first three expenditures constitutes the total variable cost (TVC), and adding to it the fixed overhead, which we call total fixed cost (TFC), we arrive at total costs (TC). Per-unit costs, shown on the

---

[1]See, for example, C. T. Horngren, *Introduction to Management Accounting*, 5th ed. (Englewood Cliffs, N.J.: Prentice-Hall, Inc., 1981), chap. 3.

TABLE 7-1. The Interpretation of Accounting Reports in Economic Terms

Costs of Production	Total Costs	Average Cost
Direct labor	$ 77,700	$52.50
Direct materials	36,260	24.50
Variable overhead	4,930	3.33
	TVC = $118,890	AVC = $ 80.33
Fixed overhead	TFC = $ 36,800	AFC = $ 24.86
Total costs	TC = $155,690	AC = $105.19

right-hand side of the table, are found by dividing the total cost figures by the output level.[2]

Explicit and Implicit Costs

The accounting process is predominantly concerned with explicit costs. These are costs that actually involve a transfer of funds from the firm to another party that had previously supplied some materials or services. These are "out-of-pocket" expenses in the current time period, since they are an actual cash outflow in payment for resources. Other cost items, however, are implicit costs, in the sense that they do not involve an actual cash outflow in the current time period.

Example: One such cost in the accounting framework is *depreciation*, which is a charge against each year's revenue of some portion of the cost of acquiring the capital equipment necessary to generate that revenue. The accounting procedures involve taking the initial cost of the asset, subtracting from this the asset's estimated scrap or salvage value at the end of its useful life, and apportioning this net cost against revenues over the life of the asset. Straight-line depreciation procedures allocate the net cost evenly over the life of the asset, while other methods, such as the sum-of-the-digits methods and double-declining-balance method, allocate proportionately more of the net cost against revenues early in the asset's life.[3] Thus the accountant charges an implicit cost against revenues each year in order to spread the explicit cost of the asset over the period during which the asset is being used in the production process.

---

[2]Simply adding variable overhead to direct labor and materials to find total variable cost, and hence AVC, may still involve error if the assignment of costs to the variable or fixed overhead categories was made on any basis other than the variability of the cost with respect to changes in the output level. In Chapter 8 we examine the "gradient method" and other cost estimation techniques which allow a more precise estimate of average variable and marginal costs. At that time we will stress the importance of examining changes in all cost categories to see that the changes were output related and not simply due to changes in factor input prices or some other reason.

[3]See Horngren, *Introduction to Management Accounting*, pp. 344-46.

Opportunity Costs and Historic Costs

Accountants are constrained by the tax laws and by the laws governing financial reporting to shareholders to express many costs in terms of the actual or historic costs paid for the resources used in the production process. For decision-making purposes, however, both accountants and economists agree that the appropriate cost concept is not the past cost at which the resource was purchased, but the current or future cost at the time in which it is involved in the decision to be made.

■ *Definition: Opportunity costs*, or alternative costs as they are often called, refer to the value of a resource in its best alternative employment. For resources that are purchased outright or hired, such as raw materials and labor inputs, there is usually little difference between historic costs and opportunity costs. The market price at which they are purchased or hired should reflect their opportunity cost, since producers must bid for these goods in their respective markets. If not willing to pay at least what the resources are worth in their best alternative usage, the firm will not be able to purchase the services of these resources.

A difference will almost certainly arise between historic cost and opportunity cost if the resources are purchased and held in inventory for some time before they are used in the production process. If the market value of those resources changes, the opportunity cost diverges from the historic cost. Given the continuing problem of inflation, input prices tend to move upwards on a more or less continuous basis, although in some cases rapid technological advances can cause the market value of resources held in inventory to decline. For decision-making purposes, the current market value of the resource is its implicit cost to the firm, and this cost should be incorporated into any decision process rather than the (either higher or lower) historic cost. Note that if the firm wanted to replenish its inventories it must pay the current market price for the resource, or alternatively, if it wanted to sell the resource to another firm, it could do so at the current market value, rather than at the historic cost of the resource.

Now let us reconsider depreciation, which is intended to represent the implicit cost of assets such as land, buildings, and equipment purchased in the past. The accountant depreciates the cost of these assets by allocating a portion of the net cost of the asset against the current period's revenues. The economist determines the opportunity cost of these services on the basis of what the land and buildings might have earned in alternative employment or on the basis of the interest which the funds tied up in those assets could have earned in alternative investment, whichever is greater. The opportunity costs of the capital tied up in land, buildings, and equipment may be quite different from the depreciation charge made against revenues, since the latter is determined on an entirely different basis. For decision-making purposes, depreciation of assets involved in the production process must be treated as the opportunity cost of those assets.

Example: The owner of a small farm might forgo $10,000 per annum in camping fees by continuing to use the land for farming rather than to take in campers. This is the opportunity cost of the land, unless the market value of the land is so high that the interest earned on the proceeds of the farm's sale would earn more. Suppose the farm could be sold for $100,000, which the farmer (supposing he owns the farm free and clear) could deposit for 15 percent interest. Thus the opportunity cost of continuing to farm the land is $15,000, this being the *best* alternative use of the resource.

The farmer's own labor must similarly be valued at its opportunity cost. If he could alternatively work for another farmer or take a job demonstrating and selling farm machinery, at say $20,000 per annum, this figure is his opportunity cost and should be included in the analysis for decision-making purposes.

Costs and Profits

The economist's concept of profit differs from that of the accountant. Both consider profit as the excess of revenues over costs, but they regard costs differently. The accountant subtracts from revenues only the costs that are actually incurred plus an allowance for depreciation of some of the previously incurred one-time expenditures, such as the cost of plant and machinery. Profits thus represent the net income to the owners of the firm; profits are their reward for having invested time and capital in the venture. The economist, on the other hand, is concerned with the wider notion of efficient allocation of resources and is thus concerned that all resources are employed where they will earn the maximum for their owners. A means of ensuring this is to consider the opportunity cost of each resource.

Example: Let us illustrate with reference to the example of a small-store owner who has $50,000 invested as equity in the store and inventory. As shown in Table 7-2, the annual sales revenues were $160,000, from which must be deducted the cost of goods sold, salaries of hired labor, and depreciation of equipment and buildings. The accounting profit to the store is thus $15,000.

In Table 7-3 we show the economic statement of profit of the same store. Note that the sales revenues, cost of goods sold, salaries, and depreciation are the same as in the preceding table. (We suppose that we have checked and found that the market values of the equipment and buildings have in fact declined by $5,000 over the current

TABLE 7-2. Accounting Income Statement for the Small-Store Owner

Sales		$160,000
Cost of goods sold	$120,000	
Salaries	20,000	
Depreciation expense	5,000	145,000
Accounting profit		$ 15,000

TABLE 7-3.   Economic Statement of Profit to Small-Store Owner

Sales		$160,000
Cost of goods sold	$120,000	
Salaries	20,000	
Depreciation expense	5,000	
Imputed salary to owner-manager	15,000	
Imputed interest cost on equity	4,000	164,000
Economic profit		$−4,000

year and that the depreciation charge, therefore, fairly reflects the opportunity costs of these resources.)

The economist, however, would add two other items relating to the implicit cost of resources that are owned by the manager. Suppose that the owner-manager could earn $15,000 as a departmental manager in a large store and that this is his best opportunity for salary. Then we would add a cost to the business of $15,000, the imputed salary of the owner-manager.[4] Similarly, the owner-manager has $50,000 equity in the store and inventory, a sum of money that could easily be employed elsewhere for financial gain. Suppose it could be banked or invested elsewhere at comparable risk and would receive 8 percent interest on the principal, or $4,000 per annum. By choosing to invest the $50,000 in the store rather than elsewhere, the owner-manager is therefore forgoing an income of $4,000 per annum, and the economist adds this as an implicit cost on the income statement. Thus the total economic costs, or the opportunity costs of all resources used in the production process, are $164,000, and in economic terms the store owner has incurred a loss of $4,000. That is, the store owner could have earned $4,000 more with the resources at his disposal if he had sold the building and inventory, invested the money at 8 percent per annum, and worked in a similar job elsewhere for a salary of $15,000 per annum.[5]

Normal and Pure Profits

■ *Definition:*   *Normal profits* are earned when total revenues equal total costs, if total costs are calculated to reflect the opportunity costs of *all* services provided. If revenues just equal these costs, then all factors are earning the same in that particular employ-

---

[4]If the owner-manager were to make drawings from the business of cash or goods, these must be accounted for. Suppose he had drawn $10,000 from the business in cash and goods over the year. This plus another $5,000 should be charged against sales revenues, in order that his opportunity cost is properly valued at $15,000.

[5]Psychic income, or the utility derived from being one's own boss in this case, should always be considered. This storekeeper should continue in his own store if the monetary value of being his own boss exceeds $4,000 per annum. Similarly, many business school professors continue to teach in business schools, rather than accept positions with substantially higher salaries in business and government, because of the psychic income associated with the academic life. (Occasional consulting work represents a nice compromise).

ment as they could earn elsewhere. If revenues exceed these costs, we say that the firm is earning a *pure*, or economic, profit. Remembering that the owners of the firm are the effective suppliers of the services of the land and buildings mentioned, you will see that an economic profit means that the owners of the firm are earning more profit than they could by investing their capital elsewhere. The accounting profit must be adjusted for the opportunity cost of the owned resources—that is, for what the firm would pay for the services of those resources if they were purchased or hired—before the alternative investment possibilities can be assessed. Accounting profit will exceed economic profit if some implicit opportunity costs are not subtracted from revenues.

This is not to say that either the accountant's or economist's view of profit is incorrect; each is designed for a different purpose. The accountant's purpose is to find, once the capital has been invested in a particular pursuit, the return to the owners of that capital. The economist's purpose is to ensure that all resources are employed in their most efficient uses. The existence of economic profit confirms this.

Note: A normal profit (when TR = TC) does not mean *no* profit. Since total costs in the economic sense include the opportunity cost of all resources used, the return on capital invested is included as a cost, rather than counted as a residual in the accounting sense. Normal profit means a *sufficient* return on the owner's investment in the firm, sufficient to prevent him or her from liquidating this investment and investing it in the next best alternative investment, since the return on the next best alternative investment opportunity is included as an economic cost of production. Normal profit, therefore, means as much profit as the owners could get elsewhere.

Normal Profits and Risk Considerations

Considering that investments are not equally risky, we need to qualify our concept of normal profits to take into account the different degrees of risk in investment opportunities. Investing money in government bonds is relatively risk free, for example, since there is virtually no risk of default in mature economies. Dividends are paid on schedule, and bonds are redeemed on the due date as long as the government exists. Investing money in the development of a new product, on the other hand, is relatively risky. Investors may not receive dividends on their investments, and in many cases they may lose all the capital they put in. Accordingly, government bonds pay a relatively low rate of interest (5 percent to 10 percent), whereas companies prospecting for oil and minerals, introducing new products, and engaging in other high-risk businesses must offer relatively high rates of interest (15 percent to 20 percent) in order to attract the required investment funds. Although investors are generally averse to risk, they are willing to take risks, but only if there is a promise of sufficiently higher returns to compensate for the risks they are taking. The extra return on high-risk investments necessary to compensate investors is known as the *risk premium*. The higher the risk involved, the larger the risk premium demanded by investors.

Since alternative investment opportunities could earn more or less, depending on the degree of risk, we must confine our considerations to alternative investments of the same or similar degree of risk, for the sake of comparability. In effect, this is the familiar *ceteris paribus* requirement: the comparison of one investment with other investments of *equal* risk. The highest return on these alternative investments of equal risk is the opportunity cost of investing in the chosen area. It follows that the opportunity cost of investing in a low-risk business is lower than the opportunity cost of investing in a relatively high-risk business. In turn, the normal profit of a low-risk business is lower than the normal profit of a high-risk business. In accounting terms, a firm in a low-risk business may be content to earn an 8 percent return on investment after taxes, whereas a firm in a high-risk industry might require a 15 percent return on investment after taxes in order to keep them in that particular business.

We turn now to incremental costs, the most important cost concept for decision making.

7.3   INCREMENTAL COST ANALYSIS

■ *Definition:*   *Incremental costs* are those costs that will be incurred as the result of a decision. Incremental costs are measured by the change in total costs that results from a particular decision's being made. Incremental costs may therefore be either fixed or variable, since a new decision may require purchase of additional capital facilities plus extra labor and materials. When we compare incremental costs with incremental revenues, that is, with the change in total revenues that occurs as a result of the decision, we can see whether a proposed decision is likely to be profitable or not. Clearly, if incremental revenues exceed incremental costs, the proposed decision will add to total profits (or will reduce losses if the total revenues generated do not cover the total costs incurred).

Note: Incremental costs are not identical with marginal costs. As defined in the preceding chapter, *marginal costs* are the change in total cost for a one-unit change in the output level. Incremental costs, on the other hand, are the aggregate change in costs that results from a decision. This decision may involve a change in the output level of 20 or of 2,000 units, or it may not involve a change in the output level at all. For example, the decision may be whether or not to introduce a new technology of producing the same output level. Knowledge of marginal costs, however, may be very important for the calculation of the incremental costs.

The incremental costs must be accurately identified. Only those costs that actually change as a result of the decision may be included, but all costs that change as a result of the decision must be included. Factors that have been lying idle, with no alternative use, do not have an incremental cost and therefore may be regarded as being costless for the particular decision at hand. Similarly, costs that have been expended in the past for machinery or plant and buildings must be regarded as *sunk* costs and should not enter the decision-making procedure unless their opportunity cost is positive. That is, unless there is a competing and profitable use for an owned resource, the incremental cost of involving that resource in the present decision will be zero.

Relevant Costs and Irrelevant Costs

■ *Definition:*   The *relevant costs* for decision-making purposes are those costs that will be incurred as a result of the decision being considered. The relevant costs are, therefore, the incremental costs. Costs that have been incurred already and costs that will be incurred in the future regardless of the present decision, are *irrelevant* costs as far as the current decision problem is concerned.

Example: The manager of a gift store thinks that he has found a miracle product that will sell rapidly and give him large profits. It is an "antenna hat" comprised of two brightly colored balls on the end of flexible springs affixed to a headband. When worn by a person, the balls swing around like the antennae of some giant insect. The manager is convinced these "hats" will sell and has purchased 5,000 of them. His cost was $1.00 each, payable $0.50 immediately and $0.50 within thirty days. He then spent $2,500 promoting these gimmicks, in newspaper advertisements and by hiring students to wear them around campus and at public events. He set the price at $4.95 and waited for his fortune to come rolling in. Three weeks have passed and he still has 4,975 of these antenna hats. His assistant manager suggested that he cut the price to $1.25 in order to get rid of what was obviously an ill-considered venture. The manager is adamant that he will never let the price fall that low since "his cost" was $1.50 per unit and he doesn't want to take a loss on this item.

But is $1.50 the relevant cost? The manager is about to make a pricing decision, and, as a result of that decision, costs may or may not be incurred and revenues may or may not be earned. The relevant costs are those that will be incurred as a result of the decision. The initial outlays of $2,500 on the antenna hats and $2,500 on promotion are irrelevant costs since they have already been incurred and cannot be retrieved. These are sunk costs. The second payment of $2,500 for the hats is also an irrelevant cost since it must be paid whether or not the price is changed and whether or not any more of the hats are sold. The relevant costs are those, if any, that will be incurred following the pricing decision. Suppose that storage costs must be incurred if the hats are not sold within another week. These costs will be incremental to a decision to maintain price at $4.95 but not incremental to a decision to cut price to $1.25, presuming that the assistant manager's judgment is correct and all units would sell at the lower price. Note that the marketability of the item is declining; it is a novelty item and must be sold before the public tires of its novelty value. Thus price should be set not with an eye on the irrelevant costs (sunk costs and committed costs) but with an eye on the incremental costs. To include the irrelevant costs in the present decision is to let an earlier bad decision cause another bad decision to be made. In business parlance, the gift-store manager should "cut his losses" and "avoid sending good money after bad."

Incremental Cost Categories

There are three main categories of relevant, or incremental, costs. These are the present-period explicit costs, the opportunity costs implicitly involved in the decision, and the future cost implications that flow from the decision. Let us examine these in turn.

Present-Period Explicit Costs.   Direct labor and materials costs and changes in the variable overhead costs, such as electricity, are fairly easy to anticipate as a consequence of a decision, for example, to increase the output level. If this increase also requires the purchase of additional capital equipment, this capital cost is incremental to the decision and should be included in full rather than apportioned in any way, notwithstanding that the equipment may have a useful life remaining after the present decision has been carried out.[6]

Thus the incremental costs of a decision will include all present-period explicit costs that will be incurred as a consequence of that decision. It will exclude any present-period explicit costs that will be incurred regardless of the present decision.

Opportunity Costs.   Items taken from inventory may not have an explicit present-period cost if the firm does not choose to replace them in inventory by current purchases. Nevertheless, the relevant cost is the opportunity cost of that item—it could presumably be sold to another firm for its market value. If an item in inventory is worthless, having no market value (because it is outmoded by a new item, for example), its opportunity cost is zero, regardless of its historic cost. The historic cost of purchasing the item is an irrelevant, sunk, cost for the purposes of the present decision.

The most common application of the opportunity cost doctrine in decision making concerns the situation in which a particular resource has one or more uses at the same point of time. In this case, if the resource is used in the production of a particular output, it precludes the production of one or more other outputs.

Example: Telarah Lite-Fab Industries produces steel gates, fences, balcony and porch railings, and similar items cut and welded from wrought iron. This firm does custom orders but also produces standard gates and railings, which are sold to retail hardware stores. The firm finds it can sell as much as it can produce of the standard gates and railings but prefers to do custom orders since the latter are invariably more profitable. At the present time the firm has no custom orders outstanding, and its labor force is producing standard items at the rate of $10,000 per week sales value. Materials cost is $2,000 per week. Suppose now that a large custom order arrives that would take a week to manufacture and would cost $4,000 in materials. What is the opportunity cost of the firm's resources presently employed in the manufacture of the standard gates and railings? Note that with the standard items the firm is making $8,000 per week over and above materials cost. It must forgo this $8,000 contribution to its other costs and profits if it takes the custom order. Thus the firm must make at least $8,000 over and above materials cost on the custom order before it should even consider accepting the order. That is, the materials cost and the opportunity cost of

---

[6]If future revenues may be expected from an item of equipment or from other capital investment, these will be incorporated into the analysis on the revenue side of contribution analysis, as we shall see in the next section.

the custom order add up to $12,000, and the firm must set its price at least that high or it would be better off sticking to the standard items.

Future Costs. Many decisions will have implications for future costs, both explicit and implicit. If the firm can form an expectation of a future cost that will be incurred or is likely to be incurred as a consequence of the present decision, that cost must be included in the present analysis. Of course, it will be incorporated in present-value terms if known for certain or in expected-present-value terms if there is a probability distribution of the future cost's occurring.

Example: A firm decides to produce a special order which it knows will cause severe wear and tear on its equipment, to the point where an overhaul will be required within one year after the job is completed. Otherwise, the equipment would serve out its useful life without a major overhaul. This overhaul is expected to cost $2,000 and will be paid one year from now. Supposing an opportunity discount rate of 15 percent, the appropriate discount factor is 0.8696, and the present value of that cost is $2,000 $\times$ 0.8696 = $1,739.20. This figure should be included as an incremental cost of deciding to produce the special order.

Example: Consider now a future cost which has a probability distribution of outcomes. Suppose a firm is considering copying another firm's design and knows that the other firm may sue for loss of business as a result. The possible legal costs and damages and the probabilities attached to each level of these costs are shown in Table 7–4. Given the congestion in the courts, it will take three years for the case to be resolved. We suppose that the firm's opportunity discount rate is 15 percent. Thus the discount factor used to find the present value of the expected costs is 0.6575.

Thus the EPV of the future legal costs is $72,325, a figure that should be included in the incremental costs of the decision to copy the other firm's design. Note that the firm should consider the possibility of such legal claims even when it does not willfully copy another firm's design. It may feel that its design is sufficiently different but that a court may nevertheless rule against it in the event of a lawsuit. In such cases

TABLE 7–4. Expected Present Value of Future Incremental Costs

Costs Expected ($)	Present Value	Probability	Expected Value ($)
0	0	0.10	0
50,000	32,875	0.20	6,575.00
100,000	65,750	0.30	19,725.00
150,000	98,625	0.25	24,656.25
200,000	131,500	0.10	13,150.00
250,000	164,375	0.05	8,218.75
	Expected Present Value		$72,325.00

the firm should calculate the EPV of the possible lawsuit and include this in its calculations.

Other future costs include labor problems, loss of future business, deterioration of supplier relations leading to higher input prices, and cash-flow problems necessitating borrowing costs. Any future cost, whether explicit or implicit, which can reasonably be expected to follow as a consequence of the current decision should be quantified in EPV terms and included in the incremental costs of the decision.

The cost concepts that were mentioned previously are summarized in Table 7–5. Note that by "relevant" or "irrelevant" we mean with respect to the decision at hand. If a cost is expected to be a consequence of the decision to be made, it is a relevant, or incremental, cost. Some subsequent (future) costs are not consequent (relevant) costs, because the firm is committed to them and they will be incurred anyway. No prior expenditures (sunk costs) are incremental costs.

7.4 CONTRIBUTION ANALYSIS

We proceed now to use the concept of incremental costs in the contribution analysis of decision problems.

■ *Definition:* The *contribution* of a decision is defined as the incremental revenues of that decision less the incremental costs of that decision. It should be interpreted as the

TABLE 7–5. Summary of Cost Concepts for Decision Making

RELEVANT COSTS	IRRELEVANT COSTS	
Incremental Costs[a]	Committed Costs[a]	Sunk Costs[b]

Present period explicit costs:
Variable:
  Direct labor
  Direct materials
  Variable overheads
Fixed:
  New equipment
  New personnel
	Managers' salaries
	
	Payments on debt
	
	Rental and lease costs
	
	Wage contracts or wages of ongoing workers
	
	All other payments that must be made regardless of the decision at hand
		Previously paid-for purchases of assets, including land, buildings, plant and equipment, and depreciation expenses based on these assets
		
		Prepaid and nonrecoverable expenses

Opportunity costs: Contribution forgone on the best alternative use of the resources involved		
Future period incremental costs: EPV of probable costs to follow in the future as a consequence of the decision		

[a]Future costs.
[b]Past costs.

"contribution made to overhead costs and profits" by the decision. Clearly, only those decisions that have a positive contribution should be undertaken; and where decisions are mutually exclusive, the one with the larger expected contribution is to be preferred. We shall illustrate contribution analysis with three common types of decision problems, but first let us clarify the notion of incremental revenues.

Incremental Revenues

■ *Definition:* *Incremental revenues* are defined as the revenues which follow as a consequence of a particular decision. We should expect incremental revenues, like incremental costs, to have an explicit current-period component, a possible opportunity component, and a possible future component.

Example: A firm bidding on a contract to supply electric light fixtures to a government office building tenders a very low bid for $265,000 and expects to avoid layoff costs of $100,000 if it wins the contract. It also expects to win future government contracts if it is the successful bidder on this contract, since this contract provides the firm with the opportunity to prove that it can supply a quality product and meet its production schedule.

The explicit current-period incremental revenues if the firm wins the contract will be $265,000. But the contract is worth much more than $265,000 to the firm. If it doesn't win the contract, it will have to lay off workers and incur subsequent severance pay and future start-up costs associated with recruiting and training totaling $100,000. If the firm does win the contract, this $100,000 is not spent and therefore stays in the bank. Avoidance of a cost as the result of a decision amounts to an opportunity revenue of the same amount.

■ *Definition:* An *opportunity revenue* is a cost avoided as the result of a decision. Although there is no actual inflow of revenues, the outflow of revenues is avoided so that money that would otherwise be spent is still sitting in the bank, and the net effect is the same. The *future* revenues associated with this pricing decision will be the expected present value of the contribution to overheads and profits associated with the future business generated as the result of winning the present contract.

Example: Suppose the firm mentioned in the preceding example feels that if it wins the present job, it has a 50 percent chance of winning a similar contract next year. Suppose further that the next contract would be for $300,000 and would have an incremental cost of $250,000. The contribution from the next contract is, thus, $50,000 (if won). Given an opportunity discount rate of 15 percent, the present value of this contribution is $50,000 $\times$ 0.8696 = $43,480. The expected present value is the present value times the probability of receiving it, or $43,480 $\times$ 0.50 = $21,740. Thus the EPV of the future revenue is $21,740, and this figure should be included in the incremental revenue calculation.

The firm's incremental revenue is the sum of the present-period explicit revenues, the opportunity revenues, and the EPV of future (consequential) revenues. Thus the contract has total incremental revenues of $265,000 + $100,000 + $21,740, or $386,740 in total. This contract would, therefore, offer a positive EPV of contribution as long as incremental costs were less than $386,740.

Note: The EPV of the contribution to be received from future business resulting from the present decision can be regarded as the *goodwill* associated with the present decision. Goodwill is the EPV of contribution from future business, and if a decision involves an increment to goodwill, the amount of that contribution in EPV terms should be included as an incremental revenue. Conversely, the present decision may cause the loss of future business. The EPV of the future contribution lost as the result of the present decision can be regarded as the *ill will* associated with this decision.

Example: Consider a construction firm that is considering bidding for a contract to move city garbage while the garbage workers are on strike. If this contract involves the possibility that the firm will lose future construction contracts because of the buyer's fear of retaliatory disruption by unionized construction workers, the EPV of the contribution expected to be lost on future jobs must be included as an incremental cost of taking the present contract to move the city's garbage.

Let us now demonstrate the application of contribution analysis in the context of three common types of decision problems.

Project A or Project B?

Example: Suppose a firm is considering adopting either project A or project B but cannot adopt both, since they use the same set of machinery and labor. Project A, as shown in Table 7-6, promises sales of 10,000 units at $2 each, with materials, labor, variable overhead, and allocated overhead costs as shown, such that there is an apparent profit of $2,000. Project B promises sales revenues of $18,000, with materials, direct labor, and variable and allocated overhead as shown. The apparent profit from

TABLE 7-6. Income Statements for Projects A and B

Project A			Project B		
Revenues (10,000 @ $2)		$20,000	Revenues (6,000 @ $3)		$18,000
Costs			Costs		
Materials	$2,000		Materials	$5,000	
Direct labor	6,000		Direct labor	3,000	
Variable overhead	4,000		Variable overhead	3,000	
Fixed overhead	6,000	18,000	Fixed overhead	3,000	14,000
Profit		$ 2,000	Profit		$ 4,000

project B is $4,000, and it would seem that project B is preferable to project A by virtue of its higher profitability.

When contribution analysis is applied to the above decision problem, however, the answer may be surprising. Consider Table 7-7, in which the incremental costs are subtracted from the incremental revenues to find the contribution of each project. Since the fixed overhead was not a cost incurred as a result of this particular decision, it is excluded from the contribution analysis, and it can be seen that project A contributes more to overheads and profits than does project B. The danger of including arbitrary allocations of fixed overhead is exemplified here. The fixed overhead was allocated on the basis of a particular criterion, in this case as 100 percent of direct labor, but if it had been included in the decision process it would have caused an inferior decision to be made. Whatever method of fixed overhead allocation is used, the danger is likely to persist. Hence we use contribution analysis, which allows an incisive look at the actual changes in costs and revenues that follow a particular decision.

Note that in this example we implicitly assumed the absence of all opportunity costs and revenues and that we proceeded as if there were neither future costs nor future revenues associated with either project. In practice, decision makers should not proceed so blithely but instead should assure themselves that *all* incremental costs and incremental revenues are included in the decision analysis. In the above example the difference between projects A and B was only $1,000. Hence, our decision to choose project A was very sensitive to the assumption of zero opportunity and future costs and revenues. Our decision would have been reversed if A had opportunity and future costs (in EPV terms) exceeding $1,000, for example. More generally, if the *net* opportunity and future revenues of project B had exceeded those of A by more than $1,000, the decision would have been reversed.[7]

TABLE 7-7. Contribution Analysis for Projects A and B

Project A			Project B		
Incremental revenues		$20,000	Incremental revenues		$18,000
Incremental costs			Incremental costs		
Materials	$2,000		Materials	$5,000	
Direct labor	6,000		Direct labor	3,000	
Variable overhead	4,000	12,000	Variable overhead	3,000	11,000
Contribution		$ 8,000	Contribution		$ 7,000

[7] Recall our discussion of sensitivity analysis from Chapter 1. A decision is sensitive to the assumptions on which it is based to the extent that a change in those assumptions would cause a different decision to have been preferable. Thus it is important to consider the dollar amount of cost variability or difference in contribution, which would cause the decision to be inappropriate. It is also useful to express this in terms of the totals, to see the *percentage* cost variability which would change the decision. In the present example, if the incremental costs of project A are understated by more than $1,000 or by more than $1,000/12,000 = 8.33 percent, and the incremental costs of project B are accurate, the decision would be reversed.

Make or Buy?

Example: The Wilson Tool Company manufactures high-quality power tools such as drills, jigsaws, and sanders. All these tools require the same roller-bearing unit, which the company manufactures in its own bearing department. Pertinent cost data for the past year of operations in that department are shown in Table 7-8.

Demand estimates indicate that the company should expand its production of some of the power tools and that an additional 7,500 bearing units will be required. The company could produce these in its bearing department but is considering having the additional units supplied by a firm that specializes in bearings. Wilson anticipates that it will require an increase of 15 percent in total direct labor costs and 12 percent in total materials costs to produce these additional units in house. No additional capital expenditure will be necessary, since some machines currently have idle capacity. A specialist bearing producer who has been approached has studied the specifications and has offered to supply the 7,500 bearing units at a total cost of $30,000, or $4 per unit. Should Wilson make or buy the additional units?

We begin by comparing the incremental costs of the two alternatives facing Wilson. The incremental costs of buying them from the specialist come to $30,000, since this is the dollar amount that Wilson must spend to obtain the additional units. To calculate the incremental costs of making the units in house, we begin by calculating the increases in materials and direct labor costs that would be occasioned by the manufacture of those units. The 12 percent increase in the total material cost would imply an incremental material cost of $4,637, and a 15 percent increase in total direct labor costs would imply a $18,959 increase in that cost category. As shown in Table 7-9, the total of these two figures is $23,596, which is less than the incremental cost of buying the units from outside. The decision to make, rather than buy, the additional units would thus appear to save the Wilson Tool Company a total of $6,404.[8]

TABLE 7-8.   Wilson Tool Company: Bearing Department Costs

	Total	Per Unit
Direct materials	$ 38,640	$ 0.56
Direct labor	126,390	1.81
Allocated overhead	252,780	3.63
	$417,810	$ 6.00
Total bearing units produced:		69,635

[8]Since the incremental revenue is the same whether Wilson makes or buys the parts, we can do the contribution analysis on the basis of the incremental costs alone. Presuming that the incremental revenues exceed the incremental costs, the "make" alternative would seem to contribute more to overheads and profits than does the "buy" alternative.

TABLE 7-9. Incremental Costs of Making the Bearing Units

	Total	Per Unit
Direct materials	$ 4,637	$0.62
Direct labor	18,959	2.53
Allocated overhead	(?)	(?)
	$23,596	$3.15

Variability of Overheads.   The above analysis, however, does not consider the possibility that some part of overhead expenses may vary with the level of production of the bearing units. It is conceivable that some overhead cost components, such as electricity, office and administration expense, and cafeteria expense, might vary to some degree as a result of producing these units in house. Rather than make arbitrary assumptions about the proportion of overheads that will vary, and since we do not have the information necessary to make a reasoned judgment, let us perform a sensitivity analysis on the decision that has been made. That is, we wish to know by how much the overhead expenses may vary before the decision to make the product would be the wrong decision. The answer is obviously that if overheads vary more than $6,404 as a result of this decision, the best decision would be to buy the product from the outside supplier. A $6,404 variation in overhead represents slightly more than a 2.5 percent variation in the allocated overhead. It is up to the decision maker to judge whether a variation of this percentage or dollar magnitude is likely to follow the decision to produce the product in house.

Longer-Term Incremental Costs.   A number of other considerations should also enter into this decision. First, there is the issue of long-term supplier relations. Since Wilson may need a specialist producer some time in the future when it may be unable to produce the bearings in house because of capacity limitations, it can perhaps establish itself as a customer of the supplier by giving this contract out at the present time, so that in future situations supply could be assured.

Second, there is the issue of the quality of the bearing units supplied by the outside firm as compared with those produced by Wilson. The decision maker would have to be assured that the units supplied from outside would be at least equal in quality to the standards desired. On the other hand, the specialist producer may be able to produce consistently higher quality bearing units, with subsequent impact upon the quality of Wilson Tools and on long-term buyer goodwill.

Third, the issue of labor relations must be considered. The decision to make the units involves an increase in the labor force, which may lead to crowded working conditions and overtaxed washroom and cafeteria facilities. The data indicate that labor efficiency is decreasing, since the incremental cost per unit to make the additional 7,500 units is $3.15 as compared with the total of $2.37 for direct materials and labor per unit shown in Table 7-8. It is conceivable that the hiring of additional labor units and the resultant increased congestion and reduced efficiency could cause a lowering of employee morale, with subsequent longer-term disadvantages to the profitability of the Wilson Tool Company.

In total, the decision maker must decide whether or not the expected present value of these eventualities, plus the possible variable components in overhead costs, is likely to exceed $6,404. If so, the decision should be to buy the product from outside.

Other Considerations.   There are several additional issues that should be considered. First, the decision maker would need to be assured of the accuracy of the estimations that are involved in this decision. If, for example, demand for the tools does not increase as predicted and Wilson purchased the roller-bearing units from outside, this would be an irreversible commitment involving considerable expense, whereas the decision to make the units in house could soon be suspended. The cost estimates are likewise subject to some doubt. These are presumably extrapolations on the estimated marginal costs of producing the units in house. The decision maker would need to be assured that these extrapolations were based on the most reasonable assumptions concerning the efficiency of direct labor and material usage and that they are, consequently, the best estimates. To the extent that there is a distribution of both demand and cost estimates, a decision based on the most likely point estimate alone may result in an outcome that is quite different from the expected value.

Another question that arises in the problem is whether or not the price quotation received is in fact the lowest-cost source of supply of these bearing units. We might assume that bids were solicited and that the lowest bid was being considered, but if this were not the case the decision maker should consult alternative sources of supply to confirm that the $30,000 price was in fact the best price at which the units may be bought from outside.

With these qualifications in mind, we turn now to the third category of decision problems in which contribution analysis is an appropriate solution procedure.

Take It or Leave It?

Example: The Idaho Instruments Company produces a variety of pocket calculators and sells them through a distributing company. The purchasing agent for a large chain of department stores has recently approached Idaho Instruments with an offer to buy 20,000 units of its model X1 at the unit price of $8. Idaho's present production level of that model is 160,000 units annually, and it could supply the additional 20,000 units by forgoing production (and sale) of 5,000 of its more sophisticated X2 model. Pertinent data relating to these two models are shown in Table 7–10. Because of the highly mechanized production process, the per-unit variable costs of each model are believed to be constant over a wide range of outputs. The sales manager for Idaho Instruments is reluctant to sell the X1 model for $8 when she normally receives $12 from the distributing company, and she has attempted to negotiate with the purchasing agent. The latter, however, insists that $8 is his only offer. Should Idaho Instruments take it or leave it?

TABLE 7-10.   Idaho Instruments Company: Per-Unit Data on Calculators

	Model X1	Model X2
Materials	$ 1.65	$ 1.87
Direct labor	2.32	3.02
Variable overhead	1.03	1.11
Fixed overhead allocation	5.00	6.00
Profits	2.00	2.40
Price to distributor	$12.00	$14.40

Since the average variable cost for both models is expected to be constant over a wide range, we can calculate the incremental cost of this decision on the basis of the average variable cost. The average variable cost is the sum of the first three components in the table, and hence 20,000 additional units of model X1 (with AVC = $5.00) will add $100,000 to the cost levels. This figure is not the total incremental cost, however, since there is an opportunity cost involved. The production of the additional 20,000 units will come partly from the idle capacity that is to be utilized and partly at the expense of 5,000 units of model X2. The opportunity cost of using the resources that previously produced the X2 are the value of those resources in that alternate use. The net value to Idaho Instruments of employing the resources in the production of 5,000 units of the X2 is the contribution made by those 5,000 units. From Table 7-10 it can be found that the contribution per unit to overheads and profits is $8.40. Hence the opportunity costs are the total forgone contribution, or 5,000 units × $8.40 = $42,000. In Table 7-11 we show the contribution analysis of this problem. The incremental revenues are $160,000, and the incremental costs add up to $142,000. Hence the contribution to overheads and profits that would follow from the decision to take the department store's offer is $18,000. Thus profits would be $18,000 greater than they would be otherwise, or losses would be $18,000 less.

An alternate method of arriving at the same contribution would be to subtract from the incremental revenues the revenues forgone when the 5,000 units of X2 were not sold at $14.40 (that is, $72,000) and subtract from the incremental cost of producing the extra units of the model X1 the decremental costs of not producing 5,000 units

TABLE 7-11.   Contribution Analysis of Calculator Decision Problem

Incremental revenues		
20,000 units of X1 @ $8.00		$160,000
Incremental costs		
Variable costs		
20,000 units of X1 @ $5.00	$100,000	
Opportunity costs (contribution forgone)		
5,000 units of X2 @ $8.40	42,000	142,000
Contribution		$ 18,000

of the model X2 (that is, \$30,000). The net adjustment as the result of these manipulations is \$72,000 − \$30,000, or \$42,000, which is exactly the opportunity cost figure we have entered in Table 7-11. The opportunity cost method achieves the same results with some economy of effort, but more importantly, perhaps, it draws the decision maker's attention to the possible alternate uses of resources.

The preceding decision is sensitive to some of the underlying assumptions, however. The first issue is that of substitutability between the units sold to the department store and those sold to the distributing company. The analysis has proceeded upon the implicit assumption that the sale of 20,000 units to the department store will be *in addition to*, and nonsubstitutable with, the 160,000 units sold through the distributing company. To the extent that some customers now buy this product through the department store rather than through the distributing company, Idaho Instruments will be forgoing an amount of \$4 per unit, or the difference in the price charged to the two wholesale buyers. If the department stores will tap a totally new market for the calculators, we can presume that total sales will increase by the entire 20,000 units and that there would indeed be a contribution of \$18,000 following this decision. On the other hand, if the sale to the department store reduces normal sales, to what degree could this happen before the decision to take the offer becomes the wrong one? Since the difference in contribution per unit is \$4, the number of units that it would take to erode that \$18,000 total contribution down to zero is \$18,000 ÷ 4 = 4,500. Thus, if in the judgment of the decision maker there are likely to be at least 4,500 units purchased from the department stores that would otherwise have been purchased from the normal distribution channels, the decision should be reversed.

An additional consideration here is that of retailer relations. Doubtless the firms in the normal distributing channels will become aware that the department stores were given a better deal, and these firms may in turn look elsewhere for their supplies. Thus any short-term gain by selling to the department store may be outweighed by longer-term losses from a deterioration of the relationship currently enjoyed with the distributing company and with other firms.[9]

A third area of concern relates to the image of Idaho Instruments' calculators. Presumably the department stores, having purchased at a relatively low cost per unit, will price below the current market price for the model X1. This reduced price may have a detrimental impact upon the quality image currently held by that model. Since many consumers judge quality on the basis of price when they have no alternate means of discovering quality or durability, the lowering of the price of the X1 may reduce the consumer's perception of its quality. Alternatively, this contract with the department store may be the beginning of a long and successful relationship with that particular buyer and may add to rather than detract from the image of the calculators and the total sales.

---

[9]In fact, if Idaho Instruments continues to favor the department store with a lower price, it may run afoul of legislation concerning price discrimination. Legal constraints on pricing are discussed in Appendix 10A.

In summary, then, the decision maker must consider all possible future ramifications of the decision and must calculate the expected present value or loss of each eventuality. The net expected present value or loss must be added to or subtracted from the immediate contribution before the final decision is made.

Multiperiod Contribution Analysis

Many decisions involve costs that will be incurred or revenues that will be received in future time periods. As discussed in Chapter 1, these costs and revenues must be converted to present-value terms in order to make them comparable with cost and revenues incurred or received in the present period. In Chapter 1 we spoke simply of "profits" in the first and subsequent periods which had to be discounted back to present value. We now know that it is the *contribution* in each future period that is important for decision making, and not profits in either the accounting or the economic sense.

The contribution of a decision in future periods is likely to be subject to uncertainty, and thus expected-present-value (EPV) analysis is involved. Thus multiperiod contribution analysis with uncertain future contributions proceeds in the by now familiar context of decision trees. The only difference is that the *expected present value of contribution* (EPVC) in each period is now the operative concept. Initial costs should now be viewed as the excess of incremental costs over incremental revenues in the current period (that is, a negative contribution). The probability distributions of contribution in future periods must be carefully estimated and placed in the appropriate branches of the decision tree. The EPVC of each decision is then calculated and compared with the EPVC of alternative decisions. The various decision criteria are then applied, using the procedures demonstrated in Chapter 2. Two of the problems at the end of this chapter involve decision trees and multiperiod contribution analysis.

7.5 SUMMARY

The cost concept of prime importance for decision making is that of incremental costs. *Incremental* costs are those that are incurred as a result of the decision under consideration. To calculate incremental costs, however, the decision maker must consider a variety of other cost concepts, such as direct and indirect, explicit and implicit, opportunity and historic, and relevant and sunk costs. Each of these cost concepts was illustrated with reference to a particular business example.

Contribution analysis seeks to ascertain the contribution to overheads and profits, or the excess of incremental revenues over incremental costs, that is expected to follow a particular decision. To calculate the contribution of a decision the decision maker must consider the present-period explicit costs and revenues arising from the decision, plus the opportunity costs and revenues associated with the decision, plus the expected present value of future costs and revenues that are subsequent to the decision. The expected present value of contribution (EPVC) of each decision alternative is then compared with the EPVC of the other decision alternatives. When uncertainty is involved, as we should expect in multiperiod contribution analysis, the risk attitude of the decision maker must be considered. A risk-neutral decision maker will simply select the decision alternative with the greatest EPVC. A decision maker who is risk averse (or risk preferring) should utilize criteria that adjust for risk, such as the coefficient of variation, certainty equivalent, and maximin.

   As before, we should be careful to conduct sensitivity analysis before plunging ahead with a decision based on EPVC calculations. Many of the consequences of a decision may be subject to a high degree of uncertainty, and our best estimates may not be especially reliable. Other issues may be assumed away, on the basis of a presumption that they will not occur. Sensitivity analysis should be undertaken to see whether or not the decision alternative selected would remain the optimal one if our underlying assumptions turn out to be in error. The assumptions most often made that cry out for sensitivity analysis fall under two broad headings, namely, data accuracy and *ceteris paribus*. Data-accuracy assumptions include the following: accuracy of the figures used and the lack of any other current-period, future-period, or opportunity incremental costs or revenues. *Ceteris paribus* assumptions include the lack of any impact on labor, customer, and supplier relations (with subsequent current or future cost or revenue implications), as well as the lack of any adverse impact on the firm's product quality, financial stability, public image, and so on.

DISCUSSION QUESTIONS

7-1. How might the accountant's calculation of indirect costs differ from the economist's calculation of fixed costs?

7-2. Explain how the economist would calculate the implicit cost of a fixed factor, such as plant and equipment, which is used in the production process.

7-3. When is the opportunity cost of an input to the production process equal to zero? If an input has several different alternative uses, how is the opportunity cost of that input determined?

7-4. Explain the economist's notions of normal and pure profits. Why wouldn't a firm wish to liquidate its investment and leave the industry if it was simply breaking even with TR = TC?

7-5. Define the *relevant costs* for decision making. When do the relevant costs include some elements of fixed costs?

7-6. Why does contribution analysis ignore the fixed overhead costs that might otherwise be included in the cost analysis of a decision?

7-7. How should future considerations be evaluated and included in contribution analysis?

7-8. In multiperiod contribution analysis, what determines the choice of the appropriate discount factors?

7-9. Explain how you would calculate the incremental cost of a decision that might lead to a future class-action lawsuit by consumers for damages caused by your product.

7-10. Explain and contrast the concepts of opportunity costs and opportunity revenues.

PROBLEMS AND SHORT CASES

7-1. The Muscle-Man Company manufactures forklift tractors, and it supplies some parts to other manufacturers of forklifts. It fabricates most of the component parts but buys the engines, hydraulic systems, wheels, and tires from suppliers. Demand estimates indicate that Muscle-Man should increase its production level from 60 forklift units monthly to 70 units monthly. Sufficient slack exists in most departments to allow this increase, except that production of 10 extra chassis assemblies could be attained only by reallocating labor and equipment from fork-assembly manufacture to chassis-assembly manufacture. The fork-assembly department currently produces 90 units monthly, and it supplies the 30 surplus units to other manufacturers at $188 each. With the expanded production level, 70 forks would be required, but the labor and equipment responsible for the remaining 20 units is thought to be just sufficient to produce the 10 extra chassis assemblies. Alternatively, the extra chassis assemblies could be purchased from a supplier, and the lowest quote is from Fenton Fabricators, for $305 per unit. The costs of the chassis and fork departments for a representative month were as follows:

| | DEPARTMENT | |
Costs	Chassis	Fork
Direct materials	$ 4,650	$ 2,070
Direct labor	6,300	4,050
Depreciation	750	500
Allocated burden of fuel, electricity, office, and other overheads (200% of direct labor)	12,600	8,100
Total	$24,300	$14,720
Production level	60	90

(a) Should Muscle-Man make or buy the ten extra chassis assemblies?

(b) What qualifications would you add to your decision?

7-2. The Crombie Castings Company produces two products, A and B, for which pertinent data are as follows for the past month:

	A	B
Sales (units)	840,000	220,000
Price per unit ($)	2.50	4.25
Materials cost ($)	386,400	105,600
Direct labor ($)	529,200	277,200
Overheads ($)	567,893	297,467

CCC's plant and labor are operating at full capacity, but the company is unable to meet the demand for product A, which is thought to be one million units per month. One way to meet the demand for A would be to reduce the output of product B and to shift resources to the production of A. For each unit reduction in the output of B, the firm could produce two units of A with the labor that is released. Note that average variable costs are constant in both production processes. Alternatively, CCC could contract out to have product A manufactured by another firm in the same industry and sold as if this product were from the CCC plant. Donald, Dodge, and Draper, a firm that holds a minor share of the same markets and has considerable excess capacity, was approached on this issue. DDD is willing to sign a contract to supply the extra 160,000 units of A at a price of $2.25 per unit.

How should CCC resolve this problem? Support your answer with discussion of the various issues involved.

7-3. Commodore Candies produces a three-pound box of chocolates which it sells at a price of $6.75 to various retail outlets. Commodore's output capacity for this product is 10,000 units per month with a one-shift operation, but it can produce more using overtime labor, which has a premium of 15 percent over regular labor cost. Variable overhead expenses would be 10 percent higher per unit of output for overtime production. Average variable costs are constant from 8,000 to 10,000 units and are then constant at the higher level. Costs of production for the current months' output of 8,000 units are as follows:

	Total Costs ($)
Raw materials	9,600
Direct labor	17,600
Variable overhead	9,200
Fixed overhead	14,500

Today Commodore is faced with a decision problem. A large retail chain has offered to purchase a bulk order of 4,000 units at $6 per unit, to be delivered within thirty days. Should Commodore take this order? Support your answer with discussion of the issues involved. Defend any assumptions that you make.

7-4. The XYZ Company produces and sells a product directly to consumers at a price of $6 per unit. Sales have been increasing at 10 percent per month, and this trend is expected to continue. Average variable costs are expected to remain constant at the current levels. The company's maximum output capacity is 200,000 with the present investment in plant and equipment.

Following is a summary record of the firm's January production and cost levels:

	January
Sales (units)	171,661
Materials ($)	211,143
Direct labor ($)	520,133
Indirect factory labor ($)	110,500
Office and administration salaries ($)	64,000
Light and heat ($)	12,116
Other fixed expenses ($)	24,680

A national mail-order company has asked XYZ to consider the following deal: 10,000 units of the product, to be ready at the end of February, at the price of $5 per unit.

(a) Should XYZ accept the order from the mail-order company?

(b) What strategy do you suggest?

(c) Support your answer with discussion of the various issues involved.

7-5. A large department store has called for bids for the following contract: A truck plus its driver must be available, given one day's notice, whenever the store's own trucks are fully utilized, to deliver goods to suburban households. The number of days for which a truck will be required is twenty, and the number of miles is expected to be 4,000 for the coming year.

You are the manager of the Clark Rent-a-Truck Company and have a number of trucks that you rent out on a day-to-day basis. One truck is a little older than the others, and it is always the last to be rented out because it does less for public relations than the new trucks. In the absence of a contract with the department store, you expect this older truck to be rented out two-thirds of the 300 "rental days" this coming year. Your normal rental charge is $25.00 per day plus $0.35 per mile.

You estimate the costs of operating the older truck to be as follows, assuming 10,000 miles of rental over the coming year:

Depreciation	$ 800
Interest on investment in truck	360
License fees and taxes	125
Insurance	440
Parking fees (permanently rented space)	300
Gasoline	1,367
Oil, grease, and preventive maintenance	600
Repairs	1,450
Allocated overheads	1,650

You can hire a driver on one-day's notice for $50 per day. A one-time cost of $400 will be involved in fitting the truck with a special loading ramp required by the contract. This ramp will not interfere with the normal use of the truck.

On the basis of this information, and making whatever assumptions you feel are necessary and reasonable, calculate your incremental costs of undertaking this contract.

7-6. Corcoran Calculators Incorporated is one of the leading manufacturers in the electronic calculator industry. Management is now considering plans for the production of the company's latest development—the minicomputer. The company already manufactures most of the parts, but the design of the new fuse trays would require the additional expenditure of $23,000 for special auxiliary equipment, which has a useful life of only two years and has no scrap value. The marketing department has estimated that sales would require the production of 4,500 fuse trays the first year and 7,000 the following year.

The company has the option of either producing these trays in house or having them supplied by an outside electronics specialist at a cost of $32.50 per tray. Corcoran would incur additional storage and carrying costs associated with this latter alternative of $26,000 during the first year and $40,000 during the following year.

The breakdown of the in-house manufacturing expenses for the 11,500 units is expected to be as follows:

		Unit Cost
Labor		$10.00
Raw materials and components		20.00
Variable overhead		4.00
Fixed cost		
Existing equipment	$3.50	
New equipment	2.00	5.50
		$39.50

The company's opportunity discount rate is 15 percent. The payments to the supplier would be made in a lump sum at the end of each of the two years. If the units were produced in house, there would be a continual outflow of funds as they are produced, although the special equipment would have to be paid for immediately.

(a) Assuming that the increased production will have a negligible effect on the present operation of the plant, what would your recommendation be on the question of making or buying the fuse trays?

(b) State any qualifications you might wish to make.

7-7. The Tico Taco Company has estimated the following total variable cost function from cost and output data pairs observed over the past ten weeks:

$$TVC = 435.85 - 1.835Q^2 + 3.658Q^3$$

where TVC represents thousands of dollars and Q represents thousands of boxes of tacos produced. TTC is currently producing 2,000 boxes weekly and is considering expanding its output to 2,200 boxes weekly. To do so, it will have to hire another taco machine operator ($400 per week) and lease another taco machine ($200 per week).

(a) Estimate the incremental costs of the extra 200 boxes weekly.

(b) State all the assumptions and qualifications which underlie your answer to part (a).

7-8. You are the manager of a ski resort. Based on industry projections of this season's demand, your competitive position, and your estimates of costs, you have set the lift ticket price at $8 per day. Because of the variability of demand between weekdays, weekends, and holidays, you hire labor on the basis of the expected demand for each particular day, based on past years' records and on current snow conditions. Extra labor is readily available on a day-to-day basis from the pool of local "ski bums."

You employ one lift attendant for every 250 tickets sold, in addition to a basic staff of four lift attendants. Ski-patrol persons are required at the rate of one for every 400 tickets sold in addition to the two patrol persons who are required regardless of ticket sales volume. All other labor employees connected with the skiing operation are required regardless of sales volume. Lift attendants are hired at the rate of $25 per day plus a free lift ticket to be used subsequently. Ski-patrol persons receive $30 per day plus a free meal in your restaurant that evening.

Your restaurant serves only one standarized meal, an "all you can eat" buffet for $3 per person. Based on expected demand fluctuations, you have hired various people on a full-time and part-time basis for the season. The $3 price represents the average cost of materials and direct labor plus a 50 percent markup to contribute to restaurant overheads and profits. Unexpected fluctuations in demand can be handled, since you keep a large inventory of supplies and can hire temporary labor at short notice. There is, however, an additional $10-per-person cost for this temporary labor, since these people are handled through an employment agency and require transportation to the restaurant. To maintain your standard of meals and service, you hire kitchen staff at the rate of one person for every 45 meals expected to be sold and serving staff at the rate of one person for every 80 meals expected to be sold.

Today you received a phone call from the Students' Association of a nearby University which is asking around various ski resorts for the following deal: Ten busloads of students (500 in total) will come to your resort on Friday of next week if they can get a lift ticket *and* a meal for $4 per person. Your expected sales for that Friday, before this possibility arose, were 1,500 lift tickets and 900 meals.

Should you give the students the deal they are asking for? Explain your decision and state any possible qualifications to that decision.

7-9. The Wyndham Wool Company is considering two alternative strategies to increase its profitability and net worth. Strategy A is to set up a string of retail outlets for exclusive distribution of Wyndham's Scottish kilts, sweaters, jackets, blankets, scarves, and so on. Plan B is to wholesale these items to a limited number of high-quality department stores. The probability distributions of contribution for each strategy are shown in the following table. Wyndham's cost of capital is 15 percent per annum.

	STRATEGY A		STRATEGY B	
	Contribution ($)	Probability	Contribution ($)	Probability
Current period	−600,000	1.0	−100,000	1.0
Year 1	200,000	0.3	50,000	0.5
	400,000	0.5	100,000	0.3
	600,000	0.2	150,000	0.2
Year 2	400,000	0.3	100,000	0.4
	600,000	0.4	200,000	0.5
	800,000	0.3	300,000	0.1

(a) Calculate the expected present value of the contribution from each of the proposed strategies.

(b) Supposing Wyndham to be risk averse, which strategy would you recommend?

(c) State all the assumptions and qualifications that underlie your recommendation. Is your recommendation especially sensitive to any of these?

7-10. The Yankee Jack Company operates a tourist service business in a New England seaside resort area. Wishing to capitalize on the expanding tourist potential of the region, the firm is considering two alternatives. The first is the creation of a wildlife and animal farm, mostly oriented to children and tourists from the big city, and the second is an amusement park, which would cater more to teenagers and young adults. The probability distributions of contribution for both alternatives are shown below. Yankee Jack has accumulated sufficient funds to finance either venture, and the money is currently earning 9 percent per annum in government treasury bills.

	WILDLIFE FARM		AMUSEMENT PARK	
	Contribution ($)	Probability	Contribution ($)	Probability
Current period	−200,000	1.0	−285,000	1.0
Year 1	50,000	0.1	100,000	0.3
	100,000	0.6	150,000	0.5
	150,000	0.3	200,000	0.2
Year 2	100,000	0.2	150,000	0.3
	200,000	0.5	300,000	0.5
	300,000	0.3	450,000	0.2

(a) Calculate the expected present value of contribution and its standard deviation for each of the two alternatives.

(b) Conduct sensitivity analysis with respect to the opportunity discount rate involved in the calculation above.

(c) Which alternative would you advise Yankee Jack proceed with, and why?

(d) State all assumptions and qualifications that underlie your analysis.

SUGGESTED REFERENCES AND FURTHER READING

Davidson, S., J. S. Schindler, C. P. Stickney, and R. L. Weil. *Managerial Accounting—An Introduction to Concepts, Methods, and Uses*, chaps. 4-6. Hinsdale, Ill.: The Dryden Press, 1978.

Greer, H. C. "Anyone for Widgets?" *Journal of Accountancy*, April 1966. (Despite its title, this paper contains an excellent discussion of relevant and irrelevant costs.)

Harrington, D. H. "Costs and Returns: Economic and Accounting Concepts," *Agricultural Economics Research*, 35 (October 1983), pp. 1-8.

Haynes, W. W., and W. R. Henry. *Managerial Economics: Analysis and Cases* (3rd ed.), chaps. 2 and 5. Dallas, Tex.: Business Publications, 1974.

Horngren, C. T. *Cost Accounting: A Managerial Emphasis* (5th ed.), chaps. 2 and 3. Englewood Cliffs, N.J.: Prentice-Hall, Inc., 1982.

————. *Introduction to Management Accounting* (5th ed.), chaps. 2-5. Englewood Cliffs, N.J.: Prentice-Hall, Inc., 1981.

Pappas, J. L., and E. F. Brigham. *Managerial Economics* (3rd ed.), chap. 8. Hinsdale, Ill.: The Dryden Press, 1979.

Simon, J. L. *Applied Managerial Economics*, chaps. 8 and 9. Englewood Cliffs, N.J.: Prentice-Hall, Inc., 1975.

Webb, S. C. *Managerial Economics*, chap. 5. Boston: Houghton Mifflin, 1976.

Appendix 7A: Breakeven Analysis: Applications and Limitations

A graphical tool of some value in decision making is the breakeven chart. When applied correctly it allows the decision maker considerable insight into the decision problem and aids in the choice of the optimal price, cost, and output levels for each product.

■ *Definition:* The *breakeven volume* is defined as that sales level for which total revenue equals total cost. Decision makers are concerned with the breakeven volume level, since it is beyond this level that revenues begin to exceed costs and the decision becomes profitable. To the extent that the breakeven point can be surpassed, the decision maker is likely to smile more broadly; the worrisome factor is usually whether or not sales volume will attain the breakeven level.

In Figure 7A-1 we show the breakeven charts under three different cost and revenue situations. In part (a) of the figure you will notice that total revenue and total cost are equal at two separate output levels. At point *A* total revenue has risen to equality with total costs, and at point *B* total revenue has fallen to equality with the

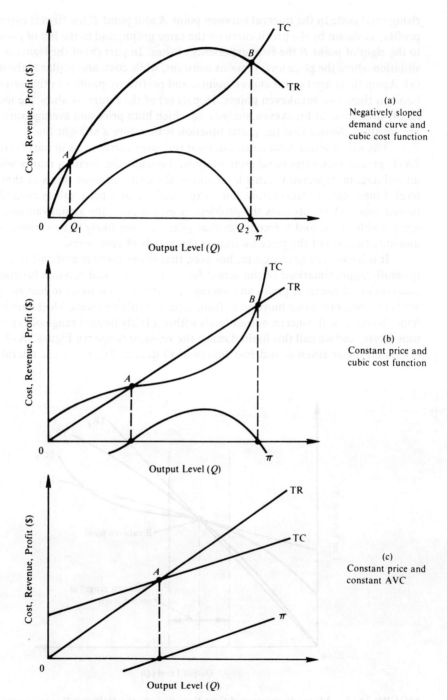

(a)
Negatively sloped
demand curve and
cubic cost function

(b)
Constant price and
cubic cost function

(c)
Constant price and
constant AVC

FIGURE 7A-1.   Breakeven Charts under Different Cost and Revenue Conditions

rising total cost. In the interval between point A and point B the firm is experiencing profits, as shown by the profit curve on the same graph, and to the left of point A and to the right of point B the firm experiences losses. In part (b) of the figure we show a situation where the price level remains constant, while costs are similar to those in part (a). Again there are two breakeven points, and profits are positive in the output range between these two breakeven points. In part (c) of the figure we show the most commonly used form of breakeven analysis, in which both price and average variable cost are constant. Notice that the profit function is therefore a straight line.

The use of linear total costs and total revenue functions, as in part (c) of Figure 7A-1, greatly facilitates breakeven analysis. Typically the decision maker will obtain an estimate of expected volume level and of the cost and price levels at that volume level. Linear extrapolation from those expected cost and price values around the expected volume level obviates the problem of ascertaining the actual variance in average variable costs, and it recognizes that prices are not likely to be variable by small amounts because of the price awareness thresholds of customers.

It is important to recognize, however, that linear revenue and cost functions are generally approximations of the actual form of the cost and revenue functions. The assumption of constant prices and average variable costs is likely to become progressively less accurate as we move away from expected volume levels. Most decision problems, however, will concern output levels within a fairly limited range of expected volume levels, and we call this limited range the *relevant range*. In Figure 7A-2 we show estimated linear revenue and cost functions (TR_E and TC_E) that are tolerably good

FIGURE 7A-2.   Linear Revenue and Cost Functions in the Relevant Range

approximations of the actual curvilinear revenue and cost functions (TR_A and TC_A) over the range of output levels in which the decision maker is interested. Within this relevant range the linear functions are a sufficient approximation of the actual functions for most decision-making purposes.

Applications of Breakeven Analysis

Breakeven analysis can be of considerable value to the decision maker when decisions must be made about the price and quality levels of a proposed product. In Figure 7A-3 a comparison is shown of the breakeven points at two different price and variable cost levels. Suppose that initially the decision maker was considering the price and cost levels represented by the curves TR and TC. The indicated breakeven sales volume is shown as Q_4. Let us suppose that the decision maker feels that it is unlikely that the product will attain that sales volume and hence is likely to incur losses. The decision maker may rectify this situation in one way or in a combination of two ways: First, the price may be raised; second, the average variable cost may be lowered. The latter adjustment has implications for the quality of the product, since lowering average variable costs presumably implies the use of lower-quality raw materials or the use of less labor input per unit of output. It can be seen that at the initial price a reduction in the average variable cost level reduces the breakeven volume to that shown as Q_3. Alternatively, an increase in the price level with costs per unit remaining unchanged

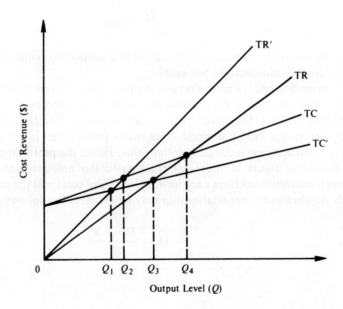

FIGURE 7A-3. Comparison of Breakeven Points at Different Price and Variable Cost Levels

would reduce the breakeven volume to output level Q_2. Finally, an increase in the price
level and a reduction in the cost level would reduce the breakeven volume to Q_1. The
decision maker must consider each of these breakeven volume points in conjunction
with the estimates of sales volume at those price and quality levels.

Algebraic calculation of the breakeven point is likely to be less time consuming
than the graphical procedure. To find the formula for the breakeven volume, recall
that it occurs where total revenue equals total costs, which may be expressed as follows:

$$P(Q) = \text{AVC}(Q) + \text{FC}$$

or

$$Q(P - \text{AVC}) = \text{FC}$$

or

$$Q = \frac{\text{FC}}{P - \text{AVC}} \tag{7A-1}$$

Since $(P - \text{AVC})$ is equal to the contribution margin per unit, we may restate this as

$$Q = \frac{\text{FC}}{\text{CM}} \tag{7A-2}$$

Thus the breakeven volume may be calculated simply by dividing the total fixed costs
by the contribution margin per unit.[1]

In multiproduct firms, where each product must attain a particular profit target
to maintain its place in the product mix and to withstand being replaced by another
profitable product, breakeven analysis can be used to find the sales volume at which
this profit target will be attained. Note that a profit target is a constant dollar value,
just as fixed costs are a constant dollar value. Hence the profit target may be added to
the fixed-cost figure to represent the total dollar amount that must be obtained
through contributions from each unit, before fixed costs and the profit target are covered. Algebraically, this relationship may be expressed as follows:

$$Q = \frac{\text{FC} + \pi}{\text{CM}} \tag{7A-3}$$

---

[1]Note that this form is applicable only for linear TR and TC functions. If either or both of these are
not linear, the contribution margin will vary with the level of output.

Having calculated the sales volume necessary to cover the fixed costs and to attain the desired target profit, the decision maker must then consider whether or not that target sales volume is likely to be achieved. If it appears quite unlikely, the decision maker may wish to revise the target profit, change either price or average variable costs, or delete this product from the product mix in favor of a more profitable product.

A third area in which the breakeven analysis may be useful is that where a particular product may be manufactured under two or more technologies of production. Suppose a firm is considering three alternate means of manufacturing a product for which the market price is established at $4.00 per unit. In Figure 7A-4 we show the three technologies under which this product may be manufactured. The total revenue function in each graph is the same, indicating that the firm does not expect to be able to influence market price by its actions. Plant A is characterized by fixed costs of $20,000 and a constant average variable cost of $2.00 per unit of output. Plant B is characterized by fixed costs of $45,000 and a constant average variable cost of $1.00 per unit. Plant C involves the much higher fixed costs of $70,000 but a low and constant average variable cost of $0.50 per unit. Using this information and equation (7A-2), one may verify that the breakeven points are 10,000, 15,000, and 20,000 units, respectively.

Suppose the decision maker's estimate of sales volume is distributed around a mean of 12,000 units. The breakeven charts of Figure 7A-4 indicate that plant A would be the most suitable choice, since its breakeven point is at the low end of this distribution. And barring an eventuality at the extreme left-hand tail of the distribution, plant A would be profitable at the likely sales levels.

In Table 7A-1 we show the profitability levels at various expected sales levels for each of the three technologies. Table 7A-1 summarizes the information given in Figure 7A-4. Plant A remains the most profitable up to the output level of almost 29,000 units, at which point it is overtaken by plant B. Plant C does not become the most profitable technology until it has an output level greater than 50,000 units.

The decision maker must use the breakeven information in conjunction with the probability distribution of expected sales levels, before deciding on the size of plant to implement. We would proceed in the way outlined in Chapter 6, namely, the calculation of the expected value of average costs in each plant, given the probability distribution of sales/output levels and a predetermined price level. Equivalently, we could assign probabilities to the expected sales levels in Table 7A-1 and calculate the expected value of profits from each plant, selecting the plant with the greatest expected value of profits. The firm should then check to see the relationship between the expected value of output (EVQ) and the breakeven output (BEQ). Clearly the EVQ should be above the BEQ or the plant should not be installed. The firm may wish to adopt a veto rule which incorporates the standard error of estimate S_e (or the standard deviation) pertaining to the probability distribution of sales/output levels. For example, unless the BEQ is less than $(EVQ - 2S_e)$, the firm will not install the plant with the greatest expected value of profit, and will choose instead the next smallest plant size. Such a rule would be interpreted as a risk averter's tradeoff between risk and return.

FIGURE 7A–4. Breakeven Charts for Different Production Technologies

TABLE 7A-1.   Profitability at Various Output Levels with Differing Technologies

Expected Sales Level	Plant A	Plant B	Plant C
10,000	Breakeven	−15,000	−35,000
15,000	10,000	Breakeven	−22,500
20,000	20,000	15,000	Breakeven
30,000	40,000	45,000	35,000
40,000	60,000	75,000	70,000
50,000	80,000	105,000	105,000
60,000	100,000	135,000	140,000

Operating Leverage.   The differences in the contribution per unit after the breakeven point are due to the extent to which fixed factors are substituted for variable factors in the production process. The greater this substitution, or the more capital intensive the technology, the greater the operating leverage of the production process. *Operating leverage* refers to the extent to which the incremental units sold contribute to overheads and profits. With linear cost and revenue functions, it is constant over the relevant range (equal to the contribution per unit); but with nonlinear total costs or total revenue functions, the operating leverage will vary as the slopes of the functions vary. Operating leverage shows the sensitivity of total contribution to changes in volume. Since the difference between total contribution and total profits is a constant (that is, fixed costs), operating leverage also shows the sensitivity to total profits to changes in volume. When a product is subject to volatile swings in sales in response to fluctuations in general economic conditions, greater leverage involves greater risk of wide variations in profits.[2]

Limitations of Breakeven Analysis

At the beginning of our discussion of breakeven analysis, the cautious note was injected that breakeven analysis is a useful tool *when correctly applied*. It is essential that the form of the total revenue and total cost functions used in breakeven analysis accurately reflect, or at least be a tolerable approximation of, the actual cost and revenue conditions. As indicated, the assumption of linear cost and revenue conditions may be a tolerable approximation within a relatively limited range of outputs but becomes progessively less accurate at higher output levels, because of the likelihood of diminishing returns to the variable factors or the necessity of reducing price in order to actually sell those higher output levels.

Second, breakeven analysis must be used in the incremental sense. That is, the total cost function must represent those costs that are incurred as a result of a decision

---

[2]Operating leverage is in fact an elasticity measure. Since it measures the relative responsiveness of profits to a change in quantity demanded, it can be calculated as the percentage change in profits over the percentage change in quantity demanded. It is the "volume elasticity of profit," if you wish.

to produce this particular product, and it must not include costs that would be incurred regardless of this decision. In the case of a firm that produces only one product, the total cost function will represent all costs incurred by the firm. If implicit costs are included at their opportunity cost value, the breakeven point will be the point of zero economic profits. Similarly, within a multiproduct firm where each department produces a single product, the total overhead costs of a particular department may be included in the total cost function in breakeven analysis. Beyond the breakeven point, the profits earned by that department will represent a contribution to the overheads and profits of the entire firm. Otherwise, in multiproduct firms, only the incremental overheads should be included and then profits are the contribution to the joint overheads and profits of the entire firm. Care must be taken, therefore, that the vertical intercept of the total cost function relates to simply the incremental and separable fixed costs associated with that particular product.

Summary

Breakeven analysis, like the decision tree, is a graphical aid to decision making. It allows the decision maker to consider the sales volumes that would be required in order to break even, given certain prices and cost structures. By reference to the estimates of the demand curve for a product of a given quality, the decision maker can see whether or not the breakeven volume can be attained. If not, the quality of the product may be upgraded or downgraded, if the breakeven volume of the product (at the changed quality and cost level) is attainable.

A simple calculation, namely the division of the fixed costs and profit target by the contribution margin per unit, allows the breakeven volume to be readily found for any combination of price and average variable costs per unit, as long as these are both constant over the relevant range.

Operating leverage measures the responsiveness of profits (or contribution to overheads and profits) to changes in sales volume. In conjunction with the breakeven volume calculation, operating leverage indicates the extent to which profits will increase as sales surpass the breakeven point.

Care must be taken with breakeven analysis to ensure that the cost and revenue functions used are sufficient approximations of the actual incremental costs and revenues.

DISCUSSION QUESTIONS

7A-1. Discuss the applications of breakeven analysis to business decision making.

7A-2. Summarize the limitations involved in the use of breakeven analysis.

7A-3. Derive an expression for the operating leverage of a particular plant, expressed in terms of the percentage changes in the appropriate variables.

7A-4. Under what circumstances is it appropriate to show the TR and TC curves as linear functions of output for breakeven analysis purposes?

7A-5. Derive an algebraic expression for the breakeven volume for the case where TR is a quadratic function of output (and TC is linear).

PROBLEMS AND SHORT CASES

7A-1. For the total revenue curve TR $= 45Q$ and the total cost function TC $= 120 + 12.5Q$, where Q represents thousands of units, perform the following.

(a) Show graphically the breakeven volume. Confirm your answer algebraically.

(b) Suppose now that a demand study estimates the demand curve to be $P = 80 - 10Q$. What do you advise?

7A-2. The Franklin Razor Company is considering the introduction of a new product that will facilitate shaving in the shower. It is considering three alternative quality levels for the product. Produced in plastic without any detailing, the product would cost $0.125 per unit over a wide range of outputs. Produced in a more expensive clear plastic material that allows intricate design work, the product would cost $0.1875 per unit over a wide range of outputs. Produced in an aluminum alloy, the product would cost $0.2225 per unit over a wide range of outputs. Fixed and setup costs would be $120,000, $180,000, and $250,000, respectively, for each of the three alternative quality treatments.

      Market research has indicated that consumers would perceive the products to contain good value when priced at $1.25, $1.49, and $1.98, respectively.

(a) Calculate the breakeven volumes for each of the three quality treatments.

(b) What other information would you prefer to have before making your recommendation?

7A-3. Suppose that the data in Table 7A-1 refer to the plant-size decision of Mainstream Motors Company, which intends to build a plant to produce extruded plastic bumper covers for the major automobile builders. Suppose the probability distribution of sales each month at the $4 price has been estimated to be as follows:

Output Level	Probability
10,000	0.01
15,000	0.05
20,000	0.18
30,000	0.45
40,000	0.25
50,000	0.05
60,000	0.01

(a) Calculate the expected value of profit from each of the three plant sizes, given this probability data.

(b) Calculate the standard deviation of profits around the expected value for each plant.

(c) Supposing management is risk averse, advise them which plant size should be selected.

SUGGESTED REFERENCES AND FURTHER READING

Horngren, C. T. *Introduction to Management Accounting* (5th ed.), chap. 2. Englewood Cliffs, N.J.: Prentice-Hall, Inc., 1981.

Davidson, S., J. S. Schindler, C. P. Stickney, and R. L. Weil. *Managerial Accounting—An Introduction to Concepts, Methods, and Uses,* chap. 6. Hinsdale, Ill.: The Dryden Press, 1978.

8 | Cost Estimation and Forecasting

8.1 INTRODUCTION

Cost estimation and forecasting for decision making are concerned with finding the shape and placement of the firm's cost curves. Knowledge of the short-run cost functions allows the decision maker to judge the optimality of present output levels and to solve decision problems using contribution analysis. We saw in Chapter 7 that the concept of incremental cost is fundamental to short-run decision making on cost issues. Incremental costs will include the variable costs, but they will also include any changes in those costs that are normally regarded as fixed costs. In any short-run situation we may experience increases in some of the fixed-cost items, since these particular facilities may meet their full capacity constraints and need to be increased. Incremental cost analysis is concerned with the variability of all cost components and therefore requires an appreciation of the degree of idle capacity in existing fixed-cost categories. When fixed-cost categories are expected to meet their full-capacity constraints, such that overtime use or additional facilities must be instituted, the decision maker must account for these costs as well as the variable costs when estimating the incremental cost of a contemplated decision.

Knowledge of long-run cost functions is important when considering the expansion or contraction of plant size and for confirming that the present plant size is optimal for the output level that is being produced. Recall that the long-run cost function shows the alternate sizes of plant available at the *present* point in time and should not be interpreted as showing the cost levels for various plant sizes that will be available in the future, since both technology and the relative factor prices are likely to change in the future, rendering the present long-run cost function inappropriate. To estimate *future* cost levels we need to forecast changes in the state of technology and changes in the factor price ratios and separate these from the expected effects of inflation in future time periods.

The remainder of this chapter is therefore organized into three main sections: (1) short-run cost estimation, (2) long-run cost estimation, and (3) cost forecasting. Under cost forecasting we examine the "learning curve" phenomenon, whereby costs per unit are seen to decline over time as the cumulative volume of production increases because of the increased productivity of the variable inputs as they better "learn" the production process.

8.2 SHORT-RUN COST ESTIMATION

In the short run we are concerned principally with the behavior of variable costs, but we must also be aware of other incremental costs, such as those changes in a fixed-cost category that would be necessitated by a particular decision. We shall discuss short-run cost estimation under four headings: simple extrapolation, gradient analysis, regression analysis, and the engineering technique.

Simple Extrapolation

■ *Definition:* *Extrapolation* means to impute values to points outside the range represented by the data base by projecting the relationship which is apparent within the data base.

The most simple method of cost estimation is to extrapolate the present level of marginal or average variable costs backward or forward to other output levels. Firms often express the belief that their marginal and average variable costs are constant over a range of output levels surrounding the current output level. Note that this belief implies constant returns to the variable factors and hence the absence of either increasing or diminishing returns in the short-run production process. If this constant efficiency situation actually exists in the production process, the simple extrapolation method is an adequate method of accurate cost estimation. However, if marginal costs are in fact increasing with additional output units, the simple extrapolation method may cause poor decisions to be made. It is a common error in business situations to assume that marginal costs are constant—in effect, assuming the absence of diminishing returns to the variable factors. It should be intuitively obvious that sooner or later diminishing returns will set in and that the decision maker must be constantly aware of this possibility.

When we have only one cost/output observation (that is, the current level), adjustment for possible diminishing returns must take place on the basis of judgment, experience, or intuition. For example, the decision maker may feel that the most reasonable presumption is that marginal costs are likely to increase by, say, 2 percent for each additional 1 percent change in the output level. Clearly, with only one set of cost/output observations, such an assumption is quite risky, since it may easily be significantly inaccurate.

Conversely, the decision maker may feel that marginal costs are more likely to fall if output is increased, or that there is no reason for marginal costs to either rise or fall, and, hence, the best estimate is that marginal costs are constant. Perhaps the best approach, in the absence of any data to the contrary, is to assume constant marginal costs for extrapolation purposes and then to examine the sensitivity of the decision made to the accuracy of that assumption.

Example: The Blissful Underwear Garment Company has an opportunity to sell 500 dozen pairs of panties to a discount store buyer who has made a flat offer of $7.00 per dozen. There has recently been a management shake-up at Blissful Underwear, and the new production manager is appalled that no data have been kept on production or cost levels for these panties and that she, therefore, has no idea what the incremental cost would be. Working quickly, she ascertains that, for the present week, 7,000 dozen pairs were produced at a total variable cost of $42,000. Thus average variable costs (AVC) are $6 per dozen at this output level, she reasons. Planned output for the next several weeks is also 7,000 dozen pairs, so fulfilling the discount store's order would expand the output rate to 7,500 per week, which is well within the plant's capacity.

FIGURE 8-1.   Extrapolation Based on Constant Marginal Costs of Output

Without any further information, the production manager has little choice but to extrapolate from the single data point she has observed. In Figure 8-1 we show the TVC, AVC, and MC curves based on an extrapolation of these curves, assuming constant MC, from the output level of 7,000 dozen to 7,500 dozen.

In the absence of any other changes in costs as a result of the decision to fulfill the discount store's order, we estimate that incremental costs will be $3,000 for the additional 500 dozen pairs. The incremental revenue, again in the absence of any other current explicit, opportunity, or future revenues, will be $3,500. Thus the contribution of this decision is expected to be positive, at $500, and the production manager is inclined to fill the order.

How sensitive is this decision to the underlying assumption of constant marginal costs? If TVC is not rising at a constant rate but, in fact, rises at an increasing rate over the next 500 dozen units of output, how much could it rise before the decision should be reversed? The answer is $3,500, at which point there would be no contribution from the decision, so it should not be taken. A $3,500 increase in TVC, bringing it to $45,500, would represent an increase in AVC to $6.0667, or fractionally more than a 1 percent increase in AVC from the earlier level. Thus the decision is very sensitive to the assumption of constant marginal costs, and we would probably advise Blissful Underwear not to fill the order unless they were very confident that TVC would, in fact, increase at a constant (or decreasing) rate.

Since output levels typically fluctuate to some degree from period to period, we should be able to find two or more cost/output observations, in which case we can conduct gradient analysis.

Gradient Analysis

■ *Definition:*   The *gradient* of a total cost curve is defined as the rate of change of those total costs over a particular interval of output levels. Gradient means slope, of course, and the gradient of total costs can be calculated as the change in total costs divided by the change in output levels. That is,

$$\text{Gradient} = \frac{\Delta TC}{\Delta Q} \tag{8-1}$$

Note: The gradient of the total cost, or total variable cost, curve is not exactly the same as *marginal costs,* since the latter is defined as the change in total costs for a one-unit change in outputs. In practice, output typically changes by discrete jumps, and we must, therefore, calculate the gradient over intervals greater than one unit. The gradient does provide us with an estimate of the marginal costs over the range of output levels, as we shall see.

Example: Suppose that Blissful Underwear accepts the order, produces the extra 500 dozen pairs, and notes that the total variable cost of producing 7,500 dozen pairs was $48,750. The gradient of total variable costs can thus be calculated as

$$\text{Gradient} = \frac{\Delta TVC}{\Delta Q}$$

$$= \frac{48,750 - 42,000}{7,500 - 7,000}$$

$$= \frac{6,750}{500}$$

$$= 13.50$$

Thus the rate of change of total variable costs, over the output interval 7,000 to 7,500 dozen, was $13.50 per unit. This is a measure of the marginal cost over that output range. In Figure 8-2 we show our best estimates of the TVC, AVC, and MC curves based on the observation of a second data point.

FIGURE 8-2.   Estimated Cost Curves Given Only Two Cost-Output Observations

Note: The single MC point shown in Figure 8-2 is plotted in the *middle* of the output interval over which it is calculated, because the gradient is a single-point estimate of the rate of change of total costs over a discrete range of output levels. It is the *average* rate of change over the output interval, or an estimate of the average MC over that range, and is, therefore, plotted in the center of that range.

Gradient Analysis with Several Observations: If we have a few more cost-output observations, we can substantially improve the estimates of the TVC, AVC, and MC curves.

Example: The new management of the Blissful Underwear Company, although planning to produce 7,000 dozen pairs per week in the next several weeks, finds that it faces a severe absenteeism problem, with weekly absentee rates ranging between 10 and 25 percent over the next three weeks, such that its output levels fall below the planned production level in each of these weeks. Total variable costs also fall, however, since absent labor is not paid for time missed, and purchases of raw materials and the use of electrical energy are also positively related to the output level. The TVC and output figures collected over the first five weeks are shown in Table 8-1 and plotted in Figure 8-3. Note that the output levels have been rearranged in ascending order, regardless of the chronology of production, in order to facilitate the calculation of the gradients over each output interval.

The AVC column in Table 8-1 is simply TVC/Q. The last three columns show the calculation of the gradients (and, hence, the estimated MC at the midpoint of each interval). When these points are plotted in Figure 8-3, we can interpolate between each adjacent pair of points and show our best estimates of the TVC, AVC, and MC curves. Note that the interpolation between the gradient values to find the MC curve indicates that the minimum point on the AVC curve must lie somewhere below 6,000 dozen pairs, since the MC curve must cut the AVC curve at the minimum point of the latter.[1]

TABLE 8-1. Cost-Output Observations and the Calculation of AVC and MC

Production Period	Output (doz.)	TVC ($)	AVC ($)	ΔTVC ($)	ΔQ (doz.)	MC ($)
Week 4	4,500	27,000	6.00			
				6,600	1,500	4.40
Week 3	6,000	33,600	5.60			
				3,775	500	7.55
Week 5	6,500	37,375	5.75			
				4,625	500	9.25
Week 1	7,000	42,000	6.00			
				6,750	500	13.50
Week 2	7,500	48,750	6.50			

[1]A smooth interpolation between the gradient values indicates that AVC is minimized at about 5,500 dozen pairs. This is open to debate, of course, since a straighter MC curve would indicate AVC minimized at a lower volume, for example. Our conclusion that AVC is minimized at 5,500 units is, therefore, sensitive to interpolation error.

FIGURE 8-3. Estimated Cost Curves Given Several Cost-Output Observations

Thus the observation of several pairs of cost-output data allows us to form a more complete estimate of the TVC, AVC, and MC curves. Each additional data point allows the shape of TVC to be seen more clearly, so that more reliable calculations of AVC and MC may be derived.

Regression Analysis Using Time-Series Data

Given a larger number of cost/output observations, we can apply regression analysis to estimate the dependence of costs upon the output level and thus obtain an estimate of the marginal cost.[2] Since we wish to estimate the cost function of a particular firm,

---

[2]The principles of regression analysis and the major problems associated with the use and interpretation of the results of this method were discussed in a self-contained section of Chapter 5. The discussion in this chapter presumes your familiarity with the earlier section.

we must use time-series data from that firm. This necessity raises some of the standard problems with time-series data: If over the period of the observations some factors have changed, the results of regression analysis will be less reliable. For example, factor prices may change because of inflation or market forces in the factor markets, or factor productivities may change because of changing technology and worker efficiency. To largely eliminate these problems the cost data should be deflated by an appropriate price index, and time should be inserted as an independent variable in the regression equation. Any trend in the relative prices or productivities will then be accounted for by the coefficient of the time variable.

Regression analysis of time-series cost data is quite susceptible to the problems of measurement error. The cost data should include all costs that are *caused* by a particular output level, whether or not they are yet paid for. Maintenance expense, for example, should be expected to vary with the rate of output, but it may be delayed until it is more convenient to close down certain sections of the plant or facilities for maintenance purposes. Hence the cost that is caused in an earlier period is not recorded until a later period and is thus likely to understate the earlier cost level and to overstate the later cost level. Ideally, our cost/output observations should be the result of considerable fluctuations of output over a short period of time with no cost/output matching problems.

Example: Suppose the weekly output and total variable costs of an ice cream plant have been recorded over a three-month period, as shown in Table 8–2. Output of the product varies from week to week because of the rather unpredictable nature of the milk supply from dairies and the impossibility of holding inventories of the fresh milk for more than a few days.

It is apparent from the data supplied that total variable costs tend to vary posi-

TABLE 8–2. **Record of Output Levels and Total Variable Costs for an Ice Cream Plant**

Week Ending	Output (gallons)	Total Variable Costs ($)
Sept. 7	7,300	5,780
Sept. 14	8,450	7,010
Sept. 21	8,300	6,550
Sept. 28	9,500	7,620
Oct. 5	6,700	5,650
Oct. 12	9,050	7,100
Oct. 19	5,450	5,060
Oct. 26	5,950	5,250
Nov. 2	5,150	4,490
Nov. 9	10,050	7,520
Nov. 16	10,300	8,030
Nov. 23	7,750	6,350

tively with the output level in this ice cream plant. But what is the *form* of the relation-ship? The specification of the functional form of the regression equation has resound-ing implications for the estimate of the marginal cost curve that will be indicated by the regression analysis. If we specify total variable costs as a linear function of output, such as TVC $= a + bQ$, the marginal cost estimation generated by the regression analysis will be the parameter b, since marginal cost is equivalent to the derivative of the total variable cost function with respect to the output level. In Figure 8–4 we show, for a given collection of data observations, the consequent average variable costs and marginal cost curves that would be generated by regression analysis using a linear specification of the relationship. Since average variable costs are total variable cost divided by output level Q, the AVC curve will decline to approach the MC curve asymptotically.

Alternatively, for the same group of data observations, if we specify the func-tional form as a quadratic such as TVC $= a + bQ + cQ^2$, the marginal cost will not

FIGURE 8–4.   Linear Variable Cost Function

be constant but will rise as a constant function of output. In Figure 8–5 we show the hypothesized quadratic relationship superimposed upon the same data observations, with the consequent average variable cost and marginal cost curves illustrated in the lower half of the figure.

Finally, if we hypothesize that the functional relationship is cubic, such as $TVC = a + bQ - cQ^2 + dQ^3$, the marginal cost estimate generated by regression analysis will be curvilinear and will increase with the square of the output level. Figure 8–6 illustrates the cost curves consequent upon a cubic expression of the cost/output relationship. Alternatively, a power function or other multiplicative relationship may be appropriate.

Which form of the cost function should we specify? Since the results of the regression analysis will be used for decision-making purposes, we must be assured that the marginal and average cost curves generated are the most accurate representations of the cost/output relationships. By plotting the total variable cost data against out-

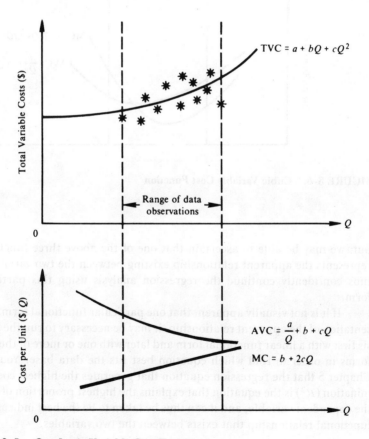

FIGURE 8–5.   Quadratic Variable Cost Function

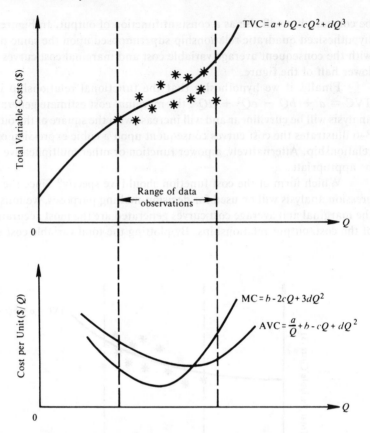

FIGURE 8-6. Cubic Variable Cost Function

put, we may be able to ascertain that one of the above three functional forms best represents the apparent relationship existing between the two variables, and we may thus confidently continue the regression analysis using this particular functional form.

If it is not visually apparent that one particular functional form is the best representation of the apparent relationship, it may be necessary to run the regression analysis first with a linear functional form and later with one or more of the other functional forms in order to find which equation best fits the data base. You will recall from Chapter 5 that the regression equation that generates the highest coefficient of determination (R^2) is the equation that explains the highest proportion of the variability of the dependent variable, and it can thus be taken to be the best indication of the actual functional relationship that exists between the two variables.

Example: Fitting a linear regression equation to the cost-output pairs shown in Table 8-2 resulted in the following computer output:

$$TVC = 1,395.29 + 0.6351Q \qquad (8-2)$$

with a standard error of estimate of 182.02 and a standard error of the regression coefficient of 0.0313. The coefficient of determination (R^2) was 0.97614.

Note that this linear regression equation explains 97.614 percent of the variation in TVC as resulting from the variation in the output level.[3]

Suppose we now wish to estimate the total variable costs at output levels of 7,000 and 11,000 units. For 7,000 units

$$TVC = 1,395.29 + 0.6351 (7,000)$$
$$= 1,395.29 + 4,445.70$$
$$= 5,840.99$$

Using the standard error of estimate we can be confident at the 68 percent level that the actual TVC will fall within the interval of $5,840.99 plus or minus $182.02 ($5,658.97 to $6,023.01), and we can be confident at the 95 percent level that the actual TVC will fall within the interval of $5,840.99 plus or minus two standard errors of estimate ($5,476.95 to $6,205.03). Thus we can be confident at the 95 percent level that TVC will be no higher than $6,205.03, given the production of 7,000 gallons of ice cream. These confidence limits allow a best-case/worst-case scenario to be developed. Of course, a highly risk-averse decision maker may wish to extend the confidence limits to plus three standard errors of estimate in order to find the TVC below which one can be 99 percent confident that actual TVC will fall.

The estimation of TVC at 11,000 units would proceed in the same way. The result must be viewed with caution, however, because it represents an *extrapolation* from the data base. The regression equation applies over the range of outputs observed and hence can be applied quite confidently for 7,000 units, a case of *interpolation*. Outside the range of the initial observations the relationship between TVC and Q may not continue to be linear but may instead be curvilinear, exhibiting diminishing returns to the variable factors, for example. Extrapolation may be undertaken, however, if we have no good reason to expect that the relationship will *not* hold outside the

---

[3]Adding extra explanatory variables will inevitably explain more of the variation in the independent variable, even if the extra variables are *not* responsible for variation in the independent variable, since the regression analysis tends to capitalize on chance. In this present case, a cubic function of the form $TVC = a + bQ + cQ^2 + dQ^3$ has $R^2 = 0.97642$ and thus explains fractionally more of the variation in TVC, although the standard errors of the coefficients are so large that one cannot have confidence in the equation's explanatory value. As a predictive equation, we could use the cubic expression, since the individual coefficients are not given any significance. For simplicity, we proceed with the simple linear specification with insignificant loss of accuracy.

range of observations, as long as we are fully cognizant that the relationship may not hold.[4]

The Engineering Technique of Cost Estimation

■ *Definition:*   The *engineering technique* consists of developing the physical production function that exists between the inputs and the output and of attaching cost values to the inputs in order to obtain a total variable cost figure for each output level. For each output level we must therefore calculate, or test for, the amount of each of the variable factors necessary to produce that output level. Attaching costs to these variable inputs we can subsequently calculate the total variable cost for each output level and hence the average variable costs and marginal costs at each output level. Let us demonstrate this in the context of a hypothetical example.

Example: Suppose a metal-stamping plant has one large machine that can be operated at five different speeds up to a maximum speed of 100 revolutions per minute (rpm). On each revolution it stamps out one unit of the product, and hence output is proportional to the operating speed of the machine. However, the requirements of materials, labor, electric power, and repairs and maintenance need not be proportional to the operating speed of the machine. In Table 8–3 we show the relationships that have been found between the output and the inputs of the variable factors, using this machine at each of its five speeds.[5]

By observing the various input components, you will notice that the ratio of materials used to output per hour increases as the operating speed of the machine is

TABLE 8-3.   Physical Requirements of a Metal-Stamping Machine at Various Operating Speeds

Operating Speed (rpm)	Output per Hour (units)	Materials Used (lb)	Labor (hours)	Power Requirements (kWh)	R&M Requirements (units)
20	1,200	1,320	20	2,585	10
40	2,400	2,880	25	4,523	20
60	3,600	4,680	27	5,262	30
80	4,800	6,720	28	6,708	35
100	6,000	9,000	30	10,954	60

[4]Throughout the regression analysis we required *ceteris paribus* to hold. Specifically, the prices of the input factors and the productivities of the factors must reasonably be expected to have remained constant over the period of data collection. The same costs and productivities must be expected to prevail over the prediction period as well.

[5]The figures at any output level should be regarded as the central tendency of the actually observed levels, since we should expect small day-to-day variations in material wastage, labor efficiency, and actual repairs and maintenance requirements.

increased, indicating increased wastage or spoilage as the machine is operated at faster speeds. Labor input, however, increases by different amounts as the operating speed is increased. It apparently requires twenty workers to operate the machine at its minimum speed, and the labor requirement increases at an irregular rate as the operating speed is increased, until at maximum speed thirty workers are required per hour of operation. Electric power requirements, measured in kilowatt-hours, increase rapidly at first, then more slowly, and then more rapidly again as maximum operating speed is attained. Repairs and maintenance requirements are indicated by an index of labor and materials necessary to maintain the machine in operating condition, and they evidently increase quite dramatically as the machine attains its maximum operating speed.

Suppose the variable inputs have the following costs per unit: Materials cost is $0.15 per pound; labor cost is $8.00 per hour; power cost is $0.0325 per kilowatt-hour; and repairs and maintenance cost is $10.00 per unit. With this information we can calculate the total variable cost of the output at various levels, as shown in Table 8-4. Dividing total variable cost at each output level by that output level, we derive the average variable cost for each output level, and the marginal cost figures are derived by the gradient method and are in effect the *average* marginal costs over each 1,200-unit interval. Note that both average and marginal costs decline at first and later rise.

In Figure 8-7 we plot these average variable and marginal cost figures against the output level. Interpolating between these observations we are able to sketch in the average variable and marginal cost curves as indicated by the engineering technique. The production process appears to be most efficient in terms of the variable factors at about 4,600 units, where average variable cost appears to reach a minimum at something like $0.37 per unit. If the speed of the machine were infinitely variable, the firm might wish to operate at this output level by running the machine at approximately 77 rpm. If the firm wishes to maximize profits rather than simply minimize costs, it will seek the output level at which marginal revenues from the sale of these output units equal the marginal cost of producing the last unit of output. Note that by multiplying the scale on the horizontal axis in Figure 8-7 by the appropriate factor, the same cost curves will be applicable for output per day, per week, or for a longer period.

Incremental costs associated with any decision to increase or decrease output

TABLE 8-4. **Costs Associated with Operating the Metal-Stamping Machine at Various Output Levels**

Output Levels (units)	Materials Cost ($)	Labor Cost ($)	Power Cost ($)	R&M Cost ($)	TVC ($)	AVC ($)	MC ($)
1,200	198	160	84	100	542	0.452	
2,400	432	200	147	200	979	0.408	0.364
3,600	702	216	171	300	1,389	0.386	0.342
4,800	1,008	224	218	350	1,800	0.375	0.343
6,000	1,350	240	356	600	2,546	0.424	0.622

FIGURE 8–7.   Estimated Cost Curves of Metal-Stamping Plant

levels will be determined on the basis of the variable costs as calculated by one or a combination of the above methods, plus an allowance for any opportunity costs that are involved and any incremental fixed costs that may be necessitated. The incremental fixed costs must be calculated on the basis of the knowledge of the production capacity of the fixed factors involved. This in turn may require an engineering-type investigation of the output capacities of particular fixed facilities. Similarly, increased costs associated with overtime use of facilities must be estimated on the basis of known overtime labor costs.

Studies of Short-Run Cost Behavior

Numerous studies of the short-run cost functions of particular business firms have been reported. Perhaps the definitive work in this area is the book by Johnston,[6] in which the theoretical and conceptual issues of cost estimation by statistical methods are examined in detail before thirty-one separate studies of statistical cost estimation are summarized by the author. With regard to short-run cost estimation, the preponderant conclusion is that marginal cost tends to be constant in the operating range of the firms studied. Hence average variable cost is constant at the same level (or is

---

[6]J. Johnston, *Statistical Cost Analysis* (New York: McGraw-Hill Book Company, 1960).

asymptotically approaching that level), and average total costs are declining because of the influence of declining average fixed costs. That is to say, in most cases a linear total variable cost function provided the best fit to the data observations.

In some cases where a curvilinear total variable cost function was hypothesized, the regression analysis generated a high coefficient of determination, but generally the linear equation provided at least as much explanatory power. Thus the general conclusion of the statistical cost studies is that marginal and average variable costs tend to be constant over the output range in which firms tend to operate, or they are sufficiently constant over that range that they may be regarded for decision-making purposes as constant. But constant MC and AVC over the range of recent output levels does not mean that we can expect these unit costs to be constant *outside* this range. For decisions that involve output levels beyond the recent range of output levels, the decision maker must consider the possibility that extrapolation of unit-cost levels is an unreliable procedure because of the possible onset of diminishing returns in the production process. The occurrence of diminishing returns in the incremental units of output should always be suspected, and if these are thought likely to occur the incremental cost figure should be adjusted accordingly.

The observation of constant marginal costs over the range of outputs observed should not be too surprising. We argued in Chapter 6 that the firm would wish to build the plant size that minimizes the expected average cost of production, given the expected output level or the probability distribution of quantity demanded at the chosen price level. This decision will typically lead to the installation of some excess capacity, allowing the firm to operate in a range somewhere below full capacity. Since full capacity is defined as the output level where average costs are minimized, the firm will typically operate somewhere around and to the left of the minimum point of the AVC curve. In Figure 8-7 note that the MC curve is virtually horizontal to the left of the minimum point of the AVC curve. If our observations of the metal-stamping plant have been restricted to output levels in the range from only 2,400 units to 4,800 units, we might well have concluded that marginal costs were approximately linear, yet the full picture shows them rising steeply as the plant approaches full capacity.

8.3 LONG-RUN COST ESTIMATION

In this section we shall outline methods by which the long-run cost curve, or the alternative short-run cost curves available at a particular point in time, may be ascertained. We shall discuss two methods of long-run cost estimation: cross-section regression analysis and the engineering technique applied to plants of various sizes.[7]

[7]G. J. Stigler has suggested a third method of estimating the long-run average cost curve based on the principle that the more efficient firms will survive and expand their market share over time. Plant sizes that allow increased market share over time are inferred to have lower average costs, while plant sizes that are associated with reduced market share over time are inferred to have higher average costs. Stigler's study

Regression Analysis Using Cross-Section Data

Since long-run cost estimation seeks to find the differing sizes of plant available at a particular point in time (while technology and factor prices remain constant), it is clear that we cannot use time-series observations to derive estimates of the long-run cost function. Observations from various plants at a particular point in time (cross-section data) may be analyzed, however, using the technique of regression analysis. Thus we would need to collect pairs of data observations relating the output level to the total cost of obtaining that output level in each plant, at a particular point in time. Care must be taken to avoid errors of measurement relating either to the actual level or rate of output in that period or to the actual level of costs that should be associated with that level of output in each plant observed.

Specification of the functional form of the equation involves the same problems for long-run cost estimation as it did for short-run cost estimation. We must choose the functional form that best fits a scatter plot of the total cost and output observations. Since we are interested in whether or not there are likely to be economies of plant size, constant returns to plant size, or diseconomies of plant size, we might initially specify the relationship as being cubic, since this relationship is consistent with the presence of increasing, constant, and decreasing returns to plant size. If there are increasing, and later decreasing, returns to plant size, the coefficients to the squared and cubed output terms will show up as significant determinants of the total cost level, with the signs of the coefficients being negative for the squared term and positive for the cubed term. If the cubed term is an insignificant determinant, the sign of the coefficient to the squared term will indicate increasing returns to plant size, if positive, or decreasing returns to plant size, if negative.

If both the squared and cubed output terms are insignificant determinants of total costs, a linear equation will give a better fit to the data. Attention should then shift to the sign of the constant term in the linear equation. If it is positive, the (long-run) total cost curve has a positive intercept, and long-run average costs (LAC), which are the ratio of (long-run) total cost to output levels, must be falling as output levels increase. Thus the data indicate economies of plant size over the range of observations. Conversely, if the intercept term is negative, LAC must be rising over the range of data observations, and we have discovered diseconomies of plant size. Finally, if the constant term is zero, we would conclude that there are constant returns to plant size over the output range observed. (In each of these three cases a positive slope term is taken for granted.)

If a power function, such as $TC = aQ^b$, best fits the data, then the size of the

---

of the U.S. steel industry inferred an LAC curve that was negatively sloping at first, then more or less horizontal for an extended range of outputs, and finally upward sloping at high output rates. This "survivor principle" suffers from several major disadvantages for practical implementation, however. See G. J. Stigler, "The Economies of Scale," *Journal of Law and Economics,* 1 (October 1958), reprinted in his *The Organization of Industry* (Homewood, Ill.: Richard D. Irwin, Inc., 1968); see also A. Koutsoyiannis, *Modern Microeconomics*, 2nd ed. (London: Macmillian, Inc., 1979), pp. 146–48.

exponent term *b* will indicate whether returns to plant size are increasing (if the exponent is less than 1) or constant (if equal to 1), or decreasing (if greater than 1).

Two major problems exist with cross-section data for estimation of the long-run average cost curve. The first arises because the observations collected may not be points on the long-run average cost curve at all.

Example: Suppose there are five plants observed, and the current output and total cost levels are as shown in Table 8-5. It seems that economies of plant size exist initially and that diseconomies of plant size prevail for the fourth and fifth largest plants, since the average cost figures decline at first and later rise as we encounter progressively larger plant sizes.

Suppose that the *actual* short-run cost curves for each of the five plants are as shown by the SAC_1, SAC_2, and so on in Figure 8-8. The observed output/average cost values are shown by the point on each short-run cost curve marked by an asterisk. Given this insight, we can see that the preceding analysis has overestimated the presence of economies and diseconomies of plant size in this instance because the observation points for each plant were not the points of tangency with the actual LAC curve. This problem is accentuated if smaller plants are operating beyond the point of tangency with the long-run average cost curve and if large plants are operating to the left of the tangency point, but it occurs whichever side of the "actual" tangency point the firms are operating on. Since we cannot expect each firm to be operating at precisely the point of tangency of the short-run average cost curve to the long-run average cost curve, the regression analysis of cross-section data is likely to produce a misleading picture of the actual economies and diseconomies of plant size that may exist. You will note that this is a case of measurement error—the assumption is that the data points are the points of tangency between the short-run average cost curves and the LAC, when in fact the data points are more likely *not* the points of tangency.

The second problem that may arise with cross-section data is that the various plants may not be operating with the benefit of the same factor prices or factor productivities. If the plants operate in differing geographical, political, and socioeconomic environments, we may expect both factor prices and productivities of the factors to differ between and among the plants. If this problem exists, regression analysis may

TABLE 8-5. **Cross-Section Estimate of the Long-Run Average Cost Curve**

Plant	Output (Q)	Total Cost ($)	Average Cost ($/$Q$)
1	1,500	7,350	4.90
2	3,500	12,600	3.60
3	6,150	18,143	2.95
4	8,750	26,688	3.05
5	11,100	43,290	3.90

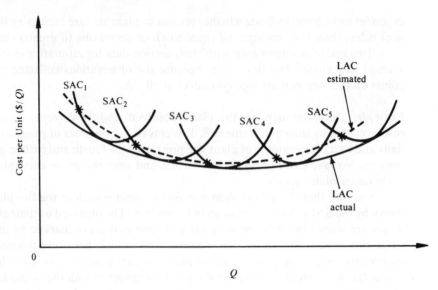

FIGURE 8-8.   Estimation of Long-Run Average Cost Curve from Cross-Section Data

indicate economies or diseconomies of plant size where the cost differences are actually due to differences in factor prices and productivities. Alternatively, the differences in these things may completely obscure the existence of those economies and diseconomies of plant size that would be seen if the influence of differing factor prices and productivities could be removed from the data.

Estimation of the long-run average cost curve presumes that all plant sizes represented are of the same vintage and therefore incorporate the same technology. Moreover, this technology should be the *latest* technology. Part of the differences in labor productivity that will most likely exist in cross-section cost-output data will relate to differing vintages of the plants observed, ranging from almost new plants to older and much less efficient plants. (Any other differences in labor productivity will relate to differences in the workers' education, training, motivation, and so on.) Regression analysis of cross-section cost-output data from plants of less than current vintage is likely to give unreliable results and should be avoided. A superior approach is to apply the engineering technique to all the different plant sizes that are currently available and that embody the latest technology.

Applying the Engineering Technique to Several Plants

The engineering technique outlined above in the context of short-run cost estimation can be used to find an estimation of the long-run cost function by applying the same analysis to a number of plants of differing sizes at a particular point in time. In the short-run cost estimation section we used the engineering technique to find the cost curves of a particular firm at a particular point in time. If we proceeded in a similar fashion with other plant sizes that are available, we would be able to trace out a series of short-run cost curves that are available to the firm at a particular point in time.

To apply the engineering technique for purposes of long-run cost estimation, we would conduct the analysis as outlined above under short-run cost estimation for each firm. To this we would add the average fixed-cost curve for each plant size, to arrive at the short-run total cost curve for each of the plant sizes. By the shape and placement of the short-run average cost curves, we could infer the presence or absence of economies and diseconomies of plant size. In Figure 8–9 we show a hypothetical case in which five different sizes of plants have been observed, and the short-run average cost curve of each has been derived by the engineering technique. The envelope curve of these short-run curves is the long-run average cost curve. It can be inferred from the figure that there are economies of plant size initially as one moves from the first plant to the second plant, followed by relatively constant returns to plant size as one progresses to the third and fourth plant, and decreasing returns to plant size with the largest plant available.[8]

Note that the construction of the long-run average cost curve by the engineering technique is predicated upon given factor productivity and factor prices. Similarly, the cost curves derived by this analysis are applicable only as long as the factor prices and

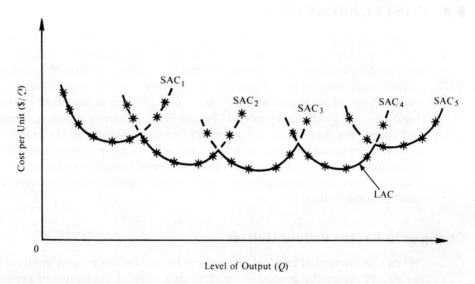

FIGURE 8–9.   Engineering Technique of Cost Estimation Used to Derive the Long-Run Average Cost Curve

---

[8]Typically we should expect discrete differences in the plant sizes that are available to the firm, rather than the infinite variability of plant sizes that is implied by a smooth long-run average cost curve.

productivities do not change. If they do, a new set of short-run average cost curves must be derived, and a new long-run average cost curve will be found.

Long-Run Cost Estimation Studies

Various studies of the long-run cost function of firms have been undertaken, and a number of these are summarized by Johnston.[9] The most common finding of these studies was that the long-run average cost curve tended to be not so much U-shaped as L-shaped; that is, there were typically significant economies of plant size at relatively low output levels, followed by an extended range of constant returns to plant size with no common tendency for costs per unit to rise at higher output levels. The absence of diseconomies of size in these production processes does not necessarily mean that they would not occur if progressively larger plant sizes were employed. The expectation that costs per unit would increase with a larger plant would presumably cause the firm to operate two smaller plants rather than build one larger plant. Thus the absence of evidence indicating diseconomies of plant size does not mean that they would never occur; it simply means that the data base does not include any plant that is experiencing diseconomies (presumably because of the foresight of the decision makers).

8.4   COST FORECASTING

Cost forecasting is necessary whenever decisions involve cost levels in future periods, such as in bidding for contracts, make-or-buy problems, or any other decision with cost implications beyond the present period. Forecasting the level of costs for various output levels in future periods requires an assessment of the likely changes in the efficiency of the physical production process, plus changes in the prices of the factors involved in the production process. Changes in the efficiency of factors of production will change the shape of the total product curve associated with the production process. If factor prices are expected to change, the relationship between the total product curve and the total variable cost curve that is derived from the total product curve will change. Hence the change in future costs will be the result of two influences, which we shall consider in turn.

Changes in Factor Productivities

When considering the physical efficiency of the production process in future periods, we should expect the productivities of at least some of the factors of production to change as time passes. Machines and equipment, for example, should be expected to become progressively more efficient in terms of output per hour (or by some other

---

[9]See Johnston, *Statistical Cost Analysis*, chap. 5.

criterion) because of the incorporation of technological advances into those machines. The increasing use of computer-controlled plant and equipment has allowed the productivity of capital equipment to increase substantially in recent years. Similarly, labor productivity may be expected to increase as time progresses because of the workers' higher level of education and increased familiarity with mechanical production processes. Conversely, changes in the attitude toward work or other sociological factors may lead us to expect reduced labor productivity in the future.

If trends have become apparent in the productivity of the factors of production, we may apply these trends as an estimate of future changes in the efficiency of the physical production process. This extrapolation of productivity trends should be modified by any changes in the productivity of any factor that may be expected to follow foreseen events of an irregular nature.

Labor productivity is typically measured as units of output per labor unit, and hence it takes the credit for increases in the productivity of capital factors such as machines and equipment. Labor productivity figures are therefore an amalgam of labor and capital productivity, and it may be quite difficult to separate the effects of each. The learning curve, introduced in Chapter 6 and discussed in a subsequent section of this chapter, is concerned with the increasing productivity of labor in conjunction with a particular set of equipment, with the familiar *ceteris paribus* requirement attached to that equipment (when interpreted strictly). Thus the average cost curve for a particular plant drifts downward as cumulative production increases. In practice, improvements are made to the firm's existing plant on an ongoing basis, so that our estimates of the learning effect will capture both the increasing productivity of labor and capital.

Changes in Factor Prices

If the costs of all inputs increase over time in the *same proportion*, then the factor combination that is initially optimal for a particular output level will remain optimal, although it will cost more dollars. If all input prices increase at the same rate, the relative prices of the inputs will stay the same, and there will be no profit incentive to substitute away from one input toward another, and thus the optimal input proportions (capital-labor ratio in the simplest case) will remain the same. Costs in a future period will therefore be equal to today's costs plus the expected percentage increase in all costs.

If market forces in the factor markets are expected to be such that the price of one factor will rise *relative* to the prices of other factors, we should expect the firm to want to substitute away from this factor and toward other factors that become relatively cheaper as a result of that price change. Thus, if labor costs are expected to increase faster than capital costs in the future, we should expect the firm to want to substitute capital for labor in order to minimize the costs of particular output levels. Historically, we have seen this to be the general case, with the increasing automation of production processes. To the extent that this process is expected to continue in future periods, the firm should expect to achieve an increasingly capital-intensive production process in the future.

Forecasting factor price changes—or, more generally, forecasting the rate of inflation—requires techniques similar to those introduced in the appendix to Chapter 5 in the context of demand forecasting. Opinion surveys, trend projections, econometric models, and leading series and other barometric indicators may be used to predict the rate at which costs of production are expected to increase in future periods.[10] Expectations of events likely to influence prices, such as supply shortages or export embargoes, must be incorporated into the cost forecasts. Given a probability distribution associated with future cost levels, we may proceed on the basis of the "expected value" of cost levels in future periods in order to obtain a point forecast of future cost levels for pricing or for other decision problems.[11]

In a socioeconomic system where inflation is endemic and relatively low rates of inflation are welcomed for their beneficial impact on business confidence, we should expect a continuing increase in nominal prices of all factors in future periods. To the extent that the firm is able to pass inflationary cost increases along to its customers and maintain the ratio of its prices to costs, the *real* cost of the resources to the firm is unchanged. Thus a current decision involving future production and costs can be made on the basis of today's cost levels modified only for expected changes in factor price ratios and for any inflationary effects that are not expected to be passed along to the purchaser. We shall see in Chapter 10 that the practice of "markup pricing" ensures that the firm will maintain its *real* contribution margin per unit under inflationary conditions. If the price must be set now but costs will be incurred in future periods, as in competitive bidding and price quotations, the price must include the expected inflation factor in order that the firm's real contribution margin will be preserved.

Estimating the Learning Curve

As discussed in Chapter 6, the learning curve relates the cost per unit to the accumulated volume of production of a particular product. We expect that the productivity of the inputs will increase as those inputs "learn" the production process, such that the cost per unit will decrease as time passes and cumulative volume increases. Evidence indicates that the cost per unit (at a particular output rate per period in a particular plant) tends to decline by a fairly stable percentage each time the cumulative volume is doubled. This rate of learning is typically around 20 percent. That is, unit costs fall approximately 20 percent each time the cumulative output level increases by a factor of 2, 4, 8, 16, 32, 64, 128, and so on. Note that for a constant output rate per period,

---

[10]See C. A. Dauten and L. M. Valentine, *Business Cycles and Forecasting*, 4th ed. (Cincinnati, Ohio: South-Western Publishing, 1974), chap. 18.

[11]Costs to be incurred in the future have a present value that is less than their future value, of course. Decisions to be made now, but which involve both costs and revenues incurred or received in future periods, should be evaluated in present-value terms.

this series of numbers indicates the number of periods before another 20 percent decline in unit costs is achieved. Thus the change in cost per unit between any two production periods, resulting from the learning effect, is most noticeable when production processes are just new, and it becomes virtually negligible as the production process matures.

The figures for the successive redoubling of output indicate that the learning curve is not a straight line; rather, cost per unit is an exponentially declining function of cumulative output. That is, the learning curve may be expressed as a power (or exponential) function of the form:

$$SAC = aQ^b \tag{8-3}$$

where Q represents cumulative volume levels, a represents the hypothetical cost of the first unit (or batch of units) produced, and b (typically a negative number) indicates the rate at which SAC will decline as output increases over time.

You will recall from Chapter 5 when we introduced regression analysis that a power function can be made linear by logarithmic transformation. Expressing our observed SAC and cumulative output values in logarithms we postulate that[12]

$$\log SAC = \log a + b \log Q \tag{8-4}$$

and use regression analysis to estimate the parameters a and b.

Example: Suppose that a manufacturing company has observed that the cost per unit of producing a particular product has declined as cumulative output increased, as shown in the first three columns of Table 8-6. The logarithms of SAC and Q are shown in the last two columns. Let us call log SAC the variable Y and log Q the variable X and postulate that $Y = a + \beta X$. The calculations to find the parameters α

TABLE 8-6. **Cost per Unit and Cumulative Volume Observations and Their Logarithms**

Date of Observation	Cost per Unit (SAC)	Cumulative Volume (Q)	Log SAC (Y)	Log Q (X)
Sept. 30	9.00	150	0.9542	2.1761
Dec. 15	7.20	275	0.8573	2.4393
March 1	6.50	350	0.8129	2.5441
May 15	5.85	500	0.7672	2.6990

[12]Your calculator may be preprogrammed to find the logarithm (and antilog) of any number. If not, find a set of log tables and think about getting a better calculator. The logs used here are to base 10. Using "natural" logs (to base e) will involve different log values but the same answers.

and β, following the example worked through in Chapter 5, are shown in Table 8-7. Note that $\alpha = 1.7418$ represents log a. To find the parameter a, we must take the antilog of 1.7418, which is found to be 55.18. Thus the power function expressing the learning curve is estimated to be

$$SAC = 55.18Q^{-0.3627} \qquad (8-5)$$

To forecast cost per unit at, for example, 1,000 units of cumulative volume, we simply substitute for $Q = 1,000$ in equation 8-5 as follows:

$$SAC = 55.18 \, (1,000^{-0.3627})$$
$$= 55.18 \, (0.0816)$$
$$= 4.50$$

Thus, we expect SAC to decline to $4.50 per unit by the time cumulative volume reaches 1,000 units.[13]

TABLE 8-7.   Calculations for Regression Parameters for Learning Curve

Y	X	XY	X^2
0.9542	2.1761	2.0764	4.7354
0.8573	2.4393	2.0912	5.9502
0.8129	2.5441	2.0681	6.4724
0.7672	2.6990	2.0707	7.2846
3.3916	9.8585	8.3064	24.4426

$$\bar{Y} = \frac{\Sigma Y}{\eta} = \frac{3.3916}{4} = 0.8479$$

$$\bar{X} = \frac{\Sigma X}{\eta} = \frac{9.8585}{4} = 2.4646$$

$$\beta = \frac{\eta \Sigma XY - \Sigma X \Sigma Y}{\eta \Sigma X^2 - (\Sigma X)^2} = \frac{4(8.3064) - (9.8585)(3.3916)}{4(24.4426) - (9.8585)^2}$$

$$= -0.3627$$

$$\alpha = \bar{Y} - \beta \bar{X} = 0.8479 - (-0.3627)2.4646$$

$$= 1.7418$$

---

[13]To be confident in the prediction, we should calculate the coefficient of determination, the standard error of estimate, and the standard errors of the coefficients. In this example, $R^2 = 0.99$, and thus the standard errors will each be relatively small. The confidence intervals around the estimated SAC will accordingly be quite narrow.

Note: Learning curves are often expressed in terms of the *percentage decline* in average costs for each consecutive doubling of cumulative volume. To find this percentage for the example here, we simply choose two output levels (one twice the other) and calculate the percentage by which SAC has declined. For example, estimating the SAC at 200 and 400 units of cumulative output from the learning curve, we have for 200 units:

$$SAC = 55.18 \, (200^{-0.3627}) = 8.076$$

and for 400 units:

$$SAC = 55.18 \, (400^{-0.3627}) = 6.281$$

Thus SAC at 400 units are

$$\frac{6.281}{8.076} \cdot \frac{100}{1} = 77.77\%$$

of what they were at 200 units, and we can see that there has been slightly more than a 22 percent decline in average costs as cumulative output doubled. We can predict that SAC will continue to decline by approximately 22 percent for the next and each subsequent doubling of the cumulative output level.

8.5 SUMMARY

Cost estimation is concerned with the levels of cost at various output levels of the firm's plant and with the relative costs of other plant sizes that are currently available to the firm. In the short-run situation we are concerned with the behavior of average variable and marginal costs, plus any other incremental costs that may be required because of the full utilization of some of the existing fixed-factor inputs. Long-run cost estimation involves the cost-per-unit levels of various plant sizes, given the current factor prices and state of technology.

Methods of short-run cost estimation discussed were simple extrapolation, gradient analysis, regression analysis of time-series data, and the engineering technique. Long-run cost possibilities may be estimated by using regression analysis of cross-section data or by applying the engineering technique to plants of various sizes. Empirical studies of cost estimation have frequently shown constant marginal costs in the short run and the absence of diseconomies of scale in the long run.

Cost forecasting requires the estimation of cost levels in future periods, in which factor productivities and prices may be different from today's levels. Trends in factor productivities that have become apparent over recent years may be used to project future changes in cost levels. Factor price changes that are real rather than simply monetary must also be forecast in order to obtain reliable indications of future cost levels for decision-making purposes.

The *learning curve*, when estimated for a particular production process, allows the cost per unit of future output levels to be predicted, based on the line of best fit to observed average cost data as cumulative volume increases. Production processes tend to become progressively more efficient in the production of an item as the experience in that production process accumulates. Unit costs tend to decline as a decreasing function of the total output, and a firm may use data collected on its past costs per unit to predict, or forecast, future costs per unit.

DISCUSSION QUESTIONS

8-1. Explain the dangers inherent in extrapolation of cost levels beyond the limits of the data base.

8-2. Why are cross-section data likely to be inappropriate for the estimation of short-run cost functions?

8-3. Why is it important to test several specifications of the cost function for their significance and goodness of fit?

8-4. Explain the engineering technique of cost estimation in terms of the production and cost theory of Chapter 6.

8-5. Outline some of the reasons why you might expect raw-material input, labor, and repairs and maintenance not to be simple linear functions of output.

8-6. Discuss the major problems that may arise in regression analysis of cross-section data to estimate the long-run average cost curve.

8-7. Explain why a linear relationship (with positive intercept and slope terms) between total costs (of different plants) and output levels (of different plants) means that the data exhibit economies of plant size.

8-8. Discuss the learning curve and the underlying reasons for its shape. What effect does this have on the firm's SAC curve?

8-9. If the productivities of all factors are expected to improve by the same proportion in the coming years, does this mean that there should be no factor substitution in future periods? Why or why not?

8-10. Summarize the issues involved in the forecasting of cost levels in an inflationary situation.

PROBLEMS AND SHORT CASES

8-1. The Rakita Racquets Company restrings tennis racquets, a business with a highly seasonal demand. The owner-manager, Ian Rakita, has kept a record of the number of racquets restrung and total variable costs for each of the past twelve months, as shown in the table on page 343.

Over the past twelve months Mr. Rakita has experienced a constant price level for all variable factor inputs, and he feels that, because of the regular turnover of employees, employee productivity and materials wastage are neither better nor worse than they have ever been.

Month	Total Variable Cost ($)	Racquets Restrung (units)
June	35,490	9,000
July	42,470	11,150
August	48,980	12,600
September	52,530	13,050
October	37,480	10,650
November	33,510	8,100
December	31,850	5,700
January	27,860	4,900
February	22,160	3,050
March	19,520	1,850
April	25,960	3,850
May	32,980	7,000

(a) Plot the total variable cost levels against output. Draw a freehand line through those observations that appear to represent the "line of best fit" to the data.

(b) From your freehand TVC cost function, derive the AVC and MC curves for Mr. Rakita's racquet-stringing operation.

(c) Suppose that demand is expected to move from its present level of 7,000 units (May) to 10,000 units next month (June). What is the incremental cost of meeting this additional demand?

(d) Explain how you would set up the data provided in order to use regression analysis to find the line of best fit. What functional form would you use?

(e) Qualify your answers with any implicit or explicit assumptions that are involved in the above analysis.

8-2. The Minical Electronics Company produces pocket calculators that are sold to various retail outlets at a price of $20. Minical feels it can sell all it is able to produce at this price. The following table indicates the physical input requirements for several weekly output levels, as compiled by the production manager, Paula Wald.

Output (units)	500	650	800	950	1,100
Labor hours	1,000	1,200	1,400	1,600	1,800
Component "packages"	750	1,000	1,275	1,575	1,895
Power (kWh)	225	400	500	650	1,000
Maintenance hours	5	15	23	28	42
Machine hours	20	25	29	32	39

The hourly wage rate paid for assembly labor is $5.50. The cost of a "package" of components is $5.00 each. (These packages each contain all the components necessary to produce one calculator. Because of imperfections in some components and breakage due to rough handling, more than one package per calculator is typically required). Power costs $0.038 per kilowatt-hour, machine hours are costed at $10 per hour, and maintenance hours cost $25 each.

(a) Using the engineering technique and gradient analysis, construct the AVC and MC curves implied by the physical input/output relationship and the prices of the imputs.

(b) At what output level are the variable inputs (combined) most efficient?

(c) What output level should the firm produce in order to maximize the contribution from this product?

8-3. The Patches Printing Company has recently expanded its product line to include a set of four-color Christmas and other Seasons Greetings cards. For the past three months it has been building up inventories and keeping records of total costs associated with the output in each month. These are as follows:

> August: 1,500 dozen cards, total cost $8,700
> September: 4,650 dozen cards, total cost $24,645
> October: 3,300 dozen cards, total cost $14,520

In the meantime PPC's market research group have conducted an investigation into the demand side of the year-end greeting card market and have arrived at the following regression equation and associated statistics:

$$Q = 8.41764 - 0.911P$$

where Q is quantity demanded in thousands of dozens per month, and P is price per dozen at the wholesale level. The coefficient of determination was 0.8652, the standard error of estimate was 0.6385, and the standard error of the coefficient was 0.3861.

(a) Estimate and plot on a graph the demand and marginal revenue curves PPC might expect to face.

(b) Plot on a graph your estimate of the average and marginal cost curves on which PPC is operating.

(c) What is the profit-maximizing price and output level you would recommend for PPC over the year-end sales period?

(d) What qualifications and assumptions underlie your analysis?

8-4. Every year the Fun in the Sun Vacations company (FSV) places an order with the Brown Bag Company (BBC) for a batch of vinyl flight bags embossed and screen-printed with FSV's logo and current promotional slogan. The size of this order has varied, being 9.000 units in 1983, 4,000 in 1984, and 6,000 in 1985. The price quoted by BBC also varies, in each case being equal to average costs plus a 15 percent markup.

Over the past two years there has been considerable inflationary pressure, and BBC finds that 1985 input prices are uniformly 12 percent above 1984 input prices and 22 percent above 1983 prices. BBC estimates that the 1985 order will require $7,000 in setup and other allocated fixed costs, and $23,000 in variable material, labor, and energy costs. The setup and fixed-cost allocation has been the same in constant-dollar terms for the past two years, although in current dollars it was less, of course. The historical cost data for the 1983 and 1984 orders is as follows. Note that dollar figures are not directly comparable because of the inflation.

Year	Quantity	Total Cost (current $)
1983	9,000	36,885.25
1984	4,000	21,428.57

This week two more orders were received, both from affiliated travel agents who want their own names added below the FSV logo and slogan. Extra setup costs of $1,000 are required for each order. Western Europe Travel (WET) wants 2,000 bags and Southern Cross Travel

(SCT) wants 1,000 bags. Each firm argues that because most of the setup and fixed costs will be charged to FSV, they should pay a lower price per unit. Each of these travel firms has made a flat offer of $5 per bag and is adamant that they will buy elsewhere if this price is not given to them. BBC feels that this auxiliary business could grow and augment its profitability in the future, and it is seriously considering these additional offers.

(a) Estimate and plot the MC, AVC, and SAC curves associated with the production of this particular line of bags, and comment on these curves.

(b) Advise BBC whether or not they should accept the additional orders, using contribution analysis to support your recommendations.

(c) What qualifications would you add to your recommendations?

8-5. A large new stadium is to be built in your city and contracts are being offered to manufacture certain items. Your company produces molded plastic items and is very interested in obtaining contracts to supply the seats for spectators. You have had substantial experience in making these hard plastic seats, ranging from garden furniture to elegant apartment furniture and including two previous contracts for hinged stadium-type seats. The major contractor for the stadium has determined that it will pay $12.50 per seat in batches of 5,000 seats. Several companies are expected to accept one or more of these contracts for 5,000 seats each. Your problem is to decide how many of these contracts your company should undertake.

Your cost estimating department has produced the following physical production requirements for various output levels.

Output Level (units)	Time to Complete (weeks)	Labor Input (hours)	Materials Required (kg)
5,000	2	500	11,000
10,000	3	1,053	23,000
15,000	4	1,724	34,500
20,000	5	2,667	54,000
25,000	6	4,167	77,500

Labor costs $10 per hour, and materials cost $2.50 per kilogram. Variable overheads are reliably estimated to be very close to 50 percent of labor cost per unit.

Rather than take these contracts, your company could instead devote its attention to making patio chairs for major chain stores and mail-order companies. Your company regularly produces these chairs whenever more lucrative contracts are not forthcoming and adds them to inventory for periodic supply to the chain stores and mail-order firms at a flat rate of $4.50 per chair. In a representative week you can produce 8,000 of these chairs with the following cost structure:

Cost Item	Cost per Week
Labor	$ 5,330
Raw materials	18,000
Variable overheads	2,670
Fixed overhead allocation	7,360

Determine how many contracts (for 5,000 seats each) your company should accept. Explain your answer fully and state explicitly any assumptions or qualifications you feel are necessary.

8-6. The Argus Boat Company manufactures aluminum paddles for use in canoes and small boats. Its demand for this product fluctuates from month to month depending upon orders received. ABC manufactures to order only, and ships the product immediately, since it has very little space for inventory accumulation. Its regular price is $10.00 per unit. Based on past demand, ABC has compiled a probability distribution of demand for next month, as shown below.

Today ABC's top salesman has asked the sales manager to authorize a special deal to a new customer: 2,000 paddles at $9.00 each. The sales manager in turn has asked the production manager for an estimate of costs per unit and has received the production data shown below. This data was derived by a careful analysis of the input requirements for various output levels and is kept in this form because costs of the inputs frequently change. The production manager advises that input costs are currently $12 per hour for labor; $3.25 per kilogram for materials; and $0.035 per kilowatt hour for electric energy. He further advises that they are expected to remain at these levels over the next month, during which time the special batch would be scheduled if the order is accepted.

In addition to the regular production costs, the special batch of 2,000 paddles will require a $3,000 setup cost for the customer's insignia to be imprinted in the metal and another $3,000 for extraordinary packing and shipping costs. Also, the salesman has just submitted his expense account, which contains $1,000 in expenses associated with a special trip to see this potential new client and to bring negotiations to their present stage. ABC's overhead costs are expected to be $24,000 next month.

(a) Derive the marginal and average cost curves from the data given and show these on a graph.

(b) Advise the sales manager about the appropriate decision, giving full supporting reasoning and calculations.

(c) State any qualifications and reservations you have regarding your recommendation.

Demand Data:

Quantity Demanded per Month	Probability
5,000	0.10
6,000	0.15
7,000	0.20
8,000	0.25
9,000	0.20
10,000	0.10

Production Data:

Units of Output	Labor (hours)	Materials (kg)	Energy (kWh)
1,000	477	500	4,885.71
2,000	807	1,000	7,600.00
3,000	1,010	1,500	9,857.14
4,000	1,140	2,000	12,000.00
5,000	1,224	2,520	13,485.71
6,000	1,280	3,050	15,071.43
7,000	1,337	3,600	17,314.29
8,000	1,478	4,180	19,400.00
9,000	1,800	4,690	22,214.29
10,000	2,407	5,320	23,600.00
11,000	3,304	5,970	25,700.00
12,000	4,434	6,660	28,200.00

8-7. The Done Brown Cookie Company produces high-nutrition "Brownie" biscuits which it sells to retailers for $22.55 per carton of 24 packets. Although demand for Brownies is not seasonal, it nonetheless fluctuates during the year. Over the past nine months of operations demand has varied between 6,000 and 10,000 cartons per month, but there is a general growth trend in sales.

The vice-president of corporate planning, Mr. Black, has put forward the proposal that the firm expand its present plant. Having investigated the financial situation of Done Brown, he suggests that the cash that the directors are considering paying out as an extra dividend would be put to better use if invested in plant expansion and renovation. He contends that running a larger plant at half capacity would be more economical than running the present plant.

The vice-president of production, Mr. Green, on the other hand, asserts that the plant is running smoothly and that sales forecasts in no way indicate that a larger plant is necessary at this time. Mr. Black, though, seems to have a convincing argument, having procured the cost figures for a competing brownie manufacturer who has a larger plant than does Done Brown. He suggests that Done Brown should model its plant after that of the competitor.

A task force has been assigned to study the question of expansion. It is to analyze costs for both firms, analyze the sales forecast, as shown below, and submit its findings to the board of directors, along with a recommended plan of action. You are the head of the task force. Is Mr. Black correct? Should Done Brown expand its plant? Support your recommendation with discussion of the issues involved. Defend any assumptions that you feel are necessary.

Sales Forecast: Average Sales per Month over the Next Year

Volume	Probability
8,000	0.05
9,000	0.20
10,000	0.50
11,000	0.20
12,000	0.05

Done Brown's Production Costs: Past Nine Months

Month	Output Level (cartons)	Materials ($)	Direct Labor ($)	Overhead ($)
April	6,000	88,500	21,000	15,200
May	7,500	107,250	24,000	17,450
June	6,500	94,900	22,100	15,950
July	8,000	113,200	24,800	18,200
August	7,000	101,150	23,100	16,700
September	8,500	118,825	28,475	18,950
October	10,000	148,500	45,000	21,200
November	9,000	126,850	32,400	19,700
December	9,500	136,075	37,525	20,450

Competitor's Production Costs: Past Nine Months

Month	Output Level (cartons)	Materials ($)	Direct Labor ($)	Overhead ($)
April	10,000	140,000	30,500	24,350
May	8,500	127,075	27,025	22,175
June	9,000	133,000	28,550	22,900
July	10,500	144,375	32,025	25,075
August	9,500	136,565	29,875	23,625
September	11,000	151,250	33,550	25,800
October	12,500	173,750	47,875	27,975
November	11,500	158,125	36,675	26,525
December	12,000	165,600	41,600	27,250

8-8. The Autoroller Company is situated near Detroit and specializes in producing ball bearings for the automotive industry. Since its inception in 1970 the company has been supplying both the Michigan and the Ohio automobile producers and has had increasing sales each year. In 1986 the company sold 600,000 units in Michigan and 200,000 units in Ohio. In 1987 the Ohio customers contracted for 400,000 units, and Michigan demand was expected to increase by 100,000 units. The Ohio customers indicated that they would need 600,000 units in 1988, and Michigan sales were expected to be 750,000 units in that year. The price per unit was increased to $8, effective January 1, 1987, for the whole of 1987. Since the Ohio customers ship other auto parts to their Michigan plants and return their trucks empty, they purchase at the same price as the Michigan customers at the Detroit plant of Autoroller.

Autoroller's president, Mr. Blydt-Hansen, was excited about the increasing demand over the years but was concerned about plant capacity and the effect on profitability. The plant's normal capacity was 600,000 units per year, but with a combination of either overtime or a second shift, both at a 50 percent premium on labor cost, demand has been met so far. A third shift was possible, and 1988 demand could be satisfied from the existing plant, although costs per unit were expected to increase further. Alternatively, Mr. Blydt-Hansen was considering whether or not to build an identical plant in Ohio. This project could be completed in time for start-up in the beginning of 1988 if a decision was reached immediately. The cost structure of the new plant in Ohio was expected to be identical to that of the existing Michigan plant.

The company accumulated the following data (all figures are thousands):

	1984	1985	1986	1987 (est.)
Sales volume	600	700	800	1,100
Total revenue	$3,600	$4,620	$5,800	$8,800
Costs: Direct labor	450	620	818	1,285
Raw materials	676	983	1,382	2,000
Variable overhead	900	1,240	1,636	2,400
Fixed overhead	1,127	1,240	1,364	1,400
Total costs	$3,153	$4,083	$5,200	$7,085
Profit	447	537	600	1,715

The company treasurer advises that hourly wages and all other costs have increased by about 10 percent per year for the last few years, and Autoroller has been able to increase its price each year. These price trends are expected to continue through at least 1988.

Advise Mr. Blydt-Hansen whether or not he should build the new plant in Ohio. Support your recommendation with discussion of all issues involved.

8-9. The Whizbang Electronic Games Company has been producing a particular machine for sale to pinball arcades for about a year. At first its costs per unit were relatively high, but these declined as total production grew, as shown below:

Total Production Since Start-up	Average Cost of Production per Unit
300	$1,000
500	870
1,000	700
1,800	540
2,400	520

(a) Estimate the learning curve for this firm, assuming that the relationship is best represented by unit costs as a power function of total production.

(b) What is the percentage of learning implied by the data?

(c) Forecast the average cost per unit when total production reaches 3,000 units.

(d) What qualifications and assumptions underlie your analysis and prediction?

8-10. The Fairway Golf Cart Company entered the American market in 1981 after production began in its Florida plant. Initially, the output rate was low, but it soon picked up as the workers learned their jobs and found ways to save time, materials, and energy in the production process. Suppose that the assembly costs during the first year were as shown below and that the variable factors will continue to become more productive as total output continues to increase.

Total Units Produced	Assembly Cost per Unit
1,000	$1,582
2,000	1,215
3,000	1,095
4,000	975
5,000	900

(a) Forecast the assembly cost per unit for each vehicle when total output reaches 10,000 units and 20,000 units.

(b) How well does the learning curve fit the data points? What are the 95 percent confidence limits to your predictions?

(c) What other qualifications should you attach to your predictions?

SUGGESTED REFERENCES AND FURTHER READING

Abernathy, W. J., and K. Wayne. "Limits of the Learning Curve," *Harvard Business Review*, 52 (September–October 1974), pp. 109–19.

Dauten, C. A., and L. M. Valentine. *Business Cycles and Forecasting* (4th ed.), chaps. 10 and 18. Cincinnati, Ohio: South-Western Publishing, 1974.

Fudenberg, D., and J. Tirole. "Learning by Doing and Market Performance," *Bell Journal of Economics*, 14 (Autumn 1983), pp. 522–30.

Harpaz, G. "Learning by Dominant Firm," *Managerial and Decision Economics*, 6 (March 1985), pp. 59–63.

Johnston, J. *Statistical Cost Analysis.* New York: McGraw-Hill Book Company, 1960.

McGuigan, J. R., and R. C. Moyer. *Managerial Economics* (2nd ed.), pp. 272–302. St. Paul, Minn.: West Publishing Company, 1979.

McIntyre, E. B. "Cost-Volume-Profit Analysis Adjusted for Learning," *Management Science*, 24 (October 1977), pp. 149–160.

Nelson, C. R. *Applied Time Series Analysis for Managerial Forecasting.* Oakland, Calif.: Holden Day, 1973.

Pegels, C. C. "Start-up or Learning Curves—Some New Approaches," *Decision Sciences*, 7 (October 1976), pp. 705–13.

Simon, J. L. *Applied Managerial Economics*, chap. 13. Englewood Cliffs, N.J.: Prentice-Hall, Inc., 1975.

Spence, A. M. "The Learning Curve and Competition," *Bell Journal of Economics*, 12 (Spring 1981), pp. 49-70.

Stigler, G. J. "The Economies of Scale," *Journal of Law and Economics*, 1 (October 1958).

Womer, N. K., and J. W. Patterson. "Estimation and Testing of Learning Curves," *Journal of Business and Economic Statistics*, 1 (October 1983), pp. 265-72.

9 Models of the Firm's Pricing Decision

9.1 INTRODUCTION

In this chapter we review the "theory of the firm," which is a series of models that attempt to explain and predict the price and output decisions of the firm. These models, which bring together the demand analysis of Chapters 3 and 4 with the cost analysis of Chapter 6, are usually covered in introductory and intermediate microeconomics courses. However, this chapter should not prove too difficult for a student who has not had these courses, since it brings together material from earlier chapters that is familiar by now. If you have taken microeconomics courses previously, this chapter will provide more than a simple review, because it takes a somewhat novel approach and introduces some more recent concepts.

The first thing to learn about the theory of the firm is that there is no single model of the firm's behavior. In fact, there are literally dozens of models of the firm, each one designed to explain or predict a firm's behavior in a particular market situation. Each model of the firm consists of four structural assumptions, which define the demand and cost conditions facing the firm, and three behavioral assumptions, which define how the firm is expected to behave in its market situation as it pursues its objective.

The Seven Assumptions of a Model of the Firm

Traditional price theory delineates four basic market forms, namely, pure competition, monopolistic competition, oligopoly, and monopoly. Pure competition consists of many firms producing identical products in an environment of full information—all firms know where to buy the cheapest inputs, and all consumers know where to buy the cheapest products. Firms operating in pure competition are called *price takers*, because the price of their product is determined by the market forces of demand and supply. Excess demand for the product will drive the market price up, and excess supply will drive the market price down. Since all firms are selling exactly the same product and consumers have full information about all firms' prices, a firm will sell nothing if it raises its price above the market price. Conversely, the firm has no incentive to reduce its price below the market price, since it is small relative to the size of the market and can sell all that it wants to at the market price.

The other three market forms are characterized by product differentiation, and the state of information is not complete. In fact, lack of information may be one of the bases for consumers' differentiating between the products of rival suppliers. Monopolistic competition consists of many firms with slightly differentiated products. Oligopoly consists of a relatively small number of firms whose products are typically substantially differentiated from each others' through some combination of product design, promotional efforts, and place of sale.[1] Monopoly consists of a single seller of a product that has no close substitutes; thus the product is highly differentiated from the products of all other firms.

Firms operating in monopolistic competition, oligopoly, and monopoly are called *price makers*, because they can adjust the price of their product up or down in order to pursue their objectives. The firm's ability to set prices derives from the differentiation of its product. Each firm can raise its price to some extent without losing all its customers, since the remaining customers believe that the product is worth the extra price being asked.

In Table 9–1 we show the four traditional market forms in terms of the underlying structural and behavioral assumptions. Note that the essential differences between the four market forms arise from assumptions 1 and 4. Thus it is the number of firms and whether or not the firms' products are differentiated that essentially characterize the firms into the four traditional market forms. The three types of price-maker markets are each characterized by differentiated products. Assumption 7 also differs across the market types, but note that this difference is related to assumption 1. When there are many firms in the market, each firm can safely expect no reactions from rivals following the adjustment of its strategic variable, since the effects of this adjustment are spread over many rivals, making an insignificant impact on each one. Conversely, in an oligopoly, where there are relatively few rivals, the firm should expect its strategic actions to have a noticeable impact on the sales of each of its rivals, and therefore expect them to retaliate in some situations, Monopolists expect no reactions because there are no rivals in their markets.

In managerial economics we are concerned with the firm's pricing problem—namely, to set its price at the level that will best serve its objective. Consequently, we

[1]An oligopoly could, in theory, have undifferentiated products. In practice a "pure oligopoly" is hard to find. Identical products means that all attributes of the product are identical across firms. Thus not only the attributes of the firms' "core" product, such as steel, but all other (peripheral) attributes of the product, including the convenience of purchasing, the delivery schedules, the product warranty, and the interpersonal relationship between the purchasing agent and the salesperson, must be equal across all firms. Even if the core product is exactly the same, it is unlikely that the buyer will not find one seller a little more convenient or a little more pleasant to buy from. The existence of imperfect information may make the buyer think there is a difference between the sellers even if there is not. If the buyer has any preference for one seller over another when prices are equal, then the products are differentiated as far as the buyer is concerned.

TABLE 9-1. Market Forms and the Seven Assumptions Underlying Them

	PRICE TAKERS		PRICE MAKERS	
	Pure Competition	Monopolistic Competition	Oligopoly	Monopoly
Structural assumptions:				
1. Number of sellers	Many	Many	Few	One
	Underlying the number of sellers is an assumption concerning barriers to entry. The absence of barriers to the entry of new firms means that there will be many firms in the market. Substantial barriers to entry in oligopoly markets limit the rivals to a few. Insurmountable barriers to entry allow the monopolist to remain the only seller of its product.			
2. Cost conditions	For all models we can assume diminishing returns in production in the short run, causing MC to rise. This is not important in oligopoly and monopoly, where constant or declining MC may prevail.			
3. Number of buyers	For all models we assume many buyers, so that the dominant force in the pricing decision will not be one, or a few, strong buyers. Variants of the oligopoly and monopoly models, known as oligopsony and monopsony, cover the strong-buyer situation.			
4. Demand conditions	Identical substitutes	Very similar substitutes	Close substitutes	No substitutes
Behavioral assumptions:				
5. Objective function	For all models we initially assume short-run profit maximization. This may be inappropriate for oligopoly, where time horizons typically extend beyond the short run, since high short-run profits may induce the entry of new competitors to cause a more competitive market for the firms later in the planning period.			
6. Strategic variable	In all models we assume the firm can adjust price and quantity supplied, although once the price is in equilibrium, pure competitors will adjust only their quantity supplied. Firms in the other three market types may also adjust their promotional efforts, product design, and distribution channels.			
7. Expectation of rivals' reactions	None, since there are many firms in both these market types. Firms are all small relative to their market, so their actions will go unnoticed by rivals.		Rivals may ignore or match the firm's actions, depending on what serves their objectives.	None, since there are no close substitutes for the monopolist's product.

are more concerned with the price-making models than with the price-taker model of pure competition. Nevertheless, the firm may face conditions approaching pure competition in some situations, so a quick review of the pure competition model is appropriate.

Price Determination in Pure Competition

In pure competition the equilibrium price is determined by the interaction of the market forces of supply and demand. There are many buyers and many sellers, each too small relative to the market to influence directly the general price level. In aggregate, however, their demand and supply decisions lead to the determination of the equilibrium market price. The market demand curve is negatively sloping, and the market supply curve is positively sloping, as shown in the left-hand part of Figure 9-1. If, at a particular price level, such as P_1, supply exceeds demand, there will be downward pressure on prices, because of the desire of firms to reduce inventories to preferred levels. Each firm reduces price in order to clear its excess inventories and thus avoid costs associated with holding those excess inventories. Since many firms will be independently reducing their prices, the market price falls. One firm alone reducing its price would not cause a reduction in the general price level, since it could sell all it wishes at the lower price without any competing firm suffering a significant loss of sales, because of the assumption that firms are small relative to the market. But the combined effect of many firms reducing their prices causes a significant loss of sales to those competitors that have *not* reduced their prices. This in turn causes those firms to suffer excess inventory, and they too will be motivated to reduce price.

Thus excess market supply leads to a reduction in the market price. The lower price causes an increase in the quantity demanded and at the same time causes the

*Note that the output scale is much smaller for the firm than for the market.

FIGURE 9-1.   Price and Output Determination in Pure Competition

firm to be willing to supply a somewhat reduced amount. Prices will continue to fall until finally supply equals demand, as shown in Figure 9-1.

Conversely, if there is excess demand at a particular price level, such as at P_2 in Figure 9-1, there will be upward pressure on prices, because of the willingness of some buyers to pay more than the market price rather than go without the product. Firms will find they can raise their price slightly yet still sell all they wish to produce, since although other firms may be maintaining their price at P_2, those firms are unable to supply all the buyers willing to purchase at price P_2, and some of the remaining buyers are willing to pay more than P_2 to obtain the product. The firms setting price P_2 then see that they too can ask for a higher price, and the combined effect is for the market price to move upward. As it does, the quantity demanded is reduced as some buyers drop out of the market, and the quantity that suppliers are willing to put on sale increases, until finally supply equals demand and no further incentive exists to raise prices. The price P^* in Figure 9-1 is thus the equilibrium price and is determined not by the actions of any one firm but by the combined effects of individual firms' actions.

Given the market price, the purely competitive firm must decide what output level to produce in order to maximize its profits. Profits are maximized when the difference between total revenues and total costs is greatest. Since the firm is small relative to its market, it can sell all it wants to at the market price, and its demand curve is therefore a horizontal line at the market price level, as shown in the right-hand part of Figure 9-1. Since the price is constant regardless of the number of units sold, marginal revenue is equal to price, and the demand and marginal revenue curves are coextensive. The short-run average cost (SAC) and marginal cost (MC) curves are added to the firm's graph, and we note that MC = mr at output level q^*. To maximize its profit the firm chooses the output level q^*, where marginal cost rises to equal marginal revenue. Producing one more unit of output would cost more than the revenue it would generate (MC > mr), and producing fewer units of output would save less cost than the revenue forgone (MC < mr). The firm's profit can be visualized as the rectangle P^*ABC, since profit is the product of the price-cost margin ($P^* - C$) times the output level $0q^*$.[2]

Note: Do purely competitive markets exist? There are certainly some markets that have many buyers and many sellers. The most difficult condition to find is that of identical products. All buyers must regard all products from the competing suppliers as identical in all respects. Buyers cannot have personal preferences for particular sellers, nor have differing expectations of quality or after-sales service, nor find it more

---

[2]Note that the purely competitive firm has no incentive to either raise or lower its price away from the market price. If it raised its price above P^* it would sell no units at all, since all its buyers would seek the product from other sellers at the market price. Lowering the price would also lead to reduced profits, since the firm would sell fewer units (because a lower mr will cut MC at a smaller output level) at a lower price, without a commensurate reduction in costs per unit. Only when there is excess market demand will the firm have a profit incentive to raise price, and only when there is excess market supply (and there is a cost of holding excess inventories) will the firm wish to reduce its price.

or less convenient to buy from one seller rather than from another. The package of attributes constituting the product must be viewed as identical in all respects.

Example: Perhaps the only market in which this condition is fulfilled is the stock exchange, at which hundreds of buyers and sellers meet anonymously (through an agent) to buy and sell a company's stock. Each share in the company has the same rights, benefits, and obligations attached (for each class of shares), and no buyer is likely to care about the identity of the previous owner. In fact, the theory of finance is based on the pure competition model.

Applications of the purely competitive model as an explanatory or predictive device will be inappropriate to the extent that the seven assumptions involved do not accord with the reality of the situation being explained or predicted. The major value of the purely competitive model is probably as a pedagogical model. It allows the theory of the firm to be introduced in a relatively simple context, free of the complications introduced by product differentiation and fewness of buyers or sellers. It thus forms a basis upon which we can build an understanding of more complex theories of the pricing behavior of firms.

9.2   PRICE DETERMINATION WHERE NO REACTIONS ARE EXPECTED

Monopolists and monopolistic competitors can safely ignore the reactions of their rivals, in the former case because there are no close rivals, and in the latter case because the firms are each small relative to the market and are expected to have insignificant impact upon each others' sales. Oligopolists may ignore the probable reactions of rivals, but they do so at their own risk. The sales and profits of oligopolists are interdependent, or "mutually dependent"—the competitive actions of one have a significant impact on the sales of the others and may provoke a competitive reaction. Recognition of mutual dependence (RMD) means that the firms recognize and take into account the probable reactions of rivals before undertaking a competitive strategy. We shall consider oligopoly pricing (with RMD) in the next section. We shall not consider "non-RMD" oligopoly pricing at all, because of the space constraints of this text and because of the topic has limited relevance to managerial economics.[3]

---

[3]These "myopic" oligopoly pricing models, such as the Cournot and Edgeworth models, do have some pedagogical value, since they demonstrate quite forcefully the implications of myopia in oligopolistic markets. In short, failure to recognize mutual dependence leads to the downward progression of prices to a price floor, as in the Cournot model, or to the fluctuation of prices between a price floor and a price ceiling, as in the Edgeworth model. A particularly thorough treatment of these classical models of duopoly (two sellers) under conditions of unrecognized mutual dependence is found in A. Koutsoyiannis, *Modern Microeconomics*, 2nd ed. (London: Macmillan, Inc., 1979), pp. 216-33.

Monopoly Markets

Monopolies exist when there is a single seller of a product in a particular market. They persist over time if the entry of new firms is prevented by *barriers to entry*. Barriers to entry are additional costs that a potential entrant must incur before gaining entry to a market. These costs may arise because the existing firm controls an essential raw material, the best location, necessary information, the right to produce the product (such as a "patent" or a government mandate), and so on. Consumer loyalty to the existing firm poses a barrier to a potential entrant, since the new firm would have to spend substantial amounts on advertising to offset it. In some cases the entry cost is infinite (where it is impossible to acquire the necessary input or permission to produce), and in other cases the cost is simply high enough to prevent a potential entrant from making a profit in the foreseeable future.

Some monopolies are *natural monopolies*, in the sense that the market would inevitably be served by a monopoly even if some other market form were to exist initially. This situation occurs when the monopolist's output capacity is large relative to the market demand. In terms of the long-run average cost (LAC) curve and the monopolist's demand curve, the quantity demanded at the monopolist's price would occur where the LAC curve is still falling. Thus a single firm will benefit from economies of plant size by expanding to supply the entire quantity demanded. If an oligopoly initially existed, the firms would have a profit incentive to merge with (or take over) each other to form a monopoly and subsequently benefit from the economies of plant size.

The profit-maximizing monopolist will wish to expand output until marginal costs rise to equal marginal revenues. Since this firm faces the entire market demand, the firm's demand curve and the market demand curve are one and the same. Thus the *market* marginal revenue curve is the *firm's* marginal revenue curve. We saw in Chapter 4 that the marginal revenue curve associated with a negatively sloping linear demand curve has the same vertical intercept on the graph and *twice* the slope of the demand curve. In Figure 9-2 we show the market demand curve (D) faced by the monopolist and the corresponding marginal revenue (MR) curve. Superimposed on these are the cost curves of the monopolist—the short-run average cost (SAC) and marginal cost (MC) curves. The profit-maximizing monopolist produces up to the point where marginal costs per unit rise to meet the falling marginal revenues. This point occurs at output level Q_m. Notice that every unit to the right of Q_m has a marginal cost greater than its marginal revenue; it therefore *will not* be produced. Conversely, every unit to the left of Q_m costs less than it earns (marginally or incrementally); it therefore *will* be produced and sold. The firm's profits can be visualized as the rectangle $P_m ABC$ in Figure 9-2.

Note: Monopolists in the real world usually do have some peripheral competition from distant and partial substitutes. The post office experiences competition from the telephone company and from such delivery services as United Parcel Service (UPS) for some of the services it provides. The electricity company competes with the gas com-

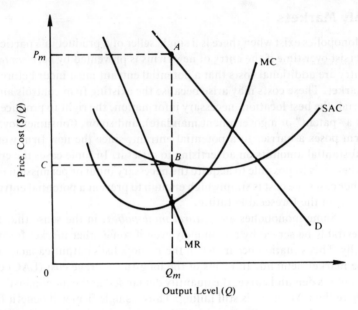

FIGURE 9-2. **Price and Output Determination for a Monopoly**

pany in some households. Bootleggers compete with the liquor control board in some areas. In all these cases, however, the extent of substitution of these products for the monopolist's product is quite small. Thus the cross elasticity of demand between the monopolist's product and the distant substitutes, over the market as a whole, is quite low.

Monopolistic Competition

In monopolistic competition markets the firm must choose price knowing that the consumer has many close substitutes to choose from. If the price is too high, in view of the consumer's perception of the value of the differentiating features of the firm's product, the consumer will purchase a competing firm's product instead. Thus the monopolistic competitor must expect a relatively elastic demand response to changes in its price level. Yet at the same time, it expects to be able to change price without causing any other firm to retaliate and, consequently, without causing a change in the general price level in the market. This is possible because the firm is one of many firms, and it expects the impact of its actions to be spread imperceptibly over all the other firms, giving no one firm any sufficient reason to react to the initial firm's price change.

Monopolistic competition is so called because it has elements of both monopoly and pure competition. The firm has a significant amount of the monopolist's pricing power by virtue of the differentiation of its product. It can change price up and down without experiencing the extreme response of pure competition. For price increases it will suffer a loss of sales, but this loss is not total, as it would be for the pure competitor. Like a monopoly, the monopolistic competitor can adjust the price upward or downward to the level which maximizes its profits. But like the pure competitor, the monopolistic competitor has many rivals in the short run, compounded by the free entry of new firms in the long run.

Example: Monopolistically competitive markets are found where a large number of vendors gather to sell similar products to a gathering of potential buyers. The weekly fruit and vegetable market in some communities may be characterized as monopolistic competition. Similarly, the gatherings of artisans selling souvenirs and other goods in tourist resorts act like monopolistic competitors.[4]

The situation of a representative firm in monopolistic competition is depicted in Figure 9–3. Since the demand curve is negatively sloping, the marginal revenue curve must lie below the demand curve, having twice the slope and the same intercept point. The monopolistically competitive firm maximizes its profits at the price and output level where marginal revenue equals marginal costs. Thus price will be set at P_1 and quantity at Q_1; profits are shown as the area P_1ABC.

The prices set by monopolistic competitors need not be at the same level. In real-world situations we should expect to find slight price differentials between and among monopolistic competitors, with some firms being able to command slightly higher prices or larger market shares because of the market's perception of greater value in the product of some firms as compared with others. Firms with more convenient locations, longer operating hours, and quick service, for example, can obtain a premium for what is otherwise the same product (e.g., brand A bread). Quality differences inherent in the product will also form the basis for price differences.[5]

---

[4]Be wary about characterizing markets as monopolistically competitive unless there are many firms in a relatively compact area and consumers could reasonably be expected to consider purchasing from any one of the firms. Note that seller location (or convenience of purchase) is a relevant attribute in the purchase decision for most consumers. Several industries have a large number of producers but are not characterized by monopolistic competition, since the markets for these industries are sparsely dispersed across the nation. There may be thousands of fast-food outlets in North America, but each one seldom competes with more than half a dozen other sellers in its local market. Similarly, there are hundreds of gas stations in and around a large city, but each one is in competition with the three or four gas stations nearest to it, rather than with every other gas station in the entire city. This spatial aspect of some industries means that, rather than being monopolistically competitive, their markets are characterized by intersecting oligopolies, with each firm competing directly with only a few nearby rivals.

[5]Price and market share differences arise in the *asymmetric* monopolistic competition model, where both cost and product differentiation are allowed to differ among firms. This is a considerably more complex model that the *symmetric* case outlined above, in which it is implicit that the "representative firm" has the same cost structure and product differentiation advantages as all other firms. The asymmetric model will not be considered here except to note that it allows greater realism, at the expense of greater complexity, by explicitly considering differing cost and product differentiation situations between and among firms.

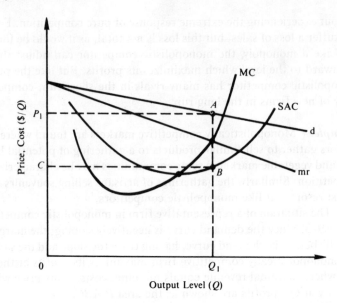

FIGURE 9-3. **Price and Output Determination for a Representative Firm in Monopolistic Competition**

9.3 PRICE DETERMINATION IN OLIGOPOLIES WITH MUTUAL DEPENDENCE RECOGNIZED

■ **Definition:** *Oligopolies* are markets in which there are only a few sellers. (The word *oligopoly* is derived from the Greek word *oligos*, meaning *few* and the Latin word *polis*, meaning *seller.*) Recall that we use the word *few* to mean a number small enough so that the actions of any one firm have a noticeable impact on the demand for each of the other firms.

Example: In the real world the great majority of market situations are oligopolies. Prominent examples are the automobile, steel, aluminum, and chemical industries. These are national and, in some cases, international oligopolies. In your local or regional area, you will notice many more oligopolies. There are probably only half a dozen new car dealerships from which you would consider buying a new automobile. Similarly, there are only a few sellers in a multitude of other lines of business in your area, and these qualify as oligopolies if the actions of any one seller have a significant impact on the sales of any other seller.

Oligopolists are mutually dependent because there are only a few of them sharing a particular market, and any one firm's sales gain, resulting from a price reduction, for example, will be accompanied by sales losses for its rivals. The rival firms must be expected to react to their loss of sales, probably by also reducing price in order to win back their lost customers. The oligopolist that ignores its mutual dependence will thus receive a rude shock when sales volume and profits do not turn out the way they were expected to. Moreover, such myopic price cutting could precipitate a "price war" which could inflict heavy financial losses on all firms. Conversely, a price increase that is ignored by rivals may lead to a substantial loss of market share and profitability, since at least some of its customers will switch to a rival firm's product.

Thus the oligopolist should attempt to predict the probable reaction of rivals to its strategic actions, and decide whether or not an action is likely to be worthwhile in the final analysis, before taking that action. The firm's expectation of its rivals' reactions is known as its *conjectural variation*. The firm's conjectural variation may be defined as the expected percentage change in the rivals' strategic variable (such as price) over the contemplated percentage change in the firm's strategic variable. Thus conjectural variation will be zero when the firm expects rivals to do nothing in reaction to its action, unity if the firm expects rivals to exactly match its action, and more than (or less than) unity if rivals are expected to adjust their strategic variables by a greater (or lesser) percentage.

The Kinked Demand Curve Model of Oligopoly

When oligopolists *do* recognize their mutual dependence, there are a variety of different conjectural variations they might make. We shall first examine the *kinked demand curve model*.[6] This model assumes that the firm's conjectural variation will be twofold: for price increases the firm expects no reaction from rivals, since the other firms will be content to sit back and receive extra customers who switch away from the firm raising its price; and for price reductions the firm expects rivals to exactly match the price reduction in order to maintain their shares of the market.

Since the firm's conjectural variation for price increases is zero, it envisages a *ceteris paribus* demand curve at all prices above the current level, this curve being more or less elastic depending primarily upon the degree of substitutability between its product and rival products. In contemplating price reductions, however, the firm envisages a different kind of demand curve, known as a *mutatis mutandis* demand curve, meaning that it takes into account all reactions induced by or concurrent with the firm's price adjustment. In this case the *mutatis mutandis* section of the demand curve represents a constant share of the total market for the product in question, because if all firms move their prices up or down in unison, their relative prices will remain the same, and we therefore expect each of them to maintain its market share.[7]

---

[6]This model was initially proposed separately by R. L. Hall and C. J. Hitch, "Price Theory and Business Behavior," *Oxford Economic Papers*, May 1939, pp. 12–45; and by P. M. Sweezy, "Demand under Conditions of Oligopoly," *Journal of Political Economy*, August 1939, pp. 568–73.

[7]Note that while the *ceteris paribus* demand curve is appropriate for "independent action" by a firm not expecting reactions, the *mutatis mutandis* demand curve is appropriate for "joint action" by firms, taking into account rivals' reactions.

In Figure 9-4 we show a firm's current price and output levels as P and Q. For prices above P, the firm envisages the relatively elastic *ceteris paribus* demand curve shown by the line dA. For prices below P, it envisages the relatively inelastic *mutatis mutandis* demand curve shown by the line AD. The demand curve facing the firm is therefore dAD, being *kinked* at the current price level. The marginal revenue curve appropriate to this demand curve will have two separate sections. The upper section, shown as dB in Figure 9-4, relates to the *ceteris paribus* section of the demand curve and therefore shares the same intercept and has twice the slope of the line dA. The lower section, CMR, relates to the *mutatis mutandis* section of the demand curve and is positioned such that it has twice the slope of the line AD, and if extended up to the price axis would share its intercept point with the line AD similarly extended.

You will note that there is a vertical discontinuity in the marginal revenue curve, shown as the gap BC in Figure 9-4. Given the foregoing, it is apparent that the length of this gap depends upon the relative slopes of the *ceteris paribus* and *mutatis mutandis* demand curves,[8] which in turn are related to the elasticity of demand under the two conjectural variation situations. If the firm is a profit maximizer, its marginal cost curve will pass through the gap BC. If P and Q are the profit-maximizing price and

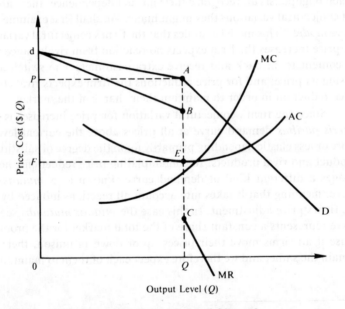

FIGURE 9-4. The Kinked Demand Curve Model of Oligopoly

---

[8]See G. J. Stigler, "The Kinky Oligopoly Demand Curve and Rigid Prices," *Journal of Political Economy*, 55 (October 1947).

output levels, this relationship implies that outputs to the left of Q would have marginal revenues exceeding marginal costs, while outputs to the right of Q would have marginal costs exceeding marginal revenues. This observation is true only if the MC curve passes through either of the points B or C or through some point in between.[9] The oligopolist's profits are shown by the rectangle $PAEF$ in Figure 9-4.

Price Rigidity in the Kinked-Demand-Curve Model. The KDC model is not a complete theory of price determination, because it is unable to tell us how the firm arrives at the initial price and output levels. Given this starting point, however, the model is able to tell us several things that are important to our understanding of oligopoly markets. First, it offers an explanation of the observed rigidity of oligopoly prices in the face of changing cost and demand conditions. Recall that in each of the models of firm behavior we have examined so far, the firms set price where marginal costs equal marginal revenue. If either costs or demand conditions change, one of these marginal curves shifts, and a new price level is required if the firm is to maximize profits under the new conditions. In the KDC case, however, the marginal cost and marginal revenue curves may shift to a considerable degree without a new price level becoming appropriate, as we shall see.

In the KDC model the firm does not wish to change price as long as the marginal cost curve passes through the gap in the marginal revenue curve. Thus costs could increase so that the MC curve moves upward until it passes through point B in Figure 9-5 without the present price becoming inappropriate. Conversely, if variable costs fall, the MC curve could sink downward until it passes through point C, and price P would remain the profit-maximizing price. As long as marginal revenue exceeds marginal costs for higher prices and is less than marginal costs for lower prices, the present price remains the optimal price. Of course, profits are smaller when costs are higher, but profits are *maximized* when the MC curve passes through the MR gap.

Now consider changes in the demand situation. In most real-world market situations, quantity demanded at the prevailing price level fluctuates up and down over time as the result of seasonal, cyclical, or random influences on the factors determining demand. But as we show in Figure 9-6, demand at price P could fluctuate over the range Q to Q' without causing the MC curve to pass outside the relevant MR gap. At quantity Q, the MR curve is shown by dBCMR, and the MC curve passes through point C. This is the extreme leftward point to which the demand curves could shift and yet still allow the MC curve to pass through the gap. The extreme rightward shift of demand, which allows P to remain as the profit-maximizing price, is found when the MC curve passes through point B', as it does at output Q'. Thus demand could fluctuate over the relatively wide range Q to Q' at price P without the firm wishing to change its price. Profits are lower when demand is lower, but are maximized at price P

---

[9] See D. S. Smith and W. C. Neale, "The Geometry of Kinky Oligopoly: Marginal Cost, the Gap, and Price Behavior," *Southern Economic Journal*, 37 (January 1971), pp. 276–82.

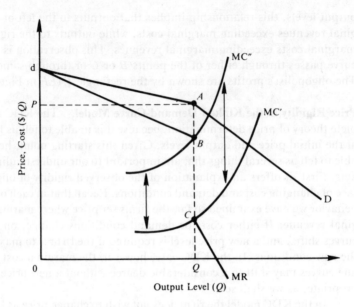

FIGURE 9-5. Price Rigidity in Oligopoly despite Changing Cost Levels

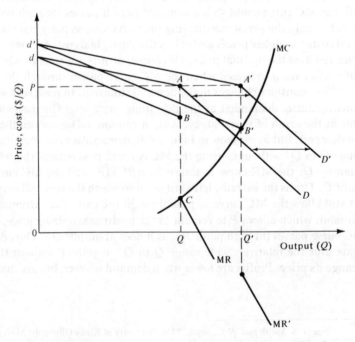

FIGURE 9-6. Price Rigidity in Oligopoly despite Changing Demand Levels

as long as the demand shift is not so large as to cause the MC curve to miss the gap in the appropriate MR curve.[10]

Price Adjustments in the Kinked-Demand-Curve Model.

Let us look briefly at a cost change that *will* lead to a change in price. As implied previously, if the change is such that the new MC curve no longer passes through the MR gap, the firm will want to change price. In Figure 9-7, we show a shift of the marginal cost curve from MC to MC′, causing it to intersect the MR curve at point *B′*. The initial price *P* is no longer the profit-maximizing price, since marginal cost exceeds marginal revenue for all the output units between *Q′* and *Q*. The new profit-maximizing price is thus *P′*, where the MC′ curve intersects the MR curve. The firm therefore raises its price to *P′* and experiences a reduction in its quantity demand from *Q* to *Q′*.

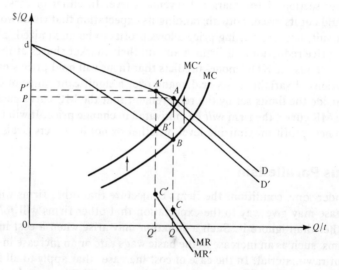

FIGURE 9-7.   A Profit-Maximizing Price Change in the Kinked-Demand-Curve Model

---

[10]George Stigler (see footnote 8), and Julius Simon, "A Further Test of the Kinky Oligopoly Demand Curve," *American Economic Review*, December 1969, each presented empirical findings to indicate that prices in oligopolies were adjusted less frequently than were prices in monopoly markets, thus appearing to refute the KDC model's prediction that oligopoly prices would be adjusted less frequently than would monopoly prices. Jack Hirshleifer, in his *Price Theory and Applications*, 2nd ed. (Englewood Cliffs, N.J.: Prentice-Hall, Inc., 1980), p. 400, points out that there are reasons to expect monopoly prices to be adjusted relatively infrequently, such as fear of attracting regulatory scrutiny and management's pursuit of their own objectives, and these reasons may have been stronger for the monopolists than was the "KDC effect" for the oligopolists. In addition, it should be recognized that the KDC model is just one model of oligopoly. Other models, such as the price leadership models and the conscious parallelism variant of the KDC model, explain how price adjustments are facilitated in oligopoly. Thus we should recognize that the KDC model does not purport to describe the conjectural variations of all oligopolists at all times. But for those firms at those times when the split conjectural variation is appropriate, it is a valuable addition to the decision maker's toolbox.

Notice that the firm raised its price independently, with the expectation that no other firm would follow its price increase; consequently, it lost part of its market share. Since the firm's price-output coordinate is now point A', it must envisage the new *mutatis mutandis* demand curve, $A'D'$, for any contemplated price reduction. Thus the firm's share-of-the-market demand curve has effectively shifted to the left as a result of its independent price increase. But the firm, being a profit maximizer by assumption, would rather increase profits than worry about market share, and hence it prefers the higher profit situation at price P', given the cost increase that upset the initial equilibrium situation.

Alternatively, we could show the demand curves shifting to the right to such an extent that the firm prefers to raise price (and lose part of its market share) in order to maximize profits. Conversely, we could show the marginal cost curve failing sufficiently or the demand situation declining sufficiently, causing the MC curve to cut the lower section of the marginal revenue curve. In either of these two cases, the firm would cut its price, notwithstanding its expectation that rivals would immediately follow suit, because cutting price allows profits to be maximized. Since all rivals match the price reduction, all firms maintain their market shares at the lower price level.

Thus the KDC model predicts that firms will hold price steady, despite the fluctuations of variable costs or demand over a significant range of cost or output levels. Outside the limits set by the requirement that the MC curve pass through the gap in the MR curve, the firm *will* be motivated to change price. It will raise or lower price to the new profit-maximizing level, whether or not it expects rivals to do likewise.

Conscious Parallelism

Under some conditions the firm's conjecture that other firms will ignore its price increase may give way to the expectation that other firms will *follow* a price increase rather than ignore it. Such a situation may arise when a cost increase applies to all firms, such as an increase in the basic wage rate or an increase in the cost of an important raw material. In the case of cost increases that apply to all firms, the individual firm may reasonably expect that all firms would like to maintain profit margins by passing the cost on to consumers. Especially if there is a history of this practice in the industry, the firm's conjectural variation for a price increase, up to the extent necessary to pass on the cost increase, may be unity.

■ *Definition:* The simultaneous adjustment of prices with the expectation that rivals will do likewise has been called *conscious parallelism.* [11] The firms consciously act in a parallel manner, given their expectation that all other firms are motivated to act in the same way.

---

[11]See W. Hamburger, "Conscious Parallelism and the Kinked Oligopoly Demand Curve," *American Economic Review*, 57 (May 1967), pp. 266–68.

The relevant demand curve for a consciously parallel price increase is the *mutatis mutandis* demand curve. As indicated in Figure 9–8, the kink in the demand curve moves up the *mutatis mutandis* section to the new price level chosen. It will kink at the level that passes on the cost increase, because the firm expects that any further price increase will not be matched by rivals and therefore expects to experience a more elastic demand response above that price level. The firm's conjectural variation is unity up to the price level that is expected to be agreeable to all firms, and it is zero for price levels above that.[12]

In terms of Figure 9–8, the firm has experienced a shift in its marginal cost curve from MC to MC′. Based on its expectation that rival firms have suffered a similar cost increase and will be raising their prices, the firm raises its price from P to P' in order to pass on the cost increase to consumers. The firm expects its price-quantity coordinate to move from point A to A', along the *mutatis mutandis*, or share-of-the-market, demand curve. If its expectation (that rivals will similarly raise prices) is borne out, it will in fact move to A', its new kinked demand curve will be d′A'D, and its new marginal revenue curve will be d′$B'$$C'$MR.

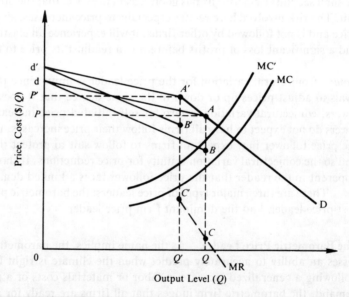

FIGURE 9–8. Conscious Parallelism in the Kinked-Demand-Curve Model of Oligopoly

Since all firms are expected to act jointly, each firm expects to maintain its share of the market at the higher price level, and, by passing on the cost increase to consumers, each firm expects to maintain its profit margin per unit (the difference between price and average costs). In the next chapter we see that the prevalent practice of *markup pricing* allows firms to practice conscious parallelism in the real world, even when they don't know how their demand curves slope away from the present price level.

Price Leadership Models

A number of oligopoly models rely upon the notion of *price leadership* to explain the upward adjustment of prices in oligopoly markets. The major difference between conscious parallelism and price leadership is that in the former situation all firms take the initiative in adjusting prices, confident that their rivals will do likewise, whereas in the latter situation one firm will lead the way and will be followed within a relatively short period by all or most of the other firms adjusting their prices to a similar degree. The price leader is the firm willing to take the risk of being the first to adjust price, but, as we shall see, this firm usually has good reason to expect that the other firms will follow suit. The risk involved here relates especially to price increases, since if the firm raises price and is not followed by other firms, it will experience an elastic demand response and a significant loss of profits before it can readjust its price to the original level.

Note: Conjectural variation for the price leader is unity, since this firm expects all rivals to adjust prices up or down to the same degree that it does. For the price followers, conjectural variation is zero for self-initiated price increases, since price followers do not expect to have all firms follow their price increases. For price decreases, the price follower may expect all firms to follow suit to protect their market shares, and so the conjectural variation is unity for price reductions. It should be immediately apparent to the reader that the price follower faces a kinked demand curve.

There are three major types of price leaders: the barometric price leader, the low-cost price leader, and the dominant firm price leader.

The Barometric Price Leader.   As the name implies, the barometric price leader possesses an ability to accurately predict when the climate is right for a price change. Following a generalized increase in labor or materials costs or a period of increased demand, the barometric firm judges that all firms are ready for a price change and takes the risk of sales losses by being the first to adjust its price. If the other firms trust that firm's judgment of market conditions, they too will adjust prices to the extent indicated. If they feel the increase is too much, they may adjust prices to a lesser degree and the price leader may bring its price back to the level seemingly endorsed by the other firms. If the other firms fail to ratify the price change, the price leadership role could shift from firm to firm over time and will rest with the firm that has sound knowledge of market supply and demand conditions, the ability to perceive a consensus among the firms, and the willingness to take the risk of sales losses if its judgment on these issues is faulty.[13]

The Low-Cost Price Leader. The low-cost price leader is a firm that has a significant cost advantage over its rivals and inherits the role of price leader largely because of the other firms' reluctance to incur the wrath of the lower-cost firm. In the event of a price war the other firms would suffer greater losses and be more prone to the risk of bankruptcy than would the lower-cost firm. Out of respect for this potential power of the lower-cost firm, the other firms tacitly agree to follow that firm's price adjustments.[14]

In Figure 9–9 we show the demand curve D as the curve faced by either firm when each firm sets price at the same level. This curve is thus a *mutatis mutandis* demand curve, predicated upon the simultaneous adjustment of the other firm's price to the same level. In price leadership situations price adjustments are more or less concurrent, and the demand curve D in this case represents a constant (half) share of the total market at each price level.[15] The marginal cost curves of the two firms are shown as MC_A for firm A, the lower-cost firm, and MC_B for firm B, the higher-cost firm. The lower-cost firm maximizes its profit from its share of the market by setting price P and output level Q, and firm B follows the lead and also sets price P.

Given that it sets price P, what output level should the higher-cost firm produce? Being a profit-maximizing firm, by assumption, it will simply choose the output level that maximizes profits, subject to the (self-imposed) constraint that its price will be the same as the price leader's. The demand curve facing firm B is the kinked line dAD. If the high-cost firm raises its price, it expects to do so alone, along the *ceteris paribus* section dA. If it sets its price below P, the other firm will match this price reduction to avoid having its sales fall dramatically. The marginal revenue curve associated with the kinked demand curve dAD is the disjointed line dBCMR. Firm B should therefore choose output level Q, since below this output level, marginal revenue exceeds marginal costs, and above this level, marginal costs exceed marginal revenue. The firms thus share the market equally at the price level chosen by the lower-cost firm.

---

[13]Barometric price leadership was first proposed by J. W. Markham, "The Nature and Significance of Price Leadership," *American Economic Review*, December 1951, pp. 891–905. For a thorough discussion of barometric price leadership, see F. M. Scherer, *Industrial Market Structure and Economic Performance*, 2nd ed. (Chicago: Rand McNally & Company, 1980), chap. 6.

[14]This agreement is likely to be ruled illegal price fixing if the firms *explicitly* agree on price levels. Price fixing is discussed in Appendix 10A.

[15]If product differentiation is *symmetric*, the share of the firms will be equal when prices are equal, and each firm would lose sales at the same rate following an independent price increase. This is a simplifying assumption, since in practice we should expect to find *asymmetric* product differentiation, whereby market shares are unequal when prices are equal, and the slopes of the firms' *ceteris paribus* demand curves are not necessarily equal.

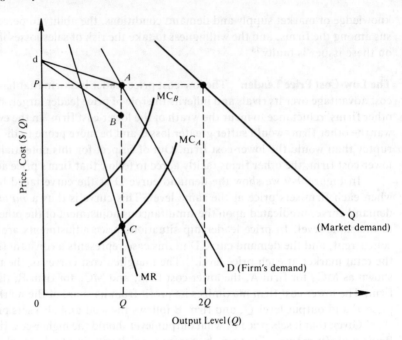

FIGURE 9-9. Low-Cost Firm Price Leadership: Simple Two-Firm, Identical Products Case

Price Leadership with Price Differentials. When product differentiation is asymmetric we should expect a range of prices among the rival firms, reflecting the different cost and demand situations facing each firm. Price leadership in this situation requires one slight modification to the preceding analysis. The price leader may adjust its price by a certain amount, and the price followers will adjust their prices by the *same percentage* as is represented by the price leader's price adjustment. Thus the relative price differentials that prevailed prior to the price changes are unchanged, and no firm expects to gain or lose sales from or to a rival. The price leader simply initiates an upward (or downward) adjustment in the entire price structure of that particular market.

In Figure 9-10 we show a situation in which three firms produce asymmetrically differentiated products. Firm A is the acknowledged price leader and sets price P_A, selling Q_A units. Firms B and C are price followers, not wishing to initiate price adjustments in case this might precipitate a price war in which the lower-cost firm A would have a definite advantage. Firm B's price is above the price leader's price, and firm C's price is below the other two prices. Firm B's product may be a higher-quality item desired by a relatively small segment of the market. This firm's higher cost level may well be the result of higher-quality inputs and more hand finishing of the product, for example. Firm C's product is both lower priced and more expensive to produce, as compared with the price leader's. The lower price may be due to the market's percep-

FIGURE 9-10.   Low-Cost Firm Price Leadership: Two or More Firms, Asymmetric Product Differentiation and Cost Conditions

tion of inferior after-sales service, an inferior location, or absence of other attributes, while the higher costs may be the result of more expensive sources of the inputs, inefficiencies in production, or a plant size too small in view of the present output level.

The price followers face the kinked demand curves shown because they expect no reaction from rivals for price increases but expect the price leader and the other price follower to match any price reductions. The price leader's demand curve is simply the *mutatis mutandis* demand curve: The price leader expects the other firms to follow both price increases and price reductions. If, for example, the price leader's costs increase, it will adjust price upward along the D_A curve. The price followers, who have probably incurred a similar cost increase, will follow the lead and adjust prices upward. But for this particular price increase they do not expect *ceteris paribus*; they expect that the other firms will be simultaneously adjusting their prices upward (or have seen them do so). Thus the kinks in the price followers' demand curves will move upward, extending the *mutatis mutandis* section of their demand curves, as in the conscious parallelism case shown in Figure 9-8.

We shall see in Chapter 10 that the common business practice of *markup pricing* allows firms to adjust prices to cost increases by a similar proportion. We turn now to the third type of price leader.

The Dominant-Firm Price Leader.   As the name implies, the dominant firm is large relative to its rivals and its market. The smaller firms accept this firm's price leadership perhaps simply because they are unwilling to risk being the first to change prices, or perhaps because they are afraid that the dominant firm could drive them out of business, for example, by forcing raw-material suppliers to boycott a particular small firm on pain of losing the order of the larger firm. In such a situation the smaller firms accept the dominant firm's choice of the price level, and they simply adjust output to maximize their profits. In this respect they are price takers, similar to pure competitors who can sell as much as they want to at the market price. Like pure competitors, they will want to sell up to the point where their marginal cost equals the price (equals marginal revenue). The dominant firm recognizes that the smaller firms will behave in this manner and that it must therefore choose price to maximize its profits with the knowledge that the smaller firms will sell as much as they want to at that price.

The first task of the dominant-firm price leader is, therefore, to ascertain how much the smaller firms will want to supply at each price level. Since each of the smaller firms will want to supply up to the point where MC = MR, and since MR = P in a situation where the individual firm is so small that it does not influence market price, each of the smaller firms will regard its MC curve as its supply curve. Note that a supply curve shows the quantity that will be supplied at each price level. At each price level the firms supply the amount for which marginal cost equals price. The MC curve therefore indicates how much the firm will supply at each price level. It follows that a horizontal aggregation of these curves will indicate the total amount that the smaller firms will supply at each price level. In Figure 9-11 we depict this aggregation of the smaller firms' marginal cost curves as the line ΣMC_s.

Knowing how much the smaller firms will supply at each price level, the dominant firm can subtract this quantity from the market demand to find how much demand is left over at each price level. This "residual" demand can be measured as the horizontal distance between the ΣMC_s and the market demand curve D at each price

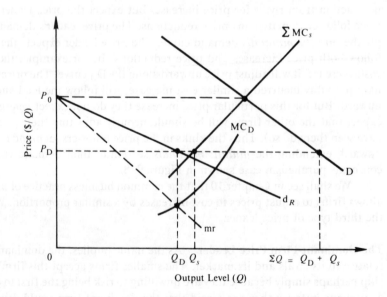

FIGURE 9-11. Price Determination by the Dominant-Firm Price Leader

level, and is shown as the demand curve d_R in Figure 9–11. Only at prices below P_0 is there any demand left for the dominant firm after the smaller firms have supplied their desired amounts. This residual demand curve is the amount that the dominant firm can be assured of selling at each price level, since the smaller firms will have sold as much as they wanted to and yet there remain buyers willing to purchase at those price levels.

The dominant firm will choose the price level in order to maximize its own profits from this residual demand. The marginal revenue curve associated with the residual demand curve is shown as the curve mr in Figure 9–11. The dominant firm's marginal cost curve is depicted by MC_D. The dominant firm therefore selects price P_D and output Q_D in order to maximize its profits. Faced with the price P_D, each of the smaller firms produces up to the point where its marginal costs equal that price, and hence the smaller firms in aggregate produce the output level Q_s. Since the residual demand curve was constructed to reflect the horizontal distance between the ΣMC_s and the D curves, the total amount supplied to the market, ΣQ, is equal to the market demand, and an equilibrium situation exists. The dominant firm thus chooses price to maximize its profits under the constraint that the smaller firms will supply the amount at that price level which will maximize their profits.

Note: An interesting long-run implication of the dominant-firm-price-leadership model is that if the chosen price allows the smaller firms to earn economic profits, the dominance of the large firm will be eroded over time. The reason for this erosion is that in the long run the small firms will expand their plant sizes in search of even greater profitability, and new firms will enter the industry—if the barriers to entry can be overcome—in search of this profitability. Unless the market grows faster than the small firms, the residual demand remaining for the dominant firm must be reduced, and the price leader will be forced to set a lower price and accept a reduced market share. Eventually, of course, the dominant firm will no longer be dominant, and the above system of market price determination will give way to some other form of price leadership, conscious parallelism, or independent price setting.

Example: Alcoa is said to be an example of a firm that was initially a monopoly, later a dominant-firm price leader, and more recently simply one of several large oligopolists in the aluminum industry.[16] Alcoa was effectively a monopoly at first because it held most of the known reserves of bauxite, from which aluminum is derived. As more bauxite was discovered, other firms entered the industry but were small in relation to Alcoa. As time passed and Alcoa's chosen price level allowed the other firms to prosper and grow, Alcoa's dominance in the industry waned to the point where it is no longer the price leader at all. Rather, Alcan has emerged as the low-cost price leader because of its cheaper source of electric power.

[16]See J. V. Koch, *Industrial Organization and Prices*, 2nd ed. (Englewood Cliffs, N.J.: Prentice-Hall, Inc., 1980), pp. 282 and 289.

9.4 PRICING FOR LONGER-TERM OBJECTIVES

The behavioral assumption of short-run profit maximization, which we have used in all the models of pricing discussed previously, may be criticized for its lack of realism in oligopolistic markets where high short-run profits may induce new firms to overcome the barriers to entry and obtain a share of the market and thus dilute future profits of the existing firms. We should expect that the time horizon envisaged by oligopolists will extend beyond the short-run period and that these firms will be likely to forgo immediate profits in order not to attract the entry of new firms. This observation suggests, of course, that a more appropriate objective function for the oligopolist is the maximization of long-term profits.

By maximization of long-term profits we must mean the maximization of the expected present value of present and future profits, since the firm will face uncertainty in the future and must employ present-value analysis to make the future profits comparable to present period profits. We argued in Chapter 1 that this objective is the equivalent of net worth maximization (in EPV terms). Thus the firm should choose the price level that maximizes the EPV of profits. A quick look at what this choice involves will convince you that the search costs of implementing this decision rule will most likely be prohibitive. Estimates must be made of the probabilities of entry in future periods, relating to each of the possible current-period price levels. Then the impact of new firms on the price level must be forecast. The growth (or decline) of the overall market, as well as the firm's share of the market in each future period, must be forecast. The firm's costs must be forecast in each of the future periods, in conjunction with the demand forecasts, before a profit forecast can be formulated. In some cases the search cost of this procedure will be considered worthwhile, but more often we should expect the search costs to be prohibitive.

It is more likely that firms wishing to maximize their long-term profits will adopt a "proxy" objective function. That is, they will pursue a policy that gives approximately the same results but is much more simple and inexpensive to administer. In the following sections we shall examine a number of such proxy policies which, it can be argued, are a short-term means of achieving the long-term objective of profit maximization.

Sales Maximization with a Minimum Profit Target

W. J. Baumol has suggested that the appropriate objective function for many firms is the maximization of sales in the short term, subject to the attainment of a certain minimum profit level.[17] First let us consider the minimum profit requirement, which

---

[17]W. J. Baumol, *Business Behavior, Value, and Growth* (New York: Harcourt Brace Jovanovich, Inc., 1967). Note that we mean sales *volume*, not sales *revenue*. Maximizing sales revenue simply means finding the point where MR = 0, and requires no reference to the firm's cost situation. This may be desirable if the firm faces an immediate cash-flow problem, but completely neglects the profit implications since it ignores the cost side. Maximization of sales volume (subject to a profit target) amounts to maximizing the firm's market share, and seems empirically more supportable.

is necessary for two main reasons: (1) a sufficient minimum profit must be forthc
ing to prevent shareholders from becoming disgruntled and voting for a new board o
directors; and (2) the value of the firm's shares on the stock exchange depend, in part,
on the current profitability of the firm, since the expectation of dividend payments has
a positive influence on the market value of the shares. If, as a result of low current
profits, the shares become undervalued in view of the firm's longer-term prospects, the
firm may be subject to a takeover bid by another firm, which again involves the risk
that managers may lose their jobs. Therefore, managers will be motivated to keep
profits at a level sufficient to stave off these two possibilities while at the same time
making sure that profits are not so large as to attract the entry of new firms.

Having determined the minimum acceptable, or target, level of profits, the firm
will wish to maximize its sales subject to this profit constraint. We can show the sales-
maximization decision on the same graph as the one for short-run profit maximization. In Figure 9–12 are displayed the familiar total revenue and total cost curves, with
the profit curve indicating the excess of total revenue over total costs at each output
level. Suppose the minimum profit constraint is the vertical distance indicated by $0\pi^*$.
The profit constraint is satisfied anywhere between output levels Q_0 and Q_2, but sales
are maximized, subject to this constraint, at output level Q_2. It is clear that this output
level is larger than the short-run profit-maximizing output level Q_1 and must be offered at a lower price than the short-run profit-maximizing price, since the firm faces
a negatively sloped demand curve.

But why is the maximization of sales volume in the short run a proxy for the
maximization of longer-term profits? The lower price level, as compared with the

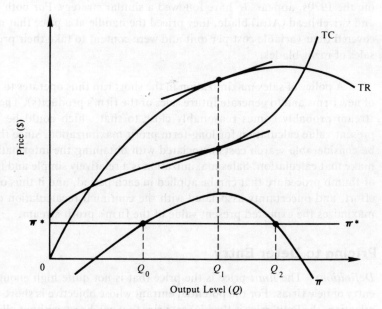

FIGURE 9–12. Sales Maximization Subject to a Minimum Profit Constraint

profit-maximizing price, has three major implications for future profits. ill tend to inhibit the entry of new firms whose costs may exceed that price ause of the extra expenses associated with overcoming the barriers to entry. it will introduce more customers to the product now and will thus operate to re repeat sales in future periods, because of the goodwill and brand loyalty that will develop over time as customers use the product. This cultivation of consumer loyalty and goodwill acts to raise one of the barriers to entry, since a potential entrant firm would need to spend even more on advertising and promotion of its own product in order to induce customers to try that product. Third, the larger market share in the short term provides a larger base for complementary sales in the longer term. This is especially important in the market for some durable consumption goods, such as automobiles and cameras, where apparently quite lucrative markets exist for specialized replacement parts and accessories.

Example: The Kodak 110 camera appears to have been priced with a view to maximizing its sales volume in the short run. When it was first introduced, it seemed to offer excellent value and became very popular as a Christmas and birthday gift, particularly for children. As every parent found out, of course, the cost of the camera was simply the start of a series of expenditures benefiting Kodak. Sales of special film cartridges, flash bulbs, developing, printing, and enlarging services, all served to keep the sales revenue flowing to Kodak. Their strategy appears to have been to get the widest possible penetration of the market with their camera, at a modest profit margin, and to rely on subsequent sales of accessory items to generate continued revenues and profitability. Gillette, who pioneered several advances in shaving equipment during the 1970s, appears to have followed a similar strategy. For both their twin-blade and swivel-head (Atra) blade, they priced the handle at a price that must barely have covered their variable cost per unit and were content to take their profits on the later sales of razor blades.

A policy of sales maximization in the short run thus operates to inhibit the entry of new firms and to generate future sales of the firm's product(s). The resultant profit stream probably comes reasonably close to that which could be attained by the present-value calculation for long-term profit maximization, since there are likely to be considerable search costs associated with obtaining the information necessary to make that calculation. Sales maximization is a relatively simple and inexpensive rule-of-thumb procedure that can be applied in each period, and it thus obviates the cost, effort, and uncertainty associated with the continual recalculation of the price that maximizes the expected present value of the firm's profit stream.

Limit Pricing to Deter Entry

- *Definition:* The *limit* price is the price that is not quite high enough to induce the entry of new firms. For the potential entrant whose objective is short-run profit maximization, the limit price is the highest price that can be set without allowing the potential entrant to make normal profits. If the potential entrant takes the longer view and would be prepared to take losses initially if it could foresee profits later, the limit price is the highest price that can be set without allowing the potential entrant's expected present value of profits to be positive.

Limit pricing may also be regarded as a proxy for long-term profit maximization. Preventing the entry of new firms serves to avoid having to share the market with new firms in the future. Thus the firm expects it future sales and the EPV of profits from the present to its time horizon to be greater if it successfully prevents the entry of new firms.

Deterring Entry of a High-Cost Firm.   In many cases the entrant firm is expected to have higher costs than the existing firms, as a result of its probable smaller scale of operation and the additional product differentiation expense it must incur to offset consumer loyalty to the existing products. Thus the established firms, at the suggestion of a price leader perhaps, choose a price that does not allow the potential entrant to earn even a normal profit at any output level. In Figure 9-13 this price is shown as P_L, which is lower than any point on the potential entrant's short-run average cost curve, SAC_e.

The demand curve D should be interpreted as the *mutatis mutandis*, or share-of-the-market, demand curve of one of the existing firms. Given that the existing firm will not wish to set a price above P_L, it faces, in effect, the kinked demand curve

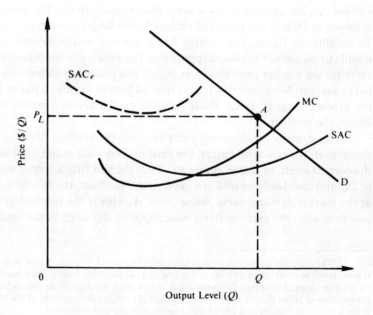

FIGURE 9-13.   Limit Pricing to Deter the Entry of a Higher-Cost Firm

P_{LA} D. Its profit-maximizing output, subject to the self-imposed constraint, is thus Q, where marginal cost and marginal revenue come nearest to being equal.[18]

Since the price set by the existing firms is less than the expected minimum cost per unit of potential entrant firms, new firms will not enter, and thus the existing firms' future market shares and profitability are protected from incursions from this quarter at least. Pursuit of a limit-pricing policy is, therefore, like sales maximization, a relatively simple short-run means of approximating a long-term objective. This is not to say that entry will not occur, since there may well be entry of a new firm if the existing firms incorrectly estimate the costs of the potential entrant, if the new firm employs the latest technology while existing firms continue to use older less-efficient plants, or if the entrant firm is prepared to take a loss for a protracted period while gaining a foothold in an expanding market.

Deterring Entry of a Low-Cost Firm. Let us now consider the case in which the potential entrant has access to the same technology and factor markets and hence has the same or lower cost structure, as compared to the existing firms. In this case there is no point in pricing below the new entrant's costs, since all firms would incur losses. Instead, the firms choose price such that the extra quantity supplied by the entry of another firm would cause the market clearing price to be depressed below the level of cost for all firms. The prospect of losses thus prevents the potential entrant from actually entering unless it expects market demand to expand over time or the existing firms to reduce output level such that price is not depressed below cost.[19]

In Figure 9–14 we demonstrate the limit price that deters entry of a potential entrant that has costs equal to or lower than existing firms. The market demand curve is shown as D, and the potential entrant firm's long-run average cost curve is shown. To simplify the figure, the existing firms' *mutatis mutandis* and *ceteris paribus* demand curves are not shown. Suppose that the existing firms follow a price leader and establish the market price shown as P_L. At this price they collectively supply ΣQ units to the market. Note that this means that all buyers willing to pay at least price P_L for the product (that is, those above point A on the demand curve) have been able to obtain the product.

The strategy for deterring entry requires the existing firms to make known the threat that, if a new firm enters, the existing firms will maintain their output levels at the current levels, or ΣQ in aggregate. Thus the new firm's output would be additional to ΣQ and could only be sold at a lower price. In effect, the new firm would be looking at the market demand curve *below* point A. This is the residual demand left for the new firm after the existing firms have supplied ΣQ units to the market. Shifting this

---

[18]The marginal revenue curve is not shown in Figure 9–3, but you should be able to figure out where it goes. It will be coextensive with the dotted line P_{LA} out to output level Q, then have a vertical discontinuity at output level Q, and then fall below the axis with twice the slope of the demand curve for output levels greater than Q. Thus the MC curve passes through the vertical discontinuity of the MR curve and the limit price is the profit maximizing price subject to this self-imposed constraint.

[19]F. M. Scherer, *Industrial Market Structure and Economic Performance*, 2nd ed. (Chicago: Rand McNally & Company, 1980), chap. 8.

FIGURE 9-14.   Limit Pricing to Deter the Entry of a Low-Cost Firm

residual section (AD) of the market demand curve over to the vertical axis, we have the demand curve d_R that is faced by the potential entrant firm. Now we see why P_L is the limit price: There is no part of the residual demand curve d_R that lies above the potential entrant firm's LAC curve. Thus the entrant could not make a profit at any output level, in any plant size.

Note: The limit price to deter the entry of a low-cost (or lower-cost) firm is, therefore, the price that causes the residual demand curve to lie everywhere below the potential entrant firm's LAC curve. There is then no plant size the entrant can select that would allow normal profits. Notice, however, that the deterrent to entry is simply the threat that existing firms will maintain their output levels, thereby allowing the new firm's output to cause the market price to fall to a lower level until demand equals supply. But at this lower price level, existing firms do not make profits either, since they have no cost advantage over the entrant. It is clear that if the new firm actually does enter the market, the established firms would be better off to reduce their output levels (and market shares) and have the price leader choose a price that would allow all firms to make at least normal profits.

Thus, if a potential entrant firm "calls the bluff" of the existing firms and does enter the market, the firms would be better off to reduce their output levels, despite their earlier threats, and to follow their price leader to a new price level that is acceptable to all. The potential entrant that foresees this and that expects to incur losses initially in any case, may not be deterred at all.

Contestable Markets.   A recent advance in the theory of markets has been made by Baumol, Panzer, and Willig.[20] Building upon earlier work demonstrating that barriers

---

[20]See W. J. Baumol, J. C. Panzer, and R. D. Willig, *Contestable Markets and the Theory of Industry Structure* (San Diego: Harcourt Brace Jovanovich, 1982).

to entry are critical elements influencing the pricing behavior of firms, they define a "contestable market" as one that may be entered by a new firm without significant cost. This potential for entry prevents the existing firms in that market from pricing to make any more than a normal profit, since doing so would attract new firms into the market that will compete with the existing firms and drive prices below cost. Pure competition and monopolistic competition markets are therefore "contestable" markets, but so too are some monopoly and oligopoly markets. If there are no significant barriers to entry but the size of plant chosen by the firms is large relative to the market, then there is only room for one firm (a natural monopoly) or a few firms in the market (a natural oligopoly). However, these monopoly and oligopoly markets are also contestable. That is, the prospect of losing their market shares because of entry by a new firm will force the existing firms to keep prices close to their average costs to avoid attracting the entry of new firms.

Example: The passenger airline industry serves literally thousands of different markets, where each market is defined as a "city pair." In larger markets, such as the New York–Los Angeles route, there are six or more different airlines offering services (an oligopoly). Most routes will be oligopolies, offering the passenger a choice between at least two or three carriers. Between other city pairs, where demand for flights is much smaller, there is a single airline offering service (a monopoly). Because the airline industry has been deregulated, any carrier may offer a service between any city pair. Entry to a particular market involves very little initial (setup) cost relative to the firm's operating costs. Note that the entrant will have operating costs that are similar to the other airlines serving the market—that is, the same landing fees, ticket sales and baggage-handling expenses, aircraft fuel and maintenance cost, and so on. The minimum efficient size for most city-pair markets involves a multiengine jetliner capable of carrying at least 100 people, which is relatively large compared to the market (at a particular time each day, for example).

    Thus there are more airlines contesting larger markets and fewer airlines contesting smaller markets. Although we might expect these oligopolies and monopolies to set prices considerably in excess of average costs, following the traditional theory of market forms, we observe rather competitive prices being set in contestable markets, to avoid attracting the entry of a new competitor into that market. Thus the firms are effectively practicing limit pricing to deter entry.

Satisficing: Achieving Targets as a Managerial Objective

Following Baumol's sales-maximization hypothesis, which represented a break with the traditional short-run profit-maximizing theory of the firm, several managerial and behavioral theories of the firm were developed. It has been suggested that firms wish to maximize the rate of growth of the firm, or alternatively, that managers wish to maximize managerial utility.[21] The "satisficing" model of firm behavior says that firms do not try to maximize anything—they simply set targets and are satisfied if they can reach those targets.[22] The targets typically relate to profits, sales or market share, worker productivity, or inventory/sales ratios, and can be seen to be either revenue- or cost-related.

The "satisficing" theory of the firm[23] is based on the proposition that firms face considerable uncertainty about costs and demands even in the short run and that they adjust prices, promotional expenditures, and other variables whenever it appears that one of their targets is not going to be attained. Once the profit target is met, for example, managers apply their efforts to satisfying the next constraint that has not yet been met, on the basis of their imperfect information systems and their imperfect expectations of the impact of the adjustments they make. In effect, satisficing managers appear to act according to short-run criteria designed to ensure the continued existence and maintained market standing of the firm they control.

The satisficing model of firm behavior is, in effect, an extension of Baumol's sales-maximization model, if we accept that a minimum-profit target is the firm's first objective. After attaining this minimum-profit level, the firm may pursue a target market share. Having attained this target, it may pursue a target inventory-to-sales ratio, and so on. In fact, all these targets are simultaneously monitored, and attention is directed primarily to whichever of these targets seems to be in jeopardy at any particular time. The targets themselves, or aspiration levels, are set by management consensus and usually reflect past achievements plus an additional margin to act as an incentive for improved performance. Thus the targets, or aspiration levels, may be consistently revised upward, as the firm becomes more and more efficient in its operation. R. H. Day has argued quite plausibly that this continued revision of aspiration levels can mean that a satisficing strategy eventually converges on the long-term, profit-maximizing strategy.[24]

Note: The above short-run proxy policies (for the maximization of the expected present value of present and future profits) may not lead to exactly the price and output levels in each period that would allow maximum EPV of profits over the firm's planning period. But these proxies would still be optimal if the amount of revenue lost (by not having the "correct" prices and output levels) is less than the search costs

[21]See E. Penrose, *The Theory of the Growth of the Firm* (Oxford: Oxford University Press, 1959); and R. Marris, "A Model of the Managerial Enterprise," *Quarterly Journal of Economics*, 77 (May 1963), pp. 185–209.

[22]H. A. Simon, "Theories of Decision Making in Economics and Behavioral Science," *American Economic Review*, 57 (March 1967), pp. 1–33. The principal-agent problem, mentioned in Chapter 1, is an outgrowth of the managerial-utility-maximization model.

[23]See R. M. Cyert and J. E. March, *A Behavioral Theory of the Firm* (Englewood Cliffs, N.J.: Prentice-Hall, Inc., 1963), and H. A. Simon, "Theories of Decision Making in Economics," *American Economic Review*, 49 (June 1959), pp. 253–83.

[24]See R. H. Day, "Profits, Learning, and the Convergence of Satisficing to Marginalism," *Quarterly Journal of Economics*, May 1967.

avoided. In such cases the firm would be better off using a relatively simplistic short-run objective function than it would by incurring the search costs and having the "correct" price and output level at all times. Thus the firm, anticipating high search costs, may actually make more profits by proceeding simplistically than by incurring the search costs and proceeding elegantly. But the firm should always attempt to evaluate the search costs necessary to obtain the required information, and it should proceed without more information only if it is persuaded that the costs outweigh the benefits that could be derived. We shall pursue this subject further in Chapter 10.

9.5 SUMMARY

In this chapter we introduced the notion that models of the firm's pricing behavior can be characterized under seven assumptions. The four structural assumptions relate to number of sellers, cost conditions, number of buyers, and degree of product differentiation. The three behavioral assumptions refer to the firm's objective function, its strategic variables, and its conjectural variation. The models of pricing behavior differ from each other only to the extent that one or more of the seven basic assumptions is different. The difference in one or more of the underlying assumptions, however, leads to a different pattern of behavior of the firm. Thus the price and output levels chosen by a firm depend upon the structural and behavioral conditions under which the firm operates.

The four basic market forms were analyzed for the pricing and output behavior of the firm in each of those market situations. Under conditions of pure competition, monopolistic competition, and monopoly, the pricing and output decision was based on a *ceteris paribus* demand curve because of the expectation that a firm's price or output adjustment would not induce any changes in any other variables. Under oligopoly we introduced the *mutatis mutandis*, or "joint action," demand curve. In the kinked demand curve model of oligopoly the firm envisages no reaction for price increases but expects rivals to match any price reductions. Given these expectations, the oligopolist faces a kinked demand curve, since the *ceteris paribus* section for price increases will be more elastic than the *mutatis mutandis* section for price reductions. The kinked demand curve offers an explanation for price rigidity despite changes in the cost and demand conditions, within limits. Outside these limits of cost and demand movements the firm will change price or output levels.

Conscious parallelism is the process by which firms separately but collectively raise prices in response to common cost or demand changes. This process allows price adjustments to be coordinated, so that no firm expects to suffer loss of market share because each firm is anticipating the price changes of its rivals. Price leadership may be provided by a firm that has a keen awareness of industry cost and market demand conditions, as well as a willingness to risk loss of market share by being the first to adjust price. The price followers accept the leader's judgment and raise prices to the same level (or by a similar proportion). The price followers thus avoid the risk of market share loss, as well as the search costs which might otherwise be spent to ascertain the price change required. Barometric, low-cost, and dominant-firm-price-leadership situations were discussed, and the pricing implications were examined.

When the firm's time horizon falls beyond the present period, a change in the objective function is indicated. The appropriate objective function for the firm facing uncertainty in future periods is the maximization of the expected present value of future profits. Given the search costs involved, however, we expect firms to pursue short-run objective functions which are, in effect, proxies for long-term profit maximization. Sales maximization subject to the attainment of a profit target, limit pricing, and satisficing were each argued to be short-run policies which could approximate the maximization of the firm's EPV of future profits over its planning period. Given the search costs avoided, of course, these policies do not need to indicate the actual prices and outputs which would maximize the EPV of future profits; they merely need to get sufficiently close to the optimal price and output levels, so that at least as much profit is earned.

With this grand tour of the theory of the firm behind us, we are now in a position to move to pricing and output decisions in actual business situations. The solution of actual business pricing and output problems is generally facilitated by, and optimized with the aid of, a sound understanding of the models of firm behavior covered in this chapter.

DISCUSSION QUESTIONS

9-1. In what single dimension does monopolistic competition differ from pure competition? In what dimension(s) does oligopoly differ from both of these?

9-2. Characterize according to the simple spectrum of market forms the markets in which the following groups of firms operate:

(a) Automobile dealerships in a large city.

(b) Colleges and universities marketing their degrees to potential students.

(c) An art dealer who wants to sell a unique painting, such as the Mona Lisa.

(d) A grain farmer selling wheat to one of forty or fifty flour-milling companies.

9-3. Given that an oligopolist envisages a kinked-demand-curve, explain why it is sometimes profit maximizing to raise prices and incur a loss of market share.

9-4. Why would you expect the price rigidity implications of the kinked-demand-curve model more likely to be observed in practice if the cost changes or demand shifts are firm-specific, rather than common to all firms?

9-5. Discuss conscious parallelism in the context of price leadership and followership. Which firms are leaders and which, if any, are followers? Should the firm expect conscious parallelism if a cost change is confined to just that firm?

9-6. Why do firms follow the price leadership of another firm? Is it simply fear of the consequences if they do not? Explain.

9-7. What is the connection between the kinked-demand-curve model and the low-cost firm price leadership model?

9-8. Explain why the objective "sales maximization subject to a minimum profit requirement" may be said to be an operational means of pursuing long-term profit maximization.

9-9. In order for oligopolists to practice limit pricing, what behavioral assumptions must be applicable?

9-10. What has the magnitude of search costs got to do with the short-run policy of satisficing and with the adequacy of any one of the proxy policies for long-term profit maximization?

PROBLEMS AND SHORT CASES

9-1. Show graphically the situation in which a purely competitive market suffers a temporary reduction in consumer demand. Summarize what happens to

(a) The price level.

(b) A representative firm's output level.

9-2. Suppose the automobile producers are confronted with an increase of 10 percent in the negotiated wage for assembly labor, yet prices of their products remain constant.

(a) Explain with the aid of graphs why the firms might not wish to increase their prices.

(b) Why might you expect these firms to raise prices at the start of the next model year, rather than during the present model year?

9-3. The Prangle Company manufactures and sells several styles of jeans which are branded as the Sizzlers. Several years ago the company introduced the stylized jean look, and Prangle sales increased dramatically. Over the past two years, however, sales have been declining steadily for their stylized jean because of the incursion of several look-alike competing products, even though the total market for stylized jeans is still expanding.

As a result of the increased supply of stylized jeans, the other companies have been selling their competitive jeans at a price below that of Prangle. Prangle's price has not changed from the original price set by the company at the introduction of the jean on the market. Prangle's price at retail was $12, with the retailer paying $9. Other firm's products are retailing for around the same price, with the retailer paying $8.

As a result of the increased supply in the market and Prangle's declining sales volume, Gail Morin, the sales manager, decided to review the cost structure to determine if the margin offered to the retailer could be widened in order to recoup some of the sales share. If she could significantly reduce the price to retailers, Prangle could recapture some of its lost market.

At the present time, variable production costs (including raw materials and labor) are constant at $4 per pair. The sales volume now is 400,000 pairs of jeans. Ms. Morin is wondering what effect a reduction in price would have on sales and on the profitability of the line. The accounting department and the market research department have estimated cost and demand figures applicable for a reduction in Prangle's price to the retailer. If the price were lowered to that of the competition ($8), demand would increase by 150,000 pairs; if the company lowered the retailer's price even further (to $7), demand is estimated to increase to 625,000 pairs. With such an increase in production the firm could more efficiently use its resources and production facilities. The advantages acquired in bulk buying of raw materials and the more efficient use of labor both help to chisel down the variable costs per pair to $3.75 per unit under the latter demand condition.

Ms. Morin has considered all of the information the market research and accounting departments have provided and is about to make a pricing decision. You are asked to advise on the following issues:

(a) Explain why the Prangle Company suffered declining sales in a market that was actually expanding.

(b) Explain the proposed price reductions in terms of the demand curve the Prangle Company is apparently facing, assuming the data are accurate.

(c) Advise Ms. Morin about the contribution-maximizing price level.

9-4. To demonstrate your understanding of the issues involved, draw the graph for and explain the price and output determination in the three-firm, symmetrically differentiated products case of low-cost firm price leadership. Now expand this model to include conscious parallelism when common cost increases are involved, with price leadership remaining in effect when market demand changes. Explain the conjectural variation of the price followers.

9-5. There are two firms in the prefabricated homes industry producing metal-frame houses. The cost structure of Struktatuff, Inc., is considerably lower than that of its rival, Steeldeal, Inc., although both firms are about the same size in terms of output capacity. The cost functions have been estimated as $TC = 160,000 + 4,850Q$ for Struktatuff, and $TC = 120,000 + 5,250Q$ for Steeldeal. These firms face the market demand curve specified by $P = 36,384 - 1.25Q$.

In past years it has become evident that Struktatuff is the effective price leader. Steeldeal twice tried to set a lower price, but each time Struktatuff undercut this price and forced a return to the price that maximized its own contribution. Product differentiation is such that when prices are equal, Struktatuff always has two-thirds of the market while Steeldeal has the remaining one-third.

(a) On separate but adjacent graphs, show the *mutatis mutandis* demand curves for both Struktatuff and Steeldeal.

(b) Show the price level that Struktatuff will prefer.

(c) Calculate the output level that will be produced by each firm.

9-6. In a dominant-firm oligopoly, the market demand curve has been estimated by the dominant firm to be $P = 100 - 1.25Q$, where Q represents thousands of units. There are twenty very small firms, who each have a cost structure estimated by $TC = 10 + 15Q + 11.25Q^2$.

(a) Show graphically the derivation of the dominant firm's residual demand curve.

(b) Suppose the dominant firm's cost structure is represented by $TC = 500 + 10Q + 0.25Q^2$. Show on your graph the profit-maximizing price the dominant firm will choose.

(c) Calculate the profits earned by the dominant firm and by each of the small firms.

(d) Comment on what you expect may happen in the long run.

9-7. In the market for introductory economics textbooks there are several competitive textbooks, whose prices range from $15.95 to $22.95. One of the established texts is the major seller and is considered to be the price leader in this field. A new text has recently become available, and its publishing company has priced it at $21.95 and expects to sell 60,000 copies. At this price the company expects to maximize contribution to its overheads and profits. The author of this text receives royalties which are a fixed percentage of total sales receipts. He feels that if the price were reduced to around $16 each, the market would demand 140,000 copies. The publisher feels that the author's perception of the market situation is unrealistic and that a lower price would *reduce* both the contribution and the royalties, as compared with the company's selected price.

(a) Explain the author's side of the argument. What is his objective function and why does he wish to select a lower price than does the publishing company?

(b) Explain the publisher's side of the argument. What is its perception of the market situation? Why does it expect both sales revenue and contribution to fall at lower prices?

9-8. The cement industry in a particular region is characterized by five firms producing what are highly similar products. Over the years these firms have found that active price competition is to be avoided, since this strategy has led to prolonged periods of low profitability. At the same time, each firm jealously guards its market share and will quickly match any price reduction by a competitor. Whenever costs increase for all firms, the firms act, as if by consensus, to raise prices concurrently to preserve their profit positions.

It has become obvious recently that a cement producer in another region is considering entering the market by building a sixth plant in the vicinity of the plants of the existing five firms. This firm would have higher costs per unit, however, because the existing five firms control all nearby sources of the basic raw material, limestone.

The existing firms have similar cost structures and find that their marginal costs per ton are virtually constant at $20 per ton. At current output levels of about 200,000 tons each per annum, the firms must cover $5 per ton in overhead costs, and they now price their cement at $32 per ton. The potential entrant's average variable costs are expected to be 20 percent higher and its total fixed costs per annum are expected to be 15 percent lower than those of the five existing firms. If entry takes place next year, the new firm is expected to gain about 10 percent of the market in the first year (pricing at $32 per ton), gradually improving its position to an equal share as a result of the very slight product differentiation involved with this product. The overall market demand for the product is expected to be constant over the next few years, and the market price elasticity of demand is quite low, at 0.2.

(a) Should the existing firms practice limit pricing to forestall the entry of the sixth firm? What price would be necessary to prevent entry?

(b) If the sixth firm does enter the industry, what price level would maximize contribution for each firm after the entrant firm achieves an equal share of the market?

9-9. Fiori Pasta Company produces high-quality pasta products. It has estimated its demand curve for its spaghetti to be $P = 39.898 - 0.03757Q$, where Q represents thousands of cartons (each containing five dozen packets of spaghetti) demanded per year by its wholesale customers. Its cost of producing this spaghetti has been estimated as $TC = 2,500,000 + 12Q + 0.01538Q^2$. Fiori is having a management meeting to reconsider its pricing strategy. Its current price for the spaghetti is $27.50 per carton. The president, Don Fiori, wants to maximize sales volume subject to earning a target profit of $500,000 per year. The vice-president of sales, Tony Fiori, wants to maximize sales revenue, since his bonus relates only to sales revenue. The vice-president of production, Gina Fiori, wants to maximize profits so they can afford to install the latest high-technology manufacturing equipment. You have been hired to give an impartial analysis of the problem facing Fiori Pasta.

(a) Calculate the profit-maximizing price and output level, and the profits at that price level.

(b) Calculate the price, output, and profit levels that would be preferred by Tony Fiori.

(c) Plot the TC, TR, and profit curves on a graph, and estimate from the graph the output level that would satisfy Don Fiori. What is the associated price level?

(d) Prepare your report for presentation at the Fiori management meeting.

9-10. Two bakeries serve a small, isolated rural community. Golden Bread Company is the low-cost price leader, and Farmer's Family Bakery is the price follower. Golden's cost function has been estimated as $TC = 8,000 + 6.5Q + 0.0047Q^2$, where TC is the firm's total cost per month and Q represents dozens of loaves of bread. The market demand curve has been estimated as $P = 24 - 0.00125Q$. The market views the products of the two bakeries as essentially similar, and so they share the market equally when their prices are equal.

Popular Bakery is a major city bakery that is considering entering the rural market. Its production facilities are large, and its average variable cost per unit is constant at a level about 20 percent less than Golden's minimum average cost. However, the additional transportation cost that Popular would have to incur would mean that its delivered cost would be about 50 percent more than its average variable cost. Popular is expected to enter the rural market if the price is at least 20 percent over its delivered cost per dozen.

(a) Show graphically (and confirm algebraically) the profit-maximizing price that Golden will set if it ignores the potential entry of the Popular Bakery Company. Calculate the firm's profits at that price.

(b) What is the limit price that will keep the Popular Bakery Company out of the rural market? What will be Golden's output and profit levels at that price?

(c) Suppose that you are the manager of Golden. What price strategy would you choose, and why?

SUGGESTED REFERENCES AND FURTHER READING

Alchian, A. A. "Uncertainty, Evolution, and Economic Theory," *Journal of Political Economy*, 58 (June 1950), pp. 211-21.

Bain, J. S. *Barriers to New Competition*. Cambridge, Mass.: Harvard University Press, 1956.

Baumol, W. J. *Business Behavior, Value, and Growth* (2nd ed.), esp. chap. 6. New York: Harcourt Brace Jovanovich, 1967.

Baumol, W. J. "Contestable Markets: An Uprising in the Theory of Markets," *American Economic Review*, 72 (March 1982), pp. 1-15.

Baumol, W. J., J. C. Panzer, and R. D. Willig. *Contestable Markets and the Theory of Industry Structure*. San Diego: Harcourt Brace Jovanovich, 1982.

Bhagwati, J. "Oligopoly Theory, Entry Prevention, and Growth," *Oxford Economic Papers*, 22 (1970), pp. 297-310.

Chamberlin, E. H. *The Theory of Monopolistic Competition*. Cambridge, Mass.: Harvard University Press, 1969.

Cohen, K. J., and R. M. Cyert. *Theory of the Firm*, esp. chaps. 15-17. Englewood Cliffs, N.J.: Prentice-Hall, Inc., 1965.

Cyert, R. M., and J. E. March. *A Behavioral Theory of the Firm*. Englewood Cliffs, N.J.: Prentice-Hall, Inc., 1963.

Demsetz, H. "Barriers to Entry," *American Economic Review*, 72 (March 1982), pp. 47-57.

Eaton, B. C., and R. G. Lipsey. "Exit Barriers Are Entry Barriers: The Durability of Capital as a Barrier to Entry," *Bell Journal of Economics*, 11 (Autumn 1980), pp. 721-29.

Flaherty, M. T. "Dynamic Limit Pricing, Barriers to Entry, and Rational Firms," *Journal of Economic Theory*, 23 (October 1980), pp. 160-82.

Francis, A. "Company Objectives, Managerial Motivations, and the Behavior of Large Firms: An Empirical Test of the Theory of 'Managerial' Capitalism," *Cambridge Journal of Economics*, 4 (December 1980), pp. 349-61.

Gaskins, D. W., Jr. "Dynamic Limit Pricing: Optimal Pricing under Threat of Entry," *Journal of Economic Theory*, 3 (September 1971), pp. 306-22.

Hall, R. L., and C. J. Hitch. "Price Theory and Business Behavior," *Oxford Economic Papers*, May 1939, pp. 12-45.

Hamburger, W. "Conscious Parallelism and the Kinked Oligopoly Demand Curve," *American Economic Review*, 57 (May 1967), pp. 266-68.

Holthausen, D. M. "Kinky Demand, Risk Aversion, and Price Leadership," *International Economic Review*, 20 (June 1979), pp. 341-48.

Kling, A. "Imperfect Information and Price Rigidity," *Economic Inquiry*, 20 (January 1982), pp. 145-54.

Loomes, G. "Why Oligopoly Prices Don't Stick," *Journal of Economic Studies*, 8, No. 1 (1981), pp. 37-46.

Markham, J. W. "The Nature and Significance of Price Leadership," *American Economic Review*, 41 (December 1951), pp. 891-905.

Osborne, D. K. "The Role of Entry in Oligopoly Theory," *Journal of Political Economy*, 72 (August 1964), pp. 396-402.

Robinson, J. *The Economics of Imperfect Competition*. London: Macmillan, Inc., 1933.

Scherer, F. M. *Industrial Market Structure and Economic Performance* (2nd ed.), chaps. 5-8. Chicago: Rand McNally & Company, 1980.

Smith, D. S., and W. C. Neale. "The Geometry of Kinky Oligopoly: Marginal Cost, the Gap, and Price Behavior," *Southern Economic Journal*, 37 (January 1971), pp. 276–82.

Stigler, G. J. "The Kinky Oligopoly Demand Curve and Rigid Prices," *Journal of Political Economy*, 55 (October 1947), pp. 432–49.

Sweezy, P. M. "Demand under Conditions of Oligopoly," *Journal of Political Economy*, 47 (August 1939), pp. 568–73.

Welch, P. J. "On the Compatibility of Profit Maximization and the Other Goals of the Firm," *Review of Social Economics*, 38 (April 1980), pp. 65–74.

Williamson, J. "Profit, Growth and Sales Maximization," *Economica*, 33, No. 129 (1966), pp. 1–16.

Appendix 9A: Further Models of Pricing Behavior

Introduction

In this appendix we examine four additional pricing models, as well as variants on these models. First, we consider the multiplant firm that operates more than one plant while serving a particular market. This firm must determine its profit-maximizing price and total output level and the cost-minimizing allocation of the total output among the plants that it operates. The cartel, a group of oligopolists acting like a monopolist, can be analyzed using the same model, since there is a central decision-making authority that sets the price and allocates production among the member firms.

Second, we consider price discrimination by a firm that can subdivide its market into separate buyers or groups of buyers. We note that the firm can, given certain market conditions, increase its profit by charging higher prices to some buyers and lower prices to others, effectively discriminating between buyers and markets on one basis or another.

Third, we consider transfer pricing. Transfer prices are the prices set for transactions between divisions or profit centers within the same firm. Since these transactions are an internal matter, they are not subject to market forces and therefore might be decided arbitrarily or for the benefit of one division or another. The optimal transfer price is the one that best serves the firm as a whole.

Finally, we consider pricing where the firms and the buyers are spread out in geographical space and the price includes the cost of transporting the item from the place of manufacture to the place of consumption. This is called "spatial" competition, and prices are quoted as "delivered prices."

The Multiplant Firm

Many firms operate more than one plant. They may have built two or more smaller plants to avoid diseconomies of plant size that would occur if they tried to serve their market from a single, much larger, plant. A second reason for multiplant operation is relatively high transportation costs for the finished goods. If the market is spread over a wide geographical area, the firm will find it more economical to operate two or more plants in two or more locations if the savings in transportation costs more than outweigh the economies of plant size forgone. Third, the firm may operate two or more plants as a result of a merger or takeover, and the costs of scrapping both plants and building another larger one more than offset the economies of plant size forgone.

The multiplant firm must determine its profit-maximizing price and total output level, and at the same time it must determine the cost-minimizing allocation of the total output among its two or more plants.

The standard profit-maximizing rule, that marginal costs should equal marginal revenue, remains applicable, but our interpretation of the marginal cost curve must reflect the fact that marginal costs now derive from two or more production sources. The relevant marginal cost curve must show the marginal cost for each incremental unit produced when the firm is free to choose the plant in which that incremental unit should be produced. Clearly, the firm will always nominate the plant that can produce the incremental unit at the lowest additional (or marginal) cost. A simple means of ensuring this result is demonstrated in Figure 9A-1.

For simplicity, we assume just two plants being operated by a particular firm. In order to make the exercise nontrivial we have assumed differing cost structures for the two plants: plant A has a higher cost structure than plant B, perhaps because of its location in a high-land-value area or another factor cost disadvantage or because of the inability of this plant to achieve the same degree of production efficiency as plant B.

The marginal cost curves of plants A and B are summed horizontally to find the curve ΣMC shown in the "firm" part of the figure. This curve shows the combined marginal costs of the firm—that is, for a particular output level, some part of the

FIGURE 9A-1. Price and Output Determination for the Multiple-Plant Firm

output will have been produced in plant A and the remainder will have come from plant B, taking care always to select the incremental unit from the plant that can produce it at lowest marginal cost. It follows that at any total output level, the marginal cost from each plant should be approximately equal, since if this were not true the last unit might be taken away from the plant with the higher marginal cost and might be produced instead by the plant with the lower marginal cost, and thus reduce the marginal cost, to the firm as a whole, of the last unit produced. The ΣMC curve thus shows the marginal cost to the firm of each successive output unit, given the ability of the firm to have that unit produced in whichever of its plants can produce it most efficiently.

The firm's profits will be maximized at the output level when the combined marginal cost just equals the marginal revenue. This is shown as output level ΣQ in Figure 9A–1, and the demand curve indicates that the firm should set price P. The intersection of the ΣMC and MR curves indicates the *level* at which marginal costs are equal to marginal revenue. If we extend a line at this level across to the cost curves of plants A and B, it will indicate how the total output ΣQ should be divided between the two plants. Marginal costs in plant A come up to this critical level at output Q_1, and in plant B marginal costs meet this level at output Q_2. Outputs Q_1 and Q_2 together add up to ΣQ by virtue of the method of construction of the curve ΣMC. Thus, when the output ΣQ is divided among the plants in this way, the marginal cost of plant A equals the marginal cost of plant B, and both of these equal the marginal revenue of the final unit sold. The firm's profit is shown as the sum of the two rectangles *PABC* (from plant A) and *PEFG* (from plant B), which show the per-unit profit margin times the number of units produced, in each of the two plants.

The above analysis of the multiplant firm applies to any market situation where a firm envisages a negatively sloping *ceteris paribus* demand curve. It is thus appropriate for monopoly, monopolistic competition, or oligopoly situations. For oligopolistic markets where mutual dependence is recognized, price may be determined by a price leader or by "conscious parallelism," rather than independently, as suggested in the preceding discussion, and the demand curve depicted in Figure 9A–1 would represent the firm's *mutatis mutandis*, or share-of-the-market, demand curve. But the rule for allocation of output between or among multiple plants remains the same. The firm should ensure that the marginal cost of the last unit produced in each plant is approximately the same and is equal to the marginal revenue obtained for those last units.

Cartel Price and Output Determination

■ *Definition:*   A *cartel* is a group of firms acting as one, determining their price and output levels from within a central administering body. Cartels are illegal in most Western countries, but a couple of major international cartels continue to exist, immune from national legislation.

Example: The International Air Transport Association (IATA) determines air fares and many elements of nonprice competition for its members, such as types of meals, beverage prices, and in-flight movie prices. During the 1970s, higher levels of excess capacity resulting from the advent of jumbo jets, as well as the vigorous competition of third world airlines, reduced IATA's market control to a significant degree. The Organization of Petroleum Exporting Countries (OPEC), undoubtedly the most powerful cartel in the late 1970s, was able to elevate the prices of petroleum products dramatically as its members jointly raised prices to the levels agreed upon. The influence of OPEC waned considerably as the "oil glut" of the 1980s induced members to offer discounts below the cartel price. As implied by these two examples, the life of cartels tends to be short and stormy. We shall see that cartels are inherently unstable because of the incentives facing each firm to cheat on the cartel agreement.

A cartel may be either profit maximizing or market sharing. The profit-maximizing cartel attempts to maximize the *joint* profits of the firms. The firms then take a share of the total profits as determined by prior agreement or as actually earned. The market-sharing cartel establishes rules that allow each firm to maintain its predetermined or historical share of the market. We examine here each type in turn.

The Profit-Maximizing Cartel. The profit-maximizing cartel has exactly the same price and output decisions to make as does the multiplant firm. The cartel is like the multiplant firm except that it does not own each of the plants; it simply controls their pricing and output decisions.

For simplicity we assume there are two members in the cartel and that the firms have differing cost structures: firm A has a higher cost structure than firm B, as shown in Figure 9A-2.

The marginal cost curves of A and B are summed horizontally to find curve ΣMC shown in the part of the figure labeled *cartel*. This curve shows the combined marginal costs of the cartel; that is, for a particular output level, some part of the output is produced in firm A and the remainder in firm B, taking care always to select the

FIGURE 9A-2. Price and Output Determination by a Joint-Profit-Maximizing Cartel

incremental unit from the firm that can produce it at the lower marginal cost. From this it follows that at any particular total output level the marginal cost from each firm should be approximately equal. The ΣMC curve thus shows the marginal cost to the cartel of each successive output unit, given the ability of the cartel to have that unit produced by the firm that can produce it most efficiently.

The cartel's profits are maximized at the output level where the combined marginal cost just equals the marginal revenue. This is shown as output level ΣQ in Figure 9A-2. The demand curve indicates that the cartel should set price P. The intersection of the ΣMC and MR curves indicates the level at which marginal costs are equal to marginal revenue. If we extend a line at this level across to the cost curves of firms A and B, we see how total output ΣQ should be divided between the two firms. In firm A marginal costs come up to this critical level at output Q_1, and in firm B they come up to this level at output Q_2. Outputs Q_1 and Q_2 together add up to ΣQ, by virtue of the method of construction of the curve ΣMC. Thus, when the output ΣQ is divided among the firms in this way, the marginal cost of firm A equals the marginal cost of firm B. Both of these equal the marginal revenue of the final unit sold. The cartel's profit is shown as the sum of the two rectangles *PABC* (from firm A) and *PEFG* (from firm B). These rectangles show the per-unit profit margin times the number of units produced, in each of the two firms.

Side Payments and the Incentive to Undercut the Cartel Price.   The two member firms may agree to keep the profits they have each earned. Alternatively, there may be a prior agreement that the more profitable firm B must give some of its profits to the less profitable firm A. This *side payment* may be thought necessary to help firm A resist the temptation to undercut the cartel price and temporarily, at least, to enjoy an elastic demand response for its product. In fact, both firms face the temptation of large sales gains and higher profits, if they can secretly undercut the cartel price. If either firm can set a price below the cartel price, while the other firm continues to set the cartel price, the price-cutting firm will face a relatively elastic *ceteris paribus* demand curve, on which there will be a lower, more profitable price. Let us illustrate, using firm A as the price cutter in Figure 9A-3.

Initially, firm A is setting the cartel price P and producing Q_1 units of output. When contemplating independent price adjustments, the firm envisages the *ceteris paribus* demand curve shown as d. Associated with that curve is the marginal revenue curve, mr, which intersects the firm's marginal cost curve, MC_A, at output level Q'. Profits at the lower price P' are equal to the area $P'A'B'C'$ and are considerably larger than the profits *PABC* available to the firm as a member of the cartel. Thus there is considerable profit incentive to leave the cartel and price independently. Firm A might require a side payment equal to the difference in these two profit rectangles in order to keep it in the cartel.

But notice that the firm would earn these extra profits only as long as *ceteris paribus* prevailed. As soon as the other firm noticed its loss of sales and ascertained that firm A was "chiseling" the cartel price, it would probably match A's price reduction in order to maintain its share of the market. Alternatively, it might undercut A's

FIGURE 9A-3.   The Incentive to Undercut the Cartel Price

price to teach it a lesson, and a price war might ensue. The extra profits are available to firm A only as long as the price reduction remains unknown to firm B. If A is able to give customers secret discounts, and if sales normally fluctuate considerably in any case, firm B might not discover the duplicity for several weeks or months, during which time A can earn extra profits, which may be worth the risk of setting off a price war or of facing other disciplinary action by the cartel.

The more firms there are in a cartel, the more difficult it is, *ceteris paribus*, for the cartel to control prices or outputs of individual firms. The more firms, the more difficult it is for cartel members to find out that they are being undercut, since the "chiseler's" sales gain is comprised of proportionately smaller sales losses for each firm. There is thus a greater inclination for individual firms to undercut the cartel price. In actual business practice the life of cartels has usually been short and stormy, ending with a rapid decline in prices after the discovery that one or more firms were undercutting the cartel price.

The Market-Sharing Cartel.   In some instances oligopolists may wish to come to an agreement regarding their share of the market as a primary objective, rather than allow the market share to be the outcome of the price-fixing agreement, as in the preceding discussion. Firms that are geographically dispersed, for example, may feel that they have a right to sales in their own territory and will want to preclude encroachment by rivals into that territory. In this case the total market would be shared on the basis of the firms' locations and the density of population (and consequent demand) in each territory. Alternatively, firms with large output capacities may feel that they deserve a larger share of the market than would be allocated to them under a joint profit-maximizing cartel agreement. The other firms may be willing to allow these firms to take more than their (joint profit-maximizing) share, rather than risk a breakdown of the cartel's price agreement.

The agreement on market share may be quite an explicit arrangement (firm A gets 15 percent of industry sales) or an implicit, general understanding among the firms concerning each one's annual output levels (firm A has a quota of about 200,000 units annually). We immediately see that problems arise in business situations, since these agreements involve an estimate of annual market demand. Different conceptions of the market, different projections about the coming year's demand, and different perceptions of the same phenomena are likely to lead to disagreements about what constitutes a 15 percent share, for example. Compromises on these issues may leave some firms feeling less happy than others and perhaps more likely to violate the agreement at a later time. Similarly, agreements on the boundaries of each firm's geographical territory may be hard to arrive at and may be quite fragile when finally made.

When business is booming, firms have little time or reason to think about how the market-sharing agreement puts them at a disadvantage. When demand slackens in periods of recession or depression, however, firms may be considerably more inclined to undercut the cartel price or to encroach upon another firm's territory and compete for sales. Such price cutting, probably in the form of secret discounts, generous trade-in allowances, or additional goods and services for the same price, soon comes to the attention of other firms. The cartel agreement would be expected to break down as other firms begin to take defensive measures to avoid losing any more of their market shares.

Cartel price and market-sharing agreements might be expected to work a lot better if the participant firms have similar cost structures and either identical or symmetrically differentiated products. In such cases a single market price and equal market shares are likely to be relatively palatable solutions to the uncertainty faced by oligopolists.

Price Discrimination

■ *Definition:* *Price discrimination* is the practice of charging different prices to different buyers or groups of buyers for essentially the same product, where these price differences do not simply reflect the cost differences associated with serving different buyers or markets. The monopolist may find it both possible and more profitable to discriminate among buyers on some basis—to charge a higher price to some buyers and a lower price to others, rather than set the same price for all buyers. Price discrimination in the "economic" sense must be distinguished from price discrimination in the "legal" sense. In Appendix 10A we briefly examine the illegal methods of price discrimination. In perhaps most instances, "economic" price discrimination is not illegal.

Note: Three major conditions must exist before it is possible and profitable to practice price discrimination. First, the buyers or groups of buyers (markets) must be *separable*. That is, it must be possible to identify and keep separate the two or more buyers or markets, in order to prevent arbitrage selling from the lower-price to the higher-price buyer or market. Second, the two or more buyers (or markets) must exhibit *differing price elasticities of demand* at any particular price level, in order to make price discrimination profitable, as we shall see below. Third, the markets must be characterized by a *lack of price competition* from rival firms, in order to prevent price levels' being eroded from the profit-maximizing levels in each market. Clearly, price discrimination is most likely to work well in a monopoly situation, where there are no rivals to worry about, but it is also feasible in oligopoly markets, where the firms coordinate their pricing strategies using conscious parallelism, price leadership, or cartel pricing.

Price discrimination has been categorized into three distinct types. *First-degree price discrimination* occurs when each buyer is forced to pay the maximum that he or she would have been willing to pay for the product. In situations where there is no price discrimination, all but one of the buyers pay *less* than they would have been willing to pay, since there is only one price at which the product is offered, and the last buyer is the one who is only just willing to pay the price asked. All other buyers (those higher on the demand curve) would have been willing to pay more but were not asked to.[1] First-degree price discrimination involves asking each buyer to pay the maximum he or she would be willing to pay or else go without the product. In practice, of course, this is a difficult pricing decision, since one cannot know the preference structures of all the potential buyers.

Example: One means of accomplishing first-degree price discrimination in practice is the so-called Dutch auction in which the price starts at a very high level and the auctioneer calls out prices at slowly reducing price levels. The first person to accept the called price as the purchase price gets the product. This person will have paid the maximum he or she would have been willing to pay, since this buyer did not know what the second-most-eager buyer would have paid and therefore must bid as soon as the price falls to the maximum level he or she would have paid. The more conventional auction, in which price is bid upward, ensures that the successful bidder pays only slightly more than the second-most-eager buyer was willing to pay, rather than the maximum he or she was willing to pay.

Second-degree price discrimination involves discriminating among groups of buyers on a time or urgency basis. Those most eager to purchase the product will pay a higher price than those prepared to wait a little longer, and so on.

---

[1]Consumer surplus is the name given to the amount of money the consumer would have been willing to pay over and above the price actually paid. In regular markets all buyers except the last one receive some amount of consumer surplus. With first-degree price discrimination all consumer surplus is expropriated by the seller from every buyer, and it is added to the producer's surplus, which is profit. For more on consumer surplus, see R. A. Bilas, *Microeconomic Theory*, 2nd ed. (New York: McGraw-Hill Book Company, 1971), pp. 97–107.

Example: An amazing example of second-degree price discrimination was the early sale of ballpoint pens, which reportedly sold for around thirty dollars each, because of their novelty and utility value. Later, as technology advanced and costs fell, and as the market became progressively more saturated, the price fell to the level we know today. Products that have undergone a similar reduction in prices in more recent years are electronic calculators and quartz-crystal wristwatches. One further example is the pricing of tickets for new-movie releases. First runs in city theaters are priced substantially above second runs in suburban theaters, and so on down the line until finally the movie appears on television for virtually no charge at all.

Third-degree price discrimination is a situation whereby the firm can charge different prices in two or more different markets at the same point in time.

Example: Examples of third-degree price discrimination are telephone and electricity price differentials between households and business establishments and a firm that charges a higher price for a particular product in a downtown store than in a suburban store. Telephone companies also practice third-degree price discrimination by separating their markets on the basis of the time of day and the day of the week. Long-distance telephone calls during business hours cost more than during early morning hours or on weekends. Business establishments are willing and able to pay the higher prices during the day, since business must be conducted when other businesses are also operating. If the prices were the same twenty-four hours a day, many home users would write letters instead. Recognizing the more elastic nature of home demand, the telephone company offers cheaper calls at less convenient hours in order to increase the use of long distance telephone calls in two ways: first, it attracts buyers who would not otherwise purchase the service; and second, it shifts some of the demand into the offpeak hours, which saves the company from building a larger plant just to handle peak traffic.

To practice third-degree price discrimination the firm must decide what its total output should be, how it should distribute this output between or among the separate markets, and what price it should set in each market, so that profits are maximized. The methodology for solving this problem is similar to that for the multiplant firm's allocation problem. The firm should distribute each successive output unit to the market in which the unit contributes most to total revenues and should continue up to the point where the marginal revenue derived from the sale of the last unit is just equal to the marginal cost of producing that last unit. Figure 9A–4 shows two market situations, A and B. Market A has the more inelastic demand situation, perhaps because of fewer competitors or higher incomes of the buyers, or simply because of different taste patterns of the buyers in that market. If the firm were to begin with its first output unit, it would certainly sell this unit in market A, at a price near P_0, since the marginal revenue of the first unit is higher there than in market B. As the firm lowers its price to sell successive units, these units too will be best sold in market A, at least initially. But when price P_1 is reached in market A, a price of P_2 in market B would generate the same marginal revenue ($=P_2$). Thus buyers in market B begin to enter the market,

FIGURE 9A-4.   Construction of the Marginal Revenue Curve for the Price-Discriminating Firm

and the firm should now allocate successive output units back and forth between markets A and B, taking care to allocate each incremental unit to the market in which it derives the greatest marginal revenue. The curve ΣMR in the "Firm" part of the figure indicates the marginal revenue to the firm when it is free to allocate each successive unit to the market in which marginal revenue is highest. It is found by the horizontal summation of the marginal revenue curves in markets A and B. Clearly, it must begin at price level P_0 and kink at price level P_2, since below this level it is the horizontal sum of both MR curves rather than just the one.

In Figure 9A-5 we superimpose the firm's short-run cost curves upon the ΣMR curve. The output level that maximizes the firm's profits is shown as ΣQ, where its marginal costs rise to equality with its declining marginal revenues. The intersection of the MC and ΣMR curves defines the *level* at which marginal revenues in each market should be equated to the firm's marginal costs. Extending a line at this level across to the graphs for markets A and B, we see that the firm should allocate Q_A units to market A and Q_B units to market B, since marginal revenues in each of these markets at these output levels have fallen to the level to which marginal costs have risen. In market A, quantity Q_A should be priced at price P_2, and quantity Q_B will be sold at price P_3 in market B. Note that the more inelastic market is charged the higher price. The firm's total profits may be calculated as the sum of the price-cost margin in each market times the quantity sold in each market. That is, profits in market A will be the shaded area $P_2C \times 0Q_A$, and in market B profits will be the shaded area $P_3C \times 0Q_B$.

The output level ΣQ, and the allocation of this output between the markets as shown, is optimal, because if another unit was produced its marginal cost would exceed the marginal revenue in either market, and if the last unit was taken from either market and sold in the other, its marginal revenue would be less than its marginal cost.

FIGURE 9A–5.   Prices and Output Determination by the Price-Discriminating Firm

Thus any different output level or allocation of output between the markets would cause the firm's total profits to be reduced.

In summary, price discrimination involves charging different prices to different buyers or groups of buyers when their demand situations differ. If markets or individual buyers can be identified and kept separate, the monopolist can increase its profits by setting different prices for each one.

Transfer Pricing

Many large firms are organized into divisions or profit centers to facilitate the efficient operation of the firm. The decentralization of decision making in this way is considered to have beneficial impact on the firm's overall efficiency and profitability, since each division manager is judged by the profit performance of his or her division or profit center. A problem can arise, however, when one division or profit center supplies a component product (or intermediate product) to another division or profit center that uses this intermediate product as the basis for the firm's finished product, which is sold to consumers. This transaction is essentially internal to the firm and does not take place in the market for that intermediate product, if indeed there is a market for it. If the "transfer" price is set at a relatively high level, the supplying division will make more profits and the buying division less, presuming there is competition of some sort in the market for the finished product. If the transfer price is set at a relatively low level, the opposite will prevail. The firm as a whole will wish to set the transfer price at a level which serves to maximize the profit of the firm as a whole, rather than at some arbitrary or negotiated level that may not best serve the firm's objective.

We shall analyze the transfer pricing problem under three scenarios, first considering the case where there is no external market for the intermediate product, then considering the existence of a purely competitive external market for the intermediate product, and finally considering the existence of an imperfectly competitive market for the intermediate product.

Transfer Pricing with No External Market.   The marginalist rule, that marginal cost equals marginal revenue, determines the profit-maximizing output and price level for the firm as a whole. But if the firm has two divisions, for example, its overall marginal cost at any output level will be the sum of the marginal costs in its two divisions. Suppose a firm has two divisions, A and B. The intermediate product is produced in division A, and then packaged and marketed by division B. We suppose that each division has an upward-sloping marginal cost curve, as shown in Figure 9A-6. The vertical sum of these two MC curves is shown as the MC_F curve, and the firm maximizes profit at the price P^* and output level Q^*.

What transfer price should be established to induce division A to produce exactly the profit-maximizing output of the intermediate product? Similarly, what transfer price will induce division B to set the market price at the level P^* such that the firm's profits are maximized? In Figure 9A-6 we show the optimal transfer price as P_T, chosen to equal division A's marginal cost at output level Q^*. As a result, division A faces a horizontal demand curve at the transfer price—it can sell as much as it wants to at that price. However, it will only want to produce Q^* units, since its marginal cost (MC_A) equals its marginal revenue (MR_A) at that output level. Thus setting the transfer price at the level P_T induces division A to produce and supply exactly the optimal amount.

From the viewpoint of division B, the net marginal revenue (NMR) from the sale of the intermediate product is equal to $MR_F - MC_B$, or the market marginal revenue minus division B's marginal cost. At output/sales level Q^*, note that $NMR = MC_A$ (because $MR_F = MC_F$ at output Q^*, hence $MR_F - MC_B = MC_F - MC_B = MC_A$).

FIGURE 9A-6.   Transfer Pricing with No External Market

That is, the marketing division's net marginal revenue equals the marginal cost of the intermediate product that it buys from division A, which is in turn is equal to the transfer price. Thus division B maximizes its profits by setting market price P^* and output/sales level Q^*. At any other price and output combination in the market for the finished product, division B's NMR would either exceed or fall short of the transfer price (its effective marginal cost of the intermediate product), and its divisional profit would not be maximized.

Thus establishing the transfer price at the level P_T provides the appropriate incentives for both divisions to produce and sell the firm's profit-maximizing output level Q^*. Each division maximizes its profits by producing Q^* units, and the overall firm's profits are also maximized. Any other transfer price may have higher profits for either division A or B, but would have lower profit for the firm as a whole, not to mention a shortage or surplus of the intermediate product.

Transfer Pricing with a Purely Competitive External Market.   Now suppose that the intermediate product is available from other suppliers as well as division A. Moreover, division A's product is identical to that of other suppliers. There will be a market price for the intermediate product determined by the forces of supply and demand in that external market. In this case the transfer price must be set equal to the market price for the intermediate product. If it is set higher, division B will prefer to buy from the external market rather than from division A. If the transfer price is set below the external market price, division A will prefer to sell to the external market rather than to division B. If, at the transfer price (equal to the market price), division A wants to produce more than division B wishes to purchase, it can sell the balance in the external market. Conversely, if division B wants to purchase more than division A wishes to produce, it can buy the remainder in the external market.

In Figure 9A–7 we show the transfer price set at the external market price P_C. Note that division A will wish to produce Q_A units, such that $MC_A = MR_A$. Division B will demand only Q^* units, since $NMR = MR_F - MC_B = P_T$ at that output level. Thus division A will sell the remainder, shown by the distance $Q_A - Q^*$, in the external market for the intermediate product. Had the competitive external market price been lower, such that $Q_A < Q^*$, division B would have purchased some from division A and the remainder from the external market.

Transfer Pricing with an Imperfectly Competitive External Market.   Now we suppose that the intermediate products are not identical across firms, and thus each supplier to the external market faces a downward-sloping demand curve in that market. In Figure 9A–8 we show the demand and marginal revenue curves for the external market in the middle panel of the figure. In the left-hand panel we show the net marginal revenue (NMR) curve for (the marketing) division B of the firm, which is responsible for setting the market price and output level in the market for the finished product. Division A again has two markets for its output—it can sell to either division B or it can sell to the external market. However, since the elasticities of demand are different

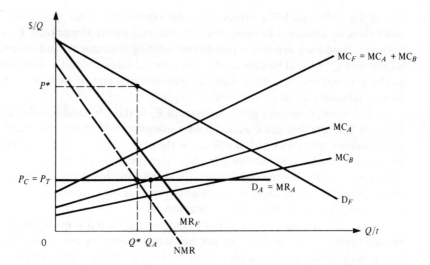

FIGURE 9A-7.   Transfer Pricing with a Purely Competitive External Market

in these two markets in this case, division A will find it profitable to practice price discrimination between the two markets.

The analysis proceeds as in the third-degree price discrimination case. The firm will sum horizontally the marginal revenue from its markets, and equate the ΣMR with its marginal cost of production MC_A. But note that from the firm's point of view it must consider only the net marginal revenue from the internal market (sales to division B), since otherwise it would be ignoring division B's marginal cost. The intersec-

FIGURE 9A-8.   Transfer Pricing with Imperfectly Competitive External Market

tion of the ΣMR and MC_A curves determines division A's total output level Q_A, which must then be allocated between the internal and external markets. By extending a horizontal line back across the panels representing the external and internal markets, we see that Q^* should be allocated to the internal market and Q_E should be allocated to the external market, such that the marginal revenue in each market equals the firm's marginal cost of production.

The optimal transfer price is shown as P_T in the left-hand panel of Figure 9A-8. Division B treats this price as a constant marginal cost of the intermediate product and demands Q^* units which it will sell at the price indicated by the demand curve for the finished product (not shown). In the external market the buyers are willing to pay a higher price, P_E, for the quantity Q_E, and thus division A discriminates against the external buyers and charges them a higher price for the intermediate product. In this way the overall profit of the firm is maximized.

Transfer pricing gets much more complicated than this example. If the demand or cost functions of the divisions are not independent, as assumed above, the issue becomes decidedly more complex. Within General Motors, for example, the demand curves of Chevrolet, Buick, and a third division producing electrical components are interdependent because their products are either substitutes or complements for each other. On the cost side, if they compete in the same input markets, their cost functions may well be interdependent as well. Multinational firms, with divisions or profit centers in different countries, must also consider the tax rates, import and export duties, and a variety of other issues that are involved. The interested reader is referred to the literature on transfer pricing for these extensions.[2]

Delivered Prices and Spatial Competition

When rival producers, and consumers, are dispersed geographically from each other, transportation costs become a significant element in the pricing decision. Either the consumer must pay the producer's price at the place of production and then incur the cost of transporting the product to the place of consumption, or the seller will incur the transportation cost and deliver the product to the consumer, charging a "delivered price." The former solution is called "f.o.b. pricing," where f.o.b. stands for "free on board," meaning that the seller may help load the item into your car or truck, if it is heavy, but then you are on your own. Clearly, this is the kind of pricing that most consumers experience. In general, where the transportation cost is trivial, or is not incremental to the consumer, or is more cheaply provided by the buyer, the buyer will

---

[2]See Joel Dean, "Decentralization and Intracompany Pricing," *Harvard Business Review*, July-August 1955, pp. 65-74; Jack Hirshleifer, "On the Economics of Transfer Pricing," *Journal of Business*, 29 (July 1956), pp. 172-84, and "Economics of the Divisionalized Firm," *Journal of Business*, 30 (April 1957), pp. 96-108; Charles T. Horngren, *Cost Accounting: A Managerial Emphasis*, 5th ed. (Englewood Cliffs, N.J.: Prentice-Hall, Inc., 1982), esp. chap. 19; and Stefan Robock, Kenneth Simmonds, and Jack Zwick, *International Business and Multinational Enterprises*, 3rd ed. (Homewood, Ill.: Richard D. Irwin, 1983), pp. 532-36.

assume that cost rather than pay the seller to provide it. Delivered prices are more common in industrial purchasing and for heavy consumer items.

The dispersion of sellers and buyers over geographical space gives rise to what is known as "spatial competition." A particular consumer may be quoted different prices by different suppliers, because of some combination of different "factory door" prices, different transportation costs per mile, and different transportation distances arising from the suppliers' differing locations. To secure a sale to a particular customer, the lucky seller must have the lowest delivered price, other things being equal.

In Figure 9A-9 we show buyers spread evenly along the horizontal axis, which measures distance, while sellers are located at the points A, B, C, and D. The vertical axis measures delivered prices. For simplicity, the base price of each firm at the factory door is the same, and the firms face the same transportation costs. The curved lines show the price to the buyer located at each point along the horizontal axis. Each buyer pays the base price plus the price of transportation services, which comprises an initial loading cost plus a freight rate per mile. Note that as the distance from the seller increases, the transportation costs, and hence delivered prices, increase at a decreasing rate. That is, the transport cost per mile diminishes as the loading cost is spread over an increasing distance traveled. The limit to each firm's sales is found where its price lines intersect with those for neighboring sellers. The buyers at each intersection point have a choice of two sellers, each quoting the same delivered price. All other buyers have one seller offering a price lower than its rivals, owing to its transport cost advantage. Note that delivered prices are a form of price discrimination, as buyers are discriminated among on the basis of their distance from the supplier.

"Basing-point" pricing is a form of delivered pricing. In this variant, the base price used by all firms is the factory door price of a particular firm at a particular location (the basing point). The agreement of all firms to set the same base price

FIGURE 9A-9.   Delivered Prices and Market Shares

amounts to an agreement to share the market based on geographic proximity of the buyers to the sellers, which we have earlier characterized as a market-sharing cartel. It is particularly effective where product differentiation is minimal or nonexistent, as in the markets for steel, grain, lumber products, and petroleum. In the past, these industries have been subject to scrutiny by the Federal Trade Commission for collusive basing-point pricing agreements.

Basing-point pricing may well be the pricing convention chosen by colluding oligopolists, but the existence of delivered pricing with similar base prices does not imply collusion, as Haddock has argued.[3] Suppliers in a purely competitive market, who will all have similar production costs and face similar transportation costs, must use a delivered pricing scheme to compete for sales in a spatial market. Their base prices will tend to be equal to their marginal and average cost of production, because of the unrestricted entry of new competitors if pure profits are earned. Noncollusive oligopolists, such as price leaders and followers, will set the base price initiated by the price leader and quote different prices on the basis of transportation cost.

In fact, an analysis of delivered pricing highlights the ways in which oligopolists may compete effectively with each other in a spatial market. Efficiency in production, leading to a lower base price than that set by rivals, will expand the firm's market, since it increase the distance from its plant that a firm can set a lower delivered price than its competitors. In Figure 9A–10 we show the impact of a reduction in firm B's base price. The dotted price lines indicate the old pricing schedule based on the higher base price. The new, lower, base price allows firm B to expand sales both to the right and the left, at the expense of firms A and C. Note, however, that it also allows firm B to be the lowest-priced supplier to the right of firm C, where it consequently steals sales from both firm C and firm D.

Similarly, increased efficiency in transportation will cause a firm's delivered price lines to be flatter, and thus lower, at any particular location, allowing it to be the lowest-priced supplier further from its plant than it was before, and thus to gain sales at the expense of rivals. Finally, in the long run, the firm may relocate to a less crowded part of the market or build a second plant in another location in order to gain market share.

In Figure 9A–10, firm B's sales in what was formerly C's and D's markets will lead to what is called "cross hauling"—firm B's trucks heading to this area will pass firm C's trucks heading in the opposite direction to service the buyers located to the left-hand side of its plant. Cross hauling is often interpreted by the courts as evidence of collusive behavior, since it might occur in market-sharing cartels (where the agreement is based on firms having no competition for their "traditional" customers).[4] It is

---

[3]David D. Haddock, "Basing-Point Pricing: Competitive vs. Collusive Theories," *American Economic Review*, 72 (June 1982), pp. 289–306. See also George J. Stigler, "A Theory of Delivered Price Systems," *American Economic Review*, 39 (December 1949), pp. 1143–59.

[4]See John S. Magee, "Cross Hauling—A Symptom of Incomplete Collusion under Basing Point Systems," *Southern Economic Journal*, 20 (April 1954), pp. 369–79.

Delivered Prices

Distance

| A's Market Share | B's Market Share | C's Market Share | B's Market Share | D's Market Share |

FIGURE 9A-10. Gains in Market Share That Result from Increased Efficiency in Production

clear that the cross hauling evident in Figure 9A-10 is due to competitive behavior. Haddock, cited above, points out some other noncollusive reasons for cross hauling. First, some buyers will prefer to buy from more than one supplier as an insurance policy against one's inability to supply at a critical time. The extra transportation cost is merely the premium paid for that insurance policy. Second, the cost of information leads to cross hauling. The buyer must incur search costs to identify the lowest-priced supplier, and where prices change frequently such that information held may not be correct, cross hauling will occur because of ignorance. Further, although it would be more profitable for firms to switch customers rather than cross haul, some cross hauling will go undetected because the managerial cost of detecting it will exceed the excess transportation costs incurred. Finally, the existence of product differentiation in a spatial market will cause cross hauling, because some buyers will pay more for what they perceive to be the superior product.

Summary

In this appendix we considered several models of the firm's pricing behavior in addition to those in Chapter 9, each one relating to a particular pricing problem that may face the firm. The multiplant firm must select the profit-maximizing price and output level, while at the same time allocating the output level between or among its two or more plants such that total costs are minimized. The technique for solving this problem involves the horizontal summation of the marginal cost curves from each of the plants to obtain a hypothetical ΣMC curve. Total output is determined where this curve cuts the firm's MR curve, and market price is read from the demand curve at this total output level. To allocate the profit-maximizing total output between the plants such that total cost is minimized, the level of ΣMC at which it equals MR is observed, and production in each plant is taken to the point where the MC in that plant rises up to the level at which $\Sigma MC = MR$.

The profit-maximizing cartel's price and output decision proceeds along the same lines. The incentive to cheat on the cartel exists for every member of the cartel, although it will be stronger for some than for others. A secret price reduction will allow any one firm to set a lower price along a relatively elastic *ceteris paribus* curve and increase its profits until the other firms discover the cheating and retaliate. The firm must weigh these additional profits against the benefits of price and output stability that are provided by the cartel. Side payments may be necessary to bribe an unhappy cartel member to remain in the cartel. Market-sharing cartels prescribe territorial limits to sales, allocate particular buyers to particular sellers, or simply prescribe output limits, and allow the prices to be determined by the individual firms. Cartels tend to be relatively short-lived, and they are more likely to break down when the members have substantial excess capacity available.

Price discrimination allows the firm that is able to separate its buyers into markets on some basis to increase its profit. First-degree price discrimination discriminates against those with higher incomes or wealth, second-degree price discrimination discriminates against those unable or unwilling to wait, and third-degree price discrimination discriminates against those with less elastic demand for the product.

Transfer pricing is involved whenever a firm is divisionalized, or organized into separate profit centers each with responsibility for its own profits. To ensure that the firm's overall profits are maximized, a centralized decision must be imposed concerning the transfer price for sales from one division to another. In general, the transfer price should equal the supplying division's marginal cost of production or the competitive market price for the intermediate product if such a market exists. If the external market for the intermediate product is imperfectly competitive, the supplying division will contribute to the maximization of the firm's profits by practicing price discrimination between the internal and external market for its output.

Delivered pricing systems occur where producers and consumers are located at different places and the consumer is charged the cost of production plus the transportation costs involved in transporting the product from the place of manufacture to the place of consumption. Given identical products, the buyer will buy from the seller with the lowest delivered price, which is not necessarily the nearest seller. Cross hauling will also occur because of lack of full information, because of product differentiation, and as a result of risk aversion.

DISCUSSION QUESTIONS

9A-1. State what the ΣMC curve represents for the multiplant firm.

9A-2. Discuss the operation of cartels and the incentive to undercut the cartel price. Does it make a difference when the products are differentiated and the "cartel price" is in reality a structure of prices around a particular level?

9A-3. Outline the principle of profit maximization as applied to a firm that operates three plants within the same market.

9A-4. In principle, explain how a firm may increase its profits by discriminating between two distinct markets for its products.

9A-5. Do you think that OPEC is still an effective cartel? Or is it a price leader instead? Why?

9A-6. Outline the three degrees of price discrimination. What is the basis of discrimination in each case? What conditions must be fulfilled to allow the firm to practice price discrimination?

9A-7. What is the transfer pricing problem? What might happen if the marketing division of the firm was required to accept whatever the manufacturing division of the firm produced at a transfer price equal to the latter's average cost of production plus a margin for profit?

9A-8. In spatial competition, why does the delivered price increase at a decreasing rate as the distance from the buyer and seller increases?

9A-9. In what ways can a firm increase its sales in a spatial market?

9A-10. What is cross hauling? List several reasons why you would expect to see cross hauling in spatial markets.

PROBLEMS AND SHORT CASES

9A-1. Analyze graphically the case of a two-plant firm that practices price discrimination in two separate markets. Assume two sets of cost conditions and two demand situations, and show the following:

(a) How the firm determines total output.

(b) Allocation of production to each plant.

(c) Allocation of output to each market.

(d) Prices in each of the two markets.

9A-2. The Thomas Tent Company has two separate markets for its midsize tent. The domestic market is characterized by the demand curve $P = 100 - 15Q$, and the foreign market is characterized by the demand curve $P = 60 - 2.5Q$, where P represents the price in dollars and Q represents thousands of units demanded. The firm's one plant has a total cost function approximated by $TC = 10,800 + 20Q + 0.1Q^2$ in the relevant range of outputs.

(a) What is the profit-maximizing output level of midsize tents?

(b) How should Thomas divide this output between the two markets?

(c) What price should be set in the domestic market?

(d) What price should be set in the foreign market?

9A-3. The Bartram Bitumen Company has two plants producing bituminous tar for its market in which it has a virtual monopoly because of the remote location of other firms producing bituminous tar. The marketing manager has estimated the firm's demand curve as $P = 68.5 - 0.005Q$; and the production manager has estimated the monthly cost functions as $TC = 5,850 + 1.5Q + 0.005Q^2$ for plant A, and $TC = 6,250 + 1.2Q + 0.003Q^2$ for plant B, where Q represents pounds of tar in all cases.

(a) Please advise Bartram about the profit-maximizing output level from both plants in total.

(b) How much of this output should come from plant A?

(c) What price should Bartram set?

(d) Demonstrate that total contribution would decline if the last 100 units to be produced in plant A could not be produced there because of a breakdown and had to be produced in plant B instead.

9A-4. Holiday Pleasure Tours is a small company that provides a two-week holiday package on a Caribbean island. It is a member of the Association of Island Tour Operators, which is effectively a cartel that sets the prices for tourist packages in the Caribbean Islands. Holiday's tour package involves air fare from New York, transfers, two weeks hotel accommodation, a rental car, and daily use of sailboats, snorkeling equipment, and so on. The cartel price for this tour is $1,600 per person, and Holiday's current quantity demanded is 400 per month. Holiday is considering a secret discount, to be advertised in the *New York Times* travel section. A market research firm has estimated that Holiday faces a *ceteris paribus* demand curve specified by $P = 2,000 - Q$, following its conjecture that quantity demanded would increase by one unit for every dollar the price is reduced. Holiday's cost function for this tour package is estimated to be $TC = 50,000 + 400Q + 0.25Q^2$.

   (a) Calculate Holiday's monthly contribution at the current price and output levels.

   (b) If Holiday were to set a lower price, what is the profit-maximizing price level, with *ceteris paribus*?

   (c) What is Holiday's expected contribution at the new price level?

   (d) What issues would you consider before advising Holiday to go ahead with the price reduction?

9A-5. General Statics Corporation is organized into a manufacturing division and a marketing division. Each division manager is responsible for his or her division's profits. The manufacturing division makes an electronic ignition system which the marketing division packages and distributes to automobile manufacturers. The firm's demand curve for this product is estimated to be $P = 1,000 - 0.625Q$, where Q represents thousands of units. The manufacturing division's marginal cost is estimated to be $MC = 200 + 0.375Q$, and the marketing department's marginal cost is estimated to be $MC = 100 + 0.5Q$.

   (a) Assuming there is no external market for the ignition systems, calculate the profit-maximizing transfer price.

   (b) Assuming there is a purely competitive external market for these ignition systems, in which the price is currently $350 per unit, how many units should be produced? How many of these should be sold internally and how many should be sold externally?

   (c) Finally, assuming that the external market demand curve is described by $P = 1,200 - 0.8Q$, what is the profit-maximizing transfer price and the optimal allocation between the internal and external markets? What price should be charged in the external market? (An answer derived from a careful graphing of the problem will suffice.)

SUGGESTED REFERENCES AND FURTHER READING

Coyne, T. J. *Managerial Economics: Analysis and Cases* (5th ed.), chap. 10. Plano, Tex.: Business Publications, Inc., 1984.

Douglas, E. J. *Intermediate Microeconomics: Theory and Applications*, esp. chaps. 8, 10, and 12. Englewood Cliffs, N.J.: Prentice-Hall, Inc., 1982.

Ismail, B. E. "Transfer Pricing under Demand Uncertainty," *Review of Business and Economic Research*, 18 (Fall 1982), pp. 1–14.

Leftwich, R. H. *The Price System and Resource Allocation* (7th ed.), chap. 11. Hinsdale, Ill.: The Dryden Press, 1979.

Mansfield, E. *Microeconomics: Theory and Applications* (5th ed.), esp. chaps. 9, 10, and 11. New York: W. W. Norton & Company, 1985.

McGuigan, J. R., and R. C. Moyer. *Managerial Economics* (3rd ed.), chap. 15. St. Paul, Minn.: West Publishing Company, 1983.

Pappas, J. L., E. F. Brigham, and M. Hirschey. *Managerial Economics* (4th ed.), chap. 11, appendix 11A. Chicago: The Dryden Press, 1983.

Seo, K. K. *Managerial Economics: Text, Problems, and Short Cases* (6th ed.), esp. chap. 16, appendix 16A. Homewood, Ill.: Richard D. Irwin, Inc., 1984.

Weismeth, H. "Price Discrimination Based on Imperfect Information: Necessary and Sufficient Conditions," *Review of Economic Studies*, 49 (July 1982), pp. 391–402.

10 Pricing Decisions in Practice

10.1 INTRODUCTION

In the preceding chapter pricing theory was discussed in the context of *certainty*, whereby firms were assumed to know the shape and location of their cost and demand curves. On the basis of these curves, the firms chose price in order to obtain their desired objective. If their objective was to maximize profit, the firms would equate the marginal cost curve with the appropriate marginal revenue curve. If the firm's objective function was other than short-run profit maximization, the cost and revenue curves were nevertheless important in the selection of the price that would facilitate the attainment of the particular objective function.

In the real-world business environment, however, firms will not be aware of the exact shape and location of their cost and revenue curves. We have argued in Chapters 5 and 8 that the firm may generate *estimated* demand and cost functions, however. By careful analysis of cost and demand data, the firm may be able to use its best estimate of the MR and MC curves to establish the price that appears to best serve its objectives.

Marginalist Pricing under Uncertainty

There are three main ways of practicing marginalist pricing under uncertainty, each of which has been outlined in preceding chapters. We shall now summarize the three methods in turn.

Given Estimated Demand and Marginal Cost Curves. Suppose we have estimated the demand curve or have derived the demand curve from an estimate of the demand function, as outlined in Chapter 5. We know that the marginal revenue curve has the same intercept value and twice the slope value as compared with the demand curve, and thus we can quickly derive an estimate of marginal revenue. Suppose also that we find marginal cost to be constant over the relevant range of output, or explained by a linear or other function of output, as outlined in Chapter 8. Setting the expression for marginal revenue equal to that for marginal cost, we can solve for the quantity level that preserves the equality. Inserting the result back into the demand curve gives us the price that, to the best of our knowledge, will maximize contribution and hence profits.

Given Estimated Price Elasticity and Marginal Costs. If we are supplied with an estimate of price elasticity for a product in the vicinity of the current price, we can use the elasticity formula ($\epsilon = dQ/dP \times P/Q$) to deduce the slope of the demand curve ($b = dP/dQ$), since we already know the values ϵ, P, and Q. We then deduce the value of the intercept term a in the demand curve expression ($P = a + bQ$), since we would then know the value of P, b, and Q. We then proceed as in the above situation to find the MR expression, and the optimal price and quantity. This method was shown in detail in Chapter 4 in the section entitled "Implications for Optimal Prices."

Given Estimates of Incremental Costs and Revenues. The incremental or contribution approach is a marginalist approach, since it is concerned with changes in both total revenues and total costs. Unlike the marginal revenue/marginal cost approach, however, the incremental approach does not require the ability to adjust output by one unit at a time. Thus demand indivisibilities and discontinuities can be handled using the incremental approach. Suppose that the following demand situation exists: As price is progressively reduced the quantity demanded will increase by discrete blocks, as a result of gaining particular orders at the lower prices. For example, at a price of $3.80 per unit we may expect to sell 12,000 units, but at $3.79 we expect to sell 14,500 as a result of gaining a particular order at the slightly lower price.

Where demand contains indivisibilities or discontinuities we cannot construct the marginal revenue function, since the total revenue curve is not continuous and therefore is not differentiable. Instead, we must compare the incremental costs and incremental revenues at each price level and choose the price that allows the maximum contribution to be made.

These methods of price determination are only as sound as the underlying information. To put our faith in the price that is indicated, we should be highly confident that both the demand and the cost estimates do in fact represent the actual situations and that the underlying *ceteris paribus* assumption can reasonably be expected to hold true. If, for example, our calculations indicate a price substantially below the prices of close rivals, we should expect those firms to react in some way and thus violate the *ceteris paribus* assumption. Because the demand and cost data are simply estimates, the actual outcomes may differ substantially from the expected outcomes. This is the nature of decision making under uncertainty, however: We must make decisions on the basis of the best information available, and if new information comes to light at a later point in time, this information forms the basis for a subsequent decision (which may involve the reversal of the initial decision).

Search Costs and Rule-of-Thumb Pricing Practices

In many cases the decision maker may expect that the cost of obtaining the estimates of the MC and MR relationships will exceed the extra revenue that might have been obtained using these estimates. Before attempting to obtain the additional information, the decision maker must expect that the additional revenues to be earned as a result of making the optimal decision (as compared with the revenues expected from the decision to be made on the basis of existing information) will exceed the cost of obtaining that information. Clearly, in many business situations the decision maker would have no such expectations. Thus it is not surprising that business decision makers, notwithstanding the elegant models of the economists, tend to adopt simple *rule-of-thumb procedures* when setting or changing prices.

Rule-of-thumb pricing procedures should be viewed as shortcut decision-making methods that economize on search costs and on the decision maker's time. These procedures usually result in a suboptimal decision being taken when that decision is compared with one that might be taken if full information were available. In terms of profits gained by the firm, however, the rule-of-thumb decision-making procedure may be optimal. Although it may never lead to the optimal decision in any specific instance, consistent decision making by a rule-of-thumb procedure may approximate the same net profit levels over the longer term. The inefficiency of rule-of-thumb decision procedures arises from the fact that some amount of profitability is lost because the optimal decision in specific instances is not taken. But to know what the optimal decision is requires additional information which in turn has search costs attached, and hence all rule-of-thumb pricing procedures need to do is *lose less* than the information would cost.

The most common rule-of-thumb pricing procedure is known as *markup pricing*, and we examine this in the next section. We will see that under a broad range of conditions it may be more profitable for the firm to practice markup pricing than to incur the search costs necessary to implement marginalist pricing. Nevertheless, the principles involved in marginalist pricing are indispensible to the optimal use of markup pricing, and the firm should periodically seek cost and demand data to confirm that its prices are at levels which best serve the firm's objectives.

Following the discussion of markup pricing, we consider a variety of pricing issues and strategies used in practice, including price positioning, product-line pricing, pricing to infer quality, temporary price "deals," pricing product "bundles," and price "breaks" (quantity discounts).

10.2   MARKUP PRICING

- **Definition:**   *Markup pricing*, also known as *cost-plus* pricing, is the practice of determining price by adding a percentage markup to the direct cost (or average variable cost) of the product.[1] Thus,

---

[1]"Full-cost" pricing is a variant of markup pricing in which the *average cost* is marked up by some percentage rate in order to determine the price per unit. Note that this practice necessarily involves an estimate of sales volume, in order to determine the value for average fixed cost to be added to the average variable cost. Since sales volume depends on price, however, the markup rate, the full-cost price, and the

$$P = \text{AVC} + X\%(\text{AVC}) \qquad (10\text{-}1)$$

where X is the markup percentage chosen. This markup, in dollar terms, is the per-unit contribution to overheads and profits, and hence choosing the size of the markup amounts to choosing the contribution margin. Thus equation (10-1) may be expressed as follows:

$$P = \text{AVC} + \text{CM} \qquad (10\text{-}2)$$

Hopefully, the markup will be large enough so that, at the actual level of sales volume, the total contributions to overheads and profits actually cover the overheads and allow a profit to be made. The size of the markup is constrained, however, by the willingness of consumers to pay the higher prices associated with a higher markup. Even a firm that has a monopoly over a certain product must acknowledge that at higher prices consumers in aggregate will buy fewer units. Oligopolists must take into account the relative prices of competitors. An individual firm will lose sales to rivals if its price is significantly above the prices of its rivals and if consumers do not think the item is worth the extra money.

Markup pricing is often thought to be simply cost based, but it is evident that the amount by which price can be marked up is highly dependent upon the demand conditions facing the firm. When asked what factors determine the size of the markup percentage, business people often respond that they choose the markup with an eye to "what the market will bear" or "in order to meet the competition."[2] These statements carry an implicit message about the price elasticity of demand facing the firm, and hence the size of the markup is both cost and demand based, contrary to the naive view that markup pricing depends upon cost alone.

Since firms tend to use markup pricing in practice, does this mean that they are ignoring the marginalist principles of pricing? No, it does not. We shall see that markup pricing is not necessarily inconsistent with the marginalist principles. In fact, if the markup rate is chosen correctly, it will give exactly the profit-maximizing price.

Reconciliation of Markup and Marginalist Pricing

For every price level which is determined by the marginalist procedure of setting $\text{MC} = \text{MR}$, there is an *implied* markup percentage. For example, if the profit-maximizing price is $6.00 and the AVC is $4.00, the implied markup is 50 percent, since $6.00 is 150 percent of $4.00. In Figure 10-1 we show this situation. In part (a), we

---

quantity demanded at that price must be determined simultaneously. Most firms using full-cost pricing have a notional "standard volume" around which they expect to produce with minor variations that result from fluctuations of demand. They use as their "full cost" the average cost at this "standard volume," and the markup rate is the rate that will bring their price into line with rivals' prices in the market, with minor adjustments to reflect differences in product quality and service.

[2] See A. Silberston, "Price Behavior of Firms," *Economic Journal*, 80 (September 1970).

FIGURE 10-1. **Marginalist versus Markup Pricing**

show the marginalist determination of price: MR = MC at output level Q_0 and the profit-maximizing price is found to be P.[3] In part (b), we show the markup approach—without benefit of data on the demand and marginal revenue curves, the firm simply applies a 50 percent markup to AVC and arrives at the *same* price P. At price P, the quantity demanded will be Q_0, and the firm will be setting the profit-maximizing price, even though it did not know where its demand curve was. (It now knows one point on its demand curve, namely point A, since consumers demanded Q_0 units at price P.)

In this case we suppose the firm using markup pricing under uncertainty was just lucky—it *happened* to apply the profit-maximizing markup implied by the marginalist approach and, thus, set the profit-maximizing price without having to spend money on search activity to estimate the shape or placement of its demand curve. How will the firm know whether its markup is profit maximizing or not? By reconciling the two approaches, we can derive a simple rule which will indicate whether or not the markup rate is profit-maximizing. To reconcile the markup and the marginalist approach to price determination we must incorporate the marginalist rule, MR = MC, into the markup pricing equation (10-1). We start by finding an expression for marginal revenue that incorporates the price elasticity. Recall from Chapter 4 that total revenue is the product of price and quantity:

$$TR = P \cdot Q$$

---

[3]Note that we show a horizontal MC curve, with AVC = MC in keeping with the empirical studies noted in Chapter 8. Constant MC over the relevant range greatly facilitate the analysis of markup pricing. The decision maker should be content that MC are constant in the situation under review before applying the simple markup-pricing rules without the modifications necessary if MC are in fact not constant over the relevant range.

Marginal revenue is the first derivative of total revenue with respect to output. Using the chain rule,[4] since P also depends on Q, we have

$$MR = P + Q\frac{dP}{dQ}$$

(10-3)

We now perform a manipulation on equation (10-3) which will allow a substitution. Multiply and divide the last term by P such that we obtain

$$MR = P + \frac{QP}{P} \cdot \frac{dP}{dQ}$$

(10-4)

Factoring out P we obtain

$$MR = P\left(1 + \frac{Q}{P} \cdot \frac{dP}{dQ}\right)$$

(10-5)

Note that the compound term in the brackets is simply the reciprocal of the expression for price elasticity. (See equation 4-16 in Chapter 4 if this is not clear). Substituting for elasticity ϵ into equation (10-5) we obtain

$$MR = P\left(1 + \frac{1}{\epsilon}\right)$$

(10-6)

Given this expression for the relationship between marginal revenue, price, and elasticity we are now ready to perform the reconciliation. Marginalist pricing requires $MC = MR$. Setting MC equal to the above expression for MR we have

$$MC = P\left(1 + \frac{1}{\epsilon}\right)$$

(10-7)

Expressed in terms of price, this may be restated as[5]

$$P = MC\left(\frac{\epsilon}{\epsilon + 1}\right)$$

(10-8)

---

[4]The chain rule of derivation is explained in Appendix A at the end of this book, in case you are not familiar with it.

[5]Note that since $MC = P(1 + 1/\epsilon)$, $P = MC[1/(1 + 1/\epsilon)]$. In the latter expression the term in parentheses can be rewritten as $[1/(1/1 + 1/\epsilon)]$, or the reciprocal of a pair of fractions. To add fractions we use their common denominator, which is the product of the denominators. In this case the common denominator of $1/1$ and $1/\epsilon$ is ϵ. The sum of these fractions is thus $(\epsilon + 1)/\epsilon$. Thus we have $P = MC\{1/[(\epsilon + 1)/\epsilon]\}$, or $P = MC[\epsilon/(\epsilon + 1)]$.

In business situations average variable costs are often constant (or viewed as constant) over the relevant range of outputs. Under such circumstances, marginal cost is equal to average variable cost. Hence we may restate equation (10-8) as

$$P = \text{AVC}\left(\frac{\epsilon}{\epsilon + 1}\right) \tag{10-9}$$

which can be rewritten as[6]

$$P = \text{AVC} + \left(\frac{-1}{\epsilon + 1}\right)\text{AVC} \tag{10-10}$$

Thus the markup rate X in equation (10-1), is equal to the negative reciprocal of one plus the price elasticity.[7]

Let us now substitute into Equation (10-10) an arbitrary value for elasticity, say $\epsilon = -5$. In this case:

$$P = \text{AVC} + \left(\frac{-1}{-5 + 1}\right)\text{AVC}$$

$$P = \text{AVC} + \left(\frac{1}{4}\right)\text{AVC}$$

$$P = \text{AVC} + 25\%(\text{AVC})$$

Thus a 25 percent markup on average variable cost is the profit-maximizing markup percentage if the elasticity value is equal to -5.

In Table 10-1 we show the profit-maximizing markup rates for a variety of other elasticity values. Note that the optimal markup rate varies inversely with the absolute value of price elasticity.[8]

Thus products with higher price elasticities of demand should be expected to have relatively lower percentage markups in order to make the maximum total contri-

---

[6]To follow this, note that $\epsilon/(\epsilon + 1) + 1/(\epsilon + 1) = [\epsilon/(\epsilon + 1)]/[\epsilon/(\epsilon + 1)] = 1$. Thus $\epsilon/(\epsilon + 1) = 1 - 1/(\epsilon + 1)$. Thus $P = \text{AVC}[1 - 1/(\epsilon + 1)]$, or $P = \text{AVC} + [-1/(\epsilon + 1)]\text{AVC}$.

[7]Note that equation (10-10) is not a formula to find the profit-maximizing price given an estimate of price elasticity at some other price, since P and ϵ vary together. Rather, equation (10-10) is the optimality condition: if the price level and its associated elasticity value are such that the equality of equation (10-10) is preserved, then the markup rate is profit maximizing. If there is an inequality, the optimal markup rate must be found by constructing the firm's demand and marginal cost curves (from the elasticity estimate) and deducing the profit-maximizing markup rate, as in Figure 10-1.

[8]Note that the formula only works for $\epsilon < -1$. But for $\epsilon > -1$, MR < 0 and hence we cannot have MC = MR, since MC must be nonnegative. The profit-maximizing markup rate is infinite for $\epsilon = -1$, because profit maximization requires MC = MR, and since MR = 0 when $\epsilon = -1$, MC = AVC must also be zero. Thus the profit-maximizing price is an infinite multiple of AVC, and it is equal to the revenue-maximizing price, when AVC = MC = 0.

TABLE 10-1.   The Profit-Maximizing
              Markup Rate Given
              Price Elasticity

Elasticity Value	Markup Rate (%)
−1	∞
−2	100
−3	50
−4	33.3
−5	25
−6	20
−7	16.7
−8	14.3
−9	12.5
−10	11.1

bution to overheads and profits. You will recall from Chapter 4 that we expect price elasticity to be higher, the greater the number of substitutes and the greater the proportion of income that is spent on that particular product. In practice we know that markups on individual items of groceries, for example, tend to be low and that on gift items they tend to be high, in keeping with the above analysis.

Do firms choose their markup with an eye to the value of price elasticity? Certainly most do not. Rather, they find their "best" markup by trial and error or by adopting the same markup that is applied by other firms or choosing the markup that brings their price into line with the price set by the price leader in their market. This is not to say, however, that marginal analysis is of limited usefulness to the decision maker. Although firms may not use marginalist analysis in choosing the price levels, they may act as if they do. Marginalist analysis may thus predict the pricing actions of firms, even if in practice they use a markup-pricing procedure. To the extent that they choose the size of the markup with reference to market conditions and to the extent that they wish to maximize the contribution to overheads and profits, the markup price level may closely approximate the price that would be indicated by marginalist procedures.

The Range of Acceptable Markup Levels[9]

Since the markup-pricing procedure avoids the search costs associated with estimating the demand curve, the markup level can vary within certain limits and still be acceptable, in the sense that the firm makes at least as much profit as it would if it first incurred the search costs and then set the MC = MR price.

Consider Figure 10-2, in which we show the total revenue (TR) curve associated

---

[9]More detail on this topic may be found in my "Pricing for Economic Objectives Given Search and Price Adjustment Costs," *Journal of Cost Analysis*, 1 (Spring 1984), pp. 59–74.

FIGURE 10-2.   The Range of Acceptable Markup Levels for the Profit-Maximizing Firm

with the actual demand curve faced by the firm. The total cost (TC) curve is shown as a straight line, reflecting constant marginal and average variable costs on top of a base comprising the total fixed costs (TFC). Profits, the vertical distance between TR and TC at each output level, are represented by the curve π. Now consider search costs. If the firm decides to spend funds to estimate the demand curve, this expenditure will shift total fixed costs and, hence, total costs upward by the amount spent on search activity. (Search costs must be regarded as a fixed cost, since they are not related to the output level.) Thus the profit curve must shift down by the same vertical distance, to that shown as π' in Figure 10-2.

   The profit-maximizing price, shown as P^* in the lower part of the figure, is found where MC = MR or where TC and TR have the same slope in the upper part of the figure. Note that this price is still the profit-maximizing price, whether or not search costs are incurred. That is, point A is the highest point on profit curve π, and point E is the highest point on profit curve π'. However, once the firm incurs the search costs, point E is the *best* it can do. If it does not incur the search costs, it might be lucky enough to set price P^* and maximize profits at point A. But note that any point on the profit curve π between B and C involves *more profit* than does point E. In terms of the demand curve in the lower part of the figure, any price between P_1 and P_2 promises more profit (without search costs) than does price P^* (after search costs have been spent). Sales can vary between Q_2 and Q_1 for prices between P_1 and P_2 and the firm will be at least as well off as (*at* prices P_1 or P_2) or better off than (*between* prices P_1 and P_2) it would be with full information and the "correct" price (where $MC = MR$).

In terms of the level of the markup, the rate applied to average variable costs could be anywhere between the low rate $(P_1 - AVC)/AVC$ and the high rate $(P_2 - AVC)/AVC$, and the firm would make more profits by *not* undertaking search activity to ascertain its demand curve. From Figure 10-2 you will note that in this example any markup between about 50 percent and 100 percent would appear to offer more profits, as compared to the alternative of incurring search costs and setting the "correct" price.[10]

Periodic Tests to Ensure Acceptability of the Markup.   The firm may wish to assure itself from time to time that its markup is in fact within the range of markup levels that allow greater profits as compared with the "correct" price after search costs have been incurred.

A simple test that should involve minimal search costs is the use of the markup rate to infer the value of price elasticity that would be required for the markup level to be profit maximizing.

Example: Earlier, in Table 10-1, we saw that a markup rate of 50 percent over AVC is profit maximizing if the price elasticity is equal to -3. Thus a firm using a 50 percent markup and wishing to maximize profits must ponder the question of whether or not its price elasticity of demand is equal to or close to the value -3. (That is, it should ask "would quantity demanded change by 30 percent if price were changed by 10 percent?") If the implied price elasticity seems *too high*, given management's knowledge of the market conditions, the markup percentage is probably *too low*, given the inverse relationship between the price elasticity and the profit-maximizing markup percentage. Thus the firm might try a higher markup and observe its impact on profit (or the contribution to profit generated by this particular product).

----

[10]The range of acceptable markups will be wider or narrower depending on the magnitude of search costs and the shape of the firm's profit curve. The greater the search costs and the flatter the profit curve, the wider will be the range of acceptable markups. The less elastic is demand in the vicinity of the profit-maximizing price or the lower is the firm's marginal and average variable cost, the flatter will be the profit curve. (You can easily verify this relationship graphically.) Thus firms with relatively elastic demand (many substitutes or a price that is high relative to incomes) will have a narrower range of acceptable markups, *ceteris paribus*.

Note: A simple formula to find what price elasticity *should* be for the current markup rate to be profit maximizing can be derived as follows. We know from equation (10-10) that the profit-maximizing markup rate is $-1/(\epsilon + 1)$. The markup rate is also measured by the difference between price and average variable cost over the average variable cost. Thus,

$$\frac{P - \text{AVC}}{\text{AVC}} = \frac{-1}{\epsilon + 1} \tag{10-11}$$

Solving for ϵ we find

$$\epsilon = \frac{-\text{AVC}}{P - \text{AVC}} - 1 \tag{10-12}$$

Example: Bonne Nuit sleeping pills are sold to retailers for $1.15 per packet, approximately 30 percent over the wholesaler's average variable cost, which is constant at $0.88 per packet. What must price elasticity be if this contribution margin represents the profit-maximizing markup? Substituting in equation (10-12), we find

$$\epsilon = \frac{-0.88}{1.15 - 0.88} - 1$$

$$= \frac{-0.88}{0.27} - 1$$

$$= -3.26 - 1$$

$$= -4.26$$

Thus, price elasticity must be something close to -4.26 if the 30 percent markup is profit maximizing. The manufacturer must now consider whether or not, for example, a 10 percent price decrease *would* expand sales by 42.6 percent. If even the most optimistic estimate is that sales would increase by only 20 percent, the markup is too low and the firm might cautiously adjust its price upward to determine the impact on profits.

Note: If the firm does adjust its price up or down as a result of its view that the markup and the price elasticity are out of alignment, it will be able to generate information on the slope of its demand curve, as long as *ceteris paribus* holds. Given this estimated slope term, it can quickly solve for the intercept term in the expression for its demand curve and subsequently derive an expression for its marginal revenue curve. Given its knowledge of average variable costs (or marginal costs if AVC is not constant), it can solve for the profit-maximizing price, the sales-maximizing price, or the limit price and adjust its markup percentage to reflect the ratio $(P - \text{AVC})/\text{AVC}$ given by the optimal price. It can then use that markup percentage in subsequent periods. As we shall see, the optimal markup percentage will remain optimal despite shifts in the demand curve and under conditions of inflation, given certain conditions. In any case, as we saw previously, the markup has only to stay within the range of *acceptable* markup rates in future periods.

Rather than change price experimentally, the firm might commission a study to estimate the price elasticity of demand around its present price. Such a study will generate information that will allow the firm to ascertain the profit-maximizing price, or the sales-maximizing price, or the limit price, as in the preceding discussion. The firm should undertake search expenditures whenever management expects the value of the information (in terms of the additional contribution generated) to more than cover the search costs of generating the information. It would seem prudent, given human fallibility, to incur these search costs *periodically*, in any case, to ensure that the firm's price does in fact best serve the firm's objective function.[11]

Markup Pricing and Iso-elastic Demand Shifts

We can show that if the firm has selected a markup rate which is profit-maximizing, it may simply maintain that markup rate despite considerable shifts in its demand curve, and the price will continue to best serve the firm's objective. Consider Figure 10-3, in which we show an initial demand situation represented by the demand curve D and marginal revenue curve MR. Given MC = AVC, the profit-maximizing price is P, implying a markup rate of about 70 percent over AVC, and the profit-maximizing output level is Q_0 units. Suppose that the quantity demanded increases by the *same percentage* at every price level—in Figure 10-3 a 40 percent increase in quantity demanded at each price level is indicated by the shift of the demand curve to D'. This is called an *iso-elastic shift* of the demand curve since it maintains the price elasticity of demand at each price level at the same value as it was before the shift. For example, the price elasticity at points A and B is the same; $\epsilon = -2.4$ at each point.

Thus the profit-maximizing price P remains the profit-maximizing price despite the shift of the demand curve from D to D'. Thus, the 70 percent markup can be applied to AVC despite shifts in the demand curve, as long as these shifts are iso-elastic and MC remains constant. Iso-elastic shifts in the demand curve are an intuitively

---

[11]Surprisingly, perhaps, a firm wishing to maximize sales subject to the attainment of a minimum profit target should *not* periodically incur search costs. To see this, note that search costs would reduce profit below the minimum level and thus place the managers' jobs in jeopardy. Managers would then have to raise the price level to restore profit to the target level. This price increase would reduce sales and thus be directly contrary to the firm's objective. Such a firm is better off lowering price to increase sales until the profit objective is just attained, and need not know any more about its demand curve. Note also that the sales maximizer's price will be lower than the profit maximizer's price, presuming that the target profit is less than the maximum attainable profit. For the same cost structure this statement implies that the sales maximizer will always use a lower percentage markup. This procedure is consistent with the sales maximizer's underlying objective (to maximize long-term profits, or the EPV of net worth) because demand elasticities are invariably higher in the long term than in the short run, since buyers have more time to adjust their purchases and their habits.

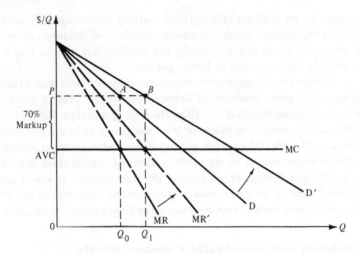

FIGURE 10-3. Constant Markup Given Iso-elastic Shifts of the Demand Curve

appealing notion and may well approximate the actual shifts that firms experience. In any case, we have seen that if the firm starts from, or periodically adjusts price to, the "correct" price (in terms of its objective function and given full information), it can afford to slip away from the "correct" price to a degree before it would be better to undertake search and reestablish the correct price. Thus, even, if demand shifts are *not* iso-elastic, the markup can be expected to remain within the optimal range over some range of demand variations at the existing price level.

Markup Pricing under Inflationary Conditions

A markup-pricing policy applied to increasing levels of variable costs per unit will lead to a commensurate increase in the price level. In Table 10-2 we show a situation where average variable costs have increased over a one-year period by 10 percent. The 40 percent markup, when applied to that cost base at the beginning of the year, resulted in a price of $8.40. The 40 percent markup applied to the higher average variable cost figure at the year's end results in a 10 percent increase also in the size of the markup, or the contribution margin. Since both components of price have increased by 10 percent, it is not surprising that price itself has also increased by 10 percent.

TABLE 10-2. Markup Pricing with Inflation

	Jan. 1 ($)	Dec. 31 ($)	Change (%)
Average variable costs	6.00	6.60	10
40% markup	2.40	2.64	10
Price	8.40	9.24	10

Thus markup pricing under conditions of inflation tends to pass the cost increase along to the consumer of the product. You will notice, however, that the increase in average variable costs was $0.60, while the increase in the price amounted to $0.84. The difference arises, of course, because the absolute amount of the contribution has risen by $0.24. Since this contribution has risen by 10 percent and the cost level has also increased by 10 percent, the contribution at the end of the period of inflation has the same purchasing power as the contribution had at the beginning of the period of inflation: It will now take $2.64 to purchase what was previously purchasable for $2.40. Thus markup pricing, as well as passing the cost increase along to the consumer of the product, also serves to maintain the purchasing power (or real value) of the firm's contribution to overheads and profits.

Note: If during this regime of inflation buyers' incomes have also gone up by 10 percent, this product will still require the same proportion of their incomes as it did before the inflation. Thus the 10 percent change in the price level is not a *real* price change in the sense that it does not cause consumers' purchasing power to be reduced, but it is a simple monetary price change resulting from the depreciation of the monetary unit. Such a price increase should not be regarded by purchasers as causing the product to become more expensive in terms of their incomes, and hence their quantity demanded should remain constant following the monetary price increase.

This situation is illustrated in Figure 10-4. Note that the demand curve has shifted vertically by a constant percentage, 10 percent in this case. This shift reflects

FIGURE 10-4. Constant Markup Given Inflationary Shifts of the Cost and Demand Curves

each consumer's willingness to pay 10 percent more for the *same* quantity demanded as before, given that consumer incomes have gone up by 10 percent. Thus the vertical intercept of the demand curve shifts up by 10 percent, while the horizontal intercept remains unchanged, so that at each quantity level, price is, therefore, 10 percent higher than before. Note that the new marginal revenue curve MR′ cuts the new marginal cost curve at the *same* output level Q_0. At the new price level, $9.24, consumers buy the same quantity as before, since both their incomes and the price have risen by the same proportion.

Note: The above analysis was conducted entirely in *nominal-dollar* terms. In *real-dollar* terms, or constant purchasing-power terms, neither the cost curve nor the demand curve has shifted. In Figure 10–5 we show two vertical scales on the graph—the inner scale is in constant-dollar terms, showing the initial price at $8.40 when AVC = $6.00. The outer scale is in nominal, or monetary, terms, reflecting the nominal cost and price levels after the inflationary period. In effect, the purchasing power of the dollar, for both the firm and its customers, has shrunk by 10 percent; it now takes 10 percent more in nominal dollars to purchase what one could before the inflationary period. Deflating the nominal price and costs by 10 percent, we find that in real terms there has been no change in price or quantity demanded.

To the extent that consumers' incomes rise *less rapidly* than the firm's average variable costs in nominal-dollar terms, use of a constant-markup rate will cause the price to rise above the profit-maximizing level. Being cognizant of this danger, the firm should consider whether or not its consumers' incomes have risen by the same

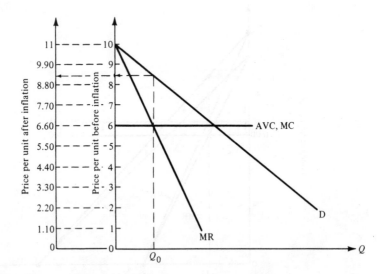

FIGURE 10–5.   Constant Purchasing Power Analysis of Price and Cost Changes under Inflationary Conditions

proportion as the firm's costs. If not, the firm should *reduce* its markup rate commensurately. Conversely, if by some chance its consumers' incomes have risen by a higher proportion than its costs, the firm may *raise* its markup rate commensurately.

Markup Pricing as a Coordinating Device

We know that a crucial element in the oligopolist's decision-making process is the decision maker's conjecture whether or not rival firms are likely to adjust prices at the same time and by similar magnitudes. To the extent that price changes are coordinated among firms, the market shares are likely to remain stable. On the other hand, if one firm raises price and rival firms do not, we expect that firm to suffer an elastic demand response and subsequently lose some part of its market share. Similarly, if all firms were to raise prices, yet one firm raised price by a significantly larger amount, that firm would be expected to lose part of its market share.

The existence of an established markup-pricing policy in a particular industry acts as a coordinating device when price changes become necessary. All firms are likely to be faced by similar changes in their cost structure, since they purchase labor and raw materials in the same or in similar markets, and if they each apply the same markup percentage to these average variable costs, their prices will rise by a similar percentage. Hence the *relative* prices of the firms will remain undisturbed at the new general level of prices. Markup-pricing policy and a common markup percentage allow a common and predictable strategy for price increases. Under conditions of conscious parallelism, each firm will expect that other firms will raise their prices to the extent of the familiar markup proportion on the change in unit costs. Thus, when a cost component changes, the firm may confidently adjust its price upward in the expectation that all rival firms will be doing likewise. An established markup-pricing procedure within an industry thus allows the decision maker to predict with a high degree of certainty the responses of rival firms to change in cost conditions.

Note: The size of the markup that will maximize profits, maximize sales subject to a profit constraint, or limit the entry of new firms will be chosen by the price leader or by the collective consensus of firms operating under conditions of conscious parallelism. Once a level of the markup is found that seems to achieve these objectives, this markup percentage will become institutionalized in the industry and be the standard percentage applied by the firms, as long as the objective functions and general market conditions do not change significantly.

This is not to imply that competing firms must necessarily mark up their average variable costs by exactly the same percentage figure. We shall see in the following section that the industry standard markup acts as a point of reference which allows the firm to bring its price into the correct "ball park," but in many cases a further price adjustment, or deviation from the standard industry markup percentage, may be desirable. Let us now turn to an examination of pricing in the context of established market situations.

10.3 PRICING IN ESTABLISHED MARKETS

In established product markets the general price level may be regarded as historically determined, in the sense that it has gravitated to the current level over a prolonged period of time and to the general satisfaction or acquiescence of the firms involved. We might therefore claim, by backward induction, that the general price level prevailing in established markets is the level that serves the objective of the price leaders or of the firms in general. In established markets we would expect the general price level to be revised upward or downward whenever deemed desirable by the price leader or by the firms in general, and this price revision may be achieved by each firm individually applying its usual markup to the new level of direct cost.

The essence of the pricing decision in established markets is therefore not so much to choose the general level of price as it is to choose the specific level of price relative to the prices of one's competitors. The price ball park is established; the firm must choose its price positioning within that ball park.

Price Positioning

The price of a product relative to the prices of its competing products should presumably be set higher or lower depending upon the presence or absence of desirable attributes perceived in that product by consumers in general.

Example: In the market for personal computers there are a variety of computers, and variations of each computer, available at a variety of prices. Those with more memory, two disk drives rather than one, and a better reputation for quality and service, command above-average prices, or a price "premium" over the average price. Conversely, those with less memory, and the absence of other desirable features, command below-average prices, or a "discount" from the average price level. The price premium, or price discount, that a particular firm may add to or subtract from the general, or average, price level will depend upon the market's appreciation of the value of the total package of attributes involved in that firm's product relative to the offerings and prices of all competitive products.

How might we determine the value of specific product attributes or the value of a total package of attributes embodied in that product? Market research techniques must be applied to find the value placed upon the presence of certain attributes or groups of attributes in a particular product. If a large sample of consumers were canvassed, their consensus regarding the extra amount they would be prepared to pay for certain features could be used as a guide for pricing variants or new models of an established product.

The maximum amount that a buyer will pay for a product is known as that buyer's "reservation price." Similarly a buyer will have reservation prices for attributes perceived to be supplied by the product. The buyer will buy the product only if the reservation price is greater than the seller's asking price. If an attribute may or may not be included in the product, such as a "luxury package" in an automobile, the buyer will only buy that attribute along with the basic product if his or her reservation price for that attribute exceeds the seller's asking price for that attribute. Buyers will be reluctant to divulge their reservation prices, since sellers would use this information to set the price just at or below the buyer's reservation price, and thus leave the consumer with little or no consumer surplus. (Consumer surplus is the difference between what the consumer had to pay for a product—the seller's asking price—and the maximum he or she would have been willing to pay rather than go without—the buyer's reservation price.)

Carefully conducted market research could supply the firm with the reservation prices (of a sample of buyers surveyed) for a particular product and for each attribute that may or may not be included in the product. Putting these in descending order essentially graphs out the sample's demand curve for that product or the attribute in question. Generalizing this information to the market as a whole, a market demand curve and associated marginal revenue curve could be derived. A profit-maximizing firm would then have a simple pricing decision—namely, price the product or the attribute such that the marginal revenue equals the marginal cost of production. An oligopolist must consider the probable reactions of its rivals if the price indicated by this analysis was significantly above or below the prices of the rivals' versions of this product or the attribute in question.

Example: One version of a particular brand of personal computer might contain 256K bytes of memory, and another might contain twice that amount. If the computers are otherwise the same, what is the appropriate price premium for the computer with the larger memory? The firm could establish the short-run profit-maximizing price or the long-term profit-maximizing price (proxied by the sales-maximizing price, for example), given information regarding the buyers' demand curve for the extra 256K bytes of memory and given its own cost data. Alternatively, rather than incur the search costs, the firm might prefer to simply mark up its average variable cost of purchasing and installing the extra 256K memory chip to arrive at the price premium for the 512K model. Should the markup rate be relatively high or low? Ask yourself whether price elasticity is likely to be relatively high or low. In the case where a prospective buyer is considering either the 256K model or the 512K model, we would probably expect relatively elastic demand for the extra 256K, and thus a relatively low markup. But if the buyer already owns a 256K computer and wants an extra 256K-byte chip installed, we would expect relatively inelastic demand and thus a relatively high markup rate for retrofitting the extra 256K. In both cases an oligopolistic seller will wish to be sure that its price premium for the computer with extra 256K, and its price for retrofitting the extra 256K, is not too far different from the prices of its rivals, other things being equal.

In general, the firm will attempt to price its product such that its position in the price range is reflective of its position in the quality range, where the word "quality" is used broadly to mean the presence of desirable attributes. Thus a product with more desirable attributes will command a higher price than one that is lacking some of the attributes desired by some buyers. Buyers will buy the product that gives them the

Pricing Analysis and Decisions

most consumer surplus for the collection of attributes that they want, namely, the product with the lowest asking price, other things being equal. Since buyers have different preferences, we should expect to see the simultaneous offering of a wide range of "quality" at a similarly wide range of prices. In fact we observe this structure in most oligopoly markets.

Example: In the market for video cassette recorders (VCRs) one can find several basic models (two video heads, twelve or fourteen preset channels, and one or two preselected programs) selling for about $250 at the time of this writing. As additional features are added, the competitive price for the product increases. A wireless remote control commands a premium over the wired type. The next step up is additional channels, and four programs over a two-week period, for which additional premiums are charged. Two more video heads with special-effects capabilities, stereo capability, and a quartz tuner each add another premium, and so on. At each "quality" level there are typically a dozen or more competing brands, and the prices tend to be similar. Each firm must consider the prices of rivals for the similar package of attributes, because buyers are aware of the availability of competing brands.

A more complicated price positioning decision must be made when the firm offers several different models of their product in a market where the "quality" demands of buyers differ. In the markets for automobiles, computers, VCRs, and so on, we find the firms each offering a "product line"—a series of related products. Some of these products are substitutes for each other, being located at different points along the "quality" spectrum, such as small cars and large cars. Other products in the product line are complementary to each other, such as a particular car and spare parts for that car. We turn now to product-line pricing.

Product-Line Price Strategy

In perhaps the majority of cases the decision maker is not simply concerned with the price of one product, but with the prices of a line of related substitute and complementary products produced or sold by that firm. Price differentials between and among these products should reflect their place in the overall product line, and the spacing of price levels should be adjusted so that the firm's objective function is maximized.[12]

The reconciliation of the markup-pricing and marginalist-pricing procedures indicates that products with a lower price elasticity should be expected to contribute a greater relative amount to overheads and profits than those with a higher price elasticity. Keeping in mind that higher price elasticities result from a product's having a variety of substitutes or being relatively expensive, we would thus expect the decision maker to consider each product in the light of its absolute cost to consumers and the

[12]See Michael Mussa and Sherwin Rosen, "Monopoly and Product Quality," *Journal of Economic Theory*, 18 (1978), pp. 301–17; and S. Oren, S. Smith, and R. Wilson, "Pricing a Product Line," *Journal of Business*, 57 (January 1984), pp. S73–S99.

availability of substitutes both within and outside that decision maker's particular price line before deciding on the appropriate markup over average variable costs.[13]

This relatively simple approach—choosing the markup rate with respect to the estimated price elasticity of demand—implicitly assumes that the demand for each of the items in the product line is *independent* of the demand for any of the other items in the product line. But items that are substitutes or complements have *dependent* demand functions. Recall from Chapter 4 that an increase in the price of one product will cause a shift outward of the demand curves for its substitutes and a simultaneous shift inward of the demand curves for its complements. In the product line case, the firm must take account of these demand interdependencies. Raising the price of one product, for example, will increase the sales of the next-higher-quality substitute, and also of the next-lower-quality substitute, but reduce the sales of the product itself and of its complements in the product line. Alternatively, improving the consumer's perception, or image, of one product in the line, as well as increasing the sales of that product, may also have positive spillover effects for sales of all other products carrying the firm's brand name.

The total contribution to overheads and profits will be maximized when the contribution from each item in the product line is chosen with respect to both its place and function in that product line and the extent of competition it faces on the market. Where products in the line are complementary goods, such as cameras, attachments, films, and projecting equipment, it may be desirable to price the basic item (cameras) with a relatively low markup in order to achieve broad penetration of the market. If the complementary products must be purchased from the same manufacturer (for example, special film cartridges), sales of these items in the future will be enhanced by greater sales of the basic item now. In some cases, total contribution from the product line may be maximized by using the basic item as a "loss leader," or promotional item, pricing it at a level below that which would be indicated by the short-term price elasticity considerations.[14]

Where two or more products in the line are substitutes, the price of the "bottom-of-the-line" product must be chosen quite carefully. Potential customers may be attracted to the store by price information and once in the store may be convinced of the virtues of more expensive products in the line. Consequently, it may enhance total contribution to price the bottom-of-the-line product somewhat lower than would be suggested by price elasticity considerations. Automobile manufacturers might be expected to price their vehicles on this basis, since potential customers are likely to be

[13]If the search costs involved in determining the value of price elasticities are relatively high, it may in fact be contribution maximizing to apply a common markup percentage to all products in a product line, as long as the revenue forgone is less than the search cost not expended. More likely, the manager will have some idea of the relative elasticities and vary the markups on that basis.

[14]"Loss leader" is generally used to mean pricing one item below full costs in order to attract customers into the store, where they will (or the store hopes they will) also buy other items at the regular prices. It is being used here in the sense of attracting a customer to the product line with (it is hoped) subsequent sales of related items at the regular prices.

attracted by relatively low advertised prices on items that are expensive in absolute terms. Once in the showroom the customer may be convinced by a salesperson to purchase a more luxurious version or a larger model (with higher contribution margins) or to "dress up" the basic vehicle with a number of higher-markup options and accessories. For obvious reasons, this type of pricing and personal selling strategy has been called "trading up."

In a line of substitutes the "bottom-of-the-line," or "entry-level," product is priced first, with an eye to the prices of rivals' similar products. If its quality is marginally better, or inferior, when compared to rivals' products at that area in quality space, it may be priced a little higher, or a little lower, than those products. This simple price positioning would then be modified to some extent if the firm takes into account the demand interdependencies. Suppose the firm wishes to promote an image of offering better value to consumers than do rival firms. It might therefore set the price below rivals' prices for the similar item, expecting this "better-value" image to be associated with its brand name and therefore shift outward the demand curves for all other products in the line, leading to increased sales for these products as well.

Another demand interdependency occurs when repeat purchases are a factor. Consumer "loyalty," the propensity of a buyer to be a repeat purchaser, is developed following the buyer's satisfactory experience with the seller's products on earlier occasions. A first-time buyer is valued, not just for the present purchase, but also for the expected value of future contributions following repeat purchases that will follow (with some probability) if the buyer in fact makes the first purchase. In cases where the seller expects the buyer to move up the product line to higher quality (more expensive) products in the future, there is an incentive to price the "entry-level" product using a lower markup than would be applied to products higher in the product line. Automobile dealers tend to follow this pattern, expecting favorable experience with their smaller (lower markup) cars to induce consumers to buy their larger (higher markup) cars in the future.

After the "lowest-quality" product in the line is priced, the next product in the line is then priced with a view to the value of the additional attributes that it contains when compared to the entry-level product, again with an eye to the prices of rivals' products at approximately the same quality level. This process continues as we move up the product line. We might expect higher markup percentages as we move up the product line, since the buyers of these items will typically have higher incomes, and may also derive more utility from quality, and thus their reservation prices will be higher, as compared with the buyers of the lower quality products. Throughout the product line, the firm will reduce the price of a particular item if it expects this to have a positive net effect on profit because of the demand interdependencies perceived to exist.

At the top of the line of substitutes we have the firm's "flagship" item, and it might be priced with yet another consideration in mind as well. Demand for this product is probably quite limited, because of its relatively high price, and thus exclusivity enters as a relevant attribute in the buyer's decision. Some buyers will pay heavily for exclusivity, or for "scarcity value," other things being equal. Antiques exemplify this phenomenon, of course, but so do limited production runs of collectors' items, and exotic automobiles like the Rolls Royce Camargue.

In pricing a line of substitutes, the firm can shift demand uphill (to the next-higher-quality substitute) or downhill (to the next-lower-quality substitute) by varying the price of any product. It can do this by raising or lowering the price of that product. Some buyers will then consider the next-higher-quality substitute to be the better deal and others will consider the next-lower-quality to be the better deal. (Buyers will select the substitute that gives them the higher consumer surplus, or the greatest difference between their reservation price and the seller's asking price.) In the short run the seller might find that quantity demanded for a particular item exceeds the supply available, or the firm's full capacity output rate, while for the adjacent levels of quality the firm has excess supply or production capacity. In this case it will increase profit to shift demand away from the more heavily demanded product toward the substitutes for which demand is lower, relative to supply or production capacity.[15]

Demand shifting up or down the product line may also be practiced in order to meet externally imposed constraints. For example, the automobile manufacturers must comply with the CAFE (corporate average fuel economy) requirement set by the EPA (Environmental Protection Agency). Larger and more powerful cars tend to consume more gas per mile than do smaller and less powerful cars in the firms' product lines. In order to meet the CAFE requirements, the firm may have to reduce the prices of its more economical models or increase the prices of its less economical models.

Example: In January 1985, Chrysler Corporation and Ford Motor Company announced increased prices for selected cars and light truck models, following the lead of General Motors, which had earlier announced its price increases. Chrysler's price hikes applied to its midsize and larger cars, as well as its "hot-selling" minivans and its light trucks. The boom in light truck sales, and the continued strong demand for larger automobiles, was also behind the price increases for these by Ford and General Motors. But prices were not increased for compact trucks, such as Ford's Ranger and GM's S-10 truck. A Ford spokesman said that stiff competition (mainly from imports) was the reason for holding the line on compact truck prices. Small-car prices were expected to hold steady because of the expected relaxation of the quota on imported Japanese cars. The Ford spokesman said options for larger engines and heavier trans-

---

[15]A similar demand-shifting strategy is known as *peak-load pricing*, whereby higher prices are set for a product during periods when the demand is strongest, and prices are reduced at "off-peak" times. Peak-load pricing is practiced by the airlines, the telephone companies, and electricity companies in some areas. In these cases the firm's product at one point in time is a substitute for itself at another point in time. Consumers who are able to defer consumption until the off-peak prices come into effect may receive more consumer surplus by doing so. Thus the firm utilizes its limited production capacity during the peak periods by supplying only those who cannot wait, or prefer not to wait, for the product or service. In effect the firm discriminates against those buyers for whom the demand is more urgent. We called this process "second-degree" price discrimination in Appendix 9A.

missions had higher than average increases, to encourage the purchase of more fuel-efficient equipment.[16]

This example indicates several things. First, General Motors is the acknowledged price leader in this market, largely because of its lower cost structure. Second, the increased demand for larger cars, minivans, and light trucks allowed the firms to jointly raise prices on these items in their product lines, while the competition from imports militated against price increases on smaller cars and compact trucks. Third, the price changes for each item in their product lines were made with an eye to rivals' prices of their similar items. Finally, an important consideration underlying the adjustments to the firms' prices was the CAFE requirement. Raising prices on less economical cars would induce some buyers, at the margin, to substitute in favor of a more economical automobile, and subsequently enable the firms to meet the CAFE requirement.

Pricing to Infer Quality

It is often claimed that pricing a product higher will make the consumer perceive it as a higher-quality item and cause sales and profits to be greater than if the product were priced at a lower level.[17] Given our knowledge of consumer behavior theory, we can think of two arguments to support this assertion.

First, if the consumer has no other means of judging quality of the product, price will be the consumer's best indicator of quality, *a priori*. Purchase of the product and subsequent experience with the product should provide other indications of quality which the consumer can use in subsequent purchase decisions. But the absence of *all* other means of estimating quality implies a situation in which the consumer cannot tell by looking, feeling, or shaking the product, or it implies a situation in which there are no consumer reports, comparative tests, word-of-mouth recommendations (or warnings), or any other information available to the consumer. Certainly, there are products for which it is difficult to judge the quality without actually using them.

Example: If your car breaks down, you could buy replacement parts made by a different manufacturer rather than by the original equipment manufacturer (OEM). The OEM parts are usually more expensive and the inference is that they are of higher quality. Objective comparison tests may show that there is no difference or even that the OEM parts are inferior to some of the cheaper alternatives. Other examples include electronic air purifiers, burglar alarms, stereo systems, brand-name aspirin, and so on.

[16]See Doron P. Levin, "Chrysler, Ford Increase Prices on Some Lines," *Wall Street Journal*, January 7, 1985, p. 5; and Amal Nag, "Auto Makers are Quietly Raising Prices Higher Than First Promised," *Wall Street Journal*, January 8, 1985, p. 39.

[17]For a recent paper on this subject and a comprehensive bibliography, see David R. Lambert, "Price as a Quality Signal: The Tip of the Iceberg," *Economic Inquiry*, 18 (January 1980), pp. 144–50.

Most of these examples beg the question, "Why doesn't the consumer do some investigating and find out more information about the quality of the product?" The consumer could shop around, read *Consumer Reports*, ask people who own or use the product, and so on. This brings us to the second argument for using price as an indicator of quality.

Second, if the search costs necessary to ascertain the quality of the product are expected to exceed the consumer's notional value of the information derived, the consumer would rationally use price as an indicator of quality rather than incur those search costs. Note that search costs include time and money; it may take you several hours to find the information, plus the cost of buying magazines, such as *Consumer Reports, Road and Track, Stereo Review*, or whichever magazine has published a comparison test on the item. Rather than spend the equivalent of $20 searching, the consumer may simply pay the extra few dollars for the more expensive item and hope to get the quality he or she seeks. Notice that it is the price difference between the higher-priced item and the lower-priced item (which are under consideration) that determines the amount of search activity the consumer should conduct. Obviously, one should search for more information when buying an automobile or a stereo system than when buying a smoke detector or barbeque fuel or other relatively low-cost items which are difficult to rank qualitatively.

This observation leads us to a consideration of the types of products for which the consumer might typically make a price-quality association. Highly technical items are an obvious candidate, since most of us don't understand why they work. Low-cost items that require high search costs to ascertain quality are another contender. Products for which quality is imperative are another.

Example: Medicines to correct ailments are often available as brand-name drugs or as generic drugs. Many people choose the higher-priced item, the brand-name drug, over the cheaper but chemically equivalent generic drug, presumably because they feel that their health is imperative and that any doubt they feel about the equivalence of the generics is easily erased by the expenditure of a few more cents or dollars. Cosmetic items to restore facial beauty, to stop the balding process, and to reverse other inevitable consequences of aging are seen as quality-imperative to many of the consumers of these items. When one's self-esteem and ego is at stake, the marketing people do not expect the consumer to respond with caution and cost-consciousness.

New products are ideal candidates for the price-quality association, as long as price is the only real indicator of quality, simply because there will be no prior information for consumers even if they do conduct search. Rather than wait until information accumulates, consumers may prefer to pay the premium price now and avoid the search costs of waiting. We examine new-product pricing in the next chapter.

Finally, people who pay triple the price for "designer" jeans and sport shirts are doubtless getting superior quality and fit as compared to the mass-market jeans and shirts available at one-third the price. But *three* times the quality? More likely, we are witnessing the *Veblen effect*, named after the classical economist Thorstein Veblen.[18]

■ **Definition:**   The *Veblen effect* is defined as the tendency of some consumers to purchase more of an item when its price is higher because of the demonstration effect such a purchase has on others (namely, that the purchaser is sufficiently wealthy, exhibits good taste, and so on). This is also known as *conspicuous consumption*, since consumers may want to become conspicuous by their consumption of the more expensive, higher-quality product. It may alternatively be argued that the devotees of designer jeans, shirts, and other designer clothing simply feel that quality is imperative for their self-esteem, image, and lifestyle and that the extra cost is simply an insurance premium to make sure they get it.

Pricing Product Bundles

Product bundling is the practice of selling two or more products together as a package deal for a single price. A series of examples will indicate how widespread product bundling is. Computer software is often bundled with the hardware and sold as a package deal. Restaurants offer "fixed menus" which include soup, main course, dessert, and coffee for a single price. Automobiles offer luxury or sports packages that must be sold in conjunction with the basic vehicle. Retailers offer free parking if you buy something at their store. Gas stations offer free games when you buy gas. Professional sports teams and symphony orchestras offer season tickets that bundle together a variety of events for a single price.[19]

The theory of pricing product bundles has been examined by Stigler, Adams and Yellen, and Schmalensee.[20] Put simply, the firm has a profit incentive to bundle products together when doing so allows the extraction of a greater degree of consumer surplus from the potential customers. In general, it is optimal to offer the products both separately and in the bundle, since some consumers will only want one of the products and would not be willing to pay the bundle price. Offering both the bundle and the separate products is known as "mixed" bundling, as opposed to "pure" bundling, where the products are only available as a package deal.

Consumer surplus is measured in dollars by the excess of the consumer's reservation price over the actual price paid for an item. If the seller raises the price by a

---

[18]See H. Leibenstein, "Bandwagon, Snob, and Veblen Effects in the Theory of Consumer Demand," *Quarterly Journal of Economics*, May 1950, pp. 183-207.

[19]Note that there will be implications for product-line pricing here, since the bundle of goods may be a substitute for a product, or another bundle of products, in the firm's product line.

[20]George, Stigler, "United States vs. Loew's Inc.: A Note on Block Booking," *Supreme Court Review*, 1963, pp. 153-157; William J. Adams and Janet L. Yellen, "Commodity Bundling and the Burden of Monopoly," *Quarterly Journal of Economics*, 90 (May 1976), pp. 475-98; Richard Schmalensee, "Commodity Bundling by Single-Product Monopolies," *Journal of Law and Business*, 25 (April 1982), pp. 67-71.

dollar, but the price remains less than or equal to the buyer's reservation price, the buyer will still buy the product but will receive one dollar less in consumer surplus. Instead, the extra dollar will be added to the producer's surplus, also known as profit. If the firm could treat each buyer separately, it would attempt to charge each buyer his or her reservation price, thus completely exhausting consumer surplus and maximizing producer surplus.[21]

In practice the seller will be unable to determine each buyer's reservation price and will simply assume that buyers have a range of reservation prices, such that there is a negatively sloping demand curve for both the products separately and collectively (the bundle). The seller will typically increase profit (over that available from pricing the products separately) by raising the prices of each product *if sold separately* and offering the bundle as a package deal at a price which is less than the sum of the prices of the components of the bundle. Thus buyers who only want one, or some subset, of the products in the bundle must pay more than they otherwise would have, and other buyers who would not have purchased all the products separately end up buying the bundle because it is the cheapest way to get the products that they do want. Raising the price of individual products will cause the firm to lose some sales, but the gain in sales resulting from the availability of the bundle typically outweighs that loss, such that the overall sales and profit are higher than if the products were priced separately.[22]

Quantity Discounts.   The theory of bundling explains why some firms offer a given product in several different sizes (such as small, medium, large, and jumbo bottles of Coke), and why some consumers buy only the small size and others pay more to buy larger sizes (but at a reduced price per unit, such as per ounce). The larger sizes can be viewed as bundles, or multiples, of the smallest size of the same product, and the buyer is given a discount for purchasing in quantity. Similarly, when a product is priced at, say, $3 each *or two for $5*, the buyer is essentially getting a discount on the second unit of the product if he or she chooses to buy that additional unit.

Why are some people induced to buy in quantity while others are not? A person will demand the extra units of the product bundled together in the larger size if the incremental cost to the consumer is less than the consumer's reservation price for those extra units.

---

[21]In Appendix 9A we referred to this practice as first-degree price discrimination. In fact, product bundling is a technique by which the seller can practice price discrimination, since it divides potential buyers into groups based on their willingness to buy one or other of the products separately, or the bundle of products, and allows the seller to discriminate against those willing to buy only one or a subset of the products.

[22]Adams and Yellen, and Schmalensee, cited in footnote 20, determine the precise conditions under which mixed bundling will be a more profitable strategy than either pure bundling or individual prices only. The distribution of customers' reservation prices is critical, as is the relationship of marginal costs to the prices chosen. They conclude that mixed bundling is a more profitable pricing strategy under a wide variety of circumstances.

Example: A consumer might be willing to pay a maximum of $1 for a 10 ounce bottle of cola, if she was very thirsty. The store price is, let us say, 70 cents. Since the asking price is less than the buyer's reservation price, the seller will make the sale. But suppose the seller also has a 20 ounce bottle of the same cola for $1.15. Will the consumer buy that one instead? Suppose that her reservation price on the 20 ounce size is $1.50, indicating she expects 50 cents worth of extra utility from the additional 10 ounces. Since the additional 10 ounces will cost her only 45 cents more, she will buy the larger size. Finally, suppose the store also has a 30 ounce size, priced at $1.75. The consumer's reservation price for the 30 ounce size is, say, $1.70, indicating her willingness to pay only another 20 cents for the additional 10 ounces. Since the additional quantity would cost her 60 cents, however, she chooses the 20 ounce size. The seller collects $1.15 from this customer, compared to only 70 cents that would have been collected if the cola had been price uniformly per ounce regardless of bottle size. Assuming that the seller's marginal cost of the extra 10 ounces is always less than the price premium attached to the larger sizes, the seller will have increased both sales and profit. Of course, more thirsty customers, or someone buying the family groceries, is likely to buy the 30 ounce size, because their reservation prices are more likely to exceed the price asked.

In summary, the firm should consider offering its products in bundles as well as separately, because bundling may be expected to increase the firm's profits. Bundling includes the packaging together of different products, the offering of the same product in different-sized containers, and the offering of quantity discounts for multiple units of the same product. Given the availability of bundles, the firm would then consider raising the prices of some or all of the individual products, of the smaller sizes, or of the single units, in order to extract more consumer surplus from those who want only part of the bundle. In practice, without full information on the distribution of consumers' reservation prices, the firm would need to conduct market research to estimate this distribution, or, if the search costs of that appear to be prohibitive, the firm would experiment by introducing product bundles and by changing the prices of individual units. If profit increases as a result of these changes, the firm may wish to fine-tune its pricing structure further until maximum profits appear to be attained.

In oligopoly markets a firm may be forced into bundling as a pricing strategy by the actions of its rivals. If the rivals offer product bundles, they will be capturing those consumers with relatively high reservation prices on the additional units included in the bundle, and the firm may feel it is necessary to seek its share of these customers. Note, however, that the existence of rivals constrains the oligopolist, to some degree, if it attempts to raise the prices of its separate products, its smaller sizes, or its single units. With the availability of substitutes, and consumer awareness of those substitutes, these price increases will meet a relatively elastic demand response. Thus the greater is the degree of similarity between the rivals' products, and the easier it is for consumers to evaluate the attributes of the products in the market, the less profitable one would expect product bundling to be.

Promotional Pricing

Promotional pricing, also known as ".dealing," involves offering the consumer a temporary price reduction by placing the product "on sale" for a specified period. Several reasons for this practice are suggested. First, the firm may have excess inventories and wish to reduce its inventory costs. Second, the firm's supplier may have provided the goods at a discount from the usual wholesale price on condition that a promotional sale be held, in an attempt to broaden the producer's share of the final market. Third, a manufacturer wishing to expand its distributional network may offer an introductory discount to a retailer to induce the latter to handle the product. Fourth, the firm may reduce prices temporarily to avoid loss of market share when other firms have placed their products on sale or undertaken major advertising campaigns. Fifth, the firm may place some products on sale as "loss leaders" to attract buyers to the seller, with subsequent increases in the demand for other items. Finally, for many firms promotional pricing is simply part of their promotional strategy designed to keep customers aware of the seller's existence and the seller's commitment to low prices.

There may be some disadvantages associated with promotional pricing, from the firm's viewpoint, and these may include the following. First, sales revenue and profit from the product may fall, if the demand is more inelastic than anticipated. This result could occur if a firm's price reduction triggered similar price reductions from its rivals. Second, some buyers may stop buying at the regular price and simply wait until the product is put on sale again, at which time they will buy several units to build a personal inventory of the item to tide them over until the product goes on sale again. Third, promotional pricing may increase the price consciousness of consumers, such that they more readily recall the price of the product and later react more elastically to price increases than they otherwise might. Fourth, it may damage the product's quality image, causing the quantity demanded at regular prices to fall as a result.

What kind of buyer is most likely to buy the product when it is priced promotionally? Blattberg[23] found that people with higher incomes, and couples with both spouses working, or with preschool children, tend to be less prone to such "deals." Furthermore, people who own their own houses and cars and consequently have relatively low storage and transportation costs tend to be more deal prone, other things being equal. Thus consumers who are prone to buying at promotional prices tend to have relatively low opportunity costs of their time, the ability to drive around to pick up a bargain, and a house in which to store personal inventories of these goods. The firm's advertising of their "sales" is thus more profitably aimed at low- to middle-income home and car owners. The myriad "flyers" that accompany the weekend newspapers delivered in the suburbs attest to the efficacy of that medium in reaching that kind of buyer.

---

[23]R. Blattberg, T. Buesing, P. Peacock, and S. Sen, "Identifying the Deal-Prone Segment," *Journal of Marketing Research*, 15 (August 1978), pp. 369–77.

Promotional pricing is frequently used on food and household convenience items that are bought frequently, such as aluminum foil, liquid detergent, headache remedies, facial tissues, and deodorant. It is also common for consumer durables that are bought infrequently, like stereo, video, and exercise equipment. What do these items have in common that makes them candidates for promotional pricing? Basic demand theory suggests that products for which demand is more elastic are better candidates for price reductions in general, since total revenue will increase more for a given price reduction. We saw in Chapter 4 that price elasticity depends on the number and availability of close substitutes, on the other hand, and the relationship of price to the consumer's income, on the other. Food and household convenience items typically have many close substitutes, causing the demand for any particular brand (or at any particular store) to be relatively elastic. Prices for stereo, video, and exercise equipment represent a relatively large proportion of the buyer's income, and thus these products also have relatively elastic demand.

Philip Nelson[24] has argued that, more important than the number of substitutes, is the number of substitutes of which the consumer is aware, and that the latter will vary with the type of product. That is, the more difficult it is to obtain information on a product and its attributes, the higher will be the search costs relative to the benefits, and the fewer substitutes the typical consumer will be informed about. Nelson categorized products into two types, those containing largely "search attributes" and those containing "experience attributes." The former can be easily evaluated prior to purchase; thus the consumer knows what he or she is getting for the price. Easily measurable or observable attributes, like size and weight of food items, design of clothing, and punctuality of airline departures fall into this category. Stereo and video equipment is similarly readily evaluated and compared on the basis of published specifications.

Experience goods contain attributes that can only be evaluated after purchase, but once evaluated will be purchased again on the basis of the consumer's recollection of the attributes. The taste of particular wines, the effectiveness of a detergent or deodorant, and the quality of paint are experience attributes. Darby and Karni[25] suggest a third category, "credence" goods, where the attributes are imperfectly evaluated even after repeated purchasing, such that the buyer tends to rely heavily on the product's projected image, brand name, and reputation. Professional services, like those of doctors, lawyers, and financial advisers, fall into this category. The quality of many goods, such as photographic film, is also difficult for many consumers to evaluate.[26]

---

[24]Philip Nelson, "Information and Consumer Behavior," *Journal of Political Economy*, 78 (March/April 1970), pp. 311–29. See also Louis Wilde, "The Economics of Consumer Information Acquisition," *Journal of Business*, 53 (July 1980), pp. S143–S158, and Nelson's comments following Wilde's paper.

[25]Michael Darby and Edi Karni, "Free Competition and the Optimal Amount of Fraud," *Journal of Law and Economics*, 16 (April 1973), pp. 67–88.

[26]This point, as well as several others made here, is attributable to Thomas Nagle, "Economic Foundations for Pricing," *Journal of Business*, 57 (January 1984), pp. S3–S26.

Since it is more difficult to evaluate the products, it follows that the consumer's cost of information to evaluate a product increases as we move from search to experience to credence items. Thus we should expect consumers to seek less information about experience items than they do about search items, and to seek less information about credence items than they do about experience items. Thus credence items effectively have fewer substitutes *that the consumer is aware of*, as compared to experience goods, and experience goods similarly have fewer substitutes than search goods. Accordingly, we should expect to see promotional pricing used more frequently in markets for search products, where a price reduction will more likely lead to a highly elastic demand response.

More generally, price competition should be expected to be a more desirable competitive strategy, as compared to advertising, for example, if consumers can more easily evaluate the attributes (or relative quality) of the products. Price competition is particularly intense in the passenger airline markets, for example, where the attributes of each firm's product are easily ascertainable, including the time of departure, whether the flight is nonstop or not, whether meals and movie are provided, type of aircraft, and so on. (Nonprice competition, including advertising and the frequent-flyer programs, is also quite intense among airlines, reflecting the more competitive environment that has prevailed following deregulation of these markets.)

10.4 SUMMARY

In this chapter we have considered the firm's pricing problem in practical market situations. Firms typically lack full information concerning their cost and revenue functions and must make a decision whether or not to incur search costs to get the cost and demand information required to set prices that are optimal in light of their objectives. If the search costs involved are expected to be less than the value of information derived, the firm should first estimate its demand and cost curves and then set the short-run profit-maximizing price, the sales-maximizing price, or the limit price, as desired.

When search costs are expected to be prohibitive, the firm may earn greater profit by proceeding in ignorance, using some proxy pricing policy that may not give the "correct" price but that also does not require search costs for its implementation, such that the firm's objective may be better served if the revenues forgone because of the "incorrect" price are less than the search costs avoided. Markup pricing is typically used in practice, as is some form of price followership, including the following of "suggested" retail prices.

We showed that markup pricing can be profit maximizing if chosen at the level commensurate with the product's price elasticity of demand. If longer-term profit maximization is desired, the markup percentage is likely to be somewhat lower than for short-run profit maximization, since long-term price elasticities tend to be higher than short-term price elasticities. As well as saving information search costs, markup pricing acts to pass cost increases along to the customer and to maintain the purchasing power, or real value, of the firm's profits, and it assists in coordinating the pricing behavior of firms in oligopolistic markets.

We saw that there will be a range of acceptable markup rates if the firm does not incur search costs and that any one of these rates will allow higher profits or greater market share as compared to setting the optimal price *after* incurring search costs. The optimal markup rate remains optimal despite shifts in costs and demand curves, under certain conditions. Periodic search activity is recommended to ensure that the markup rate remains profit maximizing.

Choosing the appropriate price level in established product markets requires an evaluation of the attributes perceived to exist in your product vis-à-vis those in competing products. In these markets the general level of prices is established, and the problem is to ensure that each product is positioned in the existing price range such that the firm's objectives are best served. The price chosen should reflect the presence, absence, or degree of desirable attributes in each product, relative to the prices and attributes offered by competing products. Product-line pricing involves essentially the same problem, except that a particular firm produces several of the competing or complementary products and must also consider the demand interdependencies. Again, attention must be paid to the relative price elasticities of demand, with allowances made for a "basic" product which has several complementary products, for the use of products as "loss leaders," and for the "entry-level" and "flagship" products in a line of substitutes.

Prices may be set higher to infer higher product quality if price is the best indicator of quality available to the buyer. This method may be applicable to new products, to highly technical products which contain what we later called "credence" attributes, and to any product where the cost of information to the consumer is high relative to the price of the product.

Product bundling can allow a firm to increase its profit by raising individual product prices and setting the bundle price at less than the sum of the prices of the component products. Some consumers will be induced to buy the bundle and consequently spend more than they would have at the prices set for each of the products separately. At the same time this strategy discriminates against those buyers who want only one, or a subset, of the products in the bundle. Setting quantity discounts is also a bundle pricing problem. Larger sizes or multiples of the product are simply bundles of the same product, and the firm can increase profit by offering the buyers a choice of small sizes (or single units) at relatively high prices per unit and larger sizes (or multiple units) at lower prices per unit.

Promotional pricing, or putting an item temporarily on sale, is also expected to increase the firm's revenues and profit, although there are some problems to be wary of. Promotional pricing, as well as price competition in general, is likely to work better for products comprised of "search" attributes, namely, attributes that are observable or measurable by the consumer at relatively low search costs. By way of corollary, products containing "experience" and "credence" attributes are less suitable for price competition, and their demand is probably better stimulated by advertising, which we consider in Chapter 13.

DISCUSSION QUESTIONS

10-1. When is it likely to be profit maximizing to use a rule-of-thumb price determination procedure rather than to determine price on the basis of estimated cost and revenue curves.

10-2. Can the markup formula linking price, average variable cost, and the price elasticity of demand be used to "plug in" the price elasticity and AVC figures to "solve for" the profit-maximizing price? Why or why not? What cost conditions are built into that formula?

10-3. Explain why there is a range of markup rates which make it preferable to avoid search costs. What does this range depend on?

10-4. Discuss the conditions under which a markup rate, if initially optimal in terms of the firm's objective, will remain optimal despite shifts in the cost and demand curves.

10-5. Explain why the presence or absence of desirable attributes in your product influences the optimal price positioning of that product in an established market.

10-6. Summarize the issues involved in product-line pricing strategy.

10-7. For what type of product is it feasible to infer higher product quality by setting a higher price? Under what circumstances, and for what objective, would it serve the firm's objective to set price *above* the short-run profit-maximizing level?

10-8. Explain how the firm may benefit from a product-bundling strategy, in the context of a computer manufacturer offering to sell the computer and various software programs separately, or the computer with several software programs as a package deal.

10-9. What considerations enter the firm's decision to offer a discount for quantity? How deep can its discount be? Explain your answer in terms of marginal costs and revenues.

10-10. Why would a firm place items temporarily "on sale"? What dangers are there in this practice? For what kind of products does promotional pricing work best? What kind of person responds to promotional pricing?

PROBLEMS AND SHORT CASES

10-1. The Ajzenkopf Company has been in operation for almost fifteen years and has enjoyed considerable success in the manufacture and sale of its glass vases.

The Ajzenkopf plant at present has a capacity of 35,000 units per year, and the facilities at the plant are highly specialized. Sales of vases are currently 29,000 units a year. The selling price is $7.00 per unit. Last month the average costs of production were determined to be as follows: average fixed costs, $1.03; average cost of labor, $1.98; and average cost of materials, $1.05. At those present price and cost levels the Ajzenkopf Company received a profit that management believed was quite acceptable.

This agreement situation came to an abrupt halt, however, when it was learned that the suppliers of raw materials were raising their prices and that there was a labor dispute which forced negotiations to begin. An agreement was reached, and the final settlement had the effect of increasing the average cost per unit of labor by 20 percent. A new contract has been signed with the suppliers of the raw materials, and the new prices of raw materials had the effect of increasing the average materials cost by 30 percent. This contract had been signed after other suppliers were contacted and no less expensive prices of raw materials could be found.

Faced with this situation, a meeting was called to determine what action should be undertaken to maintain an acceptable level of profit. It was agreed that a profit level of $75,000 was the minimum acceptable point. Two alternative suggestions were made. The first suggestion, made by the marketing manager, was to raise prices to $9.00 a unit, since he was fairly certain that this price level would reduce quantity demanded by only 8,500 units per annum. The marketing manager also offered an estimate of the average variable costs, stating that the average labor cost would be $3.10 and the average materials cost would be $1.39 at this level of output.

The plant manager proposed that the price should be reduced to $6.00. The plant manager was also fairly certain about the demand situation, stating that at this price level 32,500 vases would be demanded. He also offered his estimates of average variable costs, stating that at this level of output the average costs of labor and materials per unit would be $2.85 and $1.24, respectively. The plant manager further supported his proposal by stating that under this alternative, laborers need not be laid off and thus low labor morale would not reduce productivity of the workers.

(a) Using the information given above, derive graphical estimates of the firm's revenue and cost functions.

(b) Assuming that the firm wishes to maximize sales volume subject to obtaining a minimum profit of $75,000, what price do you suggest they charge? Discuss your answer fully. What qualifications do you wish to add to your analysis?

10-2. Regression analysis of the variations in prices and quantity demanded for Winton Garden Equipment's major product (conducted under controlled conditions in a consumer clinic by their marketing research department) provides the following results (where P is in dollars and Q represents thousands of units):

Regression equation	$Q = 49.147 - 2.941P$
Coefficient of determination	$R^2 = 0.96$
Standard error of estimate	$= 0.128$
Standard error of the coefficient	$= 0.086$

The production department has conducted its own study of weekly total variable costs and output levels over the past three months. Its results (with TVC in thousands of dollars and Q representing thousands of units) are as follows:

Regression equation	$TVC = 102.35 + 0.025Q^2$
Coefficient of determination	$R^2 = 0.92$
Standard error of estimate	$= 0.232$
Standard error of the coefficient	$= 0.003$

You are an executive assistant to the marketing manager, Derek Winton. Mr. Winton feels that the present price of $9.95 is fine. He argues that it positions our product in the upper part of the range of our competitors' prices and that the current sales level of approximately 20,000 units a week is fine in view of our full capacity limit of only 25,000 units weekly. While he agrees that a price change of a dollar or so either way would go unchallenged by competitors, he does not think such a price change would improve the contribution made by this product.

(a) What is the contribution-maximizing price? Is the associated output level feasible?

(b) How confident are you that your prediction will in fact generate a greater contribution than the present price level? Explain in detail with supporting calculations.

(c) Are there any reservations you wish to attach to your recommendation?

10-3. The Pittsburgh Plastics Company introduced a new product in January which received strong initial support and has shown a steady growth of sales in subsequent months. The initial price was set somewhat arbitrarily as a 25 percent markup over average costs. The company's objective is to maximize the contribution to overheads and profits, and it is now anxious to know whether the $6.88 price is optimal. In light of the continual growth in sales and changes in certain cost components, it has commissioned a study by Market Researchers Incorporated, who report that the price elasticity of demand is approximately −2.5 at the current (March) price and output level.

The output and cost data for the past three months are as follows:

	January	February	March
Sales (units)	*2,246*	*2,471*	*2,718*
Direct materials	$1,415	$1,557	$1,712
Direct labor	3,369	4,077	4,933
Indirect factory labor	3,000	3,075	3,154
Office and administrative salaries	2,000	2,000	2,000
Light and heat	485	470	320
Other overheads	2,100	2,100	2,100

(a) Supposing that price can be varied each month, estimate the optimal price for the month of April.

(b) What output level could be sold at the optimal price level in April?

(c) What qualifications and other considerations do you wish to add to the above pricing and output decision?

10-4. The Laura Ann Boutique purchases a line of ladies dresses from a wholesaler and pays $30 per dress regardless of quantity purchased. These dresses are marked up 33.33 percent over their invoice cost and sell quite readily. The firm's objective is to maximize contribution to overheads and profits, and management is concerned whether or not 33.33 percent is the profit-maximizing markup rate.

(a) What would price elasticity of demand have to be in order for 33.33 percent to be the optimal markup rate?

(b) Suppose Laura Ann commissions a study, costing $500, that indicates that price elasticity of demand for these dresses is $\epsilon = -3.5$. Given the present price of $40 per dress and weekly sales averaging 300 dresses, was the present markup rate within the range of acceptable markups?

(c) Was the study worth it? Will it pay for itself in the future weeks?

10-5. The Archibald Truck Service (ATS) Company has been successfully servicing and repairing large trucks and tractor trailers for several years, specializing in Kenworth, Peterbilt, and Mack tractor service. Their pricing policy on each job is to charge $25 per hour labor and the "book price" for materials and replacement parts. The labor charge represents the actual cost to ATS plus 25 percent, and the "book prices" represent the invoice cost of the materials and parts plus 25 percent. Thus, ATS effectively sets price by marking up its direct costs by 25 percent. The founder and general manager, Mr. Joseph Archibald, reasons that this relatively low price structure is the best approach, since there is a lot of repeat business in service and repair work. He would rather have more work in the present period and maximize profits over the longer term.

For a typical service and repair job his cost is $600, and he charges $750. He does, on the average, 60 jobs per month. His overhead costs are $8,000 per month. Mr. Archibald is concerned that his monthly profits are too low; he wants at least $2,000 per month and is not earning that amount at present. He has asked all his customers over the past two months to complete a questionnaire, and from this he has been able to estimate that price elasticity for his service and repair job is approximately $\epsilon = -1.1$.

(a) Construct the demand, total revenue, and total cost curves for ATS from the data given.

(b) Advise Mr. Archibald of the price level and the implied markup rate on the average service and repair job which would maximize sales volume subject to the attainment of his profit target.

(c) Explain to Mr. Archibald the conditions under which that markup rate will remain optimal despite shifts in the cost and demand curves.

(d) Give him some guidance on how he should adjust the markup rate if the conditions referred to in part (c) do not hold.

10-6.   The Napper Bag and Canvas Company, Ltd., is a specialist manufacturer of down-filled sleeping bags for sale in the camping equipment market. In this market there are several large companies with annual sales between $25 million and $30 million and many smaller companies with sales between $1 million and $5 million. Most of these companies have diversified product lines of camping equipment, including tents, cooking equipment, camping furniture, and sleeping bags with various types of filling. Napper's sales of $1.6 million last year came entirely from down-filled sleeping bags, however. Although more expensive than other materials, down has substantially more insulating value by weight and volume and commands the attention of a loyal segment of serious outdoorspeople. Only a few firms produce quality down-filled bags, but these firms face peripheral competition from other firms producing bags filled with other natural and artificial materials.

Last year Napper sold 21,000 bags directly to large department stores, catalog sales companies, and specialty sporting equipment stores. These clients typically require contracts guaranteeing prices for one year. The cost of manufacturing sleeping bags depends on the size of the bag, the materials used, and the amount of fill. A breakdown of Napper's latest manufacturing costs for a typical style is as follows:

Item	Cost per Unit
Down filling	$30.00
Other raw materials	14.40
Direct labor	8.12
Manufacturing overhead	6.09
Total unit cost	$58.61

To the manufacturing cost is added a markup of 30 percent to provide for selling, administration, financial expenses, and profit.

During the past year the cost of down increased by between 80 to 95 percent, depending on the grade and blend. Napper was able to pass this on to its customers without any apparent loss of sales or share of the market. The suppliers of down are forecasting a minimum increase of 80 percent over the next year. For Napper the average price of down will increase from the current $12 per pound to $22 per pound. It is anticipated that the cost of other raw materials will rise by 8 percent and labor by 5 percent over the next year.

George Napper, the marketing manager, is concerned about the prospects for the coming year, and you are called upon to advise him.

(a) What price level do you advise for Napper's typical style bag?

(b) Do you have any other advice for Mr. Napper concerning future marketing strategy?

10-7. The refrigerator market is characterized by a wide diversity of product offerings and a price range from less than \$400 to more than \$1,200, depending on the features of the specific refrigerator. Within this range, each manufacturer has a product line extending from the basic no-frills smaller refrigerators to the top-of-the-line luxury units.

A large chain of department stores buys various refrigerators from various manufacturers and sells them under its own brand name "Valhalla." Given the stores' reputation for quality products and after-sales service, this refrigerator line has achieved a substantial market share in the areas where it is sold. The marketing vice-president of the chain has been considering an addition to the Valhalla line. The new refrigerator, designated the Valhalla GE12456A, is made by General Electric and is similar to several sold by other major manufacturers, but it would fill a gap in the product line offered by the chain stores. The details of the Valhalla GE12456A are as follows: It is a 12-cubic-feet upright refrigerator/freezer, with two doors, a freezer at the top and freezer capacity of 3.2 cubic feet, and it has four large aluminum trays for fresh meat and vegetables (taking up the lower two shelves), fully compartmentalized inner doors, butter and cheese compartments with individual temperature controls, and "easy-glide" wheels underneath. It comes in four colors and with door hinges on either side.

The refrigerators available that would seem most competitive with the Valhalla GE12456A are as follows (apart from the details shown, they are similar in all other respects to the Valhalla GE12456A):

Make/Model	Price ($)	Total Size (cu ft)	Freezer Size	Trays	Wheels
General Electric GE12456	525	12.0	3.2	4	Yes
Westinghouse WH11521	505	11.5	2.3	3	No
Store A house brand XY-4823	485	12.0	3.0	3	No
Store B house brand BK-7742	505	12.5	3.5	4	No
RCA RC-6821	515	11.8	2.8	4	Yes
Kelvinator K-7742	535	12.5	3.5	4	No

You are asked to assist in pricing the new addition to the Valhalla line.

(a) What price level would you recommend?

(b) Explain the basis for your recommendation in detail.

(c) Outline all qualifications you feel should be made to this recommendation.

10-8. Last fall, Peripherals conducted a three-month national mail-order campaign with its line of personal accessories relating to BMW automobiles. An advertisement, complete with photographs of the items, ran for three consecutive months in the BMW Owners Club magazine and generated orders over a six-month period. All of the items sold, including tiepins, key rings, caps, T-shirts, jackets, and umbrellas, carried the BMW logo and were designed to appeal to the pride of ownership felt by most BMW owners.

Peripherals' management is wondering whether the screen-printed T-shirts were priced at the contribution-maximizing level. The price charged was $8.95, and Peripherals sold 120 units during the period. The cost per unit of these shirts was $4, regardless of volume (once the initial costs, of design and of the screens, were paid for). The design was original, showing the colors of the BMW logo in a heart shape, and words which effectively said "I (love) my Bimmer." The shirts were high quality, 50 percent cotton and 50 percent polyester, and were advertised as such. Several other BMW T-shirts were available to buyers, being advertised in automobile magazines (including the club magazine) and typically priced at $9.50 or $9.95, as well as the T-shirt which is sold at the BMW dealerships for $11.50. Each of these shirts has a different design, ranging from the simple logo with the footnote "The Ultimate Driving Machine," sold by the dealerships, to a much more complex design including a car being driven at speed. Peripherals had pretested their design at a regional meeting of the club, and it was greeted favorably by virtually everyone who saw it. These respondents were told it would be priced "competitively."

The decision to price the shirt at $8.95 was made after consideration of the following factors. First, it did not seem fair to exploit fellow club members by pricing too much above direct cost. By pricing below the competition Peripherals felt they were giving very good value to club members. Second, Peripherals guessed that demand for the shirt would be somewhat elastic at prices below the competition, since all prices were stated in print, and the lead time necessary to change prices was at least three months. No estimates of quantity demanded were attempted, but a supplier was organized to produce the printed shirts in small batches as required. Third, it was recognized that demand for T-shirts would be somewhat softer in the fall, as compared to the spring or summer.

This summer, Peripherals plans to repeat their BMW campaign. Before choosing the price for T-shirts, however, Peripherals is considering taking several "experts" to lunch in order to find their views on the appropriate price of the shirts. These people are in the custom T-shirt business and seem to be quite successful. These lunches are expected to cost Peripherals $150 in total.

Based on the $8.95 price and the 120 units sold, Peripherals calculates that price elasticity would have had to be -1.80808 in order for the price to be contribution maximizing. This figure seems higher (in absolute terms) than Peripherals would have guessed. Their best estimate, considering that this will be a summer campaign, and given their experience last fall, is that price elasticity will be unitary at the $8.95 price level. They expect sales volume to be about 25 percent greater in the summer than in the fall.

(a) Given the estimated price elasticity, and quantity demanded, at $8.95 in the summer, estimate the demand curve which Peripherals thinks it will face.

(b) What is the contribution-maximizing price suggested by the estimated demand curve?

(c) Based on these estimates, should Peripherals spend the $150 finding out what the "experts" think?

(d) Outline all assumptions and qualifications which underlie your analysis.

10-9. Emerson Electric Corporation is considering the appropriate prices for two video cassette recorders that are being made in Japan and imported (as are all VCRs at this time) with Emerson's brand name attached. These will be Emerson's first VCRs, although its name is well known in electric appliances generally. Model A being assembled for Emerson has four video heads, can record four programs in a fourteen-day period, has a varactor tuner capable of tuning ninety-nine channels, and has stereo with the Dolby feature. It does not have high-fidelity, but it has multichannel television sound (MTS) capability. Model B has six heads, can record eight programs in twenty-one days, has a quartz tuner, stereo, Dolby, high-fidelity sound, and MTS capability. Emerson has asked you to recommend price levels which will appropriately position their products in the market. They supply you with the following information on VCR models available from Quasar and some other firms that they feel will be direct competitors. They tell you that the quartz tuner is superior to the varactor tuner, because it can pick up an unlimited number of channels and tune them in very finely. Varactor tuners must be preset to a given number of channels, and consumers typically prefer more than fourteen if they receive more than that number of channels on cable. Video quality is increased by having more heads. Both video and sound signals are derived from the two or four heads, except in the case of six-head systems, where the extra two heads are used exclusively for sound. In general, video and sound quality increase with the number of heads.

Brand and Model	Price	Heads	Programs	Tuner	Stereo	Dolby	Hi-fi	MTS
Quasar VH5154	$ 520	2	4/14	Var/14	No	No	No	No
Quasar VH5254	790	4	4/14	Var/99	Yes	Yes	No	No
Quasar VH5355	799	2	4/14	Var/99	No	No	Yes	Yes
Quasar VH5346	830	2	4/14	Var/14	Yes	Yes	Yes	No
Quasar VH5655	899	4	4/14	Var/99	No	No	Yes	Yes
Quasar VH5645	950	4	8/14	Quartz	Yes	Yes	No	No
Quasar VH5845	1,000	4	8/14	Quartz	Yes	Yes	Yes	No
Akai VS303U	600	2	4/28	Quartz	No	No	No	No
Akai VS603U	900	6	8/28	Quartz	Yes	No	Yes	No
Hitachi VT65A	750	4	4/14	Var/80	Yes	Yes	No	Yes
JVC HRD725U	1,199	6	8/14	Quartz	Yes	No	Yes	No
Magnavox VR8530	699	2	4/14	Var/99	Yes	No	Yes	Yes
Magnavox VR8544	750	4	4/14	Var/99	Yes	No	Yes	Yes

(a) Considering the "quality" of model A relative to these rival products, choose the price which you think appropriately positions it in this market? Outline the reasoning behind your decision.

(b) Now select a price for model B such that it is positioned appropriately in the VCR market, and explain your reasoning.

(c) What product-line pricing considerations entered your decisions?

(d) What qualifications and assumptions underlie your decisions?

10-10. Admiral Computer Company is planning to introduce a new version of its rather successful personal computer. The new model, designated the Personal Assistant, will have 128K bytes of RAM memory standard, with upgrades to 256K and 512K at extra cost. The Word Perfect word-processing software program will run on the 128K version, but Lotus 1-2-3 requires at least 256K memory, although some users will require 512K. Word Perfect is widely available for $695, and Lotus 1-2-3 now costs $495. Admiral could buy both programs on chips and bundle them with the computer, at half the retail price. The extra 128K memory chips cost Admiral $50 each, and $20 to install if bundled with the computer, or $100 to install if retrofitted to a customer's previously purchased computer. (To upgrade from 128K to 512K would require three additional 128 chips.)

Comparable personal computers (with 128K) are currently selling in the range $1,950 to $2,950, with IBM being the most expensive, and the IBM-compatibles being in the upper half of that range. Admiral's Personal Assistant becomes IBM-compatible if an extra wafer board is installed. This board has a direct cost to Admiral of $150, and, like the extra memory, can either be bundled in for $170 or installed later for $250. Admiral has asked you to advise them what price they should set for the 128K model, the 256K model, the 512K model, the IBM-compatible version of each of these models, the 256K model with Lotus, Word Perfect, and IBM-compatibility bundled in, and the 512K model with these bundled in. Also, they want to know what price to set for the separate sale (and installation) of the Lotus and Word Perfect chips and IBM-compatibility board.

(a) Analyze this pricing problem on the basis of the information given here, and recommend prices for each product in Admiral's product line.

(b) Now suppose that IBM charges $400 for one extra 128K memory chip if it is bundled in and $750 if it is retrofitted, and its charges for the upgrade to 256K and 512K (from 128K) are $750 and $1,100, respectively. Others charge $200–300 less, citing the lower price as a positive feature in favor of their products. IBM's bundle prices tend to be about 95 percent of the sum of the prices of the products purchased separately, whereas the bundle prices of others tend to be between 70 and 80 percent of the sum of the products purchased separately. Does this factor change your recommended prices?

(c) What assumptions and qualifications underlie your analysis, and what further information would you seek, if any, before recommending the prices to Admiral?

SUGGESTED REFERENCES AND FURTHER READING

Adams, W. J., and J. Yellen. "Commodity Bundling and the Burden of Monopoly," *Quarterly Journal of Economics*, 90 (May 1976), pp. 475–98.

Alpert, M. I. *Pricing Decisions*. Glenview, Ill.; Scott, Foresman & Company, 1971.

Cohen, M., and J. Y. Jaffray. "Rational Behavior under Complete Ignorance," *Econometrica*, 48 (July 1980), pp. 1281–99.

Corr, A. V. "The Role of Cost in Pricing," *Management Accounting*, November 1974, pp. 15–32.

Earley, J. S. "Marginal Policies of 'Excellently Managed' Companies," *American Economic Review*, 46 (March 1956), pp. 46–70.

Eichner, A. S. "A Theory of the Determination of the Mark-up under Oligopoly," *Economic Journal*, 83 (December 1973), pp. 1184–1200.

Fershtman, C. "Price Dispersion in Oligopoly," *Journal of Economic Behavior in Organizations*, 3 (December 1982), pp. 389–401.

Frankel, M. "Pricing Decisions under Unknown Demand," *Kyklos*, 26, No. 1 (1973), pp. 1–24.

Fraser, R. W. "Uncertainty and the Theory of Mark-up Pricing," *Bulletin of Economic Research*, 37 (January 1985), pp. 55–64.

Lancaster, K. "Competition and Product Variety," *Journal of Business*, 53 (July 1980), pp. S79–S103.

Livesey, F. *Pricing*. London: Macmillan, Inc., 1976.

Nagle, T. "Economic Foundations for Pricing," *Journal of Business*, 57 (January 1984), pp. S3–S26.

Oren, S., S. Smith, and R. Wilson. "Pricing a Product Line," *Journal of Business*, 57 (January 1984), pp. S73–S99.

Palda, K. S. *Pricing Decisions and Marketing Policy*. Englewood Cliffs, N.J.: Prentice-Hall, Inc., 1971.

Palfrey, T. R. "Bundling Decisions by a Multiproduct Monopolist with Incomplete Information," *Econometrica*, 51 (March 1983), pp. 463–83.

Peterson, R. A. "The Price-Perceived Quality Relationship: Experimental Evidence," *Journal of Marketing Research*, 7 (November 1970), pp. 525–28.

Salop, S., and J. E. Stiglitz. "The Theory of Sales: A Simple Model of Equilibrium Price Dispersion with Identical Agents," *American Economic Review*, 72 (December 1982), pp. 1121–30.

Scherer, F. M. *Industrial Market Structure and Industrial Performance* (2nd ed.), chaps. 8, 11, and 12. Chicago: Rand McNally & Company, 1980.

Silberston, A. "Price Behavior of Firms," *Economic Journal*, 80 (September 1970), pp. 511–82.

Simon, J. L. "Unnecessary, Confusing, and Inadequate: The Marginal Analysis as a Tool for Decision Making," *American Economist*, 25 (Spring 1981), pp. 28–35.

Weston, J. F. "Pricing Behavior of Large Firms," *Western Economic Journal*, 10 (March 1972), pp. 1–18.

Appendix 10A: Illegal Pricing Practices

Introduction

Every manager should be aware of the illegality of certain business practices. Since the passage of the Sherman Antitrust Act of 1890, business in the United States has been subject to laws intended to promote competition between firms in the best interests of the public. The "public" should be understood to mean both consumers and other firms, all of whom may be injured by anticompetitive actions on the part of one firm or a combination of firms. The Sherman Act, the Clayton Act (1914), the Federal Trade Commission Act (1914), the Robinson-Patman Act (1936), the Wheeler-Lea Act (1938), the Celler-Kefauver Act (1950), and other sundry pieces of legislation specify the restraints that are imposed upon business practices. In this appendix we shall limit our purview to illegal pricing practices and thus be largely concerned with the Sherman and Robinson-Patman acts.[1]

Penalties can be harsh for violation of these laws. General Electric, Westinghouse, and several other electrical companies were fined almost $2 million (in 1960 dollars) for their part in a conspiracy to set prices collusively. Seven managers spent time in jail for their part in the conspiracy, and twenty-four others received suspended

---

[1] It would be irresponsible to ignore the other area of illegal business practices. In most economics departments a separate course will be offered, under the title Industrial Economics, or Industrial Organization, or Government and Business, that will give these matters the attention they deserve. Many books have been written on the subject, including Marshall C. Howard, *Antitrust and Trade Regulation: Selected Issues and Case Studies* (Englewood Cliffs, N.J.: Prentice-Hall, Inc., 1983); M. L. Erickson, T. W. Dunfee, and F. F. Gibson, *Antitrust and Trade Regulation: Cases and Materials* (New York: John Wiley & Sons, 1977); Peter Asch, *Industrial Organization and Antitrust Policy* (New York: John Wiley & Sons, 1983); and Frederic M. Scherer, *Industrial Market Structure and Economic Performance*, 2nd ed. (Boston: Houghton Mifflin Company, 1980).

sentences. Treble damage suits brought by injured parties may have cost the conspirators more than $300 million during the next decade.[2] More recent conspiracies uncovered have not been as wide-ranging as this one, but firms continue to find themselves in hot water for a variety of pricing activities not considered to be in the public interest. We shall discuss price fixing, price discrimination, predatory pricing, and resale price maintenance.

Price Fixing

The Sherman Act, 1890, section 1, states: "Every contract, combination . . . , or conspiracy, in restraint of trade or commerce . . . is declared to be illegal. . . . Every person who shall . . . engage in any combination or conspiracy . . . shall be deemed guilty of a felony, and . . . shall be punished by a fine not exceeding a million dollars if a corporation, or, if any other person, one hundred thousand dollars, or by imprisonment not exceeding three years, or by both said punishments, at the discretion of the court."

Price fixing, or the collusive agreement among firms as to the level of prices to be charged to customers, whether consumers or other firms, is one such "conspiracy in restraint of trade or commerce." These are known as horizontal price agreements, because all the firms involved are at the same level in the hierarchy between production and the final sale. For example, an agreement between manufacturers on the price to wholesalers, an agreement between wholesalers on the price to retailers, or an agreement between retailers on the price to consumers would each be a horizontal price agreement.

A price agreement may concern either the price or the quantity, since limiting the quantity amounts to raising the price, because the market price will tend to rise to "clear the market," or to restrict demand to the available supply. Similarly, market-sharing agreements may constitute a price agreement in the eyes of the law. Markets may be shared by the agreement to assign territorial boundaries or individual buyers (or types of buyers) to individual sellers. Or the firms may agree to simply maintain their present market shares or to produce only some of the products that they might produce, leaving the markets for other products to other firms. In competitive bid markets, the firms might take turns to submit the lowest bid, or they might bid identically.

Price fixing is illegal per se, meaning there are no avenues of defense. To use the words of Chief Justice Earl Warren, "It has been held too often to require elaboration now that price fixing is contrary to the policy of competition underlying the Sherman Act and that its illegality does not depend on a showing of its unreasonableness, since it is conclusively presumed to be unreasonable. It makes no difference whether the

[2]See John Herling, *The Great Price Conspiracy* (Washington, D.C.: Robert B. Luce, Inc., 1962); John G. Fuller, *The Gentlemen Conspirators* (New York: Grove Press, 1962); and Charles A. Bane, *The Electrical Equipment Conspiracies: The Treble Damage Actions* (New York: Federal Legal Publications, Inc., 1973).

motives of the participants are good or evil; whether the price fixing is accomplished by express contract or by some more subtle means; whether the participants possess market control; whether the amount of interstate commerce affected is large or small; or whether the effect of the agreement is to raise or decrease prices."[3]

To obtain a conviction on price fixing, prosecutors must show evidence of a conspiracy to agree on the price level or market shares. Meetings of business leaders where prices are discussed, written and reported statements made by these people, and communications between them regarding prices or market sharing are admissible evidence. The existence of meetings, followed by identical or parallel pricing behavior, has been held to be evidence of a pricing conspiracy. The exchange of price lists or of information on prices charged to particular customers is illegal per se. "Signaling" practices, such as publicly speaking of the need for a price increase or making an advance announcement of a price increase, have recently been challenged as being indicative of a conspiracy to fix prices.[4]

What about price leadership and conscious parallelism? Are these conspiracies to set prices at the same level? Not if the firms independently exercise their own judgment, each deciding independently to either raise or lower its price to a new level in its own best interests. Parallel pricing behavior by itself does not indicate a conspiracy, but there had best not be any other evidence of meetings, discussions, communications, or announcements of prices which could invite prosecution. The risk-averse decision maker will avoid discussing prices with anyone outside the firm, other than customers.

Price Discrimination

The Robinson-Patman Act, 1936, section 2, states: "It shall be unlawful . . . to discriminate in price between different purchasers of commodities of like grade and quality, . . . where the effect of such discrimination may be to substantially lessen competition or tend to create a monopoly in any line of commerce, or to injure, destroy, or prevent competition."

There are four avenues of defense against a charge of price discrimination. First, price differentials that make due allowance for differences in the cost of manufacture and in the cost of serving particular customers are allowable. Such differentials would include quantity discounts to larger buyers and any differences in transport and service costs. Second, the practice may be allowable if there is no significant injury to competition, whether actual or potential. Third, price differences that result from a reduction made in good faith to match the prices previously set by competitors may be allowable. Finally, price reductions may be permitted in response to a deterioration in the marketability of the product, such as for perishable goods, goods rendered no longer fashionable or obsolete, end-of-season sales, and distress sales.

---

[3] *U.S.* v. *McKesson & Robbins, Inc.*, 351 U.S. 305, 309–310 (1956). This passage is also found in Howard, *Antitrust and Trade Regulation*, pp. 56–57.

[4] See Howard, *Antitrust and Trade Regulation*, pp. 67–69.

In Appendix 9A we considered "economic" price discrimination. Is that illegal? It is unless one or more of the defenses mentioned in the last paragraph can be claimed. The telephone company charges rates for daytime long-distance calls that are different from the evening and weekend rates. Recall that the telephone industry was a regulated monopoly until recently, and thus there was no injury to competition. More recently, with the entry of several other suppliers of long-distance service, the new entrants have seen fit to generally follow the lead of AT&T and set higher prices for daytime use of their systems, although there have been price reductions offered in both markets. Thus we may conclude that if the firm is a monopoly it may practice price discrimination unless its actions serve to prevent the entry of a new firm. Next, if the firm is an oligopolist, it may practice price discrimination if all of its rivals similarly practice price discrimination by unspoken accord, such as through price leadership or conscious parallelism.

Predatory Pricing

Section 3 of the Robinson-Patman Act covers price discrimination "in particular localities . . . for the purpose of destroying competition, or eliminating a competitor." A large and financially secure firm might reduce prices in one region for the express purpose of impoverishing a smaller firm that contests only that regional market. Using its profits from other regional markets it can support losses in one market until the rival firm is forced to leave the market or agree to a takeover. John D. Rockefeller is alleged to have used such tactics to eliminate competitors when he built the Standard Oil monopoly during the nineteenth century.[5]

More recently, Borden, Inc., was prosecuted for their pricing of ReaLemon, a processed lemon juice product. Although ReaLemon was priced 10 to 15 cents above rival firms' prices, it was alleged that Borden's prices were predatory. The value of the ReaLemon brand name required the other firms with less well known brand names to set their prices 10 to 15 cents (about 25 percent) below ReaLemon's price in order to survive in the market, since at any lesser price difference consumers would prefer to pay a little extra for ReaLemon and be assured of the quality that they had come to expect from that product. The firms' costs were probably quite similar, although ReaLemon may have benefited from economies of plant and firm size. The resulting price-cost differentials meant that Borden could earn a reasonable profit while impoverishing rivals by reducing its price to the point that rivals' prices would be forced below costs. Thus the firm's price need not be set below rivals' prices in order to be considered predatory.[6]

---

[5]See John S. McGee, "Predatory Price Cutting: The Standard Oil (N.J.) Case," *Journal of Law and Economics*, 1 (October 1958), pp. 137–86.

[6]See Clement G. Krouse, "Brand Name as a Barrier to Entry: The ReaLemon Case," *Southern Economic Journal*, 51 (October 1984), pp. 495–502.

The ReaLemon case is perplexing because it indicates that a firm need not cut its prices below costs in order to be guilty of predatory pricing. Economic analysis suggests that a firm, even if engaged in vigorous price competition, would not wish to set price below its average variable cost, and if observed doing so might be presumed to be engaging in predatory pricing.[7] The essential element lies in the words "for the purpose of destroying competition, or eliminating a competition." If the aggressor's intent can be shown to be the reduction of competition or the elimination of a competitor, an aggressive pricing strategy may be shown to be a predatory strategy. As in a competitive sport, the object is to win the game, not injure or kill the opponent.

Resale Price Maintenance

"Fair-trade" laws, which prevented retail prices from being reduced below a minimum specified by the manufacturer, were introduced during the 1930s and finally repealed in 1975. The Miller-Tydings Resale Price Maintenance Act (1937) and later the McGuire Act (1952) had exempted from prosecution (under the Sherman Act) such *vertical* price agreements between firms, ostensibly to protect small business from the "cutthroat" competition of larger firms. Between the late 1930s and 1975 the manufacturer of a brand name or trademarked product could specify the minimum resale price at the retail level, as long as manufacturers made no *horizontal* agreement with rival manufacturers.

Since 1976, however, when the repeal of the resale price maintenance (RPM) legislation became effective, it has been illegal to specify a price at which a product must be resold. Resale prices may be "suggested" but not enforced in any way, such as by threatening to stop supplying the reseller or by raising wholesale prices, for example. If a reseller, whether wholesaler or retailer, chooses to follow the suggested list price, at his or her own volition, no offense is committed, but there must be no implicit or explicit agreement that a minimum resale price is a condition of the manufacturer's sale of the goods. The abolition of RPM removes a barrier to competition among firms and is in the general best interest of both consumers and firms, although some manufacturers are no doubt disturbed (about a possible reduction of the product's quality image) when their product is used as a "loss leader."

That the abolition of RPM is in the general best interests of firms is evidenced by the fact that RPM almost died a natural death as many resellers ignored the minimum prices and manufacturers chose not to discipline them. By 1974 only 4 percent of retail trade was conducted using RPM, and enforcement of RPM persisted in only a few lines, such as stereo equipment, cosmetics, liquor, television sets, and prescription drugs.[8]

---

[7]See P. Areeda and D. F. Turner, "Predatory Pricing and Related Practices under Section 2 of the Sherman Act," *Harvard Law Review*, 88 (February 1974), pp. 697-733.

[8]See Scherer, *Industrial Market Structure*, p. 594.

Summary

In this appendix we have briefly considered several pricing practices that may be held to be illegal by the Federal Trade Commission, which is empowered to investigate "unfair methods of competition." Price fixing, meaning a horizontal price agreement among rivals, has been illegal under the Sherman Act since 1890. Vertical price agreements that involve resale price maintenance are also illegal under the Sherman Act, although these agreements were exempted for a protracted period. The decision maker's best defense is to stay away from any such agreements and abstain from discussions with other firms concerning prices. Pricing independently, even if in conscious parallelism or as a price leader or follower, will avoid the severe fines and the jail sentences that may follow prosecution on these charges.

The Robinson-Patman Act (1936) is the major problem for managers involved in pricing decisions, since it is not as clear as the Sherman Act as to which practices are forbidden and which are permissible. Many firms, such as Borden, Inc., with their ReaLemon product, have followed what may seem to be aggressive but fair competitive practices, only to receive unwelcome attention from the Federal Trade Commission. Familiarity with the Robinson-Patman Act and recent case history is a necessary attribute of a good corporate lawyer, and access to a good corporate lawyer is necessary for aggressive pricing decisions. A general knowledge of the laws governing the competitive behavior of business is important for all managers.

DISCUSSION QUESTIONS

10A-1. What is a horizontal price agreement, as distinct from a vertical price agreement?

10A-2. Why are market-sharing agreements tantamount to price fixing? What kind of market sharing agreements may be construed as a price-fixing agreement?

10A-3. For a price-fixing conspiracy to be proven, must the Justice Department be able to produce a written and signed agreement?

10A-4. When is or is not conscious parallelism or price leadership and followership likely to be regarded as a pricing agreement.

10A-5. Under what conditions is price discrimination allowable?

10A-6. What is predatory pricing? How is predatory pricing to be distinguished from vigorous price competition?

10A-7. What is resale price maintenance? Can you think of reasons why a manufacturer would want to control the minimum price of its product at the retail level?

10A-8. What arguments, for or against resale price maintenance, can you imagine a reseller might voice in support of or in opposition to resale price maintenance.

SUGGESTED REFERENCES AND FURTHER READING

Areeda, P., and D. F. Turner. "Predatory Pricing and Related Practices under Section 2 of the Sherman Act," *Harvard Law Review*, 88 (February 1974), pp. 697–733.

Asch, P. *Industrial Organization and Antitrust Policy*, esp. chaps. 11, 15, and 16. New York: John Wiley & Sons, 1983.

Bane, C. A. *The Electrical Equipment Conspiracies: The Treble Damage Actions.* New York: Federal Legal Publications, Inc., 1973.

Calvani, T., et al. "Resale Price Maintenance: Theory and Policy in Turmoil," *Contemporary Policy Issues*, 3 (Spring 1985), pp. 1-58.

Erickson, M. L., T. W. Dunfee, and F. F. Gibson. *Antitrust and Trade Regulation: Cases and Materials.* New York: John Wiley & Sons, 1977.

Fuller, J. G. *The Gentlemen Conspirators.* New York: Grove Press, 1962.

Herling, J. *The Great Price Conspiracy.* Washington, D.C.: Robert B. Luce, Inc., 1962.

Howard, M. C. *Antitrust and Trade Regulation: Selected Issues and Case Studies.* Englewood Cliffs, N.J.: Prentice-Hall, Inc., 1983.

Issac, R. M., and V. L. Smith. "In Search of Predatory Pricing," *Journal of Political Economy*, 93 (April 1985), pp. 320-45.

Krouse, C. G. "Brand Name as a Barrier to Entry: The ReaLemon Case," *Southern Economic Journal*, 51 (October 1984), pp. 495-502.

McGee, J. S. "Predatory Price Cutting: The Standard Oil (N.J.) Case," *Journal of Law and Economics*, 1 (October 1958), pp. 137-86.

Milgrom, P., and J. Roberts. "Predation, Reputation, and Entry Deterrence," *Journal of Economic Theory*, 27 (August 1982), pp. 280-312.

Ross, T. W. "Winners and Losers under the Robinson-Patman Act," *Journal of Law and Economics*, 27 (October 1984), pp. 243-71.

Scherer, F. M. *Industrial Market Structure and Economic Performance* (2nd ed.), esp. chaps. 19 and 21. Boston: Houghton Mifflin Company, 1980.

Yamey, B. S. "Predatory Price Cutting: Notes and Comments," *Journal of Law and Economics*, 15 (April 1972), pp. 137-47.

Weismeth, H. "Price Discrimination Based on Imperfect Information: Necessary and Sufficient Conditions," *Review of Economic Studies*, 49 (July 1982), pp. 391-402.

11

New Product Pricing

11.1 INTRODUCTION

New product pricing is an area of increasing concern to many business firms. Rapid technological advances over the past two decades have spawned an ever-increasing array of new products. For example, machines that scan a person's finger to see if the fingerprint is on file are being used to prevent unauthorized entry to military bases and business offices. A machine that is already being used by a Japanese supermarket chain optimizes light, heat, water, and nutrient inputs and consequently grows lettuce (hydroponically) five times faster than normal. Electronic photography, using magnetic disks rather than conventional film, will be available by the time you read this. New plastics are becoming available that will revolutionize the automobile and a host of other products as we now know them. Artificial hearts and other organs are already being implanted, and so on.

Setting the appropriate price for a new product can present a major challenge, because almost no information exists on the demand for that product. Until it is demonstrated by the purchasing behavior of buyers, the demand for a new product may be highly unpredictable. Market research should be undertaken, but often the new product is not properly understood until it is used, and this problem renders marketing research less reliable. Even demand for the personal computer, which was no longer an unknown product to most people by the early 1980s, grew much faster than industry surveys had predicted. A more accurate prediction of demand would probably have resulted in higher prices being set initially, allowing the firms to recoup their developmental costs more quickly and expand their research into product improvements.

New products cover a wide spectrum of "newness." Advertisers may claim that a detergent is "new" simply because it is now lemon scented or is in a new container. The automobile manufacturers introduce their "new" models each year, and the resemblance to the old models is much more than superficial. In the broadest sense, a product is new if it contains a set of attributes that is different from what was previously available. New versions of existing products, such as the detergent and automobile examples mentioned, can be priced in the context of established markets. The value of their additional attributes should be used to properly position the product in the price range already existing in the market. If sellers introduce new models simultaneously, prices may not rise at all, because of competitive pressures. The firm that does not improve its product will lose market share to those that do, of course, unless it reduces its price commensurately.

In this chapter we will be concerned with entirely new products, rather than new versions of existing products. We shall be concerned with products that serve a need that was never previously served or that serve the need many times better or more effectively than it was ever served before. The examples given at the start of the chapter indicate the kind of new product that we mean. Such new products begin life with no history of consumer acceptance at existing price levels or of consumers' reactions to changes in price and other strategic variables. The demand curve for these products must be estimated "from scratch," and there are difficulties in doing so because the potential buyer does not have reference points on which to base responses to marketing surveys, rendering them less reliable. Nonetheless, surveys, consumer clinics, and market testing should be undertaken, and an estimate of the quantity demanded at various price levels should be ascertained in order to have some basis for setting the product's initial price level.

We shall first consider the initial price set for the new product, and later we shall consider the dynamic price path for the product as the firm benefits from the learning effect in production, as the market for the new product expands, and as new firms enter the market with their own versions of the new product. For simplicity of exposition we shall refer to the firm that first introduces the new product as the "innovating" firm. Firms that enter the market later with their versions of the new product are called "entrants."

11.2   SETTING THE INITIAL PRICE FOR A NEW PRODUCT

Traditionally, the appropriate initial price has been argued to be either the "skimming" price or the "penetration" price.[1] As the name implies, the skimming price skims the cream off the top of the market by initially setting a relatively high price. The penetration price, on the other hand, is set at a relatively low level, with the intent of achieving broad penetration of the market initially. We shall see that each strategy is appropriate in particular circumstances.

Price Skimming

■   *Definition:*   *Price skimming* is the choice of a relatively high price for a new product when it is first introduced, with the intent of getting as much profit from the product as possible. At the skimming price, demand will be limited to those buyers willing to

---

[1]See Joel Dean, "Pricing Policies for New Products," *Harvard Business Review*, 28 (November-December 1950).

pay the relatively high price, but the contribution to overheads and profit per unit sold will be relatively high. In fact, price skimming may be none other than short-run profit maximization. We have said the price skimmer's intent is to get as much profit as possible from the product. If the firm's time horizon does not extend beyond the short run, then the skimming price will be the profit-maximizing price. Let us pursue this topic for a moment.

In Figure 11-1 we show the firm's profit-maximizing price for the new product. This graph is familiar, of course, but is repeated here to emphasize two important points. First, the innovating firm is essentially a monopolist in the market for the new product, since there is, at least initially, no other firm with a similar product. In subsequent periods the entry of competitors with similar products will turn the market into an oligopoly, unless this development is prevented by barriers to entry, such as a patent for the new product held by the innovating firm, the unavailability of resources to potential entrants, or the unavailability of technology. A second point is that the firm's initial output capacity may be small relative to the market demand, since the risk of new product failure is notoriously high and the firm may be reluctant to commit resources to build a larger plant or may be unable to afford one until the extent of demand is demonstrated. The firm's capacity considerations are incorporated into the graph. In this case the firm is producing beyond "full capacity," defined as the output level where average cost is minimized. In the long run this firm will surely consider increasing its plant size, and the relatively high contribution from the skimming price will help the firm afford this expansion.

Thus the skimming price is appropriate when the firm's objective is to maximize its short-run profits. Such a firm does not look beyond the short run, so the potential

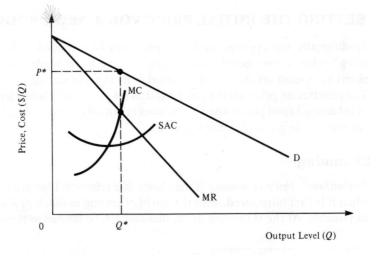

FIGURE 11-1. Price Skimming as Short-Run Profit Maximization

entry of rivals with competing versions of the product is of no concern to the firm in this case. A skimming price may also be appropriated if the firm's time horizon is longer than the short run and its objective is the maximization of long-term profit (or the EPV of net worth) over the horizon. There are essentially three situations in which the long-term profit (net worth) maximizer will choose a skimming price.

First, the long-term profit-maximizing firm will choose a skimming price if there are substantial barriers to the entry of new competitors with a similar product. If entry of new firms in subsequent periods is impossible, the firm will maximize the EPV of profit over its time horizon by setting the short-run profit-maximizing price. If the barriers to entry are not insurmountable but are nonetheless substantial, then the skimming price is the limit price, a price set just high enough to prevent the most likely entrant firm from being able to make a profit over its time horizon.

Second, if the firm expects a positive relationship between its chosen price and the quality of the product as perceived by buyers and potential buyers, it may be profit maximizing in the long term to set a relatively high (skimming) price initially. In this case the skimming price may be above or below the short-run profit-maximizing price, but it is high relative to the firm's average variable costs, or, equivalently, the markup rate is relatively high. In effect, the firm thinks that a higher price in the short run will cause the product to be perceived as a better product, and thus the quantity demanded will be higher at any given price than it would be if the product were perceived to be of lower quality. Put another way, the higher price is expected to cause an improved perception of the product, which operates to shift the demand curve for the product outward in the present and subsequent periods.

We noted in Chapter 10 that the price-quality association may be positive for new products, since there may be little alternative information on quality available to consumers, but the attributes of the product must be of the "experience" or "credence" type, rather than the "search" type that are easily ascertainable by consumers. Also, the more expensive the product is, the more search information consumers will rationally seek. Thus we might expect price skimming to be considered if the new product is a relatively inexpensive "experience" or "credence" good. We shall see below that there is a second reason why experience or credence goods may be candidates for price skimming.

Third, price skimming will be EPV-maximizing if the demand for the product is not expected to last beyond the short run, such that the question of entry of competitors is moot. "Fad" items catch the interest of the consumer briefly, and then interest fades away as the novelty value disappears. The "pet rock" enjoyed a very profitable few months before Christmas one year in the 1970s. It was reported at the time that the seller made $4 million dollars with this item, a novelty gift that was essentially a large pepple in a small cardboard box with a humorous set of instructions included. Other temporary markets, such as emergency situations where the need will soon pass, also indicate the profit-maximizing price as best strategy for the EPV-maximizing firm (although this practice may be regarded as "profiteering").

Price-skimming strategies usually result in the price being reduced in subsequent periods, as the number of buyers willing to pay the relatively high price dwindles, as the firm's cost of production falls because of the learning effect, or as rival firms enter the market with their own versions of the new product. We shall discuss the dynamic path of prices and their underlying causes later in this chapter.

Penetration Pricing

■   *Definition: Penetration Pricing* is the practice of setting a relatively low price in the current period to achieve broad penetration of the market and ensure a larger market share in subsequent periods. Of course, the firm could achieve maximum penetration by giving the product away, but giving it away would cause losses, so a minimum profit constraint is implicit in penetration pricing. In fact, penetration pricing may be nothing more than short-run sales maximization subject to a profit target, a pricing model we introduced in Chapter 9.

Penetration pricing is undertaken when the firm is concerned about the entry of new firms with competing versions of the new product in subsequent periods. It is therefore appropriate for firms with a time horizon extending beyond the short run. We argued in Chapter 9 that sales maximization subject to a minimum profit constraint was a proxy policy for the maximization of the EPV of long-term profit or net worth. Greater sales in the short run lead to greater profit in the long term because of greater repeat sales, greater sales of complementary items, and a reduced probability of entry resulting from the lower price (when compared to the short-run profit-maximizing price).

Where the firm's EPV of long-term profit is best served by setting a price that will preclude the entry of new firms altogether, it must set the limit price. The limit price may be either a skimming price or a penetration price, depending on whether it is relatively high or relatively low. In turn, the height of the price level depends on the height of the barriers to entry. Entry barriers impose higher costs on the entrant firms. For example, the entrant may incur higher fixed costs per period because of advertising expenditures necessary to overcome consumer loyalty to the existing firm. It may incur higher average variable costs because of more expensive raw material sources, royalties payable to the patent holder, and so on. Recall that the limit price is set just below the minimum average cost of the potential entrant. If the barriers to entry are relatively high and entrants are thus expected to have relatively high costs of production, the limit price will be higher and may be regarded as a skimming price. Alternatively, if barriers are relatively low and the existing firm expects little or no cost advantage over entrant firms, then the limit price will be a penetration price. The limit-pricing models for high-cost entrants and low-cost entrants were discussed in Chapter 9.

The type of product is also a factor in the decision to set either a skimming or a penetration price. In Chapter 10 we noted that products may be classified as either search, experience, or credence products depending on how difficult it is for the consumer to obtain information about the attributes of the product. We now note that price skimming will more likely be the superior strategy if the product contains predominantly experience or credence attributes, whereas penetration pricing is more likely the best strategy if the product contains mostly search attributes. Let us see why.

"Search" attributes are relatively easy for the buyer to measure. It will be more difficult for the innovating firm to build and maintain product differentiation when the new product is a search good, since entrants will easily evaluate the new product and be able to produce their own versions which consumers will recognize as essentially similar. Thus, after the entry of new firms, demand will tend to be more price elastic for search goods than for experience or credence goods. If demand is more elastic after entry, the profit-maximizing markup will be lower, and the profit per period will be lower. This outcome is inevitable once entry takes place. To avoid this dilution of future profits the innovating firm will more likely set the limit price and maximize the EPV of profit by earning a series of relatively moderate profits over its time horizon. The limit price is more likely to be a relatively low (penetration) price in the case of search goods, because the costs of the firms (after entry) are more likely to be similar, given the similarity of the products. Thus, if the new product is a search product, the EPV of profits following a penetration pricing strategy is more likely to exceed the EPV of the profits that would follow a skimming strategy.

With experience and credence products, on the other hand, it will be less difficult for the innovating firm to build and maintain product differentiation after the entry of rivals takes place. Similarly, following their entry, rivals can more easily differentiate their products with their claims and brand names. Thus (after entry) the innovating firm's demand will be less elastic, its markups higher, and its business more profitable when the product is an experience or credence good rather than a search good. In this case the EPV of profits associated with price skimming is more likely to exceed the EPV of profits associated with the penetration price, and thus price skimming is more likely to be the strategy that best serves the firm's objective.

In summary, price skimming will be appropriate when the firm's objective is short-run profit maximization, when the objective is long-term profit maximization and entry barriers are insurmountable, or when demand for the product will be short-lived. If barriers to entry are not prohibitive but are relatively high, these barriers will impose relatively high additional costs on entrants, and thus the limit price may be regarded as a skimming price since it will be relatively high. Price skimming may also be appropriate if consumers draw price-quality inferences, which may happen with experience or credence goods. If the new product *is* an experience or credence good, post-entry profits will be higher than if the new product is a search good, again militating in favor of price skimming as the best initial strategy. Penetration pricing is indicated where the firm's time horizon falls in a future period, its objective is the maximization of long-term profit or net worth, and entry of new firms is relatively easy. Given all that, the firm might still choose price skimming initially if the nature of the product is such that it can develop and maintain a high degree of product differentiation in subsequent periods.

Choosing between the Skimming Price and the Penetration Price

The choice between the skimming price and the penetration price must be made if the firm's time horizon falls beyond the short run, demand continues beyond the short run, and the barriers to entry are not insurmountable. We shall now work through an example in which the innovating firm has estimated the market demand curve for the new product, has estimated the cost structure of potential entrants, and, finally, has estimated the probability of entry in the second and third periods following the introduction of the product in the first period.

The data on the entry probabilities and demand per firm are presented in Table 11-1. Note that the entry probabilities in the third period are conditional on what happened in period 2, reflecting the reactions of potential entrants to the number of firms already in the market. The demand per firm is based on the estimated market demand curve $P = 20 - 0.001Q$ and on the presumption that the firm will maximize profits as a monopoly initially, and as the low-cost price leader after entry takes place. Assuming that the firm's marginal cost is constant at $4 per unit regardless of output, the price will be $12 per unit both before and after entry, as shown in Figure 11-2. We also assume for simplicity that the firms will share the market equally when they all set the same price. Thus the innovating firm's profit-maximizing output is 8,000 units when the firm is a monopoly and is equal to $8,000/n$, where n is the number of firms, after entry has occurred.

In Figure 11-2 we show the innovating firm initially setting the profit-maximizing price and selling 8,000 units in the first period, period t. A new firm enters in period $t + 1$, causing the innovating firm's demand curve (which is now the *mutatis mutandis* curve of a price leader) to shift inward to represent exactly half the market demand at each price level. Referring to the new *mutatis mutandis* marginal revenue curve, the innovating firm finds that $12 is still the profit-maximizing price. This result follows only because we have assumed that MC is constant and that each firm's share of the market will be constant (in this case, one-half) at various prices, as long as

TABLE 11-1.   Data for the Firm's New-Product Pricing Decision

IN PERIOD 2			IN PERIOD 3		
New Entrants	Probability	Demand per Firm	New Entrants	Probability	Demand per Firm
No firms enter	0.2	8,000	No firms enter	0.1	8,000
			One firm enters	0.7	4,000
			Two firms enter	0.2	2,667
One firm enters	0.5	4,000	No firms enter	0.3	4,000
			One firm enters	0.5	2,667
			Two firms enter	0.2	2,000
Two firms enter	0.3	2,667	No firms enter	0.5	2,667
			One firm enters	0.4	2,000
			Two firms enter	0.1	1,600

FIGURE 11-2. **Inward Shift of the Innovating Firm's Demand Curve after the Entry of One Firm**

prices are equal. Note that the price leader's *mutatis mutandis* demand curve would continue to swing inward as progressively more firms enter. The price axis intercept remains the same but the slope becomes progressively steeper, equal to n times the slope of the market demand curve, where n is the number of firms. This inward swinging of the demand curve was called an iso-elastic demand shift in Chapter 10 in the context of markup pricing. The implicit markup here is 200 percent over AVC = MC, and this markup remains profit-maximizing despite entry of competitors, given the assumptions underlying this model.

Assuming away any price-quality association, the firm has a choice of setting either the profit-maximizing price or some lower price. For simplicity we shall reduce this problem to a simple dichotomy: the firm will set either the profit-maximizing (skimming) price or the limit (penetration) price. Setting the former, it risks attracting new entrants and having to share the market in future periods. Thus its profits will be relatively high during the first period, and profits may then be relatively low in subsequent periods following the probable entry of new firms. If, on the other hand, it sets the limit price, it is able to preserve its monopoly position while earning moderate profits in each period.[2]

---

[2]To be complete, an analysis of the optimal initial price would include calculation of the EPV of contribution at a series of prices below the profit-maximizing price, with probabilities attached to the entry of one or more firms at each of these price levels. The firm might find it EPV maximizing to set the profit-maximizing price initially and induce the entry of one or more firms before switching to the limit price to inhibit the entry of any more firms.

As implied by the statement that the initial firm will assume the role of low-cost price leader if there is entry of new firms, the costs of the entrant firms are assumed to be higher than for the initial firm. In this example we assume that the entrants will each face marginal costs constant at $5 per unit and have total fixed costs per period of $12,000. The limit price is assumed to be equal to the average cost per unit of the first entrant, given that the first entrant would produce 4,000 units per period. Thus the limit price is $5 + $3 = $8. (In theory it should be fractionally less than the entrant's SAC, say, $7.99, but we shall use $8 for simplicity.) The limit price is set to prevent the entry of the first entrant, and thus no firms will enter. In markup terms, it represents a markup of 100 percent over the innovating firm's direct costs per unit.

At the limit price, $8, the innovating firm will sell 12,000 units each period, as indicated in Figure 11–2. Total contribution will be $48,000 per period, since per-unit contribution (the limit price less this firm's AVC) is $4. At the profit-maximizing price ($12), quantity demanded is 8,000 units when the firm is a monopoly, and the contribution per unit is $8, so profit is $64,000 in the first period. These profits must be discounted, however, since they are received on a more or less daily basis during the period. Assuming the period is a year and the opportunity discount rate is 10 percent and using the daily interest discount factors, we show the calculation of the EPVs of the alternate strategies in Table 11–2.

Note that after three years the EPV of the limit-pricing strategy exceeds the EPV of the profit-maximizing strategy, $125,241 compared to $113,323. If the firm has a three-year time horizon, the limit-pricing strategy is superior. If the firm has a shorter time horizon, however, the profit-maximizing strategy is superior, as can be seen by the summary results at the foot of the table. This result demonstrates quite forcefully the importance of the firm's time horizon in decision making. The longer it is, the more likely it is that the firm will be inclined to choose the limit price or any penetration price, rather than the profit-maximizing price or any skimming price, other things being equal. Similarly, the higher the probability of entry, the more likely it is that the limit price will be optimal, *ceteris paribus*.

Determining Price and Quality Jointly

In many cases the firm will face a choice concerning the level of quality that may be embodied in the new product. The new product may be introduced in a basic form or in a deluxe form, for example. It may be made of different materials (such as plastic or metal), which have different implications for the attributes that will enter the buyers' perception of product quality (such as weight and strength). It may be carefully polished by hand, or less carefully polished by machine, and so on. Higher quality typically costs more than lower quality, of course, and the firm must consider the cost of production in the light of the demand for the product at each quality level.

Essentially, the firm should choose the price-quality combination that promises the maximum EPV of profit. The EPV of profit associated with each quality level should take into account the demand curve for the product *in that quality mode*, the

TABLE 11-2. Calculating the EPV of the Skimming versus Limit-Price Strategy

Strategy A: Set profit-maximizing price, $12, in each period

PERIOD 1			PERIOD 2			PERIOD 3			ENPV CALCULATIONS		
Profit ($)	Present Value (0.9538)	Probability	Profit ($)	Present Value (0.8671)	Probability	Profit ($)	Present Value (0.7883)	Probability	NPV ($)	Joint Probability	ENPV ($)
64,000	61,043.	0.2	64,000	55,494.4	0.2	64,000	50,451.2	0.1	169,945.0	0.02	3,398.9
						32,000	25,225.6	0.7	144,720.0	0.14	20,260.0
						21,333	16,816.8	0.2	136,311.0	0.04	5,452.4
			32,000	27,747.2	0.5	32,000	25,225.6	0.3	116,972.0	0.15	17,545.0
						21,333	16,816.8	0.5	108,564.0	0.25	27,141.0
						16,000	12,612.8	0.2	104,360.0	0.10	10,436.0
			21,333	18,497.8	0.3	21,333	16,816.8	0.5	99,314.6	0.15	14,897.0
						16,000	12,612.8	0.4	95,110.6	0.12	11,413.0
						12,800	10,090.2	0.1	92,588.0	0.03	2,777.6
									Expected Net Present Value		113,323

Strategy B: Set the limit price, $8, in each period

PERIOD 1			PERIOD 2			PERIOD 3			ENPV CALCULATIONS		
Profit ($)	Present Value (0.9538)	Probability	Profit ($)	Present Value (0.8671)	Probability	Profit ($)	Present Value (0.7883)	Probability	NPV ($)	Joint Probability	ENPV ($)
48,000	45,782.	1	48,000	41,620.8	1	48,000	37,838.4	1	125,241	1	125,241

Summary

	Period 1 Present Value	Period 2 EPV	Period 3 EPV
Skimming	$61,043*	$91,565*	$113,323
Limit	$45,782	$87,403	$125,241*

*Optimal strategy if time horizon falls in the indicated period.

cost curves associated with that quality level, and the probabilities of entry occurring in subsequent periods. For each quality mode the optimal (EPV-maximizing) initial price should be determined, as we did before. Then the maximum EPVs of each quality mode should be compared, and the firm should choose the quality mode with the largest EPV. Thus the joint price-quality decision is a relatively simple (although potentially laborious) extension of the new product pricing problem.

Perhaps the skimming-versus-limit-pricing problem we examined did not seem very realistic to you. In practice, we see prices fall after the entry of new firms, but in the model the price level stayed at $12, and only the firms' sales decreased each time another new firm entered. This could well happen, of course, if the assumptions of the model fit the circumstances of the real-world situation. But it *is* a simple model. Market demand stays constant, rather than growing as we would expect in reality. The firms' costs remain constant, rather than falling because of the learning effect, as we expect in reality. Finally, the products were implicitly identical across firms, or at least symmetrically differentiated, such that the firms each had equal shares of the market when prices were equal. In reality, entrants are unlikely to win an equal share of the market immediately because of product differentiation advantages held by the first firm. (People still call copying machines Xerox machines, even if they are made by Canon or Toshiba.)

We shall now incorporate these complications into the new product price model. In the next section we consider the impact of falling production costs, changes in the market demand, and asymmetric product differentiation.

11.3   ADJUSTING PRICE OVER TIME

The innovating firm will set its initial price based on its best estimates of the market demand situation, the probabilities of future entry of rival firms, and their probable cost structures. Once the new product is on the market and time passes, the firm's estimates are either supported or refuted by the data. Unexpected shifts in market demand, unexpected entry, unexpected cost increases or decreases, and unexpected product differentiation advantages may show the initial price to have been the incorrect price, necessitating unanticipated price adjustments. Anticipated changes in demand, costs, and the number of firms will also lead to price adjustments that were anticipated by the innovating firm. Thus there are likely to be a series of price adjustments in the market for the new product as time passes, and we can call the pattern of prices over time the *dynamic price path*.

The market for a new product will be "immature" initially, in the sense that the firms will be competing vigorously for market share and have no established rules or conventions to govern or guide their competitive behavior. As markets mature, the firms learn to not provoke vigorous competition without seriously considering the consequences. They develop patterns of behavior that the other firms come to recognize and expect, and thus uncertainty about rivals' reactions is reduced as the market matures. In mature oligopolies we expect to see more price and market share stability, whereas in new product markets we expect to see price and market share instability as the combatants struggle to maintain or achieve dominance. Underlying the instability of price are changes in costs and demand conditions, which we now investigate.

The Impact of the Learning Effect on Prices

We noted in Chapter 6 that the factors of production "learn" the production process as time passes and cumulative output grows. They become more efficient, producing more output per unit of input, as a result. This increased productivity is reflected in a downward shift of the firm's cost curves, other things (particularly input prices) remaining constant. As learning continues, the cost curves continue to shift downward. We noted that the major impact of the learning effect is felt early in the product's life, since cost reductions of a given percentage are expected every time the cumulative output *doubles*. Assuming a constant output level per period of 100 units and a learning rate of 20 percent, for example, average cost would decline by 20 percent in the second period and continue to decline by another 20 percent by the end of each of the 4th, 8th, 16th, 32nd, and 64th periods, and so on. As time passes, the cost decline in any given period would become less and less noticeable.

In Figure 11–3 we show the impact of the learning effect on the new product's price, with all other things remaining constant. Note that as the cost curves shift

FIGURE 11–3.   Impact of the Learning Curve on New Product Prices with No Changes in Demand or Plant Size

downward, the profit-maximizing price also falls, since the MC curve intersects the MR curve at progressively larger output levels. These quite substantial shifts of the cost curves must reflect either a very high rate of learning or large changes in the cumulative output level.

The Impact of Economies of Plant Size on Prices

If there are economies of plant size available to the innovating firm, it may have a profit incentive to expand plant size and subsequently set a lower price in order to expand sales to match its increased productive capacity. We noted that many innovating firms start with a relatively small plant size, perhaps because they are uncertain about the demand for the product and trade off potential profit for a reduced risk of bankruptcy. Alternatively, they may not be able to afford a larger plant initially, or they may not be able to raise a loan. Once demand for the product has been demonstrated, however, the innovating firm (and its banker) may foresee that greater profit will result from operation of a larger plant.

In Figure 11-4 we show the impact on price of a change in plant size involving economies of plant size, holding other influences on price constant. Note that the firm shifts from the plant size represented by the SAC and MC curves to that represented by the SAC' and MC' curves. It is subsequently profit-maximizing to reduce price from the level P to the level P' in order to induce expansion of quantity demanded from the level Q to the level Q'.

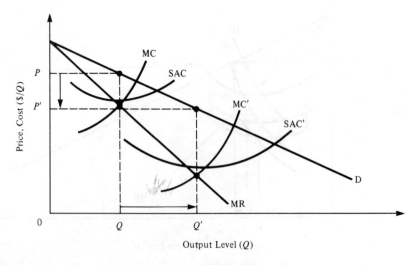

FIGURE 11-4. **The Impact of Economies of Plant Size on Product Price with No Changes in Demand or Learning**

The Impact of Entry of New Firms on Prices

Earlier we saw that the entry of new firm(s) had no impact on the product's price; it merely forced the innovating firm to share the market quantity demanded (at that price) with the entrant firm(s). This result was due to two features of the model, however. First, the innovating firm's marginal cost was assumed to be constant, and second, the firms were assumed to maintain their market share at all price levels as long as they all set the same price (following the price leader, for example). Thus the innovating firm's demand curve suffered an iso-elastic shift each time a new firm entered.

If entry causes a non-iso-elastic shift of the innovating firm's demand curve, however, prices will change following entry. Suppose that rather than swing inward from the same intercept point, the innovating firm's demand curve shifts back in a more or less parallel fashion. This kind of shift would occur if the entrants refused to follow the innovating firm's price leadership, for example, such that the firm faces a *ceteris paribus* demand curve. Such a situation is shown in part (a) of Figure 11-5. Marginal costs are shown as constant, for comparability with the "no impact on price" case depicted in Figure 11-2 earlier.

In part (b) of Figure 11-5 we show another possible combination—an iso-elastic demand shift caused by entry and a rising marginal cost curve (caused by diminishing returns in production). Again the profit-maximizing price is lower following the entry of the new firm(s). The remaining combination (namely, a non-iso-elastic demand shift and a rising MC curve) will also cause a reduction in the innovating firm's profit-maximizing price. You may graph this case for yourself.

Thus the initial conclusion that entry would not cause a price change was derived from a simplified model containing two restrictive assumptions, and one or the other of these may not fit a particular situation observed in the real world. Our purpose

FIGURE 11-5. Falling Prices Caused by the Entry of New Firms

earlier was to abstract from price changes to show that the firm's profit per period would be reduced by entry even if prices stayed the same. Now we know that if the firms set prices independently rather than follow a price leader or if there are diminishing returns in production, then prices will fall following the entry of new firms.

Shifts of the Market Demand Curve and the Product Life Cycle

Market demand for the new product is unlikely to remain static. More likely, the market demand curve will shift outward as the product becomes more widely known and appreciated. Eventually, market demand might be expected to shift inward when the tastes of consumers shift in favor of another new product that may become available and better serve their needs. The growth and eventual decline of the market demand for a new product is known as the "product life cycle."

■ *Definition:*   The *product-life-cycle* hypothesis stylizes the rate of demand for a product into three main phases, namely, the growth, maturity, and decline phases. In the growth phase, the quantity demanded per period (at a particular price level) increases rapidly. In the maturity phase the quantity demanded continues to increase and then begins to decrease. In the decline phase the quantity demanded per period falls progressively, and the product may eventually be withdrawn from the market. In Figure 11-6 the curve PLC represents a schematic representation of the product-life-cycle hypothesis.[3]

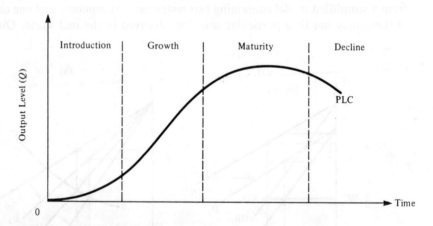

FIGURE 11-6.   The Product Life Cycle

[3]For more on the product-life-cycle concept, see P. Kotler, *Principles of Marketing*, chap. 11 (Englewood Cliffs, N. J.: Prentice-Hall, Inc., 1980); also T. Levitt, "Exploit the Product Life Cycle," *Harvard Business Review*, November–December 1976, pp. 81-94; and N. K. Dhalla, and S. Yuspeh, "Forget the Product Life Cycle Concept!" *Harvard Business Review*, January–February 1976, pp. 102-12.

In terms of the market demand for the product, the product-life-cycle hypothesis says that the market demand curve will shift outward at an increasing rate at first, then continue to shift outward at a decreasing rate, and finally begin to shift back. In the context of new products, we are largely concerned with the growth phase, in which we should expect to see entry of new firms. In the maturity phase the number of firms is more likely to have stabilized, and the price level is more likely to be relatively stable.

Given outward shifts of the market demand curve and the entry of new firms, the innovating firm might expect to garner a decreasing share of an increasing market. Whether this relationship translates to an increased quantity demanded or a reduced quantity demanded depends on the relative growth rates of market demand and the number of firms. If the market demand grows at a faster rate than the number of firms increases, the firms can expect to gain progressively larger sales volumes even if their market *shares* continue to fall with the entry of new firms. Thus the demand curve for each firm would tend to shift outward in subsequent periods, and this shift would have an upward impact on the price level.

Conversely, if the number of firms grows faster than the market demand grows, the firms will face demand curves that are shifting inward in successive periods. This kind of shift will have a depressing effect on the price of the product. This situation, with either iso-elastic or non-iso-elastic demand shifts, can be reviewed in Figure 11–5.

Thus prices are likely to fall as time passes following the introduction of a new product for any one or a combination of the following reasons: learning-curve effects, economies of plant size, and entry of new firms at a rate greater than the rate of increase of market demand. Alternatively, the price of new products might increase over time if the cost reductions were small or absent and the market demand increased at a rate faster than the rate of growth of the number of firms.

First-Mover Advantages

■ *Definition:* *First-mover advantages* are the benefits accruing to the firm that first introduces a new product that turns out to be successful. These advantages include the monopoly profits it can earn while it is still the only firm in the market, as well as the additional profits it earns from the rapid cost reductions it will experience as a result of the learning curve.

The first firm to introduce the new product is able to start sliding down its learning curve immediately and have significantly lower costs per unit by the time the first competitor's product arrives in the marketplace. It takes time to design and manufacture a competing product, even if it is a relatively close copy of the original. The second and subsequent firms must start at the *top* of their learning curves, giving the first-mover a substantial cost advantage. Now, if prices decline because the imitator has to share the market, the first-mover is more likely to be profitable despite declining prices. In Figure 11–7 we show the dynamics of pricing and costs in a hypothetical

FIGURE 11-7. Dynamic Price Paths and the First-Mover Advantage

situation. We suppose that the first-mover sets a price of $10, and it remains constant until time t_1, when entry of competing products occurs. Prices then decline over time as more firms enter and as the firms engage in price competition initially. Even if price leadership or conscious parallelism follows as the market matures, prices are likely to fall in response to falling costs for all firms.

Note that the first-mover maintains its higher profit margin through time despite the falling price level. At time t_2, for example, the price has fallen from its initial level of about $10 to about $7.40. The first-mover's costs have fallen to about $4.40 while the subsequent entrants' costs are about $5.60 per unit. Only if the subsequent entrants learn faster—that is, if they have a higher percentage of learning or if they can expand output faster—can they catch up with the first-mover firm.[4]

Thus we see firms striving to discover and launch new products for the first-mover advantages and profits that result. Unfortunately, most new products are *not* major successes and the firm's profits as first-mover with one new product may easily be eroded by its losses with several other new products that did not sell well and were soon discontinued.[5]

11.4 SUMMARY

In this chapter we have examined the pricing of new products, meaning products that are radically different from what has gone before, rather than existing products that have simply been changed or improved. We noted that it is particularly difficult to collect reliable estimates of market demand for such products, because of the lack of consumer awareness of the product and its usefulness. The innovating firm will search for information on the demand for the product initially, if it expects the value of this information to exceed the search cost. Given the high failure rate of new products, the value of information might be expected to be relatively high, and thus search activity should be seriously considered. Test marketing the new product in a limited area is a typical solution to this problem.

Price skimming will be the preferred pricing strategy if the firm's time horizon falls within the short run, if the demand for the new product will not extend beyond the short run, or if the barriers to entry are insurmountable. In these cases the skimming price will be the short-run profit-maximizing price. A skimming price is also indicated if the product is of the experience or credence type, since post-entry profit will be higher, and a higher initial price may favorably influence perceptions of the product's quality. The limit price to prevent the entry of a high-cost entrant may be viewed as a skimming price, since it will involve a relatively high markup over the innovating firm's (relatively low) unit costs.

Penetration pricing is appropriate when the innovating firm's time horizon falls beyond the short run and its EPV of profit is maximized by setting a relatively low price. This price may be the sales-maximizing price (subject to a minimum profit con-

---

[4]On the topic of first-mover advantages, see A. Michael Spence, "The Learning Curve and Competition," *Bell Journal of Economics*, 12 (Spring 1981), pp. 49-70; Richard Schmalensee, "Product Differentiation Advantages of Pioneering Brands," *American Economic Review*, 72 (June 1982), pp. 349-65; J. L. Guasch and A. Weiss, "Adverse Selection by Markets and the Advantage of Being Late," *Quarterly Journal of Economics*, 94 (May 1980), pp. 453-66; and A. Glazer, "The Advantages of Being First," *American Economic Review*, 75 (June 1985), pp. 473-80.

[5]See R. G. Cooper, "The Dimensions of New Product Success and Failure," *Journal of Marketing*, 43 (Summer 1979), pp. 93-103; J. H. Davidson, "Why Most New Consumer Brands Fail," *Harvard Business Review*, 54 (March/April 1976), pp. 117-22; W. R. Dillon, R. Cantalore, and P. Worthing, "The New Product Problem: An Approach for Investigating Product Failures," *Management Science*, 25 (December 1979), pp. 1184-96.

straint) if the firm can tolerate entry of some firms and expects to earn greater profits in future periods through repeat sales of the item and sales of goods that are complementary to it. If the EPV of profit is maximized by preventing entry and potential entrants would have little or no production cost disadvantages after entering, then the penetration price is the limit price. Search goods are more likely to be candidates for penetration pricing than are experience and credence goods, other things being equal.

After entry occurs, the resulting oligopoly may adopt low-cost price leadership if that is appropriate, or the innovating firm might initially be a dominant firm price leader. Barometric price leadership, conscious parallelism, and independent pricing along *ceteris paribus* demand curves are also possible. The latter is more likely initially while the market is still immature, and some form of price leadership is more likely as the market attains maturity. We expect the price level to decline initially because of reductions in cost that result from learning effects and economies of plant size, as well as because of reduced demand for each firm that results from the entry of new firms at a rate faster than the rate of growth of the market demand. It is possible that prices would rise over time as a result of the inability of firms to enter as fast as the market grows, where there are few or no gains from learning or economies of plant size.

The innovating firm benefits from "first-mover" advantages, which are the initial monopoly profits and an ongoing unit-cost advantage which others will find difficult to overcome. Entrants may have a steeper learning curve because they may avoid some of the pitfalls and dead ends that the innovator encountered. This statement probably is particularly true for "search" products because these products are easier to evaluate and may therefore be easier to emulate. The innovating firm faces the risk that the new product will fail to be a market success and has typically incurred high developmental costs that may not be recouped if the new product is a failure.

DISCUSSION QUESTIONS

11-1. When is a "new" product best analyzed in the context of an established product market? Why?

11-2. Why is an estimate of the demand situation particularly important for new products?

11-3. Under what circumstances is the skimming price appropriately the short-run profit-maximizing price?

11-4. Under what circumstances could a skimming price higher than the short-run profit-maximizing price be EPV maximizing?

11-5. What pricing models can we use to select the penetration price? Why?

11-6. When is the limit price a skimming price, and when is it a penetration price? Why?

11-7. How does the type of product influence the new-product pricing decision?

11-8. What factors operate to cause the price of a new product to decline as time passes?

11-9. What is the product-life-cycle hypothesis? What determines whether the innovating firm's sales volume increases or decreases as entry takes place?

11-10. What are the first-mover advantages? What risks does the first-mover face?

PROBLEMS AND SHORT CASES

11-1. The Eastman Paint Company has developed a new paint which is unique in that it allows the user to turn ordinary glass windows and doors into one-way glass. Moreover, it prevents the transmission of ultraviolet rays, a major factor in the fading of furniture fabrics, carpets, and draperies. The production manager, Arthur Eastman, has estimated the following average variable cost levels (per gallon) for the product for this year and for the next two years. Note that costs decline over time as the production process becomes increasingly streamlined.

	OUTPUT LEVEL (gallons/month)				
	2,000	4,000	6,000	8,000	10,000
Year 1	$12.61	$11.82	$11.74	$11.84	$12.07
Year 2	10.05	9.76	9.60	9.56	9.82
Year 3	9.22	9.04	8.85	8.80	9.02

The advertising manager, Ms. Lois Eastman, is excited about the prospects of the new paint. She believes that the market has long felt the need for such a product, and she has prepared a large campaign to launch the product. Several television advertisements are being prepared and a brochure is in print, all referring to the extensive test results and benefits of the new paint. The focus of the campaign is on the increased privacy afforded by the new paint, with emphasis given to the protection it provides by filtering out the ultraviolet part of the sun's rays.

The price of the new product is to be determined. Market research suggests that the demand situation will be approximated by $Q = 16 - 0.67P$ in the first year (where Q represents thousands of gallons and P is in dollars); $Q = 20 - 0.77P$ in the second year; and $Q = 17.83 - 0.87P$ in the third year. Indications are that market demand will increase in each of the first three years, but the entry of competitors with substitute paints in year 3 will cause Eastman's demand curve to shift to the left, as implied by the above specifications.

The marketing manager, Ms. Margaret Turriff, is faced with the problem of plotting price strategy over the next three years. While year 2 and year 3 prices can be determined in due time, the president of the company wants to know what type of pricing strategy Ms. Turriff intends to employ, since he is concerned that returns from this product be maximized, given the extensive research and development program that gave rise to the new product.

(a) What is the profit-maximizing price in each of the first three years, as estimated from the data given?

(b) Under what conditions would you advise the Eastman Paint Company to pursue a penetration-pricing strategy?

11-2. Quick New Products, Inc., specializes in launching new products and uses intensive television advertising campaigns to encourage high-volume sales before any other firm can enter with a competing product. QNP has a new product ready to launch called the "tender trap," a mousetrap which mice seem to love. Based on its experience, it expects to sell 20,000 units of this product in the first year at the introductory price of $9.95. Its initial cost (for the first 1,000 units) will be $14 per unit, but it expects costs to fall 20 percent for every doubling of output from that point forward. By the time it has sold 20,000 units, it expects two other rivals to be ready to imitate its product, and it expects that it will sell only 5,000 units per year in the following two years, with price gradually falling from $9.95 to $5.95. Total sales (QNP plus rivals') will be 15,000 in each of the second and third years. Its competitors will be subject to the same learning curve when they begin production as was QNP.

(a) Show graphically the dynamic price and average cost path over time for both QNP and one of its rivals (assume the rivals are similar).

(b) Explain the advantages which QNP can expect to derive as the result of being the first-mover in this market.

11-3. The Sharper Shirt Company has recently been formed by an aspiring young designer, Francine Stuart. Her first product will be a man's shirt. At this point, neither the price nor the quality decision have been made. Francine knows that at the retail level shirts typically are sold at certain fairly well defined "price points," notably $10, $13, $17, $23, and $30. Consumers have come to expect these price groupings and the salespeople prefer to deal with shirts that fit neatly into these price groups. Naturally, higher quality shirts are expected at the higher price points.

Francine is trying to decide between going for the $17-shirt market or for the $30-shirt market. She has estimated her average costs to be $6 for the $17 shirt and $12 for the $30 shirt in the first year and approximately 80 percent of these figures in the second year. Note that Sharper Shirts would receive the wholesale price of only $12 for the $17 shirt and $20 for the $30 shirt. Market research activity in the form of tentative orders from retailers has resulted in the following probability distributions of demand for each shirt over the first two years.

Sales	$17 SHIRT		$30 SHIRT	
Level	Year 1	Year 2	Year 1	Year 2
10,000	0.25	0.10	0.30	0.20
20,000	0.50	0.60	0.60	0.65
30,000	0.25	0.30	0.10	0.15

(a) Using decision-tree analysis and assuming an opportunity discount rate of 15 percent, calculate the expected net present value of each decision.

(b) Is there much difference in the comparative risk associated with each strategy, based on the data provided?

(c) Advise Ms. Stuart about which shirt she should produce and sell.

(d) State any qualifications and assumptions which underlie your answer.

11-4. Boxem-Buddies, Inc., has developed a new exercise machine that will appeal to those who like to combine an exercise program with boxing practice. After a successful market-testing program they have estimated the demand curve for this machine to be $P = 188.2351 - 0.0023Q$. Their fixed costs are expected to be $200,000 per annum, and marginal costs rise with output, as indicated by the expression $MC = 25.8634 + 0.0018Q$. The intercept of the market demand curve is expected to shift upward by 10 percent in the second year, with the slope term remaining the same. If Boxem-Buddies sets the profit-maximizing price in the first year, there will be entry of one firm at the start of the second year. Its cost curve is estimated to be $TC = 240,000 + 35Q + 0.002Q^2$. Because of its higher costs, it is expected to allow Boxem-Buddies to be the price leader. Moreover, because the innovating firm expects to gain a product differentiation advantage, the entrant will only get a third of the market when the prices are equal.

(a) What are the short-run profit-maximizing price and output levels for the machine in year 1?

(b) What is the limit price that would prevent the entry of the new firm? At that price what output would Boxem-Buddies sell?

(c) Suppose BB sets the profit-maximizing price in year 1 and the new firm enters. What price will it set as price leader? What are its output and profit levels in the second year?

(d) In retrospect, should BB have set the limit price? Explain and defend your answer with any underlying assumptions.

11-5. Waltham Wallpaper Company has developed a new type of wallpaper that is easier to apply. WWC calls their product Magicpaper. It does not need glue, nor does it need to be immersed in water before application. Instead it is more like a contact paper that sticks by itself, but Magicpaper may be removed and readjusted very easily because the "glue" does not set permanently until 24 hours after exposure to air. Because of this ease of application WWC intends to supply Magicpaper in 40-inch widths, which is expected to be a major selling feature as well. Finally, the new type of backing used on Magicpaper allows all kinds of fabric and other materials to be bonded to the front side for a far superior finish, rendering all formerly available textured wallpapers inferior by comparison.

WWC's average variable cost of producing Magicpaper is expected to be $25.00 per linear yard (40 inches wide) the first month, and this cost is expected to fall by about 20 percent each time cumulative output doubles. The output rate is fixed at 2,000 yards per month. WWC's usual markup on wallpaper of 100 percent over AVC allows its prices to be quite competitive. With Magicpaper, however, it is considering setting the initial price using a 200 percent markup, since it expects demand to support this price given the limit on output per month. Also, it expects to be the only supplier for at least a year, and it would like to recoup its rather substantial developmental costs quickly. At this price, all five of the firm's rivals are likely to respond with similar versions of this new product by the second year, at which time prices will be forced downward until markups are more competitive, probably around the 100 percent level, since this is the conventional level in the wallpaper market. Eventually, market shares tend to come out equal in any particular product line, as well.

Alternatively, WWC could employ a strategy to limit entry to the only two other firms that could afford to incur the developmental costs. This strategy would involve using a markup of 150 percent initially and then reducing markups back toward 100 percent after the firms enter. At that price, demand is expected to be 2,500 yards per month, and WWC could produce this amount using a "weekend shift." About half of the regular workers and several "weekenders" would work as long as it takes on Saturday to produce the extra 500 yards of Magicpaper. This Saturday session would initially have an incremental cost to WWC of $20,000, labor and materials included. Learning effects are expected to allow this figure to decline at the same rate as weekday production, however.

(a) Advise WWC what their EPV of contribution is likely to be if they follow the skimming-price strategy. (Assume an opportunity discount rate of 12 percent and make any other assumptions you need to, but consider the sensitivity of your answer to these assumptions.)

(b) Alternatively, what is the EPV of profits if WWC follows the moderate pricing strategy that will limit entry to just its two largest rivals?

(c) Should WWC simply start with a 100 percent markup and limit the entry of all rivals? Consider the issues involved.

(d) Summarize your recommendation to WWC.

11-6. The Knowlton Chemical Company plans to introduce its Bug Buster, a sex-lure trap that attracts all kinds of flying insects and beetles. The technology is simple—there is just one active ingredient, and this fact is public knowledge following a university researcher's publication of her research findings. Knowlton has the jump on competitors, however, since they funded the research and became privy to the findings at an earlier stage. Knowlton expects to have a monopoly on the new Bug Buster for the first year, but expects entry of two new firms in time for the second year's "bug season," and entry of three more in the third year. This entry is expected to take place because Knowlton's cost advantage over the entrants is expected to be minor, since the chemical ingredient is readily available at relatively low cost. Knowlton's estimated marginal cost of production is $4 per unit, constant across all foreseeable output rates.

On the demand side, Knowlton expects to sell 200,000 units in the first year at a proposed price of $9.99. Its marketing research team has estimated that this is the profit-maximizing price in the first year. At that price, market demand is expected to increase to 500,000 units in the second year and to approach 1 million units in the third year. (Note that there will be entry of new firms as well.) In the second and third years, the market price of the Bug Buster and its rival products would respond to supply and demand conditions, but it would tend to be fairly similar for all firms, because of the limited scope for product differentiation that exists.

(a) From the information given, deduce an expression for the market demand curve that apparently underlies the choice of the initial price.

(b) Assuming that the slope of the market demand curve stays the same, estimate the market demand curves for the second and third years.

(c) Specify the demand curve facing Knowlton in the second and third years, in your best estimation given the data supplied.

(d) Supposing that Knowlton assumes the role of low-cost price leader, what price would it wish to set in each of the second and third years, and what are its expected output levels in each of those years?

(e) What assumptions and qualifications underlie your analysis?

11-7. Hi-Techniks, Inc., has recently received a patent on a new product, an electronic cockroach deterrent. This device emits a high frequency noise that drives cockroaches out of the user's house or apartment into neighboring dwellings. Hi-Techniks plans to produce and market the product themselves, as well as to allow production by any other company that is willing to pay a royalty of $10 per unit produced, under a licensing agreement.

Hi-Techniks estimates its total cost function will be $TC = 200,000 + 80Q$, up to a maximum output rate of 40,000 units per year. Because of learning effects, average variable costs are expected to decline 25 percent in each of the second and third years. The fixed costs of competitors are expected to be about 20 percent higher, and their variable costs will be similar to those of Hi-Techniks, except for the royalty payment to Hi-Techniks.

Market demand for the product, estimated on the basis of a market survey conducted in New York City, is expected to be represented by the expression $P = 300 - 0.005Q$ and is expected to remain steady at that level for several years as market awareness of the product spreads and continues to attract new customers. Hi-Techniks expects to be a monopoly for the first year. If entry occurs, each new entrant is expected to gain $1/(n + 1)$ of the market, and Hi-Techniks will end up with $2/(n + 1)$ of the market, where n is the number of firms. Hi-Techniks expects three other firms to seek licensing agreements and enter the market after the first year, if the price set by Hi-Techniks allows them to avoid losses. No further entry is expected after these firms enter. Hi-Techniks' time horizon is three years, and its cost of capital is 15 percent per annum.

(a) What is the profit-maximizing price that Hi-Techniks could set in the first year? How many units would be sold at that price?

(b) Assuming entry of three firms at the end of the first year and that Hi-Techniks will emerge as the low-cost price leader, what price will be profit-maximizing for Hi-Techniks in the second and third years? What sales volume should Hi-Techniks expect in these years?

(c) What is the limit price that would prevent any other firm from entering the market, presuming that the royalty remains at $10 per unit, and that all three potential entrants would enter at the start of the second year if Hi-Techniks's price in the first year would allow the entrants to be profitable. (An approximate answer from a graph would suffice, or you may solve this problem algebraically.)

(d) Which is the EPV-maximizing strategy over the three-year time horizon, price skimming or penetration pricing?

(e) What assumptions and qualifications underlie your analysis?

11-8. Tropical Delights, Inc., is considering introducing a new fruit juice to the mainland market. This juice, to be called Tropic Morning, is a mixture of various tropical fruits, but TDI plans to keep the exact formulation secret. Consumer clinics conducted in Waikiki using tourists from mainland states indicate that the product will face a market demand curve in the first year of the venture specified by $P = 33.535 - 0.2828Q$, where Q represents thousands of cases, and P is the price per case of twelve bottles. Market demand is expected to increase by 20 percent per year for the next five years. TDI's cost of production is expected to be $TC = 300,000 +$

$6.25Q + 0.025Q^2$. The coefficients in this expression that determine the marginal cost are expected to decline by about 15 percent per year, because of learning effects in the production process.

Other firms are expected to enter the market with competing tropical fruit juices if TDI's product proves to be a success in the first year (that is, if the demand estimates prove to be accurate). TDI will have no cost advantages over these potential entrants, and in fact will probably have higher costs than a large rival that currently specializes in pineapple fruit and juice production. TDI's cost disadvantage would be about 20 percent, it estimates. On the demand side, however, TDI expects to establish a strong brand name identity which will make rivals' products only imperfect substitutes for Tropic Morning, such that it will retain about half the market after the expected entry of three or four rival firms, when prices are roughly equal.

The management of TDI is deliberating whether to set a skimming price or a penetration price initially. Their time horizon is three years, and their opportunity discount rate is 10 percent. You are asked to advise them on the pricing strategy they should employ.

(a) What are the arguments that might be used in favor of the skimming price? What skimming price level would you recommend?

(b) What arguments militate in favor of the penetration price? What penetration price level would you recommend?

(c) What is likely to happen to TDI's price and output level in the second and subsequent years, (1) if a skimming price is set initially, and (2) if a penetration price is set initially?

(d) Advise TDI's management as to the strategy you feel they should pursue, with supporting arguments and qualifications.

11-9. Bowers Automotive Equipment is planning to launch its new product, a pair of miniature radio transmitters that would allow the owner to locate a car that was misplaced in a crowded parking lot, or even stolen and left somewhere else. One transmitter would be hidden in the car, and the owner would activate it by a hand-held transmitter/receiver that would be carried away from the car in a pocket or handbag. The owner would then zero in on the lost vehicle by moving in the direction of strongest signal. BAE calls this product the Car Finder. Test marketing of this product has resulted in the following initial demand curve being estimated: $P = 295.6 - 0.0852Q$, where Q is the number of Car Finders.

BAE has assembled 1,500 units in the past month, and notes that average variable cost was \$40 and average fixed cost was \$60. They expect average variable costs to fall by 20 percent each time cumulative output doubles, however. They estimate that the quantity demanded initially will be 1,500 units per month at a price of \$149.95, but that the demand curve will shift to the right by about 250 units every month following the product's launch. Their present plant can produce up to 3,000 units a month, with constant marginal cost, but that output is the absolute maximum. If sales exceed 3,000 units a month, a larger plant will be required. Larger facilities and automated assembly equipment would reduce the average variable costs by 30 percent, however, and marginal costs are expected to be constant at this new level. Overhead costs would increase by 50 percent with the larger plant, which would have a maximum output rate of 6,000 units a month.

Competition is expected in the market if demand increases at the suggested rate. BAE expects Eldridge Electronics to come up with their own version of the product within six months, and Abersen Digital Systems probably will also enter the market within a year. Based on their track records, both these firms are expected to come out with a product which is better in some way, and they would therefore reduce BAE's market share to 40 percent after six months and to 30 percent after twelve months. Of course, BAE's engineers will strive to improve the Car Finder as time passes, but the better research facilities at BAE's competitors mean that the new entrants' products will probably have a competitive edge. All firms would have similar initial cost structures and would experience similar rates of learning in production.

(a) Is the proposed price the profit-maximizing price for the first month? If not, why do you think BAE chose that particular price level?

(b) Calculate the expected monthly output rates and profits for each of the first six months, presuming that the price stays at $149.95 and that Eldridge will enter the market at the start of the seventh month. Should BAE plan to build the larger plant?

(c) Speculate what would happen if Eldridge were to enter the market after six months with a superior product priced at $169.95 and capture 60 percent of the market, which continued to grow. Should BAE change its price? Calculate the monthly output rates and profits that BAE might expect over months 7 through 12. If you haven't already recommended building the larger plant, would you recommend it now?

(d) Now speculate that Abersen will enter the market after twelve months with a product superior to Eldridge's but also priced at $169.95. What would you expect to happen to Eldridges price? Should BAE change its price? Explain.

(e) Advise BAE as to the initial and subsequent prices they should set for their new product. Note all qualifications and underlying assumptions.

11-10. Yashoko Camera Company is the first to offer a new electronic camera that uses a magnetic disk to store visual images instead of film. After taking photographs in the usual way, the disk is transferred to a video player and the photographs may be viewed on the screen. Selected photographs may then be printed from this machine, in full color or in black and white.

Yashoko predicts that demand for this product will grow rapidly at first, then grow at a declining rate, and finally sales per month will begin to decline as other manufacturers bring out competing products and the market approaches saturation. The firm's demand function for the first year is expected to be $Q = 5146.7535 - 2.2584P$. The intercept term in this expression is expected to increase by 30 percent for the second year, then decrease by 10 percent for the third year, and finally decrease by another 30 percent in the fourth year.

The total variable cost function for this new product is estimated to be $TC = 100,000 + 480Q + 0.25Q^2$ for the first 2,000 units, and then the learning effect in production will cause the intercept term of this cost function to decline by 15 percent each time cumulative output doubles.

(a) Advise Yashoko as to the price level that is profit-maximizing in each of the next four years.

(b) Considering the marketing benefits of having a stable price level over a period of time, and considering Yashoko's interest in establishing their brand name and reputation as a manufacturer of high-value products, recommend a pricing strategy that might be followed.

(c) Calculate the expected sales volume and profits for each year, given your choice of price(s) in part (b).

(d) Outline all qualifications and assumptions that underlie your analysis.

SUGGESTED REFERENCES AND FURTHER READING

Cooper, R. G. "The Dimensions of New Product Success and Failure," *Journal of Marketing*, 43 (Summer 1979), pp. 93-103.

Davidson, J. H. "Why Most New Consumer Brands Fail," *Harvard Business Review*, 54 (March-April 1976), pp. 117-22.

Dean, Joel. "Pricing Pioneering Products," *Journal of Industrial Economics*, 17 (July 1969), pp. 165-79.

Dean, Joel. "Pricing Policies for New Products," *Harvard Business Review*, 28 (November-December 1950).

Dhalla, N. K., and S. Yuspeh. "Forget the Product Life Cycle Concept!" *Harvard Business Review*, January-February 1976, pp. 102-12.

Donnelly, J. H., and M. J. Etzel. "Degrees of Product Newness and Early Trial," *Journal of Marketing Research*, 10 (August 1973), pp. 295-300.

Gabor, A., and W. C. J. Granger. "The Pricing of New Products," *Scientific Business*, August 1965, pp. 141-50.

Glazer, A. "The Advantages of Being First," *American Economic Review*, 75 (June 1985), pp. 473-80.

Guasch, J. L., and A. Weiss. "Adverse Selection by Markets and the Advantages of Being Late," *Quarterly Journal of Economics*, 94 (May 1980), pp. 453-66.

Kotler, P. *Principles of Marketing* (4th ed.), chap. 10. Englewood Cliffs, N.J.: Prentice-Hall, Inc., 1980.

Levitt, T. "Exploit the Product Life Cycle," *Harvard Business Review*, November–December 1976, pp. 81-94.

Livesey, F. *Pricing*, chap. 8. London: Macmillan, Inc., 1976.

Sabel, H. "On Pricing New Products," *German Economic Review*, 11, No. 4 (1973), pp. 292-311.

Schmalensee, R. "Product Differentiation Advantages of Pioneering Brands," *American Economic Review*, 72 (June 1982), pp. 349-65.

Spence, A. M. "The Learning Curve and Competition," *Bell Journal of Economics*, 12 (Spring 1981), pp. 49-70.

12 | Competitive Bids and Price Quotes

12.1 INTRODUCTION

- **Definition:** *Competitive bidding markets* may be defined as those in which there are a number of sellers (who generally cannot or do not communicate with each other) who compete to provide a product or service to a single buyer. The buyer makes it known that he or she wishes to purchase a particular product or service, and the sellers tender their bids or quotes for the supply of that product or service. If the suppliers are quoting to a particular set of specifications, the buyer presumably chooses the lowest bid, whereas if there are quality differences in the products or services offered by the suppliers, the buyer must decide which of the offers represents the "best deal," by considering both the price and the quality differences.

  Example: Competitive bidding markets are much more common than is generally recognized. In addition to the markets for bridges, dams, highways, and buildings, the markets for a wide range of industrial components and household and personal services exhibit essentially the same features. Firms call for bids on everything from office supplies to automobile fleets. Householders call for quotes on repair jobs in the house and on their automobiles. Individuals ask the price when seeking a variety of professional services such as medical, dental, legal, and business consulting. Each supplier should expect the buyer to have obtained price quotes from other suppliers or at least to have a general awareness of the appropriate price level, and the supplier will recognize that if his or her quote is too high the business will go elsewhere. On the other hand, if the quote is too low, the supplier will get the business but it will be less profitable business than it might have been.

  The pricing problem in this type of market is essentially that the seller must choose a price high enough to provide a sufficient contribution to overheads and profits, yet low enough to ensure that a sufficient volume of work is actually obtained. In all the situations we have mentioned, however, the supplier must choose the price in an environment of considerable uncertainty about the behavior of the competitors.

When compared with the amount of price information generated by established markets, this type of market situation generates very little information, since each transaction is, in effect, a "one-shot" sale with little relationship to previous sales and with little information value for future sales.

Types of Bids and Price Quotes

Competitive bid markets are usually characterized by one of three different types of bid or price quote, although mixed-bid markets may exist. When the supplier tenders a bid price, or makes a price quote, and undertakes to complete the job for that price regardless of any variation of costs from the expected level, the bid is known as a *fixed-price bid*. Note that the supplier must estimate the costs of fulfilling the contract and that there is uncertainty involved in these cost estimates because the bid price is tendered now and the costs will be incurred later. Input prices may change, the design may prove more difficult than expected, more labor and materials might be required, and so on. Thus there is a probability distribution of cost associated with the completion of the contract, and the expected value of this probability distribution is the supplier's estimated cost level. If costs will be incurred beyond the present period, they should be expressed in expected-present-value terms. In the fixed-price case the price is determined *ex ante*, before the contract is undertaken, and the supplier faces the entire risk of cost variability, which is measured by the standard deviation of the probability distribution of costs around the expected value of costs.

Cost-plus-fee bids are the opposite case, where the bid price is determined *ex post*, after the contract is completed, and is equal to the actual costs of the job plus a fee (or profit margin) for the supplier. In this case the entire risk of cost variability is borne by the buyer, who agrees to pay whatever the actual costs turn out to be plus a fee. The fee may be a fixed amount, or it may be based on the actual costs, in which case it is usually expressed as a markup over costs. The buyer retains the right to an audit of the supplier's costs, to assure the buyer that the actual costs are fair and reasonable. Cost-plus-fee bids are common where the degree of cost uncertainty is particularly high. Repair work to automobiles, household appliances, and industrial plant and equipment typically proceeds on this basis, because the actual labor time and parts required become known only as the repair work progresses. The main problem with cost-plus-fee bids, as any consumer will appreciate, is that the supplier has little incentive to control costs. Given that the buyer's audit of the costs is time-consuming and imperfect because of the asymmetry of information, the final price to the buyer is typically higher than it would have been if the supplier had had a greater incentive to keep costs to a minimum.

Incentive bids, also known as risk-sharing bids, are the intermediate case. Here the buyer and supplier agree beforehand on a bid price but agree to share any deviation from the expected cost level in a given way. The *ex ante* bid price is based on the expected costs plus a profit margin for the supplier. A deviation of the actual costs from the expected costs is known as a cost overrun or underrun. If there is a cost overrun, the buyer pays the *ex ante* bid price plus a share of the cost overrun, and the supplier's profit margin is reduced by its share of the cost overrun. Conversely, if there is a cost underrun, the buyer's *ex post* price is the *ex ante* price less the buyer's share of the cost underrun, and the supplier's profit margin is increased by its share of the cost underrun. This is easily summarized in symbols, as follows:

$$B = C_t + \Pi_t + (1 - s)(C_t - C_a) \tag{12-1}$$

$$\Pi_a = \Pi_t + s(C_t - C_a) \tag{12-2}$$

where B is the *ex post* bid price paid by the buyer; C_t is the supplier's target costs (expected present value); C_a is the actual (*ex post*) costs; s is the supplier's share of the cost variation; Π_a is the actual profit received by the supplier; and Π_t is the target profit (expected present value) received by the supplier.

It can readily be seen that the risk-sharing case collapses to the fixed-price bid case when $s = 1$. In the fixed-price case,

$$B = C_t + \Pi_t \tag{12-3}$$

$$\Pi_a = \Pi_t + (C_t - C_a) \tag{12-4}$$

Conversely, when $s = 0$, we have the cost-plus-fee case:

$$B = C_a + \Pi_t \tag{12-5}$$

$$\Pi_a = \Pi_t \tag{12-6}$$

In what kinds of competitive bid markets should we expect fixed-price bids? Several possibilities suggest themselves. First, if suppliers are risk neutral, the risk of cost variability will mean nothing to them, and risk-averse buyers will prefer fixed-price bids. Second, if suppliers undertake many contracts of this type (incurring cost overruns on some and cost underruns on others), they can act as if they are risk neutral, because the law of averages will ensure that they will be better off using the expected-value decision criterion than any other. Third, if costs are relatively easy to control and there is consequently little or no cost uncertainty from the supplier's viewpoint, we should expect fixed-price bids. Fourth, if the supplier doesn't really care if there is a cost overrun or underrun, it may be willing to bid in this fashion. This might be the case where the value of the contract is trivial compared to the value of the supplying firm, and thus the marginal utility of the dollars involved in the cost variance is negligible. Alternatively, if the supplier is spending someone else's money and there is a principal-agent problem without proper incentives to cause the agent (manager) to act in the best interests of the principal (shareholder), the supplier may tender a fixed bid regardless of the risk of cost variability. Finally, if the buyer is extremely risk averse and will only accept fixed-price bids, the supplier will tender a fixed-price bid, even if it is also highly risk averse.

Cost-plus-fee bids will tend to predominate under the opposite conditions. If the buyer is risk neutral or can act as if it is risk neutral because it has many such contracts, suppliers will be happy to pass the risk of cost variability along to the buyer. If the buyer attaches low marginal utility to the dollars potentially involved in the cost variance, whether because of the relative triviality of the contract or because of a principal-agent problem, we should expect cost-plus-fee bids. Where there is extreme risk of cost variability, suppliers may refuse to bid in any other mode, since a cost overrun could be ruinous. Finally, if designs are speculative and quality is imperative to the buyer, such as in defense contracting, we should expect a preference for cost-plus-fee bids.

Risk-sharing, or incentive, contracts arise when cost uncertainty is relatively high but there is a perceived need to control the supplier's spending while ensuring that quality does not suffer. Defense contracting shifted to this mode, from the cost-plus-fee mode, for exactly these reasons. The share of the risk borne by each party will be determined by their relative risk aversions, the buyer's perception of the supplier's propensity to relax cost control, and competitive pressures from other suppliers willing to take a greater share of the risk at each *ex ante* bid level.[1]

The supplier's first problem is to ascertain the *ex ante* bid price that maximizes the expected present value of contribution (EPVC) to overheads and profit, assuming the supplier bears the entire risk of cost variability. Having ascertained that price, the risk-averse supplier will be willing to trade off some expected return for a reduced share of the cost variation. The supplier may wish to bid in the cost-plus-fee mode and will trade off some of the EPVC to reduce risk to zero. Thus the firm would tender a bid equal to the certainty equivalent of the EPVC-maximizing fixed-price bid, as we shall see. If the optimal strategy is a risk-sharing bid, the supplier will similarly trade off some expected profit in return for a reduced share of any cost variation and will submit a bid that is lower than the EPVC-maximizing bid level. We begin by finding the bid price level that maximizes the EPVC.

12.2 INCREMENTAL COSTS, INCREMENTAL REVENUES, AND THE OPTIMAL BID PRICE

We saw in Chapter 7 that there are three main categories of incremental costs and revenues, namely, present-period explicit costs and revenues, opportunity costs and revenues, and future period costs and revenues. Let us consider these in the context of the competitive bidding problem.

---

[1]See J. J. McCall, "The Simple Economics of Incentive Contracting," *American Economic Review*, 60 (September 1967), pp. 837–46; and F. M. Scherer, "The Theory of Contractual Incentives for Cost Reduction," *Quarterly Journal of Economics*, 78 (May 1964), pp. 257–80.

The Incremental Costs of the Contract

■ *Definition:* The *incremental costs of the contract* are all those costs, expressed in expected-present-value terms, which are expected to be incurred as a result of winning and completing the terms of the contract. Costs that have been incurred already (sunk costs) and costs that will be incurred whether this contract is won or lost (committed costs) are not incremental costs for the purpose of the pricing decision to be made.

Present-Period Explicit Costs. This category of incremental costs consists of the direct and explicit costs associated with undertaking and completing the project. Included are such cost categories as direct materials, direct labor, and variable overhead. For each of these cost categories we must be careful to include only those amounts that are expected to be paid for the purchases of materials, labor and supplies, and services required to complete production and delivery of the specified goods and services. These may be estimated on the basis of requirements for similar projects in the past, given present cost levels, plus a trend factor if one is apparent and the production will take an appreciable period of time.

In some cases an item of capital equipment must be purchased for a particular job and will have a useful life remaining after the completion of the present job. Incremental reasoning implies that the whole cost is applied to the present job and that the machine will not be part of the incremental cost on any subsequent jobs, if these in fact materialize. If ownership of the item will allow a stream of contributions to be earned in the future, the expected net present value of these contributions should enter the present decision, since they are incremental to this decision.[2]

Another consideration is the capacity utilization rate of the firm. When the firm is at or near full capacity, it must consider the additional incremental costs that will be incurred if it obtains the contract, such as overtime labor rates, outside contracting, penalty charges associated with existing contracts, and any other additional costs, and hence its minimum bid price must be higher to the extent that these costs are incurred.

Opportunity Costs. The opportunity cost of undertaking and completing a specific project is the value of the resources employed (that is, their contribution) in their best alternative usage. Hence, if plant, equipment, and personnel are lying idle, the opportunity cost of using them for a particular contract is zero. On the other hand, if these resources are currently employed in a project that will have to be set aside, delayed, or canceled, the contribution that would have been derived from this alternate project must enter the incremental costs as an opportunity cost. A firm may decide to submit a tender on a specific project and, if successful with that bid, may choose to defer

---

[2]The practice of apportioning the capital cost of an item over the present and future jobs implies a probability of unity that these future contracts will be gained. This may be an overstatement of the probabilities, of course, and may induce the firm to purchase an item, the cost of which may never be recouped. Moreover, the simple allocation of a cost over future jobs ignores the fact that a dollar received now is worth more than a dollar received in the future.

completion of another project already in process. To the extent provided by the penalty clause in the earlier contract, this decision to defer completion will cost the firm money that is an incremental cost occasioned by receipt of the latter contract. To the extent that a project in process simply is delayed and is completed later, the opportunity cost is the interest income forgone as a result of the later receipt of payment for that job.

Future Costs.   Future incremental costs may include the effects of ill will, deteriorating labor relations or supplier relations, and legal recourse by dissatisfied buyers or government prosecutors. Ill will is the EPVC of future contracts *lost* as a result of taking the present contract. There may be longer-term disadvantages, for example, in taking a contract which breaks a strike or which takes advantage of the misfortune of a competitor or other party. Future labor problems may arise if the present contract would cause the firm to operate with congestion of work space and facilities. Hard work for employees and good profits for the firm may tip the balance in favor of a labor strike for a wage increase. Supplier relations may be exacerbated by the present contract if it requires very tight deadlines and unusually stringent quality control, leading to the firm's suppliers (or subcontractors) asking for a higher price for materials and supplies needed for future contracts. Finally there is always the possibility of future legal claims for damages associated with the present contract or of prosecution under the provisions of the antitrust laws or of other legislation. To the extent that these costs can be foreseen, their EPV should be estimated and included as an incremental cost.

Example: The city's garbage collectors have been on strike for several weeks, and the mayor calls for bids for a one-week contract with an outside firm to move the garbage. Your firm, which is engaged in the construction industry, has the trucks and the personnel necessary, and you calculate your incremental present-period explicit costs to be $100,000 for the week, comprised of direct labor, fuel, repairs and maintenance, and so on.

   You are currently utilizing your equipment and work force on a day-to-day basis moving landfill to an area that will eventually be a new housing development. The contribution to overheads and profits from this job is $10,000 per week. If you win the contract to move the garbage, you must give up this contribution, and this is, therefore, the opportunity cost of winning the city's contract.

   If you win the job, you are afraid that there will be a backlash response from a company with whom you currently hold a contract for the annual removal of debris and waste products. Their labor force is strongly unionized and you feel that there is a fifty-fifty chance the firm may decide not to offer you the renewal of that contract. You reason that they may do this in order to avoid labor strife at their own plant, which they think may result if they renew the contract with the firm that helped break the city garbage workers' strike. Next year's contract with this firm is expected to contribute $20,000 to overheads and profits if it is renewed. Supposing your opportunity discount rate to be 15 percent and the cash flow to be one year away, its present value is

$20,000 \times 0.8696 = \$17,392$. Given your estimate of the probability of losing the contract at 0.5, the EPV of this future cost, or ill will, is $\$17,392 \times 0.5 = \$8,696$.

Thus the incremental cost of the job is estimated to be the sum of the present-period explicit costs, $100,000; plus the opportunity costs, $10,000; plus the EPV of the future costs, $8,696; or $118,696 in total. You would require incremental revenues to be at least this high before you would consider taking the job in order to avoid making an incremental loss on the job.

Note: Incremental costs do not include any sunk costs or costs which would have been incurred regardless of this particular pricing decision. As a result, *bid preparation costs* are technically *not* an incremental cost of the job but they are, instead, a cost of preparing to bid on the job. There are two separate decisions to be made: First, will the firm prepare and submit a bid at all; and, second, at what price level will this bid be? Bid preparation costs will include the search costs of generating information about costs, revenues, and probabilities of success at various price levels. On the basis of this information, the firm may decide not to bid at all. If it does decide to bid, the actual pricing decision will be taken after the bid preparation costs have been incurred. They are therefore *sunk* costs as far as the pricing decision is concerned and should not be included as incremental costs.[3]

The Incremental Revenues of the Contract

- *Definition:* *The incremental revenues of the contract* are all those revenues, expressed in expected-present-value terms, which are expected to be received as a result of winning and completing the contract. These revenues may be considered under the same three categories—present period, opportunity, and future revenues.

Present-Period Incremental Revenues. If the contract will be completed and the bid price received during the present period, the bid price can be included in nominal dollars as an incremental revenue. In cases where payment will be received during a future period, the bid price should be discounted at the opportunity rate to find the present value of this cash flow. In some cases, the firm will have written into the contract that it will receive some portion of the bid price (for example, one half) when the job is one-half completed. In this case, part of the bid price may be treated in nominal dollars (if it is to be received in the present period) with the balance being discounted to present-value terms.

Opportunity Revenues. Costs which can be avoided if the contract is won are known as *opportunity revenues*.

---

[3]At this point it is worth emphasizing that we are calculating incremental costs, not the actual bid price. In order to substantiate its chosen bid price the firm may wish to include various sunk costs and exclude some of its incremental costs. This is effectively a promotional decision, to be taken *after* the pricing decision.

Example: Opportunity revenues include severance pay and other costs of laying off personnel and the subsequent rehiring and retraining costs which would be incurred if the firm were forced to close down and wait until it won another contract before starting up again. Plant and equipment which will stand idle for a time must be "mothballed" to prevent its deterioration while idle. For example, machinery may need to be sprayed with oil to prevent rusting. Upon start-up, there is an additional cost of cleaning and readying the plant for use again. Another opportunity revenue which is possible is the research and development costs which can be avoided as a result of the present contract. A firm may know it has to develop a particular electronic device, for example, for the improvement of one of its existing products. If the contract currently being considered involves the development of that technology as a by-product, then winning the present contract allows future research and development expenditure to be avoided. For example, Cubic Corporation has found that some of its developments for the aerospace industry have been applicable to its products in other areas, notably elevators and fare-collection systems.

Future Revenues. The present contract may give rise to future contracts and sales, which represent the *goodwill* to be generated by the present contract. Goodwill should be regarded as the expected present value of the contribution (EPVC) which is expected to be received from subsequent contracts won *as a result* of having won and successfully completed the current contract. Care must be taken to include only *incremental* goodwill; an established firm may foresee contracts which would have been won regardless of the current contract and therefore should not consider the current contract as contributing to goodwill. On the other hand, a firm trying to enter a market may need one or more initial contracts won and successfully completed in order to be considered for future contracts. Counting the EPVC of these future contracts as an incremental revenue of the current contract allows the firm to rationally submit a somewhat lower bid than its established rivals and thus increase the likelihood of its winning the contract.

Example: The Universal Lamp Company plans to bid on a contract to manufacture and supply energy-saving fluorescent-incandescent light bulbs for a government building. At present, Universal has no work to do and will have to lay off workers within a few weeks unless it wins this contract. Universal has never manufactured these new-generation light bulbs before and knows that it must establish its credibility by demonstrating that it can manufacture a high-quality product and that it can meet the delivery schedule proposed. Its proposed bid price is $278,500, which it expects will be at least $100,000 less than the next-lowest bid, given its knowledge of recent contracts awarded and publicized. Universal feels that it must bid this low in order to win the job—any lower price difference may cause the government purchaser to opt for a more expensive, but established, supplier. If it wins the job, it is confident that it will produce a high-quality product and, therefore, make itself eligible for future contracts at higher profit margins.

Suppose that Universal will avoid layoff, mothball, and other costs, of $36,000, associated with closing down and later reopening this plant, if they win this contract. Suppose further that if they win this contract, they expect a 75 percent chance of a follow-up contract, with contribution of $200,000, to be awarded next year. The present value of that contribution (at 15 percent ODR, for example) is $173,920. The EPVC is, thus, $173,920 × 0.75 = $130,440.

This contract, therefore, promises incremental revenues of the bid price, $278,500; plus the opportunity revenues, $36,000; plus the EPVC of future sales foreseen, $130,440; or $444,940 in total. Thus the firm's incremental costs could be anything up to that figure, and it would still be incrementally profitable for Universal to complete the contract with its bid of $278,500.

The Optimal Bid Price

■ *Definition:* Given that the firm's objective is to maximize its net present worth, the *optimal bid price* will be the price level which maximizes the expected present value of contribution to overheads and profits.

To find the expected present value of each bid price, we must multiply its EPVC by the probability of winning the contract at that price level. The higher the bid price, the lower the "success probability," or the likelihood that the firm will submit the lowest bid. (For simplicity here, we assume a completely specified contract where there are no design or quality differences between tenders.)

Example: Suppose that the firm has obtained a reliable set of success probabilities, after consideration of the past bidding behavior and current capacity utilization of all its rivals. In Table 12–1 we show an assumed incremental cost (in expected-present-value terms and net of any incremental revenues other than the bid price) of $50,000. Several arbitrarily chosen bid prices and the resultant contribution and success probability for each bid price are shown in columns 2, 3, and 4. The product of columns 3 and 4 is the EPVC for each bid price level. The bid price which appears to maximize EPVC is $70,000. But this price was chosen arbitrarily from a spectrum of possible bid prices. By plotting the EPVC against bid prices and interpolating between the points,

TABLE 12-1. Expected Present Value Analysis of a Bid-Pricing Problem

Net EPV Incremental Cost [1]	Bid Price [2]	Contribution [3]	Success Probability [4]	EPVC [5]
$50,000	$ 50,000	$ 0	0.90	$ 0
50,000	60,000	10,000	0.70	7,000
50,000	70,000	20,000	0.50	10,000
50,000	80,000	30,000	0.30	9,000
50,000	90,000	40,000	0.15	6,000
50,000	100,000	50,000	0.05	2,500

we would find that the EPVC is maximized when the bid price is approximately $73,500, as indicated in Figure 12-1.

Thus the firm should bid at $73,500 to pursue the maximization of its net present worth. While it may not win this particular contract, if it bids for a large number of such contracts, the present value of its total contribution to overheads and profits, and hence its net present worth, will be maximized by continually bidding at the price which maximizes EPVC for each particular contract. It wins some and loses some, but on average it comes out ahead, as compared to any other pattern of bidding.

Aesthetic, Political, and Risk Considerations.   It is perhaps unreasonable to expect a decision maker to make a choice simply on the basis of quantifiable cost and revenue considerations. In some cases certain aesthetic considerations enter the bidding process. Suppose the project alluded to in Table 12-1 was something other than a straightforward and normal project. On the one hand, it may appeal to the artistic tastes of the decision maker; on the other hand, it may involve considerable amounts of dirty and uncomfortable work. In the first case we might expect a decision maker to choose a bid price somewhat below the expected value, since the nonmonetary gratification received by the decision maker would offset some of the monetary compensation involved in the higher bid price. But if the job is expected to be dirty, uncomfortable, or inconvenient in some nonmonetary way, we might expect the decision maker's bid to be somewhat above the $73,500 indicated by the expected-value criterion, since the nonmonetary disutility attached to the job would need to be offset by some additional monetary compensation.

A further consideration that may cause the decision maker to choose a bid price different from the one with the maximum expected contribution is the possibility that the decision maker may see personal gain in bidding at a different price level. Thus

FIGURE 12-1.   The Expected Present Value of Contribution Curve

individual decision makers within an organization may practice self-serving, or "political," behavior. This may be "functional" political behavior in that it causes certain actions that at the same time promote the organization's objectives, or it may be "dysfunctional" in that it serves the decision maker's purposes but hinders the attainment of the organization's objectives. Since it is not unlikely that the objectives of the decision maker and the organization will differ on occasion, we should not expect all decisions to reflect single-minded pursuit of company goals. Hence, if the decision maker feels there is some personal gain likely to follow a bid price above or below that indicated by the expected-value criterion, the actual bid price may well deviate from that standard.

The personal gains to the decision maker may include a wide variety of tangible and intangible benefits which the decision maker may expect to receive as the result of a particular decision's being taken. Hence, a relatively low bid price may be chosen when the decision maker feels there is something to gain by winning the contract, and conversely, a relatively high bid price may be submitted when it is felt that the purchaser owes a favor to the supplier and the supplier expects the purchaser to settle this debt. Simple friendship between the supplier and the purchaser may also cause a lower bid price to be submitted, and the reduction from the expected value bid price can be ascribed to political motivations, namely, to the supplier's recognition of the personal value of the buyer's friendship. Note that these political considerations are separate from the goodwill considerations that we include in the incremental cost calculation.

Risk Considerations

Risk considerations should be addressed under two headings. First, there is the risk of not getting the contract. Note that the probability of winning at the $73,500 bid price is somewhere between 30 and 50 percent. (A simple interpolation indicates 43 percent.) If the firm bids on contracts like this frequently, it might expect to actually win a little more than four out of every ten it bids on. Consequently, the firm should bid on more contracts than it could possibly handle at any one time, recognizing that it will win only some proportion of those. If the firm bids on many different contracts, it can afford to be risk neutral with respect to any one contract, expecting the law of averages to work in its favor.

In many situations the firm will not wish to take its chances with the law of averages. If the firm has substantial excess capacity and is facing layoffs of its workers, or worse still, is facing bankruptcy, a 43 percent chance of winning will not be good enough. In effect, the firm's time horizon has shrunk back to the immediate future, and winning the next contract becomes very important to the firm. Thus the firm will be prepared to trade off some of the expected profit for a greater chance of winning the contract. Depending on how badly it needs the contract, it will reduce its bid price in order to increase the success probability. In the worst case, it would offer to do the job at a price which simply covers its net incremental costs (its incremental costs less the EPV of any incremental revenues other than the bid price).

The second category of risk to be considered is the risk of cost variability after the contract is awarded, as discussed at the beginning of the chapter. If there is a risk of cost variability and the supplying firm is risk averse, the firm may wish to bid at a lower level while transferring some of the risk of cost variability to the buyer.

Cost-plus-Fee Bids.   As indicated earlier in the chapter, prices in some markets are typically set on the basis of *ex post* cost plus a fee or markup. In the automobile repair market this pricing convention is typical, although brake jobs, electrical tune-ups, and exhaust mufflers are often priced on a fixed-price basis, either as a temporary promotion or on a permanent basis to appeal to the risk-averse buyer. As a general rule, the greater the potential variability of cost, and the greater the risk aversion of the seller relative to the buyer, and the greater the asymmetry of information regarding costs, the more likely it is that firms will wish to bid on a cost-plus-fee basis.

Having ascertained the EPVC-maximizing bid price, the firm wishing to tender a cost-plus-fee bid must decide how much EPVC (and equivalently, how much of the bid price) it is willing to give up in order to transfer the risk of cost variability to the buyer. In Figure 12–2 we show an indifference curve in bid-price–risk-share space as an illustration. Point *A* represents the EPVC-maximizing bid price, with all the risk of cost variability being borne by the supplier. The certainty equivalent of that bid price is shown as the point *C* on the vertical axis, where the risk share borne by the supplier is zero. Thus the cost-plus-fee bid the firm should tender is $65,000, which is indicated by the firm's certainty equivalent of the EPVC-maximizing price.

Note that if the firm were to tender a cost-plus-fee bid greater than this certainty equivalent value, it would not be pursuing its objective, which we have assumed to be the maximization of its (expected present) net worth subject to its attitude toward risk.

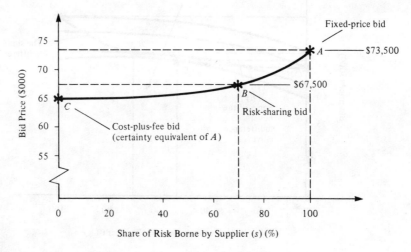

FIGURE 12–2. The Bid Price and the Risk of Cost Variation

Incentive (Risk-Sharing) Bids.   In many cases the buyer will require that each tender state an *ex ante* price and also specify the share of any cost variation that the supplier will bear. The risk-averse supplier may arbitrarily select a value of the risk share, such as 70 percent, and tender the *ex ante* price that makes the supplier indifferent between that price and that risk share, and the EPVC-maximizing price with all the risk. In Figure 12-2 we show this tender as the point *B*, indicating an *ex ante* bid price of $67,500. An arbitrary choice of risk share is unlikely to be optimal, however. The firm must be guided by the recent experience in the market. What risk share is typical? What risk share did this buyer accept last time? Unless the firm chooses its risk share with an eye to these considerations, it is likely to lose the contract to a firm that does.

In general, the optimal tender will be the combination of *ex ante* price and risk share that best serves the buyer's objectives. If the buyer's objective is to maximize net worth without regard to risk, the optimal tender is the lowest bid price regardless of risk share offered. If the buyer considers both net worth and risk, the optimal tender is the one that maximizes the buyer's utility in risk-return space. We can show the buyer's indifference curves as in Figure 12-3, where they are superimposed on the seller's indifference curve. The buyer's indifference curves must be positively sloped but convex from above, because the buyer will receive increasing marginal disutility from higher bid prices and diminishing marginal utility from larger shares of risk being assigned to the supplier. Thus the buyer's direction of preference is to the southeast, as indicated by the arrow.

Note that the buyer can rank the various tenders in terms of utility generated. Point *A*, representing the fixed-price bid of $73,500, is on the least-preferred indifference curve. The buyer prefers point *C*, the $65,000 cost-plus-fee bid, to the fixed-price

FIGURE 12-3.   The Buyer's Preferred Tender in Risk-Return Space

bid, but ranks point *B*, the $67,500 bid with 70 percent (supplier's) risk share, over both of the other two. But a bid of about $66,250 with 50 percent risk share going to the supplier (point *D*) allows the buyer to attain the highest level of utility and is thus the optimal tender for the supplier to submit.

In practice, firms rarely use the theoretical guidelines outlined here. The search costs associated with obtaining the information are typically so great that the firm is better off using a simple decision rule like markup bid pricing, which we will discuss in a subsequent section. To utilize the EPVC approach, the firm must obtain estimates of all incremental costs and revenues that are likely to follow the pricing decision. This process would usually be difficult enough, but obtaining the probabilities of success for a variety of potential bid price levels may be even more difficult. Obtaining this information would involve an analysis of all rival suppliers culminating in estimates of the probability distribution of their potential bid prices, so that the firm could deduce its success probability at each price level. Moreover, the buyer's degree of risk aversion must be estimated, and rivals' risk-share offers estimated, when the buyer requires or will accept risk-sharing tender offers. In perhaps most cases the firm will expect the search costs to be prohibitive and follow a more simple pricing decision rule. Nonetheless, the theoretical model of competitive bidding is valuable, since it identifies the concepts and variables which are important in the bid-pricing decision and allows the actual decision to be formulated in the light of these considerations.

12.3   COMPETITIVE BIDDING IN PRACTICE

In practice most firms appear to choose their bid price by applying a markup to some measure of the costs associated with the job, rather than base their bid price on the incremental costs and revenues. The firm's "cost base" is typically calculated to include all explicit costs, bid preparation costs, and an allocation of other overhead costs. No explicit calculation is usually made to include opportunity costs or other incremental costs, and costs are usually considered only in nominal dollars rather than in present-value terms. The firm will typically choose the markup percentage with an eye to its past pricing practice, modifying this "standard" markup either up or down depending upon current conditions in the market and the industry and with reference to longer-term considerations in some cases.

Markup Bid Pricing to Maximize EPVC

The firm's decision process described in the preceding paragraph may be a parallel but effectively equivalent means of arriving at the optimal bid price. Given that search costs are expected to exceed the value of the information derived, firms proceed using the markup pricing rule of thumb and keep winning enough jobs to keep them in business and sufficiently profitable. Although they do not typically include all net incremental costs in their cost calculations, they typically allow for them in a crude way by varying the size of the markup applied.

Example: Suppose a job is expected to involve future goodwill effects or that getting this job would avoid costly layoffs and subsequent rehiring and retraining expenses; the decision maker would apply a *lower* markup than normally would be applied. Conversely, if lawsuits were likely to follow a particular job or if the firm were near full capacity and getting the contract might cause labor problems sometime in the future, the markup applied might be *higher* than the standard level. The markup approach incorporates the nonmonetary considerations in the same way: we would expect to see higher markups with consequently higher bid prices to compensate for nonmonetary costs and lower markups to compensate for nonmonetary benefits.

It is clear that the firm could stumble upon the EPVC-maximizing price by using the markup approach. For example, suppose the firm calculates its "cost base" to be $61,250, comprised of direct costs and allocated overheads. A 20 percent markup on that cost base would result in a bid price of $73,500, the same as in the EPVC approach. Of course, this outcome would be sheer good luck. More likely, the firm using the simple (but inexpensive) markup pricing procedure will submit a bid which is either above or below the EPVC-maximizing price level.

How does the firm know if its markup is too high or too low? If it does not win enough contracts to keep its plant and employees operating within the desired range of capacity utilization, it will sooner or later determine that its markup rate (and hence its prices) is probably too high. Lowering the markup rate would be expected to bring improved capacity utilization with consequent larger total contribution to overheads and profits. Conversely, if the firm wins too many contracts, so that its capacity is overutilized, with all the attendant costs and problems, it will sooner or later decide to raise its markup in order to reduce demand for its services and consequently increase the profits of the enterprise. Of course, in the latter case the firm should also be considering the possibility of expanding its plant size.

Note: These capacity-utilization considerations entered the theoretical approach as well, but in the calculation of incremental costs. In the EPVC approach the potential costs of layoffs, rehiring, retraining, and so forth, which were associated with very low capacity utilization, operate to lower the total EPV of incremental costs of the potential job, and, given a structure of success probabilities, subsequently operate to lower the optimal bid price. Conversely, if the plant were near full capacity, the expected costs of future labor problems would be incorporated into incremental costs and cause the optimal bid price to be higher than it otherwise would be.

The Reconciliation of Theory and Practice

The first issue is that of information search costs. In practice these are frequently expected to outweigh the benefits of the information derived and the firm takes the completely rational decision to forgo the information and proceed using a simple decision rule such as markup pricing. This behavior is rational in that it involves pursuit of the firm's objectives. Although the markup price might be $5,000 less than the maximum EPVC price, if this simple procedure obviates spending more than $5,000 on information-search costs, the firm comes out ahead using the simple decision rule.[4]

The second issue follows from the first. Having only an imprecise view of the longer-term incremental costs, opportunity costs, goodwill, and other costs and benefits not immediately calculable but indeed consequent upon this pricing decision, the firm in practice tends to build these into a "cushion" in its markup. If these incalculable costs are larger, so too is the markup, to take into account in a rough way the probability that these incalculable costs will arise. Alternatively, if these incalculable costs are expected to be low, or if this contract will serve to enhance goodwill, the "cushion" in the firm's profit margin can be reduced by using a lower markup percentage.

Thus the markup price can be "wrong" to the extent of the information search costs that were avoided, and the markup percentage, and hence the profit margin, must take into account all net incremental costs (in EPV terms) *not* considered and *not* calculated into the cost base for the markup calculation. To the extent that overhead costs, including bid preparation costs, are included in the cost base, the markup percentage will be lower, since the markup will be simply the profit margin, rather than the contribution to overheads and profits. By way of summary, Table 12-2 shows the alternate approaches to price determination in competitive bidding situations. Notice that the cost and revenue considerations which are not incorporated in the cost base should be incorporated in the choice of the markup percentage, if the markup is to lead to a price close to (within the search cost differential of) the EPVC-maximizing price.

Note: After the firm's bid is submitted, the firm waits to learn the outcome. Suppose it loses this contract. No particular reaction is called for unless it loses "too many" contracts—that is, it finds that its probabilities were too high in the EPVC approach or that its markups were consistently too high in the markup approach. This feedback information calls for a change in the pricing level, as indicated in the bottom part of Table 12-2. Conversely, if the firm is successful "too often," it must revise its estimates of the success probabilities, revise its general price structure upward, and consider the expansion of its plant size.

Markup Bid Pricing for the Satisficing Firm

Often we notice that the practicing competitive bidder appears to exhibit the four basic features of a satisficing firm, as detailed in the behavioral theory of the firm.[5] First, the firm exhibits *bounded rationality*, calculating only its present costs and de-

---

[4]We have no reason to believe this is the general case, however. In many cases firms would profit by seeking more information, but they abstain from search activity for reasons other than the costs involved, such as ignorance of the information source and the lack of personnel qualified to lead the search.

[5]See R. M. Cyert and C. J. March, *A Behavioral Theory of the Firm* (Englewood Cliffs, N.J.: Prentice-Hall, Inc., 1963); and H. A. Simon, "Rational Decision Making in Business Organizations," *American Economic Review*, 69 (September 1979), pp. 493–513.

TABLE 12-2.   The EPVC Model and the Markup Model of Competitive Bidding

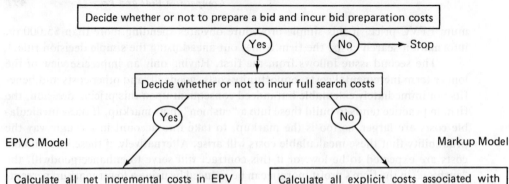

EPVC Model

| Calculate all net incremental costs in EPV terms. Include all explicit and implicit costs (including opportunity costs) now and in the future which are expected to be incurred as a result of this contract. Deduct in EPV terms all future revenues and opportunity revenues such as goodwill and costs avoided as a result of obtaining this contract. |

| Estimate the probabilities of success at each of several possible bid prices. |

| Calculate the EPVC for each of these bid prices and identify the bid price which maximizes EPVC. |

| (1) Bid at "maximum EPVC" price if this type of decision is taken frequently and if there are no aesthetic, political or other non-monetary considerations involved.
(2) Bid below the "maximum EPVC" price if indicated by the certainty-equivalent criterion or by aesthetic or political considerations.
(3) Bid above the "maximum EPVC" price if indicated by the certainty-equivalent criterion or by aesthetic or political considerations. |

| (1) If successful this time, no change is necessary unless you are successful so often that probabilities appear to be understated. If so, raise success probabilities for your next bid (and investigate plant expansion).
(2) If unsuccessful this time, no change is necessary unless you are unsuccessful so often that probabilities appear to be overstated. If so, reduce success probabilities for your next bid (and investigate plant contraction). |

Markup Model

| Calculate all explicit costs associated with this contract. Add allocated overhead charges and bid preparation costs to arrive at your "standard" cost base. |

| Apply "standard" markup percentage to this cost base to arrive at your "standard" bid price for this contract. |

| (1) Bid at this "standard" price if doing so in the past has kept your capacity utilization and profitability at preferred levels, and if there are no extraordinary incremental costs or benefits associated with this contract.
(2) Bid below this "standard" price if capacity utilization and profitability are both lower than desired, and/or if there are extraordinary incremental net benefits expected in the future as a result of this contract.
(3) Bid above this "standard" price if capacity utilization is higher and profitability lower than is desired, and/or if there are extraordinary incremental net costs expected in the future as a result of this contract. |

| (1) If successful this time, no change is necessary, unless you are receiving too many jobs for your limited capacity, in which case raise the standard markup for your next bid (and investigate plant expansion).
(2) If unsuccessful this time, no change is necessary, unless you are receiving too few jobs with subsequent underutilization of your plant, in which case reduce the standard markup for your next bid (and investigate plant contraction). |

clining to search for future costs and probability distributions. Second, it practices *selectivity* by not bidding on all contracts offered but confining its attention, instead, to those it is most likely to win and for which it has the technology and capacity. Third, it establishes *decision rules*, like standard cost bases and markup pricing, in order to facilitate and expedite the decision process. Fourth, it establishes *targets* or satisfactory levels for its most important variables, and it uses feedback information to adjust these targets and decision rules when such action becomes necessary or desirable.

We argued in Chapter 9 that "satisficing," or the pursuit of satisfactory targets, may be considered a proxy policy for the maximization of the firm's net present worth. If the targets are consistently achieved and upgraded, the firm should be expected to approach the bid price level which maximizes its EPVC without having to incur any major search costs.

Observation suggests that the main targets the bidding firm seeks to attain relate to the degree of capacity utilization and the rate of profitability. The capacity utilization target amounts to the same thing as a sales volume target and has implications for the firm's share of the market. It also has implications for the firm's cash flow and subsequent ability to meet its payroll obligations, interest expense, and other overhead costs. By striving to keep capacity utilization at or above a particular target, the firm expects to avoid the costs of retrenchment, rehiring, and retraining that would follow a plant closure and subsequent reopening. It is often apparent that the capacity utilization target takes priority over the profitability target, since firms seem to sacrifice profitability in order to attain utilization targets, but then they price to obtain their "required rate of return" on contracts when they are at or above their target rate of capacity utilization.

The markup-bid-pricing model shown in Table 12-2 is easily modified to suit the satisficing firm. Table 12-3 shows schematically the decision process for the satisficing firm.

When it first becomes aware of a call for bids on a particular contract, the firm does not immediately decide to prepare a bid. Rather, it first considers several factors of importance to the attainment of the firm's targets. Does it have the necessary technology, or could it obtain this through consultants or other subcontract work? Does it have sufficient capacity to handle this job, or could the job be partly or wholly given out to subcontractors without undue problems? Does it seem "worthwhile" to prepare a bid on this job, or alternatively, is there a strong enough chance that the firm will recoup its bid preparation costs by winning the contract?

If the answer is yes to these three basic questions the firm should go ahead and prepare its bid on the contract. If the answer is no to any one question, the firm must consider four subsidiary questions which may induce it to prepare a bid in any case. First, is the firm desperate for work, or is it considering diversification into new lines of work? An affirmative response to this question should cause the firm to reconsider preparing a bid despite not having the technology at the present time. Second, is it necessary to submit a bid in order to maintain goodwill with the buyer? If bids are requested privately, rather than being widely advertised, or if the firm feels that it should keep its name in front of the buyer, it may be important to submit a bid even

TABLE 12-3. Decision Sequence for the Satisficing Firm

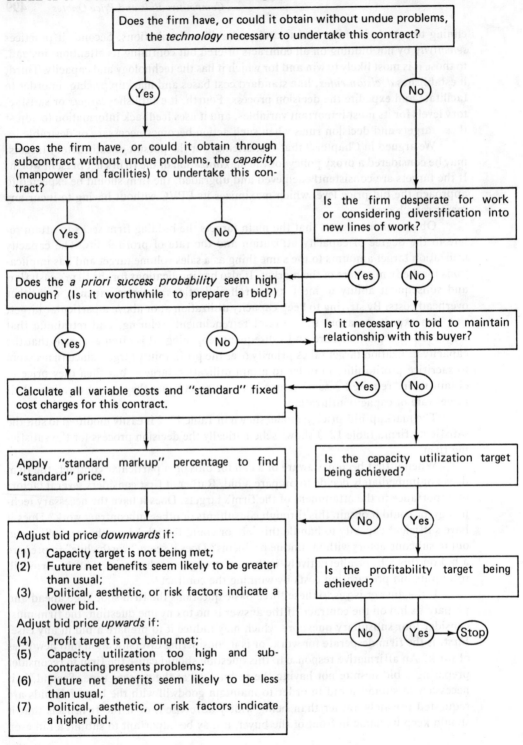

Does the firm have, or could it obtain without undue problems, the *technology* necessary to undertake this contract?

Yes

No

Does the firm have, or could it obtain through subcontract without undue problems, the *capacity* (manpower and facilities) to undertake this contract?

Yes

No

Is the firm desperate for work or considering diversification into new lines of work?

Does the *a priori success probability* seem high enough? (Is it worthwhile to prepare a bid?)

Yes

No

Yes

No

Is it necessary to bid to maintain relationship with this buyer?

Yes

No

Calculate all variable costs and "standard" fixed cost charges for this contract.

Yes

No

Apply "standard markup" percentage to find "standard" price.

Is the capacity utilization target being achieved?

No

Yes

Adjust bid price *downwards* if:

(1) Capacity target is not being met;
(2) Future net benefits seem likely to be greater than usual;
(3) Political, aesthetic, or risk factors indicate a lower bid.

Adjust bid price *upwards* if:

(4) Profit target is not being met;
(5) Capacity utilization too high and subcontracting presents problems;
(6) Future net benefits seem likely to be less than usual;
(7) Political, aesthetic, or risk factors indicate a higher bid.

Is the profitability target being achieved?

No

Yes

Stop

500

without adequate capacity to do the job. Of course, this bid should be high enough to be profitable if the firm actually wins the contract.

Regarding the prior expectation of winning the contract, two subsidiary questions must be asked if it is not considered "worthwhile" to prepare a bid. Is the firm's capacity utilization target being achieved at present and for the duration of this proposed contract? If not, the firm should prepare a bid anyway, since it will perceive that the maintenance of capacity utilization levels is of primary importance. Even if capacity utilization is satisfactory, the firm should prepare a bid if its profitability target is not being met currently or may not be met in the foreseeable future. Thus the firm will prepare a bid, despite a low prior expectation of success, if either of its capacity or profitability targets are not met. Of course, its final decision on the bid price will reflect the circumstances; for example, it will be lower if the capacity target is not met and higher if the capacity target is met but the profitability target is not.

The firm will prepare its bid on the basis of a standardized "cost base" which is calculated by the application of several basic decision rules.[6] The bid price obtained by multiplying the standard cost base by the standard markup may be called the firm's standard price for the contract. It will bid at that level if its capacity and profitability targets are being met, and if the contract appears to have no extraordinary features about it. The firm will *lower* its markup percentage and hence its bid price if capacity utilization is below the target level, if it foresees abnormal longer-term benefits to be gained by winning this contract, or if political, aesthetic, or risk considerations require a monetary tradeoff to increase the probability of success. Conversely, the firm will *raise* its markup percentage if the capacity target but not the profitability target is being attained, if future net benefits seem likely to be less than usual, or if political, aesthetic, or risk factors indicate a higher bid price. In addition, the firm would raise its markup if it did not have the capacity needed to complete the contract if won, but it was submitting a bid only to maintain the relationship currently enjoyed with the buyer. In each case the amount by which the bid price is raised or lowered from the "standard" price should be commensurate with the value to the firm of winning or losing the contract, as per the EPVC discussions earlier in this chapter.

The Targets.   What are the appropriate levels for the capacity utilization target and the profitability target? The desired rate of capacity utilization should be the same rate at which "standard" overhead charges are calculated and may be chosen, for example, to be 80 percent of full capacity.

■ *Definition:*   *Full capacity* is defined as the total number of labor-days available per year, using a single shift and the "optimal" complement of manpower. The optimal complement of labor is construed as that quantity which allows average total cost to be

---

[6]The satisficing firm may have developed a simple "costing sheet" which requires estimates of variable costs, variable overheads, bid preparation costs, and other fixed costs. The decision rules pertaining to variable overheads may be for example, 50 percent of labor costs, and the overhead charges may be the proportion of the firm's work-year devoted to this job times the firm's total fixed costs.

minimized. Thus overfull capacity can be achieved by additional workers during the single shift, overtime operation, multiple-shift operation, or subcontracting. Notwithstanding the fact that average costs are minimized at full capacity, the firm may establish its target capacity utilization at something less than full capacity in order to leave a margin for error in the event of strikes or breakdowns and to avoid the frequent disruption of normal operations associated with overtime and extra-worker operation. Note also that if the target utilization rate is achieved, the firm's overheads are completely covered, and any extra work contributes directly to the firm's profits.

The profitability target, or the firm's required rate of return, will be determined by the firm's opportunity cost of capital. Suppose the firm feels that it could obtain 20 percent before taxes at comparable risk elsewhere: It will set this as its minimum, or target, level. While higher rates of profitability may seem desirable, managers will be inclined to trade off higher profits for reduced risk. They will be content to price somewhat lower than might be possible in order to better ensure the firm's future existence in the market, not to mention the continuation of their tenure as managers.

The Standard Costs, Markup, and Price. The firm's standard cost-base calculations and its standard markup rate may be modified over time as a result of its bidding experience. The model outlined in Table 12–3 allows for adjustment in the markup rate if either of the targets is not met and for other reasons. If the firm wins virtually every contract it bids upon, we would expect it to raise its markup on subsequent bids. Rather than make each bid a special case, the firm in this happy situation may simplify its subsequent pricing decisions by raising its "standard markup" to a higher level. Conversely, if the firm finds that it is consistently not winning enough contracts to attain its capacity utilization target, it may adjust its markup rate downward to a new, more appropriate, level.

In each case, the adjustment is made to cause the firm's bid to be slightly more or less desirable and should have a noticeable effect on the quantity of work obtained. The appropriate level of the markup, and hence the price, is that level which tends to keep the firm at or above its capacity utilization target. At this target level of output, the profitability target will also be attained, except for unforeseen costs associated with jobs in process and with unanticipated increases in overhead costs. The feedback to management from past contracts won or lost allows them to judge the most appropriate levels of the standard cost base and markup levels. As before, special circumstances surrounding any particular contract will justify a deviation from the standard price.

If over a prolonged series of contracts it becomes apparent that demand for the firm's services is either too strong or too weak for its present size of plant, the firm must consider adjustment of plant size. A reasonable presumption is that the firm would choose its new plant size such that the new plant's capacity utilization target is equal to the expected value of its annual demand at standard prices. Given the new plant size and potentially different technology, the firm would need to recalculate its standard cost base and may wish to adjust its standard markup percentage in order to bring its new standard price into line with the bid prices of other firms. It would make these readjustments in the normal process of winning or losing contracts: if it wins too few it will adjust its standard markup downward, and if it wins too many it will raise the level of its standard markup.

12.4   THE VIEW FROM THE OTHER SIDE: OPTIMAL PURCHASING

Before submitting its tender, the supplier should attempt to ascertain exactly what the buyer wants. Specifications will be provided by the buyer, of course, in either general or detailed terms, but even detailed specifications are unlikely to be complete, in the sense that there will remain room for discretion on the supplier's part in the design, quality, and other aspects of the work to be carried out. Knowledge of what the supplier expects to pay, how much quality is expected at that price, whether a risk-sharing bid would be entertained, and so on would allow the supplier to tailor its tender to fit the buyer's preferences exactly and thus increase the probability of winning the contract.

To achieve a better understanding of the buyer's choice problem and how the supplier's tender may better serve the buyer's objectives, we shall look at the competitive bid problem from the buyer's perspective. The purchasing agent responsible for selecting the winning bid must go through a decision process to arrive at that decision. One such decision process is known as "value analysis."

Value Analysis for Optimal Purchasing

In general, the buyer's problem is to choose the tender that not only has an agreeable price attached to it but also includes the most desirable package of attributes in association with that price.

Example: Let us consider the purchasing decision of a householder who is contemplating having new windows installed in his somewhat older house. He receives three quotes, as shown in Table 12-4, after inviting representatives from each company to quote on the job. Notice that there is a difference not only in the prices quoted but in the qualitative aspects of the offers.

TABLE 12-4.   Details of Price Quotes on Windows

	Company A	Company B	Company C
Price	$2,200	$1,280	$1,050
Frame	Baked enamel on steel	Baked enamel on aluminum	Anodized aluminum
Glass	Two separate 5-mm panes	Double 5-mm Thermopane	Double 3-mm Thermopane
Warranty	10 years, complete	5 years, complete	3 years, complete
Delivery	12 weeks	8 weeks	6 weeks

Which quote should the consumer accept? The answer obviously depends upon a variety of considerations, including the consumer's financial liquidity, his aesthetic feelings and misgivings about the different types of materials and construction, the length of time he expects to own the house, and his attitude toward the risk and uncertainty associated with the different warranties. In the initial discussions with the buyer, the salesperson should attempt to find out exactly what the consumer wants and is prepared to pay for and should then tailor the bid accordingly. The essential consideration is whether the attributes involved in the different bids are worth as much (to the consumer) as the suppliers are asking. Clearly we cannot make the decision for this consumer, but we can say that if he chooses the bid made by company B, this decision indicates that he values the attributes provided by company B for that price more highly than he values the attributes provided by the others, relative to their prices.

Industrial purchasers are often required to rationalize their purchasing decisions in some objective manner in order to demonstrate that their purchasing policy is consistent with company objectives. A means of arriving at a purchasing decision (or for *post hoc* rationalization of a purchasing decision) is the technique known as value analysis. Using this approach the decision maker identifies the attributes that are considered desirable and which may be present in each of the bids, applies weights to those attributes in order of importance to the decision maker, ranks and scales each bidder under each attribute, multiplies the weight by the scale, and chooses the bid that has the highest weighted score.

This procedure may be illustrated in terms of the above example. In Table 12–5 we indicate that the attributes of interest to this purchaser are price, quality, delivery lag, and warranty. We presume that the purchaser values these attributes in the proportions shown by the weights. The suppliers are then ranked in terms of their performance on each attribute on a scale of 0 to 10: the better the performance, the higher the scale. Note that for price, supplier A receives a value of 1, supplier B is assigned a value of 5, and supplier C is assigned a value of 8. This reflects the fact that supplier C has submitted the lowest price, followed by the price of supplier B, with supplier A's price a greater distance above. The scale values given to each of the suppliers need not be consecutive numbers if the attributes are different by different amounts.

The buyer then scales and scores each potential supplier on each of the other attributes, as indicated in Table 12–5. Multiplying the scales assigned by the weights

TABLE 12–5. Value Analysis in Purchasing

Attribute	Weight	SUPPLIER A		SUPPLIER B		SUPPLIER C	
		Scale	Score	Scale	Score	Scale	Score
Price	7	1	7	5	35	8	56
Quality	4	8	32	7	28	1	4
Delivery	3	1	3	3	9	5	15
Warranty	2	10	20	7	14	4	8
Total score			62		86		83

for each attribute, we derive each supplier's score on each attribute, and these may be added up to find each supplier's total score over the attributes deemed desirable by the purchaser. Given this system of weighting and scaling the various attributes, supplier B has the most desirable bid, since the weighted sum of the scores is greatest.

Note: The choice of the weights assigned to each attribute is essentially arbitrary, depending upon the attitudes and judgment of the decision maker. Similarly, the ranking and then the scaling of the suppliers in terms of these attributes are at the discretion of the decision maker. Finally, other attributes may be included in the analysis, such as the supplier's previous experience with this type of project, financial stability, quality and reputation of personnel, provision of technical or consulting services, inventory charges, and shipping policy. A different decision maker may score the same three bids differently, such that supplier A or supplier C becomes the successful bidder.[7]

The importance of value analysis in purchasing is its ability to force the decision maker to rationalize and scrutinize the purchasing decision. The choice of weights, value scales, and desirable attributes must be stated explicitly and is thus subject to argumentation by the decision maker's peers and superiors. Out of the discussion should arise a consensus of those weights, scales, and attributes that are considered consistent with the firm's objectives. Purchasing decisions may thus be justified on this "relatively objective" basis, rather than merely on the basis of unstated preferences and assumptions.[8]

From the supplier's point of view it would be immeasurably valuable to obtain the criteria upon which the purchasing decision is made. With this information the supplier could tailor the bid price and other features such that the bid would score more highly and be more desirable to the buyer. In the previous case of the windows, the supplier should attempt to ascertain the likes and dislikes, willingness to pay for certain features, and other information about the prospective customer. In the industrial purchasing situation the potential supplier should attempt to judge which features the buyer regards as more or less important. In both cases the supplier will then be in a better position to supply exactly what is desired by the purchaser and will thus be more likely to be the successful bidder on the contract.

Collusive Bidding and Bid Disclosure

In the foregoing we have presumed that the firms bidding for a particular contract do so without benefit of any interaction or direct information flow between and among the potential suppliers. Where a small group of firms continually find themselves bid-

---

[7]The buyer is likely to set some minimum acceptable level or standard for each attribute which must be met in order for the seller's bid to be considered. For example, if the quality or delivery date was unacceptable or was expected to be unacceptable, the seller would be excluded from any further consideration.

[8]Value analysis is implicit in any purchasing decision. It is done explicitly in many companies for the benefits stated above.

ding against each other, it is not surprising that they will seek better information concerning each other's intended bids. Since retaliatory action cannot remove the immediate gains of a successful low bid, the firms will wish to eliminate the possibility of a rival's submitting an unexpectedly low bid. One means of achieving this purpose is to obtain prior agreement among firms about their bid prices or pricing procedures.

We might expect collusive practices to be more likely to exist in industries in which there is both the ability and the "necessity" to bid collusively. Regarding the ability to collude, where there are relatively few firms we expect firms to be able to communicate with all other firms more easily and effectively. Moreover, the fact that the actions of any one firm are more readily visible to the other firms assists in the policing of any agreement. Regarding the "necessity" to collude, where contracts are relatively few and far between and are of relatively high value, the incentive will be stronger for each firm to submit a relatively low bid in order to obtain the contract, even if doing so does not generate a profit above the fully allocated costs of operation. The longer-term result could be that all firms are pricing below full costs and that no firm earns a normal profit. As an alternative to some firms' being forced out of the industry, the firms may see collusive bidding as a necessity to avoid a degeneration of prices to unprofitable levels.

Identical Bids.   The competing suppliers for a particular contract may agree to submit identical bid prices at a level that ensures that the business will be sufficiently profitable to the successful bidder. The purchaser is then forced to select the successful bidder on some criteria other than price level. This situation is akin to nonprice competition in established market situations. The suppliers will attempt to include those attributes in their bid that are desired by the purchaser, so that at identical prices their bid appears to be the better deal. Suppliers may consider this nonprice competition to be a "more ethical" form of competition, since the successful bidder is rewarded for the expertise and efficiency involved in supplying a particular bundle of attributes at the given price, rather than for the simple ability to cut prices below what rivals are expected to bid.

Bid Rotation.   Bid rotation is a method designed to allocate the available business among the competing suppliers in proportions agreeable to all. In effect, the firms take turns in submitting the lowest bid, so that the available business is allocated around the industry. It is not necessarily allocated in equal shares among the competing suppliers, but more likely it will be allocated on the basis of historical market shares or current bargaining power.

As noted in Appendix 10A, however, collusive price fixing is illegal, and the firm may face prosecution for engaging in this practice. A second factor militating against the longer-term operation of collusive bidding in any particular industry is the profit incentive that individual firms may have to undercut the agreed price. Firms that are not getting sufficient work to obtain their desired degree of capacity utilization may break out of the agreement when an important contract is at stake. If the available business is not shared among the competing suppliers in a manner that is suitable to all, it is likely that a particular supplier will be motivated to undercut the agreed price in order to obtain the additional business.

While the exchange of information involved in collusive bidding operates to reduce the uncertainty involved in the pricing decision, the risk remains that one or more competing suppliers will operate at variance with their stated intentions. Thus it is still important to evaluate and form expectations about the probable behavior of competitors. To the extent that rivals are expected not to maintain their previous behavior pattern or are expected not to carry through with their stated intent, the decision maker may wish to adjust the bid price accordingly.[9]

Disclosure of Bids.   After the contract is awarded to the successful bidder, the bid prices of other suppliers may be disclosed to all suppliers or to the public in general. The disclosure of the bid prices generates considerable information which may be valuable to the sellers in their future bidding policies. The unsuccessful bidders will obtain information about the amount they overbid, and the successful bidder will obtain information about the amount that this bid could have been increased without losing the contract. We should expect, therefore, that disclosure of bid prices would lead to a compression of the range of bids over time, since the firms would gain an appreciation of the bid levels that are likely to be submitted by the other firms in the industry. Obviously, disclosure of bids provides information useful for the initiation and the policing of collusive bidding.

From the purchaser's point of view it may be a poor strategy to disclose the bid prices after the contract is awarded, since doing so may lead to a compression of the bid prices nearer the center of the range of bids and may facilitate collusive bidding. Such disclosure is likely to lead to an increased level of the lowest bid over time. From the purchaser's point of view it is surely better to keep the suppliers in the dark, since they are more likely to submit lower bids when they are in a greater state of uncertainty about the bids of the other firms. We should thus expect that purchasers would not wish to disclose the bids, and in some industries bid disclosure is considered an unethical procedure. Governments, which frequently purchase goods and services in this type of market, may be required to disclose bid prices, however, in order to show their constituents that the public funds involved have been spent wisely and without corruption.

12.5 SUMMARY

In this chapter we have applied the contribution approach to competitive bids and price quotes. The relevant cost concept is the incremental cost associated with the work involved in undertaking and completing the contract; and as long as the bid price exceeds this incremental cost less any other incremental revenues, some contri-

---

[9]Information concerning rival firms' bidding practices and intentions may be gleaned in conversation with rival decision makers at business and social gatherings or from industry gossip. Some people even believe in industrial espionage!

bution will be made to overheads and profits by obtaining the contract. We considered the optimal bid price from the point of view of expected-value analysis, modifying this to the extent that aesthetic, political, and risk considerations were involved.

In practice many firms use cost-plus pricing procedures in their competitive bids and price quotes. These procedures can be equivalent to the expected-value approach, and they save time and expense in the decision-making procedure. However, it is important that the decision maker attempt to justify the bid price in terms of the theoretical procedures to ensure that the objectives of the company (or the individual decision maker) are being served. We saw that the satisficing firm may expect to approach the maximization of its EPVC by pursuing capacity utilization and profitability targets.

Both the expected-value approach and the markup approach involve an implicit or explicit estimation of the probability of success at each bid price level. The major factors involved in estimating these probabilities are the probabilities of competitors' bidding at various price levels and the appreciation that the buyer will have for price and quality differences. This latter aspect was examined from the buyer's side to show the factors likely to be considered in choosing the successful bid. Potential suppliers will benefit by an appreciation of the factors considered important by the buyer. The probable bid prices of rivals may be estimated on the basis of information obtained through a collusive exchange of pricing plans, by the disclosure of price levels on previous bid prices, or by knowledge of rival suppliers' capacity utilization levels and other factors.

DISCUSSION QUESTIONS

12-1.   Outline three situations in which you have recently been the buyer in a competitive bidding or price quote situation. (Even if you received only one quote in each instance.)

12-2.   Make a list of those items that you would expect to enter the incremental cost calculation for a contract to remove the sea gulls from the vicinity of a major coastal airport.

12-3.   In calculating the incremental costs of a particular project, how would you treat the possible future cost of a lawsuit that may occur as a result of this project, where the cost of such a lawsuit may range from $10,000 to $500,000 with an associated probability distribution?

12-4.   How would you value the goodwill that is expected to be generated as a result of undertaking a particular contract? If there is expected goodwill, would you be prepared to bid lower than otherwise? Why?

12-5.   Explain why the strategy of choosing the bid price with the highest expected value is likely to generate the greatest contribution to overheads and profits over a large number of successful and unsuccessful bids.

12-6.   Outline the different types of bids that may be tendered. What is the relationship between the fixed-price bid and the other two types of bids?

12-7.   Explain how the strategy of marking up incremental costs by a standard percentage (and subsequently winning some contracts and losing some contracts) may over a period of time give equivalent results as compared with the maximum-expected-value strategy.

12-8.   Outline the factors that would cause you to use a lower markup on incremental costs (as compared with your usual markup) in a particular bidding situation.

12-9. Explain the logic behind value analysis. What is the relationship between value analysis and attribute analysis of consumer choice behavior?

12-10. Why is collusive bidding illegal? Does it hurt the customer? The competing firms? Other firms?

PROBLEMS AND SHORT CASES

12-1. The Billings Printing Company is preparing to bid for a contract to supply half a million brochures to a national mail-order company. The firm has calculated its incremental costs to be $50,000. Past experience with this type of contract has resulted in the following schedule, which shows the percentage of wins at each markup rate over incremental cost, for the past three years.

Markup Rate (%)	Contracts Won (%)
10	94
20	72
30	45
40	18
50	6

(a) Calculate the expected value of the contribution at each of the bid prices implied by the above markup rates.

(b) Interpolate between these rates to arrive at the markup rate, and bid price, that maximizes expected contribution from the contract.

(c) What assumptions and qualifications underlie your analysis?

12-2. Your company, Bright Paints, is one of several companies manufacturing a special reflecting paint used for traffic signs. Your two major customers are the state and the federal Departments of Transportation. The federal Department of Transportation has recently called for bids for 10,000 gallons of this special paint in a light blue, to be delivered within two months after signing the contract. You can foresee being able to fit in a production run of 10,000 gallons of the blue paint and have decided to bid on the job. This particular contract is absolutely standard, similar in all respects to hundreds of contracts you have bid on in the past two years.

Your pricing policy has always been to apply a markup to incremental cost to arrive at the bid price. Your markup has varied with the competitive situation perceived prior to each bid. You have assembled data on all past bids, relating the markup rate used to the percentage of times your bid was the winning one, as shown below. Incremental cost for this contract has been estimated to be $76,200.

Markup Rate (%)	Contracts Won (%)
0	95.9
10	84.8
15	65.4
20	41.3
25	15.7
30	3.0
35	0.2

(a) Why would your company have previously bid at zero markup over incremental costs? Why didn't it win all of those bids?

(b) What is the bid price that maximizes the expected contribution of the contract?

(c) Underlying your analysis is the assumption of *ceteris paribus*. Which things in particular must remain unchanged for your bid to be the optimal one?

(d) Why, or why not, is the fixed-price mode of bidding likely to be the best one to use for this contract?

12-3.   The Esna Fabricating Company manufactures valves, faucets, and similar items under contract for various industrial and commercial clients. Whenever the company has no special jobs to do, it uses its labor force and plant to produce a line of faucets which it sells to a distributor for eventual sale in hardware stores. Esna can produce 5,000 of these faucets weekly, on average, and sells them for $1.65 per unit, this representing a 50 percent markup over variable costs. This production is suspended whenever Esna wins a more lucrative contract, however. Esna is currently considering bidding for a contract to manufacture several very large pressure valves for use in the pulp-making industry. It has estimated the costs associated with this job as follows:

Direct labor (300 labor hours @ $20)	$6,000
Direct materials	8,650
Variable overhead expenses	4,270
Allocated overheads (150% of direct labor)	9,000

In addition to the above, Esna has incurred $850 in expenses to acquire the detailed specifications for examination prior to submitting its bid. If the contract is won, Esna expects to incur another $2,500 for design costs before beginning manufacture of the valves, and the manufacturing process is expected to take 300 labor hours, or three weeks of the plant's time. No new direct labor will need to be hired for the job, since the regular labor force (diverted from faucet production) is expected to be sufficient to handle the job.

Esna's bidding policy is to mark up incremental costs of each job such that the expected value of contribution is maximized. An examination of the outcomes of over 300 jobs bid for in the past two years indicates that the probability of winning the contract is related to the ratio of the bid price to incremental cost, for each particular contract, in the following way:

$$P = 2.825 - 0.115R - 1.427R^2$$

where P is the success probability and R is the ratio of the bid price to the incremental costs of each job tendered for.

(a) What are the probabilities of winning the contract at markups of 10 percent, 15 percent, 20 percent, 25 percent, and 30 percent, respectively?

(b) What price should Esna submit?

(c) Outline any reservations or qualifications you may have concerning your recommended bid price.

12-4.   Bids have been called for the fabrication of a steel watergate, and Stenson Steel is in the process of preparing to bid on this contract. The practice in your company has been to charge each contract with bid preparation costs of $2,000, which is actually about three times the actual value of time and office supplies spent on each bid but is costed this way because the company is the successful bidder only once in every three times it bids, on average. The bidding policy in the past has been to add a 15 percent margin to the incremental and allocated costs, and hence your colleague, a recent M.B.A. graduate from a rival university, insists that the appropriate bid price is $138,230, calculated as follows:

Bid preparation costs	$ 2,000
Direct materials	18,600
Direct labor	33,200
Variable overhead	14,400
Fixed overhead	52,000
Profit margin	18,030
Suggested bid price	$138,230

You are a little worried that conditions in the industry have deteriorated recently. You are aware that some of your competitors have been operating below capacity, and you suspect that demand for steel-fabricated products is likely to be depressed for the coming twelve months.

(a) What is the absolute minimum price you would bid on this contract? Explain and defend your answer.

(b) On the basis of the information given, what bid price would you recommend?

(c) What factors would you wish to investigate and evaluate before choosing the actual bid price?

12-5. A large department store has called for bids for the following contract: A truck plus its driver must be available, given one day's notice, whenever the store's own trucks are fully utilized, to deliver goods to suburban households. The expected number of days for which a truck will be required is 20, and the number of miles is expected to be 4,000, for the coming year.

You are the manager of the Clark Rent-A-Truck Company and have a number of trucks which you rent out on a day-to-day basis. One truck is a little older than the others and is always the last to be rented out because it does less for public relations than the newer trucks. In the absence of a contract with the department store, you expect this older truck to be rented out two-thirds of the 300 "rental days" this coming year. Your normal rental charge is $25.00 per day plus $0.35 per mile.

You estimate the costs of operating the older truck to be as follows, assuming 10,000 miles of rental over the coming year:

Depreciation	$ 800
Interest on investment in truck	360
License fees and taxes	125
Insurance	440
Parking fees (permanently rented space)	300
Gasoline	1,367
Oil, grease, and preventive maintenance	600
Repairs	1,450
Allocated overheads	1,650

You can hire a driver on one day's notice for $50 per day. A one-time cost of $400 will be involved in fitting the truck with a special loading ramp required by the contract. This ramp will not interfere with the normal use of the truck.

(a) On the basis of this information and by making whatever assumptions you feel are necessary and reasonable, calculate the incremental cost that would be involved in accepting this contract.

(b) What price would you bid, assuming that you wish to maximize profits and that you have no knowledge of who else will bid for this job nor of the "going rate" for this type of job?

(Outline the considerations involved and choose a bid price that would reflect *your* certainty equivalent for this gamble.)

12-6.   Your company, Canino Construction, has decided to bid on a government contract to build a bridge 50 miles from the city during the coming winter. The bridge is to be of standard government design and hence should contain no unexpected in-process costs. Your present capacity utilization rate allows sufficient scope to undertake the contract if awarded. You calculate your incremental costs to be $268,000 and your fully allocated costs to be $440,000. You expect three other companies to bid on this contract, and you have assembled the following information concerning these companies:

Consideration	Rival A	Rival B	Rival C
Capacity utilization	Near full	Sufficient slack	Very low
Goodwill consideration	Very concerned	Moderately concerned	Not concerned
Type of plant	Small and inefficient	Medium-sized and efficient	Large and efficient
Previous bidding pattern	Incremental cost plus 35–50%	Full cost plus 8–12%	Full cost plus 10–15%
Cost structure	Incremental costs exceed yours by about 10%	Similar cost structure to yours	Incremental costs 20% lower but full costs similar to yours
Aesthetic factors	Likes to utilize capacity fully	Doesn't like "dirty" jobs	Likes creative projects
Political factors	Decision maker has friends in government	Decision maker is seeking a new job	None known

Your usual bidding practice is to add between 60 percent and 80 percent to your incremental costs, depending upon capacity utilization rate and other factors. What price will you bid (a) if you *must* win the contract or (b) if you wish to maximize the expected value of the contract? Defend your answers with discussion, making any assumptions you feel are supported by the information given or are otherwise reasonable.

12-7.   Bids have been called for the construction of a turbine generator for the Milford Power Station. Your company accountant has examined the specifications and has established the following costs associated with the contract:

Bid preparation costs	$ 750
Direct materials	115,000
Direct labor	252,500
Specialized equipment required*	27,500
Variable overhead	42,000
Allocated overhead	86,750

*This equipment will not be purchased unless the contract is won. It will last for the fabrication of two more generators, should such contracts be forthcoming in the future, although there is no indication at this time that there will be a demand for any more generators like this one.

You are aware of three other companies that are likely to bid on this project. Relevant details are as follows:

Detail	Company A	Company B	Company C
Cost structure	Similar to yours	10% higher	10% lower
Previous bidding pattern	Incremental cost plus 60%	Full cost plus 15%	Full cost plus 40%
Current capacity utilization	Moderate	Very low	Near full

Your current capacity utilization is moderate, leaving sufficient capacity to handle this project. Your previous bidding practice has been to add 25 percent to full costs.

(a) What is the absolute *minimum* price you would bid on this contract?

(b) What is your *actual* bid price, on the basis of the information given?

(c) What other factors would you wish to consider or investigate before making your bid?

12-8. Fact Finders Limited, a marketing research company, has been asked by the marketing director of a large food-processing company to submit a proposal for a small market research project aimed at determining consumers' probable responses to several planned changes in marketing strategy. The proposal should outline the procedures planned and quote a price. The marketing director is not binding himself to accepting the proposal, since he is still formulating his plan of action. It would cost Fact Finders about $200 to prepare the proposal.

Fact Finders' president, Ms. Denise Jutasi, designs each project to fit individual requirements. Furthermore, the nature of the research industry is such that in general the client depends on only one or two research firms, since a certain familiarity with the client's problems is needed in the designing of the project. In addition, although price is important to the client, it is the research house's reputation for doing high-quality work that will largely influence the client's choice of research supplier. This particular client has used Fact Finders' services several times in the past, although it has also adopted other proposals in some cases in preference to the proposals suggested by Fact Finders.

Ms. Jutasi has designed a project which she believes best fulfills the client's needs, and she estimates that the incremental cost of the project could vary between $1,500 and $2,500. The wide variation in cost estimation is due to the many situational difficulties that are part of market research, including snowstorms, respondents not being home, difficulty in obtaining field staff, and unforeseen complications in other projects already in progress which could affect the one in question (for example, cause delays in starting).

The marketing director of the food-processing firm has indicated that he has allocated a budget in the vicinity of $2,500 for this project. At the top of this range, however, and dependent on the type of information the research firm will be able to obtain for him (outlined in the proposal), he may consider other methods of obtaining needed information or go with what information he has.

As a rule of thumb in calculating prices, Fact Finders uses cost plus 10 percent as a regular policy. Following are its best estimates of the probabilities with respect to the cost of the project and its chance of obtaining an acceptance by the client:

Incremental Cost of Project	Probability	Price (cost + 10%)	Probability of Acceptance
$1,500	0.2	$1,650	0.99
2,000	0.5	2,200	0.70
2,500	0.3	2,750	0.10

(a) Find the expected value of the proposal to Fact Finders at each of the three prices stated.

(b) Interpolate between the three prices shown to estimate the probability of acceptance when price is varied by $50 increments above $1,650. Would one of these price quotes be preferable to the initial three prices?

(c) How would you recommend that Ms. Jutasi deal with the risk that costs might exceed the asking price?

12-9.   Prentice Plumbing and Pipes Limited specializes in household plumbing installation and repairs. The sales manager received a call this morning to provide a written price quotation for the installation of the entire plumbing system in a new house being built by the owner (with the aid of contractors for the plumbing and electrical work). The owner has called for three or four quotes on each of the plumbing and electrical jobs.

The sales manager, David Katz, sent his estimator to the job site and has since received the following cost estimate:

Materials	$2,422
Direct labor	2,760
Standard charge for detailed quotation	100
Variable overhead (estimated incremental)	650
Allocated overhead	1,380
Estimated total cost	$7,312

Prentice's usual pricing policy is to mark up its estimated (full) costs by 12.5 percent to 25 percent, depending upon (a) how badly it needs the work to avoid employee layoffs, (b) whether or not the buyer is considering one or more other quotations, and (c) whether or not it expects the job to provide an introduction to a client who will have more jobs to be done in the future. The present demand situation for Prentice Plumbing and Pipes is quite pleasing, although Prentice does have sufficient operating capacity to handle the job under consideration. Mr. Katz intends to quote $8,775, which is approximately equal to full cost plus 20 percent markup.

Suppose that you have ascertained that the expected value of the bid price for each of the three other firms also submitting quotes on this job is $8,592, with a standard deviation of $1,032. Assuming the probability distribution of each rival's bid price to be normally distributed around the mean (expected value), find the bid price that maximizes the expected value of the contribution to overheads and profits for Prentice.

(a) Is the sales manager's price quote close enough for maximization of expected profits?

(b) What would you advise Mr. Katz, and why?

(c) Discuss the applicability of a cost-plus-fee bid on this contract.

12-10. You are the newly hired vice-president of design and marketing at Bender Fender Automotive Design and Aerodynamics, Inc. Bender Fender has grown substantially in the past few years as a result of the quest by all automobile manufacturers for greater aerodynamic efficiency. Bender Fender is one of only about a dozen firms in the world with their own wind tunnels and the capability to design and build full-scale models for the world's automobile producers. These producers regularly contract out for new designs, and some of these designs eventually go into production.

The Ford Motor Company has called for tenders for a new design. The specifications are simple: the car must seat five passengers in comfort, use existing mechanical components for the most part, and have a coefficient of drag (C_x) less than 0.20. This is an exceptionally low C_x figure for a five-passenger car, and its design represents a real challenge. Undeterred by challenges, and with you as his right-hand person, Mr. Bender tells you to prepare a bid for the Ford contract. With the aid of the company accountant, you derive the following cost data:

**Costs Associated with the
Ford Contract**

Materials	$ 40,00
Direct labor	100,000
Variable overheads	60,000
Fixed overheads	40,000
New equipment	18,500
Bid preparation costs	5,000
Design costs	30,000

Design costs will only be incurred if the contract is won. These costs are uncertain, and are shown in the table at their most likely value. Cost overruns or underruns are frequent, however, with the former being more likely. The accountant helps you construct the probability distribution of design costs from past experience, as follows:

Potential Variability of Design Costs

Costs	Probability
$50,000	0.10
40,000	0.20
30,000	0.50
20,000	0.15
10,000	0.05

The design and production of the model is expected to take a full year, with cost outlays being distributed more or less uniformly over the year. The firm's opportunity discount rate is 15 percent. Payment for the contract (the bid price) will be received in lump sum at the end of the first year. The firm's bidding practice over the past few years has been to mark up incremental costs by 30 percent, with adjustments to the markup rate to reflect current capacity utilization, profitability, foreseen future costs and revenues, opportunity costs, and so on. Mr. Bender says to bid at 30 percent over incremental costs this time because the situation is normal and there are no extraordinary features that are obvious to him.

You have been reading the trade association magazine, however, and know that if you win this contract and successfully design a car with C_x less than 0.20, you will be considered for the Automotive Designer of the Year award. To win this award would be a great boost to your career, and you think the probability of winning the award is 0.80 if you can achieve the specifications required by Ford. Moreover, if you win the award, you feel sure it will bring Bender Fender additional business in the following year, as indicated below. Assume that all cash flows relating to this future business are received and disbursed at the end of the second year.

**Incremental Contribution if
Designer Award Is Won**

| Incremental
Contribution	Probability
$200,000	0.20
150,000	0.40
100,000	0.30
50,000	0.10

You ask Mr. Bender for the firm's records concerning past contracts tendered for. After weeding out those not related to automotive design, you have the following data:

Tenders Made and Contracts Won

Markup Rate (%)	Tenders Made	Contracts Won
10	20	16
20	60	45
30	160	96
40	80	32
50	50	4

(a) Calculate the minimum bid price, such that the expected present value of contribution from the contract would be zero, if won.

(b) Calculate the expected present value of contribution at each of the bid prices suggested by the markup rates shown above, and find the price which maximizes the EPVC.

(c) Consider all the issues, assumptions, and qualifications which underlie your analysis, and choose your bid price.

SUGGESTED REFERENCES AND FURTHER READING

Alpert, M. I. *Pricing Decisions*, chap. 3. Glenview, Ill.: Scott, Foresman & Company, 1971.

Edelman, R. "Art and Science of Competitive Bidding," *Harvard Business Review*, 43 (1965), pp. 53-66.

Ekelund, R. B., Jr., and R. F. Hébert. "Uncertainty, Contract Costs and Franchise Bidding," *Southern Economic Journal*, 47 (1980), pp. 517-21.

Friedman, L. "A Competitive Bidding Strategy," *Operations Research*, 4 (February 1956), pp. 104-112.

Holt, C. A., Jr. "Competitive Bidding for Contracts under Alternative Auction Procedures," *Journal of Political Economy*, 88 (June 1980), pp. 433-45.

Kottas, J. F., and B. M. Khumawala. "Contract Bid Development for the Small Businessman," *Sloan Management Review*, 14 (Spring 1973), pp. 31-45.

Kuhlman, J. M., and S. R. Johnson. "The Number of Competitors and Bid Prices," *Southern Economic Journal*, 50 (July 1983), pp. 213-20.

Livesey, F. *Pricing*, chap. 10. London: Macmillan, Inc., 1976.

Miller, E. M. "Oral and Sealed Bidding: Efficiency versus Equity," *Natural Resources Journal*, 12 (July 1972), pp. 330-53.

Oren, M. E., and A. C. Williams. "On Competitive Bidding," *Operations Research*, 23 (November-December 1975), pp. 1072-79.

Roberge, M. D. "Pricing for Government Contractors," *Management Accounting* (June 1973), pp. 28-34.

Roering, K. J., and R. J. Paul. "An Appraisal of Competitive Bidding Models," *Marquette Business Review*, 21 (Summer 1977), pp. 57-66.

Walker, A. W. "How to Price Industrial Products," *Harvard Business Review*, 45 (1967), pp. 125-32.

13 | Advertising and Promotional Decisions

13.1 INTRODUCTION

In earlier chapters we considered *price* as the firm's strategic variable, and we discussed the implications of differing price levels for the attainment of the firm's objectives. In some markets, however, price competition may be virtually absent because of the nature of the product or the market. In these markets we find that firms usually leave the price level alone and engage in *nonprice* competition through advertising and promotional expenditures.

Nonprice competition may be favored over price competition for several reasons. First, price competition carries with it the risk of a price war in which prices tumble downward and the firms' profit margins deteriorate. Sales volumes increase, of course, but the relevant demand curve is likely to be the (inelastic) *mutatis mutandis* curve, because all prices are declining at the same time. Thus total profit typically suffers, and firms may incur losses or even suffer bankruptcy. In mature markets the firms may have had unfavorable experience with price competition in the past, and they may prefer to minimize its use as a strategic variable. As a corollary, we have the adage "Any fool can cut prices, but it takes genius to develop a good advertising campaign." With this mind-set, nonprice strategies may be considered the more appropriate forum for competition.

Second, if the firms believe that they face a kinked demand curve, they may think that it is harder to raise prices again than it is to lower them. Reducing prices is typically a joint action, as other firms follow suit in order to avoid loss of market share and future profit. Raising prices, however, may be an independent action along a relatively elastic *ceteris paribus* demand curve, unless the other firms also want to raise prices at the same time. Since raising a price independently causes a substantial loss of market share, firms may choose to avoid this problem by not reducing the price in the first place.

Third, price competition is better suited to some types of products, and nonprice competition is more effective with others. We noted in Chapter 10 that "search" products, those containing easily measurable attributes, are more likely candidates for price competition, since consumers can see that a lower price represents a substantially better value, and thus the price-cutting firm expects to face a more elastic demand. "Experience" products, which contain attributes that cannot be evaluated until after purchase, and "credence" products, which are imperfectly evaluated even after purchase, would face relatively inelastic demand curves even for independent price reductions. Thus firms are less likely to use price competition as a competitive strategy for experience or credence goods. Advertising and promotional expenditures, on the other hand, may be profitably aimed at convincing the potential buyer that these products are worth a try.

In general, products that are evaluated according to the buyer's taste, (experience products such as food, beverages, fashionable clothing, and so on), are good candidates for advertising as a competitive strategy. In 1984 McDonald's hamburger chain spent $253.9 million dollars on advertising, Burger King spent $129.4 million, Wendy's spent $73.5 million, and so on down the list, for a total of almost a billion dollars in the fast-food market alone. In the first four months of 1985, Coca-Cola spent $14.2 million advertising Diet Coke, as compared to Pepsi's $13.4 million advertising Diet Pepsi. Then there was $12.8 million spent on Coke, $7.0 million spent on Pepsi, $5.9 million spent on Tab, $5.3 million spent on Sprite, and so on down the list. Credence products, like dog food and medical, dental, and legal services, are also advertised heavily in some cases. Kibbles 'n Bits spent $8.7 million, and Purina Dog Chow spent $8.2 million on television advertising in 1984.[1] These examples indicate that advertising must work for these firms, although we shall see later that competitive advertising is like being on a treadmill—if you slow down you get left behind.

In other market situations we should expect to find firms adjusting both price and advertising expenditures simultaneously to obtain their objectives. Monopolistic competitors and oligopolists gain control over the price level as a result of the differentiation of their product: advertising and promotional expenditures are likely to increase this differentiation and hence increase the control these firms have over their market price, as well as increase the price that might be obtained for any given output level.

In the monopolistically competitive market situation the firm may presume that its actions will have an insignificant effect on each of its competitors and hence may presume that there will be no reaction from competitors to its actions. Thus we may analyze the monopolistically competitive firm's advertising and promotional decisions under the assumption of *ceteris paribus*. The same applies to the monopolist, since this firm has no existing competition from whom to expect reactions. The oligopolist, however, operating in an environment of strong interdependence of action, must expect its advertising and promotional expenditures to have a noticeable impact on competitors' sales and hence must expect these rivals to react to its advertising and promotional expenditures.

In the following sections we shall first consider the firm's optimal adjustment of

---

[1] *Wall Street Journal.* March 7, 1985; March 14, 1985; and August 16, 1985.

its advertising and promotional expenditures under conditions of *ceteris paribus*, (1) given a particular price level and (2) in a situation where both price and advertising may be adjusted simultaneously to their optimal levels. We then turn to the advertising and promotional decision under conditions of oligopoly where the reaction of rivals must be taken into account. Finally, we address the issue of the uncertainty about the impact of advertising upon the level of sales and profits.

Note: Throughout this chapter the emphasis will be on the economics of the advertising and promotional decision, and we leave to the marketing practitioners the more specialized problems of media selection, message composition, promotional mix, timing, and pattern of promotional campaigns. Throughout this chapter we shall, for simplicity of exposition, use the term *advertising* to include all elements of the promotional mix.

13.2 OPTIMAL ADVERTISING EXPENDITURES UNDER *CETERIS PARIBUS* CONDITIONS

In Chapter 4 we saw that the firm's sales or demand level was a function of several controllable variables and a variety of uncontrollable variables. The controllable variables were later termed the firm's strategic variables and may be familiar to you as the "marketing mix" of price, promotion, product design, and distribution. Since the firm's sales are a function of these variables, it follows that the firm's profits are a function of these variables, and if the firm wishes to maximize profits it should adjust these controllable variables to the point where further adjustment would make no positive contribution to profits.

The Advertising-Sales Relationship

In Chapter 4 we held all other variables in the demand function constant while varying the level of price to find the influence on demand. Analogously, we shall now examine the effect of holding all other variables (including price) constant while varying the level of advertising. Thus demand will be equal to a constant (which represents the effect of all the other variables), plus some function of advertising expenditures. In the simple linear case:

$$Q = \alpha + \beta A \qquad (13\text{-}1)$$

where Q is the quantity demanded, α and β are parameters, and A is the level of advertising expenditure. Note that this equation implies that the marginal impact on sales for additional units of advertising expenditure (i.e., the parameter β) will be constant regardless of the level of advertising expenditure. More likely we would expect diminishing returns to advertising expenditures at higher advertising levels. Thus, the advertising function may be quadratic in form, such as

$$Q = \alpha + \beta_1 A + \beta_2 A^2 \qquad (13\text{-}2)$$

where β_2 would be a negative number if there are diminishing returns to advertising. Alternatively, it might be argued that initial levels of advertising may benefit from increasing returns, since certain threshold levels of advertising expenditure must be reached in order to afford certain types of media and to penetrate the buyer's consciousness. However, we would expect that these thresholds would be soon overcome and that diminishing returns would be expected to set in for higher levels of advertising expenditure. Thus the general form of the advertising function for all levels of advertising might be expected to be cubic, such as

$$Q = \alpha + \beta_1 A + \beta_2 A^2 + \beta_3 A^3 \qquad (13\text{-}3)$$

where β_3 would be a negative number. These three types of advertising relationship are shown in Figure 13-1. Note that in all cases quantity demanded has some positive value (namely, the parameter α) when advertising is zero and that the general relationship between advertising and quantity demanded is positive. Clearly, we should not expect the relationship to be linear over a wide range of advertising levels, since this assumption neglects the probable occurrence of diminishing returns to advertising expenditures. Nevertheless, a linear advertising function may be a sufficient approximation of both the quadratic and the cubic functions over the relevant range of advertising expenditures.

The appropriate functional form of the advertising sales relationship is of course the one that provides the best statistical fit to the data in a particular case. If a firm could be assured that *ceteris paribus* held for all other significant variables, or is able to observe the changes in these other determinants, and then varies its level of advertising over a period and observes the variations in demand, it could apply regression analysis to the data generated to find which form of the regression equation best fits the observed data.[2]

The Optimal Level of Advertising for a Given Price Level

You will recall from Chapter 4 that advertising expenditure is one of the variables that are held constant while a particular demand curve is being discussed. Changes in advertising expenditures cause a *shift* in the demand curve, causing it to move to the

---

[2]See, for example, V. R. Rao, "Alternative Econometric Models of Sales-Advertising Relationships," *Journal of Marketing Research,* 9 (May 1972), pp. 177-81; and V. K. Verma "A Price Theoretic Approach to the Specification and Estimation of the Sales-Advertising Function," *Journal of Business,* 53 (July 1980), pp. S115-S137; and R. D. Carlson, "Advertising and Sales Relationships for Toothpaste," *Business Economics,* 16 (September 1981).

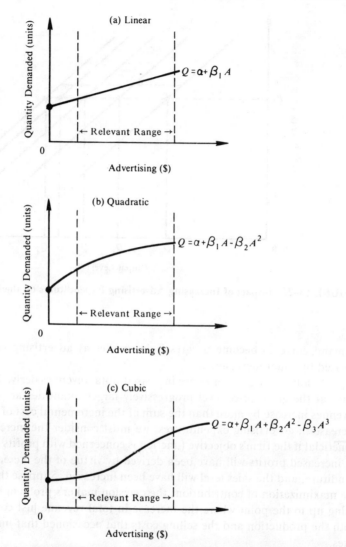

FIGURE 13-1. Possible Functional Forms of the Advertising/Sales Relationship

right when advertising expenditures are increased or to the left when expenditures are reduced. In Figure 13-2 we show the initial price and quantity coordinates as P_0 and Q_0 on demand curve D_0. Suppose now that advertising expenditures are increased from their previous level by a given amount, causing the demand curve to shift to the right to that shown as D_1. Subsequent increases in advertising expenditures would be expected to shift the demand curve farther to the right, but if there are diminishing returns to advertising expenditures we should expect these subsequent shifts of the

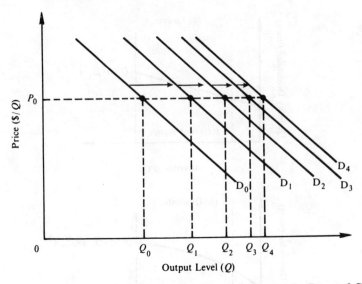

FIGURE 13-2. Impact of Increasing Advertising Expenditures on the Demand Curve

demand curve to become progressively smaller as advertising expenditures are increased by equal increments.

As advertising expenses are increased, total revenues derived are also increased, since at the given price level progressively larger quantities are demanded. If total revenues increase by more than the sum of the incremental cost of production and the increase in advertising expenditures, we must consider the increased advertising as beneficial if the firm's objective function is concerned with profits or sales levels. That is, increased profits will have been derived by virtue of the increased advertising expenditure, and the sales level will have been increased. Suppose the firm's objective is the maximization of contribution; the decision maker's problem is to increase advertising up to the point where the increase in total revenue just covers the increase in both the production and the selling costs that occasioned that increase in total revenues.

Example: To demonstrate this principle, let us suppose that the advertising function for a particular firm has been estimated as follows:

$$Q = 10,000 + 25.2A - 0.8A^2 \qquad (13\text{-}4)$$

where A represents advertising expenditures in thousands of dollars. The optimal level of advertising, using the marginalist approach, will be that level at which the last dollar spent on advertising contributes just one dollar toward overheads and profits. Thus the maximizing condition is

$$\frac{d\pi}{dA} = 1 \tag{13-5}$$

where π represents "contribution to overheads and profits." If we consider dA in one-dollar increments, the requirement for profit maximization, that is, $d\pi$, equals one dollar in order to cover the last dollar of advertising expenditure incurred. Note that to find $d\pi/dA$ we must first find how quantity demanded varies with advertising and then how profits vary with quantity demanded. That is, $d\pi/dA$ expands to

$$\frac{d\pi}{dA} = \frac{dQ}{dA} \cdot \frac{d\pi}{dQ} \tag{13-6}$$

From equation (13-4) we can find dQ/dA by taking the first derivative of the estimated advertising function with respect to the level of advertising expenditures. Hence,

$$\frac{dQ}{dA} = 25.2 - 1.6A \tag{13-7}$$

The second element on the right-hand side of equation (13-6), namely, the change in contribution over the change in output, is in fact the contribution margin on the last unit produced. Thus we can express equation (13-6) as follows:

$$\frac{d\pi}{dA} = \frac{dQ}{dA} \cdot CM \tag{13-8}$$

Since the maximizing condition is to set $d\pi/dA$ equal to one, we may restate the maximization condition as

$$\frac{dQ}{dA} = \frac{1}{CM} \tag{13-9}$$

Supposing the contribution margin to be constant at \$6 per unit, by substitution from (13-7) into (13-9) we can solve for the optimal level of advertising as follows:

$$25.2 - 1.6A = \frac{1}{6}$$
$$151.2 - 9.6A = 1$$
$$-9.6A = -150.2$$
$$A = 15.646$$

Thus in the case where the advertising function is represented by equation (13-4) and the contribution margin is constant at \$6 per unit, the profit-maximizing level of advertising is 15.646 units, or \$15,646.

Note: Where there are diminishing returns in production or a downward-sloping demand curve, we cannot expect the contribution margin per unit to remain constant regardless of output level, and hence we must specify the profit function in terms of total revenue and total costs such that we may accurately define the $d\pi/dQ$ term over all values of Q. A second problem arises where the advertising coefficient (dQ/dA) is estimated from a linear multiple-regression equation, in which case it will be the average of the marginal impact of advertising over the range of the data observations. Since we expect the marginal impact of advertising to decline as the level of advertising increases, the coefficient will overstate the effect of additional advertising at the upper end of the observations (where our interest will probably be) and should be used with caution for decision-making purposes.

Simultaneous Adjustment of Price and Advertising Levels

Where the firm is able to adjust both price and advertising, we should not expect the firm to wish to be constrained to a particular price level. The monopolistic competitor, for example, is able to adjust price without expecting retaliation from rival firms, and the monopolist has no rival firm's reactions to consider. Thus firms in these market situations may wish to adjust both prices and advertising levels simultaneously.

Note: Advertising expenditures must be regarded as a fixed cost, since they are typically independent of the current level of output and sales. Thus the average advertising expenditures, or, more broadly, average selling costs, will be graphed as a rectangular hyperbola against the output level. In Figure 13–3 we show the average selling cost curve ASC_0 for a particular level of advertising expenditures, given a particular demand situation.[3] For simplicity we shall initially assume zero marginal costs. The intersection of the marginal revenue curve with the horizontal axis therefore indicates that the profit-maximizing or contribution-maximizing output level is Q_0, to be sold at price P_0. The relevant point on the average selling cost curve is the point labeled A_0, since this is the average selling cost level at output level Q_0. There is nothing in Figure 13–3 to indicate that ASC_0 is the *optimal* level of advertising expenditure. Larger advertising budgets will cause the demand curve to shift to the right but will also cause the average selling cost curve to move upward and to the right. To find the optimal level of advertising expenditure and the profit-maximizing price, we must know to what extent additional advertising expenditures will shift the demand curve.

In Figure 13–4 we show the results of increasing the level of advertising expenditure. Starting from the initial advertising level ASC_0, which gave rise to the optimal quantity and price levels Q_0 and P_0, we suppose that advertising expenditure is increased to the level indicated by the curve ASC_1. This increase causes the demand

---

[3]This analysis follows N. S. Buchanan, "Advertising Expenditures: A Suggested Treatment," *Journal of Political Economy*. August 1942, pp. 537–57. An alternate methodology is given by R. Dorfman and P. O. Steiner, "Optimal Advertising and Optimal Quality," *American Economic Review*. 44 (December 1954), pp. 826–36.

curve to shift from MR_0 to the new marginal revenue curve MR cutting the mount... axis at the output level Q_1 (in the figure, ... equal to advertising... the point A_1A_0) at this output level $P_1 A_1$ indicates the average Selling Cost per unit...

FIGURE 13-3. The Average Selling Cost Curve

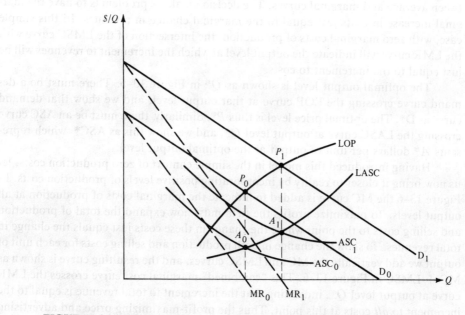

FIGURE 13-4. Optimal Prices for Successive Levels of Advertising Expenditure

525

curve to shift from D_0 to D_1. The new marginal revenue curve MR_1 cuts the horizontal axis at the output level Q_1, indicating a new profit-maximizing price level shown by the point P_1. At this output level, point A_1 indicates the average selling cost per unit.

By continuing this process we could trace a series, or locus, of optimal price points and a similar locus of average selling cost points. The locus of optimal prices for various levels of advertising expenditure is shown as the curve LOP in Figure 13-4, and the locus of the average selling costs for various advertising and demand levels is shown as the curve LASC. Each point on the LOP curve represents the optimal price-quantity combination on a demand curve relating to a particular level of advertising. (You have to imagine a series of demand curves, as in Figure 13-2 but not shown in Figure 13-4 for simplicity, that relate to a series of progressively higher advertising levels.) Similarly, each point on the LASC curve represents the advertising cost per unit of output at each optimal output level. Note that the assumption of diminishing returns to advertising expenditures is built into this model, and it is the reason for the LOP and LASC curves bending toward each other.

The LOP curve and the LASC curve in Figure 13-4 are both loci of a variable that represents an average—specifically, average revenue (or price) and average selling cost. Each of these average curves will have a curve that is marginal to it. In Figure 13-5 we show the LMR curve (locus of marginal revenue) as the curve that is marginal to the locus of optimal prices curve, and the LMSC curve (locus of marginal selling costs) as the curve that is marginal to the LASC curve. Note that the shape and placement of these marginal curves follow the general principles of the relationships between average and marginal curves. The decision maker's problem is to have the marginal increase in costs just equal to the marginal change in revenues. In this simple case, with zero marginal costs of production, the intersection of the LMSC curve with the LMR curve will indicate the output level at which the increment to revenues will be just equal to the increment to costs.

The optimal output level is shown as Q^* in Figure 13-5. There must be a demand curve crossing the LOP curve at that output level, and we show that demand curve as D^*. The optimal price level is thus P^*. Similarly, there must be an ASC curve crossing the LASC curve at output level Q^*, and we show this as ASC*, which represents A^* dollars per unit of output at the optimal output level.

Having introduced this model in the simple context of zero production costs, let us now bring it closer to reality by incorporating positive levels of production costs. In Figure 13-6 the MC curve is added to indicate the marginal costs of production at all output levels. To maximize profits the firm must now expand the total of production and selling costs to the point where the change in these costs just equals the change in total revenues. To show the change in both production and selling costs for each unit of output we add vertically the MC and LMSC curves, and the resulting curve is shown as MC + LMSC in Figure 13-6. This "combined" marginal cost curve crosses the LMR curve at output level Q^*, indicating that the increment to total revenue is equal to the increment to *all* costs at this point. Thus the profit-maximizing price and advertising levels are P^* and A^* per unit, respectively.

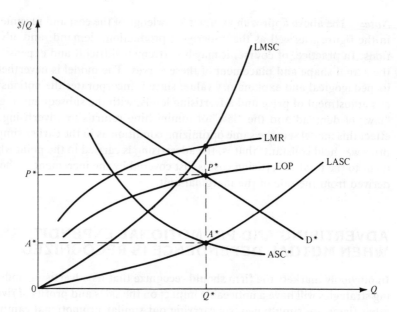

FIGURE 13-5. Establishing the Optimal Price and Advertising Levels

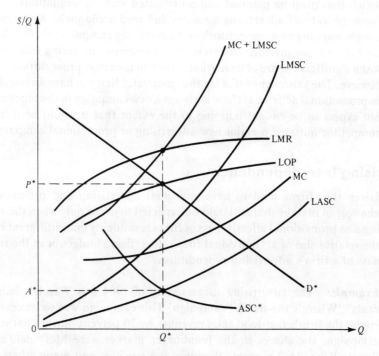

**FIGURE 13-6. Optimal Price and Advertising Levels
When There Are Both Production and Selling Costs**

Note: The above approach assumes knowledge of the cost and revenue curves shown in the figures, as well as the underlying production, demand, and advertising functions. In practice, of course, it may be extremely difficult and expensive to ascertain the actual shape and placement of these curves. The model is nevertheless useful for its pedagogical and explanatory value, since it incorporates the notions of simultaneous adjustment of price and advertising levels, with the subsequent interaction of the "law" of demand and the "law" of diminishing returns to advertising. Note that in effect this model sets the same optimizing condition as in the earlier simple case where price was held constant; that is, the advertising is carried to the point where the increment to the total advertising cost is just covered by the increment to the total revenue derived from the sale of the marginal unit.

13.3   ADVERTISING AND PROMOTIONAL EXPENDITURES WHEN MUTUAL DEPENDENCE IS RECOGNIZED

In oligopoly markets the firm should recognize that its advertising and other marketing strategies will have a noticeable impact on the sales and profits of rivals, unless the other firms are simultaneously carrying out similar promotional campaigns. Unlike price adjustments, however, promotional campaigns require a significant lead time in which they must be planned and coordinated with the availability of time and space from the various advertising agencies and media channels. As a result, if a firm is caught napping by a competitor's new advertising campaign, there will be a significant lag before it can produce its own retaliatory campaign, during which time it may have lost a significant share of its market, which in turn may prove difficult or impossible to retrieve. The existence of this lag thus motivates firms to have an ongoing involvement in promotional activity. If there is always a new campaign in the pipeline, the firm does not expect to be caught napping to the extent that it would be if it waited until a competitor initiated a major new advertising or promotional campaign.

Advertising Interdependence

Given that firms tend to have continual advertising and promotional strategies, changes in market shares should be expected to occur only when the relative advertising and promotional effectiveness of firms is suddenly made different by an increase in the relative size of an individual firm's advertising budget or in the relative effectiveness of a firm's advertising expenditures.

Example: The advertising success story of 1984 was Wendy's hamburger restaurants' "Where's the Beef?" campaign. This campaign was so successful it helped increase the firm's fast-food sales revenues by 26 percent during that year. Prior to the campaign, the shares in the hamburger market were McDonald's, 41.5 percent; Burger King, 16.2 percent; Wendy's, 9.4 percent; and many others making up the remaining one-third of the market. After the campaign Wendy's market share probably was about 12 percent, although the market may have expanded because of the barrage of competitive advertising that followed. A 26 percent increase in sales revenues translates into an extra $494 million over Wendy's 1983 sales of $1.9 billion. We saw earlier that Wendy's spent $73.5 million on advertising during 1984, and of course their materials and labor costs were higher, but profit must have been enhanced considerably by that advertising campaign. Significantly, McDonald's spent about 3 1/2 times as much on advertising, and Burger King nearly twice as much, yet these firms probably lost market share to Wendy's. (They may have held market share as a result of their counterpunching; that is, Wendy's gain in sales may have come largely at the expense of the smaller firms.) The point is that it is the *effectiveness* of the advertising, in addition to the magnitude of the expenditures, that translates into sales gains.[4]

The potential gains from a successful advertising campaign, and the benefits of larger advertising expenditures, may induce firms to continually increase their advertising budgets in search of competitive advantage. Suppose two large firms share the major part of a particular market and each budgets approximately $4 million toward promotional expenditures each year. In Table 13-1 we show the payoff matrix for the interaction of the firms' advertising strategies. When both firms spend $4 million, the net profits to each firm are $10 million. By convention, A's payoffs are shown first (followed by B's payoffs) for each combination of promotional expenditure strategies. Suppose now that Firm A contemplates increasing the promotional budget level to $6 million. If Firm B maintains its promotional budget at $4 million, A's profits will rise to $12 million while B's profits will fall to $6 million. The result of A's additional $2 million promotional expenditures will be to cause a substantial proportion of the market to switch from firm B's products to firm A's products, with associated changes in the firms' relative profitabilities.

Conversely, if firm B considered increasing advertising levels to $6 million while firm A held its advertising constant at $4 million, it would be firm B that would benefit from the change in market share that resulted. Finally, if both firms increased advertising to the higher advertising levels, the result would be as shown in the lower-right-hand quadrant of the payoff matrix, namely, that profits are reduced compared with the earlier levels of advertising expenditures. This result may be rationalized in terms of the market's becoming saturated by the products of the two firms, or we might

TABLE 13-1. Payoff Matrix for Advertising Strategies

		Firm B's Advertising Budget	
		$4 m.	$6 m.
Firm A's Advertising Budget	$4 m.	10.0, 10.0	6.0, 12.0
	$6 m.	12.0, 6.0	8.7, 8.7

[4]See "The Fast-Food War: Big Mac under Attack," *Business Week,* January 30, 1984, pp. 44-46; and *Wall Street Journal,* March 7, 1985, p. 35.

conclude that the firms' competing messages to consumers tend to offset each other's effectiveness by creating "noise" in the communication process.

Given that the firms are likely to be risk averters and that there will be a significant lag before the firm can retaliate to an increase in advertising expenditures by the other firm, we might expect each firm to wish to avoid the worst possible outcome. Thus we may expect each firm to follow a "maximin" strategy. For each firm the worst outcome associated with the smaller advertising expenditure is $6 million profit, whereas the worst outcome associated with the larger promotional budget is $8.7 million profit. The best of these worst situations is the $8.7 million profit associated with the larger promotional expenditures. Thus the maximin strategy for each firm is to increase its promotional budget to the higher level.

In this example the firms have independently increased their expenditures in pursuit of private gain, but instead they find that the result is inferior to that which was enjoyed at the earlier promotional levels. The firms are subject to what has become known as the "prisoner's dilemma."

The Prisoner's Dilemma

■ *Definition:* The *prisoner's dilemma* situation arises when two or more parties are motivated to behave in a self-serving manner, and they assume that their rivals or adversaries will act similarly. The result is that the outcome to all parties is inferior to that which could have been attained if the parties had been able to assume that their rivals would not act in a way detrimental to them.[5]

Example: This situation is called the prisoner's dilemma after the supposed situation in which two bank robbers are caught with the proceeds of a robbery, but with no more than circumstantial evidence of their being involved in that robbery. Interrogated in two separate rooms each is told that if he confesses and implicates the other he will go free as a "state's witness" while the accomplice will receive a substantial term in prison. Each prisoner knows that if they both refuse to confess they will receive a short prison term for possession of stolen goods, while if both prisoners confess, neither will be needed as a state's witness and both will receive relatively long jail sentences. Given the inability of the prisoners to communicate with each other (and since there is no honor among thieves) each will be motivated to avoid the worst possible outcome. Since the worst possible outcome is that of not confessing while the other does confess, the maximin strategy for each prisoner is to confess. Since each prisoner confesses, each ends up with a relatively long jail sentence, whereas if they had been able to communicate and coordinate their strategies they would have been sentenced to the relatively short prison term for possession of stolen goods.

The prisoner's dilemma thus applies to firms in situations of advertising rivalry. The lack of communication and coordination between parties with conflicting self-

[5]See R. D. Luce and H. Raiffa, *Games and Decisions* (New York: John Wiley & Sons, Inc., 1957), pp. 94–102; or F. M. Scherer, *Industrial Market Structure and Economic Performance* (Chicago: Rand McNally & Company, 1970), pp. 142–45 and 335–37.

interest can lead to a situation in which both parties are worse off compared with the outcomes that would have been obtained had there been communication and coordination between those firms. Referring back to Table 13-1, had the firms agreed to limit their advertising expenditures to $4 million each, their net profits would have remained at the $10 million level. In pursuit of independent profit gains, however, and without knowing whether or not the other firm was simultaneously planning an increase in the promotional budget, both firms find themselves at a reduced level of profit.

Note that when both firms have increased their promotional budget to the $6 million level, there is no incentive for either firm to reduce the advertising budget independently, since doing so would lead to a loss of market share and net profits. Similarly, larger promotional budgets promise increases in net profit levels if they are undertaken independently. When each firm fears that the other may undertake a further increase in promotional expenditures, we have the prisoner's dilemma all over again, and both firms will be motivated to spend the additional amount on promotion so that they will not be left standing still when the other's promotional campaign is launched.

Coordination of Advertising Expenditures

Is it reasonable to expect firms to coordinate their advertising and promotional expenditure levels? While firms may achieve an implicit agreement not to escalate advertising budgets beyond present levels, it is unlikely that they will achieve agreement to reduce budget levels to a point that would seem to be more efficient in terms of total profitability. In part this reluctance is undoubtedly due to the distrust that a firm may feel about reducing its own advertising expenditures while rivals may not in fact reduce theirs. Given the lead time required to prepare additional promotional campaigns, a firm that double-crosses its rivals could gain a market share advantage that might be impossible to regain.

A second factor militating against the coordination of advertising and promotional competition is that these activities are seen as an appropriate forum for the competitive instincts of rival firms, an avenue for civilized competition that should not be closed to the firms. Promotional competition requires skill and planning and the services of talented people. Price competition, on the other hand, requires little planning and not much skill on the part of the instigator, yet the impact upon the profitabilities of all firms may be significantly adverse. To avoid active competitive shifting to the price arena, firms prefer to compete on a promotional level where gains in market shares and profits are the rewards for exceptional abilities on the promotional side.

13.4 UNCERTAINTY IN ADVERTISING

In the preceding section we have presumed that the firm can foresee the result of a given expenditure on advertising and promotion. In fact, $1,000 spent this month may be very effective in influencing the level of sales, whereas a similar amount spent next month may have virtually no impact. This outcome may be the result of differences in the qualitative aspects of the advertising campaign, a different media mix, autonomous changes in consumer tastes and preferences, or similar changes induced by concurrent advertising campaigns of rival firms.

The responsiveness of consumers to television advertisements has been linked to the weather. Research indicates that changes in the weather can reduce or boost consumer response to advertisements by 50 to 100 percent. Advertisements for Campbell's soups are strategically placed prior to and during winter storms. When a storm is predicted, Campbell's ads urge listeners to stock up on soup before the weather worsens. After the storm arrives, listeners are urged to stay inside and relax with a warm bowl of soup. Similarly, demand for breakfast cereal is more responsive to advertisements when there is cloudy weather, and demand for soda pop increases with wind velocity. (Don't ask me why.) Of course the demand for many goods is seasonal, but this variation in advertising effectiveness is on a day-to-day basis. In the summer, suntan oil advertisements are more effective on hot days than on cloudy days. Thus weather predictions have begun to determine the timing of advertisements, with media service firms monitoring weather predictions across the country and then advising their clients when and where to place their advertisements for maximum impact on sales.[6]

Predictability and Probabilities

Given the uncertainty surrounding the impact on sales of a particular advertisement, the firm may be able to estimate a probability distribution of outcomes that may be expected to follow the use of an advertisement in a particular region at a particular time. However, assigning the probabilities to the possible outcomes represents no small problem. The major issue is to predict the impact of the expenditures on the purchasing behavior of consumers, of course, but underlying this issue are the twin problems of understanding consumer needs and wants and predicting competitors' simultaneous offerings to satisfy these needs and wants.

To increase the probabilities of increased sales levels for a given level of advertising, the firm should have a sound knowledge, through market research, of what tangible and intangible features the buyers want to see involved in the product. The firm's advertising and promotional expenditures should then be directed to informing the buyers of the availability of these attributes in this particular product and to persuading the buyers that the desired attributes can be *best* obtained through purchase of this product. Similarly, if market research indicates that consumers are more receptive to the advertisements at some times than at others, this knowledge should influence the timing of the advertisement.

The existence of distinct market segments implies that products and promotion

---

[6]See "Companies Look to Weather to Find Best Climate for Ads," *Wall Street Journal,* January 10, 1985, p. 29.

should be aimed at the appropriate segments of the overall market, where each segment is defined in terms of a common set of attributes desired by the buyers in that segment. The attributes that may be perceived and appreciated by consumers may be physically incorporated into the product (tangibles such as strength, durability, and other performance characteristics), or they may be intangibles that the consumer believes to exist (such as style, conferred status, and vicarious enjoyment of an agreeable lifestyle). Different attributes will be stressed (or invented) in the advertising campaigns for different segments, and some part of the persuasive element of advertising may relate to those tangible attributes that cannot immediately be verified by the consumer, as well as to the intangibles.

Once the market research has been conducted to ascertain the attributes desired by consumers and the perception of these attributes in the product vis-à-vis the competitors' products, the choice of message, medium (or media mix), and timing will be selected by specialists in the advertising area and should be confirmed by pretesting and posttesting upon representative potential buyers. In summary, the better market research is able to identify the attributes desired by buyers, and the better the product and the advertising campaign conform to the desires of the target segment(s), the more confident the decision maker can be in assigning probabilities to the various possible outcomes of a given advertising expenditure.

Advertising as an Investment

The impact of an advertising campaign may not be felt simply in the period of that expenditure but should be expected to have a residual impact which gradually attenuates over subsequent periods. Potential buyers may be only partly convinced by a particular campaign, but the current campaign may build a necessary base for future persuasion. Alternatively, the campaign may convince consumers to switch to this product, but only after they deplete their personal inventories of rivals' products. Thus a dollar spent on advertising now may lead to revenues in the same period, plus a stream of revenues in future periods. In this respect advertising can be regarded as an investment project and should compete for funds within the firm on the same basis as other investment projects with multiperiod revenue streams.

The conditions for optimal advertising expenditure considered in the earlier sections of this chapter were generated under the implicit assumption that the total impact of the expenditure would be felt in the same period. This analysis remains sufficiently accurate if the residual impact of advertising expenditure is very low or if the time period used for analysis is long enough to include the greater part of the total impact. If there is a significant residual impact of advertising expenditures in subsequent periods, the present value of the future revenues generated must be included in the decision-making process. Current advertising expenditures may exceed the short-run-profit-maximizing level to the extent of the present value of the future revenues generated, before we could say that the firm's longer-term objective of maximizing net worth was not being served.

534 *Topics in Managerial Economics*

Example: The massive advertising expenditures of the major breweries on advertising can be seen as an investment in future sales. Once won over to a particular brew, beer drinkers tend to remain loyal to that brand for a while, until they are attracted to the loyal ranks of another beer by the clever advertisements of a rival. The Miller Brewing Company's campaign focusing on the "It's Miller Time" theme convinced millions of Americans to switch to Miller beer. Later, Anheuser-Busch's "This Bud's for You" campaign took Budweiser beer to market preeminence. Table 13-2 indicates the market shares of the brewing companies and their advertising expenditures. Note the much greater advertising expenditures of Anheuser-Busch and Miller, their growing market shares, and the disappearance of smaller firms who were unable to keep up with the pace set by the market leaders. Many of the smaller firms merged in an attempt to gain the size necessary to compete with the largest two on a national basis.[7] In retrospect we can see that the huge advertising expenditures of Anheuser-Busch and Miller have led to an increasing share of the market as time progresses.[8]

Advertising to Raise Barriers to Entry

It is widely supposed that advertising and promotional efforts operate to raise or maintain barriers to the entry of potential competition.[9] Repeated messages concerning existing firms and their products are said to increase consumer loyalty to existing

TABLE 13-2. Advertising and Market Shares in the Brewing Market

| | 1977 | | 1980 | | 1984 |
Firm	Market Share (%)	Advertising Expenditure ($million)	Market Share ($)	Advertising Expenditure ($million)	Market Share (%)
Anheuser-Busch	22.9	58.7	29.0	93.8	35.0
Miller Brewing	15.2	43.2	21.5	88.5	20.7
Stroh Brewery	3.8	7.3	5.5	11.1	13.1
G. Heileman	3.9	4.7	7.5	13.6	9.2
Adolph Coors	8.0	4.3	8.0	20.9	7.2
Pabst	10.1	11.0	8.7	17.7	6.3
All others	36.1	—	19.8	—	8.6

Source: *Beverage Industry,* September 4, 1981 and February 5th, 1982; *Advertising Age,* October 9th, 1978; and *Nashua Telegraph,* June 19th, 1985.

[7]Stroh's rapid growth is largely attributable to its takeover of the F. & M. Schaefer and the Jos. Schlitz brewing companies. Heileman acquired the Falls City, Carling National, and Rainier breweries. Pabst acquired the Blitz-Weinhard and Olympia brewing companies.

[8]See "A Shrinking Beer Market Has Beer Makers Brawling," *Business Week,* August 20, 1984, pp. 59-63; "Heileman Again Goes to Battle," *Wall Street Journal,* July 5, 1984, p. 17; "Pabst Accepts Sweetened Offer of G. Heileman," *Wall Street Journal,* December 7, 1984; "Heileman Loses Bid," *Wall Street Journal,* January 18, 1985; and "Over a Barrel," *Nashua Telegraph,* June 19, 1985, p. 33.

[9]Following J. S. Bain, *Barriers to New Competition* (Cambridge: Harvard University Press, 1956), many economists have argued along these lines. For a recent view and a comprehensive bibliography, see D. Needham, "Entry Barriers and Non-Price Aspects of Firms' Behavior," *Journal of Industrial Economics,* 25 (September 1976), pp. 29-43.

products and cause consumers to be reluctant to switch to the products of new entrant firms.[10] To convince consumers that their products have comparable quality, reliability, and other desirable features, the entrant firms may need to spend more on advertising and promotion at least over the first few years, as compared with the existing firms. It has been argued that the prospect of these additional expenses in an uncertain market for their products causes potential entrants to decide against entry because of the low or negative level of expected profits.

Thus high levels of advertising by existing firms in a particular industry might be expected to allow those firms to continue to earn higher than "normal" profits, since entry is not attempted (or successfully accomplished) because of the expectations (or actuality) of significantly higher cost structures for entrant firms. Various studies have been reported in which tests were made for the empirical relationship between levels of advertising and levels of profitability. The results of these tests tend to be ambiguous.[11] Another avenue of inquiry concerns advertising's function of imparting price and quality information which can be expected to increase competition rather than inhibit competition.[12]

13.5 SUMMARY

Advertising and promotional decisions within the firm are an important adjunct to the firm's pricing decision, and in some cases they become the firm's primary strategic variable. Advertising and promotional expenditures are expected to shift the demand curve outward and cause the price elasticity of demand to be reduced at any given price level. We expect diminishing returns to additional advertising expenditures as the marginal consumer becomes increasingly more difficult to convince and the market approaches saturation.

The optimal level of advertising expenditures is that level at which the incremental cost of advertising is just equal to the incremental net revenues associated with that expenditure. If these revenues extend beyond the current time period, they must be evaluated in present-value terms for comparability with the current advertising expenditures. The general (marginalist) rule for optimality expressed previously applies both to situations where price is held constant and to situations where price is adjusted simultaneously.

In practice, several problems inhibit the application of the marginalist rule for optimal advertising. First, *ceteris paribus* is not likely to hold in many market situations as rival firms simultaneously adjust their pricing and advertising strategies. Sec-

---

[10]Notice that this argument involves the residual effects of past advertising and promotional efforts. It is the sum of these residual effects that operates to enhance consumer loyalty to existing firms' products.

[11]See the papers by Comanor and Wilson, Schmalensee, Peles, and Ayanian, that are listed at the end of this chapter.

[12]See "A New View of Advertising's Economic Impact," *Business Week,* December 22, 1975, pp. 49 and 54.

ond, the impact of advertising expenditures cannot easily be predicted with any great degree of accuracy. This unpredictability in turn is due to the uncertainty as to what potential buyers want and whether or not the selected message and media will effectively inform and persuade the buyers that this particular product best provides the desired attributes.

In oligopoly situations the level of advertising and promotional expenditures may be taken to excess because of the uncertainty facing the decision maker concerning the simultaneous actions of rivals. Even when the future impact of advertising expenditures is taken into account, oligopolists unable or unwilling to coordinate their advertising strategies may be expected to spend beyond the point where profits (short- or long-term) are maximized. They must continue to run in order to stay in the same place, since any unilateral reduction in advertising expenditures would cause them to lose some part of their market share and would reduce the present value of their future profit stream.

Advertising and promotional expenditures tend to generate a stream of future revenues as new customers finally purchase the product and current customers return to purchase more units in the future. To the extent that advertising raises barriers to entry, it also helps to avoid loss of sales to potential entrants in future periods. Advertising and promotional expenditures may therefore be considered as an investment in future revenues, and they should therefore compete with other investment projects for the funds available.

DISCUSSION QUESTIONS

13-1. Under what conditions may a firm expect *ceteris paribus* conditions to hold for changes in its advertising and promotional expenditures?

13-2. Discuss the idea of a minimum threshold of advertising and promotional effectiveness. Is it reasonable to argue the existence of such a threshold?

13-3. Why should we expect diminishing returns to (eventually) apply to advertising and promotional efforts? Outline several reasons.

13-4. What is the rule for optimal advertising expenditure in the short run, given price and average variable cost levels? Explain.

13-5. Outline the process underlying the simultaneous selection of the optimal level of advertising and the optimal price.

13-6. Why do oligopolists face a "prisoner's dilemma" problem when it comes to deciding on the level of advertising expenditures?

13-7. If firms decided to limit their advertising expenditures to a given amount, would market shares then remain stable at the present levels? Why or why not?

13-8. Outline the issues involved in attempting to predict the impact of an advertising or promotional campaign.

13-9. If there are residual impacts in future periods from this period's advertising expenditure, is it necessarily excessive to spend beyond the point where short-run incremental cost of advertising exceeds short-run incremental revenue from advertising?

13-10. Outline the issues involved in the argument that advertising and promotional expenditures raise the product differentiation barriers to entry. Would these barriers exist without advertising? Why?

PROBLEMS AND SHORT CASES

13-1. The Thompson Textile Company has asked you for advice as to the optimality of its advertising policy with respect to one of its products, product X. The following data are supplied:

Sales (units)	282,500
Advertising elasticity of demand	2.50
Price per unit	$ 2.00
Marginal cost per unit is constant at	$ 1.00
Advertising budget for product X	$ 56,000

(a) Is Thompson's advertising budget for product X at the profit-maximizing level?

(b) If not, can you say how much more or less it should spend on advertising? Discuss all relevant issues and qualifications you think are important.

13-2. The McWilliams Bottling Company bottles and markets under license a major brand-name soft drink. Prices of soft drinks are virtually dictated by the market and the preponderance of dispensing machines that require a time-consuming adjustment in order to allow price changes to be effected. In the regional market that it serves, McWilliams has noticed that quantity demanded responds to variations in the level of advertising and promotional expenditures. The firm has kept the following records of sales (units) and advertising and promotional expenditures over the past two years:

Last Year	Sales (units)	Advertising/ Promotion ($)
1st quarter	96,000	3,400
2nd quarter	103,000	4,350
3rd quarter	93,000	3,750
4th quarter	111,000	5,900
Preceding Year		
1st quarter	90,000	2,600
2nd quarter	76,000	1,850
3rd quarter	104,000	5,200
4th quarter	120,000	7,300

McWilliams's present advertising and sales (units) levels are $4,000 and 99,500 units. Contribution margin (per unit) is considered to be constant at $0.22. The marketing department at McWilliams feels that there were no significant changes in any factors that would prevent the above data from being used to reliably estimate the firm's sales/advertising function.

(a) Plot the sales data against the advertising expenditures and sketch in what appears to be the line of best fit to the data.

(b) Please advise McWilliams as to the estimated optimal level of its advertising and promotional expenditures. Explain and defend your recommendation.

13-3. Flintrock Fixtures is a small partnership that produces and markets a variety of kitchen and bathroom fixtures in ceramics, metal, and marble. The market for these products in Flintrock's area is not highly competitive, since the rival firms tend to compete in separate market segments of the fixtures market. Over the past year, one of the major partners, Charles Flint, has been experimenting with advertising and promotional levels in order to ascertain the impact of this variable on sales. Regressing monthly sales revenue against monthly advertising and promotional expenditures, Mr. Flint has obtained the following regression equation: TR = 110,482.5 + 2318.6A − 103.2A^2, where TR represents sales revenue in dollars and A represents advertising and promotional expenditures in thousands of dollars. This equation was derived from data ranging from $1,000 to $8,500 spent per month on advertising and promotion. (R^2 = 0.99, significant at the 1 percent level.) The present level of advertising and promotional expenditure is $6,000 per month, and Mr. Flint, who wishes to maximize sales revenue, wishes to increase this expenditure to $7,500 per month, which is the maximum that Rocky Spinelli, the other major partner, will agree to.

A minor partner in the enterprise, Peter Pebble, is concerned with the short-term profits of the enterprise. He argues that given the firm's pricing policy of marking up average variable costs by 100 percent, monthly profits would be increased significantly by reducing advertising and promotional expenditures. Mr. Pebble argues that a reduction of at least $2,000 per month would augment profits considerably.

Another minor partner, John Stone, argues that the longer-term profitability of the enterprise is the appropriate objective to pursue and that he supports Mr. Flint.

(a) What level of expenditure on advertising and promotion would maximize monthly sales revenue, given no limit on this level? How confident are you about the accuracy of this prediction? Explain.

(b) What level of expenditure on advertising and promotion would maximize monthly profits? Explain.

(c) Make an argument to support Mr. Stone's position.

(d) Presuming Mr. Stone to be correct in his reasoning and Mr. Pebble to be outvoted, what do you suggest Flintrock do?

13-4.   Record Breakers is a downtown store selling phonograph records and tapes. Its nearest competitor is about six blocks away, and its clientele is composed almost entirely of downtown office workers and other personnel from nearby buildings. Record Breakers has found that the sales of phonograph records vary with the number of records it places on special at $3.99 (compared with the regular price of $6.99) and with the space purchased in the city's morning newspaper for advertising these specials. The specials are intended to attract customers into the store where they will (it is hoped) also purchase one or more other records at the regular price. The greater the number of specials offered, the lower the total revenue per record, or average price of the records sold. Given any specific number of records on special, the store finds that record sales vary positively, but with diminishing returns, with the area devoted to advertising these particular records in the newspaper. Regression analysis indicates that

$$Q = 624.3 - 216.52P + 481.8S - 35.85S^2$$

where Q represents the weekly sales (units) of albums; P is average price in dollars; and S is space units (100 square inches daily for five days) in the morning newspaper. This regression equation is highly significant and explains virtually all the variation in weekly record sales.

The average variable cost per record is constant at $3 and space units in the newspaper cost $300, and this space is available in continuously variable fractions of a unit. The "average" situation is that Record Breakers will place six records on special and buy 2.5 units of advertising space each week. This combination causes the average price to be $5.75 over all records sold. The relationship between average price and number of records on special has been estimated as Av.P = 6.93 − 0.19 NS (with R^2 = 0.97, significant at the 5 percent level) over the range of one to fifteen records on special. This relationship holds independently of the units of advertising space purchased, although the latter does influence volume, as indicated by the earlier regression equation.

(a) Using graphical analysis, find the level of average price and the level of advertising space purchased that allow short-run profit contribution to be maximized.

(b) How many records should be put on special each week? Explain.

13-5. Vincenzo Pizzeria Limited operates the only pizza place in town although there are several other fast-food outlets in peripheral competition with Vincenzo. The manager, Vincenzo Fiorelli, feels that he has a virtual monopoly, since his clientele is largely comprised of fervent pizza lovers, and that selling more pizzas is just a matter of inducing people to "eat out" more often. Consequently Mr. Fiorelli holds prices constant and advertises in local newspapers and on a local television. His pizzas come in three sizes and with a variety of toppings, from "plain (tomato paste and cheese) all the way up to "deluxe" (mushrooms, peppers, olives, ground beef, pepperoni, and heaps of mozzarella cheese).

Mr. Firorelli's son Paolo has recently obtained his business degree and has joined the family business as marketing manager. Paolo is interested in maximizing profits of the enterprise, since his father has promised him half of any extra profits generated as a bonus. Paolo decides to conduct an analysis of the cost and demand conditions facing the firm. First he examines the cost structure. Given the three different sizes of pizza and the various combinations of toppings, the firm is in effect offering a very broad product line. Paolo's first task is to convert all the product offerings into the terms of a common denominator, which he calls a medium-pizza equivalent (MPE). The weights attached to each product reflect the relative variable costs of that product. Thus a medium-deluxe pizza is equal to 1 MPE, a small-deluxe pizza is equal to 0.75 MPE and a large-deluxe is equal to 1.5 MPEs, with lower weights given in each size category where the pizza is less than deluxe. The average variable cost of an MPE is $2.65, and Paolo finds this to be constant in the relevant output range. The first major decision Paolo makes is to standardize prices on all pizzas by marking up the average variable cost by 50 percent.

The marketing manager then undertakes a study of demand conditions. After examining past records and interviewing a random sample of five hundred customers and potential customers, Paolo generates the following demand function for Vincenzo's pizzas:

$$Q = 28105.1 - 5842.2P + 1061.6A - 22.5A^2$$

where Q is the number of MPEs demanded per month; P is the price of an MPE in dollars; and A is the advertising and promotional expenditures per month in thousands of dollars.

At present, prices are as indicated by the above markup-pricing policy, and advertising and promotional expenditures are running at the rate of $8,000 per month.

(a) Using graphical analysis (with algebraic confirmation of results), find the optimal price and advertising/promotional levels.

(b) How much will Paolo's monthly bonus be? (State all qualifications and assumptions, if any, underlying your answers.)

13-6. The Silk Purse Cosmetics Company operates in close competition with several other major suppliers of cosmetics and toiletries. In this market, consumers do not seem to be very price conscious: If they believe a product will help them, they tend to buy that product as long as its price lies below a limit that the consumer considers intolerable. Consequently, Silk Purse and its rivals tend to compete through their advertising and promotional expenditures, which are typically aimed at informing consumers of the virtues of their new and established products. Silk Purse's advertising and promotion budget is $25 million for this year, and it estimates that its rivals will collectively spend about $100 million this year. Silk Purse's net profits are projected to be $2.8 million this year.

The vice-president of finance is worried that the expected profits this year will not be high enough to support the continuation of Silk Purse's research and development program, given that dividends, taxes, and managerial bonuses must be paid out of profits. He suggests that a reduction of advertising to around $20 million would cause the profit situation to improve.

The vice-president of marketing argues that a reduction in the advertising budget to $20 million would cause sales to drop by $10 million, meaning a $1.7 million dollar reduction in net profits. On the contrary, she says, Silk Purse should increase advertising and promotional expenditures to $30 million. This action will increase sales by $8.5 million and net profits by $1.2 million.

The president of Silk Purse, M. C. Hogg, fears that an increase in advertising and promotional expenditures of this magnitude will very likely cause a competitive reaction from the major rivals. You are called in to advise Mr. Hogg.

(a) With the aid of a payoff matrix, explain the vice-president of marketing's argument to Mr. Hogg.

(b) How does Mr. Hogg's assessment of the situation differ from that of the marketing vice-president?

(c) What information would you encourage Mr. Hogg to obtain before making his decision?

13-7. The automobile-manufacturing industry has three major domestic producers, one minor and several minuscule domestic producers, and several major foreign producers, each supplying vehicles to the North American market. Advertising and promotional expenditures constitute a large part of the competitive effort in this industry, once the product design and price levels have been determined for each model year. With a major purchase like an automobile, the potential purchaser must feel confident about the quality of the vehicle, the efficacy of after-sales service, and the future value of the automobile at trade-in time. Advertising campaigns typically stress these factors and are also aimed at reducing postpurchase dissonance and building brand loyalty.

Suppose you are the advertising manager of one of the very small domestic auto producers. Your company's sales have been hovering perilously around one-fortieth of one percent of the entire market. Your advertising budget is $1.5 million, and your projected net profits before taxes are less than $5 million. Your advertising budget represents 10 percent of sales revenue, compared with an industry average of 7.5 percent. Net profits are low, largely because of your relatively short production runs, which do not allow overheads to be amortized over large output levels.

(a) Prepare an argument to convince the marketing vice-president that your advertising budget should be increased. Include counterarguments to his probable objections in your proposal.

(b) Outline the information you would want the marketing research department to obtain before planning your major campaigns for this year.

13-8. Concord Microwave Systems, Inc., manufactures and markets radar detectors. Their original product, the Diplomat, had been the industry standard of excellence for several years, until their new miniaturized version, the Ambassador, was introduced three years ago. This smaller version now sets the standards that the other manufacturers try to meet. Sales have been strong from its introduction, but the management of Concord is considering whether or not the advertising budget should be increased. They currently spend only $180,000 per annum, mostly in auto magazines, on advertising and promotion. They prefer to keep a relatively low profile rather than stir up opposition to radar detectors. Nonetheless, they feel that they could increase their advertising budget by about a third without raising significant opposition to their product.

Based on monthly sales and advertising data collected over the past two years, Concord's marketing research department has estimated the sales-advertising function for its miniature radar detector to be $Q = 49,973.4 + 16.111A - 0.0115A^2$, where Q represents units of quantity demanded, and A represents thousands of dollars spent on advertising. The price has been $295 ever since the introduction of the Ambassador model, and its average variable cost of production has stabilized at $200 per unit regardless of volume produced, within reasonable limits. Concord's total fixed costs amount to $2.5 million per annum, excluding advertising.

(a) Calculate the current output, total revenue, and total profit levels, based on the sales-advertising function.

(b) What is the profit-maximizing level of advertising?

(c) Calculate the output, revenue, and profit levels that Concord might expect if advertising expenditure was adjusted to the profit-maximizing level.

(d) State any assumptions and qualifications that underlie your analysis.

13-9. Meghan Alexandra Perfumes, Inc., manufactures a product line of exotic perfumes which are marketed worldwide. Sales of this perfume have been very strong, approaching a quarter of a million ounces in each of the first two years. Based on quarterly sales and advertising data Meghan has estimated the dependence of sales volume on advertising expenditures as follows:

$$Q = 52,833.98 + 248.358A - 0.0491A^2$$

where Q is ounces of the perfume, and A represents thousands of dollars spent annually on advertising. For the current year the advertising budget has been set at $950,000, over the objections of the marketing vice-president, who feels that it should be substantially higher than that. Meanwhile, others in the strategy group claim that it is already too high and simply wasteful. The wholesale price of the perfume is $9.99, and the marginal cost of production is constant at precisely one-third of that. Overheads allocated to this product amount to $400,000 per annum, not including the advertising expenditure.

(a) At the planned level of advertising, and given the same price and cost situation, what will be the quantity demanded and the total profit for this line of perfumes?

(b) What is the profit-maximizing level of advertising expenditures?

(c) Is there a significant gain in revenues and profits available by adjusting advertising expenditures to a higher level?

(d) What assumptions and qualifications underlie your answers?

13-10. Andrew Evans, Inc., produces and sells toys for babies and toddlers, and the firm has enjoyed considerable success in the past few years as the post-World War II "baby boomers" have made their own baby boom in the 1980s. Sales nationwide edged past the $4 million mark last year, and this year the president of Andrew Evans has set aside $1 million for advertising, up from $750,000 last year. The firm sells a variety of products, but it is a sufficient approximation to think in terms of an "average" product with an average price of $16 and marginal cost constant at $8 per "average" unit. The firm's overheads are $800,000 per annum, excluding advertising.

Market research has culminated in the following estimate of the firm's sales-advertising function:

$$Q = 110,386.3 + 298.674A - 0.10537A^2$$

where Q represents the units of the "average" product, and A represents thousands of dollars spent on advertising.

(a) Calculate the expected sales volume and total profit given an advertising budget of $1 million.

(b) Calculate the profit-maximizing level of advertising expenditure.

(c) At that level, what would sales volume, revenue, and profit be?

(d) What reasons can you think of for supporting the president's decision to spend $1 million on advertising?

SUGGESTED REFERENCES AND FURTHER READING

Ayanian, R. "Advertising and Rate of Return," *Journal of Law and Economics,* 18 (October 1975), pp. 479–506.

Brush, B. C. "The Influence of Market Structure on Industry Advertising Intensity," *Journal of Industrial Economics*, 25 (September 1976), pp. 55-67.

Clarke, D. G. "Sales-Advertising Cross-Elasticities and Advertising Competition," *Journal of Marketing Research*, 10 (August 1973), pp. 250-61.

Comanor, W. S., and T. A. Wilson. "The Effect of Advertising on Competition: A Survey," *Journal of Economic Literature*, 17 (June 1979), pp. 453-76.

Cubbin, J. S. "Advertising and the Theory of Entry Barriers," *Economica*, 48 (August 1981), pp. 289-98.

Dorfman, R., and P. O. Steiner. "Optimal Advertising and Optimal Quality," *American Economic Review*, 44 (December 1954), pp. 826-36.

Freidman, J. W. "Advertising and Oligopolistic Equilibrium," *Bell Journal of Economics*, 14 (Autumn 1983), pp. 464-73.

Kotler, P. *Marketing Management* (4th ed.), chaps. 7, 15, and 16. Englewood Cliffs, N.J.: Prentice-Hall, Inc., 1980.

Leffler, K. B. "Persuasion or Information? The Economics of Prescription Drug Advertising," *Journal of Law and Economics*, 24 (April 1981), pp. 45-74.

Needham, D. "Entry Barriers and Non-Price Aspects of Firms' Behavior," *Journal of Industrial Economics*, 25 (September 1976), pp. 29-43.

Nerlove, M., and K. J. Arrow. "Optimal Advertising Policy under Dynamic Conditions," *Economica*, May 1962, pp. 129-42.

Peles, Y. "Rates of Amortization of Advertising Expenditures," *Journal of Political Economy*, 79 (September-October 1971), pp. 1032-58.

Primeaux, W. J., Jr. "An Assessment of the Effect of Competition on Advertising Intensity," *Economic Inquiry*, 19 (October 1981), pp. 613-25.

Rao, V. R. "Alternative Econometric Models of Sales-Advertising Relationships," *Journal of Marketing Research*, 9 (May 1972), pp. 177-81.

Scherer, F. M. *Industrial Market Structure and Economic Performance* (2nd ed.), chap. 14. Chicago: Rand McNally & Company, 1980.

Schmalensee, R. "Advertising and Profitability: Further Implications of the Null Hypothesis," *Journal of Industrial Economics*, 25 (September 1976), pp. 45-54.

Schmalensee, R. *The Economics of Advertising*. Amsterdam: North-Holland Publishing, 1972.

Schmalensee, R. "Advertising and Entry Deterrence: An Exploratory Model," *Journal of Political Economy*, 91 (August 1983), pp. 636-53.

Simon, J. L. *Applied Managerial Economics*, chap. 7. Englewood Cliffs, N.J.: Prentice-Hall, Inc., 1975.

Spence, A. M. "Notes on Advertising, Economies of Scale, and Entry Barriers," *Quarterly Journal of Economics*, 95 (November 1980), pp. 493-507.

Telser, L. "Advertising and Competition," *Journal of Political Economy*, December 1964, p. 537.

Wiggins, S. N., and Lane, W. J. "Quality Uncertainty, Search, and Advertising," *American Economic Review*, 73 (December 1983), pp. 881-94.

14 Product Quality and Competitive Strategy

14.1 INTRODUCTION

The firm has at its disposal four main strategic variables, which marketers call the four P's—namely, price, promotion, product quality, and place of sale. We have looked at pricing in some detail in Chapters 9 through 12. Promotional expenditures, or advertising, was the subject of Chapter 13. We turn now to product quality. Place of sale can be discussed in this context as well, since product quality refers to the presence of desirable attributes in the product, and from the buyer's viewpoint place of sale translates to convenience of seller location, which is an attribute the buyer considers in the purchasing decision.[1]

In the pricing and advertising chapters we assumed the existence of a product with known attributes, and we were concerned with the optimal pricing and advertising of that product. In this chapter we go back one step further, prior to the production of the product, and consider the optimal design of the product before it is introduced to the market. That is, we consider what attributes should or should not be designed into the product in order to best serve the firm's objective function. We use the word "quality" as an index of the presence of desirable attributes in the product. Better-quality products include desirable attributes that are absent in lesser-quality products. Better-quality products also include larger amounts of desirable attributes than lesser-quality products do. For example, more fuel economy is preferred to less, and more durability is preferred to less, other things being equal.

Just as in the advertising chapter we were able to consider the joint determination of price and advertising, we shall in this chapter consider the joint determination of product quality, price, and advertising strategy. Considering all three strategies to-

---

[1]Place of sale, or distributional strategy, as a strategic *variable* to be adjusted by the firm to better serve its objectives, will not be addressed in this text: It is a topic of sufficient scope to warrant a separate course, offered by the marketing department in most business programs. Rather, we assume that the firm has an existing distributional system, which is held constant while we discuss the quality, price, and advertising decisions that are taken by the firm.

gether, in a "systems" approach, is preferable to considering them separately, since there may be a synergistic relationship among these three strategic variables.[2] Our approach in earlier chapters—treating price separately while holding advertising and quality (and all other variables) constant, and later allowing price and advertising expenditures to vary while holding quality constant—was necessary for simplicity of exposition at those points. We are now ready to consider the firm's combined quality/ price/advertising strategy.

Competitive Strategies

We shall consider product quality, as well as the joint determination of quality, price, and advertising, within a framework introduced by Michael Porter in his two recent books *Competitive Strategy* and *Competitive Advantage*.[3] In short, Porter contends that the firm should choose a well-defined "competitive strategy" in order to achieve "competitive advantage." A competitive strategy will include a combination of values for the firm's strategic variables (in this case limited to quality, price, and advertising), that best serves the firm's objective.[4] The firm's objective, Porter contends, should be the attainment of a "competitive advantage." Competitive advantage is evidenced by the firm earning greater profit than others in its industry, not just momentarily or occasionally, but on a continuing basis. This superior and *sustained* profitability will, of course, serve to maximize the firm's net worth. Although these superior profits may attract the attention of potential entrants, Porter argues that achieving competitive advantage operates to inhibit entry of new firms, and if entry does occur, the firm is insulated from competition from entrants to a large degree, and in any case holds an advantage over the other firms in competing against any entrants.

---

[2]Synergy among the determinants of demand implies a multiplicative demand function, such as $Q = a \times P^{\beta_1} \times K^{\beta_2} \times A^{\beta_3}$, where K represents the level of quality, rather than the additive demand function introduced in earlier chapters. Using logarithms, this demand function may be estimated using linear regression analysis, as we demonstrated in Chapters 5 and 8. Synergism may be said to exist if the multiplicative demand function fits the data better (has a higher R^2) than the additive demand function does.

[3]Michael E. Porter, *Competitive Strategy: Techniques for Analyzing Industries and Competitors* (New York: The Free Press, 1980); and *Competitive Advantage: Creating and Sustaining Superior Performance* (New York: The Free Press, 1985).

[4]Marketers, who call this combination of strategic variables the "marketing mix," would go into much more detail than we do here. See Philip Kotler, *Principles of Marketing* (Englewood Cliffs, N.J.: Prentice-Hall, Inc., 1980), esp. chaps. 11-18. At this point it is instructive to note the different roles of economists and marketers: Economists construct models to investigate the underlying principles and determining variables involved in the pricing, advertising, and quality choice decisions. By their nature these models are abstractions from reality, and the marketer will find them lacking as a tool for choosing the price, advertising, or quality level in a specific instance. But if the economist has provided guidance as to which variables are important and to the optimal relationships between those variables, then the marketer's task, of pricing a specific product in a specific market, will be made easier by the models of economists. See Thomas Nagle, "Economic Foundations for Pricing," *Journal of Business*, 57 (January 1984), pp. S3-S26. This paper from a symposium involving both economists and marketers indicates that rather than jealously protecting their turf, many economists and marketers are recognizing that they have much to learn from each other that will make them better economists and better marketers.

Porter identifies three generic competitive strategies. ("Generic" means that they can be pursued in any market.) One is the "cost leadership" strategy, where the firm strives to be the lowest-cost supplier and thus achieve superior profitability from an above-average price-cost margin. A second strategy is the "differentiation" strategy, where the firm strives to differentiate its product from rivals' products, such that it can raise price more than the cost of differentiating and thereby achieve superior profitability. Finally, there is the "focus" strategy, whereby the firm concentrates on a particular segment of the market and applies either a cost-leadership or a differentiation strategy. We shall consider each generic strategy in turn and examine the implications of each for product design, pricing, and advertising.

The cost of information to consumers (when they attempt to evaluate the quality of the product) is a major determinant of the optimal competitive strategy. This issue was introduced in Chapter 10 and was later discussed in the context of new products in Chapter 11. Essentially, products can be categorized as "search," "experience," or "credence" products, based on the difficulty and expense that a typical consumer faces when attempting to evaluate the quality of the product. In a nutshell, "search" products are typically prime candidates for a cost-leadership strategy, whereas "experience" and "credence" goods are typically best marketed using a differentiation strategy.

Nevertheless, within any market the firm has a choice of a cost-leadership, differentiation, or focus strategy; its selection will also depend on the strategies already adopted by its rivals. For example, in a market for "experience" goods one or more firms may have significant product differentiation advantages, leaving cost leadership as the optimal strategy for the firm to pursue in that market in order to attain competitive advantage. Or, in a market for search products, one or more of the other firms may be competing vigorously for cost leadership, and the firm's best strategy may be to adopt a focus strategy, differentiating its product to best serve a particular segment, or niche, of the market, for example.

14.2 PRODUCT DESIGN FOR A COST-LEADERSHIP STRATEGY

The strategy of cost leadership requires the firm to seek the position as the lowest-cost firm in the market or, at least, one of the low-cost producers. It may achieve cost leadership by vigorously promoting sales to benefit from the learning effect in production, economies of plant size, or pecuniary economies (quantity discounts for buying materials in larger quantities). To keep costs at a minimum, the firm will also need to continually incorporate the latest technology into its production process. Sales can be promoted both by promotional pricing and by advertising, of course, so the cost-leadership strategy has implications for the price and advertising strategies of the firm. What implications does it have for the product design strategy, or quality decision, of the firm?

To answer this question, let us first consider the circumstances under which a cost-leadership strategy is likely to be the firm's optimal competitive strategy. We can discuss these under two main headings: when the product is a search product and when the role of cost leader is vacant or may be usurped, regardless of product type.

Search Products and the Cost-Leadership Strategy

■ *Definition:*   *Search products* are products containing primarily attributes that are readily discernible by consumer information-search activity, and these *search attributes* form the basis for the consumer's purchasing decision. Weight, length, and color are search attributes, but so too are attributes that can be found out for the asking. For example, the attributes of stereo equipment, like the signal-to-noise ratio, the presence or absence of the Dolby noise reduction system, and the power per channel in watts, can be ascertained (and compared with rival products) given relatively little search cost on the part of the consumer. Similarly, the attributes of primary interest to a person wishing to take an airline flight, such as time of departure, type of aircraft, number of stops en route, meals, and movies, can be found out simply by asking a travel agent or the airline check-in person.[5]

Since search products are easily evaluated by consumers, they are easily *compared* by consumers. Consequently, if a firm's product does not measure up to the competition, it will not retain its market share at a similar price level. The firm must compensate for the lack of desired attributes by reducing the price, or it must proceed to redesign the product such that it is more competitive on the basis of quality. As a result, the firm will feel pressure to emulate the best-selling rival products in order to produce a product that has all the features other products have and does all the things that rivals' products do, since a product that is inferior will readily be identified as such by consumers and quickly lose sales to superior products.

If competition from rival firms forces suppliers to match each other's search attributes, differentiation may still take place on the basis of any experience or credence attributes that are also embodied in the products. Brand names, better service, longer warranties, more convenient locations, and so on will be used to differentiate the products, but these attributes are, by definition, not the major ones considered in the consumer's purchase decision in the case of search goods. Rather, they are minor but nonetheless significant considerations in the purchase decision. Typically, however, the opportunities for differentiating search goods are relatively limited or ineffective, since consumers' attention is directed mainly to the search attributes of the products. Thus search products will tend to be clustered closely together in attribute space, with relatively little product differentiation across competing brands.

In Chapter 9 we introduced the term "symmetric" differentiation to describe product differentiation when the firms' market shares are equal at equal prices. Essentially, each product is different, but so too are consumers' preferences. Some prod-

---

[5]See Philip Nelson, "Information and Consumer Behavior," *Journal of Political Economy*, 78 (March–April 1978), pp. 311–29.

ucts have an advantage in one or more attribute dimensions, appealing to some consumers, and other products are superior in other attribute dimensions, appealing to other consumers, such that each seller attracts an equal number of the available buyers at a given price.

To the extent that the market for a search product approaches symmetric differentiation, we should expect the firm to find advertising relatively ineffective in persuading consumers that its product is substantially different from those of its rivals, because consumers can readily evaluate the differences for the most part, and the firms have a profit incentive to keep the quality of their products competitive. In general, the responsiveness of demand to changes in advertising will be relatively low. In other words, the advertising elasticity of demand is relatively low for search products.

Price elasticity of demand, on the other hand, will be relatively high for search products, since consumers know exactly what they are getting and leap at the chance to buy the product at a "lower than normal" price. A price reduction will distinguish the firm's product from rival products and will capture many consumers from rival sellers if rivals do not react to the price reduction by similarly reducing prices. In Chapter 10 we saw that promotional pricing will work particularly well with search products.

If rivals do not match price reductions, demand will be more elastic than if they do, and even if they do match price cuts, demand will be more elastic for search goods than for experience or credence goods. When rivals match price reductions, they tend to do so with a lag, since time passes before the price cut is discovered, before the decision to match the price cut is made, and before this information is communicated to potential buyers, such that the firm initiating the price adjustment benefits from a relatively elastic demand response initially that may make the price cut worthwhile. Given the profit incentive to reduce prices, the general price level is likely to tumble downward to a level close to the firms' unit cost. We saw in Chapter 10 that the more price elastic demand is, the lower the profit-maximizing markup rate will be. Thus we expect to see relatively low markups (price-cost margins) in the market for search goods.

In such a market, where persuasive advertising is relatively ineffective and price competition keeps prices down near to the level of the firms' unit cost, competitive advantage (superior profitability) can be obtained only by having a lower cost structure than the other firms. If the firm has a cost advantage, it need not fear rivals cutting their prices below *its* costs, because its costs are lower than rivals' costs, and rivals will not wish to make a loss on any product (temporary "loss leader" situations aside). Thus a cost-leadership strategy is likely to be the best strategy for search products, other things being equal.

When the Cost-Leader Position Is Vacant

If the cost-leader role is vacant or if it may be wrested from the present cost leader, the firm's best competitive strategy may be to assume that role, even in markets for experience and credence goods. As discussed in Chapters 10 and 11, "experience" goods are those containing mainly attributes that the consumer can only evaluate after purchase, such as the taste of food or the musical quality of a concert. After experiencing the quality of the product, the buyer will store this information in memory and will use it as the basis for the purchasing decision the next time. "Credence" goods contain mainly attributes that are imperfectly evaluated even after purchase, so that the credibility of the seller, the brand name, and the firm's public image and reputation become important elements in the consumer's purchasing decision.[6]

If all rival firms are pursuing a differentiation strategy, their products will tend to be spread out over attribute space, and the firm may foresee considerable difficulty in competing on the basis of experience or credence attributes. It may take years for the firm's brand name to acquire the intangible qualities held by rival firms' brand names. The best retail locations, such as in high-class shopping areas, may all be taken. The better taste of a certain food product may be due to an ingredient or a recipe that is unavailable to the other firms. (Note that Kentucky Fried Chicken and Coca-Cola each claim their "secret recipes" are responsible for their "better taste.")

Faced with these impediments to effective product differentiation, the firm should consider a cost-leadership strategy. If it can achieve significantly lower cost levels, the firm may then choose either to follow another firm's price leadership and quietly enjoy superior profitability or to assume the role of price leader itself. Because learning effects, economies of plant size, and pecuniary economies are related to increased sales volumes, it will typically serve the low-cost firm's objective to be one of the lower-priced firms if not the price leader.

Porter cautions that attempting to usurp the cost-leadership role is fraught with danger, since it may culminate in vigorous price competition with the established cost leader(s). Particularly in the markets for experience and credence products, which may be expected to exhibit less elastic demand responses to price reductions, an attempt to displace the cost leader may cause prices to fall well below the profit-maximizing level, and thus profit will be less than anticipated. Essentially, the firm should be cautious about attempting to be the cost leader, unless there is currently no relatively-low-cost firm, or unless the existing cost leader is in a vulnerable position, assuming in both cases that cost-reduction opportunities exist. The current cost leader may be vulnerable, for example, if it has not incorporated a major new cost-saving device and is prevented from doing so by its financial limitations.

The Implications of Cost Leadership for Product Design

A cost-leadership competitive strategy has three main implications for product design. First, the firm's product must "cover the bases" that are covered by other products offered for sale in the market at similar prices. In order to be considered to have similar quality for a similar price, the firm's first concern is that it at least emulate other products available to the consumer at each quality-price level. If the firm has a line of

---

[6]Credence goods were suggested by Michael R. Darby and Edi Karni, "Free Competition and the Optimal Amount of Fraud," *Journal of Law and Economics*, 16 (April 1973), pp. 67–88.

products, as discussed in Chapter 10, this consideration applies at each price-quality point it contests. We should expect a cost leader's product line to be confined to the basic, lower-priced, lesser-quality products, since we might expect more limited demand for the higher-price-and-quality products and thus fewer opportunities for cost reduction through learning, economies of plant size, and purchasing components in large quantities.

Second, in order to reduce costs the cost leader should "trim the fat" from its products. That is, it should trim each product down to the bare essentials required at each price-quality level and not oversupply the attributes at each quality level. For example, if consumers regard the acceptable minimum horsepower of a small car to be 75, then 75 horsepower is all the cost leader's product should have. Other firms, following differentiation strategies, may wish to incorporate more horsepower in their products, but the cost leader's competitive advantage is best served by simply meeting the minimum requirements.

Third, the cost leader may see fit to engage in "product proliferation," which is the production of several competing products under different brand names. This strategy follows from the tendency of search products to be symmetrically differentiated. If they are, each brand name garners a $1/n$ share of the market at equal prices, where n is the number of competing brand names. If a firm brings out a second brand name its sales will be a $2/(n + 1)$ share of the market, which is larger than $1/n$ of the market. Even if product differentiation is not symmetric, there may be gains in overall market share from product proliferation.

Example: Proctor and Gamble has followed the product-proliferation strategy with laundry and kitchen detergents and soaps. General Motors has several different brand names of essentially the same product (Chevrolet, Buick, Oldsmobile, and Pontiac). Breweries produce rival brand name beers, in anticipation of capturing a larger share of the market. Increasing its overall share of the market should allow the firm to benefit from economies of plant size, pecuniary economies (purchasing in greater quantity), and learning curve effects, culminating in lower unit costs of production and marketing, and hence superior profitability.

Pricing and Advertising Strategies to Complement Cost Leadership

In conjunction with a cost-leadership strategy we should expect to see the firm periodically use promotional pricing and informative advertising strategies. In between its promotional-pricing campaigns we might expect the firm to assume the role of price leader. Let us discuss each of these briefly.

Promotional pricing, introduced in Chapter 10, involves placing the product temporarily "on sale" in order to stimulate its sales. If the firm is the cost leader it can better afford this strategy, since its profit margins may still be acceptable at the "sale" prices. Higher-cost firms will be less inclined to use promotional pricing, since it may reduce their profit margins to less-than-acceptable levels. Thus they will tend to use it

5

Topics in Managerial Economics

less often, and will less likely respond to the low-cost firm's "sale" with a matching price reduction. The low-cost firm may therefore expect a more elastic demand for its product than it would have if rivals' costs were similar.

Advertising will be necessary to inform potential buyers that the product is being placed on sale, to remind buyers of the quality features of the product, and to inform buyers where the product is available at the sale price. Such *informative* advertising is often little more than a picture of the item with a price attached, perhaps including the "regular" price for comparison, and perhaps also including a few words and numbers specifying features of the product.

Since search products tend to be more or less symmetrically differentiated, there is little to be gained from *persuasive* advertising—that is, attempting to persuade buyers to switch products on the basis of some feature that is only slightly better than that of competitors. Persuasive advertising that relates to experience and credence attributes would be more effective, but these attributes carry only a small weight in the buyer's purchasing decision for a search product. Thus the lack of important experience or credence attributes and the lack of strong differentiating features that can be advertised effectively mean that advertising messages for search goods are primarily informative, rather than persuasive. Since informative advertisements can be shorter and require only the facts (rather than the imagery, expensive art and camera work, and hired "celebrities" of persuasive advertising), advertising expenditures for search products will be less than for experience or credence products, other things being equal.

Finally, whether or not the cost leader periodically engages in promotional pricing, we should expect it to seek the price leadership role in order to set price at the level which best serves its own objectives. The low-cost-firm price-leadership model, introduced in Chapter 9, is appropriate for the short-run profit maximizer. If the firm's time horizon extends beyond the short run, the sales-maximizing model (subject to a minimum profit constraint) or one of the limit-pricing models, also introduced in Chapter 9, may be appropriate, depending on the height of the barriers to entry, as discussed in Chapter 11.

14.3 PRODUCT DESIGN FOR A DIFFERENTIATION STRATEGY

Michael Porter speaks of the "value chain," the series of activities within a firm that serve to create value for the customer. Each link in this chain, from the technical excellence of the design to the courtesy of the people involved in after-sales service, must be nurtured, since weak links in the value chain operate to negate competitive advantage. Value for the customer may be achieved by means of a good basic product produced at low cost and sold at a low price (cost leadership strategy) or by means of a more expensive product that more closely fits the customer's needs. In the latter case the firm's objective is to raise the value of the product to the consumer by more than the cost of production and selling is raised, and this objective is the essence of the "differentiation" strategy.[7]

Other popular authors have also advocated what may be construed as a differentiation strategy. Peters and Waterman's *In Search of Excellence* and the follow-up by Peters and Austin, *A Passion for Excellence*, contain elements of the same advice to managers.[8] In brief, they say that managers should pay particular attention to what consumers think and feel about the firm's product and strive to meet those needs. These authors contend that there are two essential ingredients in the firm's plan to create and sustain superior profit performance over the long term. First, it must take exceptional care of its customers, through superior service and superior quality. Second, it must constantly innovate in order to stay ahead of its rivals as they strive to emulate its successes. We shall find this advice to be particularly appropriate for the firm that follows a differentiation strategy.

Quality Leadership

The differentiation strategy effectively amounts to competition on the basis of quality, where "quality" is being used as a synonym for the presence of desirable attributes. In order to make the sale to any particular buyer, the product must offer the buyer greater quality relative to price than rivals' products offer, given that the buyer's reservation price is less than the asking price. Superior customer service, both point-of-sale and after-sale service (including warranty and repair work), noted by Peters, Waterman, and Austin, is simply another dimension (desirable attribute) of what we mean by quality. Innovation, which of course has implications for cost reduction, also has implications for quality, since new features must be discovered and incorporated in the firm's product to allow it to remain ahead of, or at least abreast of, its rivals.

In a sense, the firm adopting a differentiation strategy seeks to be the quality leader, at least in the eyes of its customers. It seeks to offer the target buyer the most quality for the price. Although a buyer might feel that another firm offers the "best" product (for example, Mercedes Benz), the buyer may settle for something less than the best (for example, a Toyota) because of his or her reservation-price structure. In the buyer's price-quality range the product chosen is the one that offers the most quality for the price. Thus, although there may be an acknowledged quality leader in the market, each firm strives to be a quality leader in a more limited segment of the market. Recall that the relevant perception of quality is in the eyes of the beholder. This statement implies that marketing research—as well as listening to what customers say

---

[7]See Porter, *Competitive Advantage*, chap. 2.

[8]Thomas J. Peters and Robert H. Waterman, Jr., *In Search of Excellence: Lessons from America's Best-Run Companies* (New York: Warner Books, 1982); and Thomas J. Peters and Nancy Austin, *A Passion for Excellence: The Leadership Difference* (New York: Random House, 1985). For a summary report on the latter, see *Fortune*, May 13, 1985, pp. 20–32.

about the firm's product, its salespeople, its warranty service, and so on—should be the necessary first step for a differentiation strategy.[9]

Differentiation on the Basis of Search, Experience, and Credence Products

Differentiation is only effective if at least some buyers believe that there is a significant and desirable difference between the firm's product and the product offerings of rivals. These differences may be real or imagined, tangible or intangible. The differences and the similarities that exist will relate to the perception of attribute content in the firm's product, vis-à-vis the attribute content of rivals' products.

If consumer search costs (to evaluate the attributes that are of primary importance in the purchasing decision) are relatively low, we call the products search products. If the firm's product has a definite superiority over rivals' products in its search attributes, buyers will quickly recognize this fact, and many buyers will shift their allegiance to the quality leader. Rival firms will be motivated to match these attributes as soon as they can, and the gains will be relatively short-lived. Nonetheless, there are gains to quality leadership in search attributes, since the firm that is always one step ahead of the pack will be continually gaining sales at the expense of inferior substitutes.

Experience and credence products offer substantially more opportunities for the quality leader. Recall that these products are products for which the consumer's purchasing decision is based largely on experience and credence attributes, respectively. Experience attributes, like taste, music quality, and product durability, cannot be evaluated before purchase, but having once purchased the item the consumer gains information that will form the basis for evaluating the product in the future. Credence attributes, like restaurant service, the taste of cat food, or the competence of doctors, lawyers, and other professionals, also cannot be evaluated prior to purchase, and even after repeated trials of the product the buyer is not sure about the product quality, either because it may vary next time (like restaurant service) or because it can be only imperfectly evaluated (like cat food and professional services).

Since consumers cannot completely evaluate these products prior to purchase, or even after repeated trials in the case of credence goods, there is more latitude for claims concerning the product's quality. Does Coke taste better than Pepsi? Does New Coke taste better than Classic Coke? One thing is for sure, some people will prefer one, and others will prefer the other, since tastes differ. The producer's task is to engineer the taste in such a way as to enlarge the firm's market share.

Example: In 1984 the Coca-Cola Company was suffering sluggish growth for its main product, Coke. Pepsi's sales grew at more than 7 percent per annum, compared to a lackluster 3 percent for Coke, after Coca-Cola had decided to increase the amount

---

[9]See Peters and Waterman, *In Search of Excellence*, esp. chap. 6.

of high-fructose corn sweetener and reduce the amount of sugar in Coke. (Sugar was selling for 31 cents per pound, compared to about 24 cents per pound for the corn sweeteners.) Pepsi had campaigned successfully on the basis of televised taste tests and had gained market share from Coca-Cola. On April 23, 1985, Coca-Cola announced the introduction of Cherry Coke and the replacement of regular Coke with a new Coke that had a "smoother" taste and had been overwhelmingly preferred in blind taste tests (involving 190,000 people) over the 99-year-old Coke. Turmoil followed. Pepsi issued a hastily produced advertisement implying that even Coca-Cola now agreed that Pepsi tasted better than Coke. People stockpiled the old Coke, while New Coke sales faltered. In July 1985, Coca-Cola announced it would bring back the old Coke, renamed "Classic" Coke, reversing its earlier decision in the face of unexpected pressure from consumers and bottlers. Whether it was a marketing blunder or not remains to be seen. The publicity surrounding the entire event was worth millions, and now Coca-Cola has three products in the market competing against Pepsi where it previously had only one. In September 1985 the company announced that the combined sales volume of Cherry Coke, New Coke, and Classic Coke for July and August were 10 percent above the sales volume for Coke in the same months of 1984. This increase no doubt represented a market share gain at the expense of Pepsi, but analysts felt that both Coke and Pepsi will gain market share from smaller rivals, such as RC Cola and Dr. Pepper, as a result of the intensified advertising rivalry between the two larger firms.[10]

The soft-drink market is a good example of competing firms each following differentiation strategies. Within the "sugar-based cola" segment, New Coke, Classic Coke, Pepsi Cola, RC Cola, and other minor contenders battle for supremacy, each claiming better taste. Then there is the "diet-cola" segment, the "uncola" segment (Sprite and Seven-Up), and the "different" tastes of Cherry Coke and Dr. Pepper. In the diet-cola segment, claims and counterclaims are made concerning the taste and the possible health risks of the artificial sweeteners used. The absence of caffeine is lauded as a superior feature. Note, however, that the type of sweetener and the absence of caffeine are search attributes, and the pioneering firms were quickly emulated by rivals after initially advertising these as distinguishing features of their product. Taste remains the pivotal issue in this market. Note also that "celebrities" (Bill Cosby for Coke and Michael Jackson for Pepsi) were instrumental in the advertising war between Coke and Pepsi, being used to confer credibility on the advertising claims that are not easily verifiable.

Brand Name Advantages

When products contain experience or credence attributes that are important in the consumer's purchasing decision, consumers often look to the brand name of the item as an assurance of quality. A firm's brand name can be regarded as a "stock of infor-

---

[10]See *Wall Street Journal*, December 13, 1984, p. 8; February 9, 1984; April 24, 1985; September 10, 1985, p. 8; and "Coke's Man on the Spot," *Business Week*, July 29, 1985, pp. 56–61.

mation" that has been built up by the firm in the past. It includes information concerning the experience and credence attributes in products purchased under that brand name on previous occasions, information gleaned from advertisements as to current quality attributes, the image of the firm as community-conscious or environment-conscious, a benevolent employer, and so on. Some brand names are better than others, in terms of the level of quality that they imply will be found in a product, but all are the sum total of the firm's previous efforts to build up its brand name recognition and quality image.

When a firm has an established brand name, it can introduce a new product or a new version of an existing product, and consumers will feel they already know something about the product's quality and will be more likely to purchase the product than if it were the same product introduced by a firm with a lesser brand name. This increased probability of purchase, which derives from the greater information stock embodied in the brand name, is what we mean by brand name advantage. When a product has a brand name advantage, other firms will have to offer a "compensating price differential," meaning a lower price, in order to compete effectively with that firm.

Example: ReaLemon, a well-known brand name for processed lemon juice, was priced 10 to 15 cents per quart above the prices of Golden Crown and other lesser-known brands of processed lemon juice in the late 1970s. Borden, Inc., producer of ReaLemon, was prosecuted by the Federal Trade Commission for conspiring to monopolize its market through predatory pricing. Borden had reduced the price of ReaLemon to a level that served to force its rivals' prices below their costs. (Rivals had to set their prices 10 to 15 cents lower in order to compete.) This practice was also argued to restrict new entry, since new firms would have an even greater brand name disadvantage. Whether or not Borden was fairly treated by the courts is not the issue here. Rather, the point is that the information content of the ReaLemon brand name was apparently worth a price premium of about 25 percent. If Borden had avoided this predatory pricing charge, it might have been able to enjoy superior profitability on a sustained basis as a result of its differentiation strategy.[11]

When buyers pay a price premium for a well-known brand, they are effectively paying an insurance premium to assure themselves of product quality. The consumer could avoid the premium by buying a lower-priced product with a lesser-known or unknown brand name, but at the same time the buyer would bear a greater risk of quality variation. As noted in Chapter 10, if the cost of information exceeds the price premium, the buyer may use the higher price as an indicator (or assurance) of higher quality.

Having established a brand name advantage, the firm's asking price can be higher than its rivals', and its costs are likely to be higher as well, given that higher quality typically costs more than lower quality and that part of the brand name advan-

[11]See Clement G. Krouse, "Brand Name as a Barrier to Entry: The ReaLemon Case," *Southern Economic Journal*, 51 (October 1984), pp. 495–502.

tage will derive from a relatively high level of advertising expenditures emphasizing experience and credence attributes. If the firm is able to raise price by a greater amount than cost per unit is raised by the expenses of differentiation, it will have gained a competitive advantage in the market.

The firm could conceivably cheat its customers by reducing its quality below what has come to be expected from that brand name. Thus its costs would be reduced but its price would remain at the premium level. This strategy would increase profit for only a short while, however, because the information content of the brand name will deteriorate, and it will no longer command a premium price. Firms have an incentive to maintain the quality of their brand name products, since future sales depend on the quality of products sold today. The firm's brand name is, in effect, a forfeitable "bond" that the firm stands to lose if it does not follow through with its implicit promise to maintain the quality level of its products. Firms having the most invested in a brand name will have the most to lose by cheating on quality and thus will be less likely to cheat, other things being equal.[12]

Implications of Quality Leadership for Product Design

Several implications for product design arise from the preceding discussion. First, the differentiating firm must design products that *better serve the buyer*, in that buyer's price range. Thus research into the wants and needs of target consumers, as well as feedback from existing users of the product, should be sought and then incorporated into the product's design. Prototypes of the new product or new version of the product should be constructed, tested, and exposed to consumer clinics or market tests before being put into full-scale production. A differentiating firm must have an ongoing research and development program, from which product advancements will emanate for market testing and to which ideas for product improvements will be directed from the various sources within the firm that may collect information concerning consumer preferences. These would include market research, the service department, customer complaints, public relations departments, and so on.

There are two implications that follow from this first point. Since the tastes and quality demands of buyers differ, the firm should consider *offering a product line*, with products strategically placed at intervals along the price-quality spectrum. In this way the firm is more likely to offer exactly what a particular buyer is looking for and will gain sales that would otherwise go to a rival. The firm must ensure that the cost of adding and supporting any additional product in the line is less than the incremental

---

[12]See Krouse, "Brand Name as a Barrier," pp. 498–99. Conversely, the firm will have an incentive to dissipate the information content of its brand name if the firm's planning period is shorter than the time it takes for consumers to substantially depreciate the value of the brand name. Thus, if the firm or manager has a very short time horizon or if information transmission among consumers is relatively slow and repeat purchases are relatively infrequent, then dissipating the firm's brand name advantage may be the EPV-maximizing strategy. Credence goods would be more likely than experience goods, and experience goods more likely than search goods, to suffer brand name dissipation.

revenue that this product is expected to generate. Also, the firm should consider offering one or more *product bundles*. A product bundle, as we saw in Chapter 10, is a collection of products that are complementary to each other and might be purchased separately or as a "package deal." For some buyers the bundle might offer additional convenience or some other advantage and thus allow increased sales volume at the expense of a rival firm.

Second, the quality leader must strive to be *first with new features* that allow it to differentiate its product from those of rivals. Being first is particularly important for search attributes, since these are easily evaluated by consumers, and thus differentiation is more readily established. If another firm is first with a search attribute that becomes a major determinant in the buyer's purchasing decision, the firm must also incorporate this attribute very quickly in order to avoid loss of market share. With experience and credence attributes, the advantage of being first and the urgency of emulating another firm's innovation are each probably less significant than for search goods, because the benefits of these features are not as readily apparent to potential buyers.

Third, there are longer-term benefits associated with the maintenance of quality at a particular standard, since the product's brand name becomes a stock of information about previous products that consumers will transfer to the firm's current products. Thus the *consistency of quality* is important—variations in quality from time to time tend to depreciate the brand name advantage associated with the firm's products. A firm with a brand name advantage has a longer-term profit incentive to at least maintain the standard of quality embodied in its products, because of repeat sales in future periods on the basis of the quality assurances provided by the brand name.

Pricing and Advertising Strategies to Complement Quality Leadership

If the product more closely satisfies the buyer's needs, one would expect the buyer's demand to be less elastic, or more inelastic, than it would be for a product that is not such a good match with the buyer's needs. A lower price elasticity means that the profit-maximizing markup will be higher, other things being the same. A less elastic demand means that these products will not be good candidates for promotional pricing or price competition in general. Thus the firm is likely to set the price at a relatively high level and compete on the basis of quality rather than price. If it is a quality leader, it can extract a price premium from those customers who believe that the product is worth the extra cost to them.

The firm's advertising strategy should be to reinforce the beliefs of current customers that its products are superior and to spread this belief to other potential buyers. Informative advertising is called for on all major search attributes, and persuasive advertising is called for on the major experience and credence attributes. Since experience and credence products are more amenable to the differentiation strategy, we should expect to see a preponderance of persuasive advertising associated with firms' attempts to differentiate their products. Such advertisements must be realistic to be believable, and they may involve exotic locales, well-known celebrities, and situations that are complex or humorous but above all are interesting. Because of these requirements, persuasive advertising tends to be expensive.

How much advertising should a firm do? We saw in Chapter 13 that this decision depends on the firm's sales-advertising function and its contribution margin. The rule given in Chapter 13 can be equivalently stated in terms of the firm's price and advertising elasticities of demand. Dorfman and Steiner first showed that the profit-maximizing ratio of advertising expenditure to sales revenue is given by the ratio of advertising elasticity to price elasticity. We can call this the "elasticities" rule for optimal advertising expenditures. Thus the higher the advertising elasticity, and the lower the price elasticity, the higher will be the profit-maximizing advertising budget as a proportion of sales revenue.[13]

We have argued that the price elasticity of demand will be relatively inelastic for experience and credence products, since consumers cannot easily ascertain whether or not they are close substitutes. On the other hand, we expect the advertising elasticity of demand for experience and credence goods to be relatively high, because consumers may be persuaded to try these products by advertisements that emphasize the product's brand name, the seller's reputation for quality, the assertions of famous people, and so on. Thus we see very large advertising expenditures by firms selling soft drinks and fast foods, by brewing companies, by pet-food companies, by automobile companies, and by accounting firms like H&R Block around tax return time. Firms selling goods or services which are largely composed of experience and credence attributes should be expected to have large advertising budgets relative to their total sales revenues, following the "elasticities" rule.

In conclusion, the appropriate advertising strategy to complement a differentiation strategy will require the firm to spend on advertising until it estimates that its advertising-to-sales ratio is equal to the ratio of its advertising elasticity to its price elasticity. This same prescription applies to firms following a cost-leadership strategy, of course. If their products are predominantly search products, however, we expect to see advertising as a much smaller proportion of sales revenue, because for search products price elasticity is relatively high and advertising elasticity is relatively low.

---

[13]See R. Dorfman and P. Steiner, "Optimal Advertising and Product Quality," *American Economic Review*, 44 (December 1954), pp. 826–36; or T. H. Naylor, J. M. Vernon, and K. L. Wertz, *Managerial Economics: Corporate Economics and Strategy* (New York: McGraw-Hill Book Company, Inc., 1983), pp. 230–32. In Chapter 13 we said profit would be maximized when $dQ/dA = 1/CM$, where the contribution margin, CM, equals $P - AVC$, and $AVC = MR$. Multiplying both sides by A/PQ we have $1/P[(dQ/dA)(A/Q)] = 1/(P - MC)(A/PQ)$. The term in the square brackets is the advertising elasticity of demand, which I shall call E_a. Thus $E_a = P/(P - MC)(A/PQ)$. Now, from Chapter 10 we saw that when profit is maximized, $MC = MR = P[1 + (1/E_p)]$, where E_p signifies the price elasticity of demand. This expression can be rewritten as $E_p = P/(P - MC)$. Substituting for $P/(P - MC)$ in the expression for E_a we have $E_a = E_p(A/PQ)$. Hence $E_a/E_p = A/PQ$, or the ratio of the advertising elasticity to the price elasticity is equal to the ratio of advertising expenditure to total (sales) revenue, when P and A are each set at their profit-maximizing levels.

14.4   PRODUCT DESIGN FOR A FOCUS STRATEGY

The third generic type of competitive strategy suggested by Michael Porter is the "focus" strategy, whereby the firm confines its attention to a particular segment or niche in the market and deliberately does not seek to serve the entire market. In its chosen market niche, the firm may adopt either a cost-leadership or a differentiation strategy. It may choose to be a cost leader in one niche, but follow a differentiation strategy in one or more other niches. Conceivably, the firm might be the cost leader in most of the market and yet follow a differentiation strategy in some segments. General Motors is no doubt a cost leader in most of the automobile market, yet its Cadillac Division seeks to differentiate its product to a limited target market. The major breweries have some brand name beers for sale in the vast "economy beer" segment and simultaneously have "premium" beers that sell for two or three times as much and appeal to a more limited clientele.

The Cost-Focus Strategy

A firm may adopt a cost-focus strategy when it sees that by specializing in the service of a particular type of customer, it can serve these customers at a cost level significantly below the cost levels of rivals. In any market we expect to find a variety of buyers, whose quantity demanded ranges from one or a few units to thousands or even millions of units. Many, perhaps most, of the firms will seek the business of the larger buyers, since one sales agreement with a customer of that kind produces much more sales volume and profit than one sales agreement with a smaller customer. The smaller buyers with special orders may be neglected by the larger firms, or they may be charged a relatively high price. It is on these smaller buyers that a firm might focus its cost-leadership strategy, if it can supply its goods to them at a lower price than can the other firms, whether the other firms are larger firms (perhaps following a broad-based cost-leadership strategy or a broad-based differentiation strategy) or are other small firms (perhaps following a focused-differentiation strategy).

Example: Printing is a business in which orders come in all sizes and degrees of complexity. A large buyer might want millions of copies of a brochure, and a small buyer might want 250 business cards. Large printing firms will have large and relatively expensive plant and equipment, but small printing firms will have much smaller and perhaps much older printing equipment. The large firm may charge much more for an order of 250 business cards than a smaller firm would because it has much more substantial overhead costs and perhaps its setup cost is also higher. The smaller firm may be able to set a price that allows a superior profit and still quote a lower price than its larger rival.

In Figure 14–1 we depict such a situation. The smaller plant, represented by the cost curve SAC, has lower costs per unit for small orders, whereas the larger plant, represented by the SAC' curve, has the lower costs per unit for larger orders. Undoubtedly the larger firm will quote lower prices on larger orders, and it may seek to be

FIGURE 14-1. Cost Curves to Demonstrate the Opportunity for a Cost-Focus Strategy

either a cost leader or a quality leader on those larger orders. For smaller orders, however, the smaller firm has a definite cost advantage over the larger firm. It can set a price substantially above its average costs and yet still be below the cost level of the larger firm.

Thus a cost-focus strategy involves selecting a small segment of the market and specializing in the production of the goods or services demanded by this group of customers. The firm's plant may then be limited to only that required to produce a limited range of goods, and thus costs may be kept to the lowest levels possible. If it is successful at this strategy there will be a tendency to expand productive capacity, but rather than grow larger the firm may prefer to open other small plants for cost-focus strategies in other market niches as well. This type of strategy may be appropriate if the smaller and more specialized demands of some customers are not being well served by the other firms. In markets where orders typically differ both in size and complexity, as in printing, clothing manufacture, automobile repair work, and home services (like landscaping, interior decorating, and carpet cleaning), the firm's best option for superior profitability may be to focus on the low-cost supply of goods and services to the smaller and more specialized buyers, rather than attempt to compete for the larger orders that will be hotly contested by the larger firms.

The Quality-Focus Strategy

In other markets the firm's best strategy might be to focus on a particular market segment or niche and compete on the basis of quality in that niche. If the other firms are preoccupied with the "mass market," where orders are larger or there is a concentration of buyers wanting a rather standardized product (and there is already a strong cost leader) or where there are already several firms successfully differentiating their products, there might be a profitable opportunity to cater to the buyer who wants a distinctly different version of the product or service. People with special tastes, a desire to be distinguished from others, a desire to express themselves through their purchases, or a desire to flaunt their wealth may be willing to pay substantially more for a product that more closely mirrors their tastes. The firm following a quality-focus strategy must strive to produce this good for the customer at a price premium that exceeds the additional cost of differentiation, as compared with the standard fare.

Example: Rolls-Royce automobiles claim to be the best cars in the world, and in some respects they might be. They are hand built, and attention to detail is fastidious. They are very expensive, costing as much as three exotic sports cars, or as much as ten or fifteen compact or economy cars. Accordingly, they are not very common, and a passing Rolls-Royce always attracts plenty of attention, both for itself and because it may be transporting a celebrity. The exclusiveness of owning a Rolls-Royce probably attracts as many buyers as the mechanical specifications do. If wealthy people like to show their wealth, and if celebrities like to receive attention, this car is for them.

In any market there may be opportunities for the quality-focus strategy. Custom-tailored clothes, luxurious homes, exotic automobiles, higher-quality professional services, and "better" educations, for example, are sold in markets in which some firms follow quality-focus strategies alongside the more broadly based differentiation and cost leadership strategies of others. Several smaller breweries and wineries compete with the majors by limiting their output to "premium" brands and "limited editions." Other examples abound, and they seem to illustrate that a firm can shield itself from direct competition from larger firms and from lower-cost firms by limiting its purview to a specialized niche in the overall market. In this niche it can earn above-average rates of profit if it is able to identify the wants and needs of its customers correctly, design a product to suit those customers, and attract their business at a relatively high price.

Product Design, Pricing, and Advertising for Focus Strategies

Most of the foregoing conclusions about product design, presented in the separate contexts of cost-leadership and quality-leadership strategies, apply here in the context of focused strategies of each type. Fundamental to a focus strategy is the clear and deliberate identification of the firm's target market, whereas a firm following a more broadly based cost-leadership or differentiation strategy may know less about its consumers and yet make above-average profit. The cost-focus strategist will design a product such that the costs of serving its target market are kept to a minimum, whereas the quality-focus strategist will add features to its product or service whenever it believes these features will allow price to be augmented by more than costs would be. We would expect search products to be better suited to the cost-focus firm, whereas experience and credence products are more likely optimal for the firm adopting a quality-focus strategy.

A focus strategy seems particularly appropriate for a firm attempting to enter a market for the first time. In order to gain a foothold and to avoid the direct competition of major firms, the new entrant might seriously consider focusing on a smaller, more specialized segment of the market that is relatively neglected at the present time. If successful in the chosen market segment, the new firm might later broaden its base, both to diversify its risk exposure and to allow it to expand beyond the confines of its initial clientele.

Pricing strategies for a cost-focus firm will be similar to those for the broadly based cost leader discussed previously. Price leadership (in the niche) to maximize short-run profit is possible, given the firm's lower costs, but it is appropriate only if the firm's planning period is short, if there are insurmountable barriers to entry, or if the EPV-maximizing strategy is to allow entry of some new firms at first and later restrict further entry. Pricing to maximize sales subject to a minimum profit constraint may be more appropriate if the firm expects a significant amount of repeat business and complementary sales in future periods and faces strong competition in the market niche. Limit pricing is indicated if the EPV of profits is best served by restricting the entry of new firms. Promotional pricing is indicated if the product is a search product.

Pricing strategy for the quality-focus firm will include product-line pricing, bundle pricing, and whatever short-run pricing rule best serves the firm's objective, taking into account the possibility of new entry, repeat and complementary sales, and so on.

Advertising strategy will tend to be informative if the product is a search product and to stress price if the firm follows a cost-focus strategy. In these cases, advertising expenditures will tend to be a relatively small proportion of sales revenue, following the elasticities rule. On the other hand, if the products are experience or credence goods and the firm follows a quality-focus strategy, advertising will tend to be optimal if it is mostly persuasive and if advertising expenditures are a relatively large proportion of sales revenue.

14.5 SUMMARY

In this chapter we have drawn together several threads to discuss the firm's competitive strategy in its market. A competitive strategy should include well-defined quality, pricing, and advertising policies. The firm's competitive strategy should be oriented to the firm's objective, which we presume to be the maximization of the EPV of profit over the firm's time horizon. Given the present participants in the market and the strategies they appear to be following, as well as consideration of its own strengths and weaknesses vis-à-vis those of the other firms, the firm should choose a particular type of strategy to pursue.

There are three generic strategy types—namely, cost-leadership, differentiation, and focus strategies. The two focus strategies are simply more narrowly targeted versions of the broad-based cost-leadership and differentiation strategies. We called the firm following a differentiation strategy a quality leader, for simplicity of exposition and to emphasize the fact that such a firm essentially competes on a quality basis rather than a price basis.

The type of product, classified as a search, experience, or credence product depending on the cost to consumers of evaluating the quality attributes of the product, was seen to be of major importance. Search products are typically best marketed following a cost-leadership strategy, unless the firm's product has a unique (or far superior) search attribute that rivals cannot immediately emulate, in which case a differentiation strategy is appropriate (at least temporarily). Experience and credence goods are typically best suited to a differentiation strategy, since these are less easily emulated by rivals, as well as imperfectly evaluated by consumers.

Cost leaders should "cover the bases," "trim the fat," and practice product proliferation in the design of their products, particularly if their products are search products. Their products should contain all the necessary quality attributes for a target price-quality point but none in excess of consumer requirements unless these can be provided at no cost. Producing several brand names at once may allow the cost leader to gain a larger share of the market and subsequently reduce costs. Quality leaders should offer a broad product line, offer their products in bundles as well as separately, strive to be first with new features (or respond quickly to emulate rivals), and strive to maintain the consistency of quality in order to build up their brand name advantages.

Pricing strategies to complement cost leadership include promotional pricing, profit-maximizing price leadership, pricing for sales maximization subject to a minimum profit constraint, and limit pricing, depending on which pricing strategy maximizes the EPV of the firm's profit over its time horizon. Quality leaders will be more likely to consider product line pricing and bundle pricing, and they will use the short-run pricing rule that best serves the maximization of the EPV of the firm's profit.

Advertising will tend to be informative for search products and persuasive for experience and credence products. The larger is the ratio of the advertising elasticity to the price elasticity, the larger advertising budgets will be as a proportion of sales revenue. This elasticities rule explains why we see proportionately larger advertising budgets for experience and credence goods as opposed to search goods.

Finally, we noted that a firm considering entry might best gain a foothold, or a small firm attempting to make an above-average profit might more easily do so, if it adopts a focus strategy, serving only a subset of the market with a more specialized product.

DISCUSSION QUESTIONS

14-1. Distinguish between "competitive strategy" and "competitive advantage," in terms of means and ends. How does "competitive advantage" tie in with the objective of the firm?

14-2. What issues should the firm consider before deciding to follow a cost-leadership strategy?

14-3. Why is the price elasticity likely to be relatively high, and the advertising elasticity likely to be relatively low, for search goods?

14-4. What are the implications of cost leadership for product design?

14-5. What pricing and advertising strategies are likely to best complement a cost-leadership strategy?

14-6. How do Peters, Waterman, and Austin's "two essential ingredients" fit in with Porter's two main generic strategies approach?

14-7. What issues should the firm consider before deciding to follow a differentiation strategy?

14-8. What are the implications of quality leadership for product design?

14-9. When is a focus strategy likely to be the firm's best option?

14-10. Make up a list of firms and their brand name products that appear to be following (a) a broad-based cost-leadership strategy; (b) a broad-based differentiation strategy; (c) a cost-focus strategy; and (d) a quality-focus strategy.

PROBLEMS AND SHORT CASES

14-1. Dixieland Ice Cream's profit rate has been declining over the past three years and is below average in the industry. Management has asked you to advise them as to ways that profitability may be raised. Your investigations reveal that although there is little inefficiency in production, employee productivity is relatively low, mainly because of Dixieland's reliance on relatively old equipment. In addition, product quality tends to vary perceptibly between batches as a result of the age of the equipment. Consumers think Dixieland's product is "just another ice cream," although brand name recognition is quite high. Dixieland's ice cream is marketed in all major supermarkets and food stores, and it is priced in the middle of the range of prices found there. Their relatively low advertising budget is spent largely on joint promotions with supermarket chains when Dixieland's ice cream is one of the products used for promotional pricing.

Dixieland's competitors include several like itself, some small firms competing in only some of the regional markets, and a few others that specialize in higher-quality ice cream, with a creamier taste, more chunks of real fruit, and so on. These premium-price ice creams are marketed in ice cream parlors as well as in food stores generally. An ice cream parlor typically uses a single brand name ice cream and is particularly concerned with high and consistent quality. Some ice cream parlors are owned by the manufacturers and are thus not able to use another manufacturer's product. The small firms, which market their products in only some of the food stores, accept a lower markup in an effort to achieve greater penetration of the market, but this approach causes the profit rates of most of the smaller firms to be relatively low, in turn limiting their ability to expand quickly.

(a) Discuss the competitive strategies that appear to be open to Dixieland.

(b) Based on the information given here, which strategy do you think they should adopt?

(c) What further information would you like to have before investing any money in Dixieland's stock, given that they will follow your advice?

14-2. The Ginsung Motor Company manufactures automobiles in Taiwan and has accumulated a great deal of experience supplying the home market. Recently it has been considering entering the United States market. It plans to test market some of its cars in Hawaii before expanding to the mainland states. The purpose of the test marketing program is to decide on the competitive strategy it will use in the mainland market.

Ginsung produces four different automobile lines for its home market. The smallest is its "City" commuter car, which is only seven feet long yet has adequate room for two adults and for groceries in the trunk. Interior trim is basic, the car's performance is moderate, and fuel economy is very high. Next is the "Rocker," a youth-oriented performance car that seats four without any room to spare. It has a peppier engine, is sold in several wild color schemes, and has a fairly good stereo system as standard. The "Family" model is somewhat larger, seats five adults, and has a larger engine and moderately comfortable interior trim. It is a look-alike version of the typical Japanese subcompact car. Finally, the "Executive" model is larger and seats five adults in great comfort. Interior trim is luxurious, and performance is stately and comparable to the typical American compact.

Ginsung has incorporated the latest quality control techniques into their plant. The manufacturing process tends to be relatively labor intensive because of the high productivity of the workers and the relatively low wage structure. Everyone on the management team received an M.B.A. degree at an American university or college.

(a) Outline the alternative competitive strategies that Ginsung might adopt in the mainland market, and the pros and cons of each as you see it. Which seems like the best strategy to you?

(b) What do you think Ginsung should do in Hawaii to test your hunches about the receptiveness of the American market to their products? (Consider quality, pricing, and advertising decisions.)

(c) What other information would you seek before giving your final advice about their competitive strategy for the mainland market?

14-3. Richard Koster Legal Associates is a law firm in Boston that has special expertise in immigration law, since Richard worked for the Immigration and Naturalization Service (INS) for several years before completing his law degree. At the present time the firm is involved in all kinds of civil law prosecutions and defenses, including but by no means limited to immigration cases. Acknowledging that the law business is a jungle, Richard has retained your services to advise the firm as to their future competitive strategy.

Richard is fundamentally opposed to "ambulance chasing," does not like dealing with criminals, and finds divorce proceedings unsettling. On the other hand, he does enjoy property transactions, antitrust proceedings, and dealing with immigrants who are seeking permanent resident status. In the latter area, particularly, Richard has an advantage over most other lawyers because of the knowledge he gained of immigration procedures while working for the INS and because of the contacts he still has there. In the Boston area many high-technology firms, as well as the various universities and colleges, seek Richard's assistance in getting work permits and resident alien papers for foreign nationals with special skills and expertise.

Currently, Richard feels he is being spread too thinly over several areas of law. He has to spend a great deal of time reading and conducting computerized searches whenever a case comes along that is in an area he has not considered for a while. His firm makes plenty of money, he says, but he feels that he could make at least as much and work shorter hours if he had a clearly defined competitive strategy.

(a) Which of the generic strategies do you think that this law firm should adopt, and why?

(b) What product, price, and promotion decisions should be considered in the execution of the strategy you have suggested above?

14-4. Upton College is a small liberal arts college located in upstate New York that has run into financial difficulties in recent years. The decline in the number of students since the passing of the baby boomers, the trend toward business education, and the revival of interest in science and engineering have left enrollments dwindling. Upton has lost many of its tenured faculty members because it refused to grant salary increases over the past few years in the face of this financial uncertainty. Consequently, many of the courses are covered by temporary and part-time instructors whose own education is lacking

The president of Upton College, Imelda Greer, has hired you to investigate the options and recommend a competitive strategy that they would follow. Your investigations lead to the following information: Upton still has several very good liberal arts professors who could form the base for a revival of the college as a specialist in liberal arts education. The departure of some other tenured faculty members is actually a blessing in disguise, since it opens up tenure "slots" and gives the college more flexibility in hiring new professors. There is a local demand for business education, since the nearest business school is 60 miles away. And since Upton has dormitories on campus, the reach of a business school could extend well beyond the local area. Science and engineering are another option that could save Upton, but the cost of supplying this kind of education is much higher than for liberal arts and business degrees. The administration at Upton is top-heavy and ultraconservative, with the exception of Ms. Greer, who says she would willingly fire them all and start afresh in order to save the college. Finally, the town in which Upton is located, and the surrounding countryside, are pleasant almost to the point of being idyllic.

(a) Consider the alternative strategies that Upton might follow, listing the pros and cons of each one.

(b) Advise Ms. Greer which strategy you believe Upton should follow, and what product, price, and promotion decisions should be implemented in order to ensure survival and achieve competitive advantage.

14-5. George and Sheila Boggs are retiring and moving to Florida, and will soon put their house on the market. Most of their wealth is tied up in the house, so it is particularly important that they get a good price for it. But the local real estate market is depressed, and it is a buyer's market. Hundreds of houses are for sale in the surrounding suburbs, and there are plenty of "ordinary" houses for sale at a fair price. Those that sell quickly are those that are priced to be a bargain or those that are special in some way and appeal to the tastes of a particular buyer.

A real estate agent tells the Boggses that they should simply put a low price on the house and get their money out quickly. George and Sheila want more than a fire-sale price, and they are considering doing some improvements prior to putting the house on the market. Since kitchens, bathrooms, and garages are the three most important selling points, they are considering renovating the kitchen and bathrooms and cleaning out and painting the interior of the garage. The exterior of the house could be repainted, shutters could be added for decorative effect, and money could be spent on landscaping the garden and resealing the driveway to give the house more appeal and a better first impression. George is also thinking about interior modifications: he figures that if a wall were removed upstairs the master bedroom could have a large en suite bathroom complete with whirlpool bath and sauna room. Passive solar heating and much more interior light could be introduced by adding a few skylights and enlarging existing windows. You have been asked for advice on the competitive strategy that the Boggses might use to get the maximum net income out of the house.

(a) Discuss the pros and cons of a cost-leadership strategy in this context.

(b) Discuss the pros and cons of a differentiation strategy in this context.

(c) If they follow a differentiation strategy, how much should they spend on the house prior to its sale?

(d) What do you recommend that they do?

14-6. Main Street Plumbing and Heating is a business owned and operated by Dick Watson and his wife Mary in a small Midwestern city. Dick has one full-time apprentice, and Mary works as secretary, receptionist, accountant, and public relations officer. Overhead costs are low because the business operates from the garage of the family home. Business is sporadic: There is too much work when a freezing spell bursts water pipes and too little work at other times, particularly in the summer, when the home handymen and women decide that they can do it themselves. Dick knows you are studying managerial economics and has asked for your advice on how to ensure a steady flow of work, preferably inside or summer work, with the potential of expanding the business and enjoying a greater income.

Your questions elicit the following information: There are literally dozens of "general plumbing and heating" firms in the area. Dick's costs and prices are as low as any of them. He does not advertise, except in the local yellow pages where he is listed under plumbing and heating contractors. He says that some plumbing and heating firms specialize in particular areas, such as solar-heating systems. Some work only in new construction, installing the heating, water, and sewer systems. There appear to be several opportunities open. There is no firm specializing in luxury bathroom design and installation, nor in in-ground lawn sprinkling systems, nor in fire-control systems for factories and other public buildings. Also, you perceive a need for a firm that sells plumbing tools and materials to the do-it-yourselfer where the proprietor knows plumbing and heating and is willing to dispense free advice to customers.

(a) Outline the generic strategies that are open to Dick and his wife.

(b) What strategy do you suggest, and why?

(c) Outline the product, price, and promotion decisions that must be made as part of this new strategy.

14-7. Getaway Island Tours operates a vacation planning and travel booking agency in the downtown area of a large northeastern city. They organize package tours and promote them in the local media. The winter is their busiest season, as people seek a week or two of sun and sand as a respite from the chilly winds and icy streets. A recent marketing survey indicates that the firm does not have very widespread brand name recognition and is regarded as a supplier of cheap tours with a wide dispersion of quality across tours. Potential buyers fell into two categories: those who buy largely on the basis of lowest price for air fare, hotel, and transfers and those who choose on the basis of convenient times of departure and return, known high-quality hotels, and safe, interesting, and exciting locations. Special-interest groups, such as golfers, sailers, scuba divers, and surfers, could also be identified within the latter group more readily than within the former group.

Getaway has hired your consulting firm for advice on the choice of a competitive strategy. They are currently only marginally profitable and operate from day to day, taking whatever comes along. After years in the business, however, their personnel have been to virtually every hotel on every island in the Caribbean and they have had some experience with Europe as well. They have organized tours of virtually every type for any clientele, but they have tended to dissipate their efforts over too wide a front. The big discounts at the hotels are also not available to occasional users.

(a) Discuss the various strategies that are open to Getaway Island Tours.

(b) What strategy do you suggest they follow?

(c) What product, price, and promotion decisions do you suggest they implement as part of their competitive strategy?

14-8. Stephanie Ricardo has recently taken over her family's restaurant business. For twenty-five years the Ricardo Family Restaurant has served fine family fare—nothing exotic, just good basic American food. Business has been satisfactory, but it has never been heavy enough to justify an expansion of the facilities. Now the kitchen is somewhat antiquated, the tables and chairs need replacing, the interior needs renovating, and the outside needs sprucing up. The sign outside no longer lights up at night and cannot be repaired.

Now that Stephanie is in charge she is considering the various options open to her. Since the restaurant needs refurbishing it could be reborn as any kind of restaurant, catering to any kind of clientele. Her parents would be happy if she turned it into a fine Italian restaurant—this was always her father's dream. But she is also considering the lunch and supper business of business executives from local industry. A more restricted menu would hurt her chances of capturing a sizable share of that business. Rather than a linen-tablecloth restaurant, she could alternatively pursue the breakfast and fast-food market. A franchise from a national chain of family restaurants is currently available. This chain specializes in family dining at low prices. Other options abound, and therefore Stephanie has sought your help.

(a) Outline the various strategies that are available to Stephanie.

(b) What strategy do you suggest, and what product, price, and advertising decisions should be made in pursuit of this strategy?

(c) Outline the cost and revenue implications of your proposed strategy.

14-9. Whaleback Mountain Ski Resort is surrounded by other ski resorts and is barely making ends meet. The resorts closer to the city get more of the business, and the resorts that offer superior trails and artificial snow making also have an advantage over Whaleback. Whaleback's parking lot is relatively small and cannot be expanded. On busy days skiers must park and walk along the roads to get to the chair lifts, and of course the walk is uncomfortable and tiring in ski boots. Whaleback's trails are quite good by comparison with other resorts, although a little work and the services of a ski trail designer would transform them into very high quality trails. The chalet at the base of the mountain is relatively small but very cosy and attractive. Whaleback is not set up for night skiing.

Next season will make it or break it for the present owners of Whaleback. They have a line of credit at their bank, and they are willing to spend the borrowed money to establish the resort as a viable competitor. They could simply advertise or make improvements, including snow-making equipment and trail design, and they could change their prices up or down. At present their ticket prices are lower than most other resorts.

(a) What strategies seem feasible for Whaleback Mountain?

(b) What do you advise concerning competitive strategy, and what does your advice imply for product, price, and advertising strategy?

14-10. The Billion Bytes Computer Company has grown from a start-up venture in the early 1980s to become a multimillion-dollar-sales computer company in the mid 1980s. But times are getting tougher for BBC, a; the industry shakeout threatens to extend the list of victims. BBC currently has several personal and business computers on the market, but they are not compatible with the industry-standard operating systems and have fallen behind the frontier of hardware technology.

BBC is faced with a major strategic decision. Management feels that a cost-leadership strategy is out of the question, because of economies of plant size and pecuniary economies of its major competitors. A differentiation strategy seems to be indicated, but whether this should be focused or broad based is at issue. On the one hand, BBC could focus on developing special hardware and software for engineering and scientific applications, while on the other it could go into the general market and appeal to the users who value the light weight and easy portability of their machines. Other options exist, including adoption of MS-DOS, MicroSoft's Disk Operating System, which is now the industry standard. BBC already utilizes microdisks and is working on nanodisks (less than two inches in diameter) and miniaturized disk drives and printers that would be integrated into the same carrying case as the central processing unit.

(a) Consider the differentiation strategies that exist for BBC.

(b) Is the cost-focus strategy necessarily out of the question?

(c) What strategy do you think BBC should pursue?

(d) What product, price, and promotion decisions will be involved?

SELECTED REFERENCES AND FURTHER READING

Ackerlof, G. "The Market for 'Lemons': Qualitative Uncertainty and the Market Mechanism," *Quarterly Journal of Economics*, 35 (August 1970), pp. 488–500.

Chan, Y. S., and H. Leland. "Prices and Qualities in Markets with Costly Information," *Review of Economic Studies*, 49 (October 1982), pp. 499–516.

Dixit, A. K., and J. E. Stiglitz. "Monopolistic Competition and Optimum Product Diversity," *American Economic Review*, 67 (June 1977), pp. 297–308.

Dorfman, R., and P. Steiner. "Optimal Advertising and Product Quality," *American Economic Review*, 44 (December 1954), pp. 826–36.

Gal-Or, E. "Quality and Quantity Competition," *Bell Journal of Economics*, 14 (Autumn 1983), pp. 590–600.

Griliches, Z. *Price Indices and Quality Change*. Cambridge, Mass.: Harvard University Press, 1971.

Kotler, P. *Principles of Marketing*, esp. chaps. 3, 8, 10, and 11–18. Englewood Cliffs, N.J.: Prentice-Hall, Inc., 1980.

Krouse, Clement G. "Brand Name as a Barrier to Entry: The ReaLemon Case," *Southern Economic Journal*, 51 (October 1984), pp. 495–502.

Lancaster, K. "Socially Optimal Product Differentiation," *American Economic Review*, 65 (September 1975), pp. 567–85.

Leland, H. E. "Quality Choice and Competition," *American Economic Review*, 67 (March 1977), pp. 127–37.

Levhari, D., and Y. Peles. "Market Structure, Quality and Durability," *Bell Journal of Economics*, 4 (Spring 1973), pp. 235–48.

Nagle, T. "Economic Foundations of Pricing," *Journal of Business*, 57 (January 1984), pp. S3–S26.

Naylor, T. H., J. M. Vernon, and K. L. Wertz. *Managerial Economics: Corporate Economics and Strategy*, pp. 230–32 and 264–66. New York: McGraw-Hill Book Company, Inc., 1983.

Rosen, S. "Hedonic Prices and Implicit Markets: Product Differentiation in Pure Competition," *Journal of Political Economy*, 82 (January–February 1974), pp. 34–55.

Schmalensee, R. "Market Structure, Durability, and Quality: A Selective Survey," *Economic Inquiry*, 17 (April 1979), pp. 177–96.

Schwartz, A., and L. L. Wilde. "Product Quality and Imperfect Information," *Review of Economic Studies*, 52 (April 1985), pp. 251–62.

Shapiro, C. "Premiums for High-Quality Products as Returns to Reputations," *Quarterly Journal of Economics*, 98 (November 1983), pp. 659–79.

Spence, A. M. "Product Selection, Fixed Costs, and Monopolistic Competition," *Review of Economic Studies*, 443 (June 1976), pp. 217–36.

Stigler, G. J. "The Economics of Information," *Journal of Political Economy*, 69 (June 1961), pp. 213–25.

Swan, P. L. "Durability of Consumer Goods," *American Economic Review*, 60 (December 1970), pp. 884–94.

Vander Weide, J. H., and J. H. Zalkind. "Deregulation and Oligopolistic Price-Quality Rivalry," *American Economic Review*, 71 (March 1981), pp. 144–54.

15 Capital Budgeting and Investment Decisions

15.1 INTRODUCTION

■ *Definition:* *Capital budgeting* is defined as the decision-making process concerned with the firm's decision (1) whether or not to invest financial resources and (2) how to choose between and among the available investment projects. These projects may be to replace or expand existing plant and equipment, to diversify the firm's activities, to take over another firm, to mount an advertising campaign, to put funds into bonds, or simply to hold the funds in liquid form for future investment projects. In general, the available investment projects will involve cost reduction, revenue generation, or some combination of the two. Pure cost-reduction investments include replacement of existing assets that are now relatively inefficient because of physical depreciation and technological obsolescence. Pure revenue-generating projects may be the investment in new-product development or advertising campaigns where these are treated as an investment that leads to a future revenue stream. Expansion projects typically involve both cost reduction and revenue generation, since newer plant and equipment are typically technologically superior to that being replaced.

Where there are no limits on the availability of capital, the capital-budgeting decision is simply to accept or reject each particular project. The following section establishes a number of criteria that allow the accept/reject decision to be made. But when the investments are mutually exclusive, meaning that they are alternative ways of achieving the same end or are alternative uses of available space or other resources, the available investment projects must be ranked in order of preference. The third section of this chapter establishes the criterion for ranking mutually exclusive projects. When there are limits to the availability of capital, a criterion must be established which ensures that the available capital is efficiently allocated between and among the possible projects so that the firm's objectives are achieved. Capital budgeting as an allocation problem is examined in the final section of this chapter.

You are already familiar with the basic structure of capital budgeting since it is essentially the same as the decision-making structure introduced in Chapters 1 and 2. In this chapter, we reconsider the expected-present-value decision criterion in the context of the investment decision and discuss new and related investment decision criteria. For ease of presentation, the analysis will be presented, for the most part, in terms of the firm's having full information about future costs and revenues associated with each investment decision. Thus we speak of the net-present-value (NPV) criterion, for example, rather than the *expected*-net-present-value criterion. The analysis is easily modified for uncertainty—the single-point estimates of future costs and revenues can be designated to represent the expected values of the probability distributions surrounding each expected future cost and revenue. Rather than repeat all the analysis of Chapter 1 dealing with decision making under uncertainty, this chapter introduces new material and presumes that you will have little difficulty implementing it in the context of uncertainty.

15.2   CAPITAL BUDGETING WITH UNLIMITED AVAILABILITY OF FUNDS

As stated in the introductory section, when funds are unlimited the capital budgeting decision is whether to accept or reject each available investment project. This decision must be based upon whether or not each project contributes to the attainment of the firm's objectives. In the following paragraphs we shall take the standard view that the firm's objective is to maximize its long-term profitability, or its net worth in present-value terms. In some cases, of course, the firm's time horizon may be somewhat shorter because of cash-flow or accounting profit considerations. In such cases a less profitable project may be undertaken if it promises a very short payback period or relatively large immediate gains, in preference to a more profitable project that generates its income over a longer period of time.

We shall consider five separate criteria for the accept/reject decision. We shall examine the relationships between these criteria and show why some of these criteria are superior to others.

The Net-Present-Value Criterion

You will recall from Chapter 1 that *net present value* refers to the sum of the discounted value of the future stream of costs and revenues associated with a particular project. If the net present value of a project is positive, this fact indicates that the project adds more to revenues in present-value terms than it adds to cost in present-value terms and should therefore be accepted. Symbolically, we can express the net present value as follows:

$$\text{NPV} = \sum_{t=1}^{n} \frac{R_t}{(1+r)^t} - C_0 \tag{15-1}$$

where R_t signifies the contribution to overheads and profits in each future period; C_0 represents the initial cost of the project, including installation charges and any other expenses such as increases in working capital required by the investment; r is the opportunity rate of interest; and $t = 1, 2, 3, \ldots, n$ is the number of periods over which the revenue stream is expected. Thus the revenue stream is discounted at the rate of interest that the firm could obtain in its next-best-alternative use of these investment funds at a similar level of risk. The revenue stream referred to in equation (15–1) by R_t should be regarded as the net cash flow after taxes.

■ *Definition:* Net cash flow after taxes can be defined as incremental revenues minus incremental costs, plus tax savings that result from depreciation charges that are deductible from taxable income, plus tax credits (if any) allowed against tax liability in connection with the particular investment project. If a tax credit (for example, 15 percent of the initial cost) is available for new investment, this credit will be deducted directly from the tax liability, and it thus avoids an outflow of a certain amount. Although this is not an actual inflow of cash, it is an opportunity revenue; the avoidance of what would otherwise be an outflow of cash in effect amounts to a cash inflow. Depreciation charges against revenues enter the cash-flow picture only indirectly and as a result of the tax saving that can be obtained by subtracting the depreciation charges from the income of the firm.

Example: To demonstrate this definition, suppose an investment project involves an initial cash outlay of $10,000 and will generate revenues for three years, after which time it has a salvage value of $1,000. The value of the investment project to be depreciated over the three-year life of the project is thus $9,000, and for simplicity we use the straight-line method of depreciation to allocate $3,000 to each of the three years of the project's life. In Table 15–1 we show the calculation of the cash flow after taxes, given the contribution stream indicated.

We assume that the firm is subject to the tax rate of 48 percent: The tax saving shown as $1,440 in each of the three years represents 48 percent of the depreciation figure. The cash-flow-after-taxes column shows the sum of the contribution and tax saving for each year. The next column shows the discount factors at an assumed opportunity rate of 10 percent, and the final column shows the net present value of the cash flow after taxes in each year and in total.

Note that the sum of the net present value of the cash flow after taxes is positive, and hence this investment project adds to the net present value, or net worth, of the

TABLE 15–1. Calculation of NPV of Cash Flow after Taxes

Year	Contribution	Depreciation	Tax Saving	Cash Flow after Taxes	Discount Factors	Net Present Value
0	$-10,000	—	—	$-10,000	1.000	$-10,000.00
1	5,000	$3,000	$1,440	6,440	0.909	5,853.96
2	3,000	3,000	1,440	4,440	0.826	3,667.44
3	2,000	3,000	1,440	3,440	0.751	2,583.44
						$ 2,104.84

firm. It should therefore be accepted, and the firm should continue accepting projects for implementation until it is left with only those projects that have zero or negative net present value at the appropriate opportunity rate of discount.

Different Depreciation Methods. The method of depreciation employed has important implications for the NPV of the investment project. In the example we used the *straight-line* method of depreciation, in which the difference between the initial cost of the asset and its salvage value is allocated equally to each year of the asset's life. Alternatively, we might have used a method of depreciation that accelerates the recovery of the difference between the initial cost and the salvage value, so that the depreciation expense is largest in the first year and declines each year until the asset is fully depreciated. Two such methods are the sum-of-years-digits method and the double-declining-balance method.

The *sum-of-years-digits* method, as implied by its name, adds up the digits of the years that the asset will last and each year depreciates a proportion of the amount to be recovered equal to the ratio of the number of years remaining to the sum of the digits. In the preceding example the asset is expected to last for three years, so the sum of the years' digits is $1 + 2 + 3 = 6$. Thus three-sixths, or one-half, of the total depreciation expense will be deducted in the first year; two-sixths, or one-third, will be deducted in the second year; and one-sixth will be deducted in the final year.

The *double-declining-balance* method takes twice the depreciation rate implied by the straight-line method but applies it to the undepreciated balance remaining in each year. Thus, using this method, we would recover two-thirds of $9,000 (that is, $6,000) in the first year; two-thirds of the remaining $3,000 (that is, $2,000) in the second year; and the remainder ($1,000) in the third year. Notice that both of these "accelerated" depreciation methods shift forward in time part of the net cash flow after taxes and thus increase the NPV of these dollars, since they will be multiplied by a larger discount factor when received earlier.

Example: To demonstrate this effect, let us rework the above example using the sum-of-years-digits depreciation method. In Table 15–2 we show half of the depreciation (that is, $4,500) being deducted in the first year; one-third being deducted in the second year; and one-sixth being deducted in the third year. The tax saving is now weighted toward the earlier years, which in turn have larger discount factors. Hence,

TABLE 15–2. Impact of Depreciation Method upon Net Present Value

Year	Contri-bution	Depre-ciation	Tax Saving	Cash Flow after Taxes	Discount Factors	Net Present Value
0	$-10,000	—	—	$-10,000	1.000	$-10,000.00
1	5,000	$4,500	$2,160	7,160	0.909	6,508.44
2	3,000	3,000	1,440	4,440	0.826	3,667.44
3	2,000	1,500	720	2,720	0.751	2,042.72
						$ 2,218.60

the net present value of the same project with an accelerated depreciation method can be shown to be significantly higher than it was as calculated using straight-line depreciation. In fact, the accelerated depreciation provisions of the tax laws exist primarily to encourage firms to invest in new plant and facilities for the employment multiplier impact of such investment upon the economy.[1]

The Internal-Rate-of-Return Criterion

■ *Definition:* The *internal rate of return* (IRR) is the rate of discount that reduces the present value of the income stream to equality with the initial cost. It can be shown symbolically as

$$C_0 = \sum_{t=1}^{n} \frac{R_t}{(1 + i)^t} \qquad (15\text{-}2)$$

where the only symbol different from equation (15-1) is i, which represents the internal rate of return.

Note that the internal rate of return will be that rate of discount which reduces the net present value of the income stream to zero. In the previous example we know that the internal rate of return exceeds 10 percent, since the net present value is positive at 10 percent. It will take a larger rate of discount to reduce the net present value to zero. We can calculate the internal rate of return for a given project by a process of trial and error. (This method beats attempting to solve a polynomial function of degree n.)

Example: In Table 15-3 we show the process of iteratively calculating the net present value at various discount rates, zeroing in on the rate of discount that reduces the net present value to zero. We start by testing for the value of net present value at the discount rate of 20 percent. This procedure leaves a net present value of $437.64, indicating that it requires a larger discount rate to reduce net present value to zero. We

TABLE 15-3. Calculation of the Internal Rate of Return

Year	CFAT	NPV @20%	NPV @25%	NPV @23%	NPV @23.2%
0	$-10,000	$-10,000.00	$-10,000.00	$-10,000.00	$-10,000.00
1	6,440	5,364.52	5,152.00	5,235.72	5,227.27
2	4,440	3,081.36	2,841.60	2,934.84	2,925.24
3	3,440	1,991.76	1,761.28	1,847.28	1,839.61
		$ 437.64	$ -245.12	$ 17.84	$ -7.88

then try a discount rate of 25 percent and find that the net present value at that discount rate is negative. Thus the internal rate of return lies between 20 and 25 percent. We try 23 percent and find that the net present value is $17.84. Clearly, a slightly larger internal rate of return is indicated, and we try 23.2 percent in the last column of the table to find a net present value of a mere −$7.88. Further iterations would show the internal rate of return to be precisely 23.1415873 percent.[2]

Rule: The IRR *decision rule* is that projects with an internal rate of return greater than the opportunity rate of interest should be accepted and implemented by the firm. Given the availability of investment funds, investment in various projects should be taken to the point where the internal rate of return on the last project accepted just exceeds the cost of capital (the opportunity rate of interest for that project). Note that this decision rule is equivalent to the NPV rule that says to accept any project for which the NPV (when discounted at the opportunity rate) is above zero.

Example: In Figure 15–1 we show a series of investment projects as the blocks A, B, C, D, E, and F. These investment projects are ranked in order of their internal rate of return, which represents the height of each block, and the width of each block represents the amount of capital required for the implementation of each project. The top of these blocks, shown as the heavy stepped line, is the curve relating the IRR to the level of investment expenditure.

The cost of capital to the firm is also likely to be a step function. Initially the firm will be able to utilize internal funds (undistributed profits), and the cost of these funds is their opportunity cost. That is, these could be invested elsewhere at a level of risk similar to that involved in holding the funds as undistributed profits, and the firm would wish to receive at least that rate by utilizing these funds in the proposed investment projects. After a point, however, the internal funds will be exhausted and the firm will need to borrow on the financial markets. We must expect the rate for such borrowing to exceed the opportunity cost of using internal funds, since the market will view the firm as involving at least some degree of risk. In Figure 15–1 we indicate that the firm's opportunity rate on internal funds is about 8 percent and that the firm can then borrow from the market (up to a point) at around 12 percent.

As the firm continues its borrowing in the financial market, however, the market will recognize the change in the financial structure of the firm and will at some point wish to impose a higher interest rate on loans to the firm. The greater debt-equity ratio (leverage) of the company as it continues to borrow in the market causes the firm to be a more risky proposition in the eyes of lenders. There is now a greater risk of default on the loans, and hence subsequent borrowing by the firm will take place only at a higher rate of interest. In Figure 15–1 we show the higher rate of interest demanded by bor-

---

[2]In case you are wondering how many iterations it took to find that answer, I must confess that my calculator is preprogrammed for the IRR calculation. Such calculators are becoming increasingly available at moderate cost and are, I think, an essential part of the business student's tool kit.

FIGURE 15-1.   Determining the Level of Investment Expenditure

rowers to be in the vicinity of 15 percent. The top line of the blocks, which represents the availability of funds, may thus be regarded as the cost-of-capital line. It can be seen that projects A, B, C, and D promise an internal rate of return greater than the cost of capital, while projects E and F promise lower rates of return which do not compensate for the cost of capital. Thus the firm in this particular situation would be advised to undertake projects A to D only.

Relationship between NPV and IRR

It should be firmly understood that if the internal rate of return exceeds the opportunity rate of interest, the net present value of the proposed investment project will be positive. Using the example discussed earlier, we can plot the net present value of a project against all values that may be assigned to the rate of discount, as in Figure 15-2. To construct the net-present-value curve we have three points that are known to us. Point *A* in Figure 15-2 represents the net present value at a discount rate of zero. That is, when the future stream of profits is undiscounted (or discounted at zero percent), the project will have a net present value of $4,320, as we know from Table 15-1. The second point that is known to us, also from Table 15-1, is point *B*, which indicates the net present value of the project when discounted at an opportunity rate of 10 percent. The third point known to us is point *C*, which indicates the discount rate that

FIGURE 15-2.   The Net-Present-Value Curve

reduces the net present value to zero. This is of course the internal rate of return, and we plot C at a discount rate of 23.14 percent.

■ *Definition:*   Thus the *NPV curve* is a locus of the points representing the NPV of a project and the rate at which it was discounted, for all rates of discount between zero and the IRR. Note that the NPV curve is not a straight line but is slightly convex toward the origin. We shall return to the net-present-value curve later in the chapter.

The Profitability-Index Criterion

■ *Definition:*   The *profitability index* is defined as the ratio of the present value of the future stream of net cash flows to the initial cost of the investment project. Symbolically, it may be represented as

$$PI = \frac{\sum_{t=1}^{n} \frac{R_t}{(1 + r)^t}}{C_0} \qquad (15\text{-}3)$$

Note the relationship of this criterion to the earlier formulas for the net present value and the internal rate of return. The profitability index is also called the *benefit/cost ratio* of an investment project or the *present value per dollar of outlay*. In the previous example with $r = 0.10$, the profitability index may be calculated as

$$PI = \frac{12,104.84}{10,000}$$

$$= 1.210484$$

Rule: The decision rule using the profitability criterion is to implement any invest-ment project that promises a profitability index exceeding unity. Any such project will thus add more to the present value of revenues than it will cost. It will therefore add to the present value, or the net worth, of the firm.

There is no conflict between the net-present-value, internal-rate-of-return, or profitability index for accept-reject decisions. If a project is acceptable under one cri-terion, it will be acceptable under all three. Thus any one of these criteria could be employed alone for accepting or rejecting investment projects when capital availability is unlimited. We now consider two investment criteria which are commonly used in practice.[3]

The Payback-Period Criterion

■ ***Definition:*** The *payback period* is defined as the period of time which elapses before an investment earns sufficient revenue to cover its initial cost.

Example: In Figure 15-3 we show graphically the determination of the payback pe-riod relating to the investment project we have been discussing. The initial cost of the project is shown at the $10,000 level and remains at that level over time. The undis-counted revenue stream reaches $6,440 at the end of the first year, $10,880 at the end of the second year, and $14,320 at the end of the third year. Interpolating between

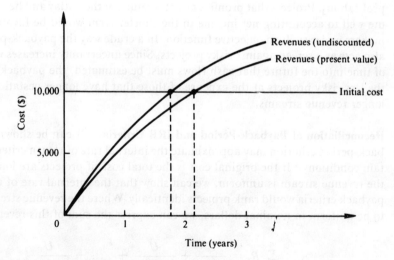

FIGURE 15-3.   The Payback-Period-Investment Criterion

---

[3]For empirical evidence of the capital-budgeting techniques and criteria actually used in business practice, you are referred to the papers by Fremgen, Klammer, Mao, and others which are listed at the end of this chapter.

points we are able to generate a curve showing the nominal dollar inflow as a function of time. This curve crosses the initial cost line at approximately 1.8 years, which is therefore the payback period.

Note that the payback-period criterion in this form ignores the time value of money. To avoid this fundamental shortcoming we could plot the present value of the revenue stream over time, and we have done so in Figure 15-3. In present-value terms, revenues amount to $5,853 in the first year, $9,521 in the second year, and $12,105 in the third year. The curve representing the present value of the revenue stream intersects the initial cost curve at approximately 2.18 years, and this is the payback period when determined by present values of the revenue stream. In either case the firm's decision rule will be to accept projects that have a payback period less than or equal to a specified period required by the firm.

A second problem is that the payback-period criterion ignores the revenues that occur after the payback period of that investment. A decision is made based simply upon whether or not the investment pays back the initial cost before the elapse of a certain period. It would thus be unable to discriminate between two investment projects that had a payback period ot, say, three years, but differed in that the net present value of one was substantially higher than the other because of a different or longer revenue stream.

Note: The payback criterion may be appropriate for decision makers or firms with short, time horizons, in which case managers are more concerned with short-term profitability. Projects that promise an early return of the outlay and hence will contribute well to accounting net income in the shorter term would be favored by decision makers under such an objective function. In a crude way the payback-period criterion also acts as a screen against risky projects. Since uncertainty increases with the length of time into the future that cash flows must be estimated, the payback period selects the less risky projects at the expense of those that have longer gestation periods and longer revenue streams.

Reconciliation of Payback-Period and IRR Criteria.   It can be shown that the payback-period criterion may approximate the internal rate of return criterion under certain conditions.[4] If the original cost is the total cost, if projects are long-lived, and if the revenue stream is uniform, we can show that the internal rate of return and the payback criteria would rank projects identically. Where the revenue stream is expected to be uniform in nominal dollars, we can express the sum of this revenue stream as

$$\sum_{t=1}^{n} R_t = \frac{U}{1 + i} + \frac{U}{(1 + i)^2} + \ldots + \frac{U}{(1 + i)^n} \tag{15-4}$$

---

[4]See M. H. Spencer, K. K. Seo, and M. G. Simkin, *Managerial Economics*, 4th ed. (Homewood, Ill.: Richard D. Irwin, Inc., 1975), pp. 449-56.

where U is the uniform annual net cash flow after taxes. The sum of the geometric progression represented by equation (15-4) is

$$\sum_{t=1}^{n} R_t = \frac{U/1 + i[1 - (1/1 + i)^n}{1 - (1/1 + i)}$$

(15-5)

which simplifies to

$$\sum_{t=1}^{n} R_t = \frac{U}{i} - \frac{U}{i}\left(\frac{1}{1+i}\right)^n$$

(15-6)

Or, in terms of the internal rate of return:

$$i = \frac{U}{\Sigma R_t} - \frac{U}{\Sigma R_t}\left(\frac{1}{1+i}\right)^n$$

(15-7)

The first term in equation (15-7) is in fact the reciprocal of the payback period, since it is the uniform annual revenue stream divided by the total revenue stream. Where the project is long-lived the second term will approach zero, since the exponent n will be large. Hence, the internal rate of return will approach the reciprocal of the payback period when projects are long-lived and the revenue stream is uniform and when there are no other capital costs during the life of the investment project. Thus decision makers using the simple payback criterion may not be too far wrong in some cases.

The Average-Rate-of-Return Criterion

■ *Definition:* The *average rate of return* is defined as the average annual revenues (undiscounted) divided by the initial cost. Symbolically,

$$\text{ARR} = \frac{\left(\sum_{t=1}^{n} R_t\right)/n}{C_0}$$

(15-8)

Example: In the example we have been using, the total (undiscounted) revenues from the project are \$14,320: the average annual revenues are, therefore, \$4,773. Hence,

$$\text{ARR} = \frac{4,773}{10,000}$$
$$= 0.4773$$

Note that this criterion ignores the time value of money and would therefore be unable to discriminate between two projects with the same initial cost and revenue totals but with differing patterns of the receipts. If we modify the ARR criterion to include the discounted present value of the revenue stream, we have

$$ARR = \frac{(12,104.84)/3}{10,000}$$

$$= \frac{4,035}{10,000}$$

$$= 0.4035$$

Note that this result is exactly the profitability index divided by three, that is:

$$\frac{PI}{3} = \frac{1.210484}{3} = 0.4035$$

This result should be no surprise, for the only difference between the PI formula and the ARR formula (using the present value of the revenue stream) is that the latter is divided by the number of years of the project's life. The additional step of averaging the income stream may obscure important cash-flow information, however. Thus the ARR criterion is seriously deficient in undiscounted form and can be regarded as inferior (or at least redundant) to the PI criterion even when the former is calculated using the present value of the revenue stream.[5]

15.3 MUTUALLY EXCLUSIVE INVESTMENTS

In many cases a firm will be considering investment projects that are mutually exclusive. For example, two or more projects may be able to perform the same function or will utilize the same space or other constrained resource, such as skilled labor within the firm. We defer discussion of investment projects that utilize the same funds to the next section, where limited availability of capital is discussed. Where investment projects are mutually exclusive, it is necessary for the firm to rank the investment projects in order of their desirability. It will then choose the project that contributes the most toward the firm's objective function.

---

[5] A variation of the ARR criterion is the accounting-return-on-investment (AROI) criterion. The latter is calculated as the ratio of accounting net income (undiscounted) to the initial cost of the project. This criterion is clearly inferior to those discussed above, since it ignores the time value of money, is subject to ambiguity resulting from the several acceptable accounting methods of calculating net income (for example, treatment of depreciation and allocation of overheads), and moreover allows sunk costs to enter the decision-making process.

TABLE 15–4. Comparison of Costs and Revenues from Two Alternative Investment Projects

	PLANT A		PLANT B	
	Cash Flow ($)	NPV @15% ($)	Cash Flow ($)	NPV @15% ($)
Initial cost	−100,000	−100,000	−60,000	−60,000
Year 1	45,000	39,150	30,000	26,100
Year 2	55,000	41,580	37,000	27,972
Year 3	50,000	32,900	28,000	18,424
Net cash flow	50,000	13,630	35,000	12,496

Example: Suppose a firm is planning to introduce a new product and has called for bids for the construction of the plant and physical facilities to manufacture that product. Let us consider two bids, which we will call plant A and plant B. Plant A is more expensive but also more efficient in terms of cost per unit and maintenance requirements, as compared with plant B. The relevant cash flows and net present values are shown in Table 15–4.

It can be seen that plant A offers the greater net present value when discounted at 15 percent. If the firm's objective is to maximize the present value of its longer-term profitability, it should thus choose plant A, since this alternative contributes more in present-value terms than does plant B.

The Superiority of NPV over IRR for Mutually Exclusive Investments

Let us now consider the relative internal rates of return of the two plants. Once again we need to find the internal rate of return by a trial-and-error procedure of zeroing in on the discount rate that reduces the net present value to zero. In Table 15–5 we perform this exercise for plant A and see that the internal rate of return is slightly more than 22.8 percent.

In Table 15–6 we perform the search procedure for the internal rate of return to plant B and find that the rate of discount that reduces the net present value to zero is slightly more than 27.2 percent. Thus the internal-rate-of-return criterion would sug-

TABLE 15–5. Calculation of Internal Rate of Return: Plant A

Year	CFAT	NPV @25%	NPV @20%	NPV @23%	NPV @22.8%
0	$−100,000	$−100,000	$−100,000	$−100,000	$−100,000
1	45,000	36,000	37,485	36,585	36,644
2	55,000	35,200	38,170	36,355	36,471
3	50,000	25,600	28,950	26,850	27,000
		$ −3,200	$ 4,605	$ −210	$ 114

TABLE 15-6.   Calculation of Internal Rate of Return: Plant B

Year	CFAT	NPV @25%	NPV @28%	NPV @27%	NPV @27.2%
0	$-60,000	$-60,000	$-60,000	$-60,000	$-60,000
1	30,000	24,000	23,430	23,622	23,580
2	37,000	23,680	22,570	22,940	22,866
3	28,000	14,336	13,356	13,670	13,608
		$ 2,016	$ -644	$ 232	$ 54

gest that plant B is preferable to plant A, and it evidently conflicts with the judgment of the net-present-value criterion.

To see why this conflict arises, let us plot the net-present-value curves of both plant A and plant B, as shown in Figure 15-4. To plot the net-present-value curve for plant A, we know that at a zero rate of discount the net present value will be equal to the net cash inflow (in nominal dollars) of $50,000. From Table 15-4 we know that at a discount rate of 15 percent, the net present value of plant A is $13,630. Finally, we know that the rate of discount that reduces the net present value to zero is approximately 22.8 percent. Similarly, for plant B we can plot its present value curve, beginning at $35,000 when the discount rate is zero, passing through $12,496 when the discount rate is 15 percent, and terminating at 27.2 percent on the horizontal axis.

It is clear that the net present value curves for the two projects intersect at approximately the 18 percent rate of discount. For discount rates below 18 percent, the net-present-value criterion would suggest project A, but above 18 percent the net-present-value criterion would suggest project B. The internal-rate-of-return criterion,

FIGURE 15-4.   Net-Present-Value Curves

since it looks at only one point on the net present value curve, would suggest project B under all opportunity rates of discount up to 27.2 percent. However, for actual opportunity rates of discount less than about 18 percent, the internal-rate-of-return criterion would suggest the investment project with the lower net present value and would thus lead decision makers to a suboptimal decision in terms of the addition to the firm's net worth, since plant A clearly has the greater net present value at these lower opportunity rates of discount.

Note: Why does this conflict arise between the net-present-value and the internal-rate-of-return criteria? It arises because of the implicit assumption that the profit stream of each project could be reinvested at the internal rate of return. To see this, note that discounting a future stream of profits is the reverse of compounding a presently held sum over the same period of time at the same rate. At higher interest rates (namely, greater than 18 percent), the net present value of plant B would compound to a greater value over the three years than would the net present value of plant A at the same interest rates. The conflict with net present value arises because the calculation of net present value implicitly assumes the reinvestment of the profit stream at the opportunity discount rate rather than at the internal rate of return.

We need the decision criterion that will always indicate the project that adds the most toward the attainment of the firm's objective function. Hence, the net-present-value criterion is superior to the internal-rate-of-return criterion for situations where mutually exclusive projects must be evaluated.

The Superiority of NPV over the Profitability Index

Let us now calculate the profitability indices for each of the projects under consideration. According to the profitability-index criterion, the plant with the higher profitability index should be chosen for implementation. The calculations are as shown in Table 15–7.

Note that the profitability index supports the judgment of the internal-rate-of-return criterion, by indicating that project B is superior to project A in this situation. However, it is inferior to the net-present-value criterion for the same reason that the IRR criterion is: It would indicate acceptance of the project that contributes the lesser amount to the net worth of the firm in at least some cases and would therefore result in decisions that are not in accord with the objectives of the firm.

TABLE 15–7.   Calculation of Profitability Index

	Plant A	Plant B
PV of revenues	113,363	72,496
Initial costs	100,000	60,000
Profitability Index	1.13363	1.20826

Note: The conflict between the profitability-index criterion and the net-present-value criterion arises because of what is known as the "size disparity" problem. Where there is a difference in the size of the initial cost or in the magnitude and time pattern of the revenue streams, the profitability-index criterion and the net-present-value criterion may rank projects differently. If the firm's objective is to maximize its net worth, the net-present-value criterion must be used, since although the profitability index indicates which project is the most efficient at generating net present value, this is a "relative" consideration rather than the "absolute" consideration of maximizing the firm's net worth.

Thus, in general, it is preferable to use the net-present-value criterion for ranking mutually exclusive projects under situations of unlimited availability of capital. Both the internal rate of return and the profitability index may indicate the acceptance of projects that are not in the best interest of the firm's objective to maximize the present value of its longer-term earnings.

Capital Budgeting Given Limited Availability of Capital

The availability of investment funds should not, in theory, ever impose a constraint upon the level of investments. We saw in Figure 15–1 that although the cost of capital may increase as the level of investment is increased, the level of investment will be carried to the point where the marginal investment project has an internal rate of return at least equal to the cost of capital. Thus, if the internal rate of return exceeds the cost of capital, if the net present value at the opportunity rate is positive, or if the profitability index exceeds unity, the project should be implemented, since it will contribute to the enlargement of the firm's net present value. Where investment projects are mutually exclusive, the problem was to choose the one project of those available that would best serve the firm's objective function. The implicit assumption was that once this choice for this particular purpose was made, the firm would continue to consider other investment projects and groups of mutually exclusive investment projects and would implement those that met the acceptability criterion. In theory, the funds are always available, although at progressively higher rates of interest perhaps, and if the net present value is positive at this higher cost of capital, the investment project under consideration should be undertaken.

In practice, however, we often find the situation of a decision maker facing a constraint upon investment funds. It is common business practice to set investment budgets for departments or divisions within the firm such that the decision-making unit faces a constraint upon investment funds. Setting investment budgets for individual departments or decision-making units or for the firm as a whole may reflect the reluctance of top management to take on additional debt, with its subsequent impact upon the leverage position and the market value of the firm's shares.

In such situations the decision maker faces an allocation problem and should proceed to select the investment projects which maximize the return from that limited supply of investment funds. The projects should be ranked in order of their NPV and implemented up to the point where the next project cannot be afforded. If any remaining projects (with positive NPV) further down the list can be afforded, by virtue of their lower initial cost levels, the decision maker should skip over the unaffordable projects and implement the remaining projects which can be afforded before the capital budget is depleted. The remaining funds, if any, should then be invested at the opportunity rate of interest.

Some Qualifications

The estimation of the future cash flows associated with investment projects involves techniques discussed in Chapters 5 and 8. Initial costs should cause few estimation problems, since they are to be incurred in the very near future and thus should be determined with relative accuracy. Future costs and revenue streams, however, are subject to uncertainty and thus may be accompanied by a probability distribution. The preceding analysis would need to be modified by insertion of the expected values of the net cash flow after taxes for each project rather than the point estimates used in the examples.

Use of probability distributions and the resultant expected value of net cash flows after taxes for each year in the future involves the law of averages and could therefore cause the net-present-value criterion to be an unsuitable decision criterion for some investment decisions. "One-shot" investment decisions may expose the investor to the risk of a very low outcome, which cannot be averaged upward by other similar projects having outcomes above their expected values. Thus we might expect the firm with a one-shot decision involving capital budgeting to apply the certainty-equivalent criterion, which allows the decision maker to place his or her own evaluation upon the risk and other nonquantifiabie aspects of the investment decision, as explained in Chapter 2.

Differing risks of differing investment projects are adjusted for by the use of differing opportunity rates of discount. Recall that the opportunity rate of discount for any project is what the investment funds involved in that project could earn elsewhere at a comparable degree of risk. Thus a firm considering a series of investment projects may discount these projects at differing opportunity discount rates if the degree of risk perceived to be associated with each project differs.[6]

15.4   SUMMARY

In this chapter we have considered the capital-budgeting decision, which is the decision to invest in plant, equipment, and other projects expected to generate a future stream of net cash flows. Given unlimited availability of capital, but typically with an

---

[6]An alternate means of adjusting for differing risks is to reduce the period over which you will recognize the revenues from the more risky projects. See J. C. Van Horne, "Variation of Project Life as a Means of Adjusting for Risk," *Engineering Economist*, 21 (Spring 1976), pp. 151–58.

increasing cost of capital, the firm should invest up to the point where the marginal investment project implemented has an internal rate of return at least equal to the cost of capital. This will mean that the project has a net present value that is nonnegative, or a profitability index of at least unity. When investment projects are mutually exclusive, the three investment criteria mentioned may give conflicting results, and we found the net-present-value criterion to be the only reliable guide if the firm wishes to maximize its net worth. Where the investment funds available are constrained, the firm would implement the projects in order of their NPV ranking, up to the point where the next project cannot be afforded. It would then implement any other affordable projects and invest the remaining funds at the opportunity rate of interest.

The techniques introduced in Chapter 2 regarding the decision-making process under conditions of risk and uncertainty must be applied to the capital-budgeting decision, since there will be a probability distribution surrounding the expected values of future cost and revenue streams. Similarly, the techniques outlined in Chapters 5 and 8 for demand and cost estimation and forecasting must be used to establish the future stream of net cash flow after taxes for each project under consideration. Finally, it should be noted that the appropriate decision criterion in any particular firm is the one that best pursues the firm's objective function. If the firm has a long time horizon and wishes to maximize the net present value of the firm, the net-present-value criterion is appropriate under most circumstances. On the other hand, if the firm's time horizon is relatively short and management is concerned with accounting profitability, market value of outstanding shares, and other considerations involving immediate or short-term cash flow, the payback criterion or the average-rate-of-return criterion may be the appropriate investment criterion in these cases.

DISCUSSION QUESTIONS

15-1. Explain in three sentences why the NPV criterion and the IRR criterion must always agree on the accept/reject investment decision, given the availability of sufficient funds.

15-2. In calculating the expected net revenue stream associated with an investment project, what factors enter the calculation?

15-3. When comparing possible investment projects, why is it important to ensure that all projects have been evaluated using the same depreciation method?

15-4. Why is the cost of capital to the firm likely to be a step function of the amount of funds demanded for investment purposes?

15-5. Under what circumstances is the use of the payback-period investment criterion appropriate?

15-6. Why is the average rate-of-return criterion inferior to the other investment criteria discussed?

15-7. Where projects are mutually exclusive, the IRR criterion may rank projects in conflict with their ranking by the NPV criterion. Why? Does this conflict invalidate the IRR criterion?

15-8. Under what circumstances might the profitability index disagree with the NPV criterion in the ranking of mutually exclusive projects? Explain.

15-9. Suppose investment projects are divisible, in the sense that any part of each project can be undertaken, with the return being proportionate to the investment. Does this factor change the analysis?

15-10. Why can the payback criteria be regarded as appropriate, in a crude way, for a risk-averse investor?

PROBLEMS AND SHORT CASES

15-1. The Omega Investment Corporation has more than half a million dollars to invest as the result of a recent windfall gain from the revaluation of a foreign currency it was holding. Failing all else, these funds can be invested in government bonds, which are considered to be risk free, at 8 percent per annum. Omega is evaluating four other investment projects as well. These projects seem to be equally risky, and Omega feels they should return at least 10 percent per annum in order to be considered an equivalent proposition to placing the funds in the risk-free bonds. The initial outlays and net cash flows after taxes (NCFAT) for each year of each project's life are as follows:

Project	A ($)	B ($)	C ($)	D ($)
Initial outlay	100,000	135,000	85,000	122,000
NCFAT				
Year 1	−12,200	26,300	56,000	−25,000
Year 2	−8,500	34,400	32,000	10,600
Year 3	76,600	48,600	18,600	48,200
Year 4	62,400	56,500	12,400	96,500
Year 5	23,500	22,000	5,500	34,000
Year 6	9,500	10,000	0	18,700

You are asked to advise Omega about which of these projects, if any, it should undertake. Explain your reasoning.

15-2. The Anderson Electronics Company is considering investing $1 million in a major advertising campaign. This expenditure will be tax deductible at the end of the year in which it is incurred, and Anderson's tax rate is 48 percent. It will take a year to produce the campaign after the million dollars is spent, and the impact of the campaign on sales is expected to be felt over the following three years. The precise outcomes are uncertain, however. The marketing research department has generated the following estimates (and associated probabilities) of incremental net cash flows after taxes that will result from this campaign for each of the three years.

Incremental	PROBABILITIES		
NCFAT ($)	Year 2	Year 3	Year 4
50,000	0.05	0.10	0.25
150,000	0.10	0.20	0.35
250,000	0.15	0.40	0.25
350,000	0.35	0.15	0.10
450,000	0.25	0.10	0.05
650,000	0.10	0.05	0.00

The probability distributions should be treated as being independent from year to year (hence no conditional probabilities), and the NCFAT figures should be regarded as arriving at the end of each year. Anderson considers this project to be about as risky as investing the funds in the bonds of a large trust company which would currently pay 12 percent per annum. Assume that Anderson's tax assessment will be finalized one year after the million is spent.

(a) What is the net present value of this investment project?

(b) What is the internal rate of return of the project?

(c) Sketch the NPV curve against various opportunity discount rates and estimate from this the NPV if the appropriate discount rate is 10 percent.

15-3. Custy Canoe and Kayak, Inc., is considering investing in a facility that would allow it to manufacture lightweight fiberglass sports kayaks. The proposed plant would involve an initial investment of $212,500 and would have an expected life of four years, after which time its expected scrap value would be $12,500. The marketing manager, Maureen Custy, expects these kayaks to become increasingly popular in future years, although other firms are likely to begin supplying competitive canoes within two or three years. Extensive market research and cost estimation studies have established the following (independent) probability distributions of the level of contribution to overheads and profits in each of the four years.

| Contributions | PROBABILITIES | | | |
($)	Year 1	Year 2	Year 3	Year 4
10,000	0.05	0.05	0.10	0.20
25,000	0.20	0.15	0.20	0.30
50,000	0.40	0.20	0.35	0.25
75,000	0.25	0.35	0.20	0.15
100,000	0.10	0.15	0.10	0.10
125,000	0.00	0.10	0.05	0.00

Note that the contribution figures do not include consideration of the tax savings resulting from depreciation. For tax purposes, depreciation is calculated using the sum-of-years-digits method. The finance manager, Michael Gable, advises that the applicable tax rate is 48 percent, and that this project should be evaluated in terms of the alternative use of these funds to establish a camping resort area for canoe enthusiasts, which he considers to be of equal risk. The resort project has an expected internal rate of return of 15 percent.

Assume that the kayak plant can be purchased and installed at the start of this year, that tax payments or refunds are due at the end of each year, that the profit contributions are received continuously throughout each year, and that the expected scrap value is realized at the end of the fourth year.

(a) Calculate the expected net present value of the kayak project, taking care to use the appropriate discount factors.

(b) Find the approximate internal rate of return of the kayak project.

(c) Recalculate the expected net present value of the kayak project, assuming this time that all cash flows take place in lump sum at the start or end of each year.

(d) Explain why there is a difference between your answers to (a) and (c).

(e) In which project (kayak or resort) should Custy Canoe and Kayak invest the funds? Explain.

15-4. Marilyn Monibaggs is considering investing in a small shop in the downtown area of a large city. Ms. Monibaggs has not been lax in her investigations but has found that only two locations are feasible. Ms. Monibaggs is considering establishing either a sportswear boutique or a sporting equipment store, and she could put either type of store at either location. Location A is initially more suitable for the sportswear boutique, but the profitability of this venture will decline in the future because of the planned establishment of a major department store and other shops nearby. After this event the sporting equipment shop would be more profitable than the sportswear shop at this location. Location B, on the other hand, is close to several competitors in both types of merchandise but is frequented by a larger number of potential customers. The initial cash outlay will be $50,000 for the sportswear store versus $60,000 for the equipment store, and Ms. Monibaggs will pay a monthly lease on the location chosen. The cash flows after taxes for each of the four alternatives have been carefully estimated as follows:

| Year | LOCATION A | | LOCATION B | |
	Sportswear	Equipment	Sportswear	Equipment
1	$-18,000	$-24,000	$-24,000	$-30,000
2	37,400	26,000	32,000	28,600
3	26,200	28,400	33,500	30,800
4	22,400	29,800	34,300	36,400
5	20,800	30,200	35,000	38,900

These figures include the initial cash outlay for inventories that was incurred at the start of the first year. Treat the other net cash flows as arriving in a continuous stream throughout each year. Ms. Monibaggs, is only interested in a time horizon of five years and considers the opportunity discount rates to be 14 percent and 15 percent for the sportswear and equipment stores, respectively, at location A; and 17 percent and 20 percent for the sportswear and equipment stores, respectively, at location B.

(a) What is the net present value of each of the four projects?

(b) Estimate the payback period for each of the four projects.

(c) Supposing Ms. Monibaggs is interested in maximizing her net worth but at the same time wants to get her (undiscounted) money back quickly in order to be ready to invest elsewhere if an opportunity arises, which alternative should she choose? Explain.

15-5. A consortium of business professors at a city university are thinking of investing in the takeout food industry. A location has been found which is considered to be highly suitable because of its proximity to thousands of downtown offices and stores, a major stadium, and two very large high schools. The professors are in the process of deciding whether they should go with hamburgers, chicken, or tacos as their product line. Extensive studies have provided the following estimated probabilities for various levels of net cash flow after taxes in each of the first three years for each of the three projects.

| NCFAT ($) | PROBABILITIES | | |
	Hamburgers	Chicken	Tacos
Year 1			
$-10,000	0.05	0.10	0.15
0	0.10	0.15	0.20
10,000	0.25	0.30	0.35
20,000	0.35	0.25	0.15
30,000	0.15	0.15	0.10
40,000	0.10	0.05	0.05

continued

NCFAT	PROBABILITIES		
($)	Hamburgers	Chicken	Tacos
Year 2			
$-10,000	0.00	0.05	0.05
0	0.05	0.05	0.10
10,000	0.15	0.10	0.15
20,000	0.20	0.25	0.20
30,000	0.30	0.35	0.30
40,000	0.20	0.15	0.15
50,000	0.10	0.05	0.05
Year 3			
$ 0	0.00	0.05	0.00
10,000	0.15	0.10	0.05
20,000	0.20	0.30	0.10
30,000	0.30	0.35	0.40
40,000	0.20	0.15	0.25
50,000	0.10	0.05	0.15
60,000	0.05	0.00	0.05

The above net cash flows after taxes do not include the initial franchise fee of $50,000 for hamburgers; $40,000 for chicken; and $35,000 for tacos. They do allow for depreciation, however. The professors' time horizon is only three years, since they are all on three-year contracts at the university and expect their research and teaching efforts to suffer so badly that their contracts will not be renewed and they will have to go elsewhere for a job. Their collective judgment is that the opportunity discount rate is 15 percent for hamburgers, 13 percent for chicken, and 16 percent for tacos. Treat the expected net cash flows after taxes as arriving continuously throughout each year and the probability distributions as being independent of each other.

(a) Calculate the expected net present value of each alternative, assuming that the franchise fee cannot be recovered at the end of the period.

(b) Estimate the payback period for each project, using the undiscounted net cash flows after taxes.

(c) Advise the professors as to which project, if any, to undertake. Support your recommendation.

15-6. You have recently been hired as an assistant investment analyst in a small corporation which promotes new products and inventions. Your boss has asked you to evaluate and rank four potential investment projects. He tells you that the capital budget for the year is $105,000 and that anything left over can be invested in government bonds at 8.5 percent per annum. The details of the four projects are as shown on page 591.

Your boss tells you that it is "company policy" to consider the expected net cash flow stream up to and including the fourth year only. He says to treat flows as if they were to arrive in lump sum on the last day of each year.

(a) Calculate the expected net present value of each project, and rank the projects in descending order.

(b) Calculate the profitability index for each project and rank them in descending order.

(c) Which projects do you recommend should be implemented if your boss wishes to maximize the expected net present value of the capital budget?

(d) What is the maximum expected net present value of the capital budget? Explain.

	PROJECT			
	A	B	C	D
Initial cost	$35,000	$28,000	$16,000	$40,000
Expected NCFAT				
Year 1	12,681	9,650	8,480	22,680
Year 2	28,323	25,462	12,624	51,070
Year 3	36,084	31,836	28,970	28,218
Year 4	20,880	42,420	14,381	8,440
Salvage value	$10,000	$ 8,000	$ 2,000	$12,000
Opportunity discount rate	12%	10%	14%	15%

15-7. A large real estate firm has half a million dollars which it wishes to invest in urban housing development projects. The available opportunities have been carefully evaluated and the four most promising projects have been thoroughly examined, with cost and demand estimates being supplied by a reliable group of consultants at a cost of $10,000. The projects are known as North, South, East, and West because of their locations relative to the firm's main office. The relevant details are as follows:

	PROJECT			
	North	South	East	West
Initial cost	$120,000	$180,000	$250,000	$285,000
Expected NCFAT				
Year 1	40,000	62,000	90,000	115,000
Year 2	42,000	75,000	88,000	140,000
Year 3	45,000	81,000	84,000	132,000
Year 4	48,000	84,000	82,000	90,000
Year 5	51,000	80,000	80,000	75,000
Salvage value	$ 30,000	$ 20,000	$ 50,000	$ 70,000
Opportunity discount rate	10%	15%	12%	18%

Each project would be developed in five yearly stages, with all accounts being paid and all revenues being received from sales on the last day of each year. The initial costs shown refer to the cost of purchasing each tract of land, and this must be paid before any activity can begin.

(a) Calculate the expected net present value of each project and rank the projects in descending order.

(b) Calculate the profitability index for each project and rank them in descending order.

(c) Which projects should be undertaken in order to maximize the net present value of the funds available?

(d) What is the maximum net present value of the funds available? Explain.

15-8. Dimmock Dry Dock Services is considering installation of a new dry dock facility. There are two competing propositions. The first plan would cover two acres of waterfront land and be capable of servicing fifteen boats at the same time. This plan would require purchase of land adjacent to Dimmock's present facility. The second plan is more modest and involves replacing the present facility with a modernized dry dock capable of handling eight boats at a time. The initial outlays and net cash flows over the firm's planning period are shown below.

	First Plan	Second Plan
Initial costs	$1,580,000	$750,000
Expected NCFAT		
Year 1	350,000	200,000
Year 2	500,000	250,000
Year 3	600,000	300,000
Year 4	600,000	300,000
Year 5	600,000	300,000
Salvage value	500,000	250,000
Opportunity discount rate	18%	15%

(a) Calculate the expected net present value, the internal rate of return, and the profitability index for each plan.

(b) Advise Dimmock Dry Dock as to which plan they should implement, supporting your analysis with explicit recognition of the underlying assumptions.

15-9. Rasta Resorts, Inc., is planning to develop some beachfront land on an eastern Caribbean island. Plan A is to build a hotel-casino for short-stay guests (up to one week), whereas plan B is to build condominiums for a clientele who would typically stay longer than one week. The hotel-casino would need to be lavishly appointed with luxury rooms, and the condominiums would optimally be somewhat more spartan. Thus there is a substantial difference in the initial cost. Plan A will cost $EC20 million (Eastern Caribbean dollars) before a single guest arrives, whereas plan B will cost only $EC6 million. Revenues from the hotel-casino are likely to be four times those from the condominiums, and operating costs of the hotel-casino are likely to be only twice those of the condominiums. Rasta Resorts personnel tell you that the hotel-casino will reach payback in five years, whereas the condominiums will reach payback in three years (in nominal terms in both cases). The resale value of these resorts, once payback is reached, will be $EC30 million for the hotel-casino and $EC10 million for the condominiums, regardless of when they are sold after payback, because of the inevitable physical depreciation of the buildings.

(a) Assuming year-end cash flows, a time horizon of five years, and opportunity discount rates of 20 percent and 15 percent for the hotel-casino and the condominiums, respectively, calculate the expected present value of each plan.

(b) Would your answer be different if the time horizon was 10 years?

(c) Advise Rasta Resorts on this decision, making explicit all underlying assumptions and reservations you might have.

15-10. Hilltop Raceway Corporation has been formed to develop a 100-acre site into a motor-racing facility. At this point the final decision has not yet been made whether it will be an oval circuit with only four banked left-hand turns or a road circuit with about ten turns both to the left and the right. The HCR management knows there is more spectator support for oval racing and that a new circuit like this would get on the Indy-car schedule as well as the stock-car schedules organized by CART (Confederation of Auto Racing Teams), which have a tremendous following. But an oval circuit would involve much greater initial costs to level the hill and install the racetrack and spectator stands. A road circuit, on the other hand, would use the terrain to advantage and be considerably less expensive to set up. The road circuit would probably attract the Indy cars but not the CART stock cars; however, it would become a regular feature on the USAC (United States Automobile Club) calendar and might possibly attract the Formula One circus after two or three years of operation. USAC events have many more competitors but fewer spectators than CART events and thus are less profitable to the promoters. Formula One events are very profitable and involve a great deal of prestige for the racetrack owners, as well as recip-rocal benefits at other race circuits around the world. The cash-flow details (in millions) are presented below. Assume year-end cash flows.

	Oval Circuit	Road Circuit
Initial cost	$50	$40
Expected NCFAT		
Year 1	15	5
Year 2	20	8
Year 3	20	15
Year 4	20	20
Year 5	20	20

Expected resale value after five years (for condominium development) is $30 million if the landscape is modified for an oval track and $50 million if the land is used for a road-racing track. The firm's cost of capital will be 17 percent if it raises $50 million but only 14 percent if it only has to raise $20 million.

(a) Calculate the expected net present value of the two alternatives.

(b) Estimate the payback period for each alternative.

(c) Advise Hilltop Raceway as to what they should do.

(d) What assumptions and qualifications underlie your advice?

SUGGESTED REFERENCES AND FURTHER READING

Ahmed, S. B. "Optimal Equipment Replacement Policy," *Journal of Transport Economics and Policy*, 7 (January 1973), pp. 71–79.

Baumol, W. J. *Economic Theory and Operations Analysis* (4th ed.), chap. 25. Englewood Cliffs, N.J.: Prentice-Hall, Inc., 1977.

Clark, J. J., T. J. Hindelang, and R. E. Pritchard. *Capital Budgeting.* Englewood Cliffs, N.J.: Prentice-Hall, Inc., 1979.

Eisner, R. "Components of Capital Expenditures: Replacement and Modernization versus Ex-pansion," *Review of Economics and Statistics*, 54 (August 1972), pp. 297–305.

Feldstein, M. S., and D. K. Foot. "The Other Half of Gross Investment: Replacement and Modernization Expenditures," *Review of Economics and Statistics*, 53 (February 1971), pp. 49–58.

Fremgen, J. M. "Capital Budgeting Practices: A Survey," *Management Accounting*, May 1973, pp. 19–25.

Hall, R. E., and D. W. Jorgenson. "Tax Policy and Investment Behavior," *American Economic Review*, 57 (June 1967), pp. 391–414.

Hirshleifer, J. "Investment Decision under Uncertainty: Choice-Theoretic Approaches," *Quarterly Journal of Economics*, 79 (November 1965), pp. 509–36.

Jorgenson, D. W. "Econometric Studies of Investment Behavior: A Survey," *Journal of Economic Literature*, 9 (December 1971), pp. 1111–47.

Klammer, T. "Empirical Evidence of the Adoption of Sophisticated Capital Budgeting Tech-niques," *Journal of Business*, July 1972, pp. 387–97.

Lorie, J. H., and L. J. Savage. "Three Problems in Rationing Capital," *Journal of Business*, 28 (October 1955), pp. 229–39.

Mao, J. C. T. "Survey of Capital Budgeting: Theory and Practice," *Journal of Finance*, May 1970, pp. 349–60.

Miller, E. "Decision-Making under Uncertainty for Capital Budgeting and Hiring," *Managerial Decisions in Economics*, 6 (March 1985), pp. 11–18.

Petty, J. W., D. F. Scott, Jr., and M. M. Bird. "The Capital Expenditure Decision-Making Process of Large Corporations," *Engineering Economist*, 20 (Spring 1975), pp. 159–72.

Van Horne, J. C. "Capital Budgeting under Conditions of Uncertainty as to Project Life," *Engineering Economist*, 17 (Spring 1972), pp. 189–99.

Van Horne, J. C. *Financial Management and Policy* (6th ed.), chaps. 4–8. Englewood Cliffs, N.J.: Prentice-Hall, Inc., 1983.

Van Horne, J. C. "Variation of Project Life as a Means of Adjusting for Risk," *Engineering Economist*, 21 (Spring 1976), pp. 151–58.

Weingartner, H. M. *Mathematical Programming and Analysis of Capital Budgeting Problems*. Englewood Cliffs, N.J.: Prentice-Hall, Inc., 1963.

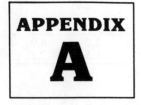

A Review of Analytic Geometry and Calculus: Functions, Graphs, and Derivatives

Functions and Graphs

A *function* is an expression of the dependence of one variable upon one or more other variables. In *general* form we may write

$$Y = f(X) \tag{A-1}$$

This expression is read, "The value of Y is a function of, or depends upon, the value of X." Note that Y is known as the dependent variable, while X is the independent variable. The value of Y may depend on more than one independent variable, of course, such that we might express in general form the functional relationship as

$$Y = f(X_1, X_2, X_3, \ldots, X_n) \tag{A-2}$$

In this multivariable function the value of Y is seen to depend upon the value of several independent variables, where n is the number of these independent variables. For example, the sales of umbrellas may be a function of the price of umbrellas, the income of consumers, the rainfall levels, the advertising expenditures of umbrella manufacturers, and the price of taxi fares.

The form of the functional dependence of Y upon the independent variables X_i, $(i = 1, 2, \ldots, n)$, remains unspecified in the expressions shown. To find the exact nature of the dependence we must examine the specific form of the function. This may take a variety of mathematical forms: for example, Y may be a linear, quadratic, cubic, quartic, or higher-order function of X (or the X's), or it may be a power function, an exponential function, or a hyperbolic function, or it may take some other form. Let us examine these in turn.

Linear Functions. The general form of a linear function is

$$Y = a + bX \tag{A-3}$$

TABLE A-1.   Values of Y for Various Values of X

Values of X	0.0	1.0	2.0	3.0	4.0	5.0	6.0
Values of Y	4.0	4.5	5.0	5.5	6.0	6.5	7.0

Example: Suppose $Y = 4 + 0.5X$. In this example, $a = 4$ and $b = 0.5$. We can array the values for Y given the values for X, as shown in Table A-1. These values indicate the specific dependence of the variable Y upon the variable X. When X is zero, the second term in equation (A-3) drops out and Y is simply equal to the parameter a. Each time the variable X is increased by one unit, the value of Y increases to the extent of the parameter b.

Let us plot the above values on a graph that has X on the horizontal axis and Y on the vertical axis. Using the pairs of observations for X and Y as coordinates, we are able to plot the equation $Y = 4 + 0.5X$ as shown in Figure A-1. Strictly, the graph of this equation would extend into three of the four quadrants, but we show only the northeastern quadrant where both variables have positive values, since for most economic applications these are the only meaningful values of the function.

Note: Notice that the graph intercepts the Y axis at the value of 4: Hence the parameter a is known as the *intercept* parameter. Similarly, the graph slopes upward and to the right at the rate of half of one unit of Y for each one-unit increase in X. The slope of the line (the vertical rise over the horizontal run) is thus equal to 0.5, precisely the value of the b parameter. Accordingly, b is often called the *slope* parameter. Thus by observing the values of the a and b terms in a simple linear function we are able to envisage the graphical form of that function.

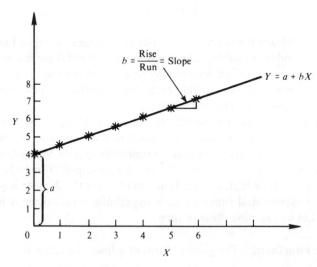

FIGURE A-1.   Graph of a Linear Function with Only One Independent Variable

For multivariable linear functions we simply extend the above analysis for the case of additional explanatory variables, such as

$$Y = a + b_1X_1 + b_2X_2 + b_3X_3 + \ldots + b_nX_n \qquad (A\text{-}4)$$

where the X_i, ($i = 1, 2, 3, \ldots, n$), represent several independent variables, and the b_i coefficients represent the influence that a one-unit change in the value of each independent variable would have on the value of Y.

Example: A simple example of a multivariable linear equation is $Y = 2 - 0.4X_1 + 0.3X_2$. Substituting values for X_1 and X_2 into this expression allows us to obtain the values for Y, as shown in Table A-2. The values in the body of the table represent the value of Y for the values of X_1 and X_2 given by the coordinates of that value. Graphing the values of Y against the values of X_1 and X_2 we obtain Figure A-2, in which it can be seen that the above equation is that of a plane. Note that the parameter a is again an intercept value, or the value of Y when the values of the independent variables are zero, and that the b coefficients represent the slope of the function as we move one unit in the direction of a particular independent variable. Note too that the sign of b_1 is negative, indicating that the value of Y declines as additional units of X_1 are added.

Quadratic Functions. The preceding linear relationships represent what are known as first-degree functions, since each of the independent variables was raised to the first power only. We move now to quadratic, or second-degree, functions, in which one or more of the independent variables will be squared, or raised to the second power, such as

$$Y = a + bX + cX^2 \qquad (A\text{-}5)$$

Hence Y is a function of the constant a plus the constant b times the independent variable X, plus the constant c times the square of that independent variable.

Example: Suppose we let $a = 5$; $b = 3$; and $c = 2$. We may calculate the values of Y for various values of X, as shown in Table A-3. Plotting these values as a graph, we

TABLE A-2. Values of Y for Various Values of X_1 and X_2

		VALUES OF X_1					
		0	1	2	3	4	5
	0	2.0	1.6	1.2	0.8	0.4	0.0
	1	2.3	1.9	1.5	1.1	0.7	0.3
Values of X_2	2	2.6	2.2	1.8	1.4	1.0	0.6
	3	2.9	2.5	2.1	1.7	1.3	0.9
	4	3.2	2.8	2.4	2.0	1.6	1.2
	5	3.5	3.1	2.7	2.3	1.9	1.5

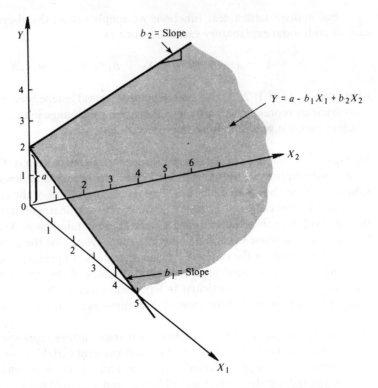

FIGURE A-2.   Graph of a Linear Function with Two Independent Variables

obtain Figure A-3, in which it can be seen that the graphical representation of a quadratic function is curvilinear, whereas linear functions are rectilinear. Notice that the parameter a remains the intercept term, but the slope depends not only upon the value of X but also upon the square of the value of X. In Figure A-3 we show a second quadratic function, $Y = 15 + 10X - 2X^2$, and it can be seen that the curvature of this function is concave from below, whereas the curvature of the first function was concave from above. This shape results from the negative sign in front of the second-degree term in the latter expression.

When there are multiple independent variables and the relationship between these variables and the independent variable is quadratic, we may express the function as follows:

$$Y = a + bX_1 - cX_1^2 + dX_2 - eX_2^2 \qquad \text{(A-6)}$$

TABLE A-3.   Values of Y for Various Values of X

Values of X	0	1	2	3	4	5
Values of Y	5	10	19	32	49	70

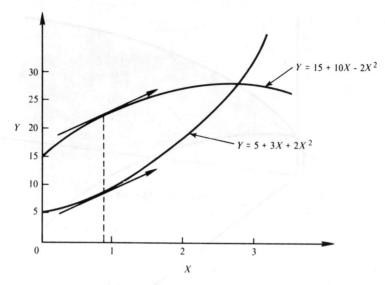

FIGURE A–3. **Graph of Quadratic Functions with Only One Independent Variable**

for the simple case in which there are only two independent variables, X_1 and X_2. This relationship is graphed in Figure A–4, where it can be seen that the negative signs preceding the second-degree terms indicate that the surface representing the function will be convex from above. Once again the parameter a is the intercept on the Y axis and takes a positive value. In other cases, of course, the parameter a may be zero or negative, just as the other coefficients may take values that are positive, zero, or negative.

Cubic Functions. We turn now to the third-degree terms in the functional relationship. Cubic functions may have first-degree, second-degree, and third-degree terms such as the following:

$$Y = a + bX + cX^2 + dX^3 \qquad (A-7)$$

When all the coefficients have positive signs, it is clear that the values of Y will increase by progressively larger increments as the value of X increases. When the signs of the coefficients differ, the graph of Y may display both convex and concave sections, may have hills and valleys, or may simply exhibit a monotonically increasing or decreasing shape, depending upon the values of the coefficients.

Example: Consider the function $Y = 25 + 10X - 5X^2 + 2X^3$. In Table A–4 we calculate the values of Y for several values of X. Plotting the values of Y against the value of X as in Figure A–5, we see that the function is monotonically increasing yet exhibits convexity from above at first, changing at the inflection point to concavity

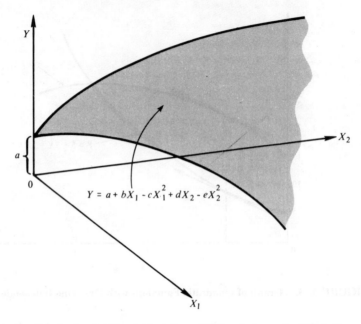

$$Y = a + bX_1 - cX_1^2 + dX_2 - eX_2^2$$

FIGURE A–4. Graph of a Quadratic Function with Two Independent Variables

from above. In the same figure we show the graph of the equation $Y = 100 + 5X - 10X^2 + 2X^3$ and note that it has sections of both positive and negative slope. This result indicates that the values of the parameters are instrumental in determining the shape of the graphical relationship. The distinguishing feature of a cubic function as compared with a quadratic function is that the former may have an inflection point (where slope changes from convexity in one direction to concavity in that direction, or vice versa), whereas the latter does not.

Cubic functions in two independent variables will produce a three-dimensional surface when graphed, as in Figure A–6. Again, the value of the parameters and the signs of these parameters and coefficients operate to determine the shape and placement of the surface depicting the functional relationship.

We could continue the examination of functional relationships with fourth-de-

TABLE A–4. Values of Y for Various Values of X

Values of X		0	1	2	3	4	5
	25 $=$	25	25	25	25	25	25
	$10X$ $=$	0	10	20	30	40	50
Calculations	$-5X^2$ $=$	0	−5	−20	−45	−80	−125
	$2X^3$ $=$	0	2	16	54	128	250
Values of Y		25	32	41	64	113	200

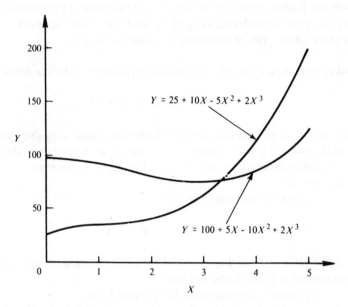

FIGURE A-5. Graph of Cubic Functions with Only One Independent Variable

FIGURE A-6. Graph of a Cubic Function with Two Independent Variables

gree and higher-degree terms influencing the value of the variable Y, but these are not necessary for an understanding of the material in this textbook. Instead we shall turn to some other types of functions that are useful to us.

Other Functional Forms.   *Exponential functions* take the form:

$$Y = a + b^X \qquad (A-8)$$

As you look at this specific form of the functional relationship, you should appreciate that the value of Y will increase monotonically as X increases, since the second term in the function assumes progressively higher degrees. An exponential function is shown in Figure A–7.

Power functions take the form:

$$Y = aX^b \qquad (A-9)$$

and can be seen from Figure A–7 to exhibit the general parabolic shape, as did the exponential and quadratic functions.

Hyperbolic functions take the general form:

$$Y = \frac{a}{X^b} \qquad (A-10)$$

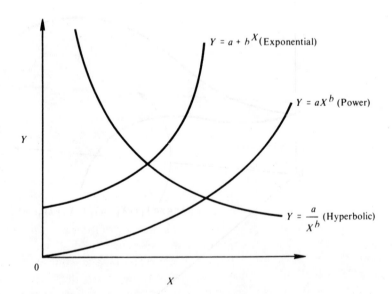

FIGURE A–7.   Graph of Other Functional Relationships between Y and X

In this case, as X grows larger the value of Y diminishes and approaches zero asymptotically, as shown in Figure A-7. You will note that hyperbolic functions are in fact power functions where the parameter b has a negative sign. That is, $Y = a/X^b = aX^{-b}$.

Note: A special case of the hyperbolic function is the rectangular hyperbola $Y = a/X$, where the parameter b takes the value unity. Hence $YX = a$ at all points on the curve. In verbal terms the product of the two variables is a constant at all levels of the two variables indicated by points on the curve. The rectangular hyperbola has applications in managerial economics such as the representation of the average-fixed-costs curve, since total fixed costs are a constant equal to the product of the number of output units and the average fixed costs at each output level.

Derivatives and Slopes

The size of the coefficient to the independent variable indicates the extent to which a marginal change in that variable influences the dependent variable. Examination of the marginal impact of one variable upon another is commonly referred to as *marginal analysis*. Economists make extensive use of marginal analysis when establishing normative rules for decision making. If Y is to be maximized, for example, the impact on the value of Y for a marginal change in the value of X is sought in order that we may decide to increase, decrease, or hold constant the value of the independent variable X. In general terms we would wish to know whether it was worthwhile in terms of the increment to Y to increase or decrease X. In terms of the graphical representations above, we are therefore interested in the slopes of the functions.

A mathematical technique that generates a slope of functions is one in which we take the first derivative (or differential) of the function. The derivative of a function shows the change in the value of the dependent variable Y given an infinitesimal change in the variable X, and is written as dY/dX, where d connotes the increment (or decrement) to each variable. For marginal analysis it is imperative that we consider small increases in the independent variable, since larger increases may incorrectly indicate the extent of change in the dependent variable. In Figure A-8 we depict a changing marginal relationship between Y and X. Suppose that the values of X and Y are as indicated by point A in that figure. The marginal relationship (or the slope of the function) is given by the slope of a tangent to the curve at point A. However, this is a correct representation of the slope of the function only for an infinitesimal change in the variable X. For larger changes such as to X_2 or X_3, the slopes of the arcs AB and AC are not accurate representations of the slopes of the function over those values of X and Y. They are in fact approximations or averages over the wider range of X and Y values. For decision-making purposes we are typically concerned with the incremental units of output (or some other variable) and hence require the more accurate marginal

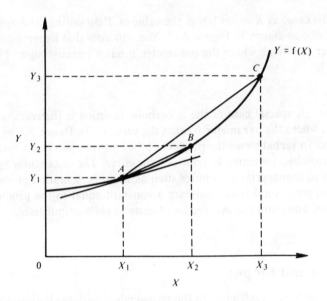

FIGURE A-8.   Change in Slope as ΔX is Increased

relationship between variables. It is therefore important that we understand the rules of derivation for use in optimization procedures.[1]

Rules of Derivation

Constants. Since the derivative shows the amount by which the dependent variable changes for a change in an independent variable and since a constant by definition does not change, it is clear that the derivative of a constant must be zero. Therefore,

$$\text{If } Y = a, \text{ then } \frac{dY}{dX} = 0$$

The Power Rule. When the function includes a term that is raised to the first or higher degree, we use the power rule, which may be stated as follows:

$$\text{If } Y = aX^b, \text{ then } \frac{dY}{dX} = baX^{b-1}$$

---

[1]These rules are stated without proof. See W. J. Baumol, *Economic Theory and Operations Analysis*, 4th ed., chap. 4 (Englewood Cliffs, N.J.: Prentice-Hall, Inc., 1976), or any good introductory calculus textbook, for formal proofs.

Example: To illustrate this rule, let us begin with a first-degree function such as $Y = aX$. Since X is implicitly equal to X^1, it is clear that the application of the power rule reduces the X term to X^0. Since X^0 equals 1, the derivative of $Y = aX$ is simply the coefficient of the X term. Thus, if $Y = aX$, then

$$\frac{dY}{dX} = 1 \cdot a \cdot X^{1-1}$$

$$= 1 \cdot a \cdot X^0$$

$$= 1 \cdot a \cdot 1$$

$$= a$$

For higher-degree terms the power function is applied similarly. Suppose $Y = a + bX^2$, then

$$\frac{dY}{dX} = 2bX^{2-1}$$

$$= 2bX^1$$

$$= 2bX$$

To demonstrate the power rule in the context of terms of various degrees, consider the function $Y = 5 + 3X + 2X^2 + 5X^3$. Treating one term at a time, $dY/dX = 3 + 4X + 15X^2$. (Is that correct? Confirm it for yourself, using the above steps.)

The Function of a Function Rule.   In the case where Y and X are related through an intermediate variable Z, to find the change in Y caused by a variation in X we need first to ascertain the impact on Z of the change in X, and then multiply this by the impact of a variation in Z upon Y. Thus,

$$\boxed{\begin{array}{l} \text{If } Y = f(Z) \text{ and } Z = f(X), \\[2mm] \text{then } \dfrac{dY}{dX} = \dfrac{dY}{dZ} \cdot \dfrac{dZ}{dX} \end{array}}$$

Example: If $Y = 4 + 6Z^2$ and $Z = 8 + 3X^3$, then

$$\frac{dY}{dX} = 12Z \cdot 9X^2$$

$$= 108ZX^2$$

The Chain Rule.   Where Y is the product of two variables X and Z which are themselves related, and we wish to find the derivative of Y with respect to X, we must consider both the "direct" influence on Y of a change in X and the "indirect" influence on Y of the change in Z that the change in X provokes. Thus,

$$\text{If } Y = ZX \text{ where } X = f(Z),$$
$$\text{then } \frac{dY}{dX} = Z + X\frac{dZ}{dX}$$

Partial Derivatives

When a function has multiple independent variables and, consequently, each independent variable is only one of a number of variables that affect the value of the dependent variable Y, we take what is known as the partial derivative of the function for each independent variable. This is equivalent to the *ceteris paribus* assumption in economics; that is, we examine the influence of one of the independent variables upon the dependent variable while holding all other variables constant. The partial derivative thus shows the impact upon Y of an infinitesimal change in one of the independent variables while all other independent variables are held constant. By convention, and to distinguish it from the derivative of functions with only one independent variable, we depict the partial derivatives by the lowercase delta (δ), rather than the lowercase d as used above. Thus if Y is a function of several variables such as

$$Y = a + bX + cX^2 + dZ + eZ^2 + fQ^3$$

then

$$\frac{\delta Y}{\delta X} = b + 2cX$$

and

$$\frac{\delta Y}{\delta Z} = d + 2eZ$$

and

$$\frac{\delta Y}{\delta Q} = 3fQ^2$$

Each partial derivative shows the marginal impact of one of the independent variables upon the dependent variable while holding constant the impact of the other independent variables.

Maximum and Minimum Values of Functions

In the above we have been concerned with "first" derivatives, which show the slope of the function as the independent variable (or *one* of the independent variables) is varied by a small amount. The first derivative thus shows the rate of change of the dependent variable relative to the specified independent variable. With curvilinear functions that rate of change will vary for different starting points in the value of X. In Figure A-9 the quadratic function $Y = -10 + 30X - 3X^2$ is graphed, and it should be appreciated that the derivative of the function is positive initially where the graph is sloping upward and to the right, but it is negative later where the value of Y decreases as additional increments of X are made. It is clear that the derivative is taking progressively declining values, being positive at first, falling to zero, and thereafter becoming increasingly negative. You may confirm this by taking the derivative of the function (that is, $dY/dX = 30 - 6X$) and substituting values for X into this expression. Clearly for values of X less than 5 the derivative is positive, but where X is equal to 5 the derivative is zero, and for values of X greater than 5 the derivative is negative.

Rule: The above discussion allows us to establish a simple rule for finding the maximum of a function. To find the value of X for which Y is maximized, we simply set the derivative of the function equal to zero and solve for the value of X. Thus where we have

$$\frac{dY}{dX} = 30 - 6X = 0$$

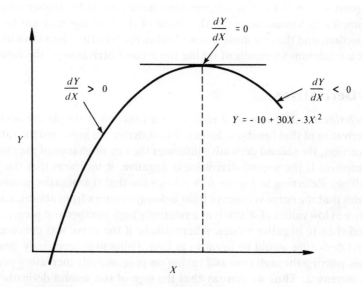

FIGURE A-9.   Changing Value of the First Derivative

Solving for X,

$$6X = 30$$
$$X = 5$$

Thus Y is at a maximum when X takes the value of 5.

Note: A zero first derivative may indicate a *minimum* of a function rather than a maximum if the function is concave from above rather than concave from below. Suppose

$$Y = 100 - 16X + 2X^2$$

The first derivative of this function is

$$\frac{dY}{dX} = -16 + 4X$$

and is equal to zero when

$$X = 4$$

Inspection of the function should indicate to you that it is a parabola that is concave from above, since for small values of X it will be falling, reaching a minimum when X equals 4, and it will rise progressively more steeply for higher values of X. In more complex functions, however, the shape of the function may not be obvious from inspection, and thus we must check whether the zero first derivative implies a maximum or a minimum by means of taking the *second* derivative of the function.

Second Derivatives

■ *Definition:*   The *second derivative* of a function is simply the derivative of the first derivative of that function. Since the first derivative indicated the rate of change of the function, the second derivative indicates the rate of change of the rate of change of the function. If the second derivative is negative, it indicates that the rate of change is falling. Referring to Figure A–9 we can see that the negative second derivative indicates that the curve is concave from below (or convex from above), since the first derivative at low values of X starts at a relatively high number and progressively falls to zero and then to negative values. Alternatively, if the curve was concave from above, the first derivative would be negative at first, rising to progressively smaller negative values, passing through zero and taking on progressively increasing positive values as X is increased. Thus we can say that the sign of the second derivative will be negative when the first derivative is set equal to zero if the function is concave from below and that the sign of the second derivative will be positive when the first derivative is set equal to zero when the function is concave from above.

Rule: The "second-order" condition for a maximum is that the second derivative must be negative, and the second-order condition for a minimum is that the second derivative must be positive.

Referring back to the function graphed in Figure A-9, where the first derivative was $dY/dX = 30 - 6X$, we may confirm that the sign of the second derivative is negative. The second derivative is equal to the derivative of the first derivative and is expressed as follows:

$$\frac{d^2Y}{dX^2} = -6$$

where the squared terms indicate that the value shown is the second derivative of the function. For the other function mentioned above, the first derivative was $dY/dX = -16 + 4X$. The second derivative of this derivative is equal to

$$\frac{d^2Y}{dX^2} = 4$$

The signs of these second derivatives confirm that the function of Y reaches a *maximum* in the first case when $dY/dX = 0$ and that it reaches a *minimum* in the second case when the first derivative is set equal to zero.

Use of Derivatives in Managerial Economics

Since one of the central aims of managerial economics is to establish rules and principles for achieving objectives, it is not surprising that derivatives may be helpful, since in many cases we are interested in maximizing profits, or minimizing costs, or optimizing some other variable.

Example: Suppose that a particular firm's cost and revenue functions are of quadratic form as follows:

$$TC = 1,500 + 50Q + 2Q^2 \tag{A-11}$$

$$TR = 250Q - 3Q^2 \tag{A-12}$$

where TC represents total costs; TR represents total revenues; and Q represents the output or sales level. Profits, represented by π, are the surplus of revenues over costs. Hence,

$$\pi = TR - TC$$
$$= 250Q - 3Q^2 - (1,500 + 50Q + 2Q^2)$$
$$= 250Q - 3Q^2 - 1,500 - 50Q - 2Q^2$$
$$\therefore \ \pi = -1,500 + 200Q - 5Q^2 \qquad \text{(A-13)}$$

represents the profit function. Assuming that the firm wishes to choose the output level that maximizes profits, we may find that output level by setting the first derivative of the profit function equal to zero for solving for Q. Thus,

$$\frac{d\pi}{dQ} = 200 - 10Q = 0$$
$$10Q = 200$$
$$Q = 20$$

The output level that appears to maximize profits is thus 20 units (where the "units" may represent single units, thousands, or millions, depending upon the initial specification of those units). To ensure that this output level represents the maximum profit rather than the minimum profit, we check the second-order condition. The second derivative of the profit function,

$$\frac{d^2\pi}{d^2Q} = -10$$

is negative, indicating that profits are indeed maximized at the output level of 20 units.

An alternative approach to finding the profit-maximizing output level using derivatives is as follows. We know that profits will be maximized when the difference between revenues and costs is greatest. In terms of Figure A-10, where the cost and revenue functions are depicted, we wish to find the output level for which the vertical separation of the two curves is greatest.

Observe that the slope (or derivative) of the cost function takes increasingly larger values as output is increased, while the slope of the revenue function takes increasingly reduced values. At some point the slopes of the two functions will be equal, and hence tangents to the two functions at that output level must be parallel lines, as shown in Figure A-10. Since a property of parallel lines is that they maintain a constant vertical separation, it must be true that as the slope of the cost function continues to increase and as the slope of the revenue function continues to decrease for larger output levels, the vertical distance between the two functions must be decreasing. Thus profits are maximized when the slopes (or first derivatives) of the functions are equal.

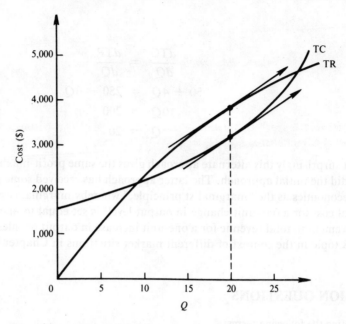

FIGURE A-10. Hypothetical Cost and Revenue Functions

To solve for the output level where the slopes (first derivatives) are equal, let us restate the cost and revenue functions:

$$TC = 1,500 + 50Q + 2Q^2 \qquad \text{(A-11)}$$

$$TR = 250Q - 3Q^2 \qquad \text{(A-12)}$$

Finding the first derivatives of these functions, equating them, and solving for Q, we have

$$\frac{dTC}{dQ} = 50 + 4Q$$

$$\frac{dTR}{dQ} = 250 - 6Q$$

Set

$$\frac{d\text{TC}}{dQ} = \frac{d\text{TR}}{dQ}$$
$$50 + 4Q = 250 - 6Q$$
$$10Q = 200$$
$$Q = 20$$

Not surprisingly this alternate approach gives the same profit-maximizing output level as did the initial approach. The latter approach has received some fame (or notoriety) in economics as the "marginalist principle," whereby marginal cost (the increment to total cost for a one-unit change in output level) is set equal to marginal revenue (the increment to total revenue for a one-unit increase in output or sales level). We discuss this topic in the context of different market situations in Chapter 9.

DISCUSSION QUESTIONS

A-1. Define the following terms:
(a) function
(b) independent variable
(c) dependent variable
(d) slope parameter
(e) constant
(f) intercept
(g) quadratic function
(h) exponent

A-2. Explain the logic of using the derivatives of a function to find the maximum or minimum of that function.

A-3. Explain the power rule of differentiation.

A-4. Explain the function-of-a-function rule of differentiation.

A-5. Explain the chain rule of differentiation.

PROBLEMS AND SHORT CASES

A-1. Rewrite $Y = f(X)$ in symbolic form as a function that is
(a) linear
(b) quadratic
(c) cubic
(d) exponential
(e) power
(f) hyperbolic

A-2. Find the first derivative, with respect to X, of the following functions:

(a) $Y = 36 + 4.5X^3$

(b) $Y = 8 - 3Z^2$, where $Z = 4 + 3X^3$

(c) $Y = 7KX$, where $X = 3 - 2K^2$

(d) $Y = -16 + 4J^2 - 6K^3$, where $J = 8 - 6X^2$ and $K = -3 + 4X^3$

(e) $Y = 3M(4N^2)$, where $M = -6 + 2X$ and $N = 4 - 2X^2$

(f) $Y = 4e^{2X}$

A-3. Solve for the maximum or minimum value of the following functions, using the second-order condition to specify whether it is a maximum or a minimum:

(a) $Y = -32 + 6X - 2X^2$

(b) $Y = 28 - 8X + X^2$

(c) $A = 4,285 - 625B + 5B^2$

(d) $K = 178 + 40J - 6J^2$

A-4. Suppose the monthly cost of maintaining a certain machine in operating order is a function of the time elapsed between shutdowns for servicing and maintenance as follows: $C = 1,400 - 30T + 0.7T^2$ where C represents cost in dollars and T represents time between services in hours. What is the optimal period between services?

SUGGESTED REFERENCES AND FURTHER READING

Baumol, W. J. *Economic Theory and Operations Analysis* (4th ed.), chaps. 2, 3, and 4. Englewood Cliffs, N.J.: Prentice-Hall, Inc., 1976.

Childress, R. L. *Calculus for Business and Economics* (2nd ed.). Englewood Cliffs, N.J.: Prentice-Hall, Inc., 1978.

Khoury, S. J., and T. D. Parsons. *Mathematical Methods in Finance and Economics*. New York: Elsevier-North Holland, Inc., 1981.

Kooros, A. *Elements of Mathematical Economics*, chaps. 1, 2, 5, 6, and 7. Boston: Houghton Mifflin, 1965.

APPENDIX B

Present Value Tables

B-1. Present Value of $1 Received at the End of N Years

B-2. Present Value of an Annuity of $1

B-3. Present Value of $1 Received throughout the Year on a Daily Basis

TABLE B-1. Present Value of $1 Received at the End of N Years

							DISCOUNT RATE							
Years Hence	1%	2%	3%	4%	5%	6%	7%	8%	9%	10%	11%	12%	13%	14%
1	.9901	.9804	.9709	.9615	.9524	.9434	.9346	.9259	.9174	.9091	.9009	.8929	.8850	.8772
2	.9803	.9612	.9426	.9246	.9070	.8900	.8734	.8573	.8417	.8264	.8116	.7972	.7831	.7695
3	.9706	.9423	.9151	.8890	.8638	.8396	.8163	.7938	.7722	.7513	.7312	.7118	.6931	.6750
4	.9610	.9238	.8885	.8548	.8227	.7921	.7629	.7350	.7084	.6830	.6587	.6355	.6133	.5921
5	.9515	.9057	.8626	.8219	.7835	.7473	.7130	.6806	.6499	.6209	.5935	.5674	.5428	.5194
6	.9420	.8880	.8375	.7903	.7462	.7050	.6663	.6302	.5963	.5645	.5346	.5066	.4803	.4556
7	.9327	.8706	.8131	.7599	.7107	.6651	.6227	.5835	.5470	.5132	.4817	.4523	.4251	.3996
8	.9235	.8535	.7894	.7307	.6768	.6274	.5820	.5403	.5019	.4665	.4339	.4039	.3762	.3506
9	.9143	.8368	.7664	.7026	.6446	.5919	.5439	.5002	.4604	.4241	.3909	.3606	.3329	.3075
10	.9053	.8203	.7441	.6756	.6139	.5584	.5083	.4632	.4224	.3855	.3522	.3220	.2946	.2697
11	.8963	.8043	.7224	.6496	.5847	.5268	.4751	.4289	.3875	.3505	.3173	.2875	.2607	.2366
12	.8874	.7885	.7014	.6246	.5568	.4970	.4440	.3971	.3555	.3186	.2858	.2567	.2307	.2076
13	.8787	.7730	.6810	.6006	.5303	.4688	.4150	.3677	.3262	.2897	.2575	.2292	.2042	.1821
14	.8700	.7579	.6611	.5775	.5051	.4423	.3878	.3405	.2992	.2633	.2320	.2046	.1807	.1597
15	.8613	.7430	.6419	.5553	.4810	.4173	.3624	.3152	.2745	.2394	.2090	.1827	.1599	.1401
16	.8528	.7284	.6232	.5339	.4581	.3936	.3387	.2919	.2519	.2176	.1883	.1631	.1415	.1229
17	.8444	.7142	.6050	.5134	.4363	.3714	.3166	.2703	.2311	.1978	.1696	.1456	.1252	.1078
18	.8360	.7002	.5874	.4936	.4155	.3503	.2959	.2502	.2120	.1799	.1528	.1300	.1108	.0946
19	.8277	.6864	.5703	.4746	.3957	.3305	.2765	.2317	.1945	.1635	.1377	.1161	.0981	.0829
20	.8195	.6730	.5537	.4564	.3769	.3118	.2584	.2145	.1784	.1486	.1240	.1037	.0868	.0728
21	.8114	.6598	.5375	.4388	.3589	.2942	.2415	.1987	.1637	.1351	.1117	.0926	.0768	.0638
22	.8034	.6468	.5219	.4220	.3418	.2775	.2257	.1839	.1502	.1228	.1007	.0826	.0680	.0560
23	.7954	.6342	.5067	.4057	.3256	.2618	.2109	.1703	.1378	.1117	.0907	.0738	.0601	.0491
24	.7876	.6217	.4919	.3901	.3101	.2470	.1971	.1577	.1264	.1015	.0817	.0659	.0532	.0431
25	.7798	.6095	.4776	.3751	.2953	.2330	.1842	.1460	.1160	.0923	.0736	.0588	.0471	.0378

(Continued)

615

TABLE B-1. *Continued*

DISCOUNT RATE

Years Hence	15%	16%	17%	18%	19%	20%	21%	22%	23%	24%	25%	26%	27%	28%
1	.8696	.8621	.8547	.8475	.8403	.8333	.8264	.8197	.8130	.8065	.8000	.7937	.7874	.7813
2	.7561	.7432	.7305	.7182	.7062	.6944	.6830	.6719	.6610	.6504	.6400	.6299	.6200	.6104
3	.6575	.6407	.6244	.6086	.5934	.5787	.5645	.5507	.5374	.5245	.5120	.4999	.4882	.4768
4	.5718	.5523	.5337	.5158	.4987	.4823	.4665	.4514	.4369	.4230	.4096	.3968	.3844	.3725
5	.4972	.4761	.4561	.4371	.4190	.4019	.3855	.3700	.3552	.3411	.3277	.3149	.3027	.2910
6	.4323	.4104	.3898	.3704	.3521	.3349	.3186	.3033	.2888	.2751	.2621	.2499	.2383	.2274
7	.3759	.3538	.3332	.3139	.2959	.2791	.2633	.2486	.2348	.2218	.2097	.1983	.1877	.1776
8	.3269	.3050	.2848	.2660	.2487	.2326	.2176	.2038	.1909	.1789	.1678	.1574	.1478	.1388
9	.2843	.2630	.2434	.2255	.2090	.1938	.1799	.1670	.1552	.1443	.1342	.1249	.1164	.1084
10	.2472	.2267	.2080	.1911	.1756	.1615	.1486	.1369	.1262	.1164	.1074	.0992	.0916	.0847
11	.2149	.1954	.1778	.1619	.1476	.1346	.1228	.1122	.1026	.0938	.0859	.0787	.0721	.0662
12	.1869	.1685	.1520	.1372	.1240	.1122	.1015	.0920	.0834	.0757	.0687	.0625	.0568	.0517
13	.1625	.1452	.1299	.1163	.1042	.0935	.0839	.0754	.0678	.0610	.0550	.0496	.0447	.0404
14	.1413	.1252	.1110	.0985	.0876	.0779	.0693	.0618	.0551	.0492	.0440	.0393	.0352	.0316
15	.1229	.1079	.0949	.0835	.0736	.0649	.0573	.0507	.0448	.0397	.0352	.0312	.0277	.0247
16	.1069	.0930	.0811	.0708	.0618	.0541	.0474	.0415	.0364	.0320	.0281	.0248	.0218	.0193
17	.0929	.0802	.0693	.0600	.0520	.0451	.0391	.0340	.0296	.0258	.0225	.0197	.0172	.0150
18	.0808	.0691	.0592	.0508	.0437	.0376	.0323	.0279	.0241	.0208	.0180	.0156	.0135	.0118
19	.0703	.0596	.0506	.0431	.0367	.0313	.0267	.0229	.0196	.0168	.0144	.0124	.0107	.0092
20	.0611	.0514	.0433	.0365	.0308	.0261	.0221	.0187	.0159	.0135	.0115	.0098	.0084	.0072
21	.0531	.0443	.0370	.0309	.0259	.0217	.0183	.0154	.0129	.0109	.0092	.0078	.0066	.0056
22	.0462	.0382	.0316	.0262	.0218	.0181	.0151	.0126	.0105	.0088	.0074	.0062	.0052	.0044
23	.0402	.0329	.0270	.0222	.0183	.0151	.0125	.0103	.0086	.0071	.0059	.0049	.0041	.0034
24	.0349	.0284	.0231	.0188	.0154	.0126	.0103	.0085	.0070	.0057	.0047	.0039	.0032	.0027
25	.0304	.0245	.0197	.0160	.0129	.0105	.0085	.0069	.0057	.0046	.0038	.0031	.0025	.0021

TABLE B–2. Present Value of an Annuity of $1

| | DISCOUNT RATE | | | | | | | | | | | | | |
Years Hence	1%	2%	3%	4%	5%	6%	7%	8%	9%	10%	11%	12%	13%	14%
1	0.9901	0.9804	0.9709	0.9615	0.9524	0.9434	0.9346	0.9259	0.9174	0.9091	0.9009	0.8929	0.8850	0.8772
2	1.9704	1.9416	1.9135	1.8861	1.8594	1.8334	1.8080	1.7833	1.7591	1.7355	1.7125	1.6901	1.6681	1.6467
3	2.9410	2.8839	2.8286	2.7751	2.7232	2.6730	2.6243	2.5771	2.5313	2.4869	2.4437	2.4018	2.3612	2.3216
4	3.9020	3.8077	3.7171	3.6299	3.5460	3.4651	3.3872	3.3121	3.2397	3.1699	3.1024	3.0373	2.9745	2.9137
5	4.8534	4.7135	4.5797	4.4518	4.3295	4.2124	4.1002	3.9927	3.8897	3.7908	3.6959	3.6048	3.5172	3.4331
6	5.7955	5.6014	5.4172	5.2421	5.0757	4.9173	4.7665	4.6229	4.4859	4.3553	4.2305	4.1114	3.9976	3.8887
7	6.7282	6.4720	6.2303	6.0021	5.7864	5.5824	5.3893	5.2064	5.0330	4.8684	4.7122	4.5638	4.4226	4.2883
8	7.6517	7.3255	7.0197	6.7327	6.4632	6.2098	5.9713	5.7466	5.5348	5.3349	5.1461	4.9676	4.7988	4.6389
9	8.5660	8.1622	7.7861	7.4353	7.1078	6.8017	6.5152	6.2469	5.9952	5.7590	5.5370	5.3282	5.1317	4.9464
10	9.4713	8.9826	8.5302	8.1109	7.7217	7.3601	7.0236	6.7101	6.4177	6.1446	5.8892	5.6502	5.4262	5.2161
11	10.3676	9.7869	9.2526	8.7605	8.3064	7.8869	7.4987	7.1390	6.8052	6.4951	6.2065	5.9377	5.6869	5.4527
12	11.2551	10.5753	9.9540	9.3851	8.8633	8.3838	7.9427	7.5361	7.1607	6.8137	6.4924	6.1944	5.9176	5.6603
13	12.1337	11.3484	10.6350	9.9856	9.3936	8.8527	8.3577	7.9038	7.4869	7.1034	6.7499	6.4235	6.1218	5.8424
14	13.0037	12.1063	11.2961	10.5631	9.8986	9.2950	8.7455	8.2442	7.7862	7.3667	6.9819	6.6282	6.3025	6.0021
15	13.8651	12.8493	11.9379	11.1184	10.3797	9.7122	9.1079	8.5595	8.0607	7.6061	7.1909	6.8109	6.4624	6.1422
16	14.7179	13.5777	12.5611	11.6523	10.8378	10.1059	9.4466	8.8514	8.3126	7.8237	7.3792	6.9740	6.6039	6.2651
17	15.5623	14.2919	13.1661	12.1657	11.2741	10.4773	9.7632	9.1216	8.5436	8.0216	7.5488	7.1196	6.7291	6.3729
18	16.3983	14.9920	13.7535	12.6593	11.6896	10.8276	10.0591	9.3719	8.7556	8.2014	7.7016	7.2497	6.8399	6.4674
19	17.2260	15.6785	14.3238	13.1339	12.0853	11.1581	10.3356	9.6036	8.9501	8.3649	7.8393	7.3658	6.9380	6.5504
20	18.0456	16.3514	14.8775	13.5903	12.4622	11.4699	10.5940	9.8181	9.1285	8.5136	7.9633	7.4694	7.0248	6.6231
21	18.8570	17.0112	15.4150	14.0292	12.8212	11.7641	10.8355	10.0168	9.2922	8.6487	8.0751	7.5620	7.1016	6.6870
22	19.6604	17.6581	15.9369	14.4511	13.1630	12.0416	11.0612	10.2007	9.4424	8.7715	8.1757	7.6446	7.1695	6.7429
23	20.4558	18.2922	16.4436	14.8568	13.4886	12.3034	11.2722	10.3711	9.5802	8.8832	8.2664	7.7184	7.2297	6.7921
24	21.2434	18.9139	16.9355	15.2470	13.7986	12.5504	11.4693	10.5288	9.7066	8.9847	8.3481	7.7843	7.2829	6.8351
25	22.0232	19.5235	17.4131	15.6221	14.0939	12.7834	11.6536	10.6748	9.8226	9.0770	8.4217	7.8431	7.3300	6.8729

(Continued)

TABLE B-2. *Continued*

Years Hence	DISCOUNT RATE													
	15%	16%	17%	18%	19%	20%	21%	22%	23%	24%	25%	26%	27%	28%
1	0.8696	0.8621	0.8547	0.8475	0.8403	0.8333	0.8264	0.8197	0.8130	0.8065	0.8000	0.7937	0.7874	0.7813
2	1.6257	1.6052	1.5852	1.5656	1.5465	1.5278	1.5095	1.4915	1.4740	1.4568	1.4400	1.4235	1.4074	1.3916
3	2.2832	2.2459	2.2096	2.1743	2.1399	2.1065	2.0739	2.0422	2.0114	1.9813	1.9520	1.9234	1.8956	1.8684
4	2.8550	2.7982	2.7432	2.6901	2.6386	2.5887	2.5404	2.4936	2.4483	2.4043	2.3616	2.3202	2.2800	2.2410
5	3.3522	3.2743	3.1993	3.1272	3.0576	2.9906	2.9260	2.8636	2.8035	2.7454	2.6893	2.6351	2.5827	2.5320
6	3.7845	3.6847	3.5892	3.4976	3.4098	3.3255	3.2446	3.1669	3.0923	3.0205	2.9514	2.8850	2.8210	2.7594
7	4.1604	4.0386	3.9224	3.8115	3.7057	3.6046	3.5079	3.4155	3.3270	3.2423	3.1611	3.0833	3.0087	2.9370
8	4.4873	4.3436	4.2072	4.0776	3.9544	3.8372	3.7256	3.6193	3.5179	3.4212	3.3289	3.2407	3.1564	3.0758
9	4.7716	4.6065	4.4506	4.3030	4.1633	4.0310	3.9054	3.7863	3.6731	3.5655	3.4631	3.3657	3.2728	3.1842
10	5.0188	4.8332	4.6586	4.4941	4.3389	4.1925	4.0541	3.9232	3.7993	3.6819	3.5705	3.4648	3.3644	3.2689
11	5.2337	5.0286	4.8364	4.6560	4.4865	4.3271	4.1769	4.0354	3.9018	3.7757	3.6564	3.5435	3.4365	3.3351
12	5.4206	5.1971	4.9884	4.7932	4.6105	4.4392	4.2784	4.1274	3.9852	3.8514	3.7251	3.6059	3.4933	3.3868
13	5.5831	5.3423	5.1183	4.9095	4.7147	4.5327	4.3624	4.2028	4.0530	3.9124	3.7801	3.6555	3.5381	3.4272
14	5.7245	5.4675	5.2293	5.0081	4.8023	4.6106	4.4317	4.2646	4.1082	3.9616	3.8241	3.6949	3.5733	3.4587
15	5.8474	5.5755	5.3242	5.0916	4.8759	4.6755	4.4890	4.3152	4.1530	4.0013	3.8593	3.7261	3.6010	3.4834
16	5.9542	5.6685	5.4053	5.1624	4.9377	4.7296	4.5364	4.3567	4.1894	4.0333	3.8874	3.7509	3.6228	3.5026
17	6.0472	5.7487	5.4746	5.2223	4.9897	4.7746	4.5755	4.3908	4.2190	4.0591	3.9099	3.7705	3.6400	3.5177
18	6.1280	5.8178	5.5339	5.2732	5.0333	4.8122	4.6079	4.4187	4.2431	4.0799	3.9279	3.7861	3.6536	3.5294
19	6.1982	5.8775	5.5845	5.3162	5.0700	4.8435	4.6346	4.4415	4.2627	4.0967	3.9424	3.7985	3.6642	3.5386
20	6.2593	5.9288	5.6278	5.3527	5.1009	4.8696	4.6567	4.4603	4.2786	4.1103	3.9539	3.8083	3.6726	3.5458
21	6.3125	5.9731	5.6648	5.3837	5.1268	4.8913	4.6750	4.4756	4.2916	4.1212	3.9631	3.8161	3.6792	3.5514
22	6.3587	6.0113	5.6964	5.4099	5.1486	4.9094	4.6900	4.4882	4.3021	4.1300	3.9705	3.8223	3.6844	3.5558
23	6.3988	6.0442	5.7234	5.4321	5.1668	4.9245	4.7025	4.4985	4.3106	4.1371	3.9764	3.8273	3.6885	3.5592
24	6.4338	6.0726	5.7465	5.4509	5.1822	4.9371	4.7128	4.5070	4.3176	4.1428	3.9811	3.8312	3.6918	3.5619
25	6.4641	6.0971	5.7662	5.4669	5.1951	4.9476	4.7213	4.5139	4.3232	4.1474	3.9849	3.8342	3.6943	3.5640

TABLE B-3. Present Value of $1 Received throughout the Year on a Daily Basis

Years Hence	1%	2%	3%	4%	5%	6%	7%	8%	9%	10%	11%	12%	13%	14%
								DISCOUNT RATE						
1	.9950	.9900	.9851	.9802	.9753	.9705	.9657	.9609	.9562	.9515	.9468	.9422	.9376	.9330
2	.9851	.9704	.9560	.9418	.9278	.9140	.9004	.8871	.8739	.8610	.8482	.8357	.8233	.8111
3	.9753	.9512	.9277	.9049	.8825	.8608	.8396	.8189	.7987	.7790	.7599	.7412	.7229	.7052
4	.9656	.9324	.9003	.8694	.8395	.8107	.7828	.7559	.7300	.7049	.6807	.6574	.6348	.6131
5	.9560	.9139	.8737	.8353	.7986	.7634	.7299	.6978	.6672	.6378	.6098	.5831	.5575	.5330
6	.9465	.8958	.8479	.8025	.7596	.7190	.6805	.6442	.6097	.5772	.5463	.5171	.4895	.4634
7	.9371	.8781	.8228	.7711	.7226	.6771	.6345	.5946	.5573	.5222	.4894	.4587	.4298	.4028
8	.9277	.8607	.7985	.7408	.6873	.6377	.5916	.5489	.5093	.4725	.4384	.4068	.3775	.3502
9	.9185	.8437	.7749	.7118	.6538	.6006	.5517	.5067	.4655	.4276	.3928	.3608	.3315	.3045
10	.9094	.8270	.7520	.6839	.6219	.5656	.5144	.4678	.4254	.3869	.3519	.3200	.2911	.2647
11	.9003	.8106	.7298	.6571	.5916	.5327	.4796	.4318	.3888	.3501	.3152	.2838	.2556	.2301
12	.8914	.7945	.7082	.6313	.5627	.5016	.4472	.3986	.3553	.3168	.2824	.2517	.2244	.2001
13	.8825	.7788	.6873	.6066	.5353	.4724	.4169	.3680	.3248	.2866	.2530	.2233	.1971	.1739
14	.8737	.7634	.6670	.5828	.5092	.4449	.3888	.3397	.2968	.2594	.2266	.1980	.1731	.1512
15	.8650	.7483	.6473	.5599	.4844	.4190	.3625	.3136	.2713	.2347	.2030	.1756	.1520	.1315
16	.8564	.7334	.6281	.5380	.4607	.3946	.3380	.2895	.2479	.2124	.1819	.1558	.1334	.1143
17	.8479	.7189	.6096	.5169	.4383	.3716	.3151	.2672	.2266	.1921	.1629	.1382	.1172	.0994
18	.8395	.7047	.5916	.4966	.4169	.3500	.2938	.2467	.2071	.1739	.1460	.1226	.1029	.0864
19	.8311	.6907	.5741	.4771	.3966	.3296	.2740	.2277	.1893	.1573	.1308	.1087	.0904	.0751
20	.8228	.6771	.5571	.4584	.3772	.3104	.2554	.2102	.1730	.1424	.1171	.0964	.0793	.0653
21	.8146	.6637	.5407	.4405	.3588	.2923	.2382	.1940	.1581	.1288	.1049	.0855	.0697	.0568
22	.8065	.6505	.5247	.4232	.3413	.2753	.2221	.1791	.1445	.1166	.0940	.0758	.0612	.0494
23	.7985	.6376	.5092	.4066	.3247	.2593	.2071	.1654	.1321	.1055	.0842	.0673	.0537	.0429
24	.7906	.6250	.4941	.3907	.3089	.2442	.1931	.1526	.1207	.0954	.0755	.0597	.0472	.0373
25	.7827	.6126	.4795	.3753	.2938	.2300	.1800	.1409	.1103	.0863	.0676	.0529	.0414	.0324

(Continued)

TABLE B-3. *Continued*

						DISCOUNT RATE								
Years Hence	15%	16%	17%	18%	19%	20%	21%	22%	23%	24%	25%	26%	27%	28%
1	.9284	.9239	.9194	.9150	.9105	.9061	.9017	.8974	.8931	.8888	.8845	.8803	.8761	.8719
2	.7991	.7873	.7757	.7643	.7530	.7419	.7310	.7202	.7096	.6992	.6889	.6788	.6689	.6590
3	.6878	.6709	.6545	.6384	.6227	.6075	.5926	.5780	.5639	.5501	.5366	.5235	.5106	.4981
4	.5921	.5718	.5522	.5333	.5150	.4974	.4803	.4639	.4480	.4327	.4179	.4036	.3899	.3765
5	.5096	.4872	.4659	.4454	.4259	.4072	.3894	.3723	.3560	.3404	.3255	.3113	.2976	.2846
6	.4386	.4152	.3931	.3721	.3522	.3334	.3157	.2988	.2829	.2678	.2535	.2400	.2272	.2151
7	.3775	.3538	.3316	.3108	.2913	.2730	.2559	.2398	.2248	.2107	.1975	.1851	.1735	.1626
8	.3250	.3015	.2798	.2596	.2409	.2235	.2074	.1925	.1786	.1657	.1538	.1427	.1324	.1229
9	.2797	.2570	.2361	.2169	.1992	.1830	.1681	.1545	.1419	.1304	.1198	.1101	.1011	.0929
10	.2408	.2190	.1992	.1811	.1648	.1499	.1363	.1240	.1128	.1026	.0933	.0849	.0772	.0702
11	.2072	.1866	.1680	.1513	.1363	.1227	.1105	.0995	.0896	.0807	.0727	.0654	.0589	.0531
12	.1784	.1590	.1418	.1264	.1127	.1005	.0896	.0799	.0712	.0635	.0566	.0505	.0450	.0401
13	.1535	.1355	.1196	.1056	.0932	.0823	.0726	.0641	.0566	.0499	.0441	.0389	.0344	.0303
14	.1321	.1155	.1009	.0882	.0771	.0673	.0589	.0514	.0450	.0393	.0343	.0300	.0262	.0229
15	.1137	.0984	.0851	.0737	.0637	.0551	.0477	.0413	.0357	.0309	.0267	.0231	.0200	.0173
16	.0979	.0839	.0718	.0615	.0527	.0452	.0387	.0331	.0284	.0243	.0208	.0178	.0153	.0131
17	.0843	.0715	.0606	.0514	.0436	.0370	.0314	.0266	.0226	.0191	.0162	.0138	.0117	.0099
18	.0725	.0609	.0511	.0429	.0360	.0303	.0254	.0213	.0179	.0150	.0126	.0106	.0089	.0075
19	.0624	.0519	.0431	.0359	.0298	.0248	.0206	.0171	.0142	.0118	.0098	.0082	.0068	.0057
20	.0537	.0442	.0364	.0300	.0247	.0203	.0167	.0137	.0113	.0093	.0077	.0063	.0052	.0043
21	.0463	.0377	.0307	.0250	.0204	.0166	.0135	.0110	.0090	.0073	.0060	.0049	.0040	.0032
22	.0398	.0321	.0259	.0209	.0169	.0136	.0110	.0089	.0071	.0058	.0047	.0038	.0030	.0024
23	.0343	.0274	.0219	.0175	.0139	.0111	.0089	.0071	.0057	.0045	.0036	.0029	.0023	.0018
24	.0295	.0233	.0184	.0146	.0115	.0091	.0072	.0057	.0045	.0036	.0028	.0022	.0018	.0014
25	.0254	.0199	.0156	.0122	.0095	.0075	.0058	.0046	.0036	.0028	.0022	.0017	.0013	.0011

Answers to the Problems

Following are brief answers to each of the end-of-chapter problems. These are typically numerical, to allow you to verify your methodology and calculations. Note that your answers may differ slightly due to rounding. In other cases, you may find that I have made a mistake. If so, please let me know, so that I can correct it as soon as possible. You can write to me at Bentley College, Waltham, MA 02254. Your help will be greatly appreciated!

CHAPTER 1

1-1. **(a)** $9,856,300.
   (b) $10,057,600 at 12%, $9,664,400 at 16%.
1-2. **(a)** $1,681.
1-3. **(a)** $273,115.
1-4. **(a)** Company A: $36,039; company B: $36,278.
   (b) Company A: $35,286; company B: $35,122.
1-5. **(a)** $2,960, using daily discount rates.
1-6. **(a)** $75,108.
   (b) $103,233.
   (c) $178,341.
   (d) No more than the NPV. In terms of your ODR.
1-7. **(a)** Project A: $67,736; project B: $76,357.
1-8. **(a)** Product A: $32,964; product B: $11,814.
1-9. **(a)** $39,500.
   (b) $36,672.
   (c) $36,523.
1-10. **(a)** Rebuild: $36,750; buy new: $37,600.
   (c) Rebuild: $34,288; buy new: $33,128.

CHAPTER 2

2-1. **(a)** Minor face-lift: expected value is $34,000; standard deviation is 24,580; coefficient of variation is 0.723. New model: EV = $34,000; SD = 60,530; CV = 1.78.

(b) EV criterion ranks them equally; CV and maximin criteria both favor minor face-lift.

(c) Minor face-lift.

2-2. (a) Hot dogs: EV = $212.50, CV = 0.356; ice cream: EV = $213.75, CV = 0.583. Risk averters, unless only very slightly risk averse, will choose hot dogs. Your certainty equivalent will indicate your degree of risk aversion.

2-3. (a) Regular store: EPV = $327,650; super store: EPV = $137,150.

2-4. (a) Lease: EPV = $12,401; buy: EPV = $11,834.

(b) Lease: SD = 7,185; buy: SD = 6,637.

(c) EV favors lease; CV favors buy; maximin favors lease; CE is ambiguous, depending on risk return trade-off. Is management willing to accept $547 more risk along with $567 more expected return?

2-5. (a) Project A: EPV = $1,044,980, SD = 1,042,376; project B: EPV = $1,294,310, SD = $1,541,660.

2-6. (a) High: EPV = $1,505; medium: EPV = $3,806; low: EPV = $-292.

(b) No, EPV of bond alternative is zero.

(c) High, low, medium.

(d) Medium, high, low.

(e) Not for a risk averter.

2-7. (a) Assuming daily cash flows, necktie A: EPV = $21,809, MIN = $875, CV = 0.485; necktie B: EPV = $33,847, MIN = $3,125, CV = 0.551; necktie C: EPV = $40,900, MIN = 5,375, CV = 0.633.

2-8. (a) Product A: EPV = $38,316, SD = 27,757; product B: EPV = $68,713, SD = 126,313; product C: EPV = $54,411, SD = 44,036.

2-9. (a) Christmas trees: EPV = $173,915, SD = 249,519; fast food: EPV = $180,161, SD = 146,543.

2-10. (a) Plan A: EPV = $36,006; plan B: EPV = $61,672.

(b) Plan A: SD = 32,874; plan B: EPV = 49,162.

CHAPTER 3

3-1. (a) The budget line will swing inward, restricting the consumer to a lower indifference curve and fewer units of the product.

3-2. (a) *Ceteris paribus* allows us to isolate the impact of one variable at a time. First the budget line swings outward, then it shifts outward, and finally the indifference curves become flatter.

3-3. (a) An advertising campaign may improve consumer perceptions of the product, thus shifting the efficiency frontier outward, and may also change tastes in favor of the attributes embodied in product X, thus steepening indifference curves. Both effects will cause the consumer to buy more, prior to a price increase. A price increase would then cut sales back, but quantity demanded would be higher than it would have been without the prior advertising campaign.

3-4. (a) Mr. A's indifference curves will be flatter than Ms. B's, and his demand curve will be more elastic in the relevant range.

3-5. (a) The consumers' choices will depend on their marginal rates of substitution between power and economy.

3-6. (a) About 97 cents.

(b) All consumers previously buying brand A, as well as some previously buying brand B, will switch to Norbert. Only those with MRS > 6.2 will continue to buy brand B.

3-7. **(b)** The market share data tells us something about the distribution of the slopes of consumers' indifference curves. Repositioning into a heavier part of this distribution will mean more customers are gained than lost. It is not clear that Snackers can do this without a price increase or a higher nutrient-calorie ratio.

3-8. **(a)** The efficiency frontier is linear across product rays B, D, and C. Plan A involves repositioning into a relatively crowded part of the market. Plan B looks more promising.

3-9. **(a)** Sportscar A. (Hint: Set the value of reliability equal to 1.)

(b) Sportscar A.

(c) Sportscar B, using the EV criterion, but sportscar A is favored by the minimax, CV, and CE criteria.

3-10. **(a)** More convenient Phoneshop.

(b) Either the more convenient or the less convenient Phoneshop, depending on the curvature (MRS) of the consumer's indifference curve.

APPENDIX 3A

3A-1. If the price of a good increases, *ceteris paribus*, the CPI will rise, and rational consumers will substitute away from that good and in favor of other products. The income effect will reinforce, partially offset, or overwhelm the substitution effect, depending upon whether the good is a superior, inferior, or Giffen good.

3A-2. Your graph should show the budget line swinging inward, causing the consumer to buy less of both products, presuming non-Giffen goods. The income effect should be negative, offsetting the substitution effect to some degree.

3A-3. The indifference curves must be drawn close together at the top (small amounts of X) and far apart at the bottom (larger amounts of X) to reflect the rapid decline of the consumer's MU of the Giffen good as more is acquired. Following a price reduction, the point of tangency between the new budget line and the highest attainable indifference curve will occur at a lower level of product X. The income effect is negative and more than offsets the substitution effect.

CHAPTER 4

4-1. **(a)** Note that the choice of scale is critical.

(b) Arc price elasticity varies from -3.03, for the price range $5 to $4.95, to -0.65 for the price range $4.55 to $4.60.

(c) Demand is elastic for prices above $4.77, unitary at $4.77, and inelastic below $4.77.

4-2. **(a)** 116,415.6.

(b) Point price elasticity is -0.437, cross-elasticity is 0.439, and advertising elasticity is 2.044.

(c) Too low, since MR is negative (regardless of MC value).

4-3. **(a)** -0.437.

(b) 1.422.

(c) Yes, to $8.40, assuming *ceteris paribus*.

(d) $7.40.

4-4. **(a)** -0.99357. Demand is very near unitary elasticity, meaning that total revenue would change only very slightly for either a small increase or decrease in price.

(b) $P = 1.585106 - 0.02649Q$.

(c) $0.89.

(d) $0.79.

4-5. **(a)** -1.21128. Demand is "elastic," meaning TR would rise if price were reduced, for example.

(b) $P = 10.862 - 0.6789Q$.

(c) No. $6.93.

(d) $5.43.

4-6. **(a)** Arc price elasticity $= -3.0768$.

(b) $4.17 and $17,210.

4-7. **(a)** No. $1.81.

(b) $1.31.

4-8. **(a)** Sales are expected to decrease by about 18.5%.

(b) Sales are expected to increase by about 4.5%.

(c) Sales are expected to decrease by about 5.5%.

4-9. **(a)** $750 and 600,000.

(b) $10,800,000.

4-10. **(a)** and **(b)** There are several price and advertising mixes that achieve both targets. I would suggest increasing advertising by 15% or a little less without any increase in price, but your answer is as good as mine.

(c) 0.949, indicating that the product is a "necessity" and that its quantity demanded will change less than in proportion to changes in income.

CHAPTER 5

5-1. **(b)** $P = 12.838 - 0.00002063Q$.

(c) $6.42.

(d) -1.00. Demand is unitary elastic, meaning that for any small price change total revenue will remain constant.

5-2. **(a)** $P = 262.389 - 1.626Q$, for the sample, and $P = 262.389 - 0.00813Q$ for the market.

(b) -2.183, -3.202, -5.183, and -10.693.

(c) $206.19.

5-3. **(a)** 5,175, 3,950, 2,925, and 1,350.

(b) $P = 230.21 - 0.026Q$.

(c) $171.36.

5-4. **(b)** $P = 40.816 - 0.505Q$; $R^2 = 0.955$.

(c) $Q = 35.2356$ hours. The 95% confidence interval is 28.03 hours to 42.44 hours, which is rather broad but should not cause a problem. Some weeks the instructor will be busier than others.

(d) $25.41.

5-5. **(a)** $2,980.

(b) $2,230.

(c) -2.0134.

(d) 6,326 to 19,332.

5-6. **(a)** -3.83, 2.59, and 0.475, respectively.

(b) $P = 239.55 - 0.000537Q$ and MR $= 239.55 - 0.001074Q$.

(c) $186.

(d) 86,826 to 112,557.

5-7. (a) $150.

(b) $200.

(c) $213.

5-8. (a) -1.08, 1.21, and 1.86, respectively.

(b) $P = 94.16947 - 0.95465Q$ and $MR = 94.16947 - 1.9093Q$.

(c) $47.08 (perhaps $46.99 would look better).

5-9. (a) The cross-elasticities are 1.666 between Hertz's compact car and the competitors' compact cars, and 1.111 between Hertz's compact cars and Hertz's subcompact cars. Thus, the competitors' compact cars are the stronger substitutes.

(b) $P = 34.93528 - 0.2772Q$.

(c) $17.47.

(d) 57.78 to 68.22.

5-10. (a) Own price elasticity is -1.14; cross price elasticities are 4.198 with respect to Sudds and 1.638 with respect to the generic beer; and income elasticity is 1.0038.

(b) $P = 14.9987 - 0.345Q$.

(c) $7.50.

(d) $8.50.

(e) 17.338 to 20.338.

APPENDIX 5A

5A-1. (a) The intercept on the vertical axis (sales) should be about 5,300, and the line should slope upward at the rate of about 4 pails per household.

(b) $S = 5,283.73 + 4.15H$.

(c) About 11,500 pails.

5A-2. (a) Sales $= 0.06976 + 3.8398$ index.

(b) Since $R^2 = 0.9992$, and the standard error of estimate (and the confidence intervals) are correspondingly very small, the index is a highly reliable indicator of sales.

(c) 1,859, 1,977, 2,094, 2,211, and 2,329.

(d) 7,139, 7,589, 8,040, 8,491, and 8,941.

5A-3. (a) They seem to be more than will be required.

(b) 1,060, 1,044, and 1,028, based on assumptions I made. Your answers will depend on the assumptions you made but should also trend downward like this, following past patterns.

5A-4. (a) 34,732 units.

(b) 32,254 to 37,210.

5A-5. (a) 52.33.

(b) No change.

(c) Yes, if one technician is fired.

(d) Yes, if one technician is fired.

(e) No.

5A-6. (a) 25,634.75.

(b) 20,169 to 23,717.

(c) 25,457.35 to 25,813.15.

5A-7. (a) $1.367 million.

CHAPTER 6

6-1. (a) Increasing MP up to about 5 divers; constant MP 6 to 12 divers; and diminishing MP after 12 divers.

(b) 5 divers, where average product (Q/L) is maximized.

(c) 14 divers, where TP is maximized.

6-2. (a) Size.

(b) Economies of plant size, since SAC declines as number of production centers increases.

(c) Mr. Panache and the other overheads were underutilized initially.

6-3. (a) For $L = 1$ through 10, $Q = 42.52, 85.76, 129.2, 172.4, 215, 256.3, 295.9, 333.4, 368.2, 400$, and the MPs are the changes in these Qs.

(b) TVC = \$200, \$400, \$600, and so on, at each of the above Q levels while TFC is \$100. Solve for AVC and SAC at each of the above Q levels. For example, for $Q = 215$, AVC = \$4.651 and SAC = \$6.976.

(d) With the 4th unit of L, when MP begins to fall.

6-4. (a) TP = 66.2, 85, 99.1, 103.6, 93.2, and 63, for $L = 1$ through 5.

(b) After the first unit.

(c) About 3.85 units, where TP is maximized.

6-5. (a) For plant 1, at output levels 30, 52, 80, and so on, SAC = \$1,000.00, \$769.24, \$625.00, and so on.

(b) Economies of plant size up to and including plant size 3, then diseconomies with plant size 4.

(c) (1) Plant 1. (2) Plant 3. (3) Given equal likelihood of demand falling at any level within the range, plant 3 has both a lower expected value of average cost and a lower standard deviation, although plant 4 is favored by the maximin criteria.

6-6. (a) For example, with $K = 3$, and for $L = 1$ through 6, SAC = \$85,000, \$45,830, \$34,650, \$32,500, \$34,170, and \$36,550.

(b) Economies of plant size are evident with $K = 3$ and 4, with diseconomies becoming evident with $K = 5$ and 6.

(c) The expected value of SAC is lowest (at about \$38,750) with plant 4, presuming that 250 cars can be produced at about \$40,000 each. Otherwise, plant 5 can handle all output levels within the range 100 to 250 with a slightly higher EV of SAC (about \$39,360) and has better potential if demand increases beyond 250.

6-7. (a) AVC at the output levels given are \$9.23, \$8.39, \$8.91, \$9.84, \$10.79, and \$12. SACs are \$18.61, \$12.59, \$11.88, \$12.30, \$12.95, and \$14.

(c) Around 150 units of the variable inputs, or 10,000 units of output, where MC begins to rise.

(d) Around 20,000 units of output, where SAC is about \$11.87.

6-8. (a) They sink downward. For example, at 20,200 units of output, AVC = \$7.43 and SAC = \$10.40.

(b) No, diminishing returns is a physical phenomenon that is independent of input costs.

(c) Again they sink downward. For example, at 22,220 units of output, AVC = \$6.75 and SAC = \$9.45.

(d) Each change increases the full capacity output level.

6-9. (b) \$87.50, \$82, and \$84.50, for plants A, B, and C, respectively.

(c) Plant B, unless demand probability distribution underestimates demand situation.

(d) About 850 units, on average.

6-10. (a) Plan A: \$630,000; plan B: \$660,000.

(b) Perhaps make 200 in house and have the other firm assemble 100, but Magnocrunch would have less control over the quality of the units assembled outside and might be training a future competitor.

APPENDIX 6A

6A-1. **(b)** About 127,000 units, using 4,500 labor hours and 1,400 machine hours.

(c) About 117,000 units, using 3,700 labor hours and 980 machine hours.

6A-2. **(b)** About 170 units.

(c) $300,000.

(d) $50,000.

6A-3. **(c)** About $112,500.

(d) Increase by $7,000 in the short run. In the long run the firm will increase K to about 1.05 and reduce L to reduce costs to about $118,500.

APPENDIX 6B

6B-1. **(a)** 2,833 pounds of fish cakes and 8,603 pounds of fish meal.

(b) $8,289.

(c) Shredding and packing processes.

6B-2. **(a)** 638.89 units of A, 388.89 units of B.

(b) $2.29.

(c) Sultanas and citrus are right at minimum limits. Munchies could buy these separately.

6B-3. **(a)** 90 sandy; 145 pebbly; 115 rocky.

(b) $868.75.

(c) All are binding.

6B-4. **(a)** Min. $0.00125A + 0.00085B + 0.0005C$, st $A > 30$; $B > 15$; $C > 10$; $2A + B + 7C > 150$; $3.3A + 5B + 2C > 300$; $A + B + C > 100$.

(b) $0.0796 per bar.

(c) Yes, it is cheaper.

6B-5. **(a)** No; product A is not worthwhile.

(b) In the assembly process only.

CHAPTER 7

7-1. **(a)** Buy. (Incremental cost, including opportunity cost, is $4,930 versus $5,995.)

7-2. **(a)** Buy, subject to qualifications, since contribution of buy alternative is $40,000 versus $24,800 for make option.

7-3. **(a)** Accept the order, subject to qualifications, since contribution is $4,910.

7-4. **(a)** Probably not. Although the contribution is positive at $963 (assuming indirect factory labor is a variable cost), this is less than 1% of the firm's profits and involves several issues that are worrisome.

(b) Build inventory while investigating either plant expansion or a price increase.

7-5. **(a)** $3,105.67. Note that there is only a $2/3$ probability that there would be opportunity costs.

628 *Appendix C*

7-6. **(a)** Although the incremental cost of making the trays is slightly more than that of buying them ($-358,932 versus $-355,918), some probable future costs are not included in the "buy" alternative. Making them in house would retain quality control and the ability to suspend production if demand does not materialize.

7-7. **(a)** $8,475.

7-8. **(a)** Yes, subject to qualifications, since incremental revenues ($2,000) exceed incremental costs ($1,262).

7-9. **(a)** Strategy A: EPV = $125,142; strategy B: EPV = $102,457.

(b) Strategy B is favored by both the coefficient of variation and the maximin criteria. If Wyndham is only slightly risk averse, however, the CE criterion may favor strategy A.

7-10. **(a)** Wildlife farm: EPV = $77,670; amusement park: EPV = $87,906, assuming risk-free ODR = 9% in both cases.

(b) Decision is sensitive to ODR chosen. At ODRs of 17% and above, the wildlife farm has the greater EPV.

(c) This depends on the ODR and Yankee Jack's degree of risk aversion.

APPENDIX 7A

7A-1. **(a)** B/E volume is 3,692.

(b) For $P = $45, $Q = 3,500$, thus B/E volume is unattainable. Advise consideration of higher price, higher quality, or promotional activity.

7A-2. **(a)** 106,667, 138,196, and 142,248, respectively.

7A-3. **(a)** $42,100, $48,150, and $38,425, respectively.

(b) 18,563, 27,845, and 32,933, respectively.

(c) A, if highly risk averse; B, if less risk averse.

CHAPTER 8

8-1. **(a)** It should look like a cubic function.

(b) AVCs are $15, $10, $8, $6.88, $6, $5.25, $4.71, $4.25, $3.94, $3.70, $3.64, $3.83, and $4.08. MCs (gradients) are $5, $4, $3.50, $2.50, $1.50, $1.50, $1, $1.50, $1.50, $3, $6, and $7.

(c) $4,000.

8-2. **(a)** AVCs are $19.17, $18.83, $18.70, $18.65, and $18.96. MCs (gradients) are $17.71, $18.12, $18.40, and $20.89.

(b) At about 920 units, where AVC is minimized.

(c) About 1,000 units, where MC = MR.

8-3. **(a)** $P = 9.24 - 1.09769Q$.

(b) SACs are $5.80, $4.40, and $5.30. Gradients are $3.23 and $7.50.

(c) $P = $6.50 and $Q = 2,500$, or thereabouts.

8-4. **(a)** SACs are $6, $5, and $5. AVCs are $4.25, $3.83, and $4.22. Gradients are $3 and $5.

(b) Do not accept, since contribution is $-2,000 and other issues are worrisome.

8-5. **(a)** 3 contracts, for 15,000 seats total, for contribution of $35,390.

8-6. **(a)** SACs are $31.52, $18.60, $13.78, $11.15, $9.47, $8.30, $7.48, $7, $6.85, $7.10, $7.63, and $8.32. Gradients are $5.68, $4.14, $3.26, $2.75, $2.45, $2.55, $3.65, $5.62, $9.38, $12.95, and $15.89.

(b) Leave it, since the expected contribution of the deal is $\$-2,384$, unless the buyer can be induced to pay the set-up cost or unless future business is expected to more than offset this deficit.

8-7. **(a)** Expected value of monthly profit from smaller plant is $13,625, compared to $28,043 from the larger plant. Standard deviations are 5,759 and 8,343, respectively. Coefficient of variation criterion indicates the larger plant, and the certainty equivalent criterion will support this unless the firm is extremely risk averse.

8-8. **(a)** Build new plant. Overtime/extra shift option has an expected loss of $\$-1,036$. Second option promises $1,493 profit, presuming all Ohio demand is served from Ohio plant.

8-9. **(a)** $SAC = 6,669.68Q^{-0.32998}$.

(b) 20.45%.

(c) $475.03.

8-10. **(a)** $711.19 and $559.92, respectively.

(b) Very well. $R^2 = 0.9964$ and $S_e = 0.0101$. Thus the 95% confidence interval is a mere 2 cents each side of the predicted cost levels.

CHAPTER 9

9-1. **(a)** Market demand shifts back and price falls.

(b) Output is cut back such that MC equals the new price level.

9-2. **(a)** Presuming a kinked demand curve, the new MC curve remains within the MR gap.

(b) Traditionally these firms raise prices at the start of the new model year and might expect conscious parallelism at that time.

9-3. **(a)** New entrants undercut Prangle's price to retailers and gained market share as retailers pushed their products to gain the higher profit margin. Also, perhaps the number of competitors increased faster than the market did.

(b) Prangle believes that it faces a kinked demand curve.

(c) Contribution is maximized at $2.2 million at a price of $8 and output of 550,000 units.

9-4. **(a)** The firms' *mutatis mutandis* demand curves are coextensive, with the same intercept and three times the slope of the market demand curve.

9-5. **(a)** Struktatuff's demand curve is $P = 36,384 - 1.875Q$ and Steeldeal's is $P = 36,384 - 3.75Q$.

(b) $20,617.

(c) 12,613 total, 8,409 for Struktatuff and 4,204 for Steeldeal.

9-6. **(a)** The supply of the small firms is represented by $S = 15 + 1.125Q$, and the residual demand curve is $P = 55.26 - 0.592Q$.

(b) $P = \$39.95$ and $Q = 26,875$ units.

(c) $108,210 and $3,180, respectively.

9-7. **(a)** Author assumes demand is relatively elastic and wants to maximize TR, since royalties depend on TR.

(b) Publisher assumes that demand is relatively inelastic, and wants to maximize profits. Inelastic demand may reflect expectation that rivals would match a price reduction.

9-8. **(a)** About $30 per ton, depending on assumptions made.

(b) $106 per ton. This is only possible if all firms raise prices to this level and is only desirable if no further entry is feared within the firms' time horizons.

9-9. **(a)** $P = \$30$, $Q = 263,455$, and profits would be $1,174,685.

    (b) $P = \$19.95$, $Q = 530,982$, and there would be a loss of $\$-2,615,491$.

    (c) $Q = 376,311$ and $P = \$26.76$.

9-10. **(a)** $P = \$16.33$ per dozen. Profits would be $\$17,778$.

    (b) $P = \$14.94$, $Q = 3,624$ per dozen, and profits would be $\$16,414$.

    (c) Set price a safe margin below the limit price, at, say, $\$14.75$ per dozen, in case the estimates of Popular's costs are inaccurate, for $Q = 3,700$ and profits of $\$16,091$.

APPENDIX 9A

9A-1. Where the combined-MC curve cuts the combined-MR curve, project this level across to each of the MC curves to find the production in each plant, and across to each of the MR curves to find the allocation to each market.

9A-2. **(a)** 10,191.

    (b) 2,599 to the domestic market and 7,592 to the foreign market.

    (c) $\$61.02$.

    (d) $\$41.02$.

9A-3. **(a)** 4,886 pounds.

    (b) 3,073 pounds.

    (c) $\$44.07$.

    (d) The contribution would decrease by $\$78.80$.

9A-4. **(a)** $\$390,000$.

    (b) $\$1,360$.

    (c) $\$462,000$.

9A-5. **(a)** $\$323.53$.

    (b) 400 units, 314 transferred to the marketing division and 86 sold externally.

    (c) Transfer price is $\$465.33$; 248 units will be transferred to the manufacturing division, and 459 units will be sold in the external market at $\$832.67$ each.

CHAPTER 10

10-1. **(b)** $\$75,000$ profits are unattainable at $\$7.95$ profit-maximizing price. Maximum profits are $\$70,000$ at output level of 24,600 units. Firm needs to shift demand curve, by promotion or product design, for example, or lower its costs, before it can achieve its objectives.

10-2. **(a)** $\$8.93$.

    (b) Confident at 95% level. Profit at lower confidence boundary on sales volume exceeds profit at the old price.

10-3. **(a)** $\$7.15$.

    (b) 2,720 units. (Hint: assume that the demand curve's slope remains the same as it shifts.)

10-4. **(a)** -4.0.

    (b) Yes, range of acceptable markups was from 21% to 50%.

    (c) No, at the profit-maximizing price of $P = \$40.71$ it will take years to recoup the search expenditure.

10-5. **(a)** $P = 1,431.82 - 11.3636Q$; $TR = 1,431.82Q - 11.3636Q^2$; $TC = 8,000 + 600Q$.

    (b) $\$772.30$, or a 28.72% markup.

10-6. **(a)** In the vicinity of $\$110$ to $\$115$.

    (b) Diversify product line, jointly promote down-filled products, develop effective substitute materials.

10-7. (a) $499 or thereabouts.

10-8. (a) $P = 17.9 - 0.05593Q$.

    (b) $10.95.

    (c) Probably not.

10-9. (a) $775, or perhaps a little higher if Emerson's brand name and quality are considered equal to Quasar's.

    (b) $1,199, or perhaps a little higher if Emerson's quality is considered equal to JVC's.

10-10. (a) Your answers will reflect your assumptions and strategy, of course. I decided to price the basic 128K model at $2,195 and then add $500 for IBM compatibility, $150 for each extra 128K chip, $600 for Word Perfect, and $400 for Lotus, when these features are to be bundled in with the product. If sold later, I would add $700 for IBM compatibility, $300 for the first 128K chip, $650 for the upgrade to 512K, $650 for Word Perfect, and $450 for Lotus.

CHAPTER 11

11-1. (a) $17.75, $17.50, and $14.50.

11-2. (a) SAC falls from $14 to $11.20, $8.96, $7.17, $5.73, and $4.59 as output doubles from 1,000 to 2,000, 4,000, 8,000, and so on. Price is constant at $9.95 up to 20,000 units, then declines smoothly to $5.95 at 50,000 units.

11-3. (a) $237,985 and $295,747 using daily discount factors (or $224,118 and $278,559 using end-of-year discount factors, which probably understates the present value significantly).

    (b) Standard deviations are 52,375 and 66,226, using daily discount factors. Thus absolute risk is greater for the $30 shirt. But relative risk, measured by the coefficients of variation, is virtually equal.

11-4. (a) $129.88 and 25,370 units.

    (b) $78.80.

    (c) $135.20; 20,827 units; $1,496,490.

    (d) No, it would suffer a loss of $1.556 million in the first year.

11-5. (a) $1,341,975 after 1 year, $1,483,733 after 2 years, and $1,542,880 after 3 years.

    (b) $948,513 after 1 year, $1,242,599 after 2 years, and $1,378,573 after 3 years.

    (c) No, it would be unable to supply the demand, given the present plant.

11-6. (a) $P = 15.98 - 0.0000299Q$.

    (b) $P = 24.94 - 0.0000299Q$ and $P = 39.89 - 0.000029Q$.

    (c) $P = 24.92 - 0.000087Q$ and $P = 39.89 - 0.0001794Q$.

    (d) $14.50 and $21.95; 116,722 and 100,028 units.

11-7. (a) $190 and 22,000 units.

    (b) $180 and $172.50; 9,600 and 10,200 units.

    (c) $124.

    (d) The limit price strategy ($4,745,953 versus $3,845,925).

11-8. (a) $21 per case.

    (b) TR-maximizing price is **$16.77**, for profits only $70,000 less than profit-maximizing price.

    (c) 1) Entry will occur, price may fall to around $16.80. 2) Entry will occur, price may fall to perhaps $15.

11-9. (a) No. $167.80 per unit. BAE's lower price is presumably intended to increase production and allow benefit from learning effects before the entry of new firms.

(b) Outputs will be 1,710, 1,960, 2,210, 2,460, 2,710, and 2,960 units. Profits will be $100,778, $145,058, $184,378, $222,168, $259,302, and $296,111, given the learning curve AVC = $421.2432Q^{-0.32192}$, where Q represents cumulative volume. No, do not build larger plant.

(c) No, assuming comparable quality/price ratio to consumer. Outputs are 1,284, 1,384, 1,484, and so on. Profits are $79,660, $93,440, $107,286, $121,193, $135,156, and $149,172. No.

(d) Both would have to reduce price, by, say, $20.

(e) Setting price at $167.80 for first six months allows higher profits. Then reduce price $20 each time there is entry.

11-10. **(a)** $1,704, $2,169, $1,968, and $1,423.

(b) The product might be introduced at a nominal price of $2,169 but sold at a "special introductory price" of $1,699 for the first year, then priced at $2,169 in the second year, reduced to $1,968 in the third year, and reduced further to $1,423 in the fourth year.

(c) Volumes are 1,310, 1,792, 1,577, and 1,000 units. Profits are $0.874 million, $2.05 million, $1.492 million, and $0.403 million in nominal terms, given SAC = $1,091.81Q^{-0.00786}$, where Q represents cumulative volume.

CHAPTER 12

12-1. **(a)** $4,700, $7,200, $6,750, $3,600, and $1,500.

(b) 23.25% markup, bid $61,625, EPVC $7,349.91.

12-2. **(a)** Desperation. Others firms' costs were lower.

(b) $87,630.

12-3. **(a)** 0.972, 0.806, 0.632, 0.452, and 0.264.

(b) $35,200.

12-4. **(a)** Incremental costs are $66,200.

(b) Your answer will depend on your assessment of the situation and your degree of risk aversion, but it should be somewhat below normal bidding policy, such as $125,000, or about 5% above full costs.

12-5. **(a)** $3,105.67.

(b) Anything above incremental cost will be better than the existing use of the truck. No need to be greedy, especially since this is an older truck and may not be as attractive to the store as would a competitor's newer truck. Also, rivals' newer trucks may have lower operating costs. There may also be future business as a result. Some additional contribution may be necessary to compensate for the extra administrative effort, and as a cushion against possible variations in costs. I would bid about $3,500, which is $175 per day, and does not seem unreasonable.

12-6. **(a)** About $396,500.

(b) About $428,000.

12-7. **(a)** $437,000.

(b) Somewhat below normal practice, say $630,000, should win the contract.

12-8. **(a)** $−396, $105, and $70, respectively.

(b) $2,450 bid price offers EPVC of $171.

12-9. **(a)** No, EPVC is maximized at a price of about $8,150. (Hint: use properties of normal distribution to estimate probabilities of firms' submitting bids at various levels.)

12-10. **(a)** $173,005.

(b) $206,857.

CHAPTER 13

13-1. (a) No, $dQ/dA = 12.62$.

(b) No, slope of the advertising function will decline as advertising increases. Thompson should make a series of increments to advertising and note sales reaction.

13-2. (a) Diminishing returns to advertising should be evident.

(b) About $7,000 per quarter.

13-3. (a) $11,233.53. Although R^2 is very high, this is an extrapolation outside the data base.

(b) About $1,625.

(c) Lagged impact of advertising on sales.

(d) Maintain advertising at current level while investigating lagged impacts.

13-4. (a) $P = \$6.56$ and $S = 5.5$.

(b) 2 records on sale per week.

13-5. (a) $P = \$4.50$ (for medium pizza) and $11,000 advertising.

(b) $563.26.

13-6. (a) V-P Finance is apparently assuming that rivals will also reduce their advertising outlays, while Marketing V-P expects *ceteris paribus* for reductions or increases in the advertising budget.

(b) Mr. Hogg expects rivals to match increases in advertising.

(c) Maintain current (maximin) advertising level while investigating rivals' attitudes toward advertising rivalry, their ability to increase advertising, and so on.

13-7. (a) Central to your argument would be that rivals will ignore your advertising increase and that sales would be responsive to increased advertising.

(b) Which attributes are desired by consumers and how much are they willing to pay for these? Will rivals react to your campaign?

13-8. (a) 52,501 units, TR $= \$15,487,730$, and profit $= \$2,307,574$.

(b) $242,812.30.

(c) 53,207 units, TR $= \$15,696,163$, and profit $= \$2,311,884$.

13-9. (a) 244,461 units and $278,112.40 profit.

(b) $1,000,079.

(c) No, only $820.20.

13-10. (a) 303,690 units and $629,522 profit.

(b) $824,115.

(c) 284,964 units, $4,559,429 revenue, and $655,600 profit.

CHAPTER 14

14-1. (a) Neither cost leadership nor quality leadership seems possible unless new equipment is purchased. New equipment should be chosen with a particular strategy in mind.

(b) Since the premium ice creams are higher priced, a quality leadership strategy, either focused to the ice cream parlors or more broadly oriented toward foodstores and the parlors, might be the best strategy. On the other hand, you might argue that given their quality reputation and proclivity for promotional pricing, they should pursue cost leadership.

(c) Cost of new equipment; relative costs of other firms; feasibility of repositioning their brand name in attribute space; feasibility of introducing a new brand name for a higher-quality ice cream; feasibility of opening one or more ice cream parlors; and so on.

14-2. **(a)** Focused cost leadership may be the best initial strategy.

   (b) Introduce the City, Rocker, and Family models first, at relatively low prices, with promotion stressing their economy of purchase and operation, targeted at young adults.

   (c) Other products available in each market segment; strategies being pursued by rivals; relative costs of rival firms; similarity of Hawaii and mainland markets; and so on.

14-3. **(a)** Focused differentiation strategy.

   (b) Immigration law services, priced at a premium, promoted directly to colleges, universities, and high-technology companies who regularly hire foreign professionals.

14-4. **(a)** A focused differentiation strategy, offering a high-quality business program (with a strong liberal arts component) in an idyllic setting, or a focused cost leadership strategy as a new business school, would seem to be prime contenders.

   (b) Establishing a new business school that specializes in liberally educated professionals seems promising. Fees should be relatively high, and the program should be promoted in business periodicals as well as through selected high schools in affluent suburbs of the major northeastern cities.

14-5. **(a)** Quick sale but low revenue.

   (b) Quick sale with higher revenue, but substantial costs involved prior to sale.

   (c) No more than they expect the sale price to be raised as a result of the improvements.

   (d) Seek information about the typical price premiums associated with each possible improvement, and the cost of making these improvements.

14-6. **(a)** Differentiation strategies seem most promising.

   (b) Open a store catering to the do-it-yourselfer, incorporating a specialty service in luxury bathrooms.

   (c) Products must include all those sought by the home handyperson, be priced slightly above hardware store prices due to the free advice available, and be promoted directly to the do-it-yourselfer in the local media. The luxury bathroom service would be featured in the advertisements and in the store itself.

14-7. **(a)** Cost focus strategies seem feasible, as do quality focus strategies. Broad-based cost leadership and differentiation strategies seem less promising.

   (b) Reposition the firm as a supplier of high-quality, special-interest tours.

   (c) The packages should be composed of direct flights with convenient departure times, quality hotels, quality recreation and sporting facilities, and so on. Prices should include a premium for this additional quality. Promotion should be targeted, by advertisements in special interest magazines, for example.

14-8. **(a)** The business lunch and dinner market and the fine Italian dining options are each quality focus strategies to a large degree. The family restaurant franchise and the breakfast and fast food market are more likely appropriate for a cost leadership strategy, since these markets tend to be more price conscious. Nonetheless, a broad-based differentiation strategy is also possible in these latter two types of restaurants.

   (b) Your answer is as good as mine.

   (c) Support your answer with an analysis of the cost and revenue implications.

14-9. **(a)** Cost leadership does not seem feasible, due to limited capacity. A focused differentiation strategy seems more promising.

   (b) Upgrade the trails, install snow-making equipment, and focus on the more affluent, enthusiast skier. Product quality must be improved, prices increased, and promotion targeted on those who want the best and are willing to pay for it.

14-10. **(a)** Unless it adopts the industry standards, a broad-based differentiation strategy seems unwise. Even then, BBC may not be able to compete with the major players. A focus strategy, utilizing the nano-disks in a portable computer, seems like a good bet.

(b) No, a focused cost leadership strategy might be possible.

(c) Adopt MS-DOS and pursue miniaturization as a focused differentiation strategy.

(d) Small portable computers, with integral disk drives and printer, sold at a premium for those who value this combination and promoted to business professionals and the college market, might be a winning combination.

CHAPTER 15

15-1. (a) Undertake projects A, B, and C.

15-2. (a) $17,792.50.

(b) 12.995339%.

(c) About $57,000.

15-3. (a) $46,343.47.

(b) About 27.4%.

(c) $17,366.37.

(e) Kayak.

15-4. (a) $53.487, $46,767, $55,900, and $41,058.

(b) Using nominal cash flows, payback periods (in months) are 17.8, 23.1, 21, and 24. Using present-valued cash flows, they are 20, 27.5, 24.6, and 30.6.

(c) It is a tradeoff between Sportswear at either location A or location B.

15-5. (a) Tacos, $20,435; chicken, $11,624; hamburgers, $9,200.

(b) In months, 24.857, 24.923, and 26.

(c) Tacos.

15-6. (a) B: $60,172; D: $48,578; A: $44,210; C: $30,405.

(b) B: 3.15; C: 2.90; A: 2.26; D: 2.21.

(c) B, D, and A.

(d) $134,787.

15-7. (a) West: $103,145; east: $86,178; south: $81,628; north: $67,963.

(b) North: 1.57; south: 1.45; west: 1.36; east: 1.34.

(c) West and south.

(d) $184,772.

15-8. (a) EPVs are $231,174 and $255,177. IRRs are 23.26% and 26.47%. PIs are 2.15 and 2.34.

15-9. (a) Plan A EPV is $EC4.02m; plan B EPV is $EC5.68m.

(b) No.

15-10. (a) Oval circuit EPV is $23.397m; Road circuit EPV is $28.864m.

(b) Using nominal cash flows, 45 months and 55.2 months. Using present-valued cash flows, 59.3 months and 62.5 months.

(c) Road circuit.

APPENDIX A

A-1. (a) $Y = a + bX$.

(b) $Y = a + bX + cX^2$.

(c) $Y = a + bX + cX^2 + cX^3$.

(d) $Y = ae^{bx}$.

(e) $Y = aX^b$.

(f) $Y = a/X^b$, or $Y = aX^{-b}$.

A-2. (a) $dY/dX = 13.5X^2$.

(b) $dX/dY = -6Z(9X^2) = -54X^2(4 + 3X^3)$.

(c) $dY/dX = 21 - 42X^2$.

(d) $dY/dX = 24(-32X + 27X^2 + 24X^3 - 36X^5)$.

(e) $dY/dX = 24(4 - 2X^2)(4 + 24X - 10X^2)$.

(f) $dY/dX = 8e^{2x}$.

A-3. (a) Y is maximized at -27.5 when $X = 1.5$.

(b) Y is minimized at 12 when $X = 4$.

(c) A is minimized at $-15,245.25$ when $B = 52.5$.

(d) K is maximized at 244,667 when $J = 3.333$.

A-4. (a) 21.42357 hours.

Author Index

Subject Index